Quest
Reading the World and Arguing for Change

Kim Stallings

University of North Carolina–Charlotte

PEARSON

Prentice Hall

Upper Saddle River, New Jersey 07458

Library of Congress Cataloging-in-Publication Data

Stallings, Kim.
    Quest : reading the world and arguing for change / Kim Stallings.
        p. cm.
    Includes index.
    ISBN 0-13-111467-0
1. English language—Rhetoric—Problems, exercises, etc.   2. Social problems—Problems,
exercises, etc.   3. Social change—Problems, exercises, etc.   4. Report writing—Problems,
exercises, etc.   5. Readers—Social problems.   6. Readers—Social change.   7. College
readers.   I. Title.
    PE1479.S62S725 2006
    808'.0427—dc22

                                                                        2005023209

Editorial Director: Leah Jewell
Senior Editor: Brad Potthoff
Assistant Editor: Melissa Casciano
Editorial Assistant: Tara Culliney
Marketing Director: Brandy Dawson
Marketing Manager: Emily Cleary
Marketing Assistant: Kara Pottle
**VP/Director of Production
   and Manufacturing:** Barbara Kittle
Production Editor: Karen Berry/Pine
   Tree Composition
Production Assistant: Marlene Gassler
Text Permission Specialist:
   The Permissions Group
Prepress & Manufacturing Manager:
   Nick Sklitsis
**Prepress & Manufacturing Assistant
   Manager:** Mary Ann Gloriande
Interior Design: Pine Tree Composition

Cover Art Director: Jayne Conte
Cover Art Design: Bruce Kenselaar
Director, Image Resource Center:
   Melinda Reo
**Manager, Cover Visual Research
   and Permissions:** Karen Sanatar
Manager, Rights and Permissions:
   Zina Arabia
Manager, Visual Research: Beth Brenzel
Image Permission Coordinator:
   Richard Rodrigues
Cover Art: Nepal, Gyoko valley, male
   climber sitting at Gyoko Ree, rear view.
   Everest in background. Melissa
   McManus/Stone/Getty Images Inc.
Composition: Pine Tree Composition, Inc.
Printer/Binder: Courier Companies, Inc.
Cover Printer: The Lehigh Press
Text Type Face: 10/12 Horley OS

Credits and acknowledgments borrowed from other sources and reproduced, with permission, in this
textbook appear on pages 629–630.

Pearson Education LTD., London
Pearson Education Singapore, Pte. Ltd
Pearson Education, Canada, Ltd
Pearson Education–Japan
Pearson Education Australia PTY, Limited

Pearson Education North Asia Ltd
Pearson Educación de Mexico, S.A. de C.V.
Pearson Education Malaysia, Pte. Ltd
Pearson Education, Upper Saddle River, NJ

10 9 8 7 6 5 4 3 2 1
ISBN 0-13-111467-0

Contents

5   Logical Reasoning, Fallacies, and Credible Evidence: Analyzing and Evaluating Arguments   135

Part Three   Joining the Official Conversation: Creating and Advancing Successful Arguments   175

6 Arguing to Educate: Advancing a Position on an Issue   177

7   Arguing to Instigate Change: Advancing a Call for Action   217

8   Arguing to Create Meaning: Advancing an Interpretation   244

Part Four The Journey So Far 279

Part Five Event Casebooks 307

Event Casebook Two   To Clone or Not to Clone   355

Event Casebook Three   What Price, Freedom?   423

Event Casebook Four   The Process and Progress of Equality   473

Memo to Instructors

The Rationale Behind This Textbook

Quest: Reading the World and Arguing for Change grew out of my experiences as a student, a writer, and a teacher of writing and the belief that *writing is absolutely necessary for personal growth and social change.* Words are powerful; a solid command of communication skills is *empowering.* Students need to discover, respect, and enjoy the power of their own written voices; I *believe* that. And I suspect I am not alone in my beliefs considering that writing courses are a required part of most general education curriculums.

Over the years, I have come to realize, however, that many (if not most) students absolutely dread required writing courses. But because these courses and the work we do in them are so important, I have made it my "mission," *my quest,* so to speak, to find ways to make writing more relevant and meaningful for my students. Almost without exception, I have found that *writing instruction is most meaningful when presented within the context of real-life experiences and situations.* Therefore, my basic approach throughout *Quest* rests on these ideas and the premise that *everything* is a text to be read and understood and questioned, and that writing is a crucial life-tool for discovery, exploration, questioning, understanding, and change.

Ideally, all reading and writing assignments within *Quest* are completed within the context of a particular world event and related social issues. As they begin their individual Quests, students may choose to study one of six significant events or series of events covered in the Event Casebook Gallery. Each of these events has impacted and continues to impact many aspects of our society and the world at large. Each event is engaging, relevant, and connected to serious social issues and problems that have yet to be solved.

While you may initially question the practicality of focusing on one event for an entire semester, for maximum growth and development, I encourage you to have faith in the process and give it a try. *Quest* is arranged in such a way as to move students through a thorough exploration of an event *from many different angles* and *for many different purposes.* One event serves as a foundation for a growing knowledge base, but students will study *many* topics related to their chosen event throughout the course. The chance for boredom is limited, while the opportunity for maximum growth and development is enhanced by this context-based thematic framework.

In addition to a context-based *thematic* framework, reading, writing, and argumentation are also taught within a meaningful context. Rather than being front-loaded with "everything you need to know about argument," *Quest* introduces students gradually to the elements of argumentative discourse *at-the-point-of-need* within a particular (and authentic) need-driven context. For instance, as students are beginning to look at an issue for multiple perspectives in Chapter 4, they are introduced to the most common types of claims and reasoning. Later, when students are working on a critical analysis of an argument in Chapter 5, their knowledge of claims and reasoning is reinforced as they are introduced to various types of evidence, warrants, and criteria for judging the credibility of a text. Learning at-the-point-of-need within a specific contextual framework enables the highest possible learning curve, particularly when students focus on a singular event and issue.

If, however, you do not believe that such a singular focus would work in your classroom, there are other more traditional options that have proven successful.

Options for Using This Textbook

Though students show the most growth and change as readers, thinkers, writers, and citizens when focusing on one event and one issue stemming from that event, you should (of course) **always** adapt this or any text to fit the requirements of your program and the needs of your students. I have often made adjustments myself—placed more emphasis on a particular assignment for one class and more emphasis on another assignment for a different class—depending on the developmental needs of my students. In terms of a thematic focus, for example, you may have students focus on:

- one event and one issue,
- one event and several issues,
- several events and one common issue, or
- several events and several issues.

Note

I have also tried (with *great* success) selecting one event for the class and then assigning several small student focus groups. Each group focused on one issue and then each individual in the group focused on one perspective related to that issue. The singular event served as a wonderful common ground for our classroom community, and regardless of which issue a group focused on, we were all able to share and provide knowledgeable feedback for one another.

Additional Options for Adapting Chapter Coverage and Assignments

- In addition to covering important critical skills, Chapters 1 through 5 serve as *invention* for Chapters 6 through 9; therefore, they may not require quite as much time and critical attention as Chapters 6 through 9.

- ○ You may decide to truncate Quests One and Two if your students are already fairly adept at critical-reading skills (I sometimes call these "mini-quests").
- ○ You may decide to combine Chapters 3 and 4 (I have sometimes simply included the history of an event or issue as one perspective among many other perspectives—the historical perspective).
- ○ You might decide Quest Five works best for you as an in-class activity spanning several days.
- ○ You may not have time to cover three argumentative essays, so you may choose to assign one, two, or all three argument essay assignments (Chapters 6 through 8).

Other Points to Consider

- ○ Chapters 1 and 2 refer students to the Event Casebooks Gallery for reading materials.
- ○ Chapters 3 through 8 ask students to *conduct their own research* and gather resources to supplement, build on, and surpass the texts found in the Casebooks (though there have been times in my own classes when research was not the primary focus—therefore, students simply used the texts in the Casebooks as supporting evidence for each Quest). Note: I sometimes have students work on gathering materials in groups, sometimes individually.
- ○ As for Chapter 9, I have sometimes eliminated the full portfolio and simply used a reflective essay as the final project.
- ○ For a variation (particularly in advanced or honors classes), Quests One through Five might serve as invention for Visi-Quests One through Five.
- ○ You might decide to use a Visi-Quest to replace one or more of Quests Six through Nine.
- ○ You might decide that the Visi-Quests work best for you as supplemental in-class activities.

> The key here—as with any text—is to modify chapter coverage and assignments to fit your needs and the needs of your students.

In my experience, students enjoy *Quest,* and because they enjoy it, their assignments do not seem like "work." Quite painlessly, students learn and grow and improve as writers, thinkers, and learners as they move from one chapter to another. But it's not all fun and games—this is a serious academic text. Each project in *Quest* meets standard academic goals for most colleges and universities, prepares students for the demands of college-level research, thinking, and writing, and also prepares students for real-life writing and their roles as active and responsible citizens.

I see this book as a journey-in-progress. For me, the journey actually began in 1997 when I developed my first Quest assignment sequence. And though this book is now ready for publication, my journey is not over—it's just changing. As I continue on, I invite you (teachers and your students) to join me. Share with one another, but also feel free to contact me—and my students—through the companion Web site and share your ideas and your discoveries with other teachers and students around the country.

Finally, I have one more invitation for you. I have included a variety of professional and scholarly texts throughout the book and in the Casebooks, and each Quest assignment is also modeled with student-produced writing samples. I am always looking for new and interesting professional texts, and I am always looking for new and excellent student models, too. If you or your students find an exceptional professional text or if a student does a particularly fabulous job on a Quest and you think it might make a good model for future editions of this book, I invite you to submit that research and/or your student's work to me for consideration. Contact information and further instructions for submission of essays and Visi-Quest projects are available on my Web site.

I look forward to hearing from you.

Supplementary Material for Instructors and Students

For more details on these supplements, available for college adoptions, please contact your Prentice Hall representative.

Instructor's Manual

A comprehensive instructor's manual is available online and includes sample syllabi, teaching tips, and other information. Please contact your Prentice Hall representative for access.

Companion Website™

A *Companion Website*™ to accompany *Quest* can be found at *www.prenhall.com/ stallings.* This useful Website contains quizzes and objectives for each chapter, additional links, and research tools.

Writer's OneKey

Use Writer's OneKey to enhance your composition classes. Everything is in one place on the Web for students and instructors, including:

- Personal tutoring available to students
- Paper review tool and research tools, including the *New York Times* archive
- Visual analysis exercises
- Mini-handbook
- And much more . . .

A subscription to Writer's OneKey can be packaged for no additional charge with each copy of this text by specifying ISBN 0-13-191824-9. See *www.prenhall.com/ writersonekey* for details.

Prentice Hall Pocket Readers

Each reading in our pocket readers has withstood the test of time and teaching, making each the perfect companion for any writing course (limit one complimentary reader per package).

To order the student edition packaged with . . .

> *Argument: A Prentice Hall Pocket Reader,* by Christy Desmet, Deborah Miller and Kathy Houff, specify package ISBN 0-13-218899-6
> *Literature: A Prentice Hall Pocket Reader,* by Mary Balkun, specify package ISBN 0-13-218995-X
> *Patterns: A Prentice Hall Pocket Reader,* by Dorothy Minor, specify package ISBN 0-13-218930-5
> *Themes: A Prentice Hall Pocket Reader,* by Clyde Moneyhun, specify package ISBN 0-13-218903-8
> *Writing Across the Curriculum: A Prentice Hall Pocket Reader,* by Stephen Brown, and *Papers Across the Curriculum,* by Judith Ferster, specify package ISBN 0-13-169642-4

The New American Webster Handy College Dictionary

To order the student edition with a dictionary at no additional cost, specify package ISBN 0-13-186218-9.

The New American Roget's College Thesaurus

To order the student edition with a thesaurus at no additional cost, specify package ISBN 0-13-186217-0.

Acknowledgments

I would like to thank the following people (in no particular order):

> Brad Potthoff and everyone at Prentice Hall
> Corey Good
> Steve Lazenby
> Sam Stallings

Marc and Margaret Luke

All of the students who allowed me to use their work and who helped me craft this textbook over the past several years

I would also like to thank the following reviewers: Lawrence J. McKenzie, West Virginia University at Parkersburg; Rachel Diehl, Drexel University; Lanell Mogab, Clinton Community College; Patrick Bettencourt, Modesto Junior College; Marti Singer, Georgia State University; Dwedor Ford, University of Arkansas at Little Rock; Michael Connaughton, St. Cloud State University; Jonathan Alexander, University of Cincinnati; Sara McLaughlin, Texas Tech University; Patricia Webb, Arizona State University; Patricia Medeiros, Scottsdale Community College; William Steven Lazenby, University of North Carolina at Charlotte; Amity Reading, University of Illinois; Jennifer Swartout, Heartland Community College; Karen Gardiner, University of Alabama; Tim Taylor, St. Louis Community College; Christy Desmet, University of Georgia; Deborah Church Miller, University of Georgia; Rebecca Whitus Longster, Purdue University; Cathryn Amdahl, Harrisburg Area Community College; Amy Banka, Drexel University; James Allen, College of DuPage; and Stacey Donohue, Central Oregon Community College.

Kim Stallings
University of North Carolina at Charlotte

Pre-Quest: A Map and a Compass

Begin with a *Question*: What Is the Quest?

> Only the educated are free.
> —Epictetus

No matter when you find yourself pursuing a higher education, whether you enroll straight out of high school, in your mid-twenties after a few years in the working world, or as a mature adult, your time spent in college will change you. The course you are enrolled in right now will change you. This textbook will change you.

College is a type of gateway experience: a *rite of passage*. Every culture has rites of passage. In Margaret Mead's *Coming of Age in Samoa*, she points out that all people, regardless of culture, come to this sort of gateway experience as adults and begin to look beyond themselves. They awaken to the rest of society. This awakening is a time to celebrate their gifts, their potentials, to look for ways to fit into their community, and come to grips with how to make their lives richer and how to make the world a better place. That's where you find yourself now. And this class, this textbook, and the journey you are about to take—the Quest—all of these are a part of *your* gateway.

Mental, Moral, and Physical Powers

Education is not just a branch, system, or stage of instruction, as we often think of it; education is *training by which people learn and develop and use their mental, moral, and physical powers*. Education is not just about college; it's about your life.

Your education did not begin when you attended orientation and registered for classes. Your education began the moment you were born. Everyone in your life is a teacher, every experience an open book. *College is another opportunity for experience.* It is a place, a moment in your life, designed in such a way that education becomes your *focus*. It is a place and a moment that prepares you to live your life as a thinking, feeling, and pro-active member of the community.

College gives you the time, space, and opportunity to open your mind and discover the world that came before you, explore the world that spins around you now, and imagine the potential for a world to come (and your place in that world). This course and this textbook provide strategies to help you question, analyze, and understand

1

the world around you, strategies for discovery and exploration and the creation of ideas that will make an impact.

Don't be surprised if this concept of education sounds important and challenging. It is, and it should be challenging. But if you believe that education is a key that opens the world for your past, present, and future, and if you believe that you can and should participate in the shape and direction of that world, then everything you experience in college, in this classroom, and beyond takes on a new level of importance. Your goal, your personal Quest, will be to learn and question, to grow and change, to think and rethink, to develop and use your mental, moral, and physical powers to make your life and your world a better place.

Developing Critical and Civic Literacy

As you begin this course, as you read this textbook, you are not simply fulfilling a general education requirement; you are beginning a Quest. A Quest is a pursuit, a search. With this textbook as your guide, you are embarking on a Quest in the pursuit of *critical* and *civic literacy*—your gateways to those mental, moral, and physical powers.

Most often, when we hear about literacy, it is in terms of the written word alone, a level of reading and writing sufficient for functioning in everyday life (also known as functional literacy). But there are many different kinds of literacy, all of which have to do with functioning in a particular environment for a particular purpose. Critical literacy moves us beyond the written word and opens up to include just about any situation you may encounter. Civic literacy is an extension of critical literacy. Together, these two types of literacies enable a broader experience of life.

Becoming critically literate means developing the ability to read not just the written word but all aspects of life and experience with a questioning eye. It is about thinking, digging below the surface and the simple answers we are often given by our friends, our parents, our schools, our government, and the media; it is about seeking understanding, meaning, and purpose. Critical literacy involves investigating, reflecting, and connecting; developing your own ideas; communicating those ideas in an effective way; and then putting those ideas into action. That's where civic literacy comes in.

Simply put, civic literacy is the level of functionality people need to participate effectively as citizens. Just as critical literacy is more than reading words—it is reading the world—civic literacy is more than simple acts such as understanding and obeying laws, voting, or filing taxes. Civic literacy is the shaping of community through the empowerment of the individual.

Being civically literate means that you are informed about the world around you, the social issues that persist in society. It means that you have a critical understanding of those issues and that you have the tools and strategies to take action, to address those issues, to work with others in the community, and to instigate change.

The pursuit of critical and civic literacy is the Quest you are beginning today with this textbook. The strategies and skills you learn and practice will help you to succeed not just in this course but in the rest of your academic career and all other aspects of your life. Critical and civic literacy are the keys to a life fully lived.

The Quest

Quest: Reading the World and Arguing for Change is designed to help you become critically and civically literate; to guide you as you examine values, assumptions, and ideologies; and then help you link that examination to your own experiences and ultimately become active in making change and shaping society.

There are common strategies you may use to help you along the way as you become more conscious of your journey and more purposeful in your direction. As you grow and discover, you may experiment and collect an *inventory of strategies and tools,* an array of choices to make and directions to take as you learn to read critically, think critically, and communicate your ideas effectively. This textbook provides you with those tools and strategies. It is a map to guide you through your Quest.

Critical and civic literacy are really just unique ways of approaching life and living an active experience of the world. They are a *process* that involves analysis and response, synthesis and sharing, growth, development, communication, and reflection. For our purposes, this process can be divided into three interconnected pathways that are vitally connected through the act of writing: *critical reading, critical thinking,* and *conversation.*

Critical Reading.   Critical and civic literacy require that we learn to *read the world around us,* so everything becomes text: all forms of media are text (magazines, newspapers, television shows, songs, movies, photographs, and works of art), events unfolding are text, people are text, and experiences are text. Critical reading involves the use of mostly informal writing strategies for analyzing and questioning. Once we learn to read the world with a critical eye, we begin to see how complex the world really is, but in the midst of that complexity, we also begin to see the *possibilities.*

Critical Thinking.   Thinking critically about what we read—*discovering and exploring our thoughts and feelings, making connections to our knowledge and experiences*— is the next step in the development of critical and civic literacy, and writing continues to be a vital tool. As we begin to respond in writing to what we see and hear, read and experience, we dig deeper for understanding. We look at the world and ourselves and reflect on what we know, what we don't know, and what we need to learn. We ask questions, seek answers, and thoughtfully begin to formulate our own opinions. We see potential for change, and we seek ways to fulfill that potential.

Joining the Conversation.   Reading the world and exploring our thoughts and feelings is the foundation of the Quest. The real journey begins as we share our discoveries, express our ideas, join the official conversation, and take action to implement change. Through our critical reading and thinking, we discover ideas that we want to share with the world. We feel the drive to communicate, the need to take action, and so we need strategies for effective communication, strategies that showcase our unique voice and ideas. Sometimes these strategies involve speaking, sometimes illustrating, and *always* these strategies involve some sort of writing.

It is through the development of effective reasoning and communication skills that you will not simply sit by and be impacted by your experiences, but you will become active and *make a true and lasting impact* on the world around you. And *that* is what critical and civic literacy are all about.

Getting Started

A Map and a Compass

Because critical and civic literacy are grounded in the real world, in real-life events and situations, this book begins by asking you to look closely at several significant events. As you begin your Quest, you will read articles about one or more different events that were heavily covered by the media. Hopefully, you will find among them a text that engages you, that piques your curiosity, that moves, angers, or inspires you. This will become your *topical focus* as you continue on your journey to critical and civic literacy.

As mentioned before, all of this exploration, questioning, and discovery is part of a process that requires strategy. The strategies you learn, practice, and master as you complete your Quest are strategies that you may use in many situations you encounter throughout your academic career and in your day-to-day life. Each strategy is modeled in this text and typically involves some type of writing. This textbook and these models are your map, examples to follow as you progress through your own personal Quest. Your topical focus will be *your compass:* it will provide you with your own unique direction.

You will soon discover that from each event, many social issues arise. After you have explored initial news reports, you will investigate various historical issues (issues with a past, a present, and a future) that continue to impact our society. In each part of your personal Quest, you will explore your event and the issues connected to it from many different angles. Through this process, you will become a sort of quasi-expert on the multiple aspects of your topic. When all is said and done, you will know

- how various social issues relate to the event and other events like it.
- the history of this type of event, the issues connected to it, and why they remain a problem.
- who these issues effect and how.
- how these issues have been addressed, what has worked, and what has not worked.

More than that, you will know what you believe to be true and *why.* It is from this *position of knowing* that you can *develop your own ideas* for tackling these issues. You can discover how to make a difference, how to make a change, and *how to use written communication as a powerful tool for education, understanding, and transformation.*

A Final Word

Remember, though your Quest is a personal journey, *you are always a part of something bigger:*

- You are a part of your classroom community.
- You are studying an event and issues that are bigger than place and time.
- Your journey begins with a discussion of one event, but many events are connected by the same issues, and many people are involved in and impacted by these events and issues.
- Many voices have spoken out in response to these events and issues in many different forums.
- Many efforts have been made to address the problems that come out of these issues, and many ideas have been shared.
- *They are still issues because those problems have not been solved.*

A conversation is going on all around you: You can probably hear it now—the whispering, sometimes the shouting. And there is silence, too. In those moments of silence, there is a place for your voice, a *need* for your voice. You can make a difference. You *will* make a difference. Just by taking the first step on your journey, you've already set a change in motion. The world is waiting for you.

Let's begin.

PART ONE

Reading Critically and Responding Thoughtfully: Establishing a Context

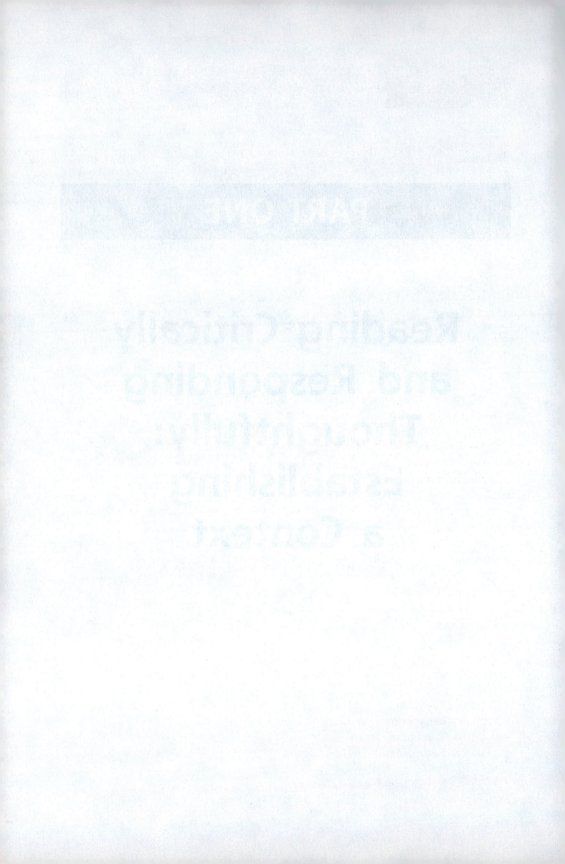

1

Multimedia Reading Strategies: Exploring an Event

Begin with a *Question*: What Happened?

"Did you hear?!" That's how it often begins—with three simple words, we're hooked; our interest is piqued. Someone, maybe a friend or family member, half-exclaims, half-whispers, *"Did you hear?!"* inviting us into a situation, calling us to become involved to one extent or another in something that is happening in the world around us.

"Did you hear?!"

"No, what happened?" We're naturally curious animals. We want to know *what happened*—give us the scoop, the details.

Sometimes that information comes to us through our own experience. We are a part of an event, participating on the inside. Other times, we are on the outside, to one degree or another, observers. Sometimes, as observers, we receive information firsthand: we see it for ourselves. Other times, we get the scoop secondhand: someone else tells us of his or her experience, or the information travels through the local grapevine (someone heard it from someone else *who said*). Most often, when an event is not a personal experience, we get our news through some sort of media (print, television, radio, or the Internet).

Print media has been a crucial part of society for centuries. The first daily newspaper was printed in London in 1702, and until the advent of television, print media was our primary source for information on local, national, and world events. But then television entered our world, and everything changed with the first reoccurring newscast in 1951.

Within the last decade or so, technology has given us the gift (or curse) of live coverage of events. No longer do we have to wait for the news to travel across the wires and make it into the morning edition of the newspaper or onto the six o'clock news. Television crews take us immediately to the scene for breaking news so that we may watch the drama unfold in real time (via satellite on television or the Internet or some other digital media device). The cameras get so close to the action and stay on the scene so long that we feel a part of even the most remote happenings. For better or for worse, this immediate news coverage draws us into the moment, up close and personal, live and in color. We stay with a developing story as the event unfolds, and often for several days afterwards. We can't help but be affected by what we see.

Is Seeing Believing?

You've probably heard comments like the following: *It's in print. It's right here in black and white, so it must be accurate. Do my ears deceive me? I know what I heard! She said so! A picture paints a thousand words. The camera doesn't lie.*

Once upon a time, philosophers like Plato and Aristotle believed in the possibility of absolute truths. In any given situation, there was a right, there was a wrong, and that was it—there was no middle ground. Thankfully, many great minds have since realized that the concept of truth is a bit more complex. In this world of ours, we recognize that there are few absolutes. Sometimes our ears *do* deceive us, and seeing *is not always* believing. We understand that in any situation, information is filtered through the lens of our experience, and there are many perspectives other than our own to consider. This is also true when contemplating the information provided by the media.

As for the stories that we read in print media, such as newspapers or magazines, an event is witnessed (or investigated) by someone who records whatever information is available to him or her and reports that information to us. The story is filtered through witnesses, through the writer's mind, through the push to meet a deadline, through the editing process, and then distilled to us in a very particular format.

This process of filtering is even more dramatic when we are witnessing a visual record of events unfolding. The media picks up on those events, captures them through the magic of technology, and brings them right into our livingrooms. From the safety and comfort of our homes, we become witnesses to history. But have you ever looked at the world through a camera lens? How much of any event is captured through a single lens? How big (wide, deep) is any picture that we see? We only see what the camera sees—never more, sometimes less. What of any event is included? What is excluded? And who decides which angle the camera will capture?

Sometimes we get so caught up in the images we see on television and the information provided in other forms of media that we forget we are witnessing a limited vision (or a collection of visions) of an event unfolding. The specific lens filters those events to us according to decisions made by someone working behind the scenes (often many people). What we read in the newspaper or see on television—even a firsthand account—*is never the whole story.* Every record is filtered through the lens of experience, and that process of filtering is inherently flawed.

The Big Picture

The *whole story* is complex. It has a history. The whole story includes everything that came before an event, the many different perspectives involved in a particular moment, and everything that happens afterwards. The whole story is like a web—a multilayered, interconnected maze of experiences. It's not something we can navigate our way through in a front-page headline or a sound bite. Unfortunately, the information we absorb seldom gets past that surface level of any event. We're informed through a series of snapshots, quick glimpses.

Why is it important to recognize (and appreciate) these media snapshots for what they are? It might not matter if all we were interested in was entertainment. But the news is much more than entertainment. The media educates us, connects us to the world, and keeps us informed. It is a record of events that have a real and lasting impact on our lives. It is history in the making.

Making Change

Here's a saying you might be familiar with: *History repeats itself.*

Is that true? *Does* history repeat itself? If so, why? Why do we see the same sorts of problems in the world today (in one form or another) that we saw last year, ten years ago, twenty-five, even fifty or a hundred years ago? What connects these events? *Are* there any common threads that the media sound bites are missing? And if it's true that history repeats itself, can that repetition, that cycle of events unfolding, be altered? Can things ever really change? And does it matter? Do the sometimes-remote events covered by the media really have an influence on *our* lives?

The simple answer is yes. And the only way for us to break the cycle of repetition is to focus our attention on the information the media (and other sources) provides us, listen carefully to what we are being told, and take a closer look. We have to learn to *read the world around us,* to ask questions, to seek answers. We have to develop an understanding of how our observations of the events experienced by others and the events we witness through the media affect us—how something that happened to someone else, in another state, on the other side of the world, even ten years ago, might impact *our* lives or *our* future.

Nothing changes if we never look below the surface. The surface does not hold understanding. In order to understand and change, we have to look carefully at an event, we have to understand what led up to a moment, we have to explore what happened from different angles, and we have to look at what changed as the result of that moment's passing.

Reading the World

In the Pre-Quest, we discussed various aspects of critical and civic literacy. We know that becoming critically literate means approaching life and living with a particular vision. It is about thinking, digging below the surface of the simple answers we are often given; it is about seeking understanding, meaning, and purpose in our lives. Critical literacy involves investigating, reflecting, and connecting, developing our own ideas, and communicating those ideas in an effective way. This critical examination leads us to the threshold of civic literacy and the steps we must take to put our ideas into action, to instigate change in the world. The first step in becoming criti-cally—and ultimately civically—literate is learning to read, not just the written word but also all aspects of life and experience.

Window on the World

Do you remember how you felt when you first learned to read a book? How did this happen? What process did you go through?

You already knew a lot about spoken language and how language helps you to ex-perience the world around you. Then you were introduced to the alphabet—the keys to the written form of our language. You learned to recognize symbols and to connect them to sounds you had heard and that you yourself had made. Then you put those symbols together, those sounds together, to form words. You recognized them as *more* sounds you had heard and made, and suddenly those abstract symbols had meaning. You began to understand how they represented every aspect of your life and your experience. By recognizing those symbols and connecting them to things in your world, you were given a window on the world. You moved beyond the limi-tations of your physical world and experiences that day. Life opened up for you, and your real education began.

Most children are excited to learn to read, but not all of us remain so excited. Not everyone is an avid reader (of the written word). But we can all be avid and active readers of life and experience.

In much the same way that learning to read written language—and maybe even in a bigger way—learning to read the world around you will open up your experience of life. Your life will become bigger and richer, your place in this world more pur-poseful and meaningful.

Learning to Read Again

In terms of critical literacy, everything is text: the images we see, the conversations in which we participate, the print media we read, and all forms of entertainment we enjoy. EVERYTHING IS TEXT. In *this* textbook, we approach the concept of read-ing in a very broad way, and it may seem a little strange to you at first.

Previously, you may have thought of reading only in terms of the written word. I want you to expand that definition and understand reading to include all forms of ex-perience. *Every situation in which we gather information may be read.* In this new way of understanding reading, it may be defined as the process of focusing on a source of information, whatever form that source may take, and examining, understanding, and evaluating what we see or hear or experience in that moment. This is a process that requires purpose and strategy.

No matter how information is delivered to us, as critical thinkers and active learn-ers, our initial purpose is to understand and then to evaluate what we see or hear.

Understanding a text, any text, requires us to look closely at the information pro-vided, to somehow decode and translate that information into the language of our own experience. This decoding and translation involves various strategies and tools that help us to question the information we gather (and the source from which it came) and make connections to other aspects of our lives and experience. We have to judge the credibility of the information and understand how it fits with what we al-ready know. We have to recognize what we do not know, and then decide how to seek answers, to fill in the gaps of our knowledge.

The Process of Reading the World

In terms of academia and your purpose in this class, the experiences you read and study are in some ways artificially contrived. The events on which you focus happened in the past, and *pieces* of those events have been selected, captured, and presented here for you to examine. For many reasons, in this and other academic courses, the texts you study are primarily print texts. But the processes you learn and practice here are meant to translate beyond the classroom, into and beyond your college ca-reer, and into the big picture of your life. Like any other experience, *this text* is only part of the story.

In this or any other situation, the process of reading begins with a conscious effort to focus on the information you are gathering. First, you must develop awareness that *no moment, no event, is truly isolated.* Every experience in life is connected in some way to everything that came before and to everything that will come after it. Once you are aware of the interconnectedness of our experiences, you can focus your attention on a single event and immediately understand that there is more going on than meets the eye.

Tools for Success: Multimedia Reading Strategies

Before you can understand anything close to the whole story surrounding an event, you must examine reports of what happened. News reports, as we discussed earlier in this chapter, take many forms and are delivered in a variety of ways. Regardless of how you find out about an event, it is important that you open your mind and take in all of the details: *you must become a scrupulous observer.* You must learn and prac-tice strategies to decode or translate what you see and experience, strategies for re-stating or recreating an event with signs or symbols that you understand. This process of examination, restating, or re-creating helps you make connections to what you al-ready know. By recognizing what you know, you also begin to recognize *what you do not know,* to see information gaps, and those gaps will raise questions for you. A big part of critical literacy is *learning to ask questions* and ultimately *seeking answers* to those questions. That's where the real adventure begins.

Reading to examine a text requires that you *actively observe* the content of a text (and remember, we are talking about text in a very broad sense of the word) and question that content. While there are many different strategies available to you, no matter what type of text you are reading, your examination should probably begin with pen in hand (and a piece of paper nearby).

Recording

To begin your examination of a text, make some sort of written record of the surface details. Be careful to avoid injecting your response into these surface details. Stay focused on recording what the text is communicating. Remember, recording as a reading strategy does not include any subjective commentary. It should be as objective and unbiased as possible. This strategy helps you to process and fully understand the information provided by any text. Following are some recording strategies demonstrated later in this chapter:

- **Summary:** Restating in your own words (in complete sentences and usually in paragraph form) the information provided by the author of a text.
- **Listing:** A brief written record of the surface details of a text (usually visual or aural media).
- **Transcription:** A verbatim written record of some form of aural media, multimedia, or interactive media.

By recording the surface details of any type of media, you can thoroughly process the information communicated by a source, and you can better articulate your understanding of that source in your own words. By articulating what you understand about a given source, you can more easily identify *what you do not understand*. With this knowledge, you can formulate good questions about what the text shows you and what it does not show you.

Questioning

A synonym for *to examine* is *to question*. In order to thoroughly examine a text, you must read with a critical eye and ask questions of the text. You begin this process of examination, as we covered in the previous section, by recording what you observe about an event or any source of information. By looking closely at the information included in a text, what you see on the surface, you begin to notice what you do not see, what you have not been shown or told. The missing information should raise questions for you: *Why hasn't the text explained this? What happened next? How did this come about? Who said such-and-such? What does all of this mean?* Once a text raises questions for you, the next step is to seek answers to those questions, to respond to the text by filling in those information gaps.

Remember, as you question a text, make a list of your questions, but do not attempt to answer them right away. As you decide the value of your questions in terms of your overall learning process, consider the following: Would knowing the answers to your questions bring you closer to an understanding of the whole story? Why weren't your questions answered in this particular source (this might have to do with purpose)?

Responding

All texts speak to us: they communicate information, they raise questions for us, they inspire a response. In order to thoroughly examine and process a text, we must engage with and speak back to the text. As a text calls, we respond, and *a conversation begins.*

Responding to a text involves answering questions raised by the text and exploring our thoughts and feelings while searching for meaning communicated by the text. There are many different strategies for responding. The type of strategy you use depends in part on your purpose for reading a text. In any case, your response should be honest and thorough. The goal of response is to move beyond the surface of a text and closer to understanding the message communicated by the text and its significance in terms of the whole story. Some response strategies include

- Dialoguing
- Free-response writing
- Simple research (or Googling)
- Discussion

Each strategy is covered explicitly in the following section.

Multimedia Reading Strategies Walk-Through

Because each type of media is unique in its presentation of information, our strategies for recording, questioning, and responding will vary according to the format of the media we are reading. Before moving on, let's take a look at an example of how these reading strategies are employed with each type of media: *print media, static visual media, aural media, multimedia,* and *interactive media.*

Print Media

If you are examining some sort of printed text (a newspaper or magazine article, a professional or scholarly essay), begin recording by making notes that summarize *in your own words* the content of the text (simply restate the information provided by the author).

Take, for example, this excerpt from the article by Mike Anton, "School War Zone" (full text is located in Event Casebook One):

> The quiet neighborhood surrounding the school exploded into chaos, with paramedics tending to victims and police surrounding the grounds. Terrified parents rushed to the school, looking for their children. Students sought refuge in nearby houses.

A record of this print media (a summary in your own words) might look something like this:

> Paramedics, police, and anxious parents encircled the school as students ran to safety in the surrounding neighborhood.

This sentence objectively sums up the content of the original paragraph without the supporting, descriptive details.

After making a record of a print source, begin questioning that source. Following are some questions you might ask of print media:

What does this particular sentence or detail mean?
What parts of the story were not covered in this source?
Is the information provided accurate?
What is the source of the information?
Who is the author?
Where was this published?
When was this published?
What was the primary purpose of this piece of information?
Who was the intended audience?

Look again at the paragraph from the article by Mike Anton. Some questions to ask of that text might be

Were there a lot of injured victims outside the school?
Why were the police simply surrounding the school—why didn't they go in to stop this massacre?
Did people in the surrounding neighborhood open their houses to the students?
How many students were able to escape?
How did parents locate their children?

Once you have made a record of your print source and you have questioned that source, you must respond to the source. There are many different strategies for response, and any of them may be used with a print source to express thoughts and feelings, to answer questions, and to move closer to an understanding of meaning communicated by the text. One that is especially useful when dealing with print media sources is *dialoguing*.

If you need an organized way of responding to a text—particularly if you are preparing to write an informative or argumentative paper using the text as support—then a dialogue is a useful response strategy.

To create a dialogue with a text, first draw a horizontal line down the center of a piece of paper. On the left-hand side at the top, write *Information from the Text*. On the right-hand side at the top, write *My Responses to the Text*. Then, in the left-hand column, record your questions. In the right-hand column, explore your thoughts and feelings and possible answers to your questions. Most dialogues (also known as double-entry journals) look something like the following:

Information from the Text	My Responses to the Text
Why were the police simply surrounding the school—why didn't they go in to stop this massacre?	This is one of the things that bothers me the most about the entire event. Police officers are sworn to protect and serve—but they waited HOURS before entering the high school that day. Why? I want to know how they could do that and live with themselves while kids were dying?

When used appropriately, a dialogue can help you organize your thoughts and generate a well-structured response to a text.

Practicum

Read the following interview with Richard Patrick. Record in your own words the main ideas presented in the article, question the article, and create a dialogue with the text. How does this process enable you to develop a more thorough understanding of the text? What did you discover about the text through this reading that you may have failed to notice had you read without this process?

Interview with an Artist

The Artist: Richard Patrick

In January 2003, Richard Patrick agreed to answer a few questions for me about the song lyrics I planned to include in this textbook. I knew from reading past interviews that Mr. Patrick was a thoughtful, humorous person, and I was excited that he agreed to speak with me. I approached the interview with several concise questions, determined not to impose on his good will any more than necessary. But I was in for a wonderful surprise.

What began as a simple fifteen-minute question-and-answer session turned into a two-and-a-half hour conversation. I walked away with twenty pages of notes, and about four weeks later, a distinct impression had formed in my mind. I sifted back through my notes and began to write. The following is what I knew I had to say.

"I'm Free, and Freedom Tastes of Reality": A Conversation with Richard Patrick

Richard Patrick is someone best known for his piercing screams in the spotlight—not his piercing intellectual insights. Though he *has* insights and has always voiced them, they are often misrepresented in media soundbites and come across as bombastic and outrageous quips. Consequently, to interviewers, to the music press, and to the fans and the general public, Richard Patrick is known as the fast-talking, hard-living, sometimes outrageous front man for the rock band Fil*ter* ("Richie needs attention in 'A' lounge! Let's GO people!!!" from Fil*ter*, *The Amalgamut*, Online Amalgamut Exclusives).

I have read many articles spanning the years between the time Richard was a guitarist for the band NIN (Nine Inch Nails) and the present. Based on those interviews, I have certain expectations of *who* and *how* Richard will be, in spite of my knowing that media images are constructed; they are masks—certainly not the real deal. But about twenty minutes into the interview, I find I have to throw out my notes. I shouldn't be surprised that my expectations were—not just incorrect—they were *wrong*. But I am surprised. I am caught off guard by the breadth and depth of our conversation (and it is a *conversation* rather than an interview).

"We are not smarter than nature. We have to learn," he tells me. "Nature is the most powerful force in the universe. When we fight nature in any way, when we impose our will and distort the natural order of things, when we refuse to learn and grow, we become unnatural. And one way or another, nature is always going to win. Knowledge and learning and growing—these *are* nature." This is Life According to Richard Patrick, or Richard Patrick's Life 101, if you will.

Don't get me wrong. Richard *is* fast-talking. Ideas come to him at light-speed, and he freely expresses those ideas. But as he is talking about the likes of Stephen Hawking, black holes, the Rape of Nanking, or the impending war in the Middle East, don't make the mistake of thinking he's off in his own little world, not paying attention. Even when he's in the midst of some deep political or philosophical rant ("I like to expound," he says with a soft chuckle), he's watching, he's listening, and he's taking in everything around him. Learning, as he says, from every possible avenue.

"What I really appreciate is what I learn from life. And I learn from everything I can, in every single way I possibly can—whether it's television, whether it's a teacher, whether it's a book, the media, anything I can learn from, I'm gonna use. Because that, to me, the sum total of ideas, thoughts, whether they're about philosophy, history, science, or religion—whatever—if it's going to make me more knowledgeable? THAT'S my higher power."

On this day, Richard is concerned about Pete Townsend, the legendary rock guitarist, co-founder of The Who and creator of the classic rock-opera *Tommy*, arrested on suspicion of possessing indecent images of children. Townsend has acknowledged using an Internet Web site advertising child pornography, but said he is not a pedophile and was only doing research for an autobiography dealing with his own childhood sexual abuse.

As our discussion of the Townsend case and the prospect of Internet policing intensifies, Richard pauses—hesitates. He wants to be sure I understand where he's coming from. "This is a tricky issue to talk about, you know? Because I'm *not* saying child porn should be accessible—*I don't* think it should be accessible. I think it's a horrible thing and I think children should be nurtured and loved and taken care of. I just don't like the way the police are going about this whole thing. It's a witch hunt."

Police arrested Townsend under the Protection of Children Act after executing two searches at a business and a home outside London where he lives. According to authorities, computers were taken from the home and were being examined for evidence. Townsend has said that on one occasion he used a credit card to download pornographic images as part of his research and that he reported what he saw to police. Allegedly, that initial report caused police to monitor Townsend's Internet usage.

Taking a long drag off a cigarette—one of his few remaining vices—Richard sighs: "You know, it's scary. I thought the Internet was supposed to be this big open thing. I mean, *what if* he just wanted to learn what something was? That's what the Internet is for—it's this enormous source of information."

It's easy to understand why this topic is so important to Richard. He values knowledge above all else. From Richard's perspective, restricting access to information is the denial of a fundamental human right. Access to information means freedom.

"The reason why I love America so much and the reason why I love at least the ideology of freedom is because it's the most natural thing," Richard explains.

"I have the raw footage from the R. Budd Dwyer (the Pennsylvania state treasurer who committed suicide on live television in 1987)," he tells me, placing this debate within the context of his own experience. "That's what brought about the song 'Hey Man, Nice Shot.' What if I went to some site just for information and—boom—somebody could be knocking at my door."

"You know, I don't like seeing snuff films—and that's really what the R. Budd Dwyer thing is—it's a snuff film. It's not like I want to sit back and look at it for pleasure. But you know, I looked at it out of curiosity; I looked at it for information, and I wrote about it. Back then, we had all the controversy—people asking, 'why are you writing about R. Budd Dwyer?' Well, why would you write a song about Hitler? Why would you write a *textbook* about Hitler?"

That begs an interesting question. Why *would* anyone write a song about Hitler or a textbook about Hitler—or the Columbine High School shooting, for that matter (which, for me at least, seems to be an underlying subtext to this conversation)? It's a question I've been asked over and over since I first proposed the idea for this textbook. Why concentrate on a violent event in human history, such as the R. Budd Dwyer suicide or the Columbine tragedy? The answer for both of us seems simple: to gain knowledge and understanding and to communicate that knowledge or understanding to a wider audience. Conversation, the free exchange of information and ideas, freedom of speech—these are things we both value on a deeply personal level.

"You don't take someone's freedom away from them. Free thought, intellectual thought, that's what nature is all about."

Much of Richard's conversation comes back to this theme of nature and what is natural versus what is unnatural. For Richard, a quest for knowledge and under-standing is a part of the natural order of life. An extension of that quest is the desire to communicate with others. How that communication takes place, the form it takes, will manifest in different ways for everyone. For me, it manifests through my writing and my teaching, my work with students. For Richard, the drive to communicate knowledge manifests through his creativity and his music.

Describing his creative process, Richard explains: "We're talking about the microphone—that's my book, you know. That's my interface. That's how I'm going to get my thoughts and emotions across. I'm using my body, my voice—my lyrics are just a small part of it. It's bizarre, because this stuff starts off in my head. I see it in my head and then my fingers get involved. So now, it's me, my brain, my fingers, and my voice—and then my ability to program and record all the instruments. All that becomes a part of the process—the creating. I have knowledge of all that stuff, so now I'm using all this knowledge and all this—*who I am*—to make this song."

For Richard, making music, the creative process, all goes back to the quest for knowledge: "by applying what I know and always seeking more knowledge—learning—I'm bettering myself. That's what's important in this life," he explains. Creating music is "the culmination of who I am as a person at a given time. You know, some people pick up a guitar and they don't know what they're doing. I'm that guy who can pick up a guitar—I don't really know how to play it, but I know how to make you feel something with it."

Of course, I'm curious how this successful musician/artist can claim that he doesn't know how to play the very instrument he's best known for playing. But it turns out that Richard *doesn't* know how to play the guitar in the conventional sense; he is a self-taught musician. He doesn't read music. In fact, he has never taken a music lesson in his life. He plays quite naturally—by instinct and intuition. For Richard, expressing himself through music is a completely natural extension of who he is and of the learning process: "Basically I'm trying to keep the pen and paper out of it. I don't want a lot of time to second-guess it; I just want to keep it close to my soul—to my identity."

He laughs, his voice full of wonder: "It's *amazing* to be able to play a guitar and literally kind of play upon this emotional, once again visceral, kind of sensory experience that people have. Hearing something and that emotional impact it has on you— you know, when you hear a violin and it's beautiful, playing Mozart. It's unbelievable to be able to control that, you know, that sense of music, that emotional *ahhhh . . . god, there it is!* It's wonderful to woo people into feeling something that you feel."

"And that's why I love America so much," he declares. Again, we're back to the idea of freedom. "If you have a good idea and you wanna be heard, there is a way."

Being heard: this is something my students struggle with, something I've struggled with at various times throughout *my* life (as a teenager, as a young woman in a male-dominated field, as a Democrat in a largely Republican community—the list could go on and on). And it's a subject that comes up quite frequently in connection with the Columbine High School shootings.

Eric Harris and Dylan Klebold, the Columbine shooters, were purported to be a part of a group of outcasts in their high school, shunned and abused by their more popular peers. Kids within such a fringe group often feel misunderstood, disenfranchised, and voiceless because their experiences are not mainstream. Within the medical community, it is common knowledge that when kids feel something intensely but do not have a healthy outlet for expression, stress builds up and comes out in other, unhealthy ways—especially through anger and aggression. As William Pollack, PhD, codirector of the Center for Men at McLean Hospital/Harvard Medical School, says, "When we don't let boys cry tears, some will cry bullets." Some speculate that Eric and Dylan fit this pattern. They didn't feel like they had a voice, but they had something they were determined to communicate or express, one way or another.

But this feeling of "voicelessness" and the drive to communicate isn't confined to boys or teens. I tell Richard that one of the biggest frustrations my students feel, and maybe most people feel in general, is that their voice doesn't matter—their vote doesn't count, so to speak. He responds: "You have to really persevere. If you wanna be heard, you have to find a way to be heard. You don't have to kill people to do it. You don't have to take people's civil rights away from them."

He recalls a few stories of his hell-raising teen years and says, "You know, when I was 17 to 21, no one took me seriously. And a lot of it had to do with the fact that I hadn't lived long enough, I hadn't learned enough, and I didn't have enough experience. But this is something that happens to every generation. It's something we all experience.

"So, if you have something to say—it's frustrating—but don't give up. You don't have to sit there and go 'no one's listening to me.' If you want to say something and you want people to take you seriously, you have to find out ways to say it. You have to find the right avenue to communicate. You know, it wasn't always easy, but I found my way. I do it with a guitar, with my singing voice. I do it with my lyrics, and I do it with interviews."

Still, it's difficult for many people to articulate what they think and feel. In fact, one thing that artists do for us is help us express what we can't on our own; they give voice to what we're feeling. That is how we connect with music; it's how music makes an impact on our lives. And Richard's fans will readily testify to the impact his music has made on their lives.

While researching this article, I joined one of the most active Filter fan sites, the FOC (Filter Online Community), created by the fans and frequented by Richard himself (note: the FOC became the official Filter message board in May 2004). This is an online environment where fans gather to discuss the music that Richard creates, as well as many other issues.

According to a long-time fan, the FOC started as an e-mail discussion group to go along with a Filter fan-created Web site known as Tinseltown. Eventually, that Web site folded, but the e-mail group stayed intact. However, that system was faulty and didn't allow for much group or community interaction between the fans, so the decision was made to create an online bulletin board.

The online community of Fil*ter* was still small at the time, but made up of fans from all around the world. That online community is no longer small and continues to grow and draw new members.

What struck me immediately about the FOC is that the people who post there are quite thoughtful and articulate. Richard's fans seem to share his quest for knowledge and understanding and information. And they have a deep respect and admiration for Richard Patrick, the man whose music has brought them together. The FOC board is filled with stories of how Richard has impacted the lives of the fans:

StoR (Chels, Scotland):

His music is the soundtrack to my life.

badassrockchick (Linda, Sweden):

I remember vividly sitting on my bed at my friend's house listening to ToR [*Title of Record*, Fil*ter*'s second album] at night before going to bed . . . bawling my eyes out to "I'm not the only one" . . . made me realize that others felt the pain too . . . that I wasn't alone . . . that there was a way to survive the hurt. . . . Because he did, Richie did, and lived to tell and share it with me . . . with all of us! And I admire him greatly for having the courage to write those songs and putting them on an album for the whole world to hear! To face his own pain in that way! Some of the lyrics Richie has written have made me shake my head in amazement because it felt like he was sitting in there, in my mind, taking notes.

RichFactWebmistress (Allison, Minnesota):

Fil*ter*'s music makes me think, too. It makes me think about us as human beings and about how we act towards one another. It lets me see things in ways I hadn't thought about before. Songs like "Columind" made me see a bit more into the Columbine incident, more than the media's spin on it or anything like that. "The Missing" made me think and feel about 9/11. "Dose" made me think about the times when I've been pressured not just by religious folks but by others trying to convince me to think like them. "Cancer" made me think about how we treat the earth and those around us.

Cynic_Elle (Laura, Canada):

As someone who became existentialist at a young age, I feel fortunate to have found Fil*ter*, whose album *Short Bus* was written with many existentialist topics. *The Amalgamut* revisited some of these ideas, on God, Religion, and Society. When it becomes frustrating that those around me don't understand the philosophies that I'm grappling with in my own mind, I feel fortunate that I can listen to Fil*ter*. Richard Patrick is empathetic; he tells me that I'm Not the Only One.

Not only does Richard Patrick endorse the FOC, he's an active member of the online community himself. The FOC board is filled with a real and honest conversation between the fans and Richard. Responding to a post in which fans expressed their gratitude for his frequent visits to the board, Richard replied,

> The pleasure is all mine . . . this board is important to me because it allows me to stay connected to the people that allow me to write and produce music. The people that hang out at this board are why I'm here . . . on the planet. . . . So keep posting and I'll keep coming back.

This is something I have never seen before, this level of personal interaction between a celebrity-status person and his or her fan base. It seems important on many levels. Like other artists, Richard offers his fans music they can relate to, but unlike other artists, through his participation in this online community, he gives the fans a forum in which *they have a voice,* and he lets them know that they are heard. As another fan and member of the FOC posted:

Iennix (Jarrod, Washington, DC):

> There is something to be said about an artist who keeps in contact with their fans not only on his website, but through the fans' own meeting places, and will answer their questions, take their concerns into thought, and more importantly joke with them—be real with them, realize that in the end it's simply two people sharing the same space in time.

And I have discovered that the interaction between Richard and his fans isn't confined to this community. Even Richard's/Filter's official Web site is run by a fan—a fan Richard has welcomed into his life as a friend and a sort of apprentice. Their connection is an interesting story.

When Filter's first hit single, "Hey Man, Nice Shot," hit the airwaves, Adam Hubka was instantly hooked. After noticing that the band's online presence was limited, Adam started a Web site. A few years later, he received a call at his home from Richard Patrick: "Richard asked me to run his new official site, and it completely blew me away. To think that the leader of my favorite band personally called me!"

Richard elaborates: "Back in '96 or '97, Adam Hubka started the Unofficial Filter Web site. Because of his hard work and determination, his site became bigger and more visited than my record company's Web site. When I figured that out, I got in touch with Adam, and now he runs the Official Filter Web site. I'd rather have my fans run things than anything else."

From that point on, Richard Patrick became an enormous part of Adam's life: "From taking me on the road with them, being able to talk to him on the phone whenever I felt the need to call—and vice versa—to helping my own band (Dualesc, *through the floods, not with them*) record a demo at his personal studio—I am eternally grateful to him . . . how many other bands bring a fan into the fold like they've done for me?"

I wonder about—and can't help but feel impressed by—this freedom that Richard seems to embrace—the free exchange with his fans, the open communication through his music and through this online environment. While this openness is in conflict with my media-fueled expectations of someone in Richard's position, it fits quite naturally with this new picture I have of him and his general philosophy of life.

As I review my notes from the interview and draw this chapter to a close, I recall something eerily appropriate that Filter fan **Cynic_Elle/Laura** posted on the FOC bulletin board:

> Listening to Filter is like Tommy's awakening in the Who's rock opera: "I'm free, and freedom tastes of reality."

This seems to sum up so much of what I have learned about Richard Patrick.

When I began this interview, I believed I was speaking with a rock star, but as I wrap up, I am experiencing one of those *ahhhh . . . there it is* moments that Richard spoke about.

To call Richard a "star" is too easy. Speaking metaphorically, stars are distant lights, untouchable, unreachable. We gaze on them at a distance. But Richard is *real*. He certainly shines, but in a very human, touchable, reachable way. Of course, the distinction is that "Richard the Star" is a media-crafted persona—"Richard the Artist" is a true expression of who he is. But it's even more than that.

Great artists are all about knowledge and learning and growing. They show us things about life and the human experience—things about ourselves that we can't readily see on our own. They show us the best and the worst of who we are. They help us to see and understand. They are seekers, always examining life for meaning, always gathering information and knowledge, and communicating what they learn. They draw us into an exchange of ideas. They make us think.

Great artists are great teachers.

Ahhhh . . . there it is!

Richard Patrick is a *natural* teacher—someone who isn't formally trained in educational theory, but someone who values knowledge above all else, who naturally gives instruction to another, who shares knowledge, who causes others to understand.

"Our gift is the mind. Because we've got this gift, we have to use it." Richard tells me as our conversation draws to a close, "I'm this little blip and I get to make music, and within my little blip life, I've got to learn and grow. This is how I'm going to better myself—by learning and knowing and by applying what I know. I apply what I know with my music, by creating.

"Knowledge—it's the most important thing on this planet."

This is Richard Patrick's Life 101.

Class dismissed.

Static Visual Media

If you are examining *a static image* (such as a photograph, a cartoon, a drawing or painting), to create a record of that source, write a description of what you see on the surface. Describe familiar objects, colors, textures, and lines. Be descriptive without interjecting personal thoughts and feelings about the content of the image.

As an example, take a look at the Student Model Reading Journal located at the end of this chapter. Created in response to Mike Keefe's political cartoon, Eagle,

Sam's record is simple, yet thorough. She concentrated on the surface details of the drawing, successfully avoiding any subjective commentary. For instance, she recorded

> The eagle's wings are spread wide and arched upwards. It is standing on some type of dark ball. The eagle's brows are drawn together and its eyes are focused sharply on something in front of it.

Here she clearly describes the position of the eagle without interpreting for meaning.

After a record has been made, it is time to question the text. Some questions that might arise from the study of visual texts are

> Why this angle?
> Why this lens?
> Why these colors?
> Why this texture?
> Why these lines?
> Were any filters used?
> Was this image altered in any way?
> What do these elements mean?
> What do we not see?
> Who is the photographer or artist?
> Where was this published?
> When was this created?
> What was the primary purpose of this image?
> Who was the intended audience?

Turning once again to Sam's model journal entry, she studied the political cartoon and asked questions such as, *Why is an eagle used in this cartoon instead of something else that represents America? Why is the eagle perched on a ball? What is the ball?* The majority of her questions focused on an attempt to understand the meaning communicated by the cartoon.

Finally, after making a record and asking questions, it is time to respond to the text. If, after making a record of a source and questioning that source, you are confused or have some sort of highly charged emotional response to the source, you may need to explore your thoughts and feelings in more detail. In this situation, a *free-response writing* is useful. Because visual texts often evoke highly emotional responses for many of us, the *free-response* strategy works quite well (but any of the response strategies covered in this chapter may be used with a visual text; the strategy you choose to use depends largely on personal preference and the goals of a particular assignment).

To create a free-response, simply write freely about a text without worrying about any particular format or any audience other than yourself. Turn off your internal critic. Do not edit your self-expression—simply write. Let the words flow from your mind, through your pen, onto the paper. This strategy for thinking on paper is like writing in a personal journal or diary. Write for as long as you have something to say. Then stop and read your response and reflect. After reviewing your initial response, you might find it useful to continue with another free-response.

Unlike other response strategies, a free-response does not require much preparation. It can be very spontaneous. All you have to do is sit down at the computer or at a desk with pen and paper and begin writing.

Practicum

Read the following photograph taken by Steve Ludlum of the World Trade Center attack. Make a record of what you see in the image, question the text, and then create a free-response to the text. How did this process of recording, questioning, and responding help you to understand this static visual image?

Static Visual Image

In a survey conducted by students around the country, more than 2,500 people were asked, What visual image stands out the most in your memory regarding the terrorist attacks of 9/11? Ninety-eight percent recalled the moment the second plane crashed into the south tower of the World Trade Center.

The following is a photograph by Steve Ludlum published in the *New York Times*.

Aural Media

If you are examining an audio text (a conversation, a radio broadcast, a song) to make a record of that text, simply write down the details of what you hear. Describe the sounds (instruments, voice, tone, volume), write down the dialogue, describe background noises, transcribe lyrics, and note any other elements that strike you.

The easiest example of a record of aural media is a transcript of a conversation. When researching, we often conduct interviews as we gather information. To ensure accuracy, it is a good idea to record all interviews and then make a written record (a transcript) of the interview at a later time.

For example, I conducted a phone interview in January 2003 with Richard Patrick (formerly a guitarist for the band Nine Inch Nails and currently leader of the rock band Fil*ter* and a part of the side project The Damning Well). Taping this conversation allowed me to concentrate on an exchange of ideas and information rather than worry about writing down everything Richard said. This allowed the conversation to move in many interesting directions, and it allowed me the time later to carefully transcribe what was said. Here is a portion of a transcript from that interview:

> *RP:* It's scary. It's like in the privacy of my own home I'm looking for information about something, you know, like the R. Budd Dwyer thing. I could access that on the Internet, and the next thing you know [voice deepens], "we've arrested Richard Patrick today because he's accessed the R. Budd Dwyer footage. Why do you think he has it? More on this on tonight's news" [laughter]. It's completely and totally Big Brother. It scares the hell outta me.
>
> *KS:* It scares me, too. I've thought about this kind of thing many times, all the way back when Timothy McVeigh and the Oklahoma bombing. I started looking into the Freemen thing, trying to understand.
>
> *RP:* Yeah. Oh, they're watching that, you know they are. And you know the feds can probably download your hard drive.
>
> *KS:* Oh, absolutely. I know I'm on somebody's watch list because I've accessed this site about a dozen times looking for information. But I'm just like, well, so watch me, then. I'm looking for information. I'm studying and trying to learn, you know?
>
> *RP:* Yeah, it's like this guy blows up a building, you wanna know why. Why'd he do it? What is his belief system? [Distant click and then a squeaking sound, a cabinet door opening; cat meows softly] [speaking away from phone] Hey, dude, you crawl in there when I'm not looking, I can't help I locked you in there. [Speaking back into phone again, chuckling.] I locked my cat in the kitchen cabinet. Hope he didn't poop in there.

This transcript highlights many interesting points that are worthy of further investigation. Because these points were not in response to the initial interview topic or questions, had they not been taped and then transcribed, they might have been forgotten. A written record of a conversation allows the opportunity for all details to surface and to be considered.

After we have a written transcript of aural media, we may study it carefully and ask questions, such as, What do I hear? What do I not hear? What was said? What was not said? In the case of songs, how does music work with lyrics? Complement? Contrast? Create meaning? What does this mean? Who is the speaker or artist? Where was this recorded or heard? When was this created? What was the primary purpose of this audio text? Who was the intended audience?

In terms of the Richard Patrick interview, some questions arise regarding the content of the interview and information gaps:

> Who is R. Budd Dwyer?
>
> What type of information would someone seek about R. Budd Dwyer on the Internet?
>
> Why would the federal government be concerned about that information?
>
> Would the federal government monitor someone who accessed a site sponsored by an organization such as the Freemen?
>
> How are the Freemen connected to Timothy McVeigh and the Oklahoma City bombing?
>
> Would investigating someone's belief system help to explain his or her actions?

In order to fully understand this source, we have to locate answers to those questions. So a useful response to a text such as this would be a simple *search* for information.

When speculation is not enough, sometimes we have to look to outside sources for additional information in order to answer questions we have about a text. This requires conducting a bit of *research*. For our purposes at this point in the Quest, we only briefly cover some basic research strategies. Research methods are covered in greater detail in Chapters 3, 4, and 5.

To continue with our example, let's return to the interview with Richard Patrick. One of the questions to emerge from an initial reading of that transcript was, Who is R. Budd Dwyer? If you do not know the answer to that question, you might ask your peers. Your peers might be able to tell you that R. Budd Dwyer was supposedly the inspiration for a song written by Richard Patrick titled, "Hey Man, Nice Shot." But beyond that bit of information, your peers probably have no idea who R. Budd Dwyer is or why Richard Patrick wrote a song referencing him. At that point, to find answers to your questions, you must consult outside sources.

A simple search on Google.com turns up 3,020 sites with information about R. Budd Dwyer. The fourth site on the list is titled "Who Was R. Budd Dwyer?" Since that is exactly your question, you click on the link to that site. That link takes you to a Web page with a brief history of R. Budd Dwyer. On that site, you discover that Dwyer was a Pennsylvania state treasurer who committed suicide during a live television conference in 1987.

Of course, you naturally question the credibility of this or any Internet site. One way to verify the credibility of this information is to check for the same facts on several sites. If most sources providing information on R. Budd Dwyer contain the same facts, you may decide those facts are accurate. There are, however, many other issues to consider when determining the credibility of a source of information, and we cover them in greater detail in Chapters 3, 4, and 5.

A word to the wise: When conducting research to answer questions, be careful to take notes and record as much information as possible about the source of your answers. In terms of a Web site, record at least the URL (Uniform Resource Locator), sometimes called the domain name. This is the World Wide Web address of a site on the Internet. The URL for the Federal Bureau of Investigation, for instance, is http://www.fbi.gov.

Practicum

Come up with a list of three to five questions related to the media coverage of an event covered in Part Five, *Event Casebooks Gallery*. Select a person to interview (a parent, teacher, friend, or coworker). Locate a tape recorder (an audio cassette or digital device) and record your interview. As you play it back at a later time, make a written transcript of the interview; then question the transcript and respond by re-searching answers to one or two of your questions.

How does this process help you to develop a deeper understanding of the initial conversation? How does it add to your understanding of the topic?

Multimedia (Visual plus Aural)

If you are examining a *moving image,* one that involves both aural text and visual text (such as a television show, a movie, or a dramatic performance), making a record of that text is a little more difficult. In this case, you should record details of what you see (people, scenery, action, special effects) *and* what you hear (background music and noises, dialogue).

Take, for example, this clip from a newscast during the initial coverage of the Columbine High School shooting. Here is a record of surface visual details (note that the detail used in this example is quite heavier than the detail you might capture *without* the benefit of stop-frame action):

> This coverage takes place on the lawn in front of a white brick and cement build-ing (presumably Leewood Elementary School in Littleton, Colorado). In the lower left-hand side of the screen, these words appear: "Breaking News, Live, 9News." Across the bottom of the screen, this text appears: "3:23, 70. . . , Jeffco, K-12 activities cancelled." In the foreground there is a white male, a reporter. He appears to be in his late twenties or early thirties. He has short-cropped, light brown hair. He is rather thin and wears a dark-colored suit, a tie, and a white button-up shirt. He is holding a microphone in his right hand and speaking into it. He is holding a white sheet of paper in his left hand and gesturing to a group of people in the background. In the background, several people can be seen sit-ting on a fence or standing in a breezeway in front of the building.

Here is a record of the audio details (a transcript of this portion of the broadcast):

> *REPORTER:* Over here, the door of Leewood Elementary School, there's a list, uh, lots of lists on the, uh, wall and the door here. You've got about, uh, twenty-five feet to go. In fact, if we can come up right over here, Bruce, see if you can stand over here. Up there on the wall you can see all the white papers that have been taped up and posted, uh, those are lists of names, of students, and where they are. So parents come here and they look on the, they look on the wall. There they can see the name, and there's actually some of those students who, who've actually been accounted for, uh, but they're at a house in the neighborhood. So

we've got the library, we've got Leewood Elementary School, and there's also groups of students, maybe fifteen or twenty, at a couple of houses just in the neighborhood, uh, that's where they ended up after the school was evacuated or after everyone left when the, uh, the shootings and the explosions, uh, went off.

This record of both visual and aural text can help you to fully process all aspects of the broadcast in a way that casual viewing cannot.

Once a record has been made, if we review our notes from the newscast, many questions arise: What was the purpose of this broadcast? How constructive was the reporter's dialogue? What information was this visual angle intended to communicate? Was the information provided appropriate for a live broadcast of an event such as this?

Sometimes our response to a text is best explored by sharing our ideas with other people and hearing their thoughts and feelings on the subject matter. If you need to share your ideas with others, to explore your thoughts and feelings in relation to other perspectives, *discussion* is a great way of responding to a text.

Either in class or outside of class, it is often useful to form discussion groups with our peers or through online discussion boards. This may prove to be more a form of conversation *about* a text than with a text, but it is very useful when you are seeking answers to questions and developing an understanding of a text. The distinct advantage of discussion over other forms of response is that you can express your ideas about a text and experience multiple responses to a text by sharing your ideas with others. Those responses may expand your understanding of the text and may answer some of the questions you raised through your own examination.

If your instructor has not already created an online bulletin board for extended class discussions, you may create your own. Many Internet services offer free online bulletin boards (such as ezboard.com or ProBoards.com). They are easy to set up, easy to use, and can be as private or as public as you want them to be.

Practicum

Scan your television channels and look for a breaking news story. When you find one, watch a few minutes of the coverage (if possible, make a video recording of the report). Make a record of what you see and a transcript of what you hear. Question the text, and then visit your class bulletin board or another online bulletin board and join a discussion on the news story (if a topic does not exist, start one on your own).

How does this process of reading, questioning, and discussing enhance your understanding of the multimedia text?

An alternative to online discussion is an in-class, small-group or whole-class discussion of the topic.

Interactive Media

Interactive media probably offers the biggest challenge for a reader. If you are examining interactive media (such as an Internet Web site or a video or computer game), you must make a record of what you see and what you hear, but you must also describe *how you interact* with the media and *how the media responds* to your interaction. The key to truly understanding this type of text is in examining that interaction.

As an example, I visited the Rock the Vote home page located at http://action .rockthevote.org. Rock the Vote is a nonprofit organization dedicated to engaging young people with the voting process and raising awareness of current social issues and opportunities for social activism.

Here is a record of interaction with this Web page in early 2004:

> The original page has a black background. The logo at the top left-hand side of the screen is white lettering with a bright red checkmark in the background. The banner across the top of the screen flashes a series of images (the one captured in this shot is a male figure waving his fingers in a "V" like the "peace" sign or "victory" sign). The words that flash in the foreground of the banner are "Rock the Vote NOW! Speak Out!" And there is a small sign-up form on the right-hand side of the banner asking for e-mail address and zip code. If a user types in an e-mail address and zip code and clicks on the button beneath the form that says Rock Me, the user is transferred to a screen that says "Thanks for joining the RTV Action Network!"
>
> Returning to the main screen, on the left-hand side of the main screen is a bar that features five links to pages that contain more information on ways to get involved with Rock the Vote, two links inviting users to register to vote and to register for peace, as well as a link to contact information for the creators of this site. On the right-hand side of the screen, there is a bar that features pictures of several celebrities associated with Rock the Vote and three links to information on outspoken musical artists supporting this organization.
>
> In the center of the main screen is information regarding a form letter being sent to President Bush through a campaign called "Take Action! Send a Message." Scrolling down the screen, there is an explanation of the purpose of the letter, a copy of the letter in full, and a form that users can fill out to immediately submit an electronic copy of the letter to President Bush in the user's name.

After recording the details of interaction with this Web page, it is easy to reflect and determine which aspects of the site were most important. It is also easier to recognize the purpose of the site.

Once a record is made, some questions may arise when dealing with interactive media: Why were these colors used? Why these words? Why this font? Why this layout? Why these graphics? Why was this link provided? How do these elements (layout, font, graphics) create meaning? What is left out? Who designed this text? Who sponsored this text? What was the primary purpose of this text? Who was the intended audience?

Regarding the Rock the Vote Web site, for example, we might want to know

> Who is the sponsor of Rock the Vote?
> Why does this campaign use celebrities as endorsements for its project?
> How effective is an e-letter?
> Would it reach the President?
> Would the President pay attention to this sort of campaign?

Response to an interactive site may take the form of a dialogue, a free-response, a discussion, or it may involve conducting a little research. But one thing about interactive media that is unique from other forms of media is that *response is an inherent part of the interaction.* By simply interacting with the Web site and following the links provided, you are responding to the site and engaging in a conversation of sorts.

For example, to respond to this Web page, you might go back and follow the links on the left- or right-hand side of the page. Or you might fill out the forms, follow the directions, and have the electronic letter submitted to the President in your name. Then wait and see what happens as a result of your interaction. Another way of responding to a Web site may be to contact those responsible for maintaining the site and ask them some of your questions. This type of direct interaction may begin an interesting and informative correspondence.

Through this online interaction, the purpose of the site becomes quite clear. The creators of this Web page intended for the reader to experience immediate involvement with a social cause. Whether or not this involvement is fruitful remains to be seen.

Practicum

Do a Google search (www.google.com) of the Internet and locate a Web site that is connected in some way to one of the events located in Part Five, *Event Casebooks Gallery.* Read the Web site, question it, and respond using one or more of the strategies discussed in this chapter (dialogue, free-response, research, and discussion).

What did you discover about the Web site after completing this activity? How does the process of reading, recording, questioning, and responding enhance your understanding of this type of media?

WRITING ASSIGNMENT   Quest One: A Reading Journal

Choose several events covered in the *Event Casebooks Gallery* that seem interesting to you (your instructor will determine how many events you should cover for this assignment). Read the Initial Reports, either local and national or national and international, for each event.

Create a reading journal in which you record, question, and respond to these reports. Your goals at this point are to practice reading strategies, explore the surface details (what happened) of several events, and, ultimately, select an event on which to focus for future Quests.

You will begin to notice that some of the initial reports provide conflicting details, and you'll notice variations in tone. An important point to consider as you complete this Quest and future Quests is, What do you believe to be true? Also consider how you can be sure that the information provided in any source is accurate.

Criteria for a Successful Reading Journal

For this assignment, read and examine initial reports of events in order to practice critical reading strategies and become familiar with the basic details generally understood about these events. The strategies learned and practiced in this assignment are used throughout the remaining Quests, so mastery at this point is important. A successful reading journal meets the following criteria:

- Create a record of each source. Each record should provide a thorough description of surface details for that source.
- Generate a list of questions about each source. The questions should demonstrate thoughtful engagement and purposeful inquiry in an attempt to understand the information provided by the source (beyond the surface detail).
- Create a response to each source. The response must be thorough and must demonstrate thoughtful engagement with the content of the source and a genuine effort to answer questions and understand the information provided by the source. It must also demonstrate the significance of that information as it relates to information provided by other sources.

In the Spotlight: A Student Model Reading Journal

The Author: Samantha Stallings

Sam Stallings is a student from North Carolina who hopes to earn a degree in criminal psychology. After graduation, her goal is to attend the FBI Academy and work for the FBI as a special agent in the National Center for the Analysis of Violent Crime.

Author's Etcetera

Sam had this to say about her experience in creating a reading journal:

> It was a lot of work, and there were times when I felt like I was looking too hard at these reports, especially the cartoon. But in the end, I understand that you don't always really "see" unless you read below the surface. The artists and authors put a lot more into these reports than you first see is there. Like with the cartoon, for example, there are so many little details that I didn't notice the first time I looked at it. "Reading" the cartoon helped me to see how every little detail works to make a much deeper meaning.

The focus of Sam's Quest was the response to terror. One source that Sam investigated as she began her Quest was an editorial cartoon by Mike Keefe published in the *Denver Post*. Here is a copy of that cartoon followed by Sam's reading journal entry.

Quest One: Reading Journal Entry for Mike Keefe's "Eagle"

Record

The focal point of the picture is the eagle. The eagle's wings are spread wide and arched upwards. It is standing on some type of dark ball. The eagle's brows are drawn together, and its eyes are focused sharply on something in front of it. The beak is pointed sharply down, and the "mouth" line is set in a flat line with a downward turn. This is an angry expression. An arrow is sticking out of the eagle. It has struck the eagle in the heart. The arrow appears to be primitive, the feathers at the end of the arrow are worn and frayed. In the center of the feathers there is a word: Terrorism. Behind the eagle is a dark cloud. The eagle's wings are rising up into the cloud. In front of the eagle the background is white, and there are words in the upper left corner: "September 11, 2001 . . . a date which will live in infamy."

Questions

Why is an eagle used in this cartoon instead of something else that represents America? Why is the eagle perched on a ball? What is the ball? Why is an arrow the weapon used to attack the eagle instead of something more powerful, like a gun or a bomb? Why is the arrow worn and frayed? Why does the eagle look mad or angry? Why are the eagle's wings raised? Is it about to fly away? Is it about to attack? Why is there a black cloud behind the eagle? Why is the arrow stabbing the eagle in the heart and not somewhere else? Why does the arrow say "terrorism"? Why are the words "September 11, 2001 . . . a date which will live in infamy" written on the white portion of the cartoon? What do these words mean?

Response

Information from the Text	My Response to the Text
Why is an eagle used in this cartoon instead of something else that represents America?	There are a lot of different symbols that could represent America and different aspects of the American culture. For instance, many cartoonists used the American flag in their 9/11 cartoons, and this often represented the government or the military in some way. The artist who created this cartoon used the eagle because the eagle represents American freedom. By showing terrorism stabbing the eagle through the heart, the artist was symbolizing the way that terrorism was an attack on the heart of an American ideal—the ideal of freedom. This ideal is more than government or military; it is something that is personal for every American citizen.
Why is the eagle perched on a ball? What is the ball?	Eagles are often shown perched on top of flagpoles that have balls at the top. This eagle could be perching on a flagpole with the American flag on it. So even though the flag is not shown, it is "implied" through this ball. And everything the flag represents is also implied. We see here that the ideal of freedom is above everything else that America stands for; it is the most visible aspect of America. But it is connected to everything else about America, too.
Why is an arrow the weapon used to attack the eagle instead of something more powerful, like a gun or a bomb?	The terrorists did not attack our country with nuclear bombs or other conventional weapons; they attacked our country with makeshift, techno-

logically sophisticated but primitive weapons: airplanes. The arrow is a very primitive weapon, often man-made or makeshift, just like the planes were.

But if you stab an eagle in the heart with an arrow, it will do the same damage that would be done if you had shot it or bombed it. The eagle will be injured and may die. America was harmed in the same way—the American ideal of freedom was injured.

Why does the eagle look mad or angry?

The eagle does not look sad or injured, he looks mad. The ideal of freedom is strong, and the eagle is strong and ready to fight back. The wings are raised, the beak lowered, the eyes narrowed and focused on something in front of it (supposedly the terrorists), and it is ready to strike back. Freedom is not about to fly away. It is about to rise up against terrorism.

Why is there a black cloud behind the eagle?

The black cloud is kind of like an angry storm. When the eagle/freedom is injured by terrorism, the eagle raises its wings, preparing to strike. The cloud represents the storm that is coming, the battle that lies ahead.

Why are the words "September 11, 2001 . . . a date which will live in infamy" written on the white portion of the cartoon? What do these words mean?

This quotation is a paraphrase of something that President Roosevelt said when Pearl Harbor was attacked. The artist included this quote to draw attention to the similarities between the attack on Pearl Harbor and the attack on the World Trade Center. Both attacks were on U.S. soil. Both were aggressive attacks, not defensive attacks. Both attacks will be remembered, and the dates when they occurred will be remembered because they were so terrible.

> **Practicum**
>
> Using the Criteria for a Successful Reading Journal, evaluate Sam's model. As you consider each criterion, refer to specific examples from the text of her journal to support your evaluation. Then, share your responses with your classmates. Do you find that your evaluations are in agreement? Or are there particular points on which you disagree?

Reflection in Action

In the past, when you were asked to complete a reading assignment, what was your process? Did you read with a pen in hand and paper nearby? How well did you comprehend what you read?

When you began this chapter, how would you have defined *reading* and *texts*? How would you define them now? How has your reading process changed? Do you feel as though your comprehension has improved?

What do you see as the connection between reading (as defined and practiced in this chapter) and your college education? What about the connection between reading and your life outside of college? Do you feel as though your new understanding of reading will have an impact on your involvement in various life events outside of the classroom? How will this new understanding help you to become a smarter media consumer?

Expanding Your Vision: A Multimedia Assignment Option

Critical Inquiry: Digging Deeper

Now that you have completed a close reading of the initial reports of your event, let's return to our original question posed at the beginning of this chapter: What happened?

Take a moment to summarize in your own words the stories told by each type of media you have studied.

Reread the local and national newspaper reports of the event. How are they similar? How are they different? Do they present the same details? Is the tone of each report similar or different? For instance, in the casebook on the Columbine High School massacre, the initial local report states that "up to 25 people were reported killed," whereas the initial national report states that there were "at least 15 and possibly 16" casualties. Which report is more accurate? How do you know?

Evaluate the effectiveness of each of these sources in your casebook. Begin by asking, What is the purpose of an initial news report of an event? Do these initial reports fulfill that purpose? If they do, how do they fulfill that purpose? If they do not, where do they fall short?

MULTIMEDIA ASSIGNMENT   Visi-Quest One: Expanding Your Vision by Rewriting History

Overview

Throughout this chapter, you have explored the initial media response to a particular event. In addition to practicing various reading strategies, you have discussed the effectiveness of these initial reports.

For this assignment, work in small groups to re-examine your initial reports and to examine several additional reports in order to evaluate their effectiveness (in terms of purpose) and to decide which "facts" presented by these reports are reliable. Create a "master list" of reliable information.

Then, working on your own, decide what type of report should have been made, the purpose of such report, the information that should have been provided, and what format that information should have taken. Then rewrite history and create your own initial report of your event. The following steps guide you through this assignment.

Step 1
- Review the initial reports in your casebook.
- Make a list of reliable "facts" as you read.
- Bring your reading notes and fact list to class.

Step 2
- Work in small groups and discuss your findings.
- Create a master "fact" list.

Step 3
- Review your fact list and decide the following:
  - What was the intended purpose and achieved purpose of each report?
  - What information should have been included in an initial report?
  - What should not have been included?
  - What format should this report have taken?
- Consider these questions:
  - What is an appropriate (ideal) purpose for an initial report of a breaking news event?
  - What information should have been provided in such a report, and why?
  - What format should this information have taken?

Step 4
- Rewrite history by creating an initial live newscast or newspaper article. Your report should detail only the facts you believe to be necessary and reliable in a format that seems appropriate.

Step 5
- Write an explanation and justification for your report. Briefly explain the purpose of your report, what information you included and why, and why you selected this format.

Criteria for a Successful Rewriting History

For this assignment, critically read the initial reports of a media event in order to distinguish between reported verifiable facts and supposition or commentary. Decide on an appropriate audience and purpose for an initial report. Then, select information to present through a particular format designed to reach a clearly defined target audience.

> *Focus:* With a clear purpose in mind, inform a select audience of specific, verifiable information at a moment of crisis. This report must not contain any supposition or commentary; it must be limited to verifiable information.
>
> *Development:* Develop your focus by presenting only verifiable information in a balanced, reasonable tone. Address the when, where, what, who, and perhaps how of the event with confirmable details. Do not address the why of an event, which in the early stages of an unfolding event relies heavily on supposition and commentary. Also include an explanation of and justification for the information you chose to present and how those choices relate to purpose and audience.
>
> *Organization:* This assignment is typically organized in some chronological pattern because it is a report of events unfolding. Some reports are organized point to point, however.

In the Spotlight: A Student Model Rewriting History

The Author: Tia Perry

In the fall semester of 2002, Tia Perry was a freshman at the University of North Carolina–Charlotte. Originally from Raleigh, North Carolina, Tia is studying nursing and plans to become a nurse practitioner or nurse anesthetist.

Author's Etcetera

As for her experience in completing Visi-Quest One, Tia recalls,

> I really enjoyed this assignment because it made me look at the different reports and views of the Columbine High School shooting with a critical eye. I had to sift through all of the excess, unnecessary, and often incorrect information presented by the media and select the facts I felt were most important for people to know at the time of an initial report.

Breaking News

Breaking news just in from the Jefferson County Sheriff's Department. Shortly after 11:00 this morning, gunfire was reported at Columbine High School in Littleton,

Colorado. There have been reports of two as-yet unidentified gunmen at Columbine. Several police units, along with the Jefferson County SWAT team, have been dispatched to the school to stabilize the situation. All possible measures are being taken to ensure the safety of everyone at Columbine. Many students are waiting at homes in the neighborhood surrounding the school, and some children are being sent to Leewood Elementary. We will keep you posted as updates arrive. For further information, parents please call 1-800-555-INFO.

Explanation and Justification

Because I felt that providing accurate information and calming fears were the only legitimate reasons for reporting an event such as Columbine as it was still underway, I chose to do my report in the form of an announcement that could be communicated over both television and radio, thereby reaching the largest audience. My intended audience was the local population of Littleton, Colorado, including parents, family, and friends of students and faculty at Columbine High School.

I felt it was best to provide only the most basic information in as brief a manner as possible. As we have learned by studying the initial reports of this event, the more detailed an initial report, the more inaccuracies occurred, so brief and to the point seemed the most effective plan. I feel very strongly that information should not be disclosed until it has been verified; early on as this event unfolded, very little information had been verified and many, many inaccurate details were made public. We know from our random surveys that these initial details, accurate or not, seem to be what people remember about this event. At the time this shooting was reported, we did know that there had been reports of gunfire, we knew where this had occurred and that there were at least two gunmen involved. We knew the police were on the scene, and we knew where students were being taken. But that is really all that could be verified, so that is the only information I included in my announcement.

It also occurred to me that providing only the barest details creates a sense of calm and control, which is important when faced with an unfolding tragedy such as this. More details and repeated details create a sense of drama and panic that serves no useful purpose. I stuck to the facts, and I was careful to avoid any descriptive language (such as "black trench coats" or "evacuated" or "taking cover") that might cause panic and unnecessary speculation.

Practicum

Using the Criteria for a Successful Rewriting History, evaluate Tia's model. As you consider each criterion, refer to specific examples from the text of her journal to support your evaluation. Then, share your responses with your classmates. Do you find that your evaluations are in agreement? Or are there particular points on which you disagree? How does the process of reading and evaluating a model assignment help you to successfully meet the requirements for the assignment yourself?

2

Reading and Writing to Form an Opinion: Examining the Blame Game

Begin with a *Question:* Why Did This Happen?

As human beings, we are natural seekers. Among other things, we are seekers of knowledge, of understanding. We like to understand how things work, how life works. We are driven to look for the *cause* in order to understand the *effect*. When good things happen, we look for someone or something to praise. When bad things happen, we look for someone or something to blame. Seldom are we willing to accept that things *just happen.*

For many of us (to one degree or another), our entire lives are built around the quest for understanding, the drive to make sense out of our experiences, to find meaning in life. We value *reason,* the *why* of any situation. Many say that what makes us uniquely human, what separates us from other animals, is the ability to reason, to understand motivations, cause, and effect, and then to act on our understanding, to do something, to change the world in some way.

As human beings, we like to be the masters of our domains, so to speak. We are movers and shakers; we take action; we like to think that we are in control of any given situation. Therefore, when we are confronted with an event that impacts or challenges us in some way, we naturally seek to understand the cause. We want to know, *Why did this happen?* We want to understand how it happened, why it happened, and who played what role. What led up to that moment in time? We want someone to take responsibility, to pay for our troubles, our confusion, our pain and suffering and loss. We want to know how we can prevent it from happening again. And so the blame game begins.

The Blame Game

Here's a scenario that's at least somewhat familiar to all of us:

> Little Johnny is playing in the livingroom with his good friend, Joe. They are bouncing a ball around the room, tossing it back and forth, even though Mom has told Johnny countless times that ball-playing is off limits inside the house. *But,* in spite of Mom's warnings, they're playing ball. It's going okay, no harm done, *until* Johnny sneezes and blinks just as Joe tosses the ball a bit to the left. Johnny reaches out in a frantic effort to catch the ball, *but* he misses, and it bounces off of the edge of a coffee table and directly into one of Mom's crystal lamps.
>
> *Phwop.*
>
> The lamp wobbles back and forth and then tips over onto the hardwood floor beneath.
>
> *Ccrrrasshh.*
>
> It shatters into a gazillion tiny pieces. Time seems to stand still.
>
> Before Johnny and Joe can take another breath, Mom is at the door, hands on her hips. She's not happy. She wants to know, *Why did this happen? Who is responsible for this?*
>
> "Johnny, what is going on in here? How did this happen? Who broke the lamp?"
>
> Johnny swallows hard, a big lump in his throat. "I don't know, Mom. It just happened."
>
> "Things like this don't just happen, Johnny. How did this lamp break? Who broke the lamp? Did you do this, Joe?"
>
> "No," Joe squeaks. "It wasn't me!"
>
> Johnny's mind races through a dozen possible explanations. The wind blew in through the open window. The dog bumped the table while wagging his tail (he was happy to see us). A ghost did it. YOU did it, Mom, when you slammed the pantry door too hard!

What happened here is fairly obvious: Johnny and Joe broke the lamp while playing with the ball inside. The evidence is clear:

- Joe is standing at a particular distance from Johnny.
- The table that held the lamp stands between the two of them.
- The ball is on the floor in the corner behind the lamp.
- The window is closed, and the dog is in the other room, asleep.

But Mom's interrogation isn't really about *what* happened; it is probably based on the desire to have someone *take responsibility* for the destruction of her rather expensive lamp. Or maybe she just wants her son to own up to the fact that he broke the rules and to understand that, in breaking the rules, something not-so-good happened. Perhaps she wants to make sure something like this doesn't happen again. Or maybe she wants to take control of a situation that has slipped—momentarily—beyond her control, to regain her sense of personal power. In any case, Mom knows *what* happened. What she doesn't know—and may never really understand—is *why* it happened. In order to understand the why of any situation, we have to dig deeper and move beyond blame.

Looking for Answers

This same simple scenario of casting blame, looking for who or what is responsible, arises with any complex event, like the events you are studying. For instance, we know the basics of what happened on September 11, 2001. The evidence is there all around us, presented through various forms of media. Sometimes it takes a little effort to bring all of the pieces of the puzzle together, but in time we can usually establish what happened in such a situation. What we don't know, what we desperately seek to find out is, *why*. Why did this happen? Events like the attack on the World Trade Center don't just happen, we say. Someone or something has got to take the blame.

When we cast blame, what we're really asking is, *Who or what is responsible?* We want someone to step forward and take responsibility. We want to make sense of the senseless, to solve the mystery. We want to understand so we can prevent such a thing from happening again. And, ultimately, we want to punish the guilty. We feel in a situation like this that someone must make retribution for our pain and suffering and loss. Identifying whoever or whatever is responsible for a tragedy like the terrorist attacks of September 11 is only a first step in a long process; in order to make change happen, we have to move beyond blame. Nevertheless, identifying cause—the responsible element or elements in any situation—is where this leg of the journey begins.

In trying to understand the events that unfold around us every day, within the finger-pointing and name-calling, we begin to see familiar issues surface. These issues, often social problems, are nothing new. The same problems tend to occur and reoccur; they've been around for quite some time, popping up in our collective consciousness again and again, unsolved, misunderstood, and persistent.

We all know that what happened at Columbine High School, for example, was not a first; many other school shootings occurred before Columbine (and many have occurred since). So, though we are driven to understand why these episodes of violence continue to happen, and we are quick to place blame, to identify the social issues and problems that fuel such events, *nothing is changing*.

There are many reasons for this lack of solution and closure. The *why* of a situation is fuzzy and confusing. It's hard to pinpoint *one* reason, a *single* cause. And when we are faced with multiple causes, a complex situation that obviously requires a complex solution (or solutions), we become overwhelmed. There probably isn't one single, simple answer for any event or social problem—certainly not one on which we can all agree. But that doesn't mean we should stop seeking.

Let's revisit our previous example with Johnny, Joe, and the lamp-breaking incident. Even in that seemingly simple and common situation, it's difficult to say exactly why it happened. Maybe it was raining outside; if so, it would be easy to blame the broken lamp on the weather (a combination of natural elements beyond our control, kids being kids—cooped up inside but wanting to play). Or maybe it's just that

Johnny and Joe were bored, so their lack of imagination drove them to play ball inside (blame it on the desensitization caused by our bleeping, blinking technoculture). Or maybe it was Johnny's belief that Mom's rule was unnecessary and not worth honoring (a lack of respect for authority). Maybe Mom has a lot of rules and ineffective consequences for breaking the rules (so her parenting skills are to blame). Maybe Johnny had seen an episode of the *Rugrats* in which Angelica and Tommy played ball inside and nothing bad happened, nothing broke, and they had fun (so he was influenced by what he had seen on television). Or maybe Joe coerced Johnny to break his mother's rule and play ball inside (so peer pressure is to blame). In truth, it could be any or all of these explanations—or something else entirely. There usually isn't one single answer to the question of why something happened, but a lot of familiar scapegoats immediately come to mind.

Another good "why" question is, *Why is blame repeatedly placed on the same people, things, situations, and/or conditions?* Is this casting of blame justified? And if it is, if we know where to rightfully place the blame for many of the problems we see, then why haven't things changed? Of all of the societal scapegoats that are continually attacked, which one, or which *ones*, seem the most logical? *Is there* one good reason (or a couple of good reasons) that gets right to the heart of what happened—more than others? In order to find the answers we seek, we have to be persistent, look closely, and think critically about what we discover.

Beyond the Scapegoat

Understanding or identifying *why* is not enough. But sometimes our search for a reason is so complicated that it overwhelms us as life goes on; ultimately, our attention shifts to other problems. As a society, as a world, the more we look away before finding a solution, the more we are left with social problems that just won't quit. It's not enough to place blame, but placing blame is certainly where this process begins.

As critical thinkers and active citizens, we have to move beyond blame and *look closely at the factors that come together* to create a given situation. We have to decide what *makes the most sense.* And we have slow down and take an honest look at our own thoughts and feelings. We have to be able to articulate what it is that we think and feel, and why. We have to understand the origins of our own beliefs before we can join the official conversation on any topic. Only then can we move on to seek answers and find solutions.

Engaging with the Issues

When asked what issues are important to them, I cannot tell you how many times I have heard my students say, "I don't know." "Nothing." "I'm not interested in anything." "This doesn't concern me." "That doesn't have any impact on my life." And every time I hear such a response, I question, *why?* Why are students so disconnected, so distanced from what is happening in the world around them? I've actually spent a lot of time thinking about this—what I see as a serious problem—and looking for answers. You see, I just don't buy it. I don't accept that students are unaffected and apathetic. I don't accept that students don't care, that they find nothing out there that is relevant to their lives and engaging enough to get them involved.

You might wonder, Why is this a problem? Why does it matter whether or not we are engaged or get involved? After all, life can and does go on even if you never pick up the newspaper or tune in to CNN. You can live and function quite happily without getting involved with anything happening beyond your backyard. But don't kid yourself into believing that what happens in the world around you doesn't matter or impact your life. It does.

You are both a product of your culture and an instrument of that culture. You are impacted by the world around you, and as you live and breathe, you have an impact on the world—*just because*. If you choose to live an unengaged life, you will continue to be impacted, usually in small, gradual ways and sometimes in big, jolting ways, by the world around you. And you'll still make an impact on the world, too, by not acting, not engaging. You see, *not choosing* is in itself a choice. It's not a very constructive choice; it's passive, but it is a choice nonetheless. However, if you become an active member of society, if you engage, then you will open up to the full potential of who you are and what you can bring to the world. You will have a greater, more powerful, and purposeful impact on the lives of those around you. That's the goal of critical and civic literacy: Purposeful engagement means being more than a sponge and doing more than simply absorbing what is going on around you.

Active Learning

When you've been asked to do research in the past, what sorts of tasks were required of you? Did you have to go to the library with some pre-assigned subject, gather books and articles that were written by "experts"? Did you have to read whatever information you found, summarize it, and report what you learned to your teacher? That's a pretty common scenario for many assignments, and there are definitely important aspects to the types of thinking skills you must practice with traditional research. After all, you have to do your homework on any topic, subject, or issue before you can do anything else. But if we stop with what someone else knows—if we do not allow questions—as author Kathleen McCormick says in her book *The Culture of Reading and the Teaching of English,* those "nagging internal voices that suggest new ways to piece together" ideas—what we're really supporting is the idea that there is no possibility of and no need for new ideas, for growth or change.

Traditional research assignments ask students to make like a sponge and soak up the world around them. This approach to learning focuses on closure, the end result. Everything is about the end product—what you got out of an event or experience rather than what you learned through the journey or what you contributed along the way. Students learn to value only what the experts have to say, what already exists. They become data processors. Questioning is not encouraged (there will be no "What does this mean?" or "Is this right?" or "What about this?"). Tentative answers are not allowed (no "I think" or "Maybe" or "Could this be?" or "Is this possible?"). With traditional research, you must show that you know what the experts have said.

Period. This assumes an absolute truth (some secret knowledge that the experts have and you've got to get from them). By employing this traditional mode of learning, educators, the media, parents, and the community at large have basically taught students not to engage. They've taught them to sit back in "their place" and quietly *absorb* what they want them to absorb.

Traditional research implies that the truth is already out there. There's nothing new under the sun. *That's why problems remain unsolved—it's a lack of creative thinking.* Let me explain.

If all you are ever asked to do is swallow and digest what other people have said and done, if you are never encouraged to question, to discuss, to challenge, and to create, to generate *new* (and maybe *better*) ideas, then what is the result? Complacency. Status quo. Societal sores that continue to fester. *No change.*

But, what if you are asked to question the information you find while researching? To "take on" and interrogate the experts? To decide for yourself *who* the experts are? To wonder? To let your imagination wander? To offer your own opinions and ideas? What if you are *expected* to get involved, to engage, and to think creatively? To share your ideas? To go public? To enact a solution? Then, the entire process of learning becomes something new, something exciting, something purposeful. It becomes a journey of discovery.

The Process of Discovery

Learning to question, to appreciate exploration, to seek discovery, is the mark of critical and civic literacy. Educated speculation is what you are after. Approaching life in this way changes things. Everything looks different, and you become empowered as a result.

With this textbook as your guide, you will do your homework (research), you will find out what the experts have to say. But you will not simply accept what they tell you without question. You will ask questions, lots of them. The experts will be interrogated and held up to close scrutiny, *and so will you,* as you respond to what you learn.

First of all, you will identify and examine and explore what you *feel* about the issues (your initial responses, what we often call a gut reaction). Then you will decide what you *think* about what the experts have to say: Does the information seem logical, supporting what you know, or is it in conflict with what you know? And you will ultimately recognize and articulate what you *believe* to be true based on what you learn through your studies: Is this right or wrong, good or bad, necessary or unnecessary? You will look at the origins of your feelings, your thoughts, and your beliefs, and you will share what you feel, think, and believe with your classmates, recognizing and appreciating that you will not always be in agreement (and that there is much to be learned and gained from examining multiple perspectives in any situation).

Beginning now and throughout the remainder of your Quest, you will not only interrogate the experts in many different ways, but you will question yourself as well. When you emerge from this journey, you will stand firm in what you believe to be true, and you will be able and willing to acknowledge what others believe to be true, supported by your close examination, your studies, and your discoveries. You will step forward knowing that you have something to say, something valuable to contribute to the official conversation. And you will be better able to listen to and think critically about what others have to say as well.

Tools for Success: Taking Inventory

The journey to critical and civic literacy requires that all situations and all information come under thoughtful scrutiny. There is no such thing as a meaningful cursory glance at a situation, an issue, or a claim regarding an issue. You have to dig in and get beneath the surface. You have to look at the complete picture and at your responses from every possible angle. The goal is to achieve a thorough understanding of a situation, of the who, what, where, when, why, and how. To do this, you begin with a close reading of a text such as you practiced in Chapter 1, where, using one or more reading strategies, you recorded surface details, you questioned the text, and you responded to the text. The next step toward a deeper understanding of a text involves a much closer examination: *taking inventory.*

As it applies to reading, an inventory is an exploration—sometimes in the form of a list, sometimes in the form of a freewrite—of the cultural, textual, and personal influences that shape your response to a situation and that shape the situation itself. Taking inventory of a text and your response to a text asks that you first *identify your reaction* to a text (and remember that our definition of text is quite broad) and then *explore that reaction* from many different angles. An inventory helps you to discover what personal and social influences, experiences, observations, and information create that response for you. It also involves exploring and ultimately explaining the personal and social influences that impact the creation of a text.

Remember, just as you are a product and an instrument of your culture and experience, the text is also a product of the culture in which it was created and an instrument of that culture. You can't really understand a text without placing it within the context of its cultural, textual, and personal inventory.

This intense exploration will help you to think critically about a text (its content, context, form, and format) to more completely (subjectively and objectively) know a situation discussed within multiple texts. It will help you to know yourself and to speak clearly and confidently about what you believe to be true. It will help you to make educated decisions and to come up with creative solutions to problems.

As we saw in Chapter 1, we begin a quest for understanding by looking at a situation. Then we listen for the issues that emerge from that situation, and we examine the talk surrounding those issues. To more closely examine the perspectives and ideas presented in that talk, we must place the conversation under a high-powered mental microscope, so to speak, and ask questions. Let's begin this process with a single text and read that text through a high-powered, questioning lens and closely examine the details; let's take inventory. Note: Before beginning your inventory, you should have completed a close reading of your text using the strategies you practiced in Chapter 1: record, question, and respond.

Inventory Walk-Through

Music videos are common texts in our culture, particularly for teenagers and young adults, but they are texts we typically enjoy as entertainment. We do not often analyze them, yet they are powerful mediums of social commentary. Musical artists often play the blame game sending messages about social problems through their music and videos to their audience. Because we do not take the time to analyze music videos as text, we sometimes misunderstand or miss altogether the message the artist intends to communicate.

As an example for our inventory, we use as a multimedia text model a music video by the rock band Pearl Jam, "Jeremy." You may listen to the song and watch the video in its entirety on the official Pearl Jam Web site located at http://www.pearljam.com.

Named for lead singer Eddie Vedder's great-grandmother Pearl's famous homemade jam, Pearl Jam set a foundation in music that would become known simply as Grunge. Pearl Jam's first album, *Ten,* released in 1991, shot up the charts and sold hundreds of thousands of albums worldwide. Pearl Jam quickly became the voice of a new, angry generation of teenagers known as Generation X.

Pearl Jam

Jeremy

At home, drawing pictures of mountain tops, with him on top
Lemon yellow sun, arms raised in a V
The dead lay in pools of maroon below

Daddy didn't give attention
To the fact that mommy didn't care
King Jeremy the wicked, oh, ruled his world
Jeremy spoke in class today (2x)

Clearly I remember pickin' on the boy
Seemed a harmless little fuck
But we unleashed a lion
Gnashed his teeth and bit the recess lady's breast
How could I forget?
And he hit me with a surprise left
My jaw left hurtin', ooh, dropped wide open
Just like the day, oh, like the day I heard

Daddy didn't give affection
And the boy was something mommy wouldn't wear
King Jeremy the wicked, ruled his world

Jeremy spoke in class today (3x)
Woo (14x)

Try to forget this . . . try to forget this . . .
Try to erase this . . . try to erase this . . .
From the blackboard . . .

Jeremy spoke in class today (2x)
Jeremy spoke in, spoke in (2x)
Jeremy spoke in class today
Woo (29x)
Woooooohhh . . . spoke in, spoke in
Woooooohhh . . . uh huh, uh huh . . .

What Is Your Initial Response?

The first step in taking inventory is to identify what you feel, your reaction to the text. Ask yourself, what effect does the text have on you? Do you feel a strong sense of compassion as you read? Does the text make you angry? Does it confuse you? Are you frustrated? Does it make you laugh, or does it make you cry? Are you frightened? Identify the primary response you have while reading the text, and then expand on your feelings as much as possible in the form of a freewrite. Note: You may have completed a free-response as a part of your initial reading strategy (record, question, respond). If you did, complete another freewrite for this inventory, and take your initial response a step further in order to more deeply explore your reaction to the text.

As an example, your initial response to the text of the music video may be something like this:

An Initial Response to "Jeremy"

First of all, I really like this video, and I've seen it a thousand times, but when I stop and think about what I feel when I watch it, I'm a little surprised. The video actually makes me feel angry and a little frustrated. I am angry because the boy in the video, Jeremy, seems so misunderstood and neglected and alone. He's just a boy, and the video shows his parents ignore him and his peers make fun of him. He seems frightened and alone, and for some reason that makes me feel angry. At the same time, it makes me feel frustrated. The situation seems so hopeless for the boy—Jeremy. The way the music builds to this frantic rush at the beginning (it starts with something like school bells chiming slowly and then builds up to a loud and frantic pace) creates a feeling of something being out of control, and that makes me feel frustrated, too. I think I feel a little afraid, too. The shots of the singer, Eddie Vedder, kind of make me afraid. He has a wild look in his eyes, seems dangerous. And when he sings "woo" over and over again, there's something scary and frantic about that sound. There's also something really sad when he almost moans "woah." And he sounds very angry when he chants "I-I-I," and then almost a calm resignation when he ends the song with "uh-huh." The images in the video are scary in a way—the quick flashes, the flashes of red, the big wolf head and eye, the classroom where everyone is dressed the same (why is that scary to me? I don't know, but it is), and then Jeremy wrapped in an American flag and all the flames near the end. And the kids at the end, all afraid and

shocked and covered with blood, it looks like they've been shot. Watching the
video is like driving by a car accident. You don't want to look, but you almost
have to.

This response was very honest and thoughtful and raised many interesting points.
Now, let's examine what lies beneath the surface of that response.

In order to understand your reaction to a text, it's important to have a clear understanding of the text itself, its various components, to understand *how* it works,
both contextually and rhetorically. Start your inventory by exploring the text as an
instrument of culture.

Practicum

Watch the video "Jeremy" in its entirety or locate (record on a VHS tape, if possible)
a music video for another song and watch it. Complete a close reading of this multimedia text using the strategies covered in Chapter 1. Then, follow the example and
write an *initial response* to the video.

Contextual Inventory

A *contextual inventory* is meant to place a given text within the *context* (the conditions or circumstances that affect something) of its cultural (social and historical)
framework. Understanding when a text was written, what was happening in the world
at the time it was written, and the culture from which a text emerged helps you to
think critically about the information provided in the text.

1. Look at the subject matter of the text: What is it about? A text can be "about"
   many different things at once.
2. What is the historical setting for the text? When was it written, and where? If
   the text was written some time ago, what do you know about the time period
   in which is was written? What was happening in the world? How is that reflected in the text? You may have to do a little research to answer these questions.
3. What are the values represented in the text? Such values are often assumed
   and taken for granted as 'normal' by the author and the intended audience.
   They may also be implied.

Now, let's take a look at a possible contextual inventory.

A Contextual Inventory for "Jeremy"

1. The music video and song are about a boy who shoots himself in front of the
   classroom or shoots his classmates (I can't tell from watching the video). He
   is neglected by his parents and taunted by his peers (we know this from the
   lyrics and the images in the video). He seems to have mental or emotional

problems. And since Jeremy is not the one singing the song, it's being sung from the perspective of someone who once teased Jeremy. It's also about this other person's reaction to what happened to Jeremy.

2. I had to do a little research to answer this question. I did a Google search and found some Web sites that explained some facts about "Jeremy." None of the sites were all that great, but I looked at enough of them to pick out the accurate information. For instance, most of the sites mentioned that this song was about a real-life incident. So I did a search on Academic Search Elite databases to confirm this, and it's true (I found an interview with Vedder where he talks about this, and I found an article published in a Texas newspaper reporting on the actual incident).

   In 1991, Eddie Vedder read about a boy in Richardson, Texas, named Jeremy Wade Delle, who committed suicide in front of a high school English class. He imagined what might have made Jeremy do such a thing, and then he wrote the song "Jeremy." Eddie Vedder has said that he could really relate to the kid, Jeremy, and he knew another kid (when he was in high school) who did something similar. This shooting happened before all the school shootings in the mid-to-late 1990s, like Columbine. Plus, Jeremy Delle didn't shoot his classmates; he just shot himself.

   Pearl Jam released the song on their first album, *Ten*. And in 1992 they made a video of the song. The video caused a lot of controversy, so they had to edit it (in one version they showed Jeremy actually put the gun in his mouth, but they took that out because it was too graphic). Then later, a boy named Barry Loukatis killed one of his classmates and used as his defense what was called "the Jeremy defense." He claimed that the video influenced him to kill his classmate. Because of all this controversy, Pearl Jam never appeared in another concept video again.

3. I think the values represented in the video are implied. The video shows problems with things that we normally value, like these things aren't the way they should be. And because they aren't the way they should be, something terrible happens.

   We value the freedom to be individuals, but the video shows that the kids at the school are all the same (they're all dressed in the same uniforms). We value freedom and democracy, but the kids in the school are doing the Nazi salute at one point in the video—when they're saying the Pledge of Allegiance. And then we value parents who are loving and who take care of their kids, but the parents in the video are shown as being neglectful, and the lyrics say that, too. We value children, but in this video, Jeremy isn't valued. He's ignored. And I think that has something to do with the most important message in this song and video. I think the biggest value represented mostly in the lyrics is that Jeremy spoke. This kind of implies that he hadn't spoken before—he didn't have a voice. But he needed to have a voice—to speak and be heard. So when he spoke, he did it in a dramatic way with a gun. I think having a voice, speaking, being heard, is what is most valued in this song and video.

This contextual inventory helped raise some important points. Most significant are that the song "Jeremy" was based on an actual event and that the boy Jeremy did not kill his classmates—he committed suicide, so the final images in the video were a bit misleading. Another important discovery is the most significant value represented in the song: having a voice and being heard.

Practicum

Complete a contextual inventory for the video you collected previously using the example of "Jeremy" as a model. First, identify the subject matter of the video; then, explain the historical setting (conduct any necessary research) and identify the values represented in the video.

Rhetorical Inventory

Another way of taking inventory is to examine the *rhetorical aspects of a text*. The *rhetoric* of a text exists in the components of that text that enable the effective presentation of ideas and information. These components vary depending upon the type of media:

- In terms of *print media,* rhetoric includes everything from words, sentences, and paragraphs, to the introduction, the organizational structure of the text, the examples used to develop the content of the text, and the particular style in which a text is written.
- For *static visual media,* rhetoric includes the people, places, and things pictured in the text; the colors (or lack of colors); the lighting effects; and textures, lines, and angles; and the focal points (what is in the foreground, what is in the background).
- The rhetoric of *aural media* includes all sounds contained in a text. Those sounds may be created by instruments, including voice and musical instruments such as guitar or piano or drums, but they may also be sounds occurring naturally in the world around us, the sounds of nature or mechanical sounds. Aural rhetoric includes the tones of all sounds, the pitch, volume, and any words spoken or sung (dialogue or lyrics).
- The rhetoric of *multimedia,* such as television, may include all of the elements of visual and aural media.
- The rhetoric of *interactive media,* such as Web pages, includes aspects of print, visual, and sometimes aural media, but also includes an interactive element (how a user manipulates a particular text and how the text responds to that manipulation).

To take inventory of the rhetorical aspects of the text, ask the following questions:

1. How are ideas and information communicated by the text, and what tools are used? How would you characterize this communication? Is the rhetoric of the text formal, highly technical, or informal and conversational?
2. Who was the intended audience for the text? To answer this question you may have to find out where it was originally published.
3. What does the author assume that you know already? Look for blanks in the text, information gaps.

Here is an example of a rhetorical inventory of "Jeremy":

A Rhetorical Inventory of "Jeremy"

1. The ideas are communicated in the video through the music (the instruments and the lyrics), Eddie Vedder's voice, and the visual images, which include the people in the video (Jeremy, his parents, his classmates, the teacher), the scenery (the woods, the classroom, the kitchen), and other things like the pictures Jeremy drew, the oversized photographs of a wolf and an eye, and traditional men's and women's clothes, the American flag, the flames. Ideas are also communicated by words and phrases that pop up in the video, like "peers" and "disturbed" and "because I said so." Eddie Vedder also communicates a lot through his presence in the video as he sings the song. So I think the song is important, and the visual images are important; together they communicate the ideas that the parents are to blame, the peers are to blame, the teachers are to blame that no one listened to Jeremy. The song says this, and the visual images show this. But the repetition of "Jeremy spoke in class today" brings a deeper level of meaning to the video. I think I'd characterize this communication as symbolic more than anything. The visual images leave a lot of room for interpretation. And I think the rhetoric of this text is highly technical and artistic. But it's also kind of minimalist: the images are simple, not crowded with lots of details.
2. This video was mostly shown on MTV. I think the audience is teenagers and young adults. MTV's audience is typically made up of fifteen to twenty-five year olds.
3. I think the artist assumes we know and recognize a lot. He assumes we will recognize Jeremy's behavior as disturbed (the crazy drawing, the expressions Jeremy makes when he is in class, the scene where he is yelling at his parents). He assumes we will have a particular idea of the way parents should behave and that we will recognize the behavior of Jeremy's parents as wrong (they seem to ignore Jeremy, and they blame each other; they don't take responsibility). I think he assumes we will understand the visual images, like the wolf and the eye. He assumes we will understand how school is supposed to be and recognize that there are problems with the system (that kids are asked to conform and when they don't, they are outcast). He assumes we will understand what it means when Jeremy is draped in an American flag. He assumes we will understand what he means by "Jeremy spoke in class today."

From this inventory, it is apparent that the lyrics and the visual images complement each other but that the repetition of the words "Jeremy spoke in class today" (which are not explicitly represented with visual images) are meant to bring a deeper level of meaning to the song and video. It also becomes apparent that the visual images were largely symbolic and that the artist assumed a great deal of knowledge on the part of the audience. There were many gaps in the text that the reader was responsible for filling based on his or her experience and understanding.

Practicum

Complete a rhetorical inventory of your video. Examine the ideas communicated by the video, explain the tools used to communicate those ideas, and characterize the style of communication. Then identify the intended audience for the video and explore the gaps in the video. What does the artist assume that his or her audience will already know?

Reader Inventory

Once you have examined a text for context and rhetorical elements, it is time to examine *your reading* of a text. Take inventory of your experience and how that shapes your reaction to a text, and explore your experience as a reader of the text and how that influences your understanding.

To take a reader inventory, begin by asking yourself these questions:

1. How are your personal values demonstrated in your response to the text? These values come from family, your religious upbringing, and your education.
2. What is your prior knowledge of the subject matter covered in the text? Do you know a lot about the subject? Not much at all? Would you call yourself a novice or an expert or something in between? Where did you acquire your prior knowledge or information on this subject? Through experience? Observation? Distanced education?
3. What are your expectations when you read such a text on this subject matter?

Take a look at this model reader inventory.

A Reader Inventory of "Jeremy"

1. My personal values are clearly demonstrated in my response to this text, particularly in my initial response. I have been taught to feel compassion for other people, so I responded in a very emotional way to Jeremy's pain. My experience with my parents has been a positive one. My parents are there for me and involved in my life, so I value them and they value me. A big part of my reaction to this video has to do with that. I am angry when I see parents neglect their children. My personal values are also demonstrated in my feelings of frustration. I have been taught to help those who are in need. I see that Jeremy is in need, but I can't do anything to help him. It's too late, so I feel frustrated.
2. My prior knowledge of music videos is just as entertainment. I watch MTV and VH1. But I haven't ever really thought about a video in depth. So this was new to me. I didn't know much about Pearl Jam or the song "Jeremy." That's why I had to do a little research. I did know about the school shooting (like Columbine), so at first this knowledge led me to kind of misunderstand the video (since it was made before a lot of the school shootings happened— and it was about a suicide instead of murder). So I guess I began this assign-

ment as a little more than a novice, but a little less than an expert. I really began it as a consumer. I think I'm a little more than a consumer now.

3. My expectations for a music video before doing this assignment were that it be entertaining and that it fit with the song and tell some sort of story about the song. This video fulfilled my expectations. It's entertaining, it's a great song, and the video is full of lots of interesting images. And it did tell Jeremy Delle's story, but it's how Eddie Vedder and Pearl Jam see that story and the causes behind it. I didn't really expect the video to show me why this happened, but it does show me lots of possibilities. I didn't expect the video to be a part of the "blame game," but it is. So in that way, it surprised me.

Practicum

Complete a reader inventory for your video. Examine how your personal values are represented in your initial response to the video. Explain your prior knowledge of the subject matter covered in the video and your expectations of this particular type of text.

Reflection

After taking thorough contextual, rhetorical, and reader inventories, you should look back at your initial response to a text and answer the following questions: How does your reader inventory conflict with the inventory of the text (contextual and rhetorical)? Does an examination of these inventories help to explain your response to the text? How so?

Making connections now will help you to read, understand, and engage with the issue on a deeper, more meaningful, and purposeful level. Sometimes it is useful to share your inventories with your peers. Lots of useful insights come out of group discussions.

Finally, here is a reflection of the experience of reading the music video "Jeremy" and completing the series of inventories.

Reflections of "Jeremy"

I think my reader inventory is only slightly in conflict with the contextual inventory. Most of that conflict comes from a lack of experience. I had experienced watching videos before—and watching this video in particular, but I had never looked very closely at a video for what the artist was saying (I had never "read" a video before). So I wasn't prepared to pick up on the significance of everything the video was communicating. I felt a lot of things when I watched this video, but I never thought about what I was feeling or why I was feeling it. It disturbed me, but I never said, "Hey, this bothers me," and I never thought about why. And the most important thing to come of this close examination, I think, is that I realized what I think Eddie Vedder is really saying. At first, it looks like Jeremy is just mentally ill—all of the crazy images. And if you look a little closer, it looks like Vedder is blaming the parents and the peers. But it goes even deeper than that. I think he's really saying that we have to listen to each other. Everyone has to have a voice. If parents don't listen and peers don't listen and other people in our lives (like teachers) don't listen, someone might be destroyed, like Jeremy was destroyed. We need a voice so much, need to be heard so much, we will find a way. Even if that way is through violence. I never would have seen that if I hadn't done this inventory.

Practicum

Complete a reflection of your inventory process. How does your reader inventory conflict with the inventory of the text (contextual and rhetorical)? Does an examination of these inventories help to explain your response to the text? How so?

Share your video and inventories with your classmates and discuss your responses and your experiences with this process. How does taking inventory help you to better understand a text?

WRITING ASSIGNMENT   Quest Two: Examining Assumptions—A Critical Inquiry Inventory

Select one of the events you studied for Quest One from the *Event Casebooks Gallery.* This will be your focus for Quest Two and possibly one or more future Quests.

The first two texts in each casebook cover the initial reports on an event. The remainder of the texts cover multiple issues connected to the event. In these texts, the authors explore possible responses to the question raised at the beginning of this chapter: *Why did this happen?* With regard to each event, common social issues are blamed, and each author makes a compelling case.

When faced with so many different—and often emotionally charged and conflicting—possibilities, as an audience (and as a society), it can be difficult to determine what you think and feel, what you believe to be true. That's why a close reading and analysis of this blame game is necessary before moving any further in your investigation.

Begin this part of your Quest by reading the multimedia sources in your casebook using the reading strategies covered in Chapter 1 (record, question, respond). (Note: Your instructor will determine how many texts you are responsible for covering in this assignment.) Then complete an inventory; explore your initial response and complete a contextual inventory, a rhetorical inventory, a reader inventory, and a reflection for each text.

As you complete your inventories, take your time. Don't rush. Your goal is discovery—to come to an understanding of your reaction to various social issues connected to your event, the texts discussing those social issues, and your own experiences that influence your reaction. In order to achieve this discovery, your responses must be honest and thorough.

After you finish this activity, you should have a much clearer understanding of the issues being blamed for your event, and you should have a clearer understanding of your thoughts and feelings about these issues. As you organize this Quest to submit it for evaluation and grading, select one text with which you strongly agree, one text with which you disagree, and one text that you really have no opinion about one way or another. Review your inventories for each of these texts. How did the process of taking inventory help you to understand your feelings about each text? Write a brief reflection in which you consider your thoughts and feelings prior to taking inventory, your thoughts and feelings after taking inventory, and the reasoning behind your selections.

Ultimately, you should be able to confidently select one or more issues you feel strongly about for the focus of your future quests.

Criteria for a Successful Inventory

For this assignment, complete a close reading and analysis of various texts engaged in the blame game surrounding your chosen event. Build on the close reading strategies practiced in Chapter 1, and begin to practice analytical strategies in order to develop an understanding of the issues raised in each text and your own reactions to those issues. Through this process, you will begin to understand the context of the text (and the issues discussed in the text), how the text works rhetorically, how rhetoric influences understanding, and how your own experience as a reader influences your understanding of a text.

A successful inventory meets the following criteria:

- Complete an initial close reading of each text (record, question, respond).
- Complete an inventory for each text that includes initial response, contextual inventory, rhetorical inventory, reader inventory, and reflection. Each section of the inventory should demonstrate engagement with the text and the issues discussed. Each section should demonstrate exploration and development of ideas (including frequent references to the original text, the event, the issues, and personal experiences).
- Demonstrate discovery by raising questions that may or may not be answered at this point in your learning process. Share insights into the issues and your response to the issues.
- Make connections between the context of each text and the rhetorical features of each text, your own personal experiences, and the broader conversation about the event at large.
- Demonstrate critical reflection skills in your selection of and commentary about a text with which you agree, a text with which you disagree, and a text about which you feel neutral.

In the Spotlight: A Student Model Inventory

The Author: Beth Horton

Beth was a freshman at the University of North Carolina–Charlotte in the spring of 2003. Her major is education, and she plans to teach in the public schools after graduation.

Author's Etcetera

Regarding her inventories, Beth said,

> This process took a long time, and at first I thought it might be busywork. But once I completed my first inventory and reread it to do the reflection, I realized how much I had learned from the process. This kind of close examination really does help you to look at a text in a new way and to discover things about the text and yourself that you wouldn't be able to do without asking and answering these questions. When we started this quest, I had no idea what my focus would be. After I finished my inventories, I knew exactly what I wanted to study for the rest of the semester.

This portion of Beth's inventory is in response to an article by Paul Valone, "Media Responsible for Copycat Teen Violence" (published in *The Charlotte Observer*, May 1999).

Cultural Inventory 1: "Media Responsible for Copycat Teen Violence"

Initial Response

I hate this article! It really upsets me for obvious, basic reasons. He's talking about me and people like me—my friends, my peers! We're teens! We consume the media he blames for these school shootings. I love the media, television and music! And speaking as a teen and a consumer, what he's saying in this article makes me angry. I'm angry that he seems to think teenagers are like these empty vessels—just waiting to be filled with media violence so we can *become* violent. I just don't think that's the answer. It's a way-too-easy cop out.

It's like the author's example of the boys watching news coverage after the shooting in Arkansas—kids who think these shootings are cool, they have problems, serious problems, already. The media isn't to blame for those problems. I think it's a basic values thing. I think something is missing in their way of looking at life and the value of life. Like that Creed song says, they don't know what this life is for. They don't know. And that seems to me to be the real problem. So I'm angry that the media keeps on getting all this blame. It's like diverting attention away from the really important issues, the real reasons all of this keeps happening.

I feel angry as I'm reading this, but I also agree with some of it. I think the people in charge of the news media could be a little more responsible about how they report things. But it isn't the media, it's the people behind the media and their lack of values. The parts of the article that discussed broadcasts being shown at later hours of the evening were absurd. Mr. Valone doesn't seem to know kids too well. It is a common fact that if kids want to see something badly enough, they will see it. It's a nice idea in a fairytale world, but in reality it would never happen. Yes, the ideas for these crimes are put "out there" when the news covers events like school shootings, but just because an idea is "out there" doesn't mean the idea will cause someone else to do something similar. We're not monkeys!

The author does make a good point that some artists have explicit lyrics and maybe those lyrics aren't appropriate for everyone to hear, but what effect do those lyrics have on school shootings? No one has ever been able to prove that there was a connection. I listen to songs with explicit lyrics, I watch the news, I watch violent movies, and I'm not going to pick up a gun and start shooting my classmates.

More than anything, after I read this article, I'm scared for the youth of today—and tomorrow. I'm scared because people like Mr. Valone don't understand teenagers, and they're looking at the wrong issues related to school shootings like Columbine. If the powers that be don't wake up and get past all this blaming of scapegoats like the media and get to some real answers, how many more Columbines will we see? So I'm scared. But I guess mostly I feel angry or frustrated that we're not getting to the real issues. This focus on media is a smoke screen. And I'm motivated. This mayhem has got to stop.

Contextual Inventory

1. This article is about the school shootings that were happening around the country in 1999. It's about the media's responsibility and the way that the people in charge of the media aren't taking any action.

2. This article was written in 1999 in Charlotte, North Carolina. This was immediately after the Columbine shooting and several others like it—at the height of what seemed like an epidemic of school-related violence. Around the same time, the rest of the country was in turmoil because of the President Clinton and Monica Lewinsky scandal. That scandal was a terrible disgrace to American pride and made us all question the values and morals we live by. We were shocked that the leader of our country could do something so disgraceful. Schools were in the media a lot because of shootings similar to Columbine. There was 24/7 news coverage of shootings like Columbine. And there was a lot of violence in all kinds of media like movies and video games and music (was Eminem popular?). The Internet was a big deal. Everyone just about had a computer. There was a problem in Kosovo—our military was involved, I think.

3. This author values people taking responsibility and taking action. He doesn't seem to value sympathy for the killers at all or the way of trying to justify or explain what those people did. He does not value doing something for money (that comment about body bags for bucks). He doesn't value the main way of reading the Second Amendment. He thinks differently than a lot of people, so I guess he values independent thinking (and probably free speech), though he thinks the Framers would never have meant for things to be the way they are now. But I think he assumes his audience will have a lot of knowledge about these different kinds of media—and the people he talks about—and that the audience will agree with him. I think he assumes his audience will share his beliefs and kind of rail up against the people in power and the media (like the media is a part of that power).

Rhetorical Inventory

1. This is a print text, so the ideas are communicated with words, written examples. The language is kind of a mixture of semiformal (educated, anyway) and conversational. I think he's a little sarcastic at times, maybe the correct term is ironic? I don't think he exactly means everything that he says exactly as he says it. But I'm not sure about this.
2. This was published in the *Charlotte Observer*, so I guess the audience was people in the Charlotte area—or in North Carolina, anyway.
3. This is a hard one to answer. I guess he assumes that we know all about the school shootings and that we know who people like T. J. Solomon are. He assumes we have seen these newscasts. He assumes we know about these different types of media. And he assumes we know about Clinton and that we have opinions about him—and that we know about Spike Lee and the NRA. He assumes we know how media works, that profits are a big factor. He assumes we have knowledge of the Constitution and of how Congress works. He assumes we'll agree that the audience will understand that media is influential. He assumes we, the audience, will not expect him to look into the psyche (?) of the killers.

Reader Inventory

1. I got angry at the author for blaming the media when I think there are other factors that are to blame, so I guess this shows I value thinking about the real cause behind something. I value honesty. I value being fair. I value looking at what motivates someone to do something, understanding behavior. And I guess that's how I think you get to justice. I value justice, I guess, because I don't like to see the wrong people or things blamed. Yeah, I think it's about justice and injustice. And I think this definitely comes from my family background. My dad is a lawyer, and he's always been really big on doing the right thing, justice. And I grew up in a kind of big family and my older brothers were always blaming things on me when I was little (things I didn't do), so I hate to see someone or something get blamed when they're really not at fault. But then when I grew up a little—and they did—my brothers also took up for me in a lot of situations. Also, I've always loved the media, movies, and music, and things like that, and I know these things are valuable. My mom made decisions about what we could or couldn't watch on TV, and I guess I just see this as a more personal thing, not a corporate thing.
2. I don't know a lot about the school shootings, only what I've recently read. I've never experienced something violent like that in my own life. And I don't know much about what goes on behind the scenes with media. But I have been a big consumer of media all of my life. So I do know about what the media puts "out there," and I've never been driven to commit some sort of violent act because of something I've seen on TV. So maybe with the media and how it effects people, I am an expert because of my experience. Like I said before, the knowledge I have of school shootings comes from reading what I have for this

class, mostly, or hearing people talk about it. My knowledge of the media only comes from being a consumer.

3. I expect someone who writes an article like this to know what he's talking about and to have his facts straight. And I guess I expect to not really agree with much of what he says—he's coming at this from a different perspective than I am. So I guess I really didn't expect to agree with him.

Reflection

I think that my values conflict with the values represented in the text. I value justice and not really placing blame but figuring out what makes someone tick—why these kids did what they did, why they didn't value life enough, why they were sad. I don't care about the money or all that name-calling. I think we have to look inside the person— these external influences aren't as important as the psychological state of the person.

I was able to see that the author of this text was not dealing with the things that I think should be dealt with. He has some good points, but I don't think he's addressing the real issues. I didn't see that before I broke things down in this detail. I think doing this inventory helped me to understand that what I am really interested in is the idea of justice. I don't think justice is served when we blame the media for violence. I think that it is an injustice to focus our attention on the media. And that is why I get angry when I read articles like this.

I see now that I am a big consumer of media and I may have my own personal bias when dealing with this topic. I also don't know very much about the inner workings of the media business, and it might be important (when seriously addressing the points raised by Mr. Valone) to find out more about who creates the media, where the funding comes from, and what sort of agenda may exist on the part of the creators or sponsors.

Practicum

Using the Criteria for a Successful Inventory, evaluate Beth's model. As you consider each criterion, refer to specific examples from the text of her inventory to support your evaluation. Then, share your responses with your classmates. Do you find that your evaluations are in agreement? Or are there particular points on which you disagree?

Reflection in Action

Before you began this chapter, did you feel you were engaged with the issues surrounding your event? How much did you feel that these issues impacted your life or the lives of those around you? After reading the articles in this chapter and completing the inventories, do you feel any more engaged? What does it take for someone to personally engage with social issues? What sort of connection must occur? In your opinion, why is it important to become actively involved in what is happening in the world around you? How can research and writing help you to get involved, to engage?

Expanding Your Vision: A Multimedia Assignment Option

Critical Inquiry: Digging Deeper

Now that you have explored the blame game surrounding your event and several examples of texts engaged in that game in your casebook, and you've explored your response to those texts and the information they provide, what do you think?

Make a list of the most relevant issues to come out of the blame game; then take a moment to reflect on each of these issues apart from the event, and then as they relate to the event you are studying. Why are these issues most relevant? Can you think of other events to which these issues are related? Current events? At this point in your studies, what do you see as the strengths and weaknesses of each issue?

Finally, pinpoint which of these issues you feel strongest about, and why. What questions do you have at this point that you would like to answer through further research?

Form groups and discuss your responses. How have your classmates answered the question, Why did this happen? What do you think about their answers?

MULTIMEDIA ASSIGNMENT   Visi-Quest Two: Expanding Your Vision by Expressing Your Opinion

Overview

You have read, discussed, and analyzed the initial media coverage of your event. You have looked into the issues that emerged in the talk that followed that event. You have explored your reaction to that event and those issues, your thoughts, and your feelings by taking a careful inventory. Now it is time to select one issue, the issue you feel is most relevant to your event, and to consider the question, *Why did this happen?*

The issue that you choose will become your primary focus for the remainder of your Quests; therefore, it is important that you feel passionately about the issue you choose. You should feel driven to join the conversation on this issue. You might feel that this issue is to blame for your event, or you might feel like it is not to blame. You might have questions and feel unsure as to whether or not the issue is to blame. Whatever your opinion at this time, you should feel engaged by this issue enough that you want to study it in greater detail.

Once you have selected your focus issue, write an unsupported opinion essay explaining your current opinion regarding that issue. This essay should be expressive and persuasive and should demonstrate your commitment to the study of your chosen issue.

In this essay, you should explain the following:

○ What have you learned about the issue you've chosen to study?
○ What are your current thoughts and feelings about the issue as it relates to your event and apart from (or beyond) that event?
○ What is your background with the issue? Did you uncover any personal connections through your cultural inventories?
○ What do you hope to learn in your future studies?

Your Goal Is to Convince Your Audience That You Have a Personal Commitment to the Study of This Issue

Step 1: Thirty-Minute Rant

What is a rant, you might ask? Well, in written form, a rant is an emotionally charged freewrite. It is an exploratory piece of writing used as a discovery tool during the writing process. A rant expresses and explores your thoughts, feelings, and opinions on a subject, yet it does not require that you support any of your ideas with evidence.

So, get busy and rant! Go back and reread your inventories, particularly your initial responses and reflections connected to your issue. Then start writing—for thirty minutes. That's right: *thirty minutes.* Settle down in front of your computer with your soda or coffee nearby, some music playing, and with your chosen issue in mind—and start writing. What do you think about the issue? What do you feel? Why does it matter to you? What do you know? What questions do you have? What do you hope to learn? Don't worry about grammar, punctuation, or finding the right word or phrase— just write. Let your thoughts and feelings flow out through your fingertips and *RANT*. For *THIRTY MINUTES*. You'll be surprised at how much you have to say.

Step 2: Testing the Waters

Bring your rant to class. Take turns in small groups reading aloud your rants. Listen to one another with a questioning ear and decide, Does this person care enough about this issue to study it in depth over the next thirteen or so weeks? If the answer is yes, then you will begin drafting your essay. If the answer is no, you will have to explore some other issues.

Step 3: The Essay

If your classmates give you the okay, complete a draft of your opinion essay. Be careful to stay focused on your issue. Develop your thoughts with explanations and examples that help to illustrate the points you wish to make.

Criteria for a Successful Opinion Essay

For this assignment, you must demonstrate a personal commitment to the in-depth study of one issue. This type of writing is expressive and persuasive, so it must retain both the balanced tone of an academic piece of writing and enough emotionally charged examples and expressions to convince the reader that you are engaged with the issue.

Focus: A focused opinion essay should demonstrate your commitment to one issue. The response should be concentrated on the four proposal questions as they relate to the issue and to your experience.

Development: This assignment is developed with details from your direct personal experience or from academic or observational knowledge. You may use anecdotes from personal experience or observation, or you may discuss and explain information you have picked up either from the media or through academic research. For this assignment, information does not have to be documented. However, you must honestly discuss how little or how much you believe you know at this point in your studies. You must qualify your presentation of information with statements such as "I have heard," or "I have read in various sources." At this point, unless your knowledge comes from direct personal experience, you must acknowledge that it is hearsay.

Regardless of which type of information you use to develop your essay, it must be selected with the goal of persuasion in mind. You must consider at all times: How can I best persuade my audience that I am committed to the study of this issue? This type of persuasion must demonstrate thoughtfulness, genuine curiosity, and concern. In the best of circumstances, some sort of emotional response will be demonstrated (sometimes this response is anger, sometimes sadness, sometimes frustration, etc.). But do not force yourself to emote.

Organization: The four questions serve as a basic organizational structure for this assignment, but you must include an appropriate introduction and conclusion, as well. A good introduction establishes the focus of the essay, grabs the reader's attention, and often establishes an organizational pattern for the remainder of the essay. An appropriate conclusion brings the essay to a close while strengthening the essay and bringing logical closure to the ideas presented in the essay.

In the Spotlight: A Student Model Opinion Essay

The Author: Jennifer Charles

Jennifer Elizabeth Charles was eighteen when she wrote her opinion essay. She chose to attend the University of North Carolina–Charlotte because, "I love Charlotte and could not even begin to imagine leaving the city. Most people think that kids who are from Charlotte and decide to stay in Charlotte for college are wimping out, but that's not the reason. I can't imagine my life in any other place."

Author's Etcetera

As for this assignment, Jennifer says,

> I had not originally recognized guns as the most important issue connected to the Columbine shootings; in fact, when I first started studying Columbine, I was looking at several of the issues, like parental responsibility and peers and media. But after completing the Quest Two Inventories, I realized that I had so much more to say about guns than I did about any other issue. It was the only issue that I actually felt passionate about and could get excited about researching. And it was the one issue I felt was directly and unquestionably responsible for the Columbine tragedy.

At the time she wrote the essay, Jennifer had very little knowledge of guns, gun control laws, and youth violence in general, but she had a very strong opinion about this issue based on personal experience (the suicide of a close friend): "That experience was what helped fuel my desire to learn about guns and teenagers."

Most People Ask: Do Guns Kill People, or Do People Kill People? I Say: People with Guns Kill People

Guns don't kill people, people kill people. This is the age-old debate, well, as old as guns and gun laws at least. There is no question that violence would exist even without guns. Violence is as old as man himself, and guns did not arrive on the scene until the thirteenth century. Guns have, however, created a new kind of severity, a level of violence in which injury and often death are immediate and irreversible.

My knowledge of guns is limited. Perhaps that is one of the reasons why I am so interested in the focus of guns. Even more limited than my knowledge of guns is my knowledge of gun laws. I know that in general gun laws are left up to the state government. I know that the National Rifle Association (NRA) is prevalent especially in the South and the Midwest. I've heard statistics that scare me, such as every ten minutes a child in America is killed by a gun. By the time you've finished reading this proposal, someone who might have made a difference in our country will have perished due to gun violence. This is all because we supposedly feel safer in our own homes when we are accompanied by a gun, and the laws agree with us. I wish I knew more about guns. If I knew more, I might be able to explain better why I feel as strongly as I do about the subject. I just know that I feel very strongly that people with guns kill other people—or themselves—and that this should not be allowed to happen.

My initial response to the gun issue related to the Columbine High School shooting was not as strong as I would have expected it to be considering my passion for it now. At first I was under the impression that guns are there, always have been, always will be, so some other cause must be to blame for the deaths of those fifteen people on that terrible day, some other cause must be to blame for youth violence in general. But after completing my Inventories, I was prompted to reconsider my initial reaction. What I realized: Yes, many different ideas can be named as possible causes for the shootings, but the bottom line is easy access to guns allowed those two boys (Eric Harris and Dylan Klebold) to kill their classmates, a teacher, and themselves with ease. I realized: No access to guns = no shootings. Plain and simple. But there's nothing plain or simple about this issue in reality; the ongoing debate is deeply complex.

Realistically, even with more or different gun laws, Harris and Klebold probably would have found a way to possess guns—they certainly seemed motivated enough. So more laws or different laws doesn't seem like the answer to me. But if there had been *better enforcement of existing laws,* Harris and Klebold may have been delayed in their actions, or they may have been caught and stopped in the planning stages. At the least, tougher enforcement of existing laws may have bought time enough for someone to come forward, for logic to set in, for a mistake to have been made. Tougher enforcement of gun laws may have prevented the deaths of thirteen innocent victims on that day in April of 1999.

I am going to pause here to tell a short story. Once upon a time, there was a girl with beautiful curly red hair named Katie. I met Katie in the seventh grade when I went to a new middle school, and we became friends. In the ninth grade when high school started, Katie was the only person I knew going to my high school, and we even had the same homeroom. We became close friends. On Friday, October 8, 1999, while her parents were attending our high school football game, Katie found her father's gun, put her headphones on, and shot herself in her left temple. The end. Easy access to a gun = the end of a beautiful life. Yes, Katie might have found another way to kill herself even without the gun if she had been motivated enough to end her life. But, then again, she may not have sought another way. Katie was not fond of physical pain. In fact, in her suicide note, Katie actually said that she chose to use a gun to end her life because it was fast and quick—a gun was her weapon of choice because she did not want her death to be prolonged or painful. Had Katie's father not owned a gun, had he not kept it in the home where Katie had access to it, she might not have shot herself that Friday night. She might be alive today.

It all comes back to this: What is to blame for incidents of violence like Katie's death and the Columbine tragedy? People. With *guns.*

People with guns kill people.

There is a lot of information that I want to find out through my investigation into this issue. I want to know: What states have the strictest gun laws, and which states have the most tolerant gun laws? What are the shooting statistics in these states, and is there a correlation between the laws and the number of deaths attributed to gun violence? What laws have changed since the Columbine shootings, if any? What direction are gun laws heading in now, especially with a Republican president? And just how deeply is this fascination with guns rooted in our culture?

I keep thinking that this problem with guns is laced with irony. As children, we are taught that we can create guns with only our hands, the pointer finger stretching out to become the long barrel of the gun, our thumb propped up as the trigger. There is a great deal of power even in this make-believe weapon. I can't help but wonder, how is this pseudo-reality transformed in our adolescent minds—during a time in our lives when we are searching, when we don't know who or what to believe, a time when we are desperate for power in a world that makes us feel powerless? By that point, we've already learned where to find the power we seek. And if that is the ultimate or the only power we know of, and we have easy access to that power, what is to stop us from embracing it? Static laws bound by dusty books won't do it. Someone has to be willing and able to enforce those laws. Maybe the question should be: *Who* is to stop us from embracing it?

Practicum

Using the Criteria for a Successful Opinion Essay, evaluate Jennifer's model. As you consider each criterion, refer to specific examples from the text of her inventory to support your evaluation. Then, share your responses with your classmates. Do you find that your evaluations are in agreement? Or are there particular points on which you disagree? How does the process of reading and evaluating a model assignment help you to successfully meet the requirements of this assignment yourself?

PART TWO

Finding and Analyzing Sources: Becoming an Expert

3

Strategies for Gathering Credible Resources: Understanding Historical Context

Begin with a *Question:*
What Is the Big Picture?

Imagine this:

Jamie and a few of her suitemates are going out for the evening. Jamie's roommate, Morgan, decides not to go with them; instead she stays in to watch a movie with a guy she likes who lives on another floor. His name is Tom. Most of Morgan's friends dislike Tom, but they do not know him very well, either. Jamie is not sure how she feels about him, but she is willing to give him a chance. It is her roommate's decision, anyway, and Jamie will support whatever Morgan chooses to do. So everyone except Morgan leaves around 7:00 for a sorority drop-in on the other side of campus.

When the girls return to the dorm around 11 p.m., their suite is eerily quiet. The television is on, some food wrappers are on the floor, but Morgan is not there. Jamie opens the door to her bedroom and finds her roommate crumpled on the floor, shaking. Her face and neck are red and swollen, her mouth is open, and she is struggling to breathe. Tom is standing over her, holding a pillow. He lifts his head in a jerky motion, glancing over at Jamie with a wild look in his eyes. He seems frantic.

The suitemates hear Jamie's cry and barge into the room. They immediately assume the worst about Tom, believing he has done something to hurt Morgan. One of the suitemates knocks Tom to the floor and drags him away from Morgan. The others kneel over their sick friend and try to get her to respond.

One of the suitemates screams at Tom, "What did you do to her? She's not breathing!"

Another yells, "It looked like you were smothering her with that pillow!"

While one of the girls calls 911, Jamie runs out into the hallway and knocks on the Resident Advisor's door. She quickly explains what happened, and the Resident Advisor rushes to Morgan and begins CPR. But it does not seem to be working. She is still struggling to breathe.

Tom is in shock on the floor in the corner of the room. The suitemates continue to yell at him, but he does not respond. He just sits on the floor with a startled look on his face, clutching the pillow. The girls are sure Tom has hurt their friend.

Jamie steps back and surveys the situation. She looks at Morgan and has a strange feeling that something like this has happened before. She wonders, *What is really going on here?*

A Little Perspective Goes a Long Way

Whenever something traumatic happens, there is often an automatic sense of isolation, a tendency to feel as if we are the first, if not the only person, to endure such an experience. This sense of isolation can lead to or intensify shock; it can immobilize us. It can delay or inhibit our response to a situation, and it can prevent us from exploring our options and moving toward an effective solution to a given problem. It can cause us to carelessly cast blame. But when we understand that we are not the first or the only to experience a particular situation, that others have walked the same or a similar path before us (or along with us), this knowledge provides us with *perspective.* It places one intense experience *within the context of other experiences* and enables us to ask more effective questions, to seek fresh answers, and to move forward rather than stall or stop or repeat the mistakes of the past.

Let's revisit our scenario with Jamie.

As the Resident Advisor continues to work to save Morgan, Jamie looks around the room, trying to imagine what happened to her friend. She notices the take-out container on the floor beside the television. Several wrappers are crumpled beside it, along with an empty container of french fries and some ketchup.

Jamie walks across the room and picks up one of the containers. Scattered along the bottom of a Styrofoam box, she finds dozens of light brown dots. *Seeds.*

Suddenly, she remembers Morgan telling her about a picnic, a sesame seed hamburger bun, a horrible allergic reaction, and an emergency trip to the hospital. Jamie knows what happened to her friend and also knows that Morgan carries an epinephrine auto-injector.

She rushes into her room and finds the auto-injector in Morgan's purse. Quickly, she injects the epinephrine into Morgan's thigh.

The suitemates yell at Jamie, "What are you doing?" The Resident Advisor continues to perform CPR.

Almost immediately, Morgan gasps and begins to breathe more easily on her own. Tom moves beside Jamie. "What happened? How did you know how to help her?" Jamie explained, "Seeds."

Sowing Seeds of Change

The scenario just described is not a perfect parallel, but it is close enough to make a point. When we talk about social problems and their possible causes, we often talk about these problems as if they were a disease. You have probably noticed this in some of the articles you have read in your casebook; for instance, in an article by Paul Valone (used for the student model writing assignment in Chapter 2), he describes teen violence as a disease and says that we, citizens of this society, must act as epidemiologists and track the source of the contagion. That is exactly what Jamie did in our example. She stepped back and surveyed the situation. She moved beyond a typical knee-jerk reaction to blame the most obvious, superficial cause (unlike her friends who blamed Tom because they did not like him in the first place and because he was standing over Morgan holding a pillow and *appeared* to be doing something menacing). But Jamie looked around at the big picture and placed the scene unfolding around her within the context of what she already knew about her friend. She noticed the seeds, and this observation helped Jamie to make connections to a story that Morgan had previously told her.

Jamie knew the history of her friend's severe allergy to sesame seeds, she knew Morgan had experienced a similar allergic reaction before, and she knew about the epinephrine shot Morgan carried in her purse. Based on her understanding of Morgan's history with allergies, she knew the cause of her roommate's illness and she knew how to respond. This is what we, as a society, as scholars, have to do as well. We have to stay away from knee-jerk reactions, we have to step back, *gain perspective,* survey the situation, and place it in *historical context.* We have to look closely to find the seeds of violence or whatever social problem we are studying. We have to develop an understanding of the history of the situation in order to find a workable solution.

Establishing Historical Context

There is very little that is brand new under the sun. Even in terms of community or world events, we find that situations are repeated with variation (the rash of school shootings and teen violence are good examples). Thanks in large part to the media, when a traumatic or dramatic event happens, we get caught up in the moment and have a difficult time stepping back and gaining perspective. Each incident, as it occurs, feels intensely unique and isolated. As a society, we look around desperately and cast blame here and there, hoping to somehow hit on a right answer, a solution, or some sort of understanding. But time and again, we ask the same questions, offer the same opinions, talk about the same solutions—and nothing changes.

Unfortunately, as a society, we tend to have a historically challenged collective memory. We react to events and situations with fervor and passion as they occur, and we forget that others may have walked a similar path before us and that there is much to be learned from the past. When we think of an incident as singular and unique, we miss the opportunity to make connections that are vital if we want to break negative cycles and someday prevent the same thing from happening again. When we do not take the past into consideration, we waste precious time casting unwarranted blame.

However, if we take the time to investigate the history of an event, if we study what happened before in similar situations, what was done in response, what worked, what did not work, we begin to see what is relevant and what is irrelevant; patterns begin to emerge. Within those patterns, we might discover common threads that will move us closer to understanding cause and effect and to developing a workable solution.

Gaining historical perspective is a lot like running a pre-employment background check. Before we employ a particular theory, we want to investigate its background. We want to look at an event and find out if anything similar has occurred before. If it has, when did it occur, and under what circumstances? Maybe this sort of event has occurred more than once in the past. If so, how often does something like this occur? How are the circumstances surrounding like-events similar and how are they different? Have cause-and-effect connections ever been made before? What has been done in response?

By understanding the history of an event, we can better understand the issues that arose from that event, and we will probably discover that it has occurred before. Knowing that a particular kind of event has been dealt with in the past should defuse the panic we feel in the present. Others have walked a similar path and survived, so there is a pretty good chance that we will be okay, too.

In studying history, we discover patterns. We remind ourselves of what has been said and done before so we do not repeat the mistakes others have already made. We are able to try new approaches and different strategies with the hope of finding better solutions.

Investigating an Event or an Issue: Seek and Ye Shall Find

In this chapter, we discussed the importance of developing a historical perspective when studying social problems, their causes, and possible solutions. It is imperative to understand the depth and breadth of an event or a social issue in order to make change happen. Historical context is not a concept we naturally understand; it is a perspective that is developed through study, analysis, and contemplation, and it requires *research*.

I find research to be exciting. When I am researching, I see myself as a detective. I am on the case, in search of clues to solve a mystery. Like any detective, I need a reliable group of informants—sources of information on any given topic. While taking this course and conducting research on your event and issue, you are a detective, too. You are on the case and in search of clues to solve *your* mystery. It is all about chasing clues, uncovering details, and bringing to light a truth (or truths) that you want to share with the world. Like any good detective, you first have to run a background check: you have to gather information to place your case in the appropriate historical context. So, Detective, where are you going to look for the information you need?

There are three major types of searches you will perform as an academic detective: *field research*, *library research*, and *Internet research*. Which search you choose depends largely on the type of information you need, and that depends upon your assignment and the resources available to you.

Field Research

Field research is investigation that involves research out in the field. No, not a field of grass but a *field of information in the broadest sense outside of the classroom and apart from traditional sources of text.* Field research is active and requires that you interview a person, that you visit a place, and that you gather information firsthand. This type of research is not especially common for academic purposes, but when it is appropriate and you have the opportunity, it can yield some interesting results.

For instance, as I put together this textbook, I ran across contact information for many of the authors of the articles and artwork I selected to include in various chapters. Anytime I came across such information, I contacted the author. Sometimes I got a response, sometimes I did not. Sometimes the response I got was helpful, insightful, and informative (and was ultimately included in this text), and sometimes it was not.

My purpose for contacting authors was to go beyond the information I had available to me from other sources. I wanted to ask them about the articles they had written or the artwork they had produced, to see if they had additional information, comments, or insights they would like to share.

All of the contacts I made regarded articles about fairly current events and information (most events occurred within the last decade). When dealing with older articles, I often found that the contact information was outdated, so I had to do a bit of research to locate current information. In these cases, field research was more of a challenge, but it was not impossible. Thanks to the Internet (and the search engine Google), I had a great deal of success tracking folks down. More often than not, I found authors and artists from all walks of life and levels of success were quite willing to correspond with me (everyone from government officials to newspaper reporters to Pulitzer Prize–winning artists to rock stars). So, do not be afraid to reach out and contact people. Authors, artists, and executives are folks just like you and me. They are often happy to speak with you and to provide you with information.

In any case, field research is a fabulous tool. Some advice: When conducting field research, take scrupulous notes, record phone calls (with prior knowledge of all parties involved), and make a record of your communication (dates, times, etc.). Just like any other kind of research, it is important to leave a paper trail when conducting field investigations (we cover this topic in greater detail later in this chapter).

Library Research

In this ever-expanding world of technology, the library is often not first on our list of resources when we begin a research project. However, it is important to remember that the library is a vital part of the academic community, and while it is true that many, if not most, sources are now available to us through the Internet, the library offers many valuable print sources as well.

One distinct advantage to resources recovered in the library over resources found on the Internet has to do with credibility. All of the sources procured by a university

library are first screened by the librarian and are considered to be respectable throughout the academic community. Many sources found on the Internet are not screened
by professionals and therefore lack credibility in the eyes of the academic community.
So, if absolute credibility is an important issue while researching, the library is the best
place to begin your work (we discuss credibility in more depth later in this chapter).

The types of print sources available to us vary from institution to institution. For
the most part, when beginning a research project, we might look first to a *reference
text* to provide general background information. For instance, if we are looking for an
overview of an event or an issue for which we have very little prior knowledge, an
encyclopedia is a good place to start. This source is available in the *reference area* of
most libraries. These texts are not in circulation but are available for use in the library during regular hours.

In addition to reference texts, the library has many *texts in circulation* that may be
checked out and taken home for an extended period of time. Fiction and nonfiction
books, collections of works by a particular author or a group of authors, and an-
thologies of critical essays are just a few examples of the types of book sources we
might find in circulation. These books may be located using an online catalog search
engine. Online catalogs replaced the dusty index files libraries used many years ago.
Most online catalog searches may be conducted using the author's last name, the title
of a book or document, or a subject keyword.

In addition to reference texts and circulating fiction and nonfiction books, most
libraries also have *collections of periodicals*. Periodicals (called so because they are
published periodically: daily, weekly, monthly, etc.) are magazines, newspapers, or
professional journals that are usually grouped according to subject matter. Periodicals are often available solely through the library in print form (or on microfilm),
particularly if you are interested in materials more than five years old. Magazines,
such as *Time, Newsweek, Rolling Stone,* and *Sports Illustrated,* are most often considered popular texts and are read by the general population of a culture. Newspapers cover current events, and most libraries subscribe to local, national, and
international newspapers. Hard copies of newspapers are kept for a relatively short
time because they do not hold up very well through normal wear and tear. However,
most libraries keep microfilm or microfiche copies of newspapers that date back as
far as the 1800s. Professional or scholarly journals are academic publications designed to be read by professionals and students in a particular field of study. These
are typically kept in bound copies and are a wonderful resource when researching
social problems.

Helpful Hint

Finding what we need in the library is often a challenging task. Many times, the best
sources are not located through the most obvious channels. Once we have exhausted
sources located through the online catalog or reference desk, another strategy that
often turns up the best information is a *search of indexes*. Most books and periodicals
contain an index.

Typically located in the back of a publication, the index is an alphabetical listing of keywords or phrases found in the text. The keywords lead us to particular pages within a text and often to the most specific and useful information.

It is also useful to pay attention to *bibliographies* included in a book or periodical. If we find an article or essay that contains useful information, locating the sources an author used in writing that article may lead us to even more useful information.

Internet Research

The Internet is one of the most valuable tools available to a researcher. There is almost nothing you cannot find on the Internet. The Internet allows us to traverse the World Wide Web, an amazing resource for academics that has revolutionized the research process. Millions upon millions of Internet Web sites are available at our fingertips twenty-four hours a day every day.

The convenience of researching on the Internet is most appealing, *but it is important to be wary.* Not all information found on the Internet is worthy of our attention. Anyone with access to a computer and Web space can create and post a Web site on any topic. For example, a twelve-year-old girl may be a big fan of the punk rock group blink-182 and may construct a Web site honoring her favorite band. That Web site may have information about the band members and may contain pages upon pages of textual references, insights, and lyrical interpretations. The interpretations may even be interesting, but that does not mean the site is a credible source for an academic project. We discuss issues of credibility in dealing with all types of sources later in this chapter, but we cannot discuss electronic sources at all without also touching on the issue of credibility. When dealing with Web sources, credibility determines where you begin your search.

The most credible Web sources are *databases.* Databases such as Academic Search Elite, Masterfile Premier, the Gale Literature Resource Center, InfoTrac, MLA Bibliograhy, and Sociofiles contain articles and essays previously published and screened by a webmaster. These sources are as credible as any we might find in print form in the library. Use them freely and without hesitation.

Many magazines, journals, and newspapers available in print form are also available through the Internet, and these sources are credible as well. An article published in the online version of the *New York Times* is just as credible as an article published in the print version of the same source.

Other credible sources include government sites (.gov), institutional sites (.edu), sites published through nonprofit organizations (.org), and sites connected to reputable organizations and institutions such as the FBI, CNN, the CIA, and the American Red Cross. But you have to be wary and think critically about these sites. They are typically deemed credible within the academic community, but you must be aware that they also have a *bias* that may skew the information presented on the site. Bias may be defined as the favoring of one side of an argument or situation, one viewpoint, or the interests of one specific individual or group. All sources have a bias, and your job as a researcher is to *recognize* that bias and be sure that it does not unfairly prejudice the information presented by the source.

As for .edu sites, be aware that student Web pages are often .edu, and the student-authors of those sites may not be experts on the subject matter covered on their sites.

Keep in mind that .com and .net sites are commercial Web sites and are not affiliated with sources that are immediately deemed credible by the academic community. But it is important to emphasize that this rule is not without exception. Many .com sites are quite credible (CNN.com, for instance). Again, *we must think critically about the information we find on the Internet and use our own judgment when determining the credibility of a source.*

Some additional top-level domains emerging on the World Wide Web include the following:

- **.aero:** for aviation-related Web sites; this is the world's first industry-based top-level Internet domain name.
- **.biz:** a commercial domain registry for small and large companies.
- **.coop:** a global domain name for business cooperatives.
- **.info:** a top-level domain used by a wide range of organizations and businesses.
- **.int:** a highly regulated top-level domain used for registering organizations established by international treaties between or among national governments.
- **.museum:** a top-level domain name created by and for the global museum community.

Tools for Success: Responsible Research Strategies

Research is all about hunting and gathering information. Once you get started, it is easy to be overwhelmed by the amount of information you find on any given subject. Therefore, it is necessary to be *scrupulously organized* as you conduct your search for information.

The most important aspect of responsible research is to have a plan and to keep accurate records. Research is a process, and it works in steps and stages, much like the writing process. The more conscious you are of your research process, the more efficient an academic detective you will be. The best way to be conscious of your process is to create a *research dossier*. A research dossier is a detailed record that is guided by your purpose for researching and contains your search plan, the information you find along the way, and your initial processing of that information. The following sections detail stages of the research process to guide you as you build your research dossier.

Step One: A Research Map and Paper Trail

Whenever you begin a journey, it is always useful to follow a map. This is true for the journey of researching, too. A map provides directions and reminds you of where you plan to go, where you have been, and the many stops you have made along your journey.

The first step in making a research map is to identify your primary purpose for researching. In order to do this, *make a list of guiding questions* you will seek to answer through your research. You have probably noticed that each chapter in this book begins with a question. That question serves as a topical focus for the chapter. Beginning a research project with a list of questions provides a focus for the research and several concrete goals to achieve. This can be an important motivator.

For instance, suppose your event is something like the move by Clear Channel Communications to censor certain songs with lyrics the company deems to have questionable content. Because this event involves the attempt to censor music, you must place this event within a historical context by researching the history of music censorship. Your list of guiding questions may look something like this:

- Has there been an attempt to censor music in the past? If so, when?
- What types of music have been the targets of censorship?
- What happened as a result of the efforts to censor music?

After creating a list of questions, but before beginning the actual search process, think of where you might seek answers to your questions. This is an important part of your research plan and will save you time and effort. Will you find answers to your questions through field research? Should you visit the library? What about the Internet?

With the topic of music censorship, you might begin your process with a little field research by questioning some adults, perhaps your parents or professors, to see if they remember any attempts to censor music in the past. The information you gather through field research may give you a specific time period on which to focus as you begin your search. Or you may begin with a basic search in an online catalog or on the Internet using subject keywords like *music* and *censorship*. Wherever you begin your search, it is useful to have a plan before you get started.

As you conduct your search for information, remember that the initial research plan is just that—a plan. It is not a guarantee for success. As you search and find or do not find what you are looking for, be prepared to adjust your plan and to generate ideas for additional resources where you might find the information you seek.

In addition to a recording a plan for where you will go with your research, it is a good idea to keep notes on where you have been. Remember the story of Hansel and Gretel? They were two kids who ventured into the dark and scary woods and left a trail of breadcrumbs to follow so they could find their way back home. These were smart kids! As a researcher, you should follow Hansel and Gretel's example. The mass of information available on any topic is often a lot like the dark and scary woods, and it is easy to get lost in the thick of so many ideas and details. So it is a good idea to leave a trail of information breadcrumbs to follow should you need a little help finding your way home and back to your sense of purpose as you conduct your search.

As you look for information, write down *where* you look and the *results* of your search. This will help you in many ways. If your research is interrupted and you must come back to it later, you will not have to repeat steps. If you meet a dead end in your search, you can look back and review what you have done and make plans to move forward in a new, more fruitful direction.

To continue with our example of music censorship, you might begin with a search of online databases such as Academic Search Elite or Masterfile Premier. The record of your search may look something like this:

Search on Academic Search Elite using the keywords *music* and *controversy*	The search produces 847 results, *way* too many. Even a cursory glance through the first 20 tells me that very few of these sources are useful. I need a more precise search term.
Conduct new search with keywords *music* and *censorship*	This time the search is considerably narrowed with 247 articles, but that is still more than I need to read.
Narrow the search again by adding another keyword: *music* and *censorship* and *history*	Returns five hits, and four of those sources seem to be exactly what I need.

If you have to stop your research at this point, when you return to it, you will have a record of where you have been and what you have found to be useful. You will not waste time repeating steps, and you will be able to get immediately to the sources you need by following your own research trail.

Practicum

Working as a whole class or in small groups, decide on a common research topic for practice throughout this chapter. Then create a research map for the investigation of that topic and locate a source for information in the library and/or on the Internet. Make a paper trail of your research process. Share your experiences and discoveries with your classmates. What problems did you encounter during your initial search? How did you overcome those problems?

Step Two: Evaluating a Source: The ABCs of Credibility

As you find sources that seem to provide important information on your topic, you must decide which sources to collect and study in depth. Since part of the reason for doing research is to *boost your credibility,* you want the information you study to be reliable; you do not want to waste your time reading a bunch of sources that are less than credible, and you do not want to be misinformed. Your goal, therefore, at this point in your research process is to conduct a surface evaluation to distinguish between a reliable and an unreliable source.

The criteria for evaluating the credibility of a source varies slightly depending on whether you are looking at traditional print sources like books and periodicals or electronic sources like databases or Web sites. Regardless of the media type, you must evaluate any potential source of information for the ABCs of credibility: *authority, bias,* and *content.*

Authority

The best information on any topic comes from sources considered to be experts or authorities on that subject. When conducting a surface evaluation, authority may be determined in a number of ways. Typically, an authority is someone who has studied a subject in depth or has had considerable experience working with or living through some aspect of that subject.

To determine whether or not an author is an authority on a subject, check the credentials of the author, her education and experience. Is she educated in her field of study? Does she have a professional degree from a respectable institution of higher learning? Is her field of study relevant to the topic you are researching? Aside from education, does the author have any particular experience (work experience or life experience) that qualifies her to write on this subject? If the author has a degree or verifiable experience related to the subject matter, then she probably qualifies as an authority. This information may not be included with your source; you may have to conduct a bit of research beyond the source in order to learn about the author's credentials.

Sometimes information on the author's education or experience is simply unavailable, but do not throw the source away just yet. In this case, look to the publisher or sponsor of your source. Is the publisher well known? Not only well-known publishing houses, but also universities, government agencies, and other educational and research institutions are often reliable publishers. Association with an educational institution or respectable organization may qualify an author as an authority.

In terms of an electronic source, you may have to look for the developer of the site or the person, business, or organization that funds the site in order to determine authority. This information often may be found at the bottom of a site's home or index page or through a hyperlink titled *About.* Some sites have corporate or institutional sponsors, so one particular author or developer is not listed. In any case, someone or some organization must take responsibility for the information provided on the site, and clear contact information must be available for the site to be deemed an authority.

If you cannot locate any information about the author's, publisher's or sponsor's credentials, then the source cannot be verified as credible, and you should probably discard it and continue your research.

Bias

Bias is a difficult thing to explain and to pinpoint within a source. Typically, bias has to do with the *way* information is presented, the *type* of information presented, and the *motives* an author or publisher has for presenting that information. Because most bias cannot be detected without a close reading of a text, when conducting a surface evaluation, bias may be determined by questioning motives. Does the author, publisher, or sponsor of the source have anything to gain, personally or financially, from the promotion of that source?

For example, if a Web site denounces current government statistics on violence in the American culture and that site is sponsored by the NRA (National Rifle Association), the information presented should be carefully questioned. The NRA certainly has something to gain from the sale of guns to wary citizens who fear for their safety in a violent society. The information presented on the site may be quite credible—remember, bias is not always a bad thing—however, it does warrant scrutiny (this goes back to purpose—the purpose of the Web site and your purpose as a researcher). The important thing is to determine whether or not the bias creates any sort of logical fallacy that may affect your credibility as a researcher.

As far as visual or multimedia sources, sometimes bias may be created by the design of a site. In terms of a Web site, for instance, the colors and pictures and background music may all work to create a sort of bias (the equivalent of tone in a print source but easier to identify in a visual or multimedia text without a close reading). We must be alert to the subtle ways in which visual and audio images work to influence us.

For example, Scott Stapp, frontman for the rock band Creed (which disbanded in 2004), began a nonprofit organization called With Arms Wide Open. Many people scoffed at the idea that this was a legitimate organization simply because Stapp was a singer in a rock band. But further investigation into the site provided interesting details worthy of our consideration. According to the Mission Statement published on the foundation's Web site:

> With Arms Wide Open was established in October 2000, with the goal to protect the lives and well-being of children by seeking to ensure healthy, loving, nurturing bonds between children and their parents through funding existing service providers and identifying and addressing service gap areas. The Foundation's intent is to raise public awareness of the importance of healthy parent–child relationships in whatever form they may arise; to provide encouraging support and education to parents; and to identify and address problematic areas that impede the development and/or maintenance of healthy, loving, nurturing parent–child relationships.

The Web site, located at www.witharmswideopen.org, began with a flash presentation that created a sort of collage with pictures of parents and their children. All of the images were loving and positive and reflected the organization's mission to affirm positive parent–child relationships. The song played in the background—"With Arms Wide Open" by Creed—was written and performed by Scott Stapp for his son, Jagger. The images—accompanied by the words and music of the song—created a bias in favor of the goals supported by the organization. The bias was not negative in this case; it did not affect the credibility of the source. In fact, the bias added to the credibility of this particular source by creating an impression that supported the organization's mission. In any case, it is important to recognize that the bias exists and how it affects the audience.

Note

Just prior to publication of this textbook, the With Arms Wide Open Web site was unavailable, and we were told that the organization was not in operation as of July 2004. This is, perhaps, another lesson in credibility and the lightning-fast rate of change on the Internet.

Content

The *content* is the most important aspect of a text to explore when deciding credibility. We look more deeply into various aspects of content and credibility in Chapter 5, but as we are initially selecting sources, there are still some content issues to consider. Before studying a source in depth, you can make several judgments about content and credibility by examining audience and purpose. You must decide *who* the text was originally intended to address and *why* the text was created?

Many times *audience* and *purpose* can be determined by looking at the publisher of a document. Was an article published in a popular magazine? Popular magazines typically have easily identifiable target audiences (*Ms.* magazine, for instance, or *Rolling Stone*). Was it published in a professional or scholarly journal (such as the *Journal of the American Medical Association* or *Chronicle of Higher Education*)? As for purpose, articles published in popular magazines are intended to inform in some general way and/or to entertain a general audience, while articles published in professional and scholarly journals are intended to delve more deeply into a subject matter and in some way advance a conversation on an issue within a particular profession.

After deciding on audience and purpose, you must evaluate how an issue is covered in a source. Does the text seem to cover the topic in depth, moderately, or is this just a general overview? Your evaluation of the *scope of coverage* will depend largely on your own purposes. For most scholarly research, however, a moderately focused or in-depth essay is more preferable than an article providing a general overview on a subject.

Depending on your own focus, another important aspect of content is *currency*. How recently was the book or article written and published? In terms of a Web site, it is important to note when the Web site was created and when it was last updated.

Timeliness matters more when dealing with issues related to science and technology, but it also counts when discussing social issues—for instance, research pertaining to television violence collected in 1960 may not be as relevant as research collected in 2000. Older materials are often most useful when gathering background information or when conducting a comparative, historical analysis on a subject. For the most part, a good rule to follow is: The more timely the research, the more credible the source.

Practicum

Conduct a quick Google search online and locate a Web site addressing some aspect of your practice research topic. Make an initial evaluation of the site based on authority, bias, and content. Is the Web site a credible source? Share your findings with your classmates. How many Web sites held up favorably to this initial scrutiny?

Step Three: Responsible Information Gathering

Once you begin to locate useful, credible information, another important step is to gather copies of that information for your own records. *Make hardcopies (photocopies) of pages and chapters in books, articles, essays, and Web pages.* Alternatively, you might turn your paper trail into a digital trail. Instead of writing down information with a pen on paper as you move through your research process, store all of your information on a floppy disk, a removable flash drive, or a writable compact disc, including information from Web sites. This is a wonderful option if your research seems geared toward electronic sources of information. Making your own copies of the information you gather enables you to take your research with you everywhere you go. The copies are yours, and you can read them when you want to, refer back to them as you work, and interact with them by writing in the margins and highlighting important points as needed.

As you gather sources, be sure to *record the necessary bibliographic information* for each source and, if possible, *write it directly on each source.* Be careful to follow the same rules for a digital trail that you would follow for a paper trail. Make and carefully label files, gather all bibliographic information, copy and save all sources, and so on.

Though the bibliographic information you need varies slightly depending on the type of source, certain information is always needed:

- all authors' names and the names of editors if any are listed
- the complete title of the source or the name of the Web site
- the title of the article or chapter within the source or the title of the Web page
- the publisher or sponsor
- the date of publication or the last update for a Web site
- the page numbers or the URL of a Web site
- the date of access of a Web site

Recording this information saves you time and trouble and possible legal problems later on in your research process.

Plagiarism

In the academic community, the ownership of ideas and information is critical. As a writer, you yourself want to receive appropriate credit for the work you create, and as a researcher, it is your job to give credit to those scholars whom you reference in your work. Giving credit where credit is due is important for many reasons, not the least of which is that acknowledging the scholars you have studied lends credibility to your own work and ideas (it shows you have done your homework and that you are knowledgeable about your field of study). Documenting the source of your information also helps you to avoid one of the most serious academic offenses: plagiarism.

What is plagiarism? Plagiarism is commonly defined as submitting the work of another as your own; directly quoting from a source without proper citation; paraphrasing or summarizing another's work without acknowledging the source; using facts, figures, graphs, charts, or information without acknowledging the source; purchasing and/or copying commercial term papers or other course work and submitting it as your own.

The penalties for plagiarism vary among institutions, but at all establishments of higher learning, plagiarism is a serious offense, typically punished by receiving a failing grade on the work in question, sometimes failing the course in which the offending student is enrolled, and occasionally suspension or expulsion from the institution.

Avoiding plagiarism is not a difficult task. All of the research steps outlined in this chapter will prevent you from accidentally plagiarizing materials you have researched. By dialoguing with the material you read, making a plan for research, recording every step you take in the process, photocopying the information you uncover, and recording all bibliographic information directly on the photocopies, you will carry with you throughout your research process all of the information necessary to give credit where credit is due.

Intentional plagiarism is another subject altogether. The only thing that can prevent intentional plagiarism is your own sense of integrity. Enough said.

Practicum

Return to one of the sources you gathered for this practice exercise and make a paper or digital copy of the source if you have not already done so. Locate and record the necessary bibliographic information for that source. Share your findings with your classmates. Was it difficult to relocate your source? Was complete bibliographic information readily available for all sources?

Step Four: Processing Information: Summary and Paraphrase

Researching is a lot like joining a conversation that is already in progress. Whenever we enter into a conversation, one of the most important things to learn is how to be *a good listener*. By reading a source of information on a topic, you are entering into a communication act with that source; you are, in a sense, listening to what the experts have to say on that topic. Psychologists and other folks who have studied the process of communication tell us that one important aspect of a good listener is *echoing.* (Remember, just as we define text in broad terms throughout our Quest, we define listening in broad terms, too; i.e., listening = hearing = reading = seeing depending on what kind of text is a part of your communication.)

A good listener goes beyond sitting quietly and concentrating while someone else is talking (verbally or in a written or visual text). A good listener *hears* what someone else is saying, *processes* that information, and then *echoes* what he has heard and understood before adding anything else to the conversation. Echoing is a way of showing respect, of declaring *I hear what you are saying.* It shows that you are paying attention and that you understand what someone else is communicating. It is an action that demonstrates respect for other perspectives. It also allows for any miscommunication to be clarified (if whatever you echo is not quite right, other people have the opportunity to restate their positions more clearly).

In terms of the academic world and your current Quest, the technique of echoing, repeating, or restating in your own words what you have learned is often called *summary and paraphrase.* You have likely heard of these tools before and have probably used them, too, in one way or another. But you may not have understood what important tools they can be in terms of communication and critical literacy. In fact, I would bet that for many of you, summary and paraphrase have in the past been dreaded exercises that seem like busywork. They have lacked purpose and meaning. Well, leave those old ideas at the door, and climb inside this new way of thinking.

In our quest for understanding an event or an issue, summary and paraphrase—the written versions of verbal echoing—are important tools and strategies. When researching an issue, these strategies are useful to demonstrate your understanding of various perspectives; they show you have done your homework and lend credibility to your own ideas by showing that you have processed the ideas suggested by experts in your field of inquiry.

The bottom line is, if other people know that you are listening to them and that you understand what they are saying, they are much more likely to listen to what *you* have to say.

Summary

A summary is a condensed version of the main ideas of all or part of a source, written in your own words—a short statement of the essential points of a text.

Generally speaking, summaries are brief, typically a paragraph or two (depending upon the length of the original text). Summaries do not include supporting information and details. They mention only the main ideas of a text.

A summary begins with an introduction to the source (the writer's name and the title of the piece, sometimes the author's credentials), followed by the main idea of the text and, if necessary, supporting ideas developed throughout the text. It should conclude with a final statement reflecting the significance of the article—not from your point of view but from the writer's.

To write a summary, it is most useful to first read through a text using whatever reading strategy you are most comfortable with (refer to the strategies covered in

Chapter 1: record, question, and respond), then *reread* the text and create a *skeleton outline* of the text.

In the margins beside each paragraph, record a few words that summarize the information covered within that paragraph. When you finish reading the entire text, you should have a neat, concise record of its main ideas. Then use that skeleton outline to create your summary.

Remember, throughout the summary, do not add your own opinions or thoughts; instead summarize what the writer has to say about the subject. You want to be careful to maintain the integrity of the original document: do not distort or alter the original views, ideas, attitudes, or their importance in the original.

Paraphrase

A paraphrase is a rewording of a particular point or points in a text. Similar to summary, paraphrasing is most typically used as a way to smoothly integrate the ideas of someone else into your own essay (to support *your* ideas).

When a writer paraphrases a section from a text (for example, when a student paraphrases a few sentences from a journal article to use in her argument paper), what she is actually doing is *translating* the original text into her own words. She's not adding her opinion, and she's not using a word-for-word quotation from the original text. However, because the ideas presented in a paraphrase are taken from someone else's text, they must be documented in order to give credit where credit is due.

Something else to remember: a summary is a concise distilling of the ideas presented in an original text, but a paraphrase might be as long as the original text, and it contains all of the ideas presented in the original text (more than just an overview of the main ideas).

To create a paraphrase, first read through the text using whatever reading strategy you are most comfortable with (again, return to the strategies in Chapter 1). Then select the portions of the text that you would like to paraphrase, reread those portions, then close the original text and write from your memory, in your own words, what you remember about the main ideas and any relevant supporting information. Read the original text again and check your paraphrase for accuracy.

Summary and Paraphrase Walk-Through

As an example, take a look at an article written by Brian Doherty for *Reason* magazine and a summary of that article.

Brian Doherty is an associate editor of *Reason*. He worked as assistant editor and reporter for *Reason* from 1994 to 1998, writing a variety of stories on topics ranging from the Americans with Disabilities Act to pollution-credit trading to the independent rock scene.

Doherty's work has appeared in the *Washington Post,* the *Los Angeles Times, Mother Jones, Spin, National Review,* the *Weekly Standard,* the *San Francisco Chronicle,* Wired Ventures' Suck.com, and dozens of other publications. He was the Warren

Brookes Fellow in Environmental Journalism at the Competitive Enterprise Institute in 1999 and served as managing editor at *Regulation* magazine from 1993 to 1994.

Doherty received a bachelor's degree in journalism from the University of Florida.

Reason is the monthly print magazine of "free minds and free markets." It covers politics, culture, and ideas through a provocative mix of news, analysis, commentary, and reviews. *Reason* provides an alternative to right-wing and left-wing opinion magazines by making a principled case for liberty and individual choice in all areas of human activity.

Author's Etcetera

In an e-mail exchange dated September 2002, Mr. Doherty shared the following information with me as I prepared this chapter:

Since this article was written in Fall 2000, Eminem has continued to record and sell millions of records. The choruses of outrage are quieting down, though. Like with all those who push cultural envelopes, Eminem has created a relatively safe space for himself to follow his muse, however outrageous and offensive he remains to many. In a world suddenly, shockingly confronted with far more serious matters, the 2002 release of his next CD, *The Eminem Show,* did not lead to any congressional hearings. Unsurprisingly, it did contain a verbal potshot at Lynne Cheney. She survived it, and so did the country. Let freedom ring!

The delicate interplay between words and actions, one person's thoughts and another person's deeds, is always a concern for a thoughtful writer. Most of my career has been spent writing about political and cultural controversies from a libertarian viewpoint, advocating the radical extension of the values of individual freedom—and individual responsibility. When plumping for a controversial or minority viewpoint, the polemical writer hopes, at best, to help change people's minds.

A decade of trying to change people's minds through words has made one thing clear: Every human being is the master of his or her own mind and actions. To look specifically at the Columbine shootings, no amount of talk about atmospheres of media violence or cruel peer bullying can even begin to adequately explain what happened there. Millions of kids live and grow within such atmospheres. The merest handful take up arms and murder others.

Individual choice and responsibility are the ultimate explanations for horrifying acts like Columbine—or any other human action. Explanations that rely on cultural causes grossly over-predict—if violent media and constant bullying had the power to compel evil actions, we'd have Columbine-level tragedies happening every day. Because human beings—even supposedly impressionable kids—are ultimately masters of their own moral fate, we don't.

In addition to my professional writing, I also ran through the '90s a small independent record label called Cherry Smash Records, which made me especially sensitive to the notion of Congress even discussing the content of popular music. While legal censorship of cultural products is extremely rare in America these days, eternal vigilance toward such matters whenever they are even being discussed is one of the prices of liberty. That's why I thought it was important to write this article.

Brian Doherty

After an initial reading of a source, the next step is to complete a skeleton outline while reading through the article a second time. Here is a model of a skeleton outline for the full text of Doherty's article.

Bum Rap

Lynne Cheney vs. Slim Shady

Cheney attacks Eminem

Would-be second lady and former head of the National Endowment for the Humanities, Lynne Cheney is no coward— and no fool. During her Senate testimony about media violence in September, Cheney didn't flinch while naming those she believes are polluting American culture with intolerable filth and vulgarity. And unlike Tipper Gore 15 years earlier, Cheney didn't finger nowheresville bands like W.A.S.P. and the Mentors as examples of pop perfidy. She attacked one of the biggest-selling recording artists around, rapper Eminem, whose birth name is Marshall Mathers and whose self-consciously sinister alter ego is "Slim Shady." Since its release in June, Eminem's latest offering, *The Marshall Mathers LP,* has sold over 7 million copies. His first CD, 1999's *The Slim Shady LP,* has moved more than 3 million units.

Cheney addresses Senate

"The time has come to get very specific, to ask individuals to be accountable," Cheney told the Senate Committee on Commerce, Science, and Transportation. "So here is a name: Marshall Mathers. In [the song] 'Kill You,' he imagine[s] the joys of murdering any woman he might come across. Wives, nuns, sluts, 'whoever the bitches might be.'"

Critics do not recognize Eminem is artist

What Cheney and a host of other critics either won't or can't acknowledge is that Eminem is not merely a bestseller; he's also one of the best pop artists of his time. He's an unparalleled verbal wizard and a master of his chosen art form: the provocation. Perhaps more to the point, *The Marshall Mathers LP* is a sophisticated, though profane, meta-pop meditation on his relationship with his fans and his responsibilities toward society.

Eminem concerned with same issues as Cheney

Eminem seems fairly obsessed with these matters and addresses them with greater wit and a deeper appreciation of the ambiguities of human life than Cheney managed. "How many retards listen to me and run up in the school shooting when they're pissed at a teacher?" he muses in the song "Who Knew." "Her, him, is it you, is it them? / Wasn't me, Slim Shady said to do it again! / Damn! How much damage can you do with a pen? / I just said it, I ain't know if you'd do it or not." On the track "I'm Back," Eminem mocks the notion that listening to "bad" music somehow relieves wrongdoers of responsibility for what they do: "I take each individual degenerate's head and reach into it / Just to see if he's influenced by me / If he listens to music he's an innocent victim / And becomes a puppet on the string of my tennis shoes."

Lyrics are controversial but ironic

Not to whitewash: Eminem does indeed rap about raping his mother and killing his wife. (Unsurprisingly, perhaps, he is involved in a defamation lawsuit with the former and divorce proceedings with the latter.) He also portrays (and sometimes advocates) violence against gays, women, boy band N'Sync, and rival rap act the Insane Clown Posse. But how seriously is anyone expected to take a CD that starts off with a faux "Public Service Announcement," the last line of which, delivered in the finest bland "official" voice, is, "Slim Shady is fed up with your shit, and he's going to kill you"?

Eminem's lyrics express struggle to understand

More than his detractors recognize, Eminem is openly torn between conflicting desires to say whatever he wants, especially if he knows it will upset all the right people, and to do the right thing and live a normal life. The *Marshall Mathers LP* is rife with such ambivalence—while he mocks the idea that the media environment excuses or explains individual perfidy, he also recognizes his own persona's sickness and sometimes blames his behavior on his mother's negligent parenting. In "Criminal," he raps, "My mother did drugs tar, liquor, cigarettes, and speed / The baby came out disfigured—It was a seed / Who would grow up just as crazy as she / Don't dare make fun of that baby—cause that baby was me / How the fuck you supposed to grow up when you weren't raised?"

Eminem struggles with same questions

Does exposure to this kind of entertainment hurt kids? Like Al Gore and Joe Lieberman, Cheney assumes it does. Oddly, if they're looking for entertainment industry allies, they need look no further than Eminem himself. He goes farther than his critics in portraying himself as possibly responsible for real-world carnage. One of *The Marshall Mathers LP*'s best tracks is "Stan," a haunting number in which a disturbed young Eminem fan writes his hero an increasingly screwy series of letters. In the end, the song's title character descends into a booze-and-pill-induced frenzy, ties up his pregnant girlfriend, stuffs her in the trunk of his car, and then drives himself and her into a river. Violence against women, nihilistic self-destruction, drunk driving—exactly what youngsters need to be protected against, right? But the point of "Stan"—spelled out in a final verse in which

Eminem, too late, responds to the letters—is that this is a seriously dreadful act which makes even Eminem "sick." And Stan is a fictional character; no critic can point to any real Eminem fan so inspired by his hero to violence or destruction.

He mocks idea anyone would want to be like him

Eminem presents such a grotesquely self-hating and negative image of himself that it's almost too obvious a joke when he mocks the idea that anyone would want to emulate him. As he puts it in "Role Model," "I slept with 10 women who got HIV / Don't you wanna grow up to be just like me? / I got genital warts and it burns when I pee / Don't you wanna grow up to be just like me?" And yet a song like "Stan" recognizes that some fans might want to, especially kids from the same kind of rootless, poor, emotionally starved background Mathers claims he rose from. (He raps in "Who Knew": "Read up / About how I used to get beat up / Peed on, be on free lunch / And change schools every three months.")

Eminem's music is art

There isn't any easy didactic message in Eminem's music to tidily support a political position about the influence of media violence. As Cheney might recognize when discussing a novel or play, such nuanced ambiguity about important questions is a touchstone of serious art. Certainly, there's far more to Eminem's output than a series of disconnected scenes of mayhem and cruelty, lacking all context and conscience. (Cheney also ignores how attractive the rapper's snaky, minimalist beats and hooks sound, apart from any issues of message. Eminem's enemies are tone deaf to his musical skills, though they're worth considering when pondering his appeal.)

The content is what makes his music marketable to kids—they relate

That said, there's no question that Eminem is marketed to children, though not in the literal terms the Federal Trade Commission and Congress fret over. Eminem's Slim Shady character is custom-made to appeal to teens, because it captures perfectly the feelings of outrage and powerlessness that often accompany—indeed, perhaps define—adolescence. Eminem is profane, rebellious, determined to be himself, to speak what he takes to be the truth about his emotions and what he sees around him. He's all the more determined to do so if it pisses off authority figures. And in a world largely dominated by modern liberal cant, the best way to outrage adults is to come across as anti-gay, anti-woman, and pro-violence. As Eminem says in "Criminal," "Half the shit I say, I just make it up to make you mad." Such an attitude speaks directly to adolescent anomie and rebellion. While it is surely annoying to adults, it isn't evil.

Content is why all kinds of kids listen to Eminem

It's also why lots of kids listen to his music—from troubled types resembling "Stan" (who says Eminem's records "help when I'm depressed") to the dutiful youngsters I saw recently when participating in the Los Angeles Coastal Cleanup, a day-long event during which volunteers picked trash out of a local waterway, Ballona Creek. Cheney and her Democratic counterparts might not believe it, but those boys and girls did their good deeds with Slim Shady tunes blasting from their boom box.

Cheney metaphor for influence of music on kids

In attacking Eminem during the Senate hearing, Cheney's central metaphor, proudly copped from Republican speechwriter Peggy Noonan, portrayed "children as intelligent fish swimming in a deep ocean." Music, movies, and video games, explained Cheney, are like "waves [that] go through [our children] again and again, from this direction and that. Cleaning up the water, the ocean our children are swimming in, is the most important environmental issue of our time." This is a terrible metaphor, implying against all evidence that human beings, even young ones, are in mindless thrall to what they see and hear. (Youngsters, no matter how many Looney Tunes they watch, are not apt to hand their dads dynamite cigars.)

Political critics of pop culture do not understand that culture

Tell those kids cleaning up Ballona Creek that the music they enjoy is "the most important environmental issue of our time." The world of popular culture concerns characters and situations that are often harsh and unpleasant. In this respect, of course, it's just like the highbrow culture that never seems to exercise the Cheneys of the world. Eminem's work is artistically and morally serious, even as it's outrageous, reckless, and often funny as hell (for those who can still laugh at punctured pomposity and the shock of taboo shattering). Cheney doesn't notice this, because the political critics of popular culture, as usual, quite literally do not know what they are talking about. Which, all questions of censorship and constitutionality aside, is reason enough to ignore them. Or, if you are more aggressive in your objections to solemn, ignorant attempts to manage other people's choices or raise other people's children, you could join Eminem and "put one of those fingers on each hand up."

After finishing a skeleton outline, it is important to review the notes you made and decide on what you believe to be the main idea communicated through the article. Then write a summary of the article. Here is an example of a summary of Doherty's "Bum Rap":

In his article "Bum Rap," Brian Doherty claims that political critics of popular culture, such as Lynne Cheney, do not understand or appreciate pop culture. According to Doherty, critics like Cheney blame the music of artists such as Eminem for negatively influencing the behavior of youth because they do not understand the message communicated by the music and they do not appreciate it as art.

This summary does everything a summary should do. It condenses the ideas of the original from several pages to one paragraph (two sentences). All supporting data was carefully excluded, but the main idea of the text was identified. It began by introducing the source (author's name and title of the text), then presented the main idea and concluded with a statement as to the significance of the article.

Practicum

Read the following article by Benjamin Soskis (until recently an assistant editor at *The New Republic;* he is now a Richard Hofstadter Fellow at Columbia University), which appeared in *The New Republic* in January 2001. Create a skeleton outline in the margins as you read. Then write a summary of the article. Share your responses with your classmates. Are your summaries similar?

George W.'s Historical Twin

I will be guided by President Jefferson's sense of purpose: to stand for principle, to be reasonable in manner, and, above all, to do great good for the cause of freedom and harmony.

—George W. Bush, December 13

If you watched George W. Bush's victory speech last Wednesday, you might have noticed a sprightly female figure with a trumpet and an hourglass flitting triumphantly among the governor's advisers. No, not Karen Hughes—it was Clio, the muse of history. Indeed, who else could have inspired our president-elect's elegant likening of himself to the sagacious Thomas J.? The nominal reason for the comparison, of course, was straightforward: Jefferson's first election, like Bush's, was marred by electoral controversy. By invoking Jefferson, Bush signaled his desire to heal a divided nation.

And yet he signaled so much more. For the manner of their elections is the beginning, not the end, of the two presidents' resemblances. Though the centuries conspire to separate them, still the two men gaze across time to recognize in each other a near-perfect likeness—one that far transcends their mutual acquaintance with Samuel Adams.

Recall, for instance, each man's upbringing, in which aristocratic privilege was tempered by hardy provincialism. Just as Jefferson emerged from the Blue Ridge frontier to acquire the social graces of Williamsburg, so, too, did Bush depart the rugged environs of West Texas for Andover and Yale, where he mastered—respectively—the pep-squad bullhorn and the Michelob funnel. Indeed, the two men shared a lifelong love of the classics: Jefferson studied Greek, Bush was one.

Both men appreciated foreign cultures and brought back to America the best the world had to offer. Jefferson, after spending five years as a plenipotentiary in Paris, became enamored with French literature, art, and cuisine. Bush is able to recollect at least one youthful weekend spent across the Mexican border; as a result, chicken chimichangas are now a staple at the governor's mansion.

But the concordances between the man from Midland and the sage of Monticello go deeper than the circumstances of their lives; theirs is an equality of minds. Both men loved language and its possibilities: Jefferson applauded the development of an indigenous American dialect, cautioned against an overly worshipful deference to the dictionary, and insisted upon the incorporation of new words—including "neologism" and "ideology"—into everyday speech. Bush, too, has bravely fought to broaden the national lexicon to accept such distinctly American colloquialisms as "subliminable" and "mistinderestimate."

Most notably, each of these men—these Americans—had, upon assuming office, authored a single, powerful book. Jefferson's enigmatic *Notes on the State of Virginia* stirred the young nation to reflect on its most vital truths; Bush's equally enigmatic *A Charge to Keep* sold well in several Amarillo, Texas, bookstores. The two works, moreover, serve as complementary chapters in a longer volume on the nation's great racial wound, a call-and-answer across the centuries. TJ: "For if a slave can have a country in this world, it must be any other in preference to that in which he is born to live and labor for another. . . . Indeed I tremble for my country. When I reflect that God is just: that his justice cannot sleep for ever: that considering numbers, nature and natural means only, a revolution of the wheel of fortune, an exchange of situation, is among possible events." GWB: "There's a trend in this country to put people into boxes. Texans don't belong in little ethnic and racial boxes. . . . As we head into the twenty-first century, we should have one big box: American."

To carry out their contemplations, each man occasionally retreated from the warfare of politics to the seclusion of a chosen idyll. Jefferson treasured his days at Monticello, where he refused to read partisan political journals and devoted himself to "my family, my farm, and my books." In similar fashion, Bush escaped the bustle of the Florida recount for the peace of his ranch in Crawford, Texas, which does not have CNN but nonetheless gets most of the good college football games.

What will history make of these twinned giants? There will be hagiographical assessments and debates over intellectual influences. (Locke or Voltaire? Olasky or Bullock?) And, of course, there will be doubters. Revisionist historians have of late downplayed Jefferson's individual genius in the creation of the Declaration of Independence. And no doubt Bush's genius will someday face a similar assault. In fact, perhaps sooner than later. Perhaps even as we speak.

WRITING ASSIGNMENT   Quest Three: Creating a Research Dossier

Overview

Building on the knowledge base you established with Quest Two and your exploration of a particular event, create a research dossier. Begin by making a research map and generating questions to answer through your research, such as, *Have any events similar to my event happened in the recent past? If so, when? What were the circumstances surrounding any past events? Has this sort of thing happened more than once?* Create a plan for your search and continue to follow the steps outlined in Tools for Success in this chapter ("A Research Map and Paper Trail," "Evaluating a Source: The ABCs of Credibility," "Responsible Information Gathering," and "Processing Information: Summary and Paraphrase").

If events similar to yours have a long history, limit your timeframe to a manageable period.

Your instructor will determine the number of sources you are required to locate for this Quest, but I recommend that you find and process *a minimum of three credible sources* for this project. If you are working in small groups, it is quite helpful for each group member to assume responsibility for locating and then sharing three sources.

Once you have located and processed credible sources, organize your research dossier in a folder, and complete an *annotated bibliography* for each source.

Each annotated bibliography should include:

- a complete bibliographic citation (MLA format)
- followed by your summary
- a statement evaluating the credibility of the source

Your annotated bibliography should be compiled in alphabetical order as a single document and should be submitted along with your complete research dossier.

Here is an example of a *formal* annotation, shown first with notes and then as it should appear in the finished research dossier:

A complete bibliographic entry in MLA style	Doherty, Brian. "Bum Rap." *Reason.* 32:7 (December 2000). *Infotrac College Edition.* Gale Group and Thomson Learning. 8 March 2002.
A summary	In his article "Bum Rap," Brian Doherty seeks to prove that political critics of popular culture, such as Lynne Cheney, do not understand or appreciate pop culture. According to Doherty, critics like Cheney blame the music of artists such as Eminem for negatively influencing the behavior of youth because they do not understand the message communicated by the music and they do not appreciate it as art.
Evaluation of credibility	Brian Doherty is an authority on the subject through study and observation and through his experience as the owner of a

record company. He writes for *Reason* magazine, which is a credible source in the academic community.

Doherty, Brian. "Bum Rap." *Reason.* 32:7 (December 2000). *Infotrac College Edition.* Gale Group and Thomson Learning. 8 March 2002.

In his article "Bum Rap," Brian Doherty seeks to prove that political critics of popular culture, such as Lynne Cheney, do not understand or appreciate pop culture. According to Doherty, critics like Cheney blame the music of artists such as Eminem for negatively influencing the behavior of youth because they do not understand the message communicated by the music and they do not appreciate it as art.

Brian Doherty is an authority on the subject through study and observation and through his experience as the owner of a record company. He writes for *Reason* magazine, which is a credible source in the academic community.

Finally, organize your research in a folder and write an *introduction* for your research dossier that introduces your event and briefly sets up the historical context for that event.

Note

Your research dossier will serve as a foundation for future research on your topic. You may reference and add to this collection of resources as you move through the following chapters and Quests.

MLA Bibliographic Citations or Works Cited

MLA (Modern Language Association) citation is a system for documenting sources of information gathered during research. There are whole books written on MLA citation, and those books provide models of just about every type of source to be found. I highly recommend that you purchase or have access to one of those in-depth books (the same information is available on the Internet at sites such as the University of Wisconsin–Madison's Writing Center Web site, http://www.wisc.edu/writing/Handbook/DocMLA.html).

Writers use MLA citations to acknowledge the sources of information used within the documents they produce, such as academic essays (this is called *in-text citation* and is covered in Chapters 4 and 5). Writers also use full MLA bibliographic citations to create a list of *works cited* or works consulted (this typically comes at the end of an essay). This is the style you will use to create the citation for your annotated bibliography for Quest Three.

MLA citations serve very practical purposes. An in-text MLA citation lets your reader know that you have included information in your text that you gathered through research. The in-text citation provides enough information to direct your reader to a particular entry on your works cited page. On the works cited page, the reader will find all of the information necessary to locate the original source if he or she wants to do any additional reading.

MLA citations are important for other reasons, too. Within the academic community, it is important to cite your sources of information to avoid plagiarism (discussed earlier in this chapter). It is important to cite your sources to give credit where credit is due; the ownership of ideas is a crucial element of our academic society. Beyond ownership, it is also important to cite the sources of your information to add to *your* credibility. Citing sources shows that you have done your homework and have consulted with experts on your subject matter. This is a good thing when trying to convince an audience to listen to what you have to say on any given topic.

MLA citations are complicated and precise. Particular information must be provided in a precise order with special attention to the details of punctuation and spacing. These details are not easily memorized. The key to successful MLA citation is to know how to use an MLA guide as a resource. MLA guides such as the University of Wisconsin–Madison Web site are reference tools to follow as you prepare your annotated bibliography or works cited or consulted. We cover the specifics of a works cited page in greater detail in Chapter 4. For our purposes at this point in the journey, we look at the creation of an individual bibliographic citation.

Though the specific information will change slightly depending on the type of source, certain information must be included in any type of citation. You gathered this information during your research process:

- all authors' names and the names of editors if any are listed
- the complete title of the source or the name of the Web site
- the title of the article or chapter within the source or the title of the Web page
- the publisher or sponsor
- the date of publication or the last update for a Web site
- the page numbers or the URL of a Web site
- data of access

For books, a basic citation is organized like this:

Author's last name, author's first name. "Chapter in quotation marks." In <u>Book title underlined</u>. Place of publication: Publisher, date of publication. Page numbers.

Of course, you will not always have a chapter in a book—sometimes you will simply use a few pages or paragraphs. You may sometimes have additional information to include, such as an editor. In that case, the editor's name follows the title of the book. Note that every line after the first is indented: that is, a bibliographic entry has a *hanging indent*.

For periodicals, a basic citation is organized like this:

Author's last name, author's first name. "Title of the article in quotation marks." <u>Title of periodical underlined</u>. Publication date, including volume number and issue number for journals: Page numbers.

The volume and issue numbers are usually illustrated numerically. For instance, if the volume number of your journal is 42 and the issue is 3, they are represented in the citation like this: 42:3.

A basic citation for electronic sources (information from databases and the World Wide Web) are organized like this:

Author's last name, author's first name. Title of work or description of site underlined. Publication date or date when the site was last updated. Name of institution or organization associated with the site and/or database. Date you accessed the site. <The URL in brackets>.

Because electronic resources are still fairly new to the academic community, there is some debate on a correct format for electronic citations. A key rule of thumb is to use the format above as a guide and provide enough information that a reader can easily locate and access the electronic source.

Criteria for a Successful Research Dossier

This assignment asks you to find information on events similar to those you have chosen to study and discover a historical context for those events or for issues surrounding those events. You must practice a systematic research process and record and organize each step in a dossier. Then you must create an annotated bibliography for at least three sources and a brief introduction to the dossier.

- Complete all four steps for the research dossier: a map, trail, evaluation of credibility (examination and explanation of how each source fulfills the ABCs of credibility), and information processing (skeleton outline and summary).
- Create an annotated bibliography for each source that follows precisely the correct format for MLA citation, summary, and evaluation.
  MLA citation must include all necessary information in the correct format.
  Summary must begin with a reference to the author and the title of the source, and must cover only the main ideas presented in the text.
  Evaluation must briefly explain whether or not the source is credible according to the ABCs of credibility.
- Include a brief introduction that connects your event to the search illustrated through the dossier and sets up the historical context for that event.

In the Spotlight: A Student Model Dossier

The Author: Jonathan Ammay

At the time he completed this assignment, Jonathan was a sophomore at the University of North Carolina–Charlotte.

Author's Etcetera

After completing Quest Three, Jonathan had the following comments to share regarding his experience:

> Researching the history of music and censorship helped me to place the events around Columbine in a broader context. It helped me make sense of arguments I hear going on even today, and it gave me information to support my own ideas and what I think is true. Now I know I don't have to panic—people have been trying to censor for a long time, and they haven't been able to succeed, but I think we still have to be on guard. It's happened before, and it will probably happen again.

This model includes the introduction to Jonathan's research dossier and an annotated bibliography for one source. The topic for Jonathan's research was an offshoot of the Columbine High School shooting: events that impacted music censorship.

Debating the Impact of Music on Youth Violence: The History of Music Censorship

During the days following the Columbine shooting, it was hard to pick up an article or tune in to a television broadcast about the event without hearing someone make a connection between the music Harris and Klebold allegedly listened to and their violent behavior. It was widely reported that they were fans of such bands as Marilyn Manson and the German rock group Rammstein. The press claimed that songs by groups such as Marilyn Manson promote violence and encourage their audience to strike out and even to kill. Influences like this were explained as a cause for the violent shooting at Columbine on April 20, 1999.

Ironically, we eventually learned that Harris and Klebold were not even fans of Marilyn Manson, but Manson was a natural target for blame nonetheless. He's high profile. He's different, and he goes against what most people would call "the norm" (just like Harris and Klebold). His stage persona might be scary to many people—the dark and menacing image he presents to the world. On the surface, the lyrics of many of his songs seem to celebrate violence and to boast a rather negative attitude about humanity and the condition of humanity in general, and that scares a lot of people.

It's human nature to attack what we fear; many people fear Manson, and so Manson came under attack. But by using Manson and others like him as a quick and easy scapegoat, we failed to look beneath the surface and examine the logical connection of music to behavior. In the midst of all the blame, lots of questions were left unasked or unanswered; for instance, how influential is any kind of music on behavior? Is there any evidence that this sort of thing has happened before? If so, under what circumstances and in response to what musical or societal influences?

Would it surprise you to know that this was not the first time that music has been blamed for behavior, that Manson is not the first artist to be accused of encouraging lascivious actions committed by an angry teen? That, in fact, music has been blamed for negative behavior for as long as music has existed, and it has been the object of attempted censorship for decades?

In order to judge the strength of the connection between music and violence/behavior, we have to place this situation in perspective. We have to know, has this happened before? If so, when? What were the circumstances under which similar incidents occured? We have to take a look at the connection between music and behavior throughout history. The following sources help to place the debate surrounding the Columbine shooting and music into a historical context.

Source One

McDonald, James R. "Censoring Rock Lyrics: A Historical Analysis of the Debate." In *Youth & Society.* 19:3 (1988): 294–313.

James R. McDonald, in his essay titled "Censoring Rock Lyrics: A Historical Analysis of the Debate," published in the scholarly journal *Youth & Society,* examines the history of censorship and rock music and evaluates the position taken by the Parents' Music Resource Center in the 1980s. Mr. McDonald examines the history of the debate regarding the influence of rock music on youth behavior, and he evaluates whether the available research data can or should contribute to the debate over censorship of rock music.

James R. McDonald has taught college courses on the topic of popular music for over ten years. He is the author of a book on the literary aspects of song lyrics, and he has published numerous articles on popular music subjects in various scholarly journals; therefore he may be considered an authority on this topic. McDonald provides examples of censorship events that span two decades, from the 1960s to the 1980s, and he documents the sources in-text and through an extensive works cited page. The article was published in 1988, so it does not cover any controversy within the last decade. In every way except currency, this article is a highly credible source.

Practicum

How does Jonathan's model fulfill the criteria for a successful annotated bibliography? Write a brief evaluation. Refer to specific examples from the text of his Quest Three to support your evaluation. Share your responses with your classmates. Do you find that you and your classmates agree? Disagree?

Reflection in Action

In your own words, explain the importance of establishing a historical context when studying events and social problems. What is the importance of historical context in terms of your specific event? How can a historical understanding of an event help when trying to find a solution to a social problem? Can you think of an event that does not have a history?

Expanding Your Vision: A Multimedia Assignment Option

Critical Inquiry: Digging Deeper

You have completed some research that places your event within a historical context, and you should have uncovered one or more past events that were similar in some way to your event. You have read about these events separately. Now let's try to pull this information together.

Make a chart to display the history of your event and events like it from the past. Your chart should include four columns: one for what happened, one for when it happened, one for who it involved, and one for why it happened (who or what was the cause)? Below each column, review your sources and record the corresponding information from each source. Be sure to note which source contained the information you include in your chart. Your chart will look something like this:

What	When	Who	Why
Information from source	Information from source	Information from source	Information from source

This visual representation should help to bring together what you know about this topic. It should provide you with a quick visual record of historical context for your event.

MULTIMEDIA ASSIGNMENT   Visi-Quest Three: Expanding Your Vision by Creating a Multimedia Timeline (PowerPoint Presentation)

Using the information you gathered while creating your research dossier, create a timeline of historical context for your event in the form of a Microsoft PowerPoint presentation, and then present your timeline to the class. Your presentation should include both textual information and visual representations that illustrate the historical context for your event.

PowerPoint Instructions

> **Note**
>
> The menu choices in PowerPoint are much like those in Microsoft Word and other Windows applications. If you understand one of these programs, you can use the same logic in using others. If you need help understanding an icon on the screen, just place the mouse pointer over that icon without pressing the button; then wait a second. The icon's name will appear in a small box next to it. This will give you additional help.

Getting Started

- Open PowerPoint.
- If you want to start a new file, choose **Blank presentation.**
- Click **OK.**
- Choose your **Slide layout** (these are preset options for text and graphics that will appear on a slide; you may change individual slides within the program and choose different layouts when adding new slides).
- Click **OK.**

> **Note**
>
> You may choose **Layout** and **Template** options from within the program. Choose **Format** and **Apply Design** to choose a background template for your slides. Choose **Format** and **Slide Color Scheme** to apply standard or customized sets of colors to the document. You may apply a color scheme to just one specific slide or to all slides in a presentation.

Slide Content

Begin replacing text by highlighting the current text on the slide. If you want to change the layout of the master slide (font, size, color, bullets, etc.), choose **View,** then **Master,** then **Slide Master.**

Adding Graphics

To use graphics, choose from options within the **Insert** menu.

For File Images

- Click **Insert.**
- Click **Picture.**
- Click **From file.**
- Find your graphic (located in My Pictures or on a floppy disk in drive A:.
- Click **Insert.** (You may have to adjust and format the graphic to fit your slide.)

For Clip Art

- ◦ Click **Insert.**
- ◦ Click **Picture.**
- ◦ Click **Clip Art.**
- ◦ Browse your collection. Choose your graphic and click **OK.**

For Organizational Charts

- ◦ Click **Insert.**
- ◦ Click **Picture.**
- ◦ Click **Organizational Chart.**
- ◦ Choose chart type and enter data into text boxes.
- ◦ Click **File** and **Exit and return to presentation** to close and view chart in PowerPoint file.

For Charts

- ◦ Click **Insert.**
- ◦ Click **Chart.**
- ◦ Enter data into the spreadsheet.
- ◦ Click **x** to close the box and return to the PowerPoint file.

Editing Graphics

- ◦ To move a graphic, click and drag the image. Be sure to have the "four-arrow" icon before moving the image.
- ◦ To resize an image, click on one of the corner handles and either pull up or pull down. If you want to keep the same proportions, hold the shift key while resizing.
- ◦ For other changes: When you click on an image, the Picture toolbar should appear (if it does not automatically appear, simply choose **Toolbars** and **Picture** from the **View** menu). From this toolbar, you may add more pictures, change the brightness or contrast of an image, or crop the borders of an image.

Using Views

Slide View

PowerPoint starts up in Slide view. You can view and make changes on a slide-by-slide basis by adding text and graphics in this mode.

Outline View

You may add information to your slides using an outline form with titles and bullets.

Slide Sorter View

You may sort and duplicate slides in this view.

Notes Page View

If you would like to use notes for your presentation, enter text in this view. Your notes will not show up on the screen during a slideshow.

Slideshow View

Use this view during the presentation.

Your Presentation

- You may play the slide show by choosing **View Show** from the **Slide Show** menu or by clicking on the **Slide Show** button at the bottom left of the screen.
- To move through the presentation, hit **Enter,** the spacebar, or the right arrow key. To move back, use the left arrow key.
- Press **Escape** to end the show before the last slide.

Slide Transition

To enable your presentation to fade in and out between slides, choose **Slide Transition** from the **Slide Show** menu. This feature also allows automatic timing of each slide.

Custom Animation

- To allow text or images to be animated on the slide, choose **Custom Animation** from the **Slide Show** menu. This allows parts of a slide to be split up so that some parts show up on the screen before others.
- When using **Custom Animations** in the **Slide Show,** you must hit **Enter,** the spacebar, or the right arrow key after every effect if you are not using timing within PowerPoint.

Printing

- If you want to print your slides, choose **Print** from the **File** menu and make your print selection.
- Choose the objects to print. You may print a slide per page or up to six slides per page. You may print your notes, as well. (Note: If you have a dark slide background, select the Black & White print option.)

Criteria for a Successful Multimedia Timeline

For this assignment, you are asked to add to the information you discovered in your research dossier and reorganize that information in the form of a multimedia timeline. You must also locate visual representations of each event to illustrate this timeline. Follow the instructions for PowerPoint outlined previously, and create a slideshow; then present that slide show to the class.

- Follow directions to create a slide show using PowerPoint.
- Include the rhetorical elements of a multimedia text (covered in Chapter 2 under Tools for Success): information presented through printed text about the event— what it was, when it happened, who it involved, and why it happened. Include visual texts that are interesting and informative (with attention to people, places, and things pictured in a visual text; colors, lighting effects, textures, lines, angles, and focal points).
- The timeline must be neatly arranged in chronological order.
- The presentation should be well-rehearsed, and you must be prepared to answer any questions posed by the audience following the presentation.

In the Spotlight: A Student Model Multimedia Timeline

The Author: Courtney Rogers

Courtney was a freshman at the University of North Carolina–Charlotte when she completed this assignment. She hopes to someday teach in the public schools.

Author's Etcetera

Courtney says that completing a PowerPoint presentation after working on her Research Dossier helped to

> bring everything together for me. I had gathered so much information on the different events, and condensing everything in the form of a timeline—plus adding the visuals— helped to put everything into perspective for me. Having all of the similar events lined up, one after another, I could see the history and where the Columbine shooting fit into the big picture. The way the media talked about Columbine—when it was happening and afterwards—it often seemed like that was the only school shooting. This timeline shows that there were lots of shootings before Columbine, and lots of shootings after Columbine, too. I like the visual aspect of the timeline—the pictures really put a human face on the tragedy. So the shooters don't become larger than life—you can see they're just kids. Somehow that makes these events even more important.

This model includes one PowerPoint slide illustrating a portion of the timeline. Each subsequent slide contained similar information about a separate shooting event and was designed in the same format.

School Shootings Timeline

February 2, 1996
Moses Lake, Washington

Barry Loukaitis, 14, dressed up like a gunslinger from the Wild West and went into his algebra class. Concealed in his long duster were two pistols, seventy-eight rounds of ammunition, and a high-powered rifle. His first victim was 14-year-old Manuel Vela, who later died. Another classmate fell with a bullet to his chest, and then Loukaitis shot his teacher in the back as she was writing a problem on the blackboard. A 13-year-old girl took the fourth bullet in her arm. Then he took hostages, allowing the wounded to be removed. Eventually a teacher rushed him and put an end to the siege. In all, three people died, and Loukaitis blamed "mood swings" and claimed the video for the song "Jeremy" by Pearl Jam had influenced him to become violent.

Practicum

How does Courtney's Visi-Quest Three fulfill the criteria for this assignment? Review the criteria listed for this assignment and make an evaluation. Offer specific examples from Courtney's project to illustrate your critique. Then share your ideas with your classmates. Do you find that you and your classmates agree? Do you disagree? Why, or why not? How does this process of reading and evaluating a model assignment help you to successfully meet the requirements for this assignment yourself?

4

Identifying Claims and Reasons: Recognizing Multiple Perspectives

Begin with a *Question*: What Are You Trying to Prove?

In the past few chapters, you began an investigation into circumstances surrounding the occurrence of a serious event. You observed that in response to that event, people want to know what happened; we search for a cause, for answers to the question of *why* something happened. The blame game begins and intensifies as social problems are identified. These problems may or may not have caused an event to happen—some seem to have a stronger causal connection to an event than others.

Events like those covered in your casebooks are very complex and multifaceted. What we ultimately must realize is that *many* social problems or issues are connected to each event (we see this in the blame game), and within each issue are many *different* ways of talking about and thinking about that issue. Every event is multidimensional; every social problem or issue is multidimensional and contains many different opinions and *perspectives.* In the quest for answers to why these events happened and how to prevent similar events from happening in the future, it is necessary to identify and understand these various perspectives and ultimately to decide which perspective we believe to be most logical. That is part of what we work on in this chapter: *identifying perspectives.*

Perspective is the evaluation of situations (events or social issues) according to a particular way of looking at them. Long ago (when Aristotle lived and breathed and maybe even more recently than that), events and social issues were discussed in terms of black and white, of either/or. There was a right way and there was a wrong way, and there was no in-between. In more recent times, scholars and philosophers have approached debate with more flexibility, acknowledging that there is often a middle ground. Currently, in this very complex world in which we live, we understand that within any event or issue there are *multiple perspectives*—many voices speaking out in black, white, gray, and every shade of the rainbow in between. A serious discussion of any event or issue is therefore much more complicated than it used to be. It is also much more interesting.

When we speak of an event such as the Columbine High School shooting, for example, each voice speaking out in the blame game offers a different perspective. One voice claims that the parents are to blame; that is one perspective. Another voice claims that peer bullying is to blame; that is another perspective. Yet another voice claims that exposure to violent media is to blame; that is another perspective. And there are others. Each answer to who or what is to blame is a different perspective. This is one way of talking about perspectives. But wait, there is more.

To make things even more complicated, each perspective in the blame game is actually a social problem or an issue, and there are multiple ways of thinking about each one of those issues. Each way of thinking about an issue is also a perspective. For example, one person may believe that the parents are to blame for the actions of their children and that they should be held accountable by our legal system; another person may believe that the parents are responsible for the actions of their *young* children but not their teens. Yet another person may believe that the parents are responsible but that they should not be held accountable by law. The list goes on and on.

When you talk about perspectives, therefore, you may be talking about an evaluation of the event and a particular way of looking at that event, or you may be talking about an evaluation of an issue and a particular way of looking at that issue. It is pretty easy to understand perspectives in terms of events. It gets a little trickier when you try to understand perspectives in terms of issues. So, from this point on, we focus our discussion of perspectives on different ways of looking at an issue.

Different Perspectives on Perspectives

Let's get visual for a moment.

Once upon a time, when we talked about perspectives, the conversation looked something like this:

Perspective 1 was on one side of an issue; perspective 2 was on the other side of an issue. The issue stood like a wall between them. The opposing perspectives usually could not hear one another, sometimes did not even know that any other perspective existed.

Then humankind progressed, and when we talked about issues and perspectives, it looked something like this:

Perspective 1 was on one side of an issue; perspective 2 was on the other side of an issue. The issue still stood like a wall between them, but there was also perspective 3, straddling both sides of the issue to one degree or another.

Thankfully, that is usually not how we look at issues anymore. We have learned to open our minds, to more freely discuss our many and various experiences, and to allow for many different opinions in response to the complexity of an issue. More recently, I have heard some people talk of issues and perspectives as salad bowls or pizza pies. Let's examine the pizza metaphor for a moment.

How is a discussion of a social issue like a pizza?

Well, the foundation of a pizza is its crust. On top of the crust, we can place a limited number of different toppings—as many toppings as the crust can hold. Once the toppings are placed on the pizza, that's it—everything is set, and the pizza is made. And so our options are limited. We can take action, cook the pizza, and then eat the pizza, or we can let it spoil.

As for social problems, the issue is like the crust of the pizza: it is the foundation for any discussion that will take place. The various perspectives are the toppings. This way of thinking allows that any discussion on an issue may contain multiple, yet a limited number of, perspectives. Once the perspectives are in place, that's it. We can take action, or we can let the issue "spoil." And when the social problem rises up again, we can start from scratch and build a new pizza/discussion.

Though this food metaphor is fairly accurate, you can see that there are still problems with this way of talking about issues and perspectives—the main problem is that there is no room for growth and change.

Going with the Flow

The pizza metaphor is problematic because issues are *always* changing, perspectives are *always* changing. The last thing we need is for an issue and its associated perspectives to get old, to spoil and be tossed away so that we must start from scratch each time a social problem arises.

Many things in the environment influence issues and perspectives on those issues, and those issues and perspectives, in turn, influence many aspects of the environment. They are never static, always active, and they rarely stand alone. Just as most events connect to other events (as you discovered in the previous chapter), most issues connect to other issues, and they all spill over into the larger pool of society. Like a river. So, maybe this is a better way of thinking about issues and perspectives:

Issues are like rivers, flowing and moving and changing all the time. The water represents the issue: always there, always moving and changing, always existing in one form or another. Communities are like the banks of the river, both shaped by its current and shaping/containing the issue/river. Everything around and within the river is in some way connected to and impacted by the river and, conversely, in some way impacts the river, just as everything around and within an issue is connected to and impacted by the issue and impacts the issue. Within the issue/river (and all around it) are many different perspectives—different ways of looking at, understanding, and experiencing the issue/river. Those on the inside of the river have different perspectives than those sitting on its banks; those on the inside, directly affected by an issue, have different perspectives than do observers.

Big and small—trees along the banks of the river, fishermen, the fish living in the river, the ducks feeding on the fish, the fish feeding on plankton, all the way down to algae and amoebas—each thing has a different perspective of the river. Some would say the water is too cold, some would say it is cool and refreshing, some would say the water is warm, some would say it is dirty, some would say it is pure and clean; some folks within the river know how to swim, some struggle against the current. And it is the same with issues, too. The people who are caught up in the middle of the experience, the people who observe from a distance, the people who come later to study what happened, those who have experienced something similar before—all of them have different perspectives based on their own experiences and their evaluation of events according to their particular way of looking at them.

Apples, Oranges, Po-tay-toe, Po-tah-toe

None of the perspectives just described are *necessarily* right or wrong—they are just different. And *none of them are complete.* Just as you must look at the past in order to understand the current events you are studying, in order to have a complete understanding of any issue, you must step outside of your own ideas and experience and consider other perspectives.

Going back to the river metaphor, to fully understand the river, we have to stand on one side of the water, then on the other; we have to stand upstream, then downstream. We have to touch our toes to the water, and then we have to climb slowly inside or jump in quickly with a splash. We have to swim with the current, against the current, ride along the river in a raft. We have to see the river at sunrise and sunset and in the middle of the afternoon. We have to experience it now and then come back later in the year to experience it again. The same is true with issues. We have to identify and explore multiple perspectives on an issue in order to fully understand the issue. We have to step outside of our worldview and see what others are thinking and feeling and saying.

Practicum

In this section, we discussed multiple perspectives in terms of two different *metaphors*. One metaphor for multiple perspectives is the pizza; another is the river. Can you think of another metaphor that describes multiple perspectives? (Remember that a metaphor is a descriptive device, a figure of speech in which one thing or action or quality is attributed to a distinctly different thing or action or quality.) Take a few moments to brainstorm a list of ideas, and then create your own metaphor to represent the concept of multiple perspectives. Share your ideas with the class.

He Said, She Said, They Said, *What?*

It used to be that when we discussed issues, we would take sides and debate issues in terms of pros and cons. But it is hard to do that anymore because no issue is ever simply a matter of "he said, she said." It is even more than "he thinks, she thinks, *they* think." It is, he thinks *because of this,* he thinks *because of that,* she thinks *because of this,* they think *because of the other,* she thinks *because of another.* There are many variations—multiple perspectives—related to any issue.

Sometimes perspectives on an issue are very different, and sometimes they are similar in some ways, sharing what we call *common ground* (points on which we agree). Making distinctions between one perspective and another is not always easy. Sometimes it sounds like perspectives are in opposition, when in fact they are not. And sometimes it sounds like perspectives are in agreement, when in fact they are not. We have to be able to identify these variations, no matter how subtle, in order to fully understand an issue.

Oppositions / *Oppositions*

When talking about perspectives, the most basic difference is *direct opposition.* Direct oppositions are like mirror images. One perspective is the mirror image of the other—the opposite—a reversed image like we see when we look in a mirror. For example, in terms of the Columbine High School shooting and the issue of media culpability, Joe thinks the media is to blame, Rachel thinks the media is not to blame. Joe's perspective and Rachel's perspective are in direct opposition with one another.

At the most basic level, this is how perspectives on issues exist and direct oppositions *are* easily identified. But remember our illustrations at the beginning of this chapter? Direct oppositions look something like our first illustration:

As we discovered already, issues and perspectives are not as simple as either/or. We have to search below this kind of surface reading of an issue and uncover the layers of perspectives that define, explain, and form a complete picture of the problem.

The Mirror Cracked

What if in talking with Joe and Rachel we discover that both of them think the media is somehow to blame, but their reasons for *why* the media is to blame or what aspect of the media is to blame are different?

What if Joe thinks the media is to blame, but his focus is on music? Rachel thinks the media is to blame, but her focus is on television? Both Joe and Rachel agree that the media is to blame (this is their common ground), but they are focusing on *different types* of media—one is focusing on music (aural) and the other is focusing on television (multimedia). The mirror has cracked. Perspectives are no longer as simple as direct oppositions, and identifying these subtle distinctions is often a challenge.

Hang on; it gets even more complicated.

Maybe Joe and Rachel both focus on the same type of media—music (more common ground), but Joe focuses on rap and Rachel focuses on rock and roll. Or they might both focus on rock, but Joe thinks the record companies are responsible and Rachel thinks the artists who write the lyrics are responsible.

Identifying and understanding perspectives can get very complicated the further you look into an issue. How do we navigate through this complexity?

Tools for Success: Introducing the Discourse of Argument— Claims and Reasons

When we express our perspectives on an issue, we step into a specialized realm of discourse known as *argumentation*. An argument is a form of expression that asserts and advances (with reasons and evidence) a position on an issue. Arguments begin with *claims,* and so that is where we begin our study of argumentation.

Simply put, a claim is a statement about a perspective on an issue. It expresses what someone believes to be true regarding something (usually a situation or condition that exists in some aspect of society). To identify a claim, we ask the question, What are you trying to prove? The answer to that question, in one form or another, is the claim that is being asserted and advanced in an argument.

Claims are made in different ways. When we are lucky, they are stated clearly and directly in an article, essay, or speech: *This is what I believe to be true.* But, this does not always (or even usually) happen. Sometimes claims are implied through the reasoning and evidence described in an argument. Sometimes we have to *infer* (to guess by reasoning) the claim based on the content of an article or argument.

Claims are the foundations of arguments, the expression of perspectives on an issue. But sometimes claims are not directly stated—instead, they are implied through a repetition or explication of ideas. For example, in a conversation with Rachel, Joe tells her that he is late to class every day no matter what time he arrives on campus because he cannot find a parking space. He tells her that Mary has the same problem. To make matters worse, the instructors on campus do not understand the dilemma, and they are penalizing students for being tardy. He complains that he paid a great deal of money for a parking sticker, but that there are no spaces available for him to use when he needs them.

Joe has not made a direct claim about parking, but Rachel can *infer,* based on the information and examples Joe has offered, that he believes parking on campus to be a serious problem for students at the University of North Carolina–Charlotte. So, what is he trying to prove? He is trying to prove that a condition exists. We know this to be true because throughout his conversation, Joe has repeatedly addressed problems that he and other students have experienced that are connected to the parking situation on campus.

Whenever a claim is not directly stated, therefore, we can look at the *overall information* offered and make an *inference.* We can ask the question, What is he trying to prove? and we can read between the lines of what Joe is saying to infer his perspective on parking on campus.

Inference requires close reading, and it takes practice. Once we are able to identify the claims that are being made regarding an issue, our understanding of that issue broadens and deepens, and we are better prepared to join the conversation of ideas.

Identifying Different Types of Claims

To get even more specific and further complicate matters, there are different categories of claims. Let's take a look at three of the most common types of claims:

> **Claims That Educate.** Sometimes claims seek to prove that a problem, a situation, or a condition exists in society. These types of claims are intended to educate a particular audience: for example, "violent content in music influences the occurrence of violent behavior in some teenagers." What is this claim trying to prove? It is trying to prove that a condition exists, that one thing causes a particular response or condition in another thing. Specifically, it is trying to convince an audience that violent musical content causes violent

behavior to occur in some teenagers. This claim presents the perspective that music influences behavior.

Claims That Motivate or Instigate Change. Some claims argue that something regarding a situation or condition should change, that some action should be taken to alter a situation or condition. These types of claims are intended to motivate an audience to adopt a particular behavior, to instigate a change: for instance, "record companies should regulate the content produced by their music artists." What is this claim trying to prove? It is trying to prove that an action should be taken to change a situation. Specifically, this claim argues from the perspective that record companies are responsible for and must take action to regulate the content of the products they distribute.

Claims That Establish Meaning. Some claims argue that a cultural artifact (a work of fiction, a poem, a song lyric, a movie or television show, an electronic text, a photograph or painting or sculpture) signifies some aspect of life and the human experience. These types of claims argue about the meaning communicated by a particular artifact. For example, if we listen to the song "Jeremy" by Pearl Jam, we might argue that Eddie Vedder intended to show through those lyrics that "the adults in Jeremy's life failed him and caused him to commit suicide." This claim seeks to prove that the song "Jeremy" communicates a particular message regarding the suicide of Jeremy Wade Dell. It is an interpretation that advances an argument regarding the meaning of an artifact—the lyrics written by Eddie Vedder and performed by the group Pearl Jam. (This type of claim is quite unique and is addressed in depth in Chapter 8.)

Practicum

1. Working in groups, generate a list of claims that might be made about an issue related to your event. Decide what types of claims you have generated: Are they claims that educate, that motivate, or that hope to instigate change? (Remember to ask and answer the question, What are you trying to prove?) If you have time, you might share your claims with the rest of the class. Have each group write a few claims on the board, and ask the rest of the class to decide whether these claims educate, motivate, or instigate change. Be sure to show how you know which type of claim each one is (for example, if a claim contains the word *should,* you would know it is designed to instigate change because it is recommending a particular course of action).

2. Think of a claim related to an issue (this might be something raised by the media while your event was in the news, or it might be something you discovered as you investigated the history of the event). Write that claim in one sentence as a clear statement. Now write a statement that is the opposite of that claim. Share your opposing claims within your group. Working together, generate a list of claims that fall between those two extremes. For instance, if your first claim is, *the music of Marilyn Manson influenced Eric Harris and Dylan Klebold to go on a shooting rampage,* and the opposite of

(continued)

that claim is, *the music of Marilyn Manson did not influence Eric Harris and Dylan Klebold to go on a shooting rampage*, think of claims that fall between these two extremes. One such claim may be, *the music of Marilyn Manson did impact the behavior of Eric Harris and Dylan Klebold in some ways, but it did not influence them to go on a shooting rampage*. Another claim may be, *the music of Marilyn Manson has a positive influence on teenagers like Eric Harris and Dylan Klebold*.

3. Your instructor may begin this exercise by writing a claim on the board. Each student should take a turn at the board and write a new claim (careful not to duplicate a previously generated claim). When you finish, you should have generated a list of twenty or more claims (depending on how many students are in your class). Each claim should represent a slightly different perspective on an issue.

Reasoning

When developing an argument, a claim is the foundation, but an argument is more than just a claim. In order to advance an argument, you must also provide *reasoning*. Reasons explain the logic behind your claim; they usually answer the question, Why? Why do you believe this (your claim) to be true?

Let's return for a moment to our example with Joe and Rachel.

Joe tells Rachel, "Parking is a serious problem on the campus."

We know what Joe's claim is—he has directly stated it. What is he trying to prove? He is trying to prove that a condition exists; therefore, we know he is arguing to educate. Joe is specifically arguing that a condition exists on campus.

But in addition to knowing what he believes to be true, we also need to know, Why does he believe this to be true? We need to know his reasoning.

Rachel asks Joe: What are you trying to prove?

Joe says: Parking is a problem on campus.

Rachel asks: Why is parking a problem on campus?

Joe replies: Parking is a problem *because* . . .

Everything that follows "because" is Joe's reasoning to explain the logic of his claim that parking is a problem on campus.

In response to Rachel's questions, Joe might say, "no matter what time I arrive on campus, I cannot find a parking space." In this case, Joe's reasoning is that the lack of available parking spaces demonstrates that parking is a problem on campus. This seems like a logical reason, but is it enough? Joe might add to his reasoning by saying, "It's also a problem because I paid for a parking sticker so that I could park on campus, but there aren't enough available spaces in the student parking lots. Every day, I end up parking across the street and walking." Joe's additional reasoning is that paying for a parking sticker entitles a student to a parking space on campus. These are just a few examples of reasons Joe might offer to explain the logic of his claim.

> **Practicum**
>
> Using one or more of the claims generated in the previous Practicum, create a list of possible reasons to explain why that claim is true. You might do this alone, in pairs, in small groups, or as a whole class, depending upon your instructor's preferences. Which reasons seem most important?

Identifying Claims and Reasons
Walk-Through

Before moving on, let's practice identifying the multiple perspectives represented within a text—the claims and reasons.

In spring of 2002, Fox News personality Bill O'Reilly aired a special news program entitled "The Corruption of the American Child." In this controversial program, O'Reilly presented information on the entertainment industry, which claimed that music and movies and television were responsible for "corrupting" children and teens. O'Reilly was subsequently attacked by many people for many reasons, most of which related to his take on music and the music industry. For instance, a reporter for the *St. Petersburg Times* claimed that O'Reilly's special was "full of hidden racism and racial profiling" and that music "has always had two goals, first, to express the angst of its generation, second, to tick off grownups." Musical artist Scott Stapp of the rock band Creed felt so strongly about O'Reilly's program that he asked to appear on *The O'Reilly Factor* to discuss the issue.

Bill O'Reilly is host of Fox News channel's *The O'Reilly Factor* and author of *The O'Reilly Factor: The Good, the Bad, and the Completely Ridiculous in American Life* and *The No-Spin Zone: Confrontations with the Powerful and Famous in America,* as well as a column appearing in *WorldNetDaily News.*

Scott Stapp is a singer/songwriter/poet/family-relations activist and philanthropist from Orlando, Florida. He is best known as the frontman for the rock band, Creed.

The full transcript is available through *Academic Search Elite, Masterfile Premier, InfoTrac,* and other online databases. Here is the bibliographic information:

O'Reilly, Bill. "Back of the Book: Interview with Scott Stapp." The O'Reilly Factor (Fox News Network). April 09, 2002.

After reading this transcript closely, we are able to identify the various perspectives represented by O'Reilly and Stapp—their claims and reasoning.

First, recall our definition of a claim: a statement about *a perspective* on an issue. The issue O'Reilly and Stapp discuss is the cause-and-effect relationship between music and its impact on youth behavior and how record sales demonstrate that impact. (It is interesting to note that both parties assume that music does, indeed, have some sort of impact on youth behavior. This is common ground for both of them.)

The argument began with the presentation of O'Reilly's television special, "The Corruption of the American Child," which Stapp viewed on television. Let's begin by identifying O'Reilly's claim.

To determine what the claim is, we may ask and answer the question, What are you trying to prove? In this brief transcript, O'Reilly's claim is implied; however, his claim is explicitly stated in the title of the television special to which Stapp is responding: *The American child is being corrupted.* What is O'Reilly trying to prove? He is trying to prove that American children are being corrupted—in this case by exposure to certain types of music. He is trying to prove that a situation exists. This is an argument to educate.

What reasoning does O'Reilly offer to explain the logic of his claim? Reasoning explains the logic behind a claim. To determine this, we ask the question, Why do you believe this to be true, or how is this true?

O'Reilly's reasoning is fairly clear:

○ He believes that there are kids who do not have parental guidance.
○ He believes that those kids are targeted by artists who deliver an "insidious message" through their music.
○ These at-risk kids are buying a lot of those albums and, as a result, they are being exposed to an "insidious message."

His conclusion is that the consequences of this exposure are troublesome.

Now let's examine Stapp's claim and reasoning.

Stapp viewed O'Reilly's television special and asked to appear on the Fox network news show, *The O'Reilly Factor,* to offer his rebuttal to O'Reilly's argument. (A *rebuttal* is a form of argument presented to contradict or nullify another, opposing argument.) So, what is Stapp's claim?

Scott Stapp begins his rebuttal by stating that O'Reilly misrepresented the impact of the music industry, that, in fact, "if you add it up, all the artists that have more of a positive message . . . [have] much more of an impact on our youth." Stapp does not dispute O'Reilly's assumption that music does have an impact on youth behavior. He argues that O'Reilly misrepresented the *kind* of impact music is having. He is trying to prove that a situation exists. This is a claim to educate.

Why does Stapp believe this to be true? He reasons that

○ O'Reilly used record sales figures to demonstrate impact and used as examples the groups Insane Clown Posse and Marilyn Manson.
○ Those two groups and others like them actually sell far fewer albums than other groups.
○ Those other groups (such as Stapp's own band, Creed) deliver a more positive message through their music.
○ Therefore, if we use record sales as an indicator, it must be true that bands like Creed have more of an impact on youth behavior than bands like Insane Clown Posse and Marilyn Manson have.

Let's pull all of this together and try to formulate the big picture. An event like the Columbine High School shooting occurred. Many social problems and issues were blamed for that event; one such issue was the effect the music the shooters listened to had on their behavior. Bill O'Reilly's perspective on that issue is that the music the shooters listened to was targeting them specifically and may have had a negative impact on their already antisocial behavior. The underlying message (implied but not explicitly stated or developed) is that this situation should cause parents concern, and something should be done to prevent artists from targeting troubled youths or to prevent youths from having access to music with a negative message. Scott Stapp's perspective on the issue is that the music is not targeting kids like the shooters specifically, and that most kids are choosing music with a more positive message. Consequently, the underlying message from Stapp is that parents need not be alarmed, that for the most part youths are making pretty sound decisions (particularly in the wake of 9/11).

So, to sum up what we now know about claims and reasons,

- A claim is a statement about a perspective on an issue.
- A claim answers the question, *What are you trying to prove?*
- Claims sometimes attempt to prove that a situation or condition exists.
- Claims sometimes attempt to prove that a situation or condition should change and perhaps explain how it should change.
- Claims sometimes argue that a cultural artifact signifies some aspect of life and the human experience.
- Sometimes claims are easily identified because the claim is directly stated. Sometimes claims are not directly stated but are implied.
- Reasons explain the logic behind a claim.
- Reasons answer the question, *Why do you believe this to be true?*

Practicum

Read the following article by Kristen Baldwin and make a claim and reasons outline. Baldwin is a staff editor for *Entertainment Weekly* magazine. Her editorial on media and the connections to youth violence was published in the May 7, 1999, edition of *Entertainment Weekly.*

In your own words, state her claim (a response to the question, What are you trying to prove?); then look for each reason she offers to explain the logic of her claim (a response to the question, Why?). Write each reason in the form of a *because* statement. Your outline will look something like this:

- What are you trying to prove?
    - **Claim:**
- Why?
    - **Reason 1:** *because*

(continued)

> ○ **Reason 2:** *because*
> ○ **Reason 3:** *because*
>
> Each statement after *because* will be an answer to the question of why Baldwin's claim is true. Share your ideas with the class.

"There's No Why"

Kristen Baldwin

What happened at Columbine High was a tragedy, an unearthly glimpse into hell, but it was not Marilyn Manson's fault. Nor was it caused by Rammstein or the videogame Doom. Yet cable news channels and network newsmagazines have filled hours with the "Violent movies-music-TV shows did this!" argument in special reports with names like "High School Terror" (*20/20*). It's no surprise. We are by nature afraid of things we can't control. When something inexplicable like Columbine ambushes us, our natural response is to talk at it, cover it so thoroughly with theories and blame that it can't leap out at us again.

But does pointing the finger at violence in entertainment ever work? Does it stop kids from blowing each other away? No. Not after Pearl, Miss. Not after West Paducah, Ky. Not after Jonesboro, Ark. After each of these instances we wailed, wept, and decried the influence of pop culture. And nothing changed.

Why? Because while graphic images can affect us—desensitize us, even—they do not, cannot, create dangerous urges in people who don't already have those urges inside them. A well-adjusted kid who watches *Natural Born Killers* over and over—as Eric Harris and Dylan Klebold reportedly did—is not suddenly going to feel the need to commit a murderous act. Movies simply don't have that much power.

Relax. I'm not letting Hollywood off the hook. I believe that a diet of violence exacerbates and inflames the antisocial, nihilistic, and even murderous emotions of kids who are mentally disturbed. It is irresponsible for entertainment aimed at children to glorify, glamorize, or diminish the impact of guns, violence, sex, etc., because there's always the chance that an unstable youngster will somehow glean—and act on—the wrong message. But what makes more sense: abolishing entertainment that may negatively influence vulnerable minds, or working harder to identify teens in need of help? Thousands of kids play Doom; only two of them went on a shooting rampage in Colorado. Is vilifying the videogame really the answer?

For the *Datelines* of the world, yes. There's only so much footage of weeping teens and bloody victims available; blaming Marilyn Manson means you can slap a clip of the shock rocker on screen. Condemning *The Basketball Diaries* is even better—producers get to run an image of Leo DiCaprio. It fills time, it looks provocative. More important, it feels good to place blame. But it doesn't get us any closer to understanding the horrific event. Maybe nothing will. One Columbine student, asked why this happened, just shook his head: "There's no why."

WRITING ASSIGNMENT   Quest Four: Critical Issue Survey and Essay

Overview

For this Quest, you will conduct a critical survey of current, multiple perspectives on an issue related to your event.

Step One

Begin by reviewing the articles from your casebook section, "Multimedia Sources." Each of the sources in that section presents multiple perspectives on what caused your event (various social problems or issues). Make a list of issues discussed in these sources, then, if you have not already done so, *select one social problem or issue* to investigate in more depth.

Step Two

Conduct additional research on that issue. Your goal is to discover the various perspectives on that issue as it relates to your event or similar events.

Your instructor will establish specific guidelines for your research; however, I recommend that you find four to six sources representing current multiple perspectives on your issue. Note that one source may present more than one perspective (much like the transcript in which one source presented multiple perspectives: O'Reilly's and Stapp's). As you locate sources, follow the same steps your followed for Quest Three (review the sections "Research Map and Paper Trail," "Evaluating a Source: The ABCs of Credibility," "Responsible Information Gathering," and "Processing Information: Summary and Paraphrase"). Remember, you are building on the foundation you established in your research dossier.

Step Three

Once you have located and processed four to six sources, then write an essay in which you present and explain at least three different perspectives on your issue. Be objective. Whereas the last Quest asked you to restate information about each source, this Quest asks you to *present information about perspectives represented in several sources* (so the focus is on the perspectives, not the sources).

Begin your essay by *forecasting:* briefly introduce the issue and the various perspectives you located. Then, in the body of your essay, explain each perspective (claim and reasoning) in greater detail, using examples from the sources you gathered. Do not quote directly from your sources; use summary and paraphrase to present the information on each perspective (document the information gathered from each source using MLA in-text citation format detailed in the following section). Conclude your essay by stating your personal perspective on the issue. Also include a works cited page (which does not have to be annotated for this Quest—just include the bibliographic citations in correct MLA works cited format).

MLA In-Text Documentation Summary and Paraphrase

As we discussed in the previous chapter, MLA (Modern Language Association) citation is a system for documenting sources of information gathered during research. Writers use MLA citations to acknowledge the sources of information used within the documents they produce, such as academic essays. This process is called *in-text citation or parenthetical reference*.

MLA citations serve very practical purposes. An in-text MLA citation lets your reader know that you have included information in your text that you gathered through research. The information documented may be in the form of a direct quotation (which we cover in Chapter 5), or it may be in the form of a summary or paraphrase. The important thing to remember is that if you use ideas, facts, words, or phrases that you gathered during the research process, you must document the source of that information within the body of your text. If you use ideas, facts, words or phrases that you gathered during the research process and you do not document the source of your information, then you have plagiarized (see "Tools for Success," Chapter 3, for a review of the consequences of academic dishonesty).

The in-text citation is brief and provides only enough information to direct your reader to a particular entry on your works cited page. The citation should come (preferably) at the end of a sentence but as close to the information documented as possible, and it should be placed before the punctuation mark.

When citing information that has been restated in the form of a summary or paraphrase, you should follow these guidelines:

> If you have mentioned the author's name in the text of your summary or paraphrase, you only need to include the page number in a citation following the information from that source:
>
>> Brian Doherty explicitly criticizes Lynne Cheney's testimony before a Senate subcommittee and claims that her analogy between environmental pollution and the effects of rap music on youth is faulty (14).
>
> If you have not mentioned the author's name in the text of your summary or paraphrase, you must include both the author's last name and the page number in a citation following the information from that source:
>
>> Lynne Cheney's testimony before a Senate subcommittee included a faulty analogy between environmental pollution and the effects of rap music on youth (Doherty 14).
>
> If your summary or paraphrase refers to a group or an organization (rather than an individual author), follow the same guidelines as you would for an individual author:
>
>> The Federal Bureau of Investigation (FBI) conducted an extensive study of various school shootings and created a list of personality indicators to help school officials predict which students might become violent offenders (7).

If your summary or paraphrase refers to a source that does not mention an author, include an abbreviated reference to the title of the source in your citation:

> Successful parenting involves the cooperation of parents and members of the community ("Parental Responsibility" 23).

If your summary or paraphrase refers to a source that does not have page numbers (like Web sites and other sources retrieved electronically), then simply list the author's last name in your citation or, if there is no author or title (which is common for electronic sources), list the Web site:

> Clear communication between parents and their children is essential for a healthy relationship, and there are many organizations around the country dedicated to this cause (witharmswideopen.org).

There are other documentation situations you may encounter when using summary and paraphrase in your text; the examples included here are simply the most common. For additional information, check out the *MLA Handbook for Writers of Research Papers* or one of the sources mentioned in Chapter 3.

MLA Works Cited

In Chapter 3, you created as a part of Quest Three an annotated bibliography. This is very similar to a works cited page. The main difference is that a works cited page does not include any summary or evaluation. The only information included on a works cited page is bibliographic references for any source mentioned in your text.

Remember, an in-text MLA citation lets your reader know that you have included information in your text that you gathered through research. The in-text citation provides enough information to direct your reader to a particular entry on your works cited page. On the works cited page, the reader will find all of the information necessary to locate the original source if he or she wants to do any additional reading.

Some important points to remember about a works cited page include the following:

- The works cited is the last page of an essay. It begins on a new page, and the title "Works Cited" is centered at the top of the page (no quotation marks).
- Each entry on the works cited page is listed alphabetically. If there is no author's last name, use the title of the source to situate it alphabetically.
- Double-space the entire works cited page.
- Each line of a citation after the first line is indented with a hanging indent.

A model works cited page is included with "In the Spotlight: A Student Model Critical Survey."

Criteria for a Successful Critical Survey

For this assignment, you are asked to locate four to six new sources following the same research process practiced in Quest Three. Then you must identify multiple perspectives on an issue that are presented in those sources and write an essay explaining each perspective. The majority of your essay must be informative (strictly an objective restating of information gathered from research), concluding with a paragraph that expresses your own current perspective on the issue.

○ A good process for this assignment includes the gathering and processing (review in Chapter 3 the sections "Research Map and Paper Trail," "Evaluating a Source: The ABCs of Credibility," "Responsible Information Gathering," and "Processing Information: Summary and Paraphrase") of four to six credible sources on *one issue* connected to your event.
○ A good critical survey essay is:
  ○ Focused on one issue and the presentation of at least three different perspectives on that issue (claim and reasoning).
  ○ Developed with clear explanations and adequate illustrations, including specific examples taken from four to six sources gathered during research. These illustrations should be in the form of summary or paraphrase; no direct quotations should be used for this assignment.
  ○ Organized with an introduction that sets up the focus on a particular issue and forecasts the organizational pattern for the remainder of the essay by introducing at least three different perspectives on that issue. The body of the essay should follow the organizational pattern forecast in the introduction. It should end with a conclusion that establishes your perspective on the issue.
  ○ Correct, with minimal grammar and punctuation errors and absolutely correct use of MLA in-text citations and a works cited page.

In the Spotlight: A Student Model Critical Survey

The Author: Jihye Choi

Jihye was an exchange student from Korea for the 2002–2003 academic year. She is a senior English major at a Korean university.

Author's Etcetera

Reflecting on the process of recognizing multiple perspectives on her issue, Jihye writes,

> This was a difficult task, but it is so important to understand how other people think about an issue. Sometimes our own perspectives cloud our vision and we cannot see that there are other ways of thinking. I feel stronger in my beliefs having experienced what others think. And I feel stronger knowing that there are many people, including experts, who agree with my way of thinking.

The Issue of Parental Responsibility
for Youth Violence

Many different social problems and issues are blamed for the occurrence of youth violence, such as the Columbine High School shooting, and there is much disagreement in the general public as to which issue is most influential. Circumstances vary in incidents of violent youth behavior, but the issue that seems to be the most consistent in all cases is parental responsibility. Every child has a parent or guardian figure; this is simply a fact of birth and the one thing that is common to all situations of youth violence.

Parental responsibility was once a consequential part of being a parent (it was assumed rather than dictated), but in the past century, society has changed to the point that the law must sometimes intervene to establish parental responsibility rules (McBride). But even the legal issue of a parent's responsibility is open to much debate. While some people feel that parents are unquestionably responsible for the actions of their children, others feel that parents are responsible to a certain extent but that outside factors have an influence on youth behavior beyond a parent's control. Still others feel that parents are not in any way responsible for the behavior of their children.

The perspective most heavily addressed in the media is that parents are completely responsible for their children's actions. According to this perspective, parents are responsible for the actions of their children until the age of eighteen (or in some states, the age of twenty-one). This assumes that parents are responsible for complete involvement in their child's life, and that they are to be firmly in control at all times (McLaughlin). This perspective is grounded in research that has shown that violent or aggressive behavior is often learned early in life. Young children spend much time with their parents, so parents have a tremendous influence on their children during those formative years. Children learn by watching their parents. They learn values and behavior (Commission). Researchers say that failure to set and monitor expectations for children is one way that parents contribute to violent youth behavior. Having a good role model who demonstrates positive behaviors will teach children to lead a non-violent life ("Raising Children").

While recognizing that parents do have a responsibility in managing their children's behavior, particularly the behavior of young children (under the age of ten), other people believe that sometimes in spite of a parent's best efforts, a child will become violent. This is due to influences beyond a parent's control. Sometimes those influences are mental disorders that affect a child's behavior. Parents have no control over some genetic factors that have been linked to violent behavior (Prothrow-Stith). Other influences include a child's peers or exposure to violence in the media or in society outside of the home (Wasserman). According to this perspective, a parent is assumed to be responsible to a certain extent, but even fulfillment of that responsibility is not a guarantee that a child will not become violent. If a parent seems to have done his or her job providing a safely structured home environment for the child through his or her formative years and the child still becomes violent, the parent is not held accountable (McLaughlin).

Finally, a third perspective regarding parental responsibility asserts that parents cannot under any circumstances be held responsible for the behavior of their children. This way of thinking assumes personal responsibility—particularly for teenagers. Kids have a mind of their own, and they are capable of choosing a form of behavior.

If they choose to behave in a violent way, then they must be held personally accountable for their actions. Parents cannot control the mind of a child much less the choices that child makes when away from the parents (Schrof).

Though I recognize the strengths in the other perspectives I have discovered through my research, my own perspective is that parents are certainly responsible for their children. I believe parents are the most important and influential people in their children's lives. Early childhood years are spent largely with parents and it is during this time that a child develops personality and behavioral traits that last a lifetime. Parents have a great deal of influence on the shaping of a child. Even as a child ages, a parent is responsible for being involved in that child's life and monitoring a child's activities and relationships. I believe much youth violence could be avoided if parents were more actively involved in the lives of their children. It's not enough to say, "how was your day" or to rush through a meal at a family dinner table. Real quality time must be spent with a child every day, and a child must have rules to follow and expectations clearly established. This is more than a parent's responsibility. It is a parent's moral duty.

Works Cited

Commission for the Prevention of Youth Violence. "Youth Violence, Setting the Stage." *Youth Violence in America*. The American Medical Association. December 2000.

McBride, Michael, et al. "Parenting on Trial." *Time*. 147:21. 20–23.

McLaughlin, Abraham. "If kids get in trouble, parents may feel the heat." *Christian Science Monitor*. 90:56. 63–65.

Prothrow-Stith, D. *Deadly Consequence*. New York: HarperCollins, 1991.

Raising Children to Resist Violence: What You Can Do. 1996. American Psychological Association. March 16, 2003. <www.apa.org/pubinfo/apa-aap.html>.

Schrof, Joanne M. "Who's Guilty?" *U.S. News & World Report*. 126:19.

Wasserman, Gail A., et al. "Prevention of Serious and Violent Juvenile Offending." *Juvenile Justice Bulletin*. Washington, D.C.: U.S. Department of Justice. 2003.

Practicum

How does Jihye's model fulfill the criteria for a successful critical survey? Write a brief evaluation. Refer to specific examples from the text of her essay to support your evaluation. Share your responses with your classmates. Do you find that you and your classmates agree? Disagree?

Reflection in Action

In your own words, explain the following terms:

○ perspective
○ argument

- ○ claim
- ○ reasons

Based on your understanding of the information covered in this chapter, how are these terms related?

Look back over the research you completed for your Quest Four. Explain your issue and the perspectives you have identified using the river metaphor that we discussed at the beginning of this chapter. How does this metaphor work when applied to your issue?

Expanding Your Vision: A Multimedia Assignment Option

Critical Inquiry: Digging Deeper

We encounter arguments and make claims ourselves every day in a variety of forums. You have investigated various claims made about an issue connected to your event. Most of the claims you have identified were made in printed text, probably in the form of an article or essay. But claims are made and arguments are advanced in other forms, too, through other types of media. Can you think of any visual texts that assert claims about your issue? Multimedia texts (such as a television program) or aural texts? What about interactive texts? Make a list of different texts that you might encounter that assert claims on various issues. Then consider, How does a visual text assert a claim? How does a multimedia text or aural text assert a claim? What about an interactive text? What tools are used in place of statements? Share your ideas with the class.

MULTIMEDIA ASSIGNMENT   Visi-Quest Four: Expanding Your Vision by Creating an Issue Brochure

Using the information gathered during your Quest Four research, create a two-sided, three-fold brochure that presents your issue, three perspectives on your issue, and your own perspective. Your brochure should be an informative document that incorporates both textual information and visual details that represent your issue.

Brochure Instructions

Though there are many templates available for the creation of brochures, the instructions for this assignment are designed using the word processing program Microsoft Word. They are simple and should be adaptable to most any word processing program.

Getting Started

Setting Up Two Pages

Open a new Word document and immediately name it and save it on a floppy disk. Then press Enter until your cursor has moved down the screen from the first page to the second page. You will not need more than two pages for this assignment.

- In the toolbar at the top of your screen, click on **File.**
- Click on **Page Setup.**
- In the dialogue box that pops up, click on the tab for **Paper Size.**
- Click on the circle beside **Landscape.** Then click **OK.**
- Again, in the toolbar at the top of your screen, click on **Format.**
- Then click on **Columns.**
- In the dialogue box that pops up, click on the image for **Preset / Three.**
- Click **OK.**

Note that you may have to adjust the margins, too.

Panel Content

This is difficult for some people to visualize, so be sure to carefully follow these instructions. Do not confuse your left side and your right side. It is important that certain information be included on certain panels. Otherwise, your brochure will not align properly when you assemble the finished product.

Page One, Left Side Panel

This panel will contain information on the inside flap of your folded brochure. This panel should include your works cited information. Select the font and font size of your choice and type in your works cited information. Pay attention to details, correctness, and format as you would with a regular works cited page.

Page One, Middle Panel

This panel will be the back panel of your folded brochure. It should contain the presentation of your perspective on your issue. Again, pay attention to font size. If you include any visual images, be sure to size them and place them carefully. This can be a tricky process. Be patient. Remember that a brochure is a multimedia document that contains both print text and static visual images. The design of the brochure—its visual appeal—is important.

Page One, Right Side Panel

This panel will be the front of your brochure where you present your issue. This panel serves the same purpose that an introductory paragraph serves in an essay. You must capture the audience's attention, and you must establish the focus of your document. Attention to visual details and placement is important. The layout of the first page is shown below.

Page one will be set up like this:

This is the inside flap and will contain your Works Cited page	This is the back of your brochure and will contain information on your perspective	This is the front panel of your brochure and will introduce the issue

Page Two, Left Side Panel

This panel will be the inside left of your folded brochure. It should contain information on one perspective for your issue.

Page Two, Middle Panel

This panel will be the inside middle of your brochure. It should contain information on one perspective for your issue.

Page Two, Right Side Panel

This panel will be the inside right of your brochure. It should contain information on one perspective for your issue. The layout of the second page is shown below.

Page two will be set up like this:

This is the inside left panel and will contain information on one perspective for your issue	This is the inside middle panel and will contain information on one perspective for your issue	This is the inside right panel and will contain information on one perspective for your issue

Printing and Assembling Your Brochure

If you have the capabilities to print a two-sided document, that is the easiest way to proceed. If you do not, print the two pages on separate sheets and place them back-to-back—the top right of page one back-to-back with the top left of page two. Secure them in place with a little bit of glue or tape. Then carefully fold to create a three-panel brochure. Fold the right side in first, just past the inside margin of the left panel, and then fold the left side over the right.

Criteria for a Successful Issue Brochure

For this assignment, you are asked to create a visual and textual representation of various claims on your issue. Follow the directions for creating an issue brochure and transfer the information you gathered during your research to a highly visual brochure format. This brochure must include printed text and visual images, and special attention to the layout of each panel (font, color, size, spacing) must be observed.

- A good issue brochure is correctly created and assembled according to the instructions provided.
- A good issue brochure is
  - Focused on one issue and the presentation of at least three different perspectives on that issue.
  - Developed with clear explanations and adequate illustrations, including specific examples taken from four to six sources gathered during research. These illustrations should be in the form of summary or paraphrase; no direct quotations should be used for this assignment. A brochure must also include visual images that correspond with the text on a given panel and should be designed according to a visually appealing format with attention to font, color, size, and spacing.
  - Organized with a front panel that grabs the audience's attention (is visually engaging) and introduces the focus on a particular issue. Each of the inside panels should present a separate perspective on the issue. The inside flap should present the works cited, and the back panel of the brochure should present your perspective on the issue.
  - Correct, with minimal grammar and punctuation errors and absolutely correct use of MLA in-text citations and a works cited page.

In the Spotlight: A Student Model Issue Brochure

The Author: Ian Heggan

Ian plans to major in architecture. He hopes to one day own and operate his own design company.

Author's Etcetera

Ian had no prior experience with this type of multimedia project, so he initially found the assignment to be quite a challenge:

Before tackling this assignment, I could barely type an essay in a word processing program, much less make something like a brochure. It was a real challenge for me to complete all the research and process it and then pull everything together into the format of a brochure. The research was challenging because there are so many sources out there on this topic, but a lot of them say the same things. So I had to look long and hard to find multiple perspectives on this issue. Then processing the sources was a challenge, too. But pulling it all together in the brochure was the biggest challenge of all. I have to say it was worth all of my time and effort. I'm really proud of the finished product, and I feel like it's a realistic way of communicating this kind of information. It's something I might do again in the future.

The Front Panel of Ian's Brochure

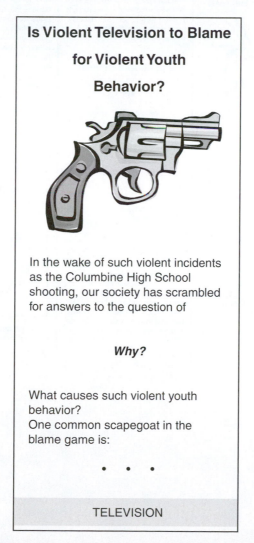

Is Violent Television to Blame for Violent Youth Behavior?

In the wake of such violent incidents as the Columbine High School shooting, our society has scrambled for answers to the question of

Why?

What causes such violent youth behavior?
One common scapegoat in the blame game is:

• • •

TELEVISION

The Inside Panels of Ian's Brochure

Some People Believe:

Television causes violent behavior in children.

For many years, researchers have attempted to show a cause and effect relationship between television watching and aggressive behavior in children. Based on the findings in these studies and basic cognitive developmental learning theories, many people believe that watching violent television programs influences youth to commit violent crimes (Centerwall). This perspective operates on the assumption that children learn through imitation (Withecomb). It also assumes that excessive exposure to violence on television desensitizes children to real-life violence (Mudore).

Then there are those people who believe that television viewing is a positive thing. That it can actually be used in a way to prevent violent behavior.

Some People Believe:

Television has a positive influence on behavior.

This perspective asserts the connection between television viewing and behavior but places an emphasis on the positive outcome. Television can be a learning tool and can actually educate an audience on how to avoid violent behavior and how to respond to instances of violence in a positive, constructive way (Klite).

Another perspective on this issue is that television does not influence behavior at all. This viewpoint sees television as purely entertainment and acknowledges that the healthy human mind—regardless of age and experience—is capable of distinguishing between fantasy and reality (White). Those who accept this perspective also counter that television is used as a scapegoat, and this attack on television is often used to divert the public's attention away from the real issues (such as government's desire to control the information that people consume) (Fowles).

Some People Believe:

Television does not influence behavior.

The Side Flap of Ian's Brochure

Works Cited

Centerwall, Brandon S. Television
and Violent Crime. <u>Public
Interest</u>. Spring 1993. 56–72.

Fowles, Jib. The Whipping Boy.
<u>Reason</u>. March 2001. 27–34.

Klite, Paul. Media can be antibiotic for
violence. <u>Quill</u>. 88:3. 32–35.

Mudore, Constance Faye. Does TV
Violence Kill? <u>Current Health</u>.
26:6. 24–27.

White, Timothy. The Real Bottom Line
Is Human Accountability.
<u>Billboard</u>. 111:19. 3–8.

Withecomb, Julie L. Causes of
Violence in Children. <u>Journal
of Mental Health</u>. 6:5.
433–453.

The Back Panel of Ian's Brochure

As a heavy consumer of television media, with a solid eighteen years of experience as a consumer, I cannot deny that television has an impact on my life and my perception of the world. But impact is a very different thing from influence. I am impacted by the medium of television, but my behavior is not influenced by television. Based on my experience and my observation of other television consumers throughout my life, I do not believe that television can be blamed for youth violence. If viewing violent television programs caused violent behavior, youth violence would be much more common. I believe there are other factors that influence violent behavior. Our energies should be concentrated on those other factors.

Practicum

How does Ian's Visi-Quest Four fulfill the criteria for this assignment? Review the criteria listed for this assignment and make an evaluation. Offer specific examples from Ian's model to illustrate your critique. Then share your ideas with your classmates. Do you find that you and your classmates agree? Do you disagree? Why, or why not? How does this process of reading and evaluating a model assignment help you to successfully meet the requirements for this assignment yourself?

5

Logical Reasoning, Fallacies, and Credible Evidence: Analyzing and Evaluating Arguments

Begin with a *Question*: Who Should We Believe?

A newspaper headline screams: "MEDIA RESPONSIBLE FOR COPYCAT TEEN VIOLENCE!" Another roars: "HOLLYWOOD IS NOT TO BLAME!" A professional publication declares: "VIDEO GAMES INCREASE AGGRESSION!" Another proclaims: "EVERYTHING YOU KNOW ABOUT VIDEO GAME VIOLENCE IS WRONG!" One group of politicians argue: "GUN CONTROL LAWS CAN PREVENT TRAGEDIES LIKE THE ONE AT COLUMBINE HIGH!" Another group contends: "STRICTER GUN LAWS WOULD NOT HAVE STOPPED THE COLUMBINE GUNMEN!" "THE PARENTS ARE TO BLAME!" "SUBURBS AND SMALL TOWNS BREED KILLERS!" "MARILYN MANSON'S LYRICS PULLED THE TRIGGER!"

Voices, voices everywhere! How are we to think?!

With so many conflicting ideas bombarding us from every direction, day in and day out, trying to sort through and find answers to the social problems we face is a difficult task, to say the least. It is so difficult, in fact, we often simply tune out all of the voices and disengage from the problems that surround us and the questions those problems raise.

It is not that we do not care; we do care. It is just that the media chatter can be overwhelming. But instead of tuning out and turning away, we need to think critically about the conversations that rage around us on the topics of racism, militia groups, youth violence, and other pressing social issues.

The fact is, social problems will continue to rise up again and again until we *listen carefully, look closely, sort through all of the questions, the possible answers, the shouting, arguments, and debate,* and make sense of what we are being told. If you have any doubts, check out the statistics on youth violence and school shootings after Columbine, an event covered by and debated through the media 24/7 for weeks.

Time magazine reported in a March 2001 issue, "The Columbine Effect," that from May 13, 1999, through March 7, 2001, there were more than twenty violent, Columbine-like attacks and plots executed or uncovered in U.S. schools. That is more than twenty attacks in less than twenty-two months, the first attack occurring less than three weeks after the Columbine incident. This just goes to show that the media roar may fade, but problems like youth violence still hum persistently up and down the streets of our cities, the halls of our schools, the sidewalks of our neighborhoods. You have seen similar examples related to your own events as you conducted research for Quest Three.

As students of life and citizens of a global society, we have to analyze these social problems, test the experts who come forward with commentary and solutions, and decide *what we believe*. Ultimately, we have to join the conversation ourselves—that is the only way anything will ever really change. But when the many viewpoints presented by the media seem like a shouting match, where do we turn? When even experts do not agree, to whom do we listen? Out of all of the many voices we hear on any given subject, how do we *know* who the experts are? Whom do we trust? *What do we believe?*

What Kind of Proof Do You Have?

As you have discovered through your research, in this complex world in which we live, nothing is as simple as either/or. Every issue has a history, and within that history exist multiple viewpoints or perspectives. Each perspective has inherent strengths as well as weaknesses.

For each perspective, there are typically a few major players who are outspoken regarding their views and well covered in the media. These are the folks we read about most often in the paper and hear about on the news. Their opinions are strong and often articulated with passion and style and grace. They get our attention: we listen, we read, and they inspire us with their enthusiasm. They make us feel; they move us.

What these players say may sound good, but do their words have substance?

As critical thinkers on the journey to critical and civic literacy, we have to step back and scrutinize what is being said as well as how it is being said. We have to ask, How many of these spokespeople are *experts*? Have they *done their homework?* What kind of *proof* do they offer in support of their ideas?

Doing Your Homework

You have already done a great deal of homework on your event and an issue related to your event, and you are well on your way to becoming a sort of "quasi-expert." You researched the historical background of your event, you narrowed your issue to a specific focus, and you gathered information to represent many ideas and opinions within that focus.

You have also completed a cursory evaluation of each source and determined which sources appear to be reliable and which sources do not. Now you must look closely at the ideas presented in your sources: What is being said, and who is doing the talking? Identify the major players, analyze and evaluate what they have to say, and draw your own conclusions. It is time to take on the so-called experts and put them to the test. How many of them will pass as credible?

Reasons and Supporting Evidence

Opinion vs. Argument

It is often said that opinions are like bellybuttons. Some are in, some are out, but we all have one. Opinions are what we think or believe about something for our purposes, what we think about a social problem or issue. Much of what we read or hear in the popular media regarding any issue is simply opinion. It is often through the exchange of opinions in the media that we educate ourselves on social issues—it is how we become "informed." There is a certain danger to that, obviously, since anyone can form and voice an opinion on any topic. How do we distinguish between the laymen, the people just like the rest of us, who have an opinion on a subject and the experts? And how do we determine which experts to believe?

You have already practiced evaluating sources for credibility. You looked at credentials to determine authority, you looked for an indication of bias, and you skimmed the content of a source to judge scope of coverage and currency. But this is just a surface evaluation, an initial screening to determine which sources to collect for further study. To really judge the credibility of an argument, you have to go below the surface and analyze.

Let's pause for a moment and review what we know about argument. An *argument* is a form of expression that asserts and advances (with reasons and evidence) a position on an issue. Arguments begin with claims. A *claim* is a statement about a perspective on an issue. It expresses what someone believes to be true regarding something (usually a social problem that exists in some aspect of society). To identify a claim, we ask the question, *What are you trying to prove?*

When developing an argument, a claim is the foundation, but an argument is more than just a claim. In order to advance an argument you must also provide *reasoning*. Reasons explain the logic behind your claim; they usually answer the question of why.

Remember Joe and Rachel from Chapter 4? Joe's claim was that parking is a problem on campus because

1. "No matter what time I arrive on campus I cannot find a parking space."
2. "It's also a problem because I paid for a parking sticker so that I could park on campus, but there aren't enough available spaces in the student parking lots. Every day, I end up parking across the street and walking."

As it turns out, Rachel agrees with Joe and thinks his reasoning is sound. But what if an argument does not express logical reasoning or if the audience for that argument does not accept the reasoning *alone* offered in explanation of a claim?

Though Joe's claim and reasoning seem logical, in developing an argument, for most audiences a claim and reasons are not enough. Most audiences want to know what proof Joe has beyond his claim and reasoning that this situation is a problem and that his observations are accurate. An audience may want to know, Is this situation a problem for anyone besides Joe? Or does the purchase of a parking sticker guarantee parking on campus? As Joe's extended audience, we do not know the answer to these questions, because Joe has not provided us with any information beyond his own experience and observations. To successfully make an argument, in addition to a claim and reasoning, Joe must offer something more in support of his claim and reasoning: Joe must offer *evidence*.

Argument Is All About the Evidence

Argument is similar to opinion in that it begins with what someone believes about an issue, but *argument is more than opinion*. An argument takes opinion and builds on it. It is like a Power Bar for opinion—a nutritional supplement. An argument takes those very good points (claim and reasons) made by writers and makes them stronger by offering *proof*—verifiable evidence to support those points:

- To show that a writer has done her homework and has based her ideas on sound reasoning and evidence.
- To show that there are experts in a particular field who have studied an issue and have gathered documented evidence that a particular idea is valid or invalid.

Refer back to the article by Kristen Baldwin, "There's No Why," in Chapter 4. An initial evaluation of this article by a group of my students was fairly positive. By searching the *Entertainment Weekly* Web site, they learned that Kristen Baldwin had worked as a writer and an editor for this magazine for many years. Since the focus of the magazine is entertainment and this group's issue involved popular entertainment, they decided to accept the publication as an authority. They concluded that there was no unacceptable motive-related bias on the part of Baldwin and that the article was current in relation to the event (the Columbine High School shooting). The students liked many of the points Baldwin raised and felt the article would help them with their future research. But when asked to take a closer look at the article, they were surprised both by what they found and what they did not find.

Baldwin's piece is certainly well written and engaging. However, though it contains many of the same points addressed by scholars and experts in this field of study, it is entirely one person's opinion: Kristen Baldwin's. For what it is, an opinion editorial, there is nothing wrong with it. The article is a great *starting point* for an inquiry into the topic of media violence, so the students were right about that. Baldwin raises some interesting points worthy of further investigation, but on its own, there are some problems.

Baldwin's article presents a claim that may be stated as, *Pointing the finger at violence in entertainment does not stop kids from behaving violently* (see paragraph two). What is she trying to prove? She is trying to prove that a situation exists that the action of blaming violent media for violent behavior is futile and will not prevent more violent behavior. She is arguing from the perspective that violent entertainment does not cause violent behavior.

Her reasoning is also clear. As to the question of why, she responds, "because while graphic images can affect us—desensitize us, even—they do not, cannot, create dangerous urges in people who don't already have those urges inside them." Blaming the entertainment media, she reasons, does not solve the problem of youth violence.

In an informal discussion on the topic of entertainment and violence, this editorial is fine, particularly if you believe as Baldwin does. If you already support the perspective that violent entertainment does not cause violent behavior, then this might provide enough information to satisfy you, reinforcing what you already believe to be true. But as a serious academic piece, it has no credibility because all we have to go on is what Baldwin says: her claim and her reasoning.

It is dangerous that we, the audience, so often form or reinforce our own opinions based on pieces like this without further inquiry. After all, what do we know about Kristen Baldwin? How does she qualify as an expert in this field? This is not to say that Baldwin is not knowledgeable on the subject of media violence, but what has she offered in the way of proof to demonstrate her expertise? *How do we know what she knows?* All she has done in this article is state and briefly explain her opinion. If we do not share this opinion, we will not give a great deal of consideration to what she has to say. If we *do* share this opinion, what information have we based our ideas on? How informed is *our* opinion? Are we informed beyond op-ed articles in publications like *Entertainment Weekly?* Before we settle for an opinion, we need to see *evidence.*

Types of Evidence

Evidence takes many shapes and comes in many forms. The most commonly accepted form of evidence is information offered by verifiable experts in a particular field of study. This information may show up as *quantitative data* (facts, statistics, surveys, and measurements) gathered through various types of research, or as *qualitative data* (inferences and opinions) offered by experts.

In our earlier example, Joe presented a claim that parking is a problem on campus, and he offered reasoning to explain the logic of that claim: no matter what time he arrives on campus, he cannot find a parking space. If Joe wanted to strengthen his argument, what sort of evidence might he offer as support?

He might offer quantitative data:

- ○ He might keep a log of what time he arrives on campus for a period of time and whether or not he is able to find a parking space.
- ○ He might poll other students to provide statistical evidence of the extent of this problem.
- ○ He might check with parking services for the number of parking spaces available on campus, then check with the Registrar's office for the number of commuter students attending classes at various times throughout the day. From the combination of that information, he might be able to show that there are more students commuting to classes at certain times than there are parking spaces available.

All of this information would be considered quantitative.

He might also include some qualitative evidence:

- ○ He might interview other students about their experiences with parking on campus.
- ○ He might interview the head of parking services to see what her interpretation of the data Joe collected might be.

These are just a few examples of the ways in which Joe might support his argument with different kinds of evidence. Providing evidence that supports his ideas strengthens Joe's argument and makes him seem more credible to his audience. It shows he has done his homework and he knows what he is talking about.

In terms of argument, we do not have to take the author's word alone for anything because the author *shows* us (through the presentation of evidence) the truth of what he or she believes. For example, an author would not just say, "The media is responsible for teaching kids to kill." A credible author provides evidence, verifiable proof (data gathered in scientific studies, quotes from scholarly articles or essays written by experts in the field of cognitive development or behavioral psychology or sociology), that the media is responsible for teaching kids to kill.

It is important for *you* as a writer of arguments to offer support for *your* ideas. You cannot assume that an audience will have any detailed knowledge of your subject or that an audience will naturally agree with what you believe to be true. You must convince them to believe you, or at the very least to listen to what you have to say. In order to get your audience's attention, to earn their respect and trust, *you must establish your own credibility* by providing evidence garnered from experts in support of your reasoning.

As an audience, you must demand the same of anyone who presents you with an argument on an issue. You must demand that the so-called experts who deliver information to you through the media, in government, in the educational system, in our communities, have a clear claim, sound reasoning, and evidence from credible sources to support their ideas.

Practicum

Go back to the claim and reasons outline you created for Baldwin's editorial in Chapter 4. Look carefully at each reason and come up with examples of the types of evidence Baldwin could have offered as support. How much evidence would she have to offer to prove her claim is valid? Where would she locate this information?

Tools for Success: Analyzing Reasoning and Evaluating Evidence

As we do our homework on an issue and gather information to form our own opinions and build our own arguments, we must look closely at each source of information we find and put those sources to the test. When studying an issue and creating our own arguments, we must gather the best information available on our subject. As researchers, our goal is to present star witnesses to testify on our behalf as we build the case for our arguments.

When creating an argument, we present a claim and reasoning to explain the claim, and then we present evidence to support our reasoning. The evidence we present should come from expert, credible sources. But how do we know that evidence is credible?

You have already thought a great deal about credibility. As you gathered sources for Quests Three and Four, you evaluated the credibility of each source. You determined whether or not they appeared to be worthy of your time and attention. But this was just a cursory evaluation. To truly determine the value of a source, you have to look closely at and analyze the argument presented by the source. You have to identify the claim that is being made and the reasoning offered to explain the claim, and you have to evaluate the quality of the evidence presented in support of that reasoning. You must analyze the reasoning to determine whether or not it is logical and evaluate the evidence for STAR quality (discussed later in this chapter).

Fallacies and Illogical Reasoning

When creating an argument, it is easier than you might think to slip into patterns of illogical reasoning. In the academic world, faulty reasoning is known as *fallacy;* fallacy occurs when the quality of reasoning used to explain a situation is unsound. This is a sure way to ruin your credibility.

There are many different kinds of fallacy, most stemming from a problem with *inductive reasoning* (when the characteristics of a sample are applied to a whole group). All fallacies can destroy an argument. For our purposes, we cover ten of the most common fallacies.

Ad Hominem

This type of fallacy occurs when the *person* presenting an argument is attacked instead of the argument itself; it is often used as a diversion tactic. An *ad hominem* fallacy might be an attack against someone's character, appearance, ethnicity, or personal circumstances. Here are some examples:

- You can't tell me not to smoke; you can't even control your own addictions.
- Of course Colin Powell is against gun control! He's a career military man!
- Parents should not determine what type of music their teens can listen to because they (the parents) are too old.

Ad Populum

With this type of fallacy, a claim is accepted as true simply because most people the majority believe it to be true. Often the fact that most people have positive feelings associated with the claim is substituted in place of actual evidence for the claim. Here are some examples:

- Most people are trying a low-carb diet and losing weight, so it must be healthy.
- CNN reported that most people support the Patriot Act, so it must be a good thing.
- None of my friends registered to vote, so there's no reason why I should register to vote either.

Begging the Question

If an arguer makes a statement that assumes the very question being argued has already been proven to be true, then the arguer is guilty of begging the question. Here are some examples:

- Charlie has never lied to us, so what he says must be true.
- *Bill:* God must exist.
  Jill: How do you know?
  Bill: Because the Bible says so.
  Jill: Why should I believe the Bible?
  Bill: Because the Bible was written by God.
- We do not need more gun control laws because multiple laws already exist.

Doubtful Cause

This type of fallacy occurs when it is implied that because one event follows another event, the first event must have been caused by the second. However, the proximity of events does not guarantee a cause-and-effect relationship. Here are some examples:

- I forgot to take my vitamins on Tuesday and woke up with a cold on Wednesday; that's the last time I forget to take my vitamins!
- Statistics show that people who listen to classical music live longer than people who listen to jazz. If you want to live longer, listen to classical music.

- Juvenile crime has been on the rise since the early 1970s when women began to work outside of the home.

False Analogy

A false analogy occurs when a description compares one thing with another but with no proof of connection between the two things being compared. Here are some examples:

- Students are like nails. Just as nails must be hit on the head in order to make them work, so must students.
- If we decide to attack country X, we should probably do it in January. We attacked Iraq in January, and look how well that turned out.
- Gay marriages are like using cream in your coffee—as the cream weakens the coffee, so gay marriage weakens society.

Faulty Appeal to Authority

This type of fallacy occurs when an author or speaker attempts to support a claim by citing the opinions of so-called "experts" who may not have any expertise related to that claim. Here are some examples:

- On a routine visit to your doctor, she tells you not to support a particular political candidate.
- A celebrity appears in a commercial advertisement telling you to buy a particular brand of dog food because it is the healthiest for your dog.
- In an essay arguing that parents should be held legally responsible for crimes committed by their children, a student quotes from an anonymous .com Web site to support her reasoning.

Hasty Generalization

This type of fallacy occurs when someone claims that all members of a particular group share the characteristics attributed to a few members within that group. Here are some examples:

- Tim is lazy; he is a teenager; therefore, all teenagers are lazy.
- Eric Harris and Dylan Klebold wore long, black trench coats to school the day of the Columbine High School massacre. Therefore, anyone wearing a long, black trenchcoat to school may be a threat. No one should be allowed to wear long, black trenchcoats to school.
- In light of Janet Jackson's controversial Super Bowl Half-Time Show performance in 2004, no female singers should be allowed to perform at televised events like the Super Bowl.

Non Sequitur

This is the fallacy of irrelevance in which the claim is not adequately explained by the reasoning. Here are some examples:

- Jane is wearing red, white, and blue—the colors of the American flag; therefore, Jane must be patriotic.
- Eric Harris and Dylan Klebold listened to the music of Marilyn Manson, and they committed mass murder; therefore, the music of Marilyn Manson will cause other teens to behave violently.
- If a child is bullied when he is in elementary school, he will become violent as a teen, but when a child is not bullied, he will not become violent as a teen.

Prejudicial Language

The fallacy of prejudicial language occurs when highly emotive terms are used to designate value or moral goodness to the acceptance of a claim, when the words chosen for an argument are chosen for their *emotive* meaning rather than their *cognitive* meaning. Here are some examples:

- A *reasonable* person would agree that the *Lord of the Rings* is the best motion-picture trilogy ever made.
- Not only is parental responsibility required by law, it is a *sacred obligation*.
- MTV's voter *propaganda* is biased in favor of *left-wing* politics.

Slippery Slope

This type of fallacy occurs when an argument purports that taking one step will inevitably lead to another, often undesirable step without offering sufficient evidence that this will indeed happen. Here are some examples:

- If I make an exception for you, then I have to make an exception for everyone.
- If we pass laws against fully automatic weapons, then it won't be long before we pass laws against all weapons and begin to restrict other rights, and finally we will end up living in a communist state. Thus, we should not ban fully automatic weapons.
- If we allow women to have legal abortions, we are encouraging unprotected sexual intercourse.

Practicum

Think of examples of fallacies and illogical thinking related to the issue (or issues) you researched for previous Quests and the information you have already gathered. Come up with several examples for each type of fallacy and take turns writing your ideas on the blackboard. Have the rest of the class practice identifying the types of fallacies you have created.

STAR

Just as an attorney seeks out and presents star witnesses to testify on behalf of his client when trying a court case, anyone presenting an argument should present the best evidence available in support of his or her claim and reasoning. Evidence offered in support of any argument should meet certain criteria. It should be *sufficient, typical, accurate,* and *reliable.* It should be STAR quality.

Sufficient

In order to determine whether or not the evidence offered in support of reasoning is sufficient, ask, Does the argument offer *enough* evidence in support of each reason? When a claim is particularly controversial, more than one piece of evidence may be required in support of the reasoning offered to explain the claim. Determining how much is enough can be tricky and really depends on the audience for the argument. Good questions to ask when considering sufficiency include, Who is the intended audience for this argument? How difficult will it be for them to accept this claim and reasoning? How much proof are they likely to need before they are convinced?

The *connection* between the claim and reasoning and evidence must be sufficient and *sufficiently explained,* as well. Providing evidence for the sake of evidence is worthless. Evidence should directly support the reasoning offered to explain a claim. This is particularly important. I have seen many writers, particularly student writers, offer evidence as support for reasoning that did not quite fit. The evidence may be highly credible and look fantastic on its own, but if it is not clearly related to the reasoning and claim that is being made, then it is not sufficient.

Typical

Sometimes when making a particularly controversial argument, evidence may be difficult to locate. If only one piece of evidence is found to support a particular line of reasoning, the temptation is to use that evidence. But we have to ask, Is the evidence offered in support of the reasoning and claim typical of other information that is available? When we offer support for a reason, that support serves as a representation of other, similar evidence. It implies that other sources believe this point to be true. But if other evidence is not available, it is dishonest to present the one and only piece of support as if it were common. Evidence should be representative, an example of like-minded thinking. If no other evidence is available, an author should either say so in the text (which may weaken an argument) or develop another line of reasoning.

Accurate

Another question to ask when evaluating the credibility of evidence has to do with the way in which the evidence is presented and used in support of an argument. You have to evaluate. Whether the supporting evidence is presented accurately and without bias.

In terms of individual pieces of evidence, check to see that the information is presented within the *correct context* and that statistics and data are accurately interpreted. If statistics are not explained (where they came from, under what circumstances they were gathered, how they were interpreted, and how they relate to the reasoning in this particular argument), then they cannot be trusted.

Also check to see that the information is presented throughout the source in a fair and impartial tone, and that the author has attempted to address (or at least acknowledge) multiple perspectives. The overuse of temperamental or emotional language to influence an audience can create an *unfair bias,* and bias interferes with the accuracy of a source. Naturally, strong, vivid language is an important part of an effective argument, but that language should remain balanced and fair. A credible text does not berate, belittle, disparage, or attack a person rather than an issue. Beware of overly emotive language and personal attacks disguised as evidence.

Bias can also occur when a source presents only one perspective on an issue or situation, giving the impression that there are no alternate viewpoints. As an example, look at the following excerpt from Brent Baker's 1994 book *How to Identify, Expose & Correct Liberal Media Bias* (note that not all bias is liberal bias—that is simply the particular emphasis in this publication). In this passage, Baker analyzes two newscasts, one following the Los Angeles riots (in 1991, following the acquittal of four Los Angeles police officers of charges resulting from the videotaped beating of motorist Rodney King, South Central Los Angeles erupted in a violent and deadly outburst of arson, shooting, and looting that engulfed the city for a period of several days) and another on the topic of child poverty.

Identifying Bias in News Stories

To demonstrate how to detect bias, take a look at two examples of biased network news stories.

First, here's an ABC *World News Tonight* story from May 3, 1992, days after the Los Angeles riots:

> *Anchor Forrest Sawyer:* The death toll in the Los Angeles rioting rose to forty-six today, and that makes it the nation's bloodiest civil unrest in seventy-five years. Now that the smoke is clearing, L.A. residents are arguing over who is to blame. As Tom Foreman reports, many say that blame goes all the way to the top.
>
> *ABC News reporter Tom Foreman:* As the clean-up continues, the federal government is being swept into the circle of blame for failing to address inner-city problems and leaving poor people in despair.

Rep. Maxine Waters: Absolutely desperate, absolutely angry, and justifiably so. Nothing is working for them. The systems aren't working.

Foreman: In recent years, as federal funding for social services has fallen, many have disappeared. Gone are programs for job training, health care, child care, and housing.

Bruce Johnson, L.A. resident: A lot of black people don't have no jobs or nothing else, you know.

Foreman: Bruce Johnson once worked at a federally funded job. The funding dried up. He has been without steady work since. His wife Pat was getting a federally funded education. That's over too.

Pat Johnson: I think the government stinks. You want me to be honest, I think it stinks. Like I say, they promise you everything, it give us nothing, you know.

Foreman: Some people believe the President has not recognized any social motive for the violence.

President George Bush, May 1, 1992: It's not a message of protest. It's been the brutality of a mob. Pure and simple.

Foreman: People here say the President should listen.

Woman on street: Who's going to listen? I bet they listen now. They listen now, won't they. If this is where you have to get their attention, damn it, get it. Any way you can.

Foreman: Increasingly, people are saying that all of the violence had very little to do with Rodney King. Instead it was the desperate call of a community fighting for change. Tom Foreman, ABC News, Los Angeles.

Foreman's story reflected bias by spin, bias by selection of sources, and bias by commission. Foreman's spin on what caused the riots (the federal government failed to address inner-city problems and that the riots were a "desperate call of a community fighting for change"), matched the liberal spin at the time. Conservatives believed the individuals who committed the violent acts were responsible, not societal pressures.

Except for a George Bush soundbite, which Foreman used to back his thesis that Bush "doesn't get it," the other four soundbites supported the liberal view on what caused the riots. Bias by commission came in Foreman's declaration as a fact beyond dispute that "federal funding for social services has fallen, many have disappeared. Gone are programs for job training, health care, child care, and housing." That's a ludicrous assertion, since federal funding for virtually every social program grew faster than inflation during the 1980s.

Second, here's a March 23, 1992, *CBS Evening News* story on child poverty:

Anchor Connie Chung: A new snapshot today of the health and well-being of children in this country. For a growing number of them, it's not a pretty picture. Eric Engberg reports on the young face of poverty in America.

CBS News reporter Eric Engberg: The way America treats its children from newborns to teens has deteriorated to danger levels according to a study out today. This premature baby, born to a cocaine-using mother in a Washington hospital, weighed one pound, ten ounces at birth. Such underweight births, often a precursor to serious health problems, are on the rise across the country.

Dr. Victor Nelson, Greater SE Community Hospital: Here over the last few years, we have doubled this to almost fifteen percent.

Engberg: Other yardsticks for measuring child well-being compiled by the child advocacy group Kids Count point to trouble. While the death rate for infants has declined, the teen years have gotten more dangerous. Violent teen deaths climbed eleven percent in five years. Reason: soaring rates for murder and suicide. More children are having children; there were 76,000 more babies born to single teens in 1989 than in 1980. The number of children living in single-parent families has grown by two million in the decade. The study found one in five children was poor, an increase of twenty-two percent during the eighties.

Douglas Nelson, Annie E. Casey Foundation: And if we don't turn these numbers around in the decade, we, I mean every American regardless of age or their family status, we're going to be in deep trouble.

Engberg: As child poverty has grown, social workers have encountered more homeless children.

Marlys Wilson, social service worker: They forget how to laugh, they just sit, they cry a lot. We have a lot of kids that cry. They've lost a sense of trust.

Engberg: Americans are very aware that something is wrong in the way children are treated. A poll released with today's survey found that adults, by a margin of two to one, think today's kids have it worse than their parents did. Eric Engberg, CBS News, Washington.

Engberg's story demonstrated five types of bias. First, bias by story selection. A liberal organization released a study with a liberal theme and CBS considered it newsworthy. Second, bias by labeling. The Annie E. Casey Foundation and the Center for the Study of Social Policy are liberal advocacy groups. Engberg failed to properly identify them. Third, bias by commission. Without citing any statistical source, Engberg insisted, "social workers have encountered more homeless children." He also cited, without any balancing counterpoint, the Casey Foundation's claim that child poverty increased 22 percent in the 1980s. In fact, even the Children's Defense Fund, a left-wing lobby for increased welfare dependency, calculated that the percentage of children in poverty declined from 22.3 percent in 1983 to 19.6 percent in 1989.

Fourth, bias by omission. In building a case for how the welfare of children deteriorated in the '80s, Engberg excluded critics like Heritage Foundation analyst Robert Rector, who told the *New York Times* the report was "pure mental rubbish" that "ignores $150 billion in welfare; so it doesn't look at the children's standard-of-living conditions." Census Bureau statistics don't consider substantial non-cash welfare benefits such as housing assistance and Medicaid. The exclusion of critics like Rector brings us to Engberg's bias by selection of sources. All three espoused the same point of view.

Baker's analysis covers several different types of bias specific to reporting the news, but for our purposes, we concentrate on two specific types of bias: *bias by commission* and *bias by omission*.

- ◦ **Bias by commission:** When an argument asserts a position as if there were no other perspectives to consider, this is bias by commission. A non-biased argument respectfully presents multiple perspectives on an issue and offers evidence for each perspective.
- ◦ **Bias by omission:** When an argument recognizes multiple perspectives but fails to offer key information on one or more perspective, thereby creating a false appearance of weakness, or when an argument fails to present evidence in support of a particular reason (perhaps because there is no evidence or the available evidence is not particularly credible), this is bias by omission. A non-biased argument acknowledges the strengths of alternate perspectives and presents evidence for each reason.

Bias may also have to do with personal or corporate gain. In Baker's example, it is possible that the news stations reporting these stories had some stake in the political agendas they were supporting through these reports. By hearing only one point of view, the audience is left with the impression that there are no other perspectives to consider and that the problems identified in the broadcast are monodimensional.

Reliable
When evaluating credibility, check to see that the evidence offered as support is from a respectable authority. How do you know? Where did this evidence come from? Is the supporting evidence attributed to a credible source? How do you know the source is credible? Look for documentation (in-text, parenthetical references and a works cited page, a bibliography, or footnotes) to help you make this judgment.

As we discussed in Chapter 3, an authority may be someone who has studied a subject in depth or someone who has had considerable experience working with or living through some aspect of that subject.

To determine whether or not an author has presented evidence from an authority on a subject, check the credentials of the source of that evidence, his or her education and experience. Is the information generated by a professional or organization recognized in a particular field of study—either by academic degree, professional affiliation, or experience?

Finally, it is important to note that the evaluation of evidence is directly related to the warrant of an argument. This evaluation helps us to identify implicit and explicit warrants and to test their validity. If the evidence offered is not sufficient, is not enough to support a claim and reasoning, or if the connection between the claim, reasoning, and evidence is not sufficiently explained, then the audience will not accept the substantive warrant underlying the argument. If the evidence offered is not typical of other, similar evidence, then the audience will not recognize the exigency of the situation and will not accept the motivational warrant underlying the argument. And if the evidence is not presented accurately and without bias, or is not reliable, the audience will not accept the underlying authoritative warrant. Therefore,

solid evidence meeting STAR criteria is essential for the development of a successful argument.

So, there you have it: common fallacies to watch for and the criteria for STAR evidence. Now, let's put this formula to the test.

Analyzing and Evaluating Argument Walk-Through

While conducting initial research into the issue of violence in the media, a group of
students came across an essay by Lieutenant Colonel Dave Grossman. They had noticed Grossman's name mentioned in several other sources as an expert on the subject of the effects of media violence on behavior, so they were pretty excited to find
an original essay by Grossman.

After a surface evaluation to determine whether or not they should further study
the source, the group of students decided that Grossman was credible. They discovered that he is a former West Point psychology professor and Army Ranger. He re-
tired from the Army in February 1998 to become a full-time writer, trainer,
consultant, and speaker. He is an Airborne Ranger infantry officer, prior-service
sergeant, and paratrooper with more than 23 years of military experience. He is widely
recognized as an expert on the psychology of killing.

Based on all of this information, Grossman did not appear to be biased in a negative way, and the content of the article was moderately comprehensive (plus he had
listed in-text citations throughout the essay and included a works cited page). Grossman looked good. But what happened when the students took a closer look and put
Grossman's argument to the test?

Before we answer that question, take a look at this essay by Grossman.

Teaching Kids to Kill

Michael Carneal, the fourteen-year-old killer in the Paducah, Kentucky, school shootings, had never fired a real pistol in his life. He stole a .22 pistol, fired a few practice
shots, and took it to school. He fired eight shots at a high school prayer group, hitting eight kids, five of them head shots and the other three upper torso (Grossman
& DeGaetano, 1999).

I train numerous elite military and law enforcement organizations around the
world. When I tell them of this "achievement," they are stunned. Nowhere in the
annals of military or law enforcement history can we find an equivalent achievement.
Where does a fourteen-year-old boy who never fired a gun before get the skill and the
will to kill? Video games and media violence.

A Virus of Violence

First we must understand the magnitude of the problem. The murder rate does not accurately represent our situation because it has been held down by the development of ever more sophisticated life-saving techniques. A better indicator of the problem is the aggravated-assault rate—the rate at which human beings are attempting to kill one another. And that rate went up from around 60 per 100,000 in 1957 to over 440 per 100,000 by the mid-1990s (Statistical Abstracts of the United States, 1957–1997).

Even with small downturns recently, the violent-crime rate is still at a phenomenally high level, and this is true not just in America, but also worldwide. In Canada, per-capita assaults increased almost fivefold between 1964 and 1993. According to Interpol, between 1977 and 1993 the per-capita assault rate increased nearly fivefold in Norway and Greece, and in Australia and new Zealand it increased approximately fourfold. During the same period it tripled in Sweden and approximately doubled in Belgium, Denmark, England-Wales, France, Hungary, the Netherlands, and Scotland. In India during this period the per-capita murder rate doubled. In Mexico and Brazil violent crime is also skyrocketing, and in Japan juvenile violent crime went up 30 percent in 1997 alone.

This virus of violence is occurring worldwide, and the explanation for it has to be some new factor that is occurring in all of these countries (Grossman, 1999b). As in heart disease, there are many factors involved in the causation of violent crime, and we must never downplay any of them. But there is only one new variable that is present in each of these nations, bearing the same fruit in every case, and that is media violence being presented as "entertainment" for children.

Killing Unnaturally

I spent almost a quarter of a century as an Army infantry officer, a paratrooper, a Ranger, and a West Point psychology professor, learning and studying how we enable people to kill. Most soldiers have to be trained to kill.

Healthy members of most species have a powerful, natural resistance to killing their own kind. Animals with antlers and horns fight one another by butting heads, while against other species they go to the side to gut and gore. Piranha turn their teeth on everything, but they fight one another with flicks of the tail. Rattlesnakes bite anything, but they wrestle one another.

When we human beings are overwhelmed with anger and fear, our thought processes become very primitive, and we slam head on into that hard-wired resistance against killing. During World War II, we discovered that only 15 to 20 percent of the individual riflemen would fire at an exposed enemy soldier (Marshall, 1998). You can observe this phenomenon in killing throughout history, as I have outlined in much greater detail in my book, *On Killing* (Grossman, 1996), in my three peer-reviewed encyclopedia entries (Grossman, 1999a, 1999b, and Murray and Grossman,

1999), and in my entry in the *Oxford Companion to American Military History* (1999) (all posted at www.killology.com).

That was the reality of the battlefield. Only a small percentage of soldiers were willing and able to kill. When the military became aware of this, they systematically went about the process of "fixing" this "problem." And fix it they did. By Vietnam, the firing rate rose to over 90 percent (Grossman, 1999a).

The Methods in This Madness

The training methods that the military uses are brutalization, classical conditioning, operant conditioning, and role-modeling. Let us explain these and then observe how the media does the same thing to our children, but without the safeguards.

Brutalization

Brutalization, or "values inculcation," is what happens at boot camp. Your head is shaved, you are herded together naked, and you are dressed alike, losing all vestiges of individuality. You are trained relentlessly in a total-immersion environment. In the end, you embrace violence and discipline and accept it as a normal and essential survival skill in your brutal new world.

Something very similar is happening to our children through violence in the media. It begins at the age of eighteen months, when a child can begin to understand and mimic what is on television. But up until they are six or seven years old they are developmentally, psychologically, and physically unable to discern the difference between fantasy and reality. Thus, when a young child sees somebody on television being shot, stabbed, raped, brutalized, degraded, or murdered, to them it is real, and some of them embrace violence and accept it as a normal and essential survival skill in a brutal new world (Grossman & DeGaetano, 1999).

On June 10, 1992, the *Journal of the American Medical Association (JAMA)* published a definitive study on the effect of television violence. In nations, regions, or cities where television appears there is an immediate explosion of violence on the playground, and within fifteen years there is a doubling of the murder rate. Why fifteen years? That is how long it takes for a brutalized toddler to reach the "prime crime" years. That is how long it takes before you begin to reap what you sow when you traumatize and desensitize children. (Centerwall, 1992).

JAMA concluded, "the introduction of television in the 1950s caused a subsequent doubling of the homicide rate, i.e., long-term childhood exposure to television is a causal factor behind approximately one-half of the homicides committed in the United States, or approximately 10,000 homicides annually." The study went on to state, "if, hypothetically, television technology had never been developed, there would today be 10,000 fewer homicides each year in the United States, 70,000 fewer rapes, and 700,000 fewer injurious assaults" (Centerwall, 1992).

Today the data linking violence in the media to violence in society is superior to that linking cancer and tobacco. The American Psychological Association (APA), the American Medical Association (AMA), the American Academy of Pediatrics (AAP), the Surgeon General, and the Attorney General have all made definitive statements about this. When I presented a paper to the American Psychiatric Association's (APA) annual convention in May 2000 (Grossman, 2000), the statement was made: "The data is irrefutable. We have reached the point where we need to treat those who try to deny it, like we would treat Holocaust deniers."

Classical Conditioning

Classical conditioning is like Pavlov's dog in Psych 101. Remember the ringing bell, the food, and the dog that could not hear the bell without salivating?

In World War II, the Japanese would make some of their young, unblooded soldiers bayonet innocent prisoners to death. Their friends would cheer them on. Afterwards, all these soldiers were treated to the best meal they had had in months, sake, and the so-called "comfort girls." The result? They learned to associate violence with pleasure.

This technique is so morally reprehensible that there are very few examples of it in modern U.S. military training. But the media is doing it to our children. Kids watch vivid images of human death and suffering, and they learn to associate it with laughter, cheers, popcorn, soda, and their girlfriend's perfume (Grossman & DeGaetano, 1999).

After the Jonesboro shootings, one of the high school teachers told me about her students' reaction when she told them that someone had shot a bunch of their little brothers, sisters, and cousins in the middle school. "They laughed," she told me with dismay, "They laughed." We have raised a generation of barbarians who have learned to associate human death and suffering with pleasure (Grossman & DeGaetano, 1999).

Operant Conditioning

The third method the military uses is operant conditioning, a powerful procedure of stimulus-response training. We see this with pilots in flight simulators, or children in fire drills. When the fire alarm is set off, the children learn to file out in orderly fashion. One day there is a real fire, and they are frightened out of their little wits, but they do exactly what they have been conditioned to do (Grossman & DeGaetano, 1999).

In World War II we taught our soldiers to fire at bull's-eye targets, but that training failed miserably because we had no known instances of any soldiers being attacked by bull's-eyes. Now soldiers learn to fire at realistic, man-shaped silhouettes that pop up in their field of view. That is the stimulus. The conditioned response is to shoot the target, and then it drops. Stimulus-response, stimulus-response, repeated hundreds of times. Later, when they are in combat and somebody pops up with a gun, reflexively they will shoot and shoot to kill. Of the shooting on the modern battlefield, 75 to 80 percent is the result of this kind of training (Grossman & Siddle, 1999).

When children play violent video games, especially at a young age, they receive this same kind of operant conditioning in killing. In his national presidential radio address on April 24, 1999, shortly after the Littleton high school massacre, President Clinton stated, "A former lieutenant colonel and professor, David Grossman, has said that these games teach young people to kill with all the precision of a military training program, but with none of the character training that goes along with it." The result is ever more homemade pseudosociopaths who kill reflexively and show no remorse. Our kids are learning to kill and learning to like it. The most remarkable example of this is the Paducah, Kentucky, killer who fired eight shots and got eight hits on eight different milling, scrambling, screaming kids (Grossman & DeGaetano, 1999). Where did he get this phenomenal skill? Well, there is a $130-million lawsuit against the video game manufacturers in that case, working itself through the appeals system, claiming that the violent video games, the murder simulators, gave that mass murderer the skill and the will to kill.

In July 2000, at a bipartisan, bicameral Capitol Hill conference in Washington, D.C., the AMA, the APA, the AAP, and the American Academy of Child and Adolescent Psychiatry (AACAP) issued a joint statement saying that "viewing entertainment violence can lead to increases in aggressive attitudes, values and behavior, particularly in children. Its effects are measurable and long lasting. Moreover, prolonged viewing of media violence can lead to emotional desensitization toward violence in real life. . . . Although less research has been done on the impact of violent interactive entertainment [such as video games] on young people, preliminary studies indicate that the negative impact may be significantly more severe than that wrought by television, movies, or music."

Role Models

In the military your role model is your drill sergeant. He personifies violence, aggression, and discipline. The discipline, and doing it to adults, is the safeguard (Grossman, 1996). The drill sergeant, and hero figures such as John Wayne, Audie Murphy, Sergeant York, and Chesty Puller, have always been used as role models to influence young, impressionable teenagers.

Today the media are providing our children with role models, not just in the lawless sociopaths in movies and in television shows, but in the transformation of these schoolyard killers into media celebrities. In the 1970s we learned about "cluster suicides" in which television reporting of teen suicides was directly responsible for numerous copycat suicides of other teenagers. Because of this, television stations today generally do not cover teen suicides. But when the pictures of teenage killers appear on television, the effect is tragically similar. If there are children willing to kill themselves to get on television, are there also children willing to kill your child to get on television?

Thus we get the effect of copycat, cluster murders that work their way across America like a virus spread by the six-o'clock local news. No matter what someone has done, if you put his or her picture on television, you have made that person a celebrity whom someone, somewhere, may emulate. This effect is greatly magnified when the role model is a teenager, and the effect on other teens can be profound. In Japan, Canada, and other democracies around the world it is a punishable criminal act to place the names and images of juvenile criminals in the media because they know that it will result in other tragic deaths. The media has every right and responsibility to tell the story, but do they have a "right" to turn the killers into celebrities?

Unlearning Violence

On the night of the Jonesboro shootings, clergy and counselors were working in small groups in the hospital waiting room, comforting the groups of relatives and friends of the fifteen shooting victims. Then they noticed one woman sitting alone.

A counselor went up to the woman and discovered that she was the mother of one of the girls who had been killed. She had no friends, no husband, no family with her as she sat in the hospital, alone. "I just came to find out how to get my little girl's body back," she said. But the body had been taken to the state capital, for an autopsy. "I just don't know how we're going to pay for the funeral. I don't know how we can afford it."

That little girl was all she had in all the world, and all she wanted to do was wrap her little girl's body in a blanket and take her home. Some people's solution to the problem of media violence is, "If you don't like it, just turn it off." If that is your only solution to this problem, then come to Jonesboro and tell her how this would have kept her little girl safe.

All of us can keep our kids safe from this toxic, addictive substance, but it will not be enough if the neighbors are not doing the same. Perhaps the time has come to consider regulating what the violence industry is selling to kids, controlling the sale of violent visual imagery to children, while still permitting free access to adults, just as we do with guns, pornography, alcohol, tobacco, sex, and cars.

Fighting Back: Education, Legislation, Litigation

We must work against child abuse, racism, poverty, and children's access to guns, and toward rebuilding our families, but we must also take on the producers of media violence. The solution strategy that I submit for consideration is, "education, legislation, litigation."

Simply put, we need to work toward legislation that outlaws violent video games for children. In July 2000, the city of Indianapolis passed just such an ordinance, and every other city, county, or state in the United States has the right to do the same. There is no Constitutional right to teach children to blow people's heads off at the local video arcade. And we are very close to being able to do to the media, through litigation, what is being done to the tobacco industry, hitting them in the only place they understand—their wallets.

Most of all, the American people need to be informed. Every parent must be warned of the impact of violent visual media on children, as we would warn them of some rampant carcinogen. Violence is not a game, it is not fun, it is not something that we let children do for entertainment. Violence kills.

CBS President Leslie Moonves was asked if he thought the school massacre in Littleton, Colorado, had anything to do with the media. His answer was, "Anyone who thinks the media has nothing to do with it is an idiot" (Reuters, 2000, March 19). That is what the networks are selling, but we do not have to buy it. An educated and informed society can and must find its way home from the dark and lonely place to which it has traveled.

References

Centerwall, B. (1992). "Television and violence: The scale of the problem and where to go from here." *Journal of the American Medical Association, 267*: 3059–3061.

Grossman, D. (1996). *On Killing: The Psychological Cost of Learning to Kill in War and Society.* New York: Little, Brown, and Company.

Grossman, D. (1999). "Aggression and violence." In J. Chambers (Ed.), *Oxford Companion to American Military History.* New York: Oxford University Press (p. 10).

Grossman, D. (1999a). "Weaponry, Evolution of." In L. Curtis & J. Turpin (Eds.), *Academic Press Encyclopedia of Violence, Peace, and Conflict.* San Diego, CA: Academic Press (p. 797).

Grossman, D., & Siddle, B. (1999b). "Psychological effects of combat." In L. Curtis & J. Turpin (Eds.), *Academic Press Encyclopedia of Violence, Peace, and Conflict.* San Diego, CA: Academic Press. (pp. 144–145).

Grossman, D. (2000, May). "Teaching kids to kill, A case study: Paducah, Kentucky." Paper presented at the American Psychiatric Annual Meeting, Chicago, IL. Interpol International Crime Statistics, Interpol, Lyons, France, vols. 1977 to 1994.

Marshall, S. L. A. (1978). *Men Against Fire.* Gloucester, MA: Peter Smith.

Murray, K., and D. Grossman (1999). "Behavioral Psychology." In L. Curtis & J. Turpin (Eds.), *Academic Press Encyclopedia of Violence, Peace, and Conflict.* San Diego, CA: Academic Press.

Reuters Wire Service (2000, March 29). "CBS airing mob drama deemed too violent a year ago." *Washington Post.*

Statistical Abstracts of the United States, 1957–1997.

Note: This essay is reprinted here as originally published; however, I want to note that there are several MLA documentation errors: The Grossman & DeGaetano in-text reference is not included in the Works Cited; the Grossman & Siddle reference does not need a "b"; "a" and "b" should differentiate the two Grossman 1999 publications.

A Group Analysis and Evaluation of Grossman's Argument

Grossman's claim is that video games and media violence teach kids to kill. He is trying to prove that a condition exists and he is arguing to educate. His reasoning is primarily based on his experience in the military and a connection he sees between the effects of military training on soldiers and similar effects of exposure to violent media on children. Grossman spent years training soldiers to kill using the techniques of brutilization, classical conditioning, operant conditioning, and role models, and he believes that video games use these same techniques to influence children. Therefore, he says, video games teach kids to kill in the same way that the military teaches soldiers to kill. This is an interesting argument. But what proof does he offer that this is true? Follow along as a group of students evaluate the logic of Grossman's reasoning and determine whether or not Grossman's evidence has that STAR quality.

Initially, the students were impressed by Grossman's works cited page, which lists ten sources. Upon closer examination, however, they were surprised to find that six of those ten sources are Grossman's previous publications. For the most part, Grossman cites his own work as evidence to support his reasoning and claim. The students identified this as a problem.

Grossman's argument is highly controversial, yet he bases the majority of his argument on his own experience and observations and an analogy. He hopes that his audience will recognize the similarities he has observed between the training of a soldier for combat and the experiences of a child exposed to violent media such as video games. But what if his audience does not accept that these two situations are analogous? What if that is not enough?

If Grossman's audience does not accept the logic of his analogy, his argument will fall apart. Additional information from credible sources—if such information is available—should have been offered to support Grossman's observations. Without additional support, his reasoning appears illogical.

The majority of Grossman's argument is based on his experience in the military and a connection he sees between the effects of military training on soldiers and similar effects of exposure to violent media on children. If his audience does not accept this reasoning, they will not accept his argument without a great deal of outside evidence from experts. But Grossman does not provide adequate evidence outside of his own experience. The evidence provided in support of his reasoning draws entirely on the analogy between training soldiers and teaching kids to kill. The success of this argument depends on the audience's willingness to accept Grossman's experience and observations as universal. The student group decided that for most audiences, this would not be adequate. Additional evidence from outside experts is necessary to adequately support this line of reasoning, but since Grossman does not provide any additional support, he creates a *false analogy*.

In terms of the *connection* between the claim and reasoning and evidence, the students thought that Grossman does a pretty good job explaining how soldiers were trained for combat, but they thought Grossman falls short when explaining the connection between that training and what happens when children are exposed to violent media; again, this weak connection creates illogical thinking and a false analogy. Most of the argument seems to rest on the military examples. If an audience does not naturally understand the other side of that argument/analogy (the effects of repeated exposure to violent media on children) or if an audience does not accept the analogy (does not see the situation involving the training of soldiers as analogous with the situation of children playing video games), then Grossman's explanations are insufficient.

As to whether or not the evidence presented is typical of other information available on this subject, the students were left with the impression that it may not be typical because six of the ten sources cited in Grossman's essay are from works previously published by Grossman himself, and Grossman does not offer any additional outside evidence as support. The subsequent impression that is created is that Grossman is the only source available on this topic. If other information were available, why did Grossman not provide that information in support of his ideas? Without additional information, the exigency of the situation remains unclear, and there is no evidence of a direct connection between exposure to violent video games and violent youth behavior. This creates the fallacy *doubtful cause.* Grossman wants his audience to accept a cause-and-effect relationship, but beyond his analogy, he offers no proof to demonstrate such a relationship exists.

In terms of bias, again, the student group found it particularly troubling that six of the ten sources offered as evidence are previous articles and books written by Grossman. They felt that Grossman may be an expert on combat killing and training soldiers to kill, but he has no apparent education or experience directly related to child psychology. If his audience does not accept him as an expert, they will not accept his argument, and another fallacy is created: *faulty use of authority.* Therefore, Grossman should have provided his audience with outside evidence beyond his own experience and publications to support the chain of reasoning presented in his argument.

Also troubling is Grossman's use of statistics. Grossman does not provide adequate context for the statistics he offers as support. The source itself is credible, but there is no context for that information in the essay, so we cannot be sure it is used accurately as support for his claim and reasoning.

Additionally, after conducting a little outside investigation, the students discovered that one of Grossman's sources was presented out of context. Brandon Centerwall did indeed conduct studies into the relationship between media violence and violent behavior in children, but his studies were focused on the effects of *television violence* on children, not interactive violent play such as video games. Taken out of context, this evidence loses its power (assuming there is a difference between passive viewing and interactive play). Plus, Grossman presents only one perspective on his issue, and this creates a *bias by commission.* There are many other perspectives to consider, and he should have addressed some of those perspectives to enhance his credibility.

Finally, the student group felt since Grossman was not a verifiable expert in child psychology he should have offered sufficient sources from other verifiable experts in the field to support his argument. However, in terms of the sources Grossman did offer outside of his own the students only found one to be credible: Brandon Centerwall wrote an article for the *Journal of the American Medical Association*. A quick search on Google reveals that he is a faculty member at the University of Washington where he is a clinical assistant professor of epidemiology. He has conducted a great deal of research into the relationship between media violence and violent behavior. This appears to be a credible source.

Centerwall's research is on the subject of the effects of television violence on violent behavior, but it is not connected to the effects of video games on behavior. Because some audiences may question the difference between passive viewing of violence and interactive violent play, this source may not be reliable within the context of this particular argument and, as stated earlier, creates a *false analogy*.

Of the other three sources cited as evidence in Grossman's essay, the student group discovered that one is a book written in 1947, another is an anonymous news story printed in the *Washington Post*, and another is a collection of statistics prepared by the United States Census Bureau. Here are the details of their evaluation of these sources:

- The source listed on Grossman's works cited as *Men Against Fire* is actually *Men Against Fire: The Problem of Battle Command* and is a first-person account of combat leaders in World War II. The author, S. L. A. Marshall, is not well known, but the group discovers a little information by conducting a simple search on Google. They find that Marshall was a lieutenant colonel in the Army who worked in the Historical Division of the General Staff to develop methods of combat research. They also find that this book was actually written in 1947. So, while Marshall may have been an authority on training soldiers for combat, it would be a stretch to say he was an authority as a source supporting an argument about the connection between video games and violence. This is another *faulty use of authority*.

- The anonymous story was released through Reuter's Wire Service and published in the *Washington Post*. The *Washington Post* is considered credible within the academic community, but in terms of supporting the argument that Grossman is developing, it is weak. It is a brief news report used only in the conclusion of this essay and is not directly connected to the support of Grossman's claim. This is an example of the fallacy *non sequitur*, the fallacy of irrelevance.

- The Statistical Abstracts is generally considered to be a credible source for data compiled by experts working for the government (the Census Bureau). In terms of an authority, this appears to be a credible source for providing statistics on various aspects of the American culture.

This group's experience is a good example of why it is important to put our experts to the test. Grossman is widely recognized and cited as an expert on the topic of media violence and behavior, but a close examination of his essay leaves the audience with many questions. In fact, one student asked, "I wonder if these people who quote Grossman as an expert have really looked at his evidence?" If Grossman cannot offer evidence from any other sources to back up what he is saying, maybe there is a problem with his argument. This is not to say that Grossman's argument is entirely faulty, but rather that his argument—the reasoning presented to explain his claim—is not developed with adequate evidence.

After finding this source to be problematic, this group was forced to search for additional experts on his topic. Grossman's article, though it looked promising at first, was not enough.

Practicum

1. The student group we followed in analyzing Grossman's essay identified several fallacies in the essay. Working with a partner or in small groups, review the essay for additional fallacies. Make a list, and be sure to reference specific examples of each type of fallacy in the text. Then share your findings with the class.

2. Return to the discussion of the transcript of *The O'Reilly Factor* in Chapter 4. Look for fallacies in the arguments presented by both O'Reilly and Stapp. How might these fallacies have been avoided? If you have not done so already, locate a copy of the transcript. Read and identify the evidence offered by both parties and make an evaluation using the STAR criteria. Share your findings with one another.

3. Consider for a moment how fallacies might be presented in multimedia texts. Consider television commercials, for example. Can you think of any advertisements that use faulty reasoning to sell a product or a service? How is credible evidence presented in multimedia texts? Think of some examples and share your ideas with the class. Try using the STAR criteria to evaluate evidence found in multimedia texts.

WRITING ASSIGNMENT   Quest Five: Critical Analysis Essay

Put your sources to the test. Pick an article from Quest Four (or from your casebook) that seems very credible, and analyze it in depth according to STAR criteria. Identify any logical fallacies. Then present your findings in the form of an essay. Outline the argument, claim, and reasoning, then evaluate the argument and explain whether or not the evidence is sufficient, typical, accurate, and reliable. Finally, explain what led you to choose the source or sources initially and how your analysis supports or changes your initial judgment of the quality of the source. Use direct examples from the source or sources to illustrate your evaluation.

Step One

Reread your source and create a chart to sort your analysis. Make a table with three columns. Above the table, write the claim asserted by the source. In the left column, record reasons offered to explain the claim. In the middle column, record evidence offered in support of each reason. In the right column, record the source of that evidence.

Claim:

Reasons	Evidence	Source

This organized and highly visual record will help you evaluate the quality of the evidence, both individually and overall.

Step Two

Examine the evidence chart according to STAR criteria. Write an explanation of your reasoning. Identify and explain any fallacies.

Step Three

Based on your findings, make an evaluation and write your essay. Remember to consider these questions: What have you learned from this process? Are you surprised? Was your initial evaluation accurate? Based on your close examination, what problems do you see with determining whether or not a particular perspective is credible? Which perspective seems to be the most credible after conducting this evaluation?

Your essay should focus on the analysis of one or more source. Develop your essay with examples from the source and your interpretation of those examples. It should be organized using STAR criteria as a guide, and it should be free of grammar and punctuation errors. Follow MLA style for format and documentation, and include a works cited page at the end of the essay if you address more than one source or if you refer to outside sources as a part of your evaluation process.

Criteria for a Successful Critical Analysis Essay

For this assignment, you are asked to identify the claim and reasoning presented in an argument and to evaluate the evidence offered as support. Based on your analysis, evaluate the overall credibility of the source and present your evaluation in the form of an essay. A successful critical analysis essay is:

- Focused on the analysis of the evidence in one or more sources located during Quest Four.
- Developed by identifying the claim, reasoning, evidence, and any fallacies, and by addressing STAR criteria (evidence must be sufficient, typical, accurate, and reliable). All points are illustrated with examples from the text. All illustrations are explained in your own words.
- Organized in a logical pattern (either according to reasons in the order they are presented in the essay or according to STAR). The essay begins with an

introduction that establishes the focus of the evaluation, and the conclusion summarizes the evaluation of the source or sources covered in the analysis.
  ○ Correct, with few grammar or punctuation errors. The essay must be formatted according to MLA style, in-text, parenthetical references must be cited for each direct quote from a source as well as each summary and paraphrase, and a correct works cited page must follow the essay.

MLA In-Text Documentation of Direct Quotes

In Chapters 3 and 4 you worked with in-text documentation of summaries and paraphrases. Another way to provide information in your essay is to use a direct quote from a source (to take information word-for-word directly from a source and place that information in the body of your text within quotation marks).

Direct quotations are especially effective when they are used selectively. Quote directly from a source when the original text is particularly powerful or unique. Keep quotations brief; remember that your ideas and words are most important. Information taken from a source should not dominate your essay; it should be used as support for your ideas. Also, when quoting directly from a source, be accurate. Reproduce the original source precisely.

When using a direct quotation, you must integrate the quote smoothly into the body of your text. You may do this in one of two ways. The first way is to introduce the source in the body of your text by using the name of the author (with or without credentials) and/or the title of the source, as in the following two examples.

> Psychologists Craig A. Anderson, of Iowa State University of Science and Technology, and Karen E. Dill conducted two studies of 227 college students. They found that "students who more frequently played violent video games during junior high and high school were more likely to have engaged in aggressive delinquent behavior" (14).

> In their article, "Video Games Increase Aggression," published in the *Journal of Personality and Social Psychology,* psychologists Craig A. Anderson, of Iowa State University of Science and Technology, and Karen E. Dill reported on two studies they conducted of 227 college students. They found that "students who more frequently played violent video games during junior high and high school were more likely to have engaged in aggressive delinquent behavior" (14).

Another way to use a direct quotation is to integrate the quotation with your own wording and cite the author parenthetically:

> Gun control advocates often fail to publically recognize the fact that "guns are used for self-defense an estimated 2.5 million times per year" (Barr 1).

If the direct quote is more than four lines, you must set it off from the main text, and the style of documentation changes slightly. Begin the actual quotation on a new line and indent the entire quotation ten spaces from the left margin. Do not use quotation marks. Introduce the quote with a colon and end it with a period followed by the parenthetical reference:

Jonathan Freedman, a University of Toronto psychologist, recently completed a review of the American Medical Association's studies regarding the effects of television violence on behavior. According to Dr. Freedman, conducting studies in more realistic settings would not alter the results in any significant way:

> The field experiments show almost nothing. The contrast between the way it's described, in terms of overwhelming evidence, and the reality is just remarkable. It's not that 60 percent of them get good results and 40 percent of them don't—it's more like 25 percent get supportive results and 75 percent either get nothing or get mixed results. (15)

Again, these are just a few of the most common situations you will encounter when citing direct quotations. If you need additional assistance, please consult your MLA handbook or one of the online references.

Remember that the information provided in a parenthetical reference will lead your reader to a full citation on the works cited page.

In the Spotlight: A Student Model Critical Analysis Essay

The Author: Natalie Legra

Natalie was a freshman at the time she completed this assignment. In addition to pursuing a degree at the University of North Carolina–Charlotte, Natalie also worked as a translator for Carolinas Medical Center in the emergency clinic.

Critical Analysis of a Source from Quest Four

In a quest to learn how to ensure the credibility of articles in the media today, I chose "The Men of Columbine: Violence in Masculinity in American Culture and Film" to undergo the ultimate test. It was published from *The Journal for the Psychoanalysis of Culture and Society,* in the fall 2000 edition. The author of this complex article, Hilary Neroni, has a B.A. from Clark University in Worcester, MA. She has an M.A. and PhD from the University of Southern California in the School of Cinema and Documentary Film. Neroni has also taught various courses including Film Studies, Women's Studies, and Critical Theory. At first glance, this article did seem fairly credible, and after reading it in full text it sparked my curiosity. Therefore, I chose to analyze this article to decide if after immense scrutiny it is actually credible, or if it is just an opinionated article based on thought-provoking reason.

In this article, Neroni claims that masculinity is characterized by violence, both by the media and, in a greater spectrum, by society as a whole. She states three major reasons in the article, each one describing the way masculinity is exerted through violence. Her first reason is that men use violence to represent the superiority of their masculinity. She supports this reasoning by using examples of dangerous professions, such as the police or marines, who are judged by the amount of violence they experience, handle, or witness. Marines are considered to be the toughest and bravest group of all, because they are present in extreme situations of violence. By experiencing this violence, such as putting their life on the line more so than others do, they are considered to be more "manly." It is by their exuberance of the epitome of a non-fearing, courageous man, that they are placed within a certain rank of supremacy in their given field. Neroni quotes Cynthia Enloe to support her reasoning, who firmly believes that the risking of life is a behavior that is indulged by men in order to prove how masculine they really are. This greatly relates to Columbine as Neroni further explains, due to the criticized police who were called to duty the day of the shooting. One of the parents complained that the officers did not put their lives on the line, and that he was greatly disappointed that they did not make a greater effort to face the violence and be men, police officers. She feels that Dylan and Eric believed that violence is a signifier of masculinity due to the fact that they viewed themselves as violent masculine figures.

Neroni's second reason is that men use violence as a way to regain their lost masculinity. She believes that some men just rebel against their own castration and loss of masculinity in society. She elaborates with the example of Eric and Dylan, who as she believes, were reclaiming their lost masculinity and power, which had been taken away by their taunting peers. She quotes James Gilligan in her article, who states that, "Violence towards others, such as homicide, is an attempt to replace shame with pride" (4). Neroni also mentions Mark Bracher, who says "Since violence, in our society at least, is strongly coded as masculine, the violent behavior of such men functions not only as an attempt to destroy that which threatens their claim to this identity but also as an act that performs this identity and reclaims it" (4).

Thirdly, Neroni discusses the way violence works. She reasons that "men use violence as an economic exchange between men" (1). She mentions Rene Girad, who says, "Only violence can put an end to violence, and that is why violence is self-propagating. Everyone wants to strike the last blow . . . it is an attempt to destroy the masculinity and patriarchal order of one group while protecting your own" (4). Most importantly, she notes how this fits into the Columbine incident. In the news, we constantly hear that Dylan admitted on tape that he felt hated by the people that always made fun of him and made him feel inferior. Even Eric stated that he was tired of everything that he had been put through, and said, "I don't care if I live or die in the shootout, all I want to do is kill and injure as many pricks as I can" (4). Neroni fits this perfectly into her reasoning noting that both boys felt this was the only "economic exchange" to "return the attack" (4). The most striking words she uses to further support her reasoning include "It is not surprising that Klebold and Harris videotaped themselves before the big day trying to further solidify and control their identities, what they did was meant to transform their emasculated bodies into immortalized all-American males" (4). Also, every bit of evidence she used to support all three reasons was quantitative.

When it comes to sufficiency, I think Hilary Neroni used the right amount of information and sources needed to launch her claim and support her reasoning. In her development of all three reasons, she uses at least two different authors or scholars and quotes them. She also provides a sufficient amount of explanations to get her point across and to make sure the reader understands what she is trying to say. Everything she uses to support her main idea is related directly to her claim. For instance, when she is proving that society has placed the more violent man as a symbol for supreme masculinity, she not only quotes Cynthia Enloe that "the risking of death is in the name of a larger cause," but also further breaks it down and says on her own, "When a man is violent, he puts his life at risk, and when he does this, he asserts his independence, the indication of masculinity par excellence" (1). Then she continues to give an even more detailed example of Dale Todd and what he expected of the police who were called to duty on the day of the shooting. She even uses his quote: "When 500 officers go to a battle zone and not one of them comes away with a scratch, then something's wrong . . . I expected dead officers, crippled officers, disfigured officers, not just children and teachers" (2). She lets you see that she is not the only person that feels this way and provides the reader with sufficient information to understand and grasp the quality of her own words.

With regards to being typical, I believe this article is just that. Neroni uses various authors and people to back up her claims, and they all have the same opinions. For instance, all her sources of information have some background in psychology, and they all agree and coincide with one another. In a more detailed example, Gilligan, Enloe, and Bracher all believe that masculinity plays a major part in the way men behave. It is because of this that I believe her article is typical, because she provides support of her claim and reasoning from various sources that all relate exactly to her claim and remain on the topic at hand.

Deciding whether or not this article is accurate is rather tricky. Neroni only used examples that supported her ideas. Never once did she use somebody else's opinion and never tried to explain why she felt it was not right by providing reasonable evidence. I don't exactly want to say that she is biased because she provides several credible sources of evidence, which in light of agreeing with each other, offer a uniquely different insight into her article. Also, she fails to explain how she collected her evidence, and what caused her to turn to these specific sources in particular. It might have been helpful to understand why she thought they were credible. The lack of this information forces the reader to do a little bit of research. With all this in mind, I still believe the evidence offered in this article is fairly accurate, given that she did provide the names and locations of all the sources she used.

This article contains several quotes, coming from people such as James Gilligan, Mark Bracher, Cynthia Enloe, and Jonathan Alter. After doing research on Gilligan I found that he "has been on the faculty of the department of psychiatry at the Harvard Medical School since 1996, and is the director of the Center for the Study of Violence" (www.edge.org 1). Furthermore I learned that he is active with the Academic Advisory Council of the National Campaign Against Youth Violence. As far as Cynthia Enloe is concerned, she has had several publications pertaining to sexual politics, and is also a director in the Women's Studies Program at Clark University (www.radcliffe.edu 1). Mark Bracher is a professor of English (PhD) at Vanderbilt University and has extensive experience in psychoanalytic cultural criticism, and has written several articles and books (www.dept.kent.edu 1). Jonathan Alter has a B.A.

in History with honors from Harvard, and he is the *Newsweek* senior editor who has won a long list of awards because of his work (www.newsweekmediakit.com 1). I think that it is reasonable to say that all these people have a great amount of credibility to their name. They have all been in their field of study for a long time and have not only used their knowledge to write, but have been recognized and praised. They have helped in promoting the well-being of youth, and, in some cases, adults, and continue to do so. Neroni didn't pick just any random group of people to mention in her article. Instead, it shows that she has done her homework. That is why I believe that this article is reliable.

I conclude that "The Men of Columbine: Violence and Masculinity in American Culture and Film" by Hilary Neroni is credible. I found no evidence of illogical, fallacious reasoning in any part of the article. Neroni provides plentiful and sufficient examples and evidence to back up her claim, and she has chosen her sources extremely well. I think the few flaws in her writing such as not including views that do not pertain to her opinions, or perhaps not introducing her sources in more detail are way too minuscule to even bring into the greater picture. Obviously, the intended audience for this paper—professionals in the field of psychology—would be more readily familiar with her sources than a freshman college student. With all of that in mind, I believe that Neroni has asserted a reasonable claim developed by clear reasoning with great eloquence and professionalism, and by this I have decided that I find this article credible and intellectually stimulating.

Works Cited

2000–2001 Radcliffe Institute Fellows: Cynthia Enloe. Radcliffe Institute for the Advanced Study at Harvard University. 28 Oct 2003. http://www.radcliffe.edu/fellowships.current/2001/enloe.htm

Hilary Neroni. University of Vermont. 29 Oct 2003. http://www.uvm.edu/~english/hneroni.htm

Neroni, Hilary. "The Men of Columbine: Violence and Masculinity in American Culture and Film." *Journal for the Psychoanalysis of Culture and Society* 5:2 Fall 2000 Academic Search Elite. EBSCOhost. J. Murrey Atkins Library, Charlotte, NC.E.-Recources. Article A6798273 3 Oct. 2003.

Newsweek U.S.: Jonathan Alter. Editor Bios. 29 Oct 2003. http://www.newsweekmediakit.com/us/bios_alter.html

The Third Culture: James Gilligan. Edge Foundation Inc. 27 Oct 2003. http://wwwledge.org/3rd_culture/bios/gilliganj.html

---

Practicum

How does Natalie's model fulfill the criteria for a successful critical analysis? Write a brief evaluation. Refer to specific examples from the text of her essay to support your evaluation. Share your responses with your classmates. Do you find that you and your classmates agree? Disagree?

Reflection in Action

When you began this chapter, how many sources had you gathered on your issue in your Quests Three and Four? How many did you believe to be credible?

How has your understanding of the difference between opinion and argument changed?

In your own words, explain why credibility is important and how it is connected to argumentation.

How can we use the STAR criteria in our day-to-day lives as we encounter various issues in the media?

Expanding Your Vision: A Multimedia Assignment Option

Critical Inquiry: Digging Deeper

A good example of a visual representation of opinion is an editorial cartoon. Political cartoons are a unique visual medium, so in some ways it is like comparing apples to oranges when we compare a cartoon to written rhetoric. Many people would argue that political cartoons *are* arguments (and in some ways I would argue that point, too—it is difficult to apply the same rules to visual media and written media). But what cartoons generally offer is an *interpretation* of an issue, an opinion unsupported by verifiable evidence. As an academic argument, they do not usually cut muster. What would it take for a visual text to communicate a supported argument?

Take a look at some of the editorial cartoons in your casebook. Can you identify the claim that each cartoon is making? Is there any reasoning offered to explain the claim? How are the claim and reasons represented visually in the cartoon? Is this representation effective? If so, why?

What types of evidence could be added to a visual text to transform an opinion into a supported argument? Brainstorm a list of ideas and share them with the class.

MULTIMEDIA ASSIGNMENT   Visi-Quest Five: Expanding Your Vision by Creating a Critical Analysis of a Multimedia Argument

Multimedia arguments are quite common, and we encounter them frequently in the form of advertisements. Locate an advertisement related to the one of the issues covered in the event casebooks. Complete a critical analysis of that text. Identify and describe the claim, the reasoning, any evidence offered as support, and the warrant connecting these aspects of the argument. Analyze the evidence in terms of STAR criteria, and then present your findings in the form of an essay.

Before you begin, let's review how the various elements of argument are represented in a multimedia text (previously covered in "Tools for Success" in Chapter 2). A multimedia text contains more than one form of media. For this assignment, you will analyze print advertisements (originally published in newspapers and magazines) that contain printed text and static visual images.

In terms of printed text, advertisements have a very limited amount of space; therefore, text is selected very carefully and is usually concise. An advertisement may include words, sentences, or in rare instances, paragraphs. A great deal of attention is given to font style and size and layout (the placement of text on the advertisement).

As for visual images, advertisements include photographs and artistic renderings of people, places, and objects. Visuals also include the consideration of colors, lighting, texture, lines, angles, and focal points (foreground images and background images). Again, layout is a key consideration.

To create a multimedia argument, these various rhetorical elements, print and visual, are used to communicate claim, reasoning, and evidence. Many times, the claim and reasoning is implied. The creator of the advertisement targeting a specific audience relies on that audience to interpret the claim and reasoning from the information provided in the ad. Sometimes the claim and/or reasoning are explicitly stated.

Evidence is offered in the form of printed text data, statistics, and facts such as contact information, and it is offered in the form of visual images and illustrations. Again, the visual images often are open to some amount of interpretation, and the creator of the argument assumes that his or her target audience will understand the meaning implied through the combination of printed text and visual images.

Typically, advertisements in the form of Public Service Announcements (or PSAs) typically communicate one of two claims: either a claim intended to educate an audience about the existence of a particular social problem or a claim intended to motivate an audience to take a specific course of action to address a social problem.

When evaluating a multimedia argument such as an advertisement, the criteria must become a bit flexible. A text such as an advertisement operates in a very limited space and contains a limited amount of information. What is sufficient in terms of this format? The answer to that may be determined by considering purpose and audience. If the purpose of a PSA is to educate, the advertisement must provide enough information to suggest an idea for future study. If the purpose of the PSA is to motivate an audience to take a particular action, the advertisement must provide enough information to direct that audience to initiate action. When analyzing a multimedia argument, we must ask, in terms of printed text, Is enough information provided? Do the visual images adequately support the claim and reasoning?

Aside from offering *sufficient* support, the evidence offered in a PSA should be typical of other evidence available, and that typicality must be easily recognized. The actual content of a PSA is minimal, so context must be rather obvious. Bias may be recognized in terms of motives (Does the agency producing the advertisement have something personal or financial to gain?) and tone (Is the ad fair and balanced in its presentation of information?).

We still look for evidence of authority in a PSA, and this may be communicated through printed text (such as contact information or expert testimony), or it may be communicated through some sort of visual image that represents authority.

NOTE: Several PSAs are included in Chapter 7.

For this assignment, describe the advertisement, then address the rhetorical elements of multimedia texts: analyze and evaluate the overall argument for effectiveness in terms of authority, bias, and content. Use direct examples from the source to illustrate your evaluation (provide descriptions or explanations of various visual elements as necessary).

Step One

Read your source and make a chart to sort your analysis. Above the chart, record the claim presented in the source and the visual elements that represent that claim. Then create a table with five columns. Label the columns as in the following example. Then record information (probably in the form of descriptive details) in the appropriate column as you analyze your source.

Claim: **Represented by:**

Reason	Represented by	Evidence	Represented by	Warrant

This organized and highly visual record will help you evaluate the quality of the evidence both individually and overall.

Step Two

Examine the chart according to STAR criteria. Remember to consider the layout and design of the advertisement. The colors and pictures, even the font and spacing and layout, are all important to your evaluation.

Step Three

Based on your findings, make an evaluation and write your essay. Remember to consider these questions: What have you learned from this process? Are you surprised? Was your initial evaluation accurate? Based on your close examination, what problems do you see with determining whether or not a particular perspective is credible? Which perspective seems to be the most credible after conducting this evaluation?

Your essay should focus on the analysis of one multimedia source for authority, bias, and content. Develop your essay with examples from the source and your interpretation of those examples. It should be organized, and it should be free of grammar and punctuation errors. Follow MLA style for format and documentation, and include a works cited page at the end of the essay if you refer to outside sources as a part of your evaluation process.

Criteria for a Successful Critical Analysis of a Multimedia Argument

For this assignment, you are asked to identify the claim and reasoning presented in a multimedia argument and to evaluate the evidence offered as support. Based on your analysis, evaluate the overall credibility of the source and present your evaluation in the form of an essay. A successful critical analysis essay is:

- Focused on the analysis of the evidence presented in one multimedia argument.
- Developed by addressing STAR criteria (evidence must be sufficient, typical, accurate, and reliable) and considering the unique rhetorical features of a multimedia text. All points are illustrated with examples from the text. All illustrations are explained in your own words.
- Organized in a logical pattern first describing the features of the multimedia argument, then explaining how those features fit the STAR criteria. The essay begins with an introduction that establishes the focus of the evaluation, and the conclusion summarizes the evaluation of the source or sources covered in the analysis.
- Correct, with few grammar or punctuation errors. The essay must be formatted according to MLA style, in-text, parenthetical references must be cited for each direct quote from a source as well as each summary and paraphrase, and a correct works cited page must follow the essay.

In the Spotlight: A Student Model Critical Analysis of a Multimedia Argument

The Author: Shannon Luke

Shannon's major is English, and she hopes pursue a career in public relations.

Author's Etcetera

After completing this assignment, Shannon shared her reflections:

When I first looked at this advertisement, I was pretty impressed. It does make an emotional impact on the audience. The idea that everyone should be able to protect themselves, and that some people can't, made me think this was a good PSA. But then I looked closer and realized that there really wasn't any information provided at all on this advertisement. It really bothered me that the organization sponsoring this ad didn't even list their name. That seems shady to me. I think I've learned more than anything that I can't let an emotional response to something cloud my judgment.

www.keepandbeararms.com

Critical Analysis of a Multimedia Argument

Though it is not stated on the advertisement, this Public Service Announcement was produced and distributed by the Keep and Bear Arms organization. It contains three lines of text and two photographic images. These rhetorical elements communicate the claim, reasoning, and evidence for this argument.

The claim presented by this advertisement is explicitly stated: Everyone has a right to self-defense. The purpose of this claim is to educate. It seeks to prove that a condition, a right, exists (in this case, the right to self-defense). The reasoning is also explicitly stated: 1. Politicians tell us to run away, and 2. Some of us find such advice hard to follow. Evidence is offered in the form of visual images and textual formatting. Much of the evidence is open for interpretation.

Regarding the first reason, politicians tell us to run away from criminals, there is no evidence offered as support; therefore we cannot evaluate credibility. The *implication* is that "politicians" are usually considered authorities, but these authorities give us bad advice, to run away from criminals.

As for the second reason, some of us find such advice hard to follow, the evidence offered is a photographic image of an empty wheelchair. The audience is intended to understand that people who use wheelchairs cannot run away from criminals.

Additional evidence illustrates the message implied by the claim. The photographic image of the gun in the hip holster implies that the handgun is a form of self-defense that people who cannot run away (such as people confined to wheelchairs) are entitled to. This is their "right." The word "right" is meant to remind the audience of the second amendment of the United States constitution and the right to bear arms.

The layout of the advertisement carries quite a few implications, as well. The picture in the foreground is a human torso (clothed). The belt and gun and hip holster are prominent. In the background, the chest and abdomen area of the torso contain a transparent, ghost-like photographic image of an empty wheelchair. The fact that the wheelchair photo is transparent—not vivid, realistic, or life-like—seems to suggest the loss of life. This loss of life would indicate that someone who could not run away as politicians advise died because s/he had no means of self-defense.

Along the top of the advertisement, there is a black strip with white lettering and the text about the politicians. This is placed on top to immediately address the opposition politicians and their agenda. It sets up an us vs. them dynamic right away. Directly below this is black text on top of the ghost-like image of the wheelchair. The black text is bold and strong against the faded photograph. At the bottom of the advertisement, the claim is stated. The word "everyone" is in all capital letters and is underlined. This is intended to emphasize that all people are entitled to self-defense, but that the politicians have ignored some people who cannot follow their advice and run away from criminals. Again, the word "right" is used to suggest the second amendment.

In terms of evidence, this advertisement offers no data, no statistics, no expert testimony, and no contact information. The content of this advertisement is limited to photos and the three lines of text. The photos do seem directly connected to the text and the reasons offered in support of the claim; so in terms of what is included, this is credible, but is it sufficient? If the goal of this advertisement is to educate, it does plant an idea in the mind of the audience. It suggests something for future study (the idea that some people cannot run in self-defense, so they need access to other means of self-defense like firearms). However, if the goal of this advertisement is to motivate or instigate change, there is no information provided for how an audience should take action. Based on this lack of information, in good faith I assume the purpose is to educate more than suggest action.

Based on other sources I have encountered on the topic of gun rights, the information presented in this advertisement is typical in some ways and atypical in others. It is typical in that people who believe the second amendment promises the right to bear arms, including hand guns, also believe that politicians are pretty much the enemy. It is not typical in that I have never run across another source that suggested an appropriate response to criminals is to run away, nor have I run across another source that discusses self-defense for people with disabilities. Because that is the actual focus of this advertisement, I would have to say the evidence presented is not typical. How many people with disabilities are faced with situations that require self-defense, is a firearm the only or best method of self-defense for a disabled person, and what about the rest of the population? If this is true for people with disabilities, does it also apply to other groups of people as well?

As for accuracy, this source may be biased. Two perspectives are presented in this advertisement—that of the politicians and wheelchair-bound people who cannot run away. The language "tell us" and "some of us" is meant to create a sense of unity to imply that we are all in this together everyone. The speaker and the audience are unified against the politicians. The only evidence offered, however, is in support of one position (that of the people who cannot run away). This creates a bias by omission.

Since such a limited amount of information is provided on the advertisement, it is difficult to evaluate reliability. However, authority is implied by the mention of politicians, people who are typically thought of as authorities, but these authorities are considered wrong in this advertisement. Authority is also implied with the picture of the gun. Guns are symbols of power. Because the advertisement says that the audience has a right to do a particular thing, the audience is also empowered as an authority. However, in terms of overall credibility, I'm not sure that implied authority suggests that the information provided in the advertisement is reliable.

Because no information was offered on the advertisement, I accessed the keepandbeararms.com website and learned a little about this organization. According to this site, keepandbeararms.com is:

> a grassroots movement of the people, by the people, and for the people. It is a call to action, a call for self-education, and a 21-gun salute to the many good men and women who fought and died to bring America into being.
>
> This web site is about helping lawful people maintain their abilities to protect themselves and the people they love effectively from anyone who would do them harm through legal, private ownership and use of guns. We also stand for the repealing of all gun laws which infringe on the civil rights of peaceable women and men to defend their own lives and property. (About Us).

On a very small link at the bottom of the page, various contact information is available for officers in this organization and creators of the website. It appears to be a legitimate organization, though heavily biased in support of gun ownership. I have to wonder why the organization did not list its name or contact information on the advertisement.

Finally, there are three warrants underlying this argument: Substantive, motivational, and authoritative. First of all, because there is no verifiable evidence offered and much of the reasoning is implied, the audience must recognize that reasoning and then accept it as logical; therefore, a substantive warrant underlies the majority of this multimedia argument. If the audience does not recognize or agree with the implied reasoning, the argument will fall apart. Additionally, the audience is expected to recognize the exigency of this situation based on the implied reasoning and the emotional appeal created through the use of particular visual images. This is a motivational warrant. If the audience does not accept the situation as urgent, the argument will fall apart. And lastly, the argument is most dependent on the audience's willingness to accept keepandbeararms.com as an authority on the necessity for disabled people to have access to firearms in order to protect themselves from harm. This is an authoritative warrant, and if the audience does not accept the organization as an authority on this matter, the argument falls apart.

Though the claim and reasoning may be worthy of consideration, no contact information and no verifiable evidence was included on the advertisement. After careful analysis, I have to say that this multimedia argument is not a credible source of information on gun rights.

Works Cited

"About Us." Keep and Bear Arms.com: Gun Owners Homepage. 2002. NetSalon Corporation. April 28, 2003.

"Notice: Seeking Physically Disabled Gun Owners." *Keep and Bear Arms: News and Editorials.* May 28, 2002. NetSalon Corporation. April 28, 2003. <www.keepandbeararms.com>.

Practicum

How does Shannon's Visi-Quest Five fulfill the criteria for this assignment? Review the criteria listed for this assignment and make an evaluation. Offer specific examples from Shannon's model to illustrate your critique. Then share your ideas with your classmates. Do you find that you and your classmates agree? Do you disagree? Why, or why not? How does this process of reading and evaluating a model assignment help you to successfully meet the requirements for this assignment yourself?

PART THREE

Joining the Official Conversation: Creating and Advancing Successful Arguments

6

Arguing to Educate: Advancing a Position on an Issue

Begin with a *Question*: What Do You Believe to Be True?

Let's recap your journey so far. You began your Quest some time ago by looking closely at one or more events. To begin with, you scrutinized the initial media coverage. You filtered through all of the information and misinformation that flooded all forms of media—television, print, and electronic—and ultimately decided what you believed to be true. You looked closely at the blame game that played out during and after an event, and you conducted a cursory examination of the major scapegoats identified as possible causes. Then you stepped back and examined an event from a historical perspective. You conducted extensive research, and you focused on the current, major perspectives on a social problem, issue, or issues connected to an event. You identified and examined *claims* made by those who are a part of the official conversation, and finally, you identified, analyzed, and evaluated the *reasoning* and *evidence* presented in one source.

This in-depth study was necessary. It was a matter of gaining historical, social, and personal perspective. Historically, you understand the background of your event. You know where it comes from, how it is similar to and different from like events, how that type of event has evolved over time. Socially, you know what the current perspectives are on an issue or several issues connected to your event, and personally, you have a much clearer understanding of what you think and feel, and why. At this point in your journey, it is safe to say that you have a fairly thorough understanding of both the event and at least one issue that is closely tied to that event. So what now? What to do and where to go with everything you know?

Coming Home

In your preliminary studies, you recorded and examined your initial response to an event, and you explored your assumptions surrounding various issues that were blamed for that event. When you began to research, you were aware of your opinions, and you were filled with questions you hoped to answer. As you conducted your research, you managed to answer some of your questions, and new questions emerged along the way. Your initial opinions about your issue or issues were reformed, reshaped, and strengthened with your growing understanding and broadened personal perspective. *Now it is time to bring everything you have learned back to the official discussion and take a position on what you believe to be true.*

Some people say that you can't come home again. I do not believe that is entirely true—at least, it is not entirely accurate. You *can* come home again, but you cannot expect everything to be the same. Home may be basically the same, *but you have changed.* You return to a familiar place with new knowledge and experiences. And upon your return, because of all you bring with you, home will *seem* very different; *it will be* and *become* a very different place because of what you bring back with you. So, it is time to return to home base in terms of your Quest, time for you to turn your opinions into an official, academically sound argument and to join the official conversation of ideas.

Joining the Conversation

Becoming an active participant in a conversation already in progress is sometimes intimidating, but there is no reason for you to feel intimidated. The moment you began reading about your event and social problems connected to the event, you became a part of the conversation. You have been listening, learning, and politely waiting for your turn to speak. That time has come. The next step in the process is nothing to be intimidated by. You are already here. You are welcome, and we cannot *wait* to hear your ideas. It is time for you to find and use your voice and to make a difference.

The news that you are already a part of the conversation should be comforting, but for many students, it is very intimidating. It is not uncommon for those who speak freely during the initial phases of their Quest to suddenly freeze, become speechless, and develop an acute case of what we might call *academic-speak-itis.* This is an ailment caused by a fear of the unknown, the fear of a new and largely intimidating audience based on perceptions and expectations. Symptoms include frustration, anxiety, and writer's block (which often degenerates into procrastination, late work, and poor grades); silent sufferers of academic-speak-itis typically have strong opinions and ideas on a given issue but have difficulty formulating words or phrases to articulate those opinions and ideas. Causes are a misunderstanding of academic expectations, the "ivory tower" syndrome, and difficulty recognizing what it means to join the conversation. Treatment is to learn the expectations of an academic audience and to practice the basics of argumentation; to look closely at how arguments are made; to understand the features of a good, strong argument; and to know how to use that understanding of argumentation as a framework to shape and communicate ideas and knowledge to a particular audience.

There is nothing mystical or magical about academic writing and argumentation. Once you look closely at how arguments are shaped, what constitutes a good argument, and how to move from opinion to argument while maintaining a unique sense of voice and purpose, you see that this is really nothing new, nothing to fear. Academic argumentation is simply a slightly different forum for discussion—maybe a more purposeful spin on something you have been doing all of your life.

Playing by the Rules

The rules governing a conversation in the general public (in a popular publication, for instance) and the rules governing an academic conversation are usually a little different. For the most part, articles published for the general public do not have strict requirements. But as a part of the *academic community,* you are expected to

- communicate your ideas clearly
- explain your ideas thoroughly
- support your reasoning with evidence from credible sources
- provide documentation for those sources (to verify for your reader the origins of your evidence).

This is not to say that academic arguments are completely distinct from other parts of the official conversation. Unfortunately, however, many people see the writing produced in a college classroom as something produced solely for the classroom with no practical purpose in the real world. But, as usual, it is a mistake to place such limits on vision and understanding. The bottom line is that *you should be able to take what you learn about argumentation in this class and use it in many situations to strengthen and advance the official conversation in wonderful ways.*

What you learn and practice of academic argumentation will help you to find and use your voice in the most effective ways possible. The rules of academic argumentation will help you to be taken seriously anywhere. People will listen to what you have to say because your claim will be clear and understandable. They will be able to follow your well-organized and purposeful reasoning, and based on your presentation of evidence from credible sources, it will be clear that you know what you are talking about. Your audience will listen to you, they will respect you, and you will impact the world around you as a result.

Academic argumentation will help you to bring a new strength to the official conversation and *that is how real and lasting change will happen.* Others, in order to compete and to remain a part of the conversation, will have to reshape their arguments and rise to the occasion. Their claims will have to be clearer, their reasoning stronger, and their evidence more credible.

So, What's on Your Mind?

You have read and thoroughly studied and analyzed an event and one or more social problems or issues connected to that event, and you have formed your own opinion. Now it is time for you to turn that opinion into an official argument and join the public conversation. It is a bit like joining a game that is already in progress—a game with lots of rules and regulations, with referees and an audience that has some pretty tough expectations. But remember what we have been saying all along: *Your voice matters.* You have something to say, something valuable to contribute, and people *will listen* to what you have to say. You simply need to build your case strategically and state your ideas clearly and confidently. Creating an argument really *is* a bit like playing a game. It is all about strategy. Let's begin by reviewing what we already know.

The Building Blocks of Argumentation

- An *argument* is a form of expression that asserts and advances (with reasons and evidence) a position on an issue.
- The foundation of every argument is a *claim*. A claim is a statement about a perspective on an issue.
  - Claims sometimes attempt to prove that a situation or condition exists.
  - Claims sometimes attempt to prove that a situation or condition should change and sometimes suggest *how* it should change.
  - Claims sometimes attempt to prove that a cultural artifact signifies a particular meaning.
- A claim is similar to an opinion in that it states what someone believes about an issue, but an argument is more than opinion.
- An argument builds on opinion by offering *reasons* (reasons explain the logic behind your claim and answer the question *why*) and proof or *evidence* (verifiable quantitative or qualitative information from experts in a given field of study).
- Evidence can take many shapes and comes in many forms. This information may show up as
  - *quantitative data* (facts, statistics, surveys, and measurements) gathered through various types of research, or
  - *qualitative data* (inferences and opinions) offered by experts.
- By offering verifiable evidence to support a claim and reasons, a writer shows that she has done her homework and that there are experts in a particular field who have studied an issue and have gathered documented evidence that a particular idea is valid or invalid.

Claims, reasons, and evidence: these are the building blocks of any argument. But they will not hold together and stand up to scrutiny without a few additional ingredients: *purpose* and *audience*. You have to have a clear understanding of your purpose and your audience in order to create an effective argument. A clear understanding of these elements will determine the strategy you use to construct your argument. An argument developed with a particular strategy in mind will hold together and withstand scrutiny.

Purpose: What Are You Trying to Prove?

Before you begin to construct your argument, you must survey the current landscape. What is the conversation already in progress, and where do your ideas fit in? What is it that you hope to prove?

Is your primary purpose to educate or to call attention to or define a social problem? Do you want to prove a situation or condition exists (or does not exist)? Or do you want to generate concern and motivate, to show the exigency of a social problem? Is your purpose to inspire individuals or a group to take action, to change a situation or condition? Do you have a particular plan of action that you want to recommend? Or is your purpose to create meaning from a cultural artifact? Do you want to form an interpretation? *What is your purpose?*

Before you begin to build your argument, you must have a clear understanding of what it is that you hope to achieve: this is your purpose. Your purpose largely determines the reasoning you provide to build your argument, as well as the types of evidence you offer as support. Purpose directs you in terms of strategy and how your argument comes together, how it looks, how it sounds.

From here on out in this chapter we concentrate on the achievement of one particular purpose: *arguing to educate*. In the following chapters, we concentrate on arguing to instigate change and arguing to create meaning. For now, let's turn our attention to the task of proving that a situation or condition exists—arguing to educate a particular audience.

A clear understanding of your purpose for advancing an argument is only one part of the equation for success. In addition to purpose, you must also know your audience. Who are you speaking to? *Understanding your audience is perhaps the most important part of constructing an argument. Knowing whom you are speaking to and what it takes to get them to listen, to pay attention, is the most crucial element of strategy.*

Audience: Don't Talk to Strangers

Know your audience. Who is your audience? Why are you speaking to them? What do you hope to achieve? Arguments do not exist in a vacuum; arguments are conversations, so you are speaking *to* someone—even across space and time—discussing an issue with someone or several someones. Remember what your mother said: *Don't talk to strangers.* This very wise advice works away from the playground—it applies to argumentation, too. Know whom you are talking to. Know what they know. Know what they believe to be true.

Of course, except in very rare circumstances, you cannot have personal knowledge of each individual in your audience. To some extent, *you have to make generalizations.* While it is true that in most situations, generalizations are risky and illogical, this is an exception to that rule of logic. In an attempt to determine strategy, it is possible and it is necessary to "read" your audience and to make a few generalizations.

How can you get to know your audience? Begin by describing your *target audience.* Who are they? Who needs to hear what you have to say? Will you address a group of parents? Will you address a particular community like a neighborhood watch association or the residents of a particular apartment complex in an inner city? An organization such as Mothers of Murdered Offspring or S.A.V.E. (Students Against Violence Everywhere)? Will you address government officials? Teenagers? A prison population? Decide whom you will address, and write down what you already know about this group of people (age range, education level, likely political affiliation, religious background, etc.). Then make a list of questions you need answers to. If you know the answers, write them down. If you do not know the answers, do a little research. You might even conduct a brief survey if your audience is easily accessible.

Note

Some vital statistics are available through the U.S. Census Bureau online at http://factfinder.census.gov/servlet/BasicFactsServletor or through many additional federal agencies at http://www.fedstats.gov. Other organizations and government agencies provide useful statistical information as well—check your library for local resources.

Practicum

Conducting a brief survey:

1. Once you have identified a particular target audience, think of where you might locate a sampling of that audience. For example, if your intended audience is young adults between the ages of 17 and 21, college dorms are a good place to conduct your survey. If your intended audience is working adults and parents, you might speak to people in your neighborhood or poll customers at the local grocery store.

2. Make a list of several questions related to your topic (these should be questions that are easily answered in a two- to five-minute interview). Then poll a sampling of your intended audience. Your purpose is to get to know your audience in a general way—

who they are, what they know, what they believe, how strong their opinions are on a particular subject. For example, if the event you are studying is the Oklahoma City bombing, your may ask questions such as, *Do you remember this event?* and *Who or what is to blame for this event?* You might ask questions related to a specific issue, such as gun control or the threat of militia groups. The questions you ask are intended to give you a basic idea of what your target audience believes to be true regarding your topic. (Also gather information such as sex, race, age, educational level, political affiliation, etc., but do not gather names or any personal information. Explain that you are conducting a survey for a school project, and assure the people you approach that the results of the survey are confidential.)

3. Gather a reasonable sampling (20 to 30 responses to five to eight questions). Then make a summary of the information you gathered. Bring that to class and share with your classmates. You will use this information as you prepare to write your argument.

At the Intersection of Purpose and Audience: Controversy

Once you have completed an audience survey, study the information you have gathered and begin to formulate some general ideas about your audience. What can you determine from the results of your survey? What do these folks know about your event and/or issue? What is their experience? Generalize. Now, how can you use that information to help you construct your argument?

For example, if your event is the Columbine High School shooting and 81 percent of those surveyed remembered details of that event, you know that you do not have to spend a lot of time reviewing basic, background information. If 55 percent of those surveyed believe that media coverage of the event was adequate to good, you know that the majority of your audience favors the media, and an argument that does not favor the media will be pretty controversial. If 89 percent of those surveyed believe that Marilyn Manson has a negative influence on youth behavior, you know that it will be a challenge to argue that music does not influence behavior.

The fuel for your argument and the map for how your argument will come together have to do with the intersection of audience and purpose—that intersection is called *controversy*. Controversy will ultimately determine your strategy for bringing together your argument successfully. Strategy depends on the level of controversy surrounding your claim, your position regarding an issue. The level of controversy depends on your audience and their *assumptions*.

Identifying Audience Assumptions: Warrants

Assumptions are connected to our most basic beliefs about life and living. They underlie just about everything that we say and do in our lives—all of our decisions, our motivations. For the most part, assumptions are so deeply ingrained in our lives as a part of our value systems that we do not consciously recognize them. They are fundamentally connected to our most basic beliefs and values, those springing from the very core of our family, our social culture, the presence or absence of religion in our lives—whatever it is that guides our behavior and our understanding of life.

In terms of argumentation, assumptions can be thought about in several different ways, but they are usually called *warrants*. When an author puts together an argument s/he is operating on the assumption that the audience will recognize and accept the connection between his or her claim, reasoning, and evidence. That underlying connection is known as a warrant. A warrant is like an unspoken guarantee that all of the pieces of an argument fit together logically—that the reasoning is logical, the evidence is credible, and that the situation is exigent and demands attention.

Put simply, warrants are the implicit or explicit connections linking the claim, reasoning, and evidence for any argument. We can often identify these underlying warrants or connections by asking, *What must an audience believe to be true in order to* accept this evidence *as support* for this reasoning? Generally, there are three broad categories of warrants: substantive, motivational, and authoritative

- *Substantive* warrants are based on traditional forms of logical reasoning: Does the audience understand *how* the evidence offered supports the reasoning behind the claim?
- *Motivational* warrants depend on appeals to an audience's needs and values: Will the audience appreciate the *exigency* of the situation as demonstrated through the reasoning and evidence?
- *Authoritative* warrants rely on expert testimony and the strength of evidence from credible sources: Will the audience recognize the *credibility of sources* presented as evidence?

As an example, let's look again at Joe's argument regarding parking on campus from Chapters 4 and 5:

- Joe's **claim:** Parking is a problem on campus.
- Joe's first line of **reasoning:** No matter what time he arrives on campus, he cannot find a parking space.
- Joe's supporting **evidence:** Over a period of several weeks, he keeps a log of his arrival time on campus and documents how long he must wait to find a parking space. For a period of two weeks, five days a week, Joe arrives on campus at various times and records how long it takes him to find a parking space. Regardless of what day of the week it is, and no matter what time he arrives on campus, it takes him between ten and thirty minutes to find a parking space, which results in his tardiness to class every day.

In order to accept the connection between Joe's claim, this line of reasoning and the evidence he offers as support, his audience must understand how his evidence supports the reasoning behind his claim—his audience must accept the substantive warrant connecting his evidence and reasoning. They must understand that Joe's evidence demonstrates a parking problem on campus, that the documentation of his difficulty in finding a parking space illustrates a situation beyond his immediate control, that the time of his arrival to campus has nothing to do with the availability of parking spaces, and that this example is representative of a pervasive problem. If an audience does not accept these implicit connections as logical, Joe's argument falls apart.

Let's say that Joe adds some additional evidence to his argument. In support of the same reason,

> Joe polls more than 200 commuters regarding their experiences with parking and presents testimony that 88 percent of those polled have suffered some sort of penalties because of tardiness to class when they were unable to find a parking space.

Joe is counting on his audience to understand the importance of being on time and doing well in school. He is counting on them to relate to the value of an education, to accept that the parking problem has an extensive impact on the student population, and therefore to recognize the exigency of this situation. In this example, the underlying warrant is motivational. The audience must accept that the problem Joe details is widespread and urgent enough to demand attention. If an audience does not accept the problem as urgent and does not place a value on promptness, learning, and earning good grades, Joe's argument falls apart.

Finally, suppose Joe decides he needs another type of evidence to support his reasoning:

> Joe might add information from an interview with the director of parking services, who admits that the university needs to create more parking spaces on campus and that there are more commuters than there are available parking spaces.

This aspect of Joe's argument is based on an authoritative warrant. In order to accept Joe's argument, an audience must recognize the director of parking services as a credible expert in the matter of parking on campus. If an audience does not accept this person as an expert, Joe's argument falls apart.

So, a warrant is the underlying implicit or explicit connection between a claim, reasons, and evidence that holds an argument together. Identifying warrants is an excellent tool to use when examining arguments presented by experts in any given field. Recognizing the warrant that connects a claim, reasoning, and evidence enables us to pinpoint the major strengths or flaws in a given argument.

Practicum

Warrants may seem difficult to understand and identify when you first begin thinking about them, but they are actually a part of just about everything we say and do. Before moving on, let's take a moment to examine some common arguments that we encounter in the world around us every day and practice identifying warrants.

    Read each of the following (a bumper sticker, a button, and a t-shirt). Identify the claim, any supporting reasons or evidence, and the underlying warrant or warrants. Then share your ideas in small groups or as a whole class. Do you find that you agree with your classmates? Disagree?

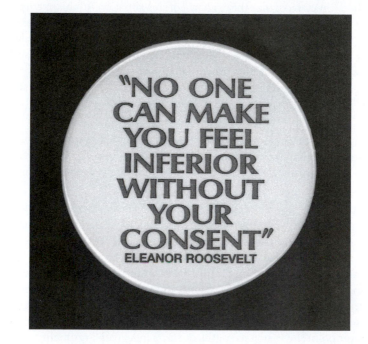

Recognizing warrants or assumptions is important when analyzing an argument someone else has presented, but this is also an important aspect of developing a strategy for communicating your own argument

Choosing an Effective Strategy

Depending on the level of controversy surrounding your claim (the intersection of your purpose and your audience), the development of that claim into an effective argument may be guided by three different persuasive elements: *logos, ethos,* and/or *pathos:*

Logos = Logic
Ethos = Ethics/Credibility
Pathos = Emotions

These three persuasive elements date back to Aristotle and have been used to describe and create arguments for centuries. For our purposes, we use these terms to define *strategies* for creating and developing an argument depending upon the level of controversy generated by a particular claim and a particular audience. An argument will be dominated by one strategy or another, but all three persuasive elements are typically present in any given argument.

Notice that each persuasive element also corresponds with a particular type of warrant:

Logos = Logic = Substantive Warrants
Ethos = Ethics/Credibility = Authoritative Warrants
Pathos = Emotions = Motivational Warrants

If an argument is not very controversial for a particular audience, that audience is likely to accept the argument based on a solid claim and logical reasoning (i.e., the audience will accept the argument based on a substantive warrant). If an argument is mildly controversial, or if an audience is split or undecided on a particular issue, that audience will need a solid claim and logical reasoning, but the success of such an argument will depend largely upon the evidence offered in support of the reasoning and the claim (an authoritative warrant underlies this type of argument). But when an argument is highly controversial and based on an emotionally charged issue, the audience is typically quite resistant to new ideas and information. This type of argument is challenging and delicate—it requires a certain finesse. At best, you *may* get your audience to listen to what you have to say. In order to achieve even the attention of your audience, you must provide a solid claim, logical reasoning, and credible evidence, but your success will depend upon your ability to connect with your audience's needs and values (i.e., this type of argument is held together by a motivational warrant).

Let's look at how logos, ethos, and pathos shape the creation of an argument.

Logos. Whether you are arguing to educate, to motivate or instigate change, or to create meaning, if it is likely that your audience will share your basic assumptions about your claim, then your argument is not very controversial. It can be logos- or logic-driven. Basically, to make a successful logos-driven argument, you must provide *sound reasoning* and some *evidence to support your reasoning* (though not a lot). Your goal is to show that *you are reasonable and your argument is logical.* For the most part, your claim and reasoning will be enough, though part of being reasonable is acknowledging (briefly) other perspectives. The evidence will offer further support for your reasoning, but the reasoning itself will be the key to your success.

For example, Courtney decided to advance an argument to educate her audience: that music cannot be blamed for youth violence. Her audience is made up of 15 to 20 year olds, 75 percent of whom believe that music has an impact on their lives but does not significantly influence their behavior, so in this situation the level of controversy is pretty low. Based on their own experience, most of Courtney's audience already believes that music does not directly influence behavior, so it will not take much to convince them that music cannot be blamed for youth violence.

To create a successful argument in this situation, Courtney must state her claim and reasoning, and then provide a few credible examples. She may not have to bring in a great deal of evidence from experts—it may be enough to create *scenarios* (a synopsis of a specified situation, real or imagined) as support. As usual, the audience brings its own common experiences and assumptions to the conversation, and that—along with the reasoning Courtney provides—should be convincing enough.

Here is another brief example of a logos-driven argument: Janice wants to argue the claim that active parental involvement in a child's life can prevent violent youth behavior. Her purpose for creating this argument is to educate her audience, to define active parental involvement, and to show how active parenting can prevent violent youth behavior (such as the Columbine High School shooting).

The target audience for Janice's argument is a PTA group (Parent–Teacher Association). The members of the PTA are already active to one extent or another in the lives of their children (after all, they are attending an extracurricular school event in order to hear what Janice has to say). Most of the parents are fairly educated (78 percent have a college degree), and most are concerned about the possibility of violence in the schools (89 percent are worried about an event similar to the Columbine High School shooting and believe it could happen at their school). Because her audience shares her concern for school-related violence, and because they obviously value parental involvement, Janice's claim is not very controversial. She does not have to provide a great deal of outside evidence to convince her audience to believe what she has to say. The success of her argument depends largely on the presentation of her claim and reasoning. She must offer sufficient information to define and illustrate active parenting, and she must show that active parenting, as she has defined it, prevents youth violence. Her audience may believe attending a PTA meeting is evidence of active parenting. Janice must show them (perhaps with examples and scenarios) that active parenting involves consistent, positive *interaction* with a child and must also show how that interaction may prevent youth violence.

Courtney's and Janice's situations are not typical. More often than not, you will find that your audience does not so easily or completely accept the assumptions behind your argument. You may find instead that your ideas challenge your audience's basic assumptions about some aspect of life, thereby making your argument more controversial.

Ethos.   When your argument is more controversial for your audience, it will be primarily *ethos-driven. This means you must work harder to establish credibility.* In order to capture your audience's collective ear, to hold their attention, and to hopefully convince them that you are right, you must show you have done your homework by providing a good bit of evidence. A clear claim is important, and logical reasoning is necessary, but unlike in a logos-driven argument, in an ethos-driven argument, that is not enough. Whereas with a logos-driven argument, the logic of your reasoning is the key to your success, with an ethos-driven argument, you must concentrate on providing adequate evidence from credible sources to support your reasoning. Too little evidence, and your audience will not trust you. Too much ethos takes away from your credibility, as well, so balance is the key.

Let's say that Todd's audience is made up of the parents of teenagers and that 84 percent of them are in the midst of dealing with the turbulent teens and believe that music has a strong influence on the behavior of youth. Todd wants to argue that music does not cause instances of youth violence, so his argument is pretty controversial for this audience. He must provide a clear claim and logical reasons, and he must establish his credibility with more evidence from credible sources. He will have to *show his audience* that he has done his homework. Reasoning is still important, but the evidence from sources that Todd's audience will recognize as credible is the key to his success. Showing that he knows the background of an issue, and that other credible people (experts in a particular field) agree with him are the cornerstones of his strategy for building an ethos-driven argument. Most arguments fall into this category.

Here is another example of an ethos-driven argument. A student, Rebecca, wants to argue the claim that militia groups have quietly grown in popularity since the Oklahoma City bombing and pose an increasing threat across the United States. Her purpose for writing this essay is to call attention to the growing threat of militia groups in the United States. She is arguing to educate. So how controversial is this argument? That depends on her audience.

Rebecca's intended audience is primarily made up of 17- to 23-year-old college students attending a southern university in a major U.S. city. Based on her initial survey, Rebecca knows that the majority of her audience, 68 percent, knows what a militia group is but that 87 percent do not know what a militia group does. These college students have no direct knowledge of militia groups, and the limited understanding they do have is based on what they have heard in the media. Rebecca also learns through her survey that while only 23 percent of her audience believes that militia groups exist in their area, 56 percent believe such groups might present a real threat to the general public.

Rebecca decides that her primary purpose is educating her audience about the existence of militia groups in all fifty states and the current operating status of such groups. Because the majority of her audience does acknowledge the possible threat of militia groups, Rebecca believes her argument is not overly controversial, *but since she is not an expert on militia groups, without a sufficient amount of outside evidence, her audience will not readily accept what she has to say.* She must provide verifiable evidence from credible sources to support her claim. Her argument will be best developed using clear reasoning and a sufficient amount of credible supporting evidence. She must define and explain what a militia group is and what it does, and then she must provide evidence of the existence and expansion of such groups across the United States and testimony from experts in law enforcement regarding the threat to public safety such groups pose.

Pathos.   If your argument challenges the basic assumptions of your audience in a significant way, you are suddenly playing a high-stakes game. When dealing with highly sensitive and controversial ideas, your argument may be *pathos-driven*. This means that you must not only provide logical reasoning and credible evidence but you also must present your ideas and evidence in such a way as to *appeal to and connect with*, on some level, your audience's emotions, needs, and values. You must *use* your audience's needs and values strategically as you present your radical ideas to help them listen to what you have to say and accept a new way of thinking that may ultimately alter their core system of beliefs in some fundamental way.

A word of caution: If your argument is highly sensitive, chances are *you* have very strong feelings about this, too, and you must keep them in check. Remain fair and balanced. Above all else, think *strategy.*

A pathos-driven argument is difficult to create effectively. Too much pathos creates a flaming argument (imbalanced tone), which can edge even the soundest argument into the pitfalls of fallacy. Again, the key is to know your audience. Provide logical reasoning and credible evidence but also *find a way to connect to your audience on an emotional level through their needs and values.* Sometimes the best way to do this is by establishing a *common ground,* by focusing on a set of beliefs or values that you have in common with one another. Or, if your audience is hostile, it may help to diffuse the situation by acknowledging your understanding of *their beliefs* first, even if you do not share them. This demonstrates respect and creates an empathetic bond between the writer or speaker and the audience. Then, once you have your audience's attention, you might advance your position by carefully introducing more controversial and challenging perspectives.

For example, Carmen's claim is that "easy access to guns enabled the lethal youth violence that otherwise might have been avoided at Columbine High School." As she prepared to develop this claim, Carmen reviewed her initial audience survey and learned that the majority of her audience (made up of both teens and their parents) strongly supported the Second Amendment right to bear arms, yet most also acknowledged that we have a serious problem with violence in our culture. Immediately, she knew that her argument was fairly controversial.

Carmen conducted a follow-up survey with more detailed questions and learned that 98 percent of her audience supported the Second Amendment in theory, but only 32 percent had even a cursory knowledge of the gun laws governing our right to bear arms and how those laws related to the problem of youth violence. Based on this information, Carmen decided the best strategy for developing her argument would be to *diffuse the emotions surrounding her claim by establishing a common ground with her audience.* She would demonstrate her respect for the ideals of the Second Amendment and then educate her audience by walking them through a detailed exploration of gun laws throughout history before defining the root of the problem as she understood it: faulty, unenforceable laws.

By demonstrating a common-ground respect for the Second Amendment, Carmen instantly gained the respect and attention of her audience and diffused some of the emotion connected to this volatile subject. Then, by offering credible information and a detailed analysis of gun laws throughout history, Carmen showed she had done her homework and that she is knowledgeable on this subject matter. Her audience was guided through a framework of logical reasoning and supporting evidence that built a solid, credible argument worthy of their attention.

Sometimes, some arguments so completely challenge an audience's basic assumptions about life and living that they will not listen to the first bit of reasoning, they will not consider the first piece of evidence as support. Therefore, on a personal level, they completely shut down, turn off, tune out. When faced with that sort of challenge, many arguers simply give up and remain silent. But there is a way to proceed with even the most controversial argument.

Here is another example of a pathos-driven argument. Leah wanted to argue the claim that "the parents of youths who commit violent crimes—such as the Columbine High School shooting—are responsible for those crimes."

From the outset, Leah knew that her argument was quite controversial for her intended audience. Results from her initial survey showed that 87 percent of her audience (made up of 17- to 23-year-old college students) believed that the parents of shooters Dylan Klebold and Eric Harris *were not* responsible for their crime. Leah, however, firmly believed that the lack of parental involvement was a key factor in such violent episodes, and she believed that lack of involvement was negligence on the part of the parents. Therefore, she felt the parents were responsible for the crimes committed by their children. In spite of her audience's resistance, she was determined to speak out on this none-too-popular position.

In order to do this, Leah searched for common ground with her audience. She decided the best strategy would be to tap into the emotional need we all have for a positive relationship with our parents. Most of her audience had recently moved out on their own, away from their parents for the first time. While this newfound independence was a positive experience for the majority, almost everyone admitted to occasional pangs of homesickness. So, by reminding her audience of the loving aspects of a parent–child relationship, she hoped to create an empathetic bond with her audience and to remind them of the impact that parents have on the lives of their children. Then, using logical reasoning and credible evidence, while maintaining a reasonable pathos, she planned to ease her audience into and through her position on parenting.

To establish that empathetic connection with her audience, Leah planned to begin her argument with a personal narrative that demonstrated the benefits of a healthy, positive parent–child relationship. She began her essay by telling a story of what her birth meant to her parents and by sharing examples of the bond that she experienced with them while growing up. Then she introduced the issue of youth violence as connected to parenting by telling of her own experience when she first learned of the Columbine massacre (an experience she had discovered to be common among most of her audience members). She continued to develop her argument by introducing testimony from credible experts as she defined positive parenting and parental negligence and showed through various common scenarios the impact that both types of parenting might have on youth behavior. She maintained a balance throughout her essay and a connection to the common ground she had initially established with her audience. The result was an emotionally powerful and strongly supported argument.

As you can see from the examples in this chapter, creating a solid argument is all about strategy. Many factors come into play. The foundation of any argument is its claim, its logical reasoning, and its evidence. But the glue that holds it all together is a driving purpose for communication and a thorough knowledge of audience.

A Reminder

No argument is entirely logos-, ethos-, or pathos-driven. Every argument includes some logic, some ethics, and some appeal to emotions. The *degree* to which each element is required in your essay is what varies, and this is tied to your purpose, your audience, and the level of controversy surrounding your claim.

Tools for Success: Planning and Creating an Effective Argument

You have a pretty clear understanding of purpose and audience and how to determine the level of controversy surrounding an argument. You know the basics of creating a sound argument *in theory,* but what about putting that theory into practice?

As you begin to build your argument, you know you need a claim, but *how do you make one?* And what qualities distinguish an *effective* claim from an *ineffective* one? You know you need to provide logical reasons to explain the *why* of a claim but, *which reasons do you cover* (to avoid writing a book), and *how can you be sure you have answered your audience's questions sufficiently?* Finally, you know you need to provide evidence in support of your reasoning and you have found a great deal of evidence, but *how do you use the evidence to support your argument effectively?* Let's look at some simple guidelines for creating an effective argument.

Making Claims

A claim answers the question, *What are you trying to prove?* This is the thesis for your argument. In one statement (usually a sentence or two, but no more than a paragraph), tell your audience the main point your argument will communicate. An effective claim *clear, concise,* and *balanced* in tone. What does that mean?

- A *clear* claim is stated directly—no hemming or hawing, no beating around the bush, no worn-out or tired clichés. It is a clearly articulated statement of your main idea.
- A *concise* claim is not weighed down by extra wording. It does not contain supporting details. It demonstrates a purposeful use of language to directly communicate your main idea.
- A claim with a *balanced tone* does not contain overly emotive language; if necessary, it contains qualifiers (such as *typically, sometimes, many times, often*). It is an even, as-close-to-objective-as-possible declarative statement.

Providing Reasoning

Once you have established your claim, you must identify and explain reasons to demonstrate the logic of your claim. Your reasons answer the question, *Why?*

This is a difficult part of an argument to anticipate. It is often a challenge to identify the reasoning behind our own claims. After all, it is very clear to us; we have somehow managed to internalize our reasoning. The trick to creating an effective argument, though, is to *anticipate the questions your audience might have* and to answer those questions—to lead your audience through *your pattern of reasoning* in such a way that they might be able to draw the same conclusions that you have drawn and accept your argument to be true.

Supporting with Evidence

At this point, you have stated your claim, and it is clear, concise, and balanced in tone. You have provided reasons to explain the logic of your claim, but your audience needs more than your reasoning. Your audience needs verification: *evidence.*

Evidence answers the questions, *How do you know this to be true? What proof do you have?* You have heard the old saying, seeing is believing. Well, your audience is a bunch of skeptics. For the most part (unless you can establish yourself as an expert on a given topic), they are not going to simply take your word for it when it comes to accepting a claim and reasoning. Part of your responsibility in creating an argument is to offer evidence from credible outside sources (typically from experts in a given field) in support of your reasoning and your claim.

Remember, there is strength in numbers. Your audience wants to know that there are other reasonable, educated folks who have thought long and hard about the same issues, who have studied those issues, and who have reached the same conclusions that you have reached. You must *prove* to your audience that what you say is true: *you must show them what you know.*

This is where you really begin to utilize the materials you have gathered in your previous Quests. After completing the extensive research for Quests Three and Four, you have collected a tremendous amount of resources. You have uncovered many voices speaking about dozens of perspectives, and you might feel a bit overwhelmed. You have a lot of material to sort through and choose from as you search for just the right piece of evidence. The key here is to be selective.

The first rule of evidence in argumentation is that *your evidence should be directly connected to your reasoning, which in turn should directly support your claim.* Do not use a piece of evidence just because it sounds good or seems impressive or because you cannot find anything better in the information you have gathered. Do not use a piece of evidence by default because you cannot find exactly what you are looking for. If you do not already have the information you need to support your reasoning, *conduct additional research until you find what you need.*

Another rule of evidence is to *use only the most credible sources.* Do not use evidence you cannot verify as credible (remember the lessons from Chapter 5 regarding STAR). No matter how fabulous the quote you have found, no matter how seemingly perfect for your argument, if you cannot verify the credibility of the source, do not use it. Keep looking. *Your reputation is at stake.* Using less-than-credible evidence will destroy your ethos.

Testing Your Warrants

Once you have created your claim and reasoning and have located evidence to support that reasoning, you should test the logical connections underlying the argument you have constructed. With your audience in mind, examine each reason and the evidence offered as support, and ask yourself, What am I asking my audience to accept? Have I provided everything my audience will need in order to accept the logical connection(s) I have established here?

Identify the type of warrant(s) connecting your reasoning and evidence. Is it substantive, motivational, or authoritative? Based on what you know about your audience, will your audience accept an implicit warrant? Or should you address the warrant explicitly and offer additional evidence as support? This final test will help you to be sure that you have presented a sound argument with the particulars of your audience in mind.

Using Sources Effectively

Finally, perhaps the most important rule of evidence in the academic world: *Handle your sources responsibly.* Use proper documentation format to avoid plagiarism, to demonstrate credibility (yours and your source's), and to give credit where credit is due.

Once you have found the evidence you need to support your reasoning, your next big challenge is incorporating that information from an outside source into the text of your essay. This must be done skillfully. There are several important points to remember: Use a *tagline* to introduce your source, *interpret* your quotation, and *make necessary connections* for your reader.

A tagline introduces your quotation to your audience and establishes the credibility of your source.

An interpretation explains for your reader your understanding of the evidence you are providing.

An explanation clarifies connections for your reader between your claim, reasoning, and evidence.

This combination of tagline, quotation (or summary or paraphrase), interpretation, and explanation creates a *full thought cycle*. If any one part of the cycle is missing, the reader is left with questions. For instance,

- If no tagline is presented, in response to the quotation, the reader wonders, Who says so, and why should I care?
- If no quotation (or summary or paraphrase) follows, the reader wonders, Where is your proof?
- If no interpretation follows the quotation, the reader wonders, What does this mean?
- If no explanation follows, the reader wonders, So what?

Skillful use of sources in a full thought cycle leaves no gaps in logic and reasoning for the reader to fall into and strengthens your argument so that it may bend to scrutiny but will not break.

Planning and Creating an Effective Argument Walk-Through

Let's follow a student, Christina, as she plans and creates her argument paper. Christina has completed her previous Quests on the issue of parental responsibility. Christina believes that parents *are not* to blame for the actions of their teens. She plans to advance an argument to educate her audience. Based on her knowledge of her audience, she knows that this claim will not be very controversial. But because she is not a parent, nor is she an expert in any field of study related to parenting, she knows that the success of her argument will largely depend upon both the logic of her reasoning and the evidence she provides in support of her claim and reasoning, so her argument will be primarily ethos-driven. With this in mind, she is ready to begin building her argument essay. The first step is to make a claim.

Making Claims

Christina knows that an effective claim will be *clear, concise,* and *balanced* in tone. She conducts a brief freewrite to generate ideas, and her first attempt at a claim looks like this:

A draft of Christina's claim:

> Despite a parent's best intentions and the instillment of such values and morals, a good child can "go bad." Parental involvement, whether in high or low volumes, is not to blame.

As part of a class workshop, Christina puts her claim on the blackboard and her peers make the following evaluation:

This statement moves into supporting details and should not be a part of the main claim.

This statement is too wordy—unclear.

Unclear—to blame for what?

> Despite a parent's best intentions and the instillment of such values and morals, a good child can "go bad." Parental involvement, whether in high or low volumes, is not to blame.

Through class discussion, Christina realizes that there are some definite problems with her first claim. But her classmates provide enough suggestions that she is able to modify it and create another claim:

Claim One	**Claim Two**
and the instillment of such values and morals	This is removed entirely from the introduction and saved for the body of the paper where supporting details are covered
whether in high or low volumes	This statement is reworded to be more direct: *the degree of parental involvement*
not to blame	This statement is changed to more directly reference the previously unnamed "blame": *not to blame for youth violence*

Christina's revised claim:

> Despite a parent's best intentions, a good child can "go bad." The degree of parental involvement is not to blame for youth violence.

This claim works. It is clear, concise, and balanced in tone. Christina is ready to move on.

Providing Reasons

Christina writes at the top of a sheet of paper,

> The degree of parental involvement is not to blame for
> youth violence.

She recognizes that her audience will want to know *why*. She responds by generating the following list of reasons:

> The degree of parental involvement is not to blame for youth violence *because*
> 1. We have many examples of parents who are actively involved in their children's lives, yet those children exhibit violent behavior.
> 2. Many other factors influence the behavior of children once they reach a certain age.
> 3. There are cases in which two or more siblings raised in the same home by the same parents with the same amount of parental involvement exhibit different kinds of behaviors—one sibling may be violent while the other is not.
> 4. We have many examples of children who never exhibit violent behavior in spite of the fact that they have no parental involvement in their lives.

Once she has a list of reasons to explain the logic of her claim, Christina must decide if she needs to include all of her reasons. She knows she needs to select the *best reasons* and that her selection will have something to do with whether or not she can support her reasoning with evidence and whether or not her audience is likely to accept that reasoning and evidence. She also knows she needs to decide on a *pattern of organization* for her reasoning that is most logical and effective.

To make Christina's argument, it might not be necessary to include reason 2 (that many other factors influence the behavior of children). It might be enough to simply cover reasons 1, 3, and 4. This depends in large part on the audience and the level of controversy that this claim might generate. If her audience is likely to be threatened by her claim, she might need to include a discussion of all four reasons. While she is fairly certain that her audience is not challenged on any fundamental level by her claim, she decides to use all four reasons to demonstrate the breadth of her knowledge on her subject matter and to add to her credibility.

As for an organizational pattern, again, Christina's goal is to guide the audience through the logic of her argument so that the audience can reach the same conclusions she reached. Each reason should lead logically to the next reason, like steps in a staircase. Miss a step, the reader tumbles and falls.

Christina decides that it is most logical to begin her argument with reason 1, since it is most directly connected to the claim. Reason 4 naturally follows because it addresses what would be the opposite side of the same coin, so to speak. Reason 3 does not fall last in her organizational pattern by default. It could easily be covered after reason 1, since it expands on the idea of involved parents, but it could also be covered after reason 4 as a sort of middle ground, a way of introducing unexplained variables, which leads naturally into reason 2.

So, after testing this proposed organization with her classmates, Christina decides to use the following pattern:

Claim: The degree of parental involvement is not to blame for youth violence. (I know this to be true *because*)

Reason 1: We have many examples of parents who are actively involved in their children's lives, yet those children exhibit violent behavior.

Reason 2: We have many examples of children who never exhibit violent behavior in spite of the fact that they have no parental involvement in their lives.

Reason 3: There are cases in which two or more siblings raised in the same home by the same parents with the same amount of parental involvement exhibit different kinds of behaviors—one sibling may be violent while the other is not.

Reason 4: Many other factors influence the behavior of children once they reach a certain age.

Note

1. Reasons, like claims, should be clear, concise, and balanced in tone. At some point during the writing process, the reasons Christina outlined must be reworded, but while drafting, the emphasis is on content, on getting ideas down on paper in an organized manner and thoroughly developing those ideas.

2. Again, as Christina demonstrated, many of your decisions as to reasons and organization have to do with your audience and the level of controversy generated by your claim. Your goal is always to find the best, most effective strategy for communicating your ideas to a given audience.

Supporting with Evidence

Once Christina has her claim and reasons, she spends a great deal of time sorting through the mass of evidence she gathered during her previous Quests. To begin with, she discovers information that sounds great, but she is unsure whether or not it is directly connected to her claim and reasoning. For example, Christina's claim is that the degree of parental involvement is not to blame for youth violence. The reason she must support is that many other factors influence the behavior of children once they reach a certain age. One piece of evidence she collected is from an article titled "Young and Depressed," which says, "Psychological disorders like depression, anxiety, obsessive compulsive behaviors, etc., affect over 3 million adolescents in this country."

This is a staggering statistic and seems quite impressive, but it is not directly connected to the reason she needs to support. Yes, it does detail evidence about something that influences a child's behavior aside from a parent, but her reason is focused on *factors that influence the behavior of children once they reach a certain age* and how this demonstrates that *the degree of parental involvement is not to blame for youth violence.*

After discussing this with her peers, Christina decides that a better piece of evidence would be from psychiatrist Alvin Poussaint of Harvard Medical School who says that "kids have a mind of their own. And also they are influenced by the outside world and by their friends" (Blakemoore). This is a good place to begin to support her reason, but it is not enough. She decides she might also bring in some evidence from a study published in the *Journal of Leisure Research* that states, "Finally, our analyses show that juveniles experience a decreasing parental influence when they get older . . . 13–15 year old girls indicate as often as 13–15 year old boys that their parents no longer intervene in their leisure activities (83% for both sexes)" (Zeijl). Then she might look for expert testimony regarding the types of activities teens are involved in and the way those various activities influence the behavior of kids.

Remember

Do not settle for less than the best. If you search through your resources and cannot find the evidence you need, go back to the computer, the databases, the library, and research some more!

Another problem Christina faces as she searches for evidence is selecting information from only the most credible sources. For example, she finds what seems to be a useful quote from an online source, www.keepkidshealthy.com: "Teenagers usually begin spending more time with their friends and less time with their family, which allows their friends to have more of an influence on them." This source seems to provide useful information; it even says exactly what Christina wants to say in support of her reason, but she knows nothing about the author of the Web site—a dotcom website (which immediately raises concerns in the academic world because dotcom means it is a commercial site).

Christina knows that no matter how fabulous the quote she found, no matter how perfect for her argument, if she cannot verify the credibility of the source, she cannot use it as support in her essay. But this quote is so perfect, she returns to the Web site and searches until she finds the information she needs. Fortunately, this particular site provides information about the author, and he seems to be a credible source for information on adolescents and teens:

> Vincent R. Iannelli, MD, FAAP, is a board certified pediatrician in Dallas, Texas. He is a member of the Dallas County Medical Society, Texas Medical Association and is a Fellow of the American Academy of Pediatrics. In addition to having a Pediatrics practice in a suburb of Dallas, he is currently an Associate Professor of Pediatrics at the UT Southwestern Medical School.

Based on this information, it appears that this is a credible source, but Christina still wonders if it is the best she can find. Will her audience accept this dotcom source as credible? Ultimately, she decides that her audience will accept the site as credible as long as she provides the professional credentials of Dr. Iannelli within the body of her text.

Testing Warrants

Christina has already worked to build a strong connection between her reasoning and her evidence. She has constructed each aspect of her argument with her audience in mind, but she wants to be sure that her argument is solid. In order to do this, she must check the connection between each reason and the evidence offered as support for that reason by identifying the underlying warrant and asking herself, Will the audience recognize my reasoning as logical, my evidence credible, and the situation addressed as exigent?

For example, Christina's claim, again, is that the degree of parental involvement is not to blame for youth violence. One of her reasons is that many other factors influence the behavior of children once they reach a certain age. The evidence offered in support of that reason is from psychiatrist Alvin Poussaint of Harvard Medical School, who says that "kids have a mind of their own. And also they are influenced by the outside world and by their friends" (Blakemoore).

The primary warrant connecting this reason and supporting evidence is authoritative. Her audience must recognize Poussaint as credible. Christina is sure that the majority of her audience will accept a Harvard Medical School psychiatrist as an expert in the field of developmental psychology. Therefore, she feels that this part of her argument is sound. She continues this evaluation throughout the remainder of her essay and decides that she has created an argument that her audience will understand and accept on every level.

Using Sources Skillfully

Using in her own writing the information Christina found in her research is a tricky thing. There are many points to consider as she begins to incorporate her research materials into her essay. She must be sure to balance the information she uses as support with her own ideas. Christina knows that information gathered through her research should be used to support and supplement her ideas, but that *her ideas* should always remain the central focus of her essay. So, she must carefully pick and choose the quotations she uses. She must be selective and use only the information that is absolutely necessary to reinforce points she is making and to lend credibility to her argument.

Incorporating information from an outside source into the text of her essay is a big challenge. Christina knows that there are several important points to remember: she must use a tagline to introduce her source, interpret her quotation, and make necessary connections for the reader.

Christina's first attempt looks something like this:

> Parents cannot always control their teenagers and the decisions they make. "Once the teenage years arrive, parental controls slip away and old sanctions that once constrained unacceptable behavior no longer work." "Anyone who thinks that parents have total control over their teenage children is not parenting a teenage child." Teenagers usually do what they want to do and are very stubborn when it comes to following directions or doing what they are told.

But there are several problems. First of all, she dropped a quotation into her essay without fully incorporating it into her text, and she strung together multiple quotations:

> "Once the teenage years arrive, parental controls slip away and old sanctions that once constrained unacceptable behavior no longer work." "Anyone who thinks that parents have total control over their teenage children is not parenting a teenage child."

Christina had to be reminded of why she needs evidence to support her argument—to offer proof from credible experts that what she says is true—to *support her argument*. So, what she has to say should be the bulk of her text; any quotations work like scaffolding—to help hold together and strengthen her ideas.

In order for Christina's audience to recognize that a quotation is from a credible expert, she must introduce the source of her quote and tell why that person is an expert. This lends credibility to her source and, ultimately, to Christina (because she is demonstrating that she has done her homework and that she recognizes the experts in a given field). So, to properly use the quotation in the example above, Christina must provide what we call a *tagline* and introduce her source.

A tagline is like an introduction for a guest speaker. As the host for this guest speaker, it is Christina's responsibility to properly introduce the speaker, to let her audience know who the speaker is, why he or she is speaking, and why this speaker is worth listening to:

> Parents cannot always control their teenagers and the decisions they make. According to Michael DeSisto, counselor and author of the book *Decoding Your Teenager*, "Once the teenage years arrive, parental controls slip away and old sanctions that once constrained unacceptable behavior no longer work."

The tagline provides us with the author's name, Michael DeSisto, so we know who is speaking, and it provides us with his professional credentials (he is an expert in this field of study, a counselor, and the author of a book). Based on this information, Christina's audience will recognize that this is a credible source worthy of their attention. They will also recognize Christina as a credible researcher, and the validity of her ideas will be strengthened.

Reminder

As we covered in Chapters 3, 4, and 5, you must also cite sources of information when you summarize and paraphrase.

Aside from providing a tagline, Christina must also *provide her own commentary— her interpretation or understanding* of the quoted material. She cannot assume that her audience will understand the quotation as she understands it. To avoid confusion and to demonstrate her own understanding, she must always offer a paraphrasing of the quotation:

> Parents cannot always control their teenagers and the decisions they make. Teenagers often do what they want to do and are very stubborn when it comes to following directions or doing what they are told. According to Michael DeSisto, counselor and author of the book *Decoding Your Teenager*, "Once the teenage years arrive, parental controls slip away and old sanctions that once constrained unacceptable behavior no longer work." They are at a stage in their development when they want to assert their independence.

Finally, Christina knows that she must never use a quotation without *explaining its significance in relation to her reason and to the claim she is attempting to prove.* She cannot assume that her audience will automatically understand the importance of the quotation or how it supports her ideas. She must provide an explanation of the thought processes that led her to select the material as support for her argument:

> Parents cannot always control their teenagers and the decisions they make. Teenagers often do what they want to do and are very stubborn when it comes to following directions or doing what they are told. According to Michael DeSisto, counselor and author of the book *Decoding Your Teenager*, "Once the teenage years arrive, parental controls slip away and old sanctions that once constrained unacceptable behavior no longer work." Teens are at a stage in their development when they want to assert their independence. No matter how much their parents try to control or influence their teens' decisions and actions with rules and established consequences for breaking those rules, sometimes rules are not enough. If a teen thinks that a particular rule is unreasonable, he or she may decide to break that rule—regardless of the consequences. For most teens, independence is a number one priority.

After combining her reasoning with a tagline, a quotation, an interpretation of that quotation, and an explanation of how everything connects to her main point, Christina has completed a full thought cycle and is ready to move on to her next point. She is well on her way to developing a convincing argument essay.

Practicum

The time has come for you to create your own argument essay. But you are not alone. You are a member of a community, and the best way to get started in this process is to work together as a part of that community as you begin your essay. This practicum is designed as a class workshop that may take place over the span of one or more class periods.

Pre-Workshop: One-Hour Freewrite.

Find a comfortable place to sit down where you will not be disturbed. Clear your desk of all Quest materials and focus on what you know, what you think, what you feel, and what you have learned this semester. For this portion of the practicum, write nonstop for one full hour.

You have read and studied your event for quite some time. For the most part, you have been pretty quiet—your participation in the conversation has been limited. Now is your chance to speak out. What is it that you want to say? What do *you* believe to be true? What do you want to educate your audience about?

Once you have finished this freewrite, put it down and walk away. Then come back to it and reread it. Somewhere in this writing you will find the beginnings of your claim. Using the guidelines covered in this chapter, create a claim to share with the class. (Your teacher may decide to have you work in small groups rather than as a whole class in order to complete Workshops 1 and 2 in a single class period.)

Workshop 1

As a class, take turns writing your claims on the blackboard. Have your classmates evaluate your claim. Is it clear from your claim that you are arguing to educate your audience? Is your claim clear? Is it concise? Is it balanced in tone? If there are problems with clarity, conciseness, or balance, have your classmates make suggestions to help you reword your claim. Then evaluate the level of controversy surrounding your claim. In terms of your audience, is it mildly controversial? Pretty controversial? Or is it highly controversial? Based on this discussion, you should be able to determine a strategy for developing your argument as either logos-driven, ethos-driven, or pathos-driven.

Workshop 2

At the top of a sheet of paper, write your claim. Then write the question, *Why?* Generate a list of responses to the *because* clause—reasons to explain your claim. Remember to consider your audience (who they are, what they know, what they believe to be true) and the level of controversy while completing this exercise. Once you have a list of three or more reasons, take turns with your classmates writing those reasons on the blackboard. Have your classmates evaluate your reasons and suggest possible organizational patterns. When your classmates have questions you have not addressed in your reasons, have them make suggestions.

Post Workshop: Reason and Support Outline

Now that you have your claim and reasons, go through the sources you collected during Quests Three and Four and locate evidence to use as support. If you need additional evidence, conduct more research (be sure to follow the guidelines for responsible research as covered in Chapters 3 and 4). Make an outline of your organizational pattern, leaving adequate space beneath each reason. Then, as you find evidence you would like to use as support, add it to the outline beneath the appropriate reason.

If you have time, bring your outline to class and share with your classmates. Have them evaluate your evidence and the implicit warrant. Is each piece of evidence from a credible source? Does each piece of evidence directly support your reason and claim? Have classmates make suggestions, when necessary, on ways to strengthen your use of evidence. If you determine that your evidence is not strong enough, go back to your research or go back to the Internet, databases, or library, and continue searching.

Once you have completed this practicum, you are ready to begin writing your argument essay.

WRITING ASSIGNMENT   Quest Six: Advancing an Argument to Educate

Write an essay in which you advance a position on an issue related to your event. Create an argument that will educate your audience about a situation or condition that exists.

Your completed essay should advance a clear, concise claim. It should provide sound reasoning to develop that claim. It should be organized strategically and should provide adequate evidence for each reason (depending on the level of controversy generated by the claim). The evidence provided should be from credible sources and should directly support your reasoning. All information from outside sources should be properly integrated into the body of your text and should be documented according to MLA guidelines. A complete works cited page should follow your essay.

You have already completed several important steps in the process of creating a written argument. You created a freewrite, a claim and reasons outline, and you located evidence to support your reasoning. The next step is drafting.

Making a Rough Draft

Complete a rough draft of your argument paper. This draft should be as close to a finished product as you can produce on your own (that means you should have a thoughtful introduction, clearly organized and developed body paragraphs, a conclusion, and a works cited page).

Peer Review

Bring your rough draft to class for a peer review session. Your instructor will provide guidelines for your comments and suggestions. Remember: Be honest. Your comments are important to the success of your peers' papers.

Revising Your Draft

Study the comments and suggestions made by your peers during peer review, and revise your rough draft. Before handing it in to your instructor for his or her comments and suggestions, color-code your revision:

- Gather a set of three highlight markers, one yellow, one blue, and one orange.
- Highlight your claim in yellow. Write in the margin of your paper: CLAIM.
- Highlight each of your reasons in blue. Write in the margin of your paper beside each reason: REASON.
- Highlight your evidence in orange. Write in the margin of your paper beside each piece of evidence: EVIDENCE. (You may want to simply bracket the ev-

idence in orange rather than highlight all of it. Be sure to include all direct quotations, paraphrased information, and summaries.) Indicate where and how you have shown your audience that your evidence is credible.

Criteria for Evaluating a Successful Argument Essay

For this assignment, you are asked to assert a position on an issue connected to your event and advance that position with a claim, reasoning, and evidence.

- A successful argument essay focuses on the advancement of one claim. That claim must be clear and concise, and must have a balanced tone.
- The purpose of the argument must be clear. In this case, the essay must clearly develop an argument to educate a particular audience about a situation or condition that exists related to an issue and/or event.
- A successful argument essay addresses a specific target audience. It is well developed according to a particular strategy with that audience in mind. It provides logical reasoning and sufficient, typical, accurate, and reliable evidence in support of that reasoning. All evidence is effectively integrated into the text of the essay using a full thought cycle.
- A successful argument essay is organized overall and within paragraphs. It has an interesting introduction that establishes the focus of the essay, and it has an appropriate conclusion.
- A successful argument essay provides correct in-text parenthetical documentation of all sources and a complete and correct works cited page. It is free of grammar and punctuation errors.

In the Spotlight: A Student Model Argument Essay

The Author: Meghal Bhatt

Born in Mumai, India, and raised just outside of Toronto, Canada, Meghal was enrolled in English 1102 during the spring of 2003. His major is mechanical engineering.

Author's Etcetera

Meghal had this to share about his writing experience:

> The essay and the portfolio essentially grew out of the confidence that I had developed over the course of the semester in my own ability to present a strong argument. Reading many articles, penned by experts and opinion casters, had helped me to get completely immersed in the issue of effects of techno culture on adolescents and young adults. Having
> *(continued)*

evaluated all sorts of perspectives, as well as identifying the biases and preconceptions I brought to each, had grounded my argument as a claim of fact and provided me with some great support material that I feel is the strength of this paper: the research process that preceded the actual development and shaping of the paper. By following the process set out by the professor over the course of the semester I felt that the final paper was much more objective and well defined. Following the process helped to curb tendencies to rush into the final paper and inject unsupported personal biases into the same. I have learned through this assignment that the writing process can become a lot easier, fluid, and interesting by engaging in a thorough research process. Great research material not only allows the writer to have several sources to reference from, but also challenges the writer to see what model arguments exist on the subject, and how to break out of the mold and present a unique voice to the readers.

Toys for Boys: The Virtual Reality of the Video Gaming Industry

America's love affair with video games began in the early sixties as young males took to the emerging technology in droves. Small groups of computer enthusiasts, those on the cutting edge of research and development initiatives in Information Technology, and self-styled techno geeks, traded, tweaked and played simple pixel graphics games based on algorithmic mathematical models. Programmers, computer engineers, and those with a flair for technology around the United States began tinkering with existing technologies to create something fun, and challenged their programming abilities, without much care for patents or profits (Van Buren para. 2). The development and pursuit of video games for much of the sixties and seventies was largely conducted in the homes of enthusiasts and research labs of scientists.

This demographic of video gamers changed drastically in the mid eighties when a number of major corporations began adapting sophisticated programming languages, originally developed for expanding computer technology markets in industry, to video games and took advantage of the reduced prices of silicon-based computer moulds to make and market gaming consoles and accessories. The entry of video games in the commercial market was also brought on by the vast potential for expansion that existed. Any home that had a television set and young boys interested in interacting with characters on screen could serve as a target consumer and young boys were definitely the target. The gender bias associated with video and computer games has existed since the initial phase of game activity in the early 1980s, with young males being the targeted market (Ward Gailey 84). Characters in video game releases at the outset, like the immensely profitable *Super Mario Brothers* by Nintendo™, had a cartoony feel, and plot lines designed around tales familiar and interesting for many young boys, stomp over freakish monsters and rescue the fair maiden from the dragon.

The existence of a large potential market and virtually no regulation or rating systems for gaming titles created an ideal economic outlook for game makers and an environment the economist would describe as ripe for perfect competition. The result was that major console manufacturers (Sony, Nintendo, Microsoft, and, Sega) engaged in intense competition for profits, jockeying for market share and third-party developer relationships (Van Buren para. 2). This environment of increasing competition between video game systems continued throughout the nineties and arguably intensified, fueled by extraordinary leaps in computer technology and with computers and televisions becoming mainstays in the modern American home. In order to secure the male gaming market and capture greater market shares major game makers continued to test the limits of visually graphic content and interactive violence that could be packaged into their products. Social science researchers, Derrick Janushewski and Myna Truong, in their paper "Video games and violence," provide a widely accepted definition of violence as being "to cause pain or death onto other beings" (Janushewski 3). The most successful video game releases of the early 1990s can be categorized as violent and were immensely popular with the almost exclusively male gaming community. Games like Rampage, Bionic Commando, Street fighter, Altered Beast, Duck Hunt, and mainstays like Mortal Combat and Legend of Zelda, that still produce profitable releases, were probes that confirmed for game makers that the market responded positively to interactive violence. Experts and gamers alike accept that since their inception most video games have depicted and utilized violent content to cement their position in the gaming markets.

Even the most conservative surveys indicate that gaming markets have grown to encompass a large portion of the American population and are overwhelmingly dominated by males. Dr. van Buren reports that in the year 2000 video games were played by 60% of American residents over six years of age (Van Buren para. 22). The disparity that existed at the outset in terms of the gender-based demographics of gamers has changed slightly over time to include more female gamers, but still young male gamers continue to dominate game purchase decisions. The "Console facts report" in 2002, by the Interactive Digital Software Association, states that females influenced only 25% of console purchase decisions (Console Facts). Another widely recognized report by the Children Now society, titled "Fair Play," concluded that "overall there were very few girl-friendly games . . . most popular video games don't appeal to girls, females don't use power mowers as much as males," further highlighting the disparities. In the words of Sharon Schuster, the President of the American Association of University Women Educational Foundation, "When it comes to computer games and software, girls want high-skill, not high-kill" (Glaubke 7).

The idea of high-kill pioneered in the games of the 1990s gained an added intensity at the eve of the new millennium, through the exponential improvements in computer technology and riding that progressive wave the video gaming industry too has secured a colossal market for its products. Most products of these game makers are largely consumed by and specifically directed towards male gamers, particularly those that depict explicit violence are made graphically attractive making the "virtual" seem virtually real.

For the case against game makers of targeting male gamers with specific products, take the example of the latest industry trends. In a Billboard magazine report on gaming industry trends, columnist and industry analyst Brian Garrity, reports that, "The computer gaming industry generated $10.3 billion [in the year 2002] surpassing the record high of $9.4 billion from the previous year. Unit video game software sales were up were up by 15%, led by titles including: Grand Theft Auto: Vice City, Madden NFL 2003, Halo and Tom Clancy's Splinter Cell" (Garrity 38). In an industry where sales are at an all time high, most of the recognizable popular titles seem to have in common the obvious and exclusive appeal to male gamers. Three out of the top four share (not including Madden NFL and steering clear from the hotly debated topic of the violent nature of football) a particular genre, Action based first person shooters (FPS), modeled around an unchanged formula of the early gaming greats like Doom, Quake and Duke Nukem. The list goes on to include Command and Conquer: Tiberian Sun, Hitman-2, and other FPS clones. In an article, "A room full of Doom," published in *Time* magazine, journalist David S. Jackson reports about his experience at the Electronic Entertainment Expo '99, just months after Columbine, "If the gamemakers wouldn't defend their industry, their customers were happy to try," and cites candid conversations with gamers like Paul Good, 30, a visual artist and avid gamer, who says, "When the world p——— you off and you need a place to vent Quake is a great place for it. You can kill somebody and watch the blood run down the walls, and it feels good" (Jackson 65). Facts, figures and frank admissions by experts, analysts and gamers alike overwhelmingly indicate that the gaming industry caters FPS games specifically for the male gamer.

Even more evidence for this directed approach of game makers of FPS games comes from analyzing the content, in particular the characters involved in game play. In almost all FPS games, the gamer controls male characters that exude machismo and the handful of playable female characters and virtually all non-playable female characters serve as cinematic props to satisfy the sexual fantasies of young males. The Fair Play report indicates that both male and female characters were stereotypically hypersexualized, with 20% of females being fitted in to voluptuous, unrealistic and disproportionate body types and one in three male characters shown as extremely muscular. The report also indicates that female sexuality was often accentuated with highly revealing clothing and males were shown to be highly aggressive and dominant (Glaubke 4). The use of traditionally accepted behavioral and sexual tendencies of both genders incites increased participation from males in FPS gaming and also indicates the gaming industries awareness of and tremendous success with this approach.

In addition to capitalizing on expected male behavioral tendencies, another lure of video gaming has been the stunningly real graphics of the games. Complex gaming systems bring previously unknown levels of interactivity and literally expand the realm of possibilities for the gamer. Coupled together, the graphics and added interactivity are a major cause for the tremendous success of video games in recent times, in comparison to other educational and entertainment pursuits available as alternatives.

One of the gamers I interviewed in preparation for this article was Parth Desouza. While Parth's virtual character lay imprisoned in a military brig for ten excruciating minutes, obscenities seemed to be spewing out of him like rainfall in the Cherapungi, and his fingers twitched frantically on the disabled controller to induce the slightest movement on the screen. "I hate it when this happens," howled twenty-year-old Parth, "I thought I had disabled this feature."

Inquiring further about the course of action that had led Parth's virtual character to be placed "behind bars" on screen and disabled his controller for a few minutes, the explanation I heard was: "I basically tossed a frag [fragmentation] grenade into a group of friendly units defending our forward position. It was a mistake! I am still learning the controls, but Command and Conquer penalizes you for that!" Still fresh in my mind are news from just two days ago in Kuwait, where over the course of the war campaign on Iraq, Sgt. Hasan Akbar had been charged for tossing a grenade into a tent full of sleeping marines that had resulted in the death of two officers and wounded fourteen others (www.cnn.com). Here was a game, Command and Conquer: Tiberian Sun, which had the capacity to allow the gamer control of fighting men, reenacting battles of present, past and future, and also had the virtual capability of allowing dangerous situations to play out in the realm of virtual reality. The games of today can mimic life and even generate true to life situations with the greatest of ease.

The sophisticated graphics and added interactivity are often combined easily with behavioral tendencies to produce an even greater "gaming experience" and hook the gamer. Take the case of the most popular game on *Billboard*'s "Top Video Games" list: Grand Theft Auto: Vice City. Most parents detest the game and have trouble coming to terms with it having only a 17+ rating. Lauren Sandler, a writer for the reputable *New Republic Magazine,* calls it a "partner in misogyny in the world of video play" (Sandler 7). In a statement published Connecticut Sen. Joseph Lieberman stated with much concern: "Games like 'Grand Theft Auto' are particularly troubling because they go beyond celebrating violence generally and actually reward players for engaging in organized crime, murdering innocent people and other forms of perverse, antisocial behavior" (Leland). The cautionary words of the good Senator and outspoken critics are wasted on the young fellas that chose to go out and buy the game, catapulting its sales to new records since its release in the last quarter of 2002.

One such avid gamer I met engaging in an adventure in the virtual realm was Jay McCwen, a sixteen-year-old high school junior. Jay sped expertly around the crowded virtual streets of "Vice City" in his speedster, raking in every possible point he could for hit-and-run maneuvers on helpless pedestrians. The tally of points in the far corner continued to increase, like jackpot tickers in a Las Vegas casino, as more and more bloodied virtual bodies lay strewn across the television screen. He paused the game for just a minute to grab a sip of his cola and a bite out of the microwave snack. I peered intently at the pixel graphic snapshot on screen and admired the skill of the graphics designers who had created the stunning visual.

As a testament to the attention to detail of the game's programmers, on the corpse-littered virtual street one of the meticulously animated bodies carried a leather satchel and a cell phone, immediately recognizable as a downtown businessman. Within seconds the snack was finished, the carnage resumed once more and Jay sunk back into his virtual world. Into a place here he could banish morality, forego thinking about the repercussions of his actions, and merely focus on maxing out the points tally. Beside him lay the cover of the video game, Playstation II's Grand Theft Auto: Vice City, rated M for mature (17+).

Hold on just one moment. Jay is sixteen, the game is rated M. And M means for mature individuals 17 years of age and older. So how did he get access to it? According to an investigation conducted under the auspices of Ohio Attorney General Betty Montgomery, children of state employees were sent out to purchase restricted video game titles at major retailers (like Kmart, Target, Blockbuster, Hollywood Video, Meijer, Media Play, Best Buy and Wal-mart) to test enforcement of policies that prohibit sale of gaming titles marked with an M to minors. Andrew Welsh-Higgins, in his article "Buying violent video games is child's play," written to report on the investigations findings states, "Children as young as 7 brought the games without being challenged 22 times out of the 28 attempts" (Welsh Higgins 4). To my surprise and dismay, investigating existing rating and enforcement systems for restricted gaming titles further led me to discover that the Entertainment Software Rating Board (ESRB), the agency that puts the ratings on these games, functions only as advisory board and not an enforcement agency. In other words, the game ratings are meant to function only as cautions for consumers and retailers, intended to sway market response away from buying FPS titles marked M and theoretically put a dent in earnings for the game makers. Chances are unless the teen encounters a concerned clerk or visits the store with informed parents, he will probably not be carded before making the purchase. Jay looks every bit the average pre-teen, and if I must admit, not too "mature." Maybe he played the odds and succeeded; at 22 of 28 they are certainly in his favor.

FPS Video games are fast becoming staples in the modern American home, where young males like Parth and Jay, self-professed avid gamers, are being specifically targeted for consumption by makers of video games. History, market forces, lack of regulation and the gamers own inherent behavioral patterns clearly form too strong a wall for any change to take place in this pattern. For now, expect little change in policy or practices of game makers or in the coming years listing of the top video games. All indications are that the lions share of the gaming products will utilize visually violent, three dimensionally animated, seemingly real interactive FPS titles to entice their predominantly male clientele.

Works Cited

"Console Facts." Interactive Digital Software Association. 2001 survey. IDSA. February 6, 2002. http://www.idsa.com/consolefacts.html.

DeSouza, Parth. Personal Interview. 13 Apr 2003.

Garrity, Brian. "Gaming sales lost 10% last year." *Billboard Magazine* 115.38 (2003).

Glaubke, Christina R. et al. "Fair Play? Violence, Gender and Race in Video Games." *Children Now.* December 2001. 11 March 2003. http://www.childrennow.org/media/video-games/2001/.

Jackson, David S. "A room full of Doom." *Time Magazine.* 153 (1999): 65–67.

Janushewski, Derrick and Truong, Myna. "Video games and Violence." Fall 1999. McMaster University. 18 March 2003. <http://www.socsci.mcmaster.ca/soc/courses/stpp4C03/ClassEssay/videogames.htm#6>.

Leland, John. "Bigger, Bolder, Faster, Weirder." *The New York Times.* October, 27, 2002. April, 13, 2003. <http://www.nytimes.com/2002/10/27/fashion/27GRAN.html?ex=1119067200&en=76362abfb6273e33&ei=5070&oref=login>.

McEwen, Jay. Personal Interview. 12 Apr 2003.

Sandler, Lauren. "Game Boy." *The New Republic.* 227:7 (2003).

Van Buren, Cassandra. "Video Games." March 2002. Technology Futures Inc. 12 March 2003. <http://www.tfi.com/pubs/videogames.html>.

Ward Gailey, Christine. "Mediated Messages: Gender, Class and Cosmos in Home Video Games." *Journal of Popular Culture.* Volume 27 (1993): 81–97.

Welsh Higgins, Andrew. "Buying video games is child's play." December 2000. *The Cincinnati Enquirer.* 14 March 2003. <http://enquirer.com/editions/200/12/13/loc_buying_violent_video.html>.

Practicum

How does Meghal's model fulfill the criteria for a successful argument essay? Write a brief evaluation. Refer to specific examples from the text of his essay to support your evaluation. Consider Meghal's strategy for communicating with his imagined audience: *parents of children and young teens.* Why did he begin with an informative overview of the history of video games? Why did he wait until the fifth paragraph to directly state his claim? Why did he end his essay with narratives about Parth and Jay? Share your responses with your classmates. Do you find that you and your classmates agree? Disagree?

Reflection in Action

You have spent many weeks researching an issue. You began by looking at an event and an issue that came out of the talk surrounding that event. You focused on one issue and became a sort of quasi-expert on that issue. Now that you have joined the official conversation, looking back, what can you say about the experience? How did the earlier Quests prepare you to make your own argument? What do you feel your argument contributes to the official conversation on your issue?

Who was the intended audience for your essay? How did that audience shape the development of your essay? Was your essay logos-driven, ethos-driven, or pathos-driven? How would a different audience have changed the development of your argument? Select another potential audience and describe how you would present your claim to that audience and why. What changes would you make?

Expanding Your Vision: A Multimedia Assignment Option

Critical Inquiry: Digging Deeper

One of the most common arenas for public argument is the courtroom. Many court cases argue to educate a jury regarding a situation or condition—the guilt or innocence of a particular person in the commission of a crime.

Have you ever witnessed or participated in a court case? What do you know about arguments in court? How are claims presented? How are reasons and evidence offered and substantiated? Are courtroom cases logos-, ethos-, or pathos driven? Can you think of any specific examples of high-profile cases you have followed in the media or watched on television?

Take a moment to write down what you know about argumentation in a court of law. Then consider the following questions: If your argument were to be presented in this format, how would that work? Are you aware of any real-life court cases connected to your issue? If so, what do you know about them? Outline your argument in terms of defense, prosecution, and witness testimony. Share your ideas with the class.

MULTIMEDIA ASSIGNMENT   Visi-Quest Six: Expanding Your Vision with a Courtroom Drama

For this assignment, you will create a class court and put some aspect of an issue related to your event on trial.

Step One

Divide the class into teams based on events. As a group, generate a list of claims and narrow your selection down to one claim that puts an issue on trial as guilty and a rebuttal claim that argues the same issue is not guilty (for instance, the "Columbine" group may decide to focus on the claim that obscene lyrics are responsible for influencing youth to commit violent actions, so the rebuttal claim would be that obscene lyrics do not influence youth to commit violent actions).

Step Two

Each team should divide into three groups. One group will represent the prosecution and adopt the "guilty" claim. One group will represent the defense and adopt the "not guilty" claim. The third group will be the jury and decide on a set of criteria for judging the effectiveness of an argument. Each group must then work to plan the presentation of its case. Each group must be prepared to provide reasoning and to present evidence from "expert witnesses" who will testify at the trial (taken from the research gathered during Quests Three, Four, and Six). Groups should decide on a primary spokesperson and witnesses. Each group should rehearse its arguments in advance of the trial.

Step Three

Place the issue on trial. Following a traditional court/debate format, the jury will present its criteria and establish rules that the prosecution and defense must follow. Then both the prosecution and the defense will present opening statements. The prosecution will present its case first, followed by the defense. Both sides will present closing arguments, and the jury will deliberate and decide who presented the most convincing argument. The jury will announce its verdict to the class, and an open discussion may follow.

Criteria for a Successful Courtroom Drama

For this assignment, you are asked to work in groups to present an argument using a legal courtroom format. You must work together with your classmates to decide on an argument. Then your group must select a prosecution team, a defense team, and a jury. Each team must work together to complete specific duties. Then the group must present its case to the class. A successful courtroom drama meets the following criteria:

Groups

- Will work together cooperatively and each individual will participate equally in all aspects of this assignment.
- Will complete all aspects of the assignment thoroughly and in a timely manner.

Presentation

- Following a traditional legal courtroom format, each team will present a clear claim, logical reasoning, and supporting evidence from expert witnesses.
- Expertise and credentials of witnesses will be clearly stated.
- Reasoning will be clearly explained.
- Evidence will fulfill STAR criteria.
- Each team will present a compelling introduction.
- Each team will present a compelling conclusion.
- The jury team will provide a set of criteria before the presentation begins.

○ The jury will evaluate the presentation according to that criteria and will announce and explain its judgment, offering specific examples from the trial. (Note: The jury's verdict will not influence the evaluation of this assignment.)

Note

Because of the interactive nature of this assignment, it was difficult to provide a clear and useful model in print form for this textbook; therefore, there is not a Visi-Quest Six included in this chapter.

7

Arguing to Instigate Change: Advancing a Call for Action

Begin with a *Question*: How Can We Change Things?

> The important thing is this:
> To be able at any moment to sacrifice what we are for what we could become.
>
> —*Charles DuBois*

In the 1990s, there was a very popular television program starring Tim Allen called *Home Improvement*. The lead character, Tim "The Tool Man" Taylor, was big on fixing things. His efforts to change his world—to add "more power!"—were often misguided and comical, but there was more to this character than comedy. In the midst of all of the hijinks and silliness, the exploding kitchen devices and droopy, toolbelt-heavy jeans, something admirable, maybe even amazing, was happening.

Day in and day out, season after television season, regardless of the problems he faced, Tim Taylor looked at the world around him with imaginative eyes and always sought ways to make it better. Yes, it is true that many (if not most) times his efforts at improvement went comically awry, but he never gave up. He never lost his vision for change.

Though it might seem strange to philosophize about a television character, the determination and vision demonstrated by the character of Tim Taylor are lessons we can all learn from:

○ Never give up.
○ We do not have to accept things as they are.
○ Always look for a better way.

We can also learn from Tim's mistakes. Tim Taylor was often impulsive. He did not take the time to think his ideas through; he did not have a plan—he just took action. But if we want to bring real and lasting change to our world, we have to have a plan.

How Change Happens

Imagine that you are at home in your bedroom; you are sitting on the floor, relaxing, watching television. You wiggle around, shifting side to side. You are not very comfortable, but you are watching a great movie. You look to your left, and there is your bed. Your big, comfortable bed with the big, fluffy pillows and the nice, soft blankets. You look back at the television set. Too bad you cannot see the TV from your bed; that would be a much more comfortable viewing space. What were you thinking, anyway, when you arranged your room this way? You certainly were not thinking about the best setup for watching TV.

During a commercial break, you spend some time looking around your room and it occurs to you: if you move your bed to the other side of the room and then put your television set on top of the bookcase, you could sit in your big, comfortable bed with the big, fluffy pillows and the nice, soft blankets, and you could watch TV without getting a cramp in your neck! What a great plan! But the bed is heavy. If you try moving it yourself, you will probably scratch the floor, and your landlord would not be happy about that. You need someone to help you, so you decide to give your neighbor a call. You tell him what you plan to do, and he gladly offers to help you make these changes to your room.

This is an example of how change happens in everyday life. We experience an uncomfortable situation, identify the problem, come up with a solution to that problem, make a plan for change, and, if necessary, enlist the help of others to make that change happen. This is a process we go through regularly. It is so natural for us that we do not really think about it as a process at all. We just do it. We make changes to improve our lives. It is simple. So, if change is so easy and so natural for us, why is it so difficult for us as a people, as society, to make changes when it comes to social problems? What would happen if we applied the same process or processes we use to make changes and improvements in our personal lives to larger social problems?

> Some men see things as they are and say, "Why?"
> I dream of things that never were and say, "Why not?"
>
> —*George Bernard Shaw*

Thinking Globally; Acting Locally

We began this semester by talking about the importance of critical and civic literacy. Everything you have studied to this point, all of the assignments you have created, have helped you to develop the skills and strategies necessary to live a critically and civically literate life. The next step in this journey is to take action, to use all of the information you have gathered and the ideas you have developed, and formulate a plan to instigate a positive change in the world.

For some time now, you have been studying an event and one or more social problems or issues related to that event. You understand the situation, and you have identified a particular problem within that situation. You are already halfway through the process! Now you have to take the next step (and you may have already begun this part of the process, as well). You have to come up with a solution to the problem or to some aspect of the problem. Just as you must when dealing with a small change such as the arrangement of your bedroom, when dealing with change on a larger scale, such as a social problem, you must focus in on a reasonable response to the problem.

The response in our example was to make a plan and enlist the help of a neighbor to enact that plan, but that was not the only possible (or likely) response to the problem. In a similar situation, you could simply get up, turn off the TV, and walk out. You could decide not to watch the movie because you are so uncomfortable, but to go out and do something else. That response would provide a temporary solution to the problem, but the next time you wanted to watch TV, you would be faced with the same situation again. Or, you could look around your room and decide, *I don't like this room, I want to move.* That would be a solution to the problem, too, though not a very reasonable one. You cannot up and move every time you feel uncomfortable. But these are responses we see on a larger scale all the time. People identify a problem and then walk away from it, ignore it, and come back to face it again and again without making any changes. Or, they identify a problem and go on with their lives, leaving it behind, unaddressed, thinking, "That is someone else's situation to deal with; I have moved on."

The key to making change happen is to think logically about the problem, to study and inventory your available resources, to think creatively about how those resources might be used to solve the problem, then to make a focused, logical plan of action. But even the best plans cannot be enacted without a little help. Just as in our example with the bedroom, once you have thought your plan through thoroughly, you have to share your plan with other people. Most often, that communication takes the form of a proposal.

Proposals for Change

Proposals are a specialized form of communication designed to bring about change. They are a form of argumentation, perhaps the most difficult and demanding kinds of arguments to make.

In our daily lives, we make casual proposals all the time. We walk around saying things like, "you should," "they need to," or "we ought to," without giving the whole process much thought. But when we seriously want to bring about some sort of change, we must survey the situation and come up with a strategy and a solid plan before we make a proposal. For instance, say you would like to ask your boss for a raise. You would not simply walk into her office and say, "You should give me a raise." You would think about the best, most reasonable approach to take with your boss, the strategy most likely to convince her that you *do* need and deserve a raise; then you would present your proposal in just the right time and place to—hopefully—bring about the results you desire (more money). The same is true when making a proposal related to a social problem.

When making a formal proposal (most often in writing), you have to pull out all the stops and utilize every strategy available to you.

- You must make a claim (tell your audience what needs to be changed).
- You must provide reasoning for that change (explain why a change needs to happen).
- You must provide evidence as support for your reasoning (show proof that a change is needed).
- You must provide a plan of action (detail what needs to be done in response to the problem).
- You must convince your audience that your plan will work (explain how your plan solves the problem).

Whereas most arguments are driven by one persuasive element (though all three elements are often present to one extent or another), proposals are *driven by all three persuasive elements:* logos, ethos, and pathos. The success of your proposal depends on your demonstration of logical reasoning, credibility, and an emotional connection with your audience: it must appeal to their needs and values.

In the real world, most proposals addressing social problems are generated by nonprofit organizations in order to garner financial support (legally, a nonprofit organization is one that serves the public interest without declaring a profit). These proposals are detailed plans for projects, also called *campaigns,* which typically have one (or more) of the following three purposes:

- to inform and educate
- to change public thoughts and feelings about an issue or problem
- to motivate behavior

The audience for a campaign may vary but is ultimately what determines the content and structure of a campaign.

Practicum

Take a look at the campaigns in the following text (you may want to review the elements of multimedia arguments covered in the Chapter 5, Visi-Quest). Analyze them for claim, reasons, and evidence. Speculate on the purpose of each campaign and the intended audience. Examine the warrants behind each.

Utilizing words and images, how do these campaigns instigate change? Do they inform? Do they instigate change in thoughts and feelings? Do they motivate behavior?

Discuss your responses to these questions in small groups.

Mad Libs

The Author: The Ad Council and U.S. Department of Homeland Security

According to the Ad Council and the U.S. Department of Homeland Security, numerous strides have been made in the area of preparedness. The percentage of parents who stocked emergency supplies to prepare for a possible terrorist attack has increased significantly and the proportion of parents who have created a family communications plan has increased. However, despite these remarkable results, most Americans have still not taken basic steps to prepare.

In order to continue to encourage all Americans to prepare themselves, their families and their communities, the U.S. Department of Homeland Security has sponsored new public service advertisements that empower Americans to prepare for and respond to potential terrorist attacks and other emergencies. The following is one of several new advertisements focusing specifically on encouraging parents to develop a family communications plan.

Leave Me Alone

The Author: Office of National Drug Control Policy, National Youth Anti-Drug Media Campaign

With overwhelming bipartisan Congressional support, in 1998, the White House Office of National Drug Control Policy (ONDCP) launched a historic initiative to encourage kids to stay drug-free. The campaign targets youth ages 9 to 18, especially vulnerable middle-school adolescents, their parents, and other adults who influence the choices young people make.

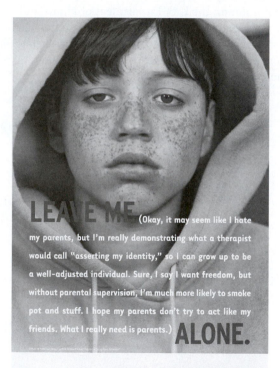

Text: LEAVE ME (Okay, it may seem like I hate my parents, but I'm really demonstrating what a therapist would call "asserting my identity," so I can grow up to be a well-adjusted individual. Sure, I say I want freedom, but without parental supervision, I'm much more likely to smoke pot and stuff. I hope my parents don't try to act like my friends. What I really need is parents.) ALONE.

To get the word out across every economic and cultural boundary, the campaign uses a mix of modern communications techniques—from advertising and public relations to Interactive media—and all possible venues—from television programs to after-school activities—to educate and empower young people to reject illicit drugs. The campaign also teams up with civic and nonprofit organizations, faith-based groups, and private corporations to enlist and engage people in prevention efforts at school, at work, and at play.

If You Don't Vote, You Don't Count

The Author: Drum Major Institute Organization

Originally called the Drum Major Foundation, DMI was founded by Harry Wachtel, lawyer and advisor to Rev. Dr. Martin Luther King Jr. during the turbulent years of the civil rights movement. DMI was relaunched in 1999 by New York attorney Bill Wachtel, Harry's son, and Martin Luther King III. Today, led by President Fernando Ferrer (former borough president of the Bronx, New York City Council Member, and candidate for mayor of New York City), DMI is committed to adding a strong progressive voice to compete in the marketplace of ideas.

The Ad Council officially endorsed the following campaign created by DMI to increase voter turnout: "If you don't vote, you don't count." The PSA ran on twenty-three network-affiliated television stations, reaching four million homes across the United States in the two weeks leading up to the November elections. A print version ran on the side of 120 public telephone kiosks throughout New York City as well.

Author's Etcetera

Andrea Batista Schlesinger, executive director for DMI, had this to say about the organization's mission:

> Thanks for the opportunity to talk about DMI. Our mission statement is as follows—anything you want to pick out would be great:

> The Drum Major Institute for Public Policy is a non-partisan, non-profit organization dedicated to challenging the tired orthodoxies of both the right and the left. The goal: progressive public policy for social and economic fairness. DMI's approach is unwavering: We do not issue reports to see our name in print or hold forums for the sake of mere talk. We seek to change policy by conducting research into overlooked but important social and economic issues, by leveraging our strategic relationships to engage policymakers and opinion leaders in our work, and by offering platforms to amplify the ideas of those who are working for social and economic fairness.

He paid the ultimate price to win
our right to vote.

Are you going to give that right away?

If you
don't vote,
you don't count.

DRUM
MAJOR
INSTITUTE FOR PUBLIC POLICY

Keeping the dream alive   drummajorinstitute.org

Get Ready Now

The Author: The Office of Homeland Security and the Ad Council

The creation of the Department of Homeland Security (DHS) is the most significant transformation of the U.S. government since 1947, when Harry S Truman merged the various branches of the U.S. Armed Forces into the Department of Defense to better coordinate the nation's defense against military threats.

DHS represents a similar consolidation, both in style and substance. In the aftermath of the terrorist attacks against America on September 11, 2001, President George W. Bush decided that twenty-two previously disparate domestic agencies needed to be coordinated into one department to protect the nation against threats to the homeland. The new department's first priority is to protect the nation against further terrorist attacks. Component agencies analyze threats and intelligence, guard our borders and airports, protect our critical infrastructure, and coordinate the response of our nation for future emergencies.

Besides providing a better-coordinated defense of the homeland, DHS is also dedicated to protecting the rights of American citizens and enhancing public services, such as natural disaster assistance and citizenship services, by dedicating offices to these important missions.

Text: "After a terrorist attack your first instinct may be to run. That may be the worst thing you could do." Mario Polis, Firefighter, Ladder 106, FDNY. Knowing what you should do in a terrorist attack isn't just a matter of common sense. It takes some reading, some learning and some planning. That goes for people who live in small communities, too. Readiness is for every American family, business and school. The terrorist threat is real and we can't afford to go unprepared. Learn to put together an emergency supply kit, how to make a family communication plan, and how you should respond to an act of terror. All of that information is clearly explained at www.ready.gov. If you prefer, you can call 1-800-BE-READY (1-800-237-3239) for a free copy of the brochure, Preparing Makes Sense. Get Ready Now.

In the wake of September 11, the American public is fearful of terrorist attacks, but there is a distinct lack of knowledge about what to do in the likely event of future emergencies. To address this information gap, the Department of Homeland Security sponsored a public education media campaign that will empower American citizens to prepare for and respond to emergencies including natural disasters and potential terrorist attacks. The campaign provides individuals with specific actions they can take to protect themselves and their families, through multimedia public service advertising informational materials (fulfillment) and public relations efforts.

The print advertisement on p. 225 was a part of this campaign when it was launched in February 2003.

The universe is transformation; our life is what our thoughts make it.

—*Marcus Aurelius*

Tools for Success: Proposing a Plan for Change

You have probably heard the saying, "Don't rock the boat." In general, folks will do almost anything to maintain the status quo. This is not so hard to understand. We humans desire peace and tranquility in our lives, and we like to know what to expect. Sometimes it is easier to put up with a less-than-ideal situation than to deal with the consequences of change, even if that change is for the better. We have been talking about this in one way or another all semester. We recognize that there are problems in our society, we even talk about those problems, but we rarely *do* anything to make a change. We rarely take action.

Change is difficult. Deciding what needs to be changed is often a challenge, but even when we have a pretty good idea of *what* to change, planning *how* to make that change happen and *getting support* from other people to *implement* (and follow through on) a *plan for change*—well, that is where the real challenge lies.

Proposing a change requires a great deal of planning, strategy, and finesse. As you know, a proposal is an argument to instigate change—the most difficult kind of argument to make with any success. Just as you do for any other argument, to make a proposal, you must have a clear purpose and you must know your audience. You must make a claim and provide logical reasoning to explain the claim and evidence in support of that reasoning. You must utilize the three persuasive elements of strategy as you build your argument: logos, ethos, and pathos. That seems like a tall order to fill! And it *is*—tough, but it is not impossible. If we are ever going to make our world a better place and truly address the social problems we have been studying, persuasion is a necessary skill that we *all* need to develop.

When addressing social problems, many different kinds of proposals are made with many different purposes, but no matter what the specific purpose, *a proposal always recommends that a plan for change be put into action.* Sometimes that plan is to *educate,* to make a particular audience more informed about a situation or condition. Sometimes it may be to *develop community-based programs,* or sometimes a plan may be intended to *change laws* at the federal, state, or local levels. These are just a few examples; there are countless other types of proposals with a multitude of purposes. The campaigns included in this chapter, for instance, focus on providing information. They are Public Service Announcements (PSAs) created with the assumption that education is the first step toward enacting change. Each PSA that you analyzed in this chapter is a campaign for social change that began with a written proposal.

PSAs are commonly known as advertisements that serve the public interest. A PSA is a proposal-in-action, *instigating change by educating the public.* In terms of proposal-generated projects, PSAs are unique in that they typically address *individuals* in a community as agents for change. PSAs often are aired through television or radio broadcasts, but many are also distributed through print media and electronically (via Web sites).

For the remainder of this chapter, we focus our attention on this specialized form of problem solving and the proposals that generate support for them.

To Serve the Public's Interest

PSAs focus on one or more of the following: to inform, to change thoughts or feelings on an issue, or to motivate behavior. They typically answer the questions, *What does this have to do with me? Why should I care? What can I do? How can I get involved?*

Before the PSAs in this textbook were created and put into action, someone somewhere, probably an employee working for a nonprofit organization, recognized a social problem and came up with an idea to address that problem—in this case, a PSA to educate and motivate a particular audience. He or she then wrote a formal proposal and submitted it to someone within an organization to garner support (financial and/or creative) for the development of the PSA. The initial proposal was an argument that told a particular audience: "This problem exists in society; here is a way to address the problem; this is what we need to do and how we need to do it; these are the outcomes we can expect."

Based on the effectiveness of the argument presented in the original proposal, the logic of the plan, the credibility of the supporting evidence, and the strength of the emotional appeal, someone made the decision to support the production of each PSA we have seen. The key to putting a good idea into action was a convincing proposal.

Qualities of a Successful Campaign

Proposals for campaigns addressing social problems are adopted or rejected based on the potential effectiveness of the campaign. Not every campaign proves to be successful. Before you write a proposal for a campaign, you need to have a clear understanding of what makes a successful PSA.

In terms of PSAs, how do we determine whether or not a proposed campaign is worth pursuing? It is useful to understand the *qualities* of an effective PSA campaign:

- As with any argument, a successful campaign should have a *clearly defined purpose:* to inform, to challenge thoughts and feelings about an issue, and/or to motivate behavior. A PSA often does all of these things, but one or the other is the ultimate guiding purpose.
- A successful campaign should *address a clearly defined audience.* Remember, a PSA is a form of communication, and as with any type of argument, the audience largely determines the strategy used to create the proposed campaign.
- A successful campaign should *clearly communicate one idea* (that is, the claim). This idea may be directly stated, or it may be implied.
- A successful campaign should *provide logical reasoning* that answers the *why* or *how* questions a claim raises. These reasons may be communicated visually, with text, or through audio. Sometimes reasons are implied—made through association (for instance, we might hear "The Star Spangled Banner" playing in the background of a radio PSA; we associate this song with patriotism, so hearing it may remind us indirectly that we should take a particular action because it is our duty as American citizens).
- A successful campaign should *provide support for reasoning,* and because a PSA is limited in terms of available space, it may offer links (addresses, phone numbers, Web sites, contact names) for more supporting information. This supporting information should establish credibility for the campaign, and it may be provided in the form of visual imagery, text, or, when appropriate, audio.
- A successful campaign should *appeal to an audience's needs and values* in an honest way. Appeals should not be manipulative or heavy-handed. The purpose of an appeal is to establish an emotional connection with the audience. Whereas with commercial advertisements, an audience is being sold a tangible good or service, with a PSA, it is being sold on an idea or ideal, and the emotional connection replaces the tangible item or service that the audience gets from buying into the campaign. Appeals may be accomplished through visual imagery, text, or audio.
- Format and construction of the PSA should be high quality, imaginative, and attractive to the audience.

Before moving on, let's take a closer look at a way of understanding emotional appeals.

When discussing an appeal to needs, we often reference the hierarchy of needs established by Abraham Maslow, a humanist psychologist. Maslow described personality through a hierarchic theory of needs, which has five levels:

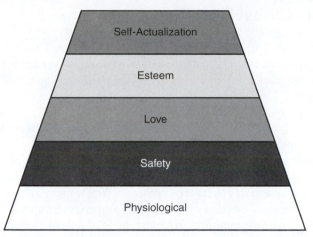

The bottom level, physiological needs, includes the most basic elements necessary for our survival as humans (food, water, shelter, sex for continuation of the human species). The second level, safety, addresses our need to live in a safe environment, healthy and free from harm. The third level, love, addresses our need for loving relationships with other people, companionship, friendship, our love for our family and our children, as well as romantic love. The fourth level, esteem, deals with our need to feel good about who we are, our desire for acknowledgment from outside sources that we are successful, and our emotional esteem. The fifth level, self-actualization, concerns a higher level of consciousness, a spiritual enlightenment and fulfillment.

We use this hierarchy to help us understand what humans need and where we place the most value. In terms of argument and persuasion, when we appeal to an audience's need, we establish an emotional connection with the audience because these basic needs are common to all people. If an audience has a need, it will value whatever helps in meeting that need. If audience members need food to satisfy a physiological need, they will value someone who feeds them. If they need to feel good about themselves, they will value a service that helps them to do that.

It is important to recognize that if our most basic needs are not being met, if we are hungry or live in an unsafe environment, we will not be concerned with issues of self-esteem or "being all we can be." Our most basic needs must be met before our concerns advance in the hierarchy.

Making a Proposal

In order to succeed, a proposal must convince the audience of two things: that a problem or need of significant magnitude exists and that the author of the proposal has the means and imagination to solve the problem or meet the need. Many organizations have their own guidelines for formatting proposals, but for the most part, proposals follow a similar pattern of organization and development.

Arguing for Change Walk-Through

A proposal typically begins with a clear *statement of purpose*. This is very similar to the claim in any argument. The statement of purpose explains *what you are trying to prove* (in this case, that you have a plan to address a situation or condition that is in need of change).

Let's say you have spent the last few months researching the causes and effects of bullying. Through your research, you discovered a fair amount of evidence that involvement in some sort of structured physical activity—such as Tae Kwon Do—improves self-esteem in adolescents and lessens the negative effects of bullying. You believe that participation in Tae Kwon Do classes is a good way to address the social problem of bullying and its effects on adolescents. You want to inform the public of your discoveries in the hopes that you will motivate them to involve their children in Tae Kwon Do (or a similar activity). Your statement of purpose might be:

> In order to foster the development of self-esteem and positive peer relationships, I propose the development of a public service announcement campaign geared toward troubled adolescents and their parents that informs them of the positive benefits of studying Tae Kwon Do.

Following a statement of purpose, a proposal provides *background information* about the author (who he or she is, what the author knows about the social problem, why he or she is qualified to address the problem, and information about his or her training or background). Because a background statement establishes your credibility, you must provide details about your experience related to the social problem you are attempting to address. You may provide details regarding your education. For instance,

> I am a student at a major U.S. university, and, following rigid academic guidelines, I have just completed a thorough investigation into the social problem of bullying. I have conducted research on the history of bullying and its causes and effects.

You may provide details regarding your own expertise with Tae Kwon Do:

> My friends and I have studied Tae Kwon Do for seven years at the Trinity Tae Kwon Do Martial Arts Academy, and I have earned a second-degree black belt. I have won several awards at local and regional martial arts competitions, including the Chevalier Martial Arts Competition where I received a gold medal in kumite in the women's 18- to 34-year-old intermediate division.

You may provide details regarding your experience working with children and adolescents in a structured environment:

> I have worked with children through various church organizations over the past five years (including Sunday School at First United Methodist Church and the Youth Group and Choir), and I have worked for two summers as a camp counselor for a local youth retreat, Camp Thunder.

All of this is the type of information you should include in a background statement. Such information qualifies you as someone who is educated through research and experience to address this particular social problem.

A proposal then provides a *problem statement* or *needs assessment* (details regarding what the problem is and why help is needed). This critically important section of a proposal is similar to other types of written arguments in that you are establishing the reasoning behind your claim. As with any argument, each reason must be supported by credible evidence. This evidence should meet STAR criteria; it should be sufficient to demonstrate that a problem or need exists; it should be typical, accurate, and reliable; and it should clearly illustrate the exigency of the problem.

Let's say that through your research into the social problem of bullying, you have gathered evidence that *bullying is a problem many adolescents face.* You have statistical data to offer as support. You also have expert testimony from notable child psychologists that a negative result of bullying is low self-esteem. This becomes your formal problem statement.

You have gathered statements from experts (as well as statistical data from scientific studies) that kids with low self-esteem are more likely to experiment with drugs, to do poorly in school, to have difficulties developing healthy peer relationships, and to consider suicide. These same experts claim that kids with self-esteem problems need outside intervention in order to raise their self-esteem.

Additionally, you have gathered evidence from a few long-term studies that shows involvement in some form of structured physical activity raises self-esteem in adolescents and counteracts the effects of bullying. Tae Kwon Do is a structured physical activity that many youth enjoy. Therefore, you believe that participating in Tae Kwon Do with a group of peers might raise the self-esteem of troubled adolescents and counteract the negative effects of bullying.

This expert testimony and evidence forms your needs assessment—clearly this is a problem in need of a solution. This is the reasoning behind your claim. You have information from objective, credible sources to support each reason.

A proposal then clearly states the *objectives of the project* (what the project hopes to achieve). This section of the proposal is a concise description of the project's purpose and how that purpose addresses a target audience.

Because your proposal is for the production and distribution of a PSA campaign, the objectives of the project are

1. to inform adolescents and their parents that there are steps they can take to raise self-esteem.
2. to convince adolescents and their parents of the positive benefits of participating in a structured activity such as Tae Kwon Do.
3. to motivate adolescents to try Tae Kwon Do.

You have evidence that your target audience typically enjoys structured interaction with peers in an emotionally neutral environment (evidence that you provide in this portion of your proposal). Tae Kwon Do classes will provide that sort of structured interaction (you may include a description of an actual Tae Kwon Do class, maybe a class plan provided by a local instructor of Tae Kwon Do), and meetings at a public location such as a local park will provide a neutral environment.

This information should demonstrate that your plan adequately meets the needs of your intended audience.

Remember

Objectives are outcomes (what you hope to achieve), not methods (how you hope to achieve the outcome).

Finally, a proposal includes a section describing the *methodology* (how a proposal will be implemented). This section should describe the activities to be conducted to achieve the desired objectives. It should also include the rationale for choosing a particular approach.

For this section of your proposal, you outline a specific plan for the PSA. You include a complete description of the campaign—what form it will take, what visual images you plan to use, what text you plan to include—everything from color, to size, to font. For example, if the focal point of your PSA is a photo essay following a troubled adolescent as he deals with the effects of bullying, enrolls in a Tae Kwon Do class, and undergoes positive changes, you would describe all of this in the methodology section of your proposal. Describe each picture you imagine and what it should communicate to the audience. Describe the text you would like to include, what the text will look like, where it will be positioned, and how this design informs and motivates your intended audience.

This detailed methodology should create a complete picture of how your project will function and how it will address the social problem and achieve the goals you have outlined in your proposal.

WRITING ASSIGNMENT   Quest Seven: Create a Proposal to Instigate Change

Develop a plan for a PSA to address a social problem, and then write a proposal to generate support (financial and/or creative) for the implementation of that plan (the PSA).

Note

This assignment requires that you create a *plan* for a PSA, but you will not develop or create the actual PSA.

The heart of this assignment is the *proposal* for the PSA. Remember, your job is to convince an audience that a problem or need of significant magnitude exists and that your plan has the means and imagination to solve the problem or meet the need.

Step One

Before you begin drafting your proposal, brainstorm a list of possible solutions for a social problem that might be effectively addressed through a PSA. Select one solution, and develop a plan for a PSA.

Consider the following questions as you plan your PSA:

What is the primary purpose of PSA: to inform, to change thoughts and feelings, or to motivate behavior?

Who is the intended audience for the PSA?

How controversial will this PSA be for your audience based on the projected level of controversy?

How can you best get your audience's attention?

What kind of visuals might you use in this PSA?

What information must be provided to establish credibility?

Step Two

Before you begin to draft, gather all necessary supporting evidence for the proposal's problem statement or needs assessment and objectives of the project.

Create a draft of your proposal. Remember to adequately develop each section of the proposal with appropriate reasoning, evidence, and explanations. As with any argument, document all information gathered through research using correct MLA citation format for parenthetical references and works cited.

Step Three

Share your draft with your peers for feedback, then revise your proposal and submit it in a folder.

Criteria for Evaluating a Successful Proposal

This assignment asks you to identify a social problem and design a plan to address that social problem through the development of a PSA campaign. Then you must create a proposal to garner support for the development of that campaign. A successful proposal meets the following criteria:

- It contains the following sections: statement of purpose, background, problem statement or needs assessment, objectives of the project, and methodology.
- The statement of purpose clearly and concisely explains what the author is trying to prove.

- The background section provides specific and detailed information about the author of the proposal (education and experience) and establish his or her credibility.
- The problem statement or needs assessment provides specific details regarding what the problem is and why help is needed. Reasoning is supported by evidence from credible sources that meet STAR criteria (sufficient, typical, accurate, reliable).
- The section outlining the objectives of the project details and explains exactly what the project hopes to achieve (its purpose) and how the project addresses a specific audience.
- The methodology section describes and explains how the project will be implemented.
- All reasoning is supported by sufficient evidence. All evidence is documented through correct parenthetical references and a works cited page.
- The proposal is free of grammar and punctuation errors.

In the Spotlight: A Student Model Proposal

The Author: Bailey Watson

Bailey is a double major in Spanish and social work, a field she chose because she wants to help others. She has always been involved in community service organizations, and she feels she has an insight into our world that most people her age do not. She tries hard not to take anything for granted.

Author's Etcetera

Of this assignment, Bailey said

> This was the most challenging project we attempted all semester, but it was also the most meaningful. We walk around all the time saying this needs to change or that needs to change, but we don't do anything to make a change happen. This project helped me to understand the steps you have to take to make changes, and it helped give me tools I will use in the future.

Proposal for a Public Service Announcement Campaign Addressing Television Violence

Statement of Purpose

The amount of televised violence viewed by a person can have a definite effect on that person's behavior. The more violent acts a person views on television, the more aggressive that person's behavior will become. This is especially true when it comes to children. Therefore, I propose the development of a Public Service Announcement educating parents on the negative effects of media violence on youth behavior.

Background

My name is Bailey Watson, and I am an undergraduate at the University of North Carolina at Charlotte. I am a double major in Spanish and Social Work, and I have studied the issue of media violence for some time from a variety of perspectives. Aside from significant exposure to televised violence throughout my own childhood and adolescence, over the past five months I have conducted extensive research into the topic of media violence and the effects of media violence on children. After gathering and processing more than thirty sources on this topic, I have authored three research papers for two different college courses (Introduction to Sociology and Writing in the Academic Community). All three papers earned excellent scores.

Problem Statement or Needs Assessment

The American Medical Association, the American Academy of Pediatrics, the American Psychological Association, and the Center for Media Education all support my opinions about the effects of media violence on children. According to a report issued by the American Academy of Pediatrics, "[d]estructive behavior in real life follows television and movie violence like night follows day" (AAP). When children view violent behavior on television, they tend to either mimic the actions or reproduce them.

The media provides most of us with an understanding of what the world is like, or rather, what the world should be like. In today's technologically advanced world, we have cameras and media everywhere. Even prisoners are allowed the privilege of watching television. It has become a necessity in the United States. Many Americans have even stopped reading the newspapers. We have developed the philosophy, "Why read when we can watch the news?" (Murray 2). Without TV, what would we do? Many of us even fall asleep with the TV on.

The media influences almost everything we do. For example, what we wear, our hairstyles, the type of car we drive, and even the kinds of food we eat—all of these things are impacted by television. It would be nice to think that we all develop our own personal sense of fashion, but that's simply not true. From the media we develop personal values and often times we develop strong stereotypes. Depending on what type of show is being watched, we learn how to develop personal relationships with family and friends. We learn about religion and sexuality from television. The downside is that we also learn how to behave violently and surprisingly, "programs especially designed for children, such as cartoons, are the most violent of all programming" (Murray 1).

Violence in the media is a terrible problem in the United States. According to media experts and scholars David Gordon and John Kittross, authors of the book *Controversies in Media Ethics*, "[v]iolence in American society seems to be an epidemic that is increasing, perhaps fueled in part by the apparent growth in its acceptability or normality" (191). The media tends to glorify violence and create a false sense of reality that is easily accepted by children and alienated individuals. Violent acts can be found in all types of media, and in a recent study, it was determined that

> [t]he most violent periods were between 6 to 9 a.m. with 497 violent scenes (165.7 per hour) and between 2 to 5 p.m. with 609 violent scenes (203 per hour). Most of this violence is presented without context or judgment as to its acceptability, and most of this violence in the early morning and afternoon in viewed by children and youth. (Murray 1)

Notice that these are the times when most children are either just waking up to get ready for school or just getting home. This information is not insignificant.

CNN reported that, according to a report issued by the American Medical Association, "[v]iolent crime among 13- to 17-year-old teenagers climbed 126 percent from 1976 to 1992, and TV violence is partially responsible" (Price). Watching violent acts taking place on television makes violence seem like a logical solution to many of life's problems, and, in fact, "portrayals of violent incidents in both news and entertainment programming seem ever more prevalent, often shown as an acceptable solution to problems and too often failing to show any real consequences resulting from the violent acts" (Gordon and Kittross 191–192). This is a problem that must be addressed.

Objectives of the Project

My Public Service Announcement will address the parents of young children. I would like to introduce this Public Service Announcement in the form of an informative pamphlet to be handed out upon entering a physician's office. Pamphlets will also be distributed to the parents of children enrolled in elementary and middle schools through PTA meetings. Most parents believe that teachers and physicians are intelligent people with good intentions and will therefore be more likely to accept the information offered in the pamphlet as true.

The purpose of this pamphlet will be to inform parents of the dangers of exposing their children to televised violence. The goal will be to convince these parents that viewing violent media is harmful to their children and that they, the parents, should be monitoring the programs their children watch on television.

Methodology

On the front cover of the pamphlet, it will say, "Do you care about your children?" in a Copperplate Gothic Bold font. The letters will be black and bold to draw the parents' attention. When parents see this, they will immediately be drawn to open the pamphlet because most parents do care about their children and will do anything they can to make sure that they are safe. Surrounding the words on the cover will be a picture of several very innocent children of different ethnicities (to demonstrate that this applies to all people). Parents will be greatly affected by this portrayal of happy, healthy, and seemingly perfect kids. The background will be a warm yellow color. This will inspire a warm and friendly feeling in the reader.

Upon opening the pamphlet, parents will see a picture of a young child staring attentively at a television. Most parents have witnessed their children watching television in the same manner. This will create a sense of familiarity, an emotional tie between the reader and the issue at hand. The child's face will be neither happy nor sad, thus leading the reader to question what the child is watching on television, which is exactly what the Public Service Announcement hopes to achieve. The background will be the same warm yellow color used on the cover page.

"What Is Your Child Watching?" will be the first thing written on the inside of the pamphlet in a Copperplate Gothic Bold font. Again, the letters will be black and bold to draw the parents' attention. Many parents don't monitor what their children are watching on television. They do not realize what a serious problem televised violence really is, so the first purpose of the pamphlet will be to educate parents about the issue of media violence. The inside of the pamphlet will also include statistics from the American Medical Association and the Federal Trade Commission, such as:

> [a report by the American Medical Association] finds that while the entertainment industry has taken steps to identify content that may not be appropriate for children, the companies in those industries still routinely target children under 17 in their marketing of products their own rating systems deem inappropriate or warrant parental caution due to violent content. (Federal Trade Commission 1–2)

If parents feel as if their child is being threatened, they will be motivated to learn more about this issue and take action to protect their children. No healthy parent wants a child to be harmed. It is a parent's number one instinct to protect their children at all costs. So, the second purpose of the pamphlet will be to motivate parents to take action.

Although there are many steps that the entertainment industry can take (and has taken) to regulate which products children are able to purchase and view, it is up to parents to monitor the types of media their children have access to. It is up to the parents to take action. Therefore, the last page of the pamphlet will list the various actions that parents can take to address this issue, such as becoming familiar with the television ratings system and installing a V-chip on every television in their home. The printed text will be in a Copperplate Gothic Bold font. The background will be white. This stark black and white color scheme will appear very matter-of-fact.

Because it is so important for parents to understand the meanings of the various ratings and descriptors, the pamphlet will explain the rating system developed by the TV Parental Guidelines Board (in affiliation with National Parents and Teachers Organization) and how it works. For example, a program labeled "TV Y" is appropriate for all children, and a program labeled "TV Y7" is appropriate for children ages 7 and up who have "acquired the developmental skills needed to distinguish between make-believe and reality" (TV Parental). But a program labeled "TVY7 fv" may contain fantasy violence that is "more intense or more combative than other programs in this category" (TV Parental). This information will be explained in a bulleted list so that it is easily scanned and understood.

By alerting parents to the problem created by televised violence, by showing how that violence is a threat to their children, and by offering easy steps parents can take to protect their children from that threat, this pamphlet will be successful.

Works Cited

AAP Committee on Communications. "Media Violence." *Pediatrics.* 95:66. June 1995.

Federal Trade Commission. *Marketing Violent Entertainment to Children.* 2000. 26 Mar. 2003 <http://www.ftc.gov/opa/2000/09/youthviol.htm>.

Gordon, David A., and John Michael Kittross. *Controversies in Media Ethics.* 2nd ed. Longman Inc., 1999. 191–92.

Murray, John P., Ph.D. *Impact of Televised Violence.* 25 Mar. 2003 <http://www.ksu.edu/humec/impact.htm>.

Price, Lisa. "Parents Must Ration TV to Cut Teen-age Violence." CNN-Online. 1996. 17 Feb. 2003 <http://www.cnn.com/HEALTH/9609/09/nfm/ama.violence/>.

The TV Parental Guidelines. *National Parent/Teacher Association.* 2001–2002. 26 March, 2003. <http://www.pta.org>.

Practicum

How does Bailey's model fulfill the criteria for a successful proposal? Write a brief evaluation. Refer to specific examples from the text of her model to support your evaluation. Share your responses with your classmates. Do you find that you agree with your classmates? Disagree?

Reflection in Action

How is a *proposal* for change different from an *action* for change? How is it related to an action for change? How does making a proposal help when putting a plan into action?

How might you use proposal-writing skills later in life? Can you imagine a situation in which you might write a formal proposal?

How will your knowledge of proposals help you to better evaluate the PSAs (and other solutions to problems) you encounter in the world around you?

Expanding Your Vision: A Multimedia Assignment Option

Critical Inquiry: Digging Deeper

Let's look closely at a PSA and practice evaluating it using the criteria for an effective campaign detailed earlier in this chapter.

The mission of Adults & Children Together (ACT) Against Violence is to prevent young children from learning aggressive/violent behavior. This campaign is based on social science research that shows that children learn violent and aggressive behavior from various sources (parents, friends, media, environment, etc.) and, in turn, act with aggression/violence themselves. This campaign shows that adults' everyday behavior greatly affects the children around them. The campaign's ad messages remind parents and other caregivers that their everyday reactions and interactions teach children to deal with life's daily hassles in either positive or problematic ways.

The following PSA is a part of this anti-violence program.

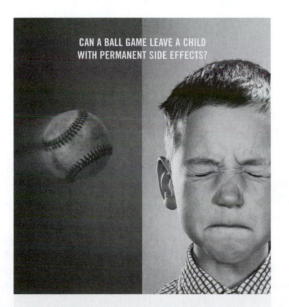

CAN A BALL GAME LEAVE A CHILD
WITH PERMANENT SIDE EFFECTS?

React to sports with rage and kids learn aggressive behavior. Keep your cool
and kids learn to do the same. To learn more about preventing aggressive or violent behavior,
call 877-ACT-WISE for a free brochure. Or visit ACTAgainstViolence.org.

 You're always teaching. *Teach carefully.*

MetLife Foundation
ACT Against Violence is a joint project of the American Psychological Association
& the National Association for the Education of Young Children.

1. Does this campaign have a *clearly defined purpose?*

   Yes. Clearly, the primary purpose of the campaign is to raise the audience's awareness of the ways in which adult behavior influences child development and behavior.

2. Does this campaign *address a clearly defined audience?*

   Yes. The audience is probably young, employed adults with children.

3. What is the *one idea* that this campaign communicates (the claim)?

   The main idea (or claim) communicated by this PSA is that *you're always teaching. Teach carefully.* This is a proposal to raise awareness.

4. Does this campaign provide *logical reasoning?*

   Yes. The campaign begins by posing the question: Can a ball game leave a child with permanent side effects? The campaign then answers that question with the following logical reasoning: 1) React to sports with rage and kids learn aggressive behavior. 2) Keep your cool and kids learn to do the same.

5. Does this campaign *establish credibility* by offering *supporting evidence* or links to evidence?

   Yes. The most dramatic piece of evidence is the photograph of the young boy wincing as a baseball moves toward the side of his head. This picture establishes an emotional connection with the audience by appealing to our need for love and safety (see Maslow's hierarchy of need). The intended audience—parents with young children—typically loves and wants to protect its children. The campaign also provides a great deal of contact information so that concerned parents might take action; we are provided with a phone number, a Web address, and references to several highly credible organizations: the American Psychological Association, the National Association for the Education of Young Children, Metlife Foundation, the Ad Council, and Act Against Violence.

6. Does this campaign *appeal to the audience's needs and values* in a non-manipulative way?

   Yes. This campaign clearly appeals to both the audience's need for love and the need for safety.

7. Is the format and construction *high quality?* Are *visuals appealing?*

   Yes, the photograph is a high-quality, digitally enhanced/manipulated photograph. The boy's facial expression is clearly frightened, anticipating pain. The speeding baseball represents violence and the potential for injury and damage. A sense of urgency is evident. The boy needs someone to protect him.

   The text is concise and informative. It is appropriate for the nature of this campaign.

   After analyzing this campaign according to the criteria established in "Tools for Success," we may judge this as an effective PSA.

Practicum

Do a brief search through current popular magazines and locate an example of a PSA currently circulating in some form of media. Bring your example to class. Working in small groups, evaluate each PSA with the criteria covered in "Tools for Success."

Write out your evaluation, clearly and concisely, explaining your judgments. Then present your PSA and evaluation to the class.

After a class discussion, consider the following questions before you move on: What did you learn through this analysis and sharing? How many different ways do these campaigns fulfill the criteria for a successful PSA?

MULTIMEDIA ASSIGNMENT Visi-Quest Seven: Expanding Your Vision by Creating and Presenting a Model PSA

Using the proposal you wrote in response to the assignment covered earlier in this chapter, put your plans into action and create a PSA to address a social problem. Use one of the multimedia formats previously covered in this textbook (PowerPoint, a brochure created in Word, a flier, etc.). Create the PSA and then present it to the class.

Step One

Divide the class into several small groups. Within each group, share your PSA proposals. Discuss the strengths and weaknesses of each proposal; then select one PSA to create. Write a justification for your selection.

Step Two

Work together as a group to create a model of the PSA.

Step Three

Present your completed PSA to the class. Each member of the class should evaluate all PSAs using the criteria covered in "Critical Inquiry: Digging Deeper."

Share and discuss your evaluations. Which PSAs were most successful, and why? How did the proposal help your group to create your PSA?

Criteria for a Successful PSA

- As with any argument, a successful PSA campaign should have a *clearly defined purpose:* to inform, to challenge thoughts and feelings about an issue, and/or to motivate behavior.

- ○ A successful campaign should *address a clearly defined audience.*
- ○ A successful campaign should *clearly communicate one idea* (that is the claim). This idea may be directly stated, or it may be implied.
- ○ A successful campaign should *provide logical reasoning* that answers the *why* questions a claim raises. These reasons may be communicated visually, with text, or through audio. Sometimes reasons may be implied—made—through association.
- ○ A successful campaign should *provide support for reasoning,* and because a PSA is limited in terms of available space, it may offer links (addresses, phone numbers, Web sites, contact names) for more supporting information. This supporting information should establish credibility for the campaign, and it may be provided in the form of visual imagery, text, or, when appropriate, audio.
- ○ A successful campaign should *appeal to an audience's needs and values* in an honest way. Appeals should not be manipulative or heavy-handed. The purpose of an appeal is to establish an emotional connection with the audience. Appeals may be accomplished through visual imagery, text, or audio.
- ○ A successful campaign is visually appealing and engaging. It is correct and does not contain careless errors in grammar or punctuation.

In the Spotlight: A Student Model PSA

The Authors: Brandon Bowlin, Alie Maughan, and Kelli Dover

Brandon, Alie, and Kelli worked together during the fall 2003 semester. Their topic of study was the Oklahoma City bombing.

Author's Etcetera

Brandon had this to say about his group's Visi-Quest Seven project:

> One thing that we recognized over and over as we worked on our different Quests this semester is that real, credible information on the Oklahoma City bombing seemed to be disappearing right before our eyes. There are a lot of conspiracy theories circulating "out there," and it's not hard to see why. After reading about Timothy McVeigh and his beliefs about the government, we decided that his biggest problem was that he did not see any other course of action. And we realized when we conducted our survey for Quest Six, SO MANY people think certain things need to change, but they have no idea how to take action. That's where our idea for littlebrother.org came from. It would be great if there were an easily accessed site and organization to help people take action on just about anything. This was a great project. We learned a lot all semester, but it seemed like this project gave us a chance to express ourselves in a satisfying way.

Are your rights slipping away right before your eyes?

Don't

Let

That

Happen

Need help understanding The Patriot Act? Have an opinion on public policy but don't know your Congressman's address? Want to get involved in the upcoming election, but don't know who to contact?

little brother knows

Visit our website. www.little-brother.org We're here to help.

little brother **is a non-profit organization operated by the little people for the little people with liberty and justice for all who take action**

Practicum

How does this group's Visi-Quest Seven fulfill the criteria for this assignment? Review the criteria for this assignment and make an evaluation. Offer specific examples from the model to illustrate your critique. Then share your ideas with your classmates. Do you find that you agree with your classmates? Do you disagree? Why, or why not? How does this process of reading and evaluating a model assignment help you to successfully meet the requirements for this assignment yourself?

8

Arguing to Create Meaning: Advancing an Interpretation

Begin with a *Question*: What Is the Relationship Between Art and Life?

Does life imitate art, or does art imitate life?

All of us have undoubtedly heard this question asked at some point in our lives. It's a bit like that age-old riddle: *Which came first, the chicken or the egg?* Of course, as you would expect, there are countless theories on the connection between life and art, art and life. Philosophers since Plato have debated the question. And out of the centuries-old debate, we have produced many fabulous ideas, but we still have no definitive answers. This is probably because, as with most debates, there *are no* definitive answers one way or the other.

The part of the debate we most often hear about concerning modern artifacts (television programs, movies, music, and more recently, video games and the Internet) has to do with life imitating art. This is the argument that art influences life to one degree or another, specifically behavior, *precisely* the behavior of adolescents and teenagers in connection to acts of violence and other illicit behaviors such as drug usage and promiscuity.

Many experts argue that various forms of media influence and even inspire the violent behavior exhibited by kids and teens—for example, those who were responsible for school shootings like the Columbine High School massacre. Other experts argue that media does not influence behavior—not to the extreme, in any case—and that violence cannot be attributed to artifacts such as the music of Marilyn Manson or Eminem or video games like Doom. Still others find a middle ground on this argument, believing instead that media has the potential to influence or impact our lives, but that other forces play a more influential role.

So, while most of the conversation on this subject is centered on the idea that art may or may not influence life, what happens when we turn this question upside down and ask; How does life influence the creation of art?

244

Imitation or Representation?

To begin this discussion, let's reframe the question, When studying the relationship between life and art, are we looking for *imitation*, or are we looking instead for *representation?* More precisely, *re*-presentation?

What is the difference between imitation and *re*presentation? At first glance, it may seem that there is not a very clear distinction between these two labels, but there is. Imitation is the attempt to replicate, to duplicate. *Representation* is the attempt to symbolically interpret, to signify, to *re*-present some aspect of life in order to communicate meaning.

Plato argued in his writing, *The Republic,* that art is essentially imitation. He believed that the artistic process is really nothing more than craftsmanship, and the goal of art is to copy or reproduce aspects of life (this is a simplified explanation of Plato's arguments; if you have time and are interested in further study, you might look more closely at *The Republic*). Imitation is the effort to mimic life in the form of an artifact. Mimesis as an exclusive artistic theory is not widely ascribed to today (even Plato's student Aristotle disagreed with him and thought art to be more than imitation).

Most philosophers believe that art *is* more than an attempt to copy some aspect of life. Art is more commonly believed to be a *representation of life* created for various purposes (to find meaning, to communicate understanding, to teach, etc.). Ascribing to this distinction, art is the *signification* of experience. An artifact, such as a story about the Oklahoma City bombing, for instance, would not simply record the minute-by-minute events of that day (*could not* entirely, because there are far too many perspectives to truly imitate). A story about the bombing would *re*-present select moments from that event in an attempt to communicate the significance of the experience from one or more perspectives.

So, if we view art as a *re*-presentation of life, what, exactly, is represented? How is it represented, and why? For what purpose?

Art as a Representation of Life

Artifacts represent everything about life and living—from experiences, events, questions, and fears to the gamut of emotions, hopes, dreams, the personal, and the political. For our purposes, we look at various aspects of social issues as represented in art.

Social problems, such as the many issues that arose from the Columbine tragedy, the terrorist attacks of September 11, 2001, and the Gulf War, include and embody multiple features of the human experience and are natural subjects for artistic representation. We find issues of classism, racism, ethnocentrism, ethics, sexism, relationships, adolescent angst, violence, and political agendas explored in just about every expressive medium. And from the fictional and poetic to the visual and musical, our lives are filled with artistic representations of the social issues that concern us. Consider the publishing industry, which is enormous; we read millions of books (novels and short story collections) and subscribe to countless magazines and newspapers every year. Then there is the "entertainment" industry—we are mass consumers of both movies and music.

But getting back to the idea of art as a representation of life, more specifically, a representation of social issues, we have to ask, What aspects of social issues are represented through these artifacts? How do these representations look? And, ultimately, what do they tell us? What do they mean?

Digging Below the Surface of Life and Art

Human beings are expressive creatures and have always been driven to create. We are seekers. We know there is more to life than meets the eye, so we constantly look for ways and means to help us make sense of experience, to find meaning in life. Art helps us to do that, beginning with the creative process.

As creators, artists have observed something in life, some sort of meaning that exists below the surface of events and experience, and have expressed those observations through the creation of fiction, photographs, lyrics, or some other type of artifact. In the act of creation, interpretation has already taken place. An artifact represents an aspect of life as seen through the eyes of an artist and communicated within a particular genre. And every genre, because of the unique form it takes, imposes certain rules or restrictions on representations within that genre.

Because what an artist creates is more than a replication of life, it is a representation of life and experience in a particular form, various artistic elements are used to construct that artistic representation and to shape an artist's message, such as characters and themes, images and symbols. The message that a work of art communicates is coded or embedded in those elements. Therefore, when reading an artifact for meaning, we have to decode and interpret what we see or hear or feel. Essentially, this means that we have to take apart a piece of art and examine its individual elements, then put it back together again in order to understand it. This taking apart (analysis) and putting back together (synthesis) is called *interpretation.*

Unlocking the Message and the Meaning

Coming up with an interpretation is a bit like taking apart your computer's hard drive to get a look at the inside parts, studying how they fit together, and then reassembling it so that the technology still works. But this is not a perfect analogy because when we take apart a computer and put it back together, it must be restructured exactly as it was before in order to function properly—there is one right way.

When we take apart an artistic representation, however, examine the individual parts, and put it back together, there is no one, set outcome. We may each walk away with a different understanding of how the artifact works and what it means. And that is okay. It is fabulous, even. Interpretation depends on the individual and the life experience he or she brings to the art. That is probably why artistic representations of social issues inspire so much debate.

But before we get into the idea of conflicting interpretations, how do we develop a solid understanding of our own? *How do we put the pieces of our analyses together and synthesize them to form a complete interpretation?*

Tools for Success: Description + Association + Context = Interpretation

Once you have completed an initial reading of an artifact and you have examined the individual and distinct elements that make up that artifact, it is time to form an interpretation, to answer the question, *What does this artistic representation mean to me?* A simple equation will help you to formulate your own interpretations:

Description + Association + Context = Interpretation.

Description

The first step in pulling together an interpretation is description. In your own words, describe the literal elements that make up the artifact. If you are reading a story or a play, summarize what happens in the story, who the main characters are, and what actions they take throughout the story. For example,

> A rhinoceros appears in a small town and rampages through the streets. Later, several other rhinoceroses appear and run through the streets of the town. A citizen of the town (a man) becomes a rhinoceros and joins the other beasts. ("Rhinoceros" by Eugene Ionesco)

Describe the setting in which the story takes place. Do not try to read any meaning into any of these elements; simply summarize the events, people, places, and happenings as they literally appear in the story.

If you are reading a poem or the lyrics to a song, describing the literal is a bit trickier. Still, you should summarize only what is actually happening in the poem or song. Describe who is speaking—if that is obvious—and what is being said. If there is any action, describe it. Do not attempt to translate metaphors. Describe them as they are in the poem or song.

> The speaker, "I," walked down the sidestreets of a supermarket in California. He walked under the trees. He had a headache. He was self-conscious. He was looking at the full moon. ("A Supermarket in California" by Allen Ginsberg)

Finally, if your artifact is a photograph or painting, simply describe what you see. Describe the people depicted—who they are, what they look like, what they are doing. Describe any inanimate objects. Describe the setting. Be as detailed as possible in your descriptions, but keep it on the literal:

> There is a ladder-back chair standing up against a wall. It is brown. Paint is chipping off of it. The seat cushion is torn, and yellowed-stuffing is hanging off to one side.

The literal description *is not the meaning communicated by the artistic representation,* but it will contribute to your understanding of the meaning. So, it is important to articulate what you literally see or read or hear before digging any deeper into meaning and what the literal may represent.

Association

After reading for the literal meaning, it is time to dig deeper and ask questions. What are the literal aspects of the artifact associated with? One way to approach the activity of association is to think in terms of *denotation* and *connotation*.

Denotation is the dictionary definition, the literal (which you have already described). *Connotation* is the association with what something implies apart from its primary meaning. For instance, the denotation of the word *bullet* is a small, round piece of lead fired from a rifle or pistol. The connotation of the word *bullet* may be danger, destruction, violence, and death. A bullet may also be thought of as a small piece of a larger apparatus that is inactive until forced into action—bullets on their own, outside of a gun, are harmless pieces of metal.

A good way to approach the activity of association is to make a radial diagram (sometimes known as a bubble diagram). Draw a bubble in the center of a piece of paper and write a word or phrase from your description of the text inside the bubble. Then draw a line extending out from the center bubble and make a new bubble. Inside it, write the first association you make with that core word (the first connotation that comes to mind). Repeat this process for each association you make.

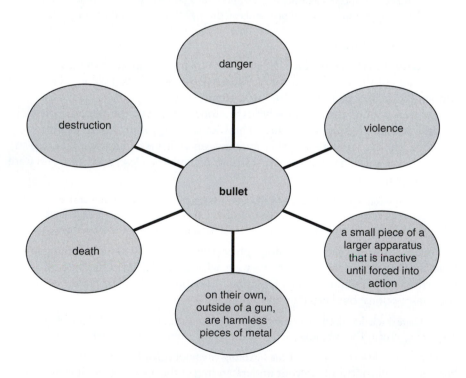

Make a radial diagram for words or phrases in the text or in your description. You may begin to notice patterns in and between your diagrams.

The process of association may *seem* a little more challenging when dealing with a photograph or painting, but that is because we are not accustomed to analyzing photos. We do not often look for more than the literal in a photograph, thinking instead that what we see is what we get. So, when you begin to explore associations, do not refer to the photograph itself; instead, use your written description as a guide.

Context

Once you have worked through your description of the literal aspects of a text and you have made associations and explored any evident patterns, it is important to place that information within a given *context*. Understanding and placing an artifact within an appropriate context—that is, what preceded or followed the creation of the artifact historically or personally—is the final, necessary step you must take before articulating meaning. Placing any associations you might have made about that text within its historical context helps you to produce a more accurate and informed interpretation.

When thinking about the historical context of a given artifact, consider these questions: What do you know about the era in which the artifact was created? Do the associations you have made make any more or any less sense historically? Understanding historical context probably requires a bit of research to find out simple information, such as when the artifact was created and what was going on in the world prior to its creation. And understanding the historical context of an artifact may not always change your interpretation.

Aside from the historical context, you may want to consider the artifact within a more personal context. What do you know about the artist, his or her life experience, background, education, political affiliations, beliefs, and so on? Has the artist ever offered any commentary (explanation, interpretation) about the artifact? What happens when you examine an artifact within the context of the artist's personal life and experience? Does this context shed any new light on the associations you have made?

For instance, how does knowing that Richard Patrick interprets "American Cliché" as "a song about the politics of the bus ride when you're, like, six" affect your understanding of the song? Does this artist commentary add a new dimension to your own interpretation? Does it complement or is it in conflict with associations you made based on your own experience?

Interpretation

Once we understand the literal, generate a list of possible figurative associations, and place the artifact in some sort of historical or personal context, it is time to bring everything we have learned together and ask, What does this mean? It is time to form an *interpretation*.

If description, association, and context are tools of analysis (breaking down a text into its various parts), then interpretation is synthesis (assembling the parts of a text into a whole). The first step in interpretation or synthesis is to look for *patterns of repetition*.

Begin by examining your associations. Do you see any similar words or phrases, images or symbols? For instance, do you see a pattern of warm associations repeated with variations (sun, fire, light, heat, red, orange, etc.)? Group together the words or phrases with similar associations.

Next, look for *oppositions*. Do you see a pattern of opposing associations? Warm images versus cold images? Light images versus dark images? Things associated with peace and things associated with destruction? Categorize and group together the opposing words or phrases you have identified.

When we see patterns of repetition or opposition in a text, those patterns are usually not accidental; they are meant to communicate something significant. Go back to the original text, now, and read it again with those patterns in mind. How do the patterns you have identified and their associated meanings work within the text as a whole? What overall impression is created? Somewhere in that impression lies the meaning you have been searching for.

Through the synthesis of the literal and the figurative within a given context, we create an interpretation and come to understand what an artistic representation means.

Interpretation Walk-Through

Let's do a quick analysis and synthesis of Richard Patrick's "American Cliché" and see if we can formulate an interpretation. Description + Association + Context: How does it all add up? Here is the full text of the song:

American Cliché

Last seat on the bus
Who you gonna trust
Which one do you follow
Last seat on the bus
Don't make such a fuss
This much should make you hollow
'Cause every time you make yourself the reason
Is every time you make yourself beaten
Yeah

Yeah, this is an American cliché

American, American
Get on the bus
Yeah, this is an American cliché
American, American
Get on the bus

First seat on the bus
Who you gonna trust
Which one do you make follow
First seat on the bus
Don't make such a fuss
Which one do you make hollow
Now every time you make your friend the reason
And every time you make your friend beaten, yeah

You want a way to be the same
You want a way to be the same
You want a way to be the same Oh no

Description

The speaker in this song is an omniscient voice addressing a specific or general "you." The speaker is observing a situation.

In the first stanza, the "you" is getting on a bus, and there is one seat left. The speaker tells the character of "you" that he or she faces a dilemma: Who will "you" trust and which one will "you" follow? The "one" is not defined (because "you" is getting on a bus, we assume that "one" refers to someone already on the bus). It is clear that "you" must make a choice, and that choice will have consequences. The speaker directs "you" not to complain. Complaining—drawing attention to "you"— is self-defeating.

In the chorus, the speaker claims that this situation is an American cliché (a situation so common in America that it is overused, tired, hackneyed).

In the second stanza, the "you" is getting on the bus and is able to take the first seat (no one else is on the bus at this point?). The situation has changed. The speaker asks again who "you" will trust, but this time "you" will make someone else follow rather than be a follower. It is clear that "you" still faces a dilemma, but the dilemma has changed the focus from "yourself" to "your friend."

The lyrics conclude with a repetition of the phrase: "You want a way to be the same." The speaker tells "you" that he or she wants a way to be the same (to be just like everyone else, to not stand out, to conform).

The sung version of the lyrics contains a repetition of the phrase "Shackled God" at the end. This is not included in the print version of the lyrics. (God is shackled by whom? By what?)

Association

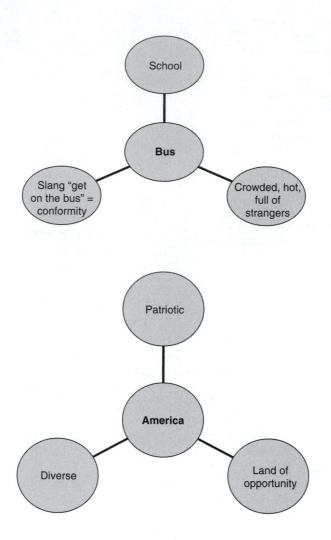

If space is a problem, or if you prefer a more structured format, another way to organize associations is by using a chart:

Bus	Transportation for school, city transportation, crowded, full of strangers, stuffy, Rosa Parks, "get on the bus" = conformity
America	Red, white, and blue, patriotic, diverse, fast food, freedom, land of opportunity
Cliché	Everyone does it, overdone, overused, loss of meaning from overuse
Hollow	Empty, sad, should hold something but doesn't

Context

Historical

- This song was written post-Columbine.
- One aspect of culture to be blamed for the Columbine High School shooting and other school shootings was cliques in the school or negative peer relationships. Outcasts were said to have been bullied by the popular kids. These "outcasts" were known for their lack of conformity.
- America is typically associated with ideals such as freedom and diversity, but it is also associated with social conformity.
- Buses are historically associated with the Civil Rights Movement and protests, particularly Rosa Parks, the Freedom Riders, and Montgomery, Alabama.

Personal

- This song was written as a part of the album *The Amalgamut*. Of that album, Richard Patrick said, "I'm not about preaching, but if there's a message to this music it's that we live in a country that gives us the freedom to dream big and the diversity to do it each our own way. People died for that freedom, and that means none of us has the right to waste our lives. You can call that patriotic if you want. I don't put labels on it. I just know that I'm an American, 13th generation, and proud of it. I recently discovered I have some Cherokee blood in me, and I'm proud of that heritage too. All I can do is be the best I can be, and that's what has made this country great from the beginning." It's an explanation aptly summed up in the album's title, combining the amalgamation of the American melting pot with the gamut of its diversity. "It's also about being a mutt," Patrick adds with a grin. "Because in this country, that's what most of us are" (officialfilter.com).
- Of the song "American Cliché," Richard Patrick said, "American Cliché," that's the song about the bullies. It's about the politics of the bus ride when you're six years old. It's about the political juxtaposition you find yourself in on a school bus. When you get on that bus and you are faced with the reality that you have to fit in with this community, how do you do that? How do you fit in? What if you can't? What happens then? Well, sometimes, things like Columbine happen."

Note

Many artists do not offer an interpretation of their own work as Richard Patrick did. But this, again, is *one* interpretation. If your understanding of these lyrics is different from the artist's intentions, that is okay—as long as you can justify your interpretation with the text of the lyrics and outside examples and explanations. Richard Patrick himself said, "[the students interpreting these lyrics] are coming up with a different interpretation. So now we've got a bunch of good stuff going on. Whether it's far-fetched or whether it's close to home, we've got 'em thinking. And that's what's important."

Interpretation

Repetitions

> Who you gonna trust
> Don't make such a fuss
> This much should make you hollow
> This is an American cliché
> Get on the bus
> You want a way to be the same

Repetitions with Alterations

> Last seat → First seat
> Which one do you follow → which one do you *make* follow
> Make *yourself* the reason → make *your friend* the reason
> Make *yourself* beaten → make *your friend* beaten

Other Oppositions

Ideal	Real
American →	Cliché
Freedom →	conformity
Diversity →	conformity
Land of opportunity →	loss of meaning
Should hold →	empty/hollow

Crowded/Full	Empty
Bus	bus
Bus	"you"

Stranger → friend
Trust → fuss

Based on the literal description of the lyrics, the figurative associations, the historical and personal context for this artifact, and the patterns I have identified, my interpretation follows:

> There are many oppositions in this song. These oppositions create a sense of conflict. The biggest opposition lies in the difference between the ideal and the real. The American cliché is the ideal of freedom and independence and diversity, but the reality is conformity. The decision to conform or not to conform creates internal conflict within an individual (and maybe within a society). That conflict makes us hollow, unfeeling, empty of emotions.
>
> Conformity is an American cliché. This struggle to conform begins in childhood and is supported through the educational system.

Practicum

Work through your own interpretation of one of the following artistic representations. Complete the entire equation: Description + Association + Context = Interpretation. Share your discoveries with the class.

The Artist: Richard Patrick, Filter

Richard Patrick is the singer, songwriter, and programmer for the rock band Fil*ter*. Drawn to music from an early age, Patrick started playing guitar at around nine years old. "I knew at five years old I had to be a guitar player." Over the years, he moved from band to band, including several years with the controversial Nine Inch Nails, until he finally came into his own as an artist and formed the commercially successful Fil*ter*.

Fil*ter*'s music has been described by Patrick as "Realcore," meaning that the band's music addresses real-life issues in an honest way. The following song, "Columind," is from Fil*ter*'s third album, *The Amalgamut* (Reprise Records, 2002). It was written in direct response to the Columbine High School shooting. (Note: A more detailed interview with Richard Patrick is included in Chapter One).

Author's Etcetera

I had the pleasure of speaking with Richard Patrick at length in January 2003. This is what he had to say about the Columbine tragedy and the song "Columind":

Obviously, you remember Columbine. Did you watch the media coverage on that day?

Yeah, I watched it as it was happening. You know, "this just in, there's something going on in a school outside of Denver, Colorado," and I remember thinking when that kid [Patrick Ireland] jumped out of the window, "oh my God, this is real!"

What media images stand out for you?

The kids running out of the building, the SWAT teams approaching the building, and then this poor bloodied kid jumping out of a window. I mean, it sent a huge amount of horror right through my system. Because it was real.

How did you feel about the media coverage?

I loved the fact that it was covered so well. I didn't love the horror I was seeing, but we live in a world where news is instantaneous. When I turn on CNN, I

(continued)

wanna see what's going on in the world. I wanna see who did it, I wanna know why, I wanna know it's been stopped—I wanna know everything about it. So in my mind, they did a good job. The media coverage, to me, was exactly what it was supposed to be.

How do you feel about the media blame game?

We as humans wanna blame things, and that's okay as long as it gets to the solution. The fact that Marilyn Manson or Fil*ter* or anybody gets blamed keeps us sharp, because freedom—especially freedom within the arts, especially freedom within the press, the things my grandfather fought for—these things can be taken away.

How do you feel about the connection between music and behavior?

Yeah, music has an impact, but there's a line between impact and influence, and that line is rational, logical thought. It's amazing as an artist to be able to play the guitar and literally kind of play upon this emotional, visceral kind of sensory experience that people have—you know, when you hear something and that emotional impact it has on you, like when you hear a violin and it's beautiful, playing Mozart. It's unbelievable to be able to control that, you know, that sense of music, that emotional "ahhhh, there it is!" It's wonderful to woo people into feeling something that you feel. But when a person hears a song and commits a crime or does something heinous, that's completely his or her choice. Because, see, there's a difference between feeling something and doing something. If people are allowed to walk this planet and say this band made me do it, I guarantee you, the cheeseburger will tomorrow. To not acknowledge the personal responsibility in a thing like the Columbine shootings, that, to me, is a just a huge loss of accountability.

Why did you feel compelled to write "Columind"?

Writing this song was like trying to figure out the human psyche, you know? What makes a guy wanna kill people? Once in a while humans go nuts; they go absolutely spastic. And you figure, statistically, it should happen maybe more than it does, you know—you've got 300 million possibilities, and most of us are just trying to go through life and be all right. But what is that insanity? What is that mind set? What gets a person to the point where he can just blow away his classmates like they're nothing? So, musically, I tried to come from the standpoint of their insanity. You know, with the lyrics or the way I scream it or the anger from the guitar, it's heavy and dark and big and ominous sounding. I tried to sonically approximate the place where they came from when they decided to do all this.

How do you feel about the lyrics appearing in this textbook apart from the music?

I feel like you're not getting the complete picture. I feel like you're not getting all of the information, which makes it very tough for you to understand what I'm trying to say. Looking at the lyrics apart from the music, you're getting one seventieth of what I'm doing as an artist. And when I say one seventieth, I mean that there are seventy tracks on our mixing console and each one of those tracks in an instrument—the lyrics [are] one track, my voice is one track; it's one seventieth of the total package. So, you put all those tracks together, all seventy of them, and you have this four-minute song, and that's the best we can do to try and convey the insanity of that particular day.

Columind

What do you think you did here kid?
You're living like some rich kid bitch?
The scratch that makes you flinch
The scratch that you can't itch

What do you think you got done here man?
You're putting on a show
What do you think you got done here kid?
Did you reach your killing goal?

Shame, you got everything,
you want everything
Shame, you need everything,
you kill everything

Oh Christ, look at them bleed
Oh, what makes this sick disease?
Oh God, they're on their hands and knees
Oh, look at me, I'm about to be free

Now when it's all over
Listen to this shit man
Now when it's all over
We won't even care, we won't care

Shame, you got everything,
you want everything
Shame, you need everything,
you kill everything

The Artist: Pray for the Soul of Betty

Pray for the Soul of Betty is a self-proclaimed "NYC Homegrown Rock n Roll" band made up of four accomplished musicians: Hamboussi (drums), Joao Joya (guitar), Constantine Maroulis (vocals), and C.R. Taylor (bass).

An Indie band determined to define their own path in an industry dictated by monster corporations, Betty's music (like the band members) is passionate, spiritual, and full of reflections on the human experience.

The following songs are from their self-titled debut release: *Pray for the Soul of Betty*.

Find out more at the band's website: www.prayforthesoulofbetty.com.

. . . *the Day*

Why don't you pick today to be the day
That you decide for the first time not to lie

The adults are dead
Overfed and programmed
Thoughts that fill your head
Are the world's eye

You can't let it go

And if you can't find your way to a better world
Set your will inside
All the answers
There within your mind

I've been to the ends of the earth and
I've seen what it means to be dead end
This land is the best for the best man
Rise up, pick your line, end distraction

Why don't you pick today to be the day
That you decide for the first time this is your life

You can't let it go

And if you can't find your way to a better world
Set your will inside
All the answers
There within your mind

I've seen what it takes to be free
Man, be bold, let go of the railing
These things can be had with a strong hand
Take what you want, it's yours, you can't let it go
It's time.

Suicide

Hey what'd you say?
An empty day?
Won't you be brave?
You're everywhere
You disappeared though . . .

A grave mistake
For Heaven's sake
You did it all for Jesus
Did you think it all would please us?

If you step outside
I'll warm you from your suicide
This pain in your eyes
Don't do anything
Just pray for something better
There's always something better

I'll take you home
Forgive me, for trespassing

Hey, what'd you say (what'd you say)
Do you think you could stay (it's a beautiful day)
Did you do it all for Jesus?
Did you think it all would please us?

If you step outside
I'll warm you from your suicide
This pain in your eyes
Don't do anything
Just pray for something better
There's always something better

I can feel you inside
you got time to make up your mind
Don't turn your back to the sun
'Cause baby you're gonna burn
My baby's gonna burn down

If you step outside
I'll warm you from your suicide
This pain in your eyes
Don't do anything
Just pray for something better
There's always something better

I'll take you home . . .

I can feel you inside
you got time to make up your mind
Turn your back to the sun
'Cause baby, babe you're gonna burn. . . .

The Artist: A Perfect Circle: Billy Howerdel and Maynard James Keenan

Led by vocalist Maynard James Keenan and guitar tech Billy Howerdel, A Perfect Circle is a rock and roll super group formed in 1999. A Perfect Circle released their debut album, *Mer de Noms,* in 2000. *Thirteenth Step* followed in 2003. The following lyrics are from the band's third album, *Emotive*—released in 2004.

Counting Bodies Like Sheep to the Rhythm of the War Drums

don't fret precious, i'm here.
step away from the window. go back to sleep.
safe from pain and truth and choice and other poison devils.
see, they don't give a fuck about you like I do.
count the bodies like sheep.
counting bodies like sheep to the rhythm of the war drums.
go back to sleep.

I'll be the one to protect you from your enemies and all your demons.
I'll be the one to protect you from a will to survive and and a voice of reason.
I'll be the one to protect you from your enemies and your choices, son.
they're one in the same.
I must isolate you.
isolate and save you from yourself.
Sleep.
Sleep.
Sleep.

The Artist: Willie Nelson

Willie Nelson is an American guitarist and country singer, originally from Abbott, Texas. He reached his greatest fame during the outlaw country movement of the 1970s, though he had already become famous as a 1960s songwriter. Nelson stirred quite a controversy with the following song, "Whatever Happened to Peace on Earth," written after watching the news on Christmas Day, 2003. He has said that he hopes it stirs passion in anyone who hears it.

What Ever Happened to Peace on Earth

There's so many things going on in the world
Babies dying
Mothers crying
How much oil is one human life worth
And what ever happened to peace on earth

We believe everything that they tell us
They're gonna' kill us
So we gotta' kill them first
But I remember a commandment
Thou shall not kill
How much is that soldier's life worth
And whatever happened to peace on earth

(Bridge)
And the bewildered herd is still believing
Everything we've been told from our birth
Hell they won't lie to me
Not on my own damn TV
But how much is a liar's word worth
And whatever happened to peace on earth

So I guess it's just
Do unto others before they do it to you
Let's just kill 'em all and let God sort 'em out
Is this what God wants us to do

(Repeat Bridge)
And the bewildered herd is still believing
Everything we've been told from our birth
Hell they won't lie to me
Not on my own damn TV
But how much is a liar's word worth
And whatever happened to peace on earth

Now you probably won't hear this on your radio
Probably not on your local TV
But if there's a time, and if you're ever so inclined
You can always hear it from me
How much is one picker's word worth
And whatever happened to peace on earth

But don't confuse caring for weakness
You can't put that label on me
The truth is my weapon of mass protection
And I believe truth sets you free

(Bridge)
And the bewildered herd is still believing
Everything we've been told from our birth
Hell they won't lie to me
Not on my own damn TV
But how much is a liar's word worth
And whatever happened to peace on earth

The Artist: Bruce Springsteen

One of the world's most popular performers for almost three decades, Bruce Spring-steen has often been the voice of America in rock music. From early songs such as "Born to Run" and "Born in the U.S.A." to the more recent album *The Rising,* he has always managed to catch the spirit of the nation musically and lyrically.

On September 11, 2001, America was thrust into strange, uncertain times, and on a nationally broadcast benefit concert for the victims of the September 11 tragedy, Springsteen rose to the occasion, delivering a powerful rendition of "My City of Ruins." It did not seem to matter that the song had originally been written to chronicle the deterioration of Asbury Park, New Jersey, Springsteen's old stomp-ing grounds. Suddenly, the song's lyrics took on new meaning, making a powerful statement and giving it a life of its own. Many of the songs on *The Rising* were writ-ten post-September 11. The following song seems to best capture the spirit of that terrible event.

You're Missing

Shirts in the closet, shoes in the hall
Mama's in the kitchen, baby and all
Everything is everything
Everything is everything
But you're missing

Coffee cups on the counter, jackets on the chair
Papers on the doorstep, you're not there
Everything is everything
Everything is everything
But you're missing

Pictures on the nightstand, TV's on in the den
Your house is waiting, your house is waiting
For you to walk in, for you to walk in
But you're missing, you're missing
You're missing when I shut out the lights
You're missing when I close my eyes
You're missing when I see the sun rise
You're missing

Children are asking if it's alright
Will you be in our arms tonight?

Morning is morning, the evening falls I have
Too much room in my bed, too many phone calls
How's everything, everything?
Everything, everything
You're missing, you're missing

God's drifting in heaven, devil's in the mailbox
I got dust on my shoes, nothing but teardrops

WRITING ASSIGNMENT Quest Eight: Write an Argument to Create Meaning

Write an interpretive argument paper in which you advance a claim about the meaning of an artistic representation of your issue (a song lyric). Your paper must focus on one claim, developed with sufficient reasoning that is supported by examples from the text (properly integrated into the body of your paper and documented according to MLA standards). Your paper must also be organized according to your claim and reasoning and free of grammatical and mechanical errors.

Criteria for Evaluating an Interpretive Argument Essay

For this assignment, you are asked to create an interpretation of an artifact—an artistic representation of a social problem or issue. Then you are to advance that argument of interpretation with reasoning and evidence. A successful argument of interpretation meets the following criteria:

- A successful interpretation presents and advances a claim that suggests an interpretation of the meaning signified by an artifact.
- A successful interpretation develops that claim with logical reasoning.
- A successful interpretation supports all reasoning with evidence from the text of the artifact. That evidence meets STAR criteria.
- A successful interpretation is organized (either point-to-point or according to the organization of the artistic representation).
- A successful interpretation has no grammar or punctuation errors, and all supporting evidence is correctly documented according to appropriate MLA style for parenthetical citations and a works cited page.

In the Spotlight: Student Model of an Interpretive Argument Essay

The Author: Marianne Moller

Marianne is from Copenhagen, Denmark. She is currently studying at the University of Copenhagen, where her major is English.

Author's Etcetera

Marianne had this to share about her experience writing this essay:

> I have analysed and interpreted various kinds of text, but this is my first real attempt at studying song lyrics. In my experience, doing thorough analyses and interpretations often leads to a deeper appreciation of the text in question, and this was the case with "The Missing." I began the process by listening closely to the whole album and then writing down all the thoughts and ideas that the lyrics gave me on a hard copy of the text. I've found that it is a good way of linking the different ideas together, and it helps me keep the text in focus. It is often difficult not to get carried away by all the thoughts that a text inspires, and even though an interpretation allows a relatively wide range of freedom to introduce different ideas, it is always crucial to keep the actual words and the analysis in mind. The attention to detail is part of the analysis, but it is also important to the interpretation, because without it, the analysis would be useless as a tool to help with the interpretation.
>
> I looked at the song on its own, in the context of the album, in the context of the other albums, and finally, in the context of recent events in the world. This gave me different ideas about what the song means to me, and that is what I've tried to convey with my essay. Despite the aforementioned freedom that an interpretation allows, I also had to maintain some degree of academic objectivity, and this was probably the hardest part, seeing as I am biased in my opinion about Fil*ter*'s qualities. I have enjoyed doing this interpretation because it allowed me to look closer at a song that I like and use my knowledge about language and literature to think about it in another way than I usually would. It confirmed my theory that "The Missing" is a song with a message, has much more to it than it appears at first glance, and that is a very rewarding experience.

The Missing

Interpretations of texts are, by definition, more or less subjective. They will be influenced by the person who is interpreting and his or her experiences, knowledge, and general outlook on life. Meanings change as we go along, and events will invariably shape us and our thoughts. With this in mind, present essay is by no means an exhaustive or final interpretation of Richard Patrick's lyrics for the Fil*ter* song, "The Missing," but merely a suggestion for an interpretation in which I shall be looking at a few features I find the most interesting in the lyrics. We all read texts how we want

to read them, and one of Patrick's talents is writing lyrics that most people can identify with. Some music speaks to people in a way that defies description. This is what
good music means to me. Fil*ter*'s music has this quality. It contains a range of emotions and an insight that is remarkable, so for someone who is willing to listen, there
is almost certainly a message or something else to be gained, something to learn or
something to inspire.

Let us start by looking at the time frame and the context of the song. The album,
The Amalgamut, on which "The Missing" can be found, was released in the summer of 2002, relatively shortly after the events of 9/11; events that shocked the world
and will leave repercussions for a long time to come. Those events will affect the way
we look at the world, how we express ourselves through art, and how we interpret
pieces of art. In the light of this, the lyrics for "The Missing" can be seen as a way of
representing and describing the eerie atmosphere of insecurity and helplessness,
which the world saw in the aftermath of 9/11:

> What now, the cross has been greased
> But I don't feel the heat
> Nor the peace in the street
> Everybody feels hit
> So just bury it in the pit
> With the best of the sick ideological shit. (Patrick, *Amalgamut*)

Clearly, this verse refers to religion. If the cross in the first line represents a religion—
Christianity—what this seems to be suggesting is that religion is not a solution to
the abovementioned insecurity. "So just bury it in the pit / With the best of the sick
ideological shit," where "it" is the cross, can be interpreted as an agnostic rejection
of religion. It appears that the "I" of the lyrics does acknowledge the existence of a
god or gods, but he does not believe in their intentions (Patrick, *Amalgamut*).

It is still being debated whether the terrorist acts of 9/11 were in fact terrorism in
the name of religion, but they were indeed acts caused by a clash of ideologies. However, it could be argued that the ideologies that clashed were freedom and religion.
At times of crises, people often turn to religion for help and answers. Of course, this
has more than one explanation, but what I want to focus on here is the insecurity
caused by a fear of being alone. It is well known that by joining a group, most people will feel less insecure, but what happens in many cases is that the spirit of the
group takes over people's ability to act and think for themselves. We all want to belong somewhere, but often that entails abandoning the individual. The lyrics of "The
Missing" are not written by a man who has turned to religion, but the employment
of religious terminology makes the listener think about how religion influences us
and how it is often used as a weapon of war:

> He says turn the other cheek
> But that seems kind of weak
> I just want to beat up
> Beat up the meek. (Patrick, *Amalgamut*)

The idea of "turning the other cheek" is Biblical, as is the expression "the meek." Turning the other cheek implies accepting what has happened . . . it is a sign of resignation and it is "weak." The "I" wishes for some sort of action. This could be revenge, but most likely, the wish to "beat up the meek" is just an expression of frustration with "the meek", i.e., people who do not react with anything but resignation, and not so much a declaration of war. However, it also touches on the problem of how easy it is to interpret passages from the Bible (or indeed any other religious or ideological text) in order to use them as means of explaining or justifying the most horrible of actions. The power of words is immense because people understand them any way they want to. Someone who believes strongly enough in a cause needs only guidelines, in the form of words and conventions, and no logical reasons for committing atrocities. Someone who has been told since childhood that the only true words are those of any given religious text or any given person will not think twice about justice or reason. That person is not free. Beliefs shape people and any paradigm can be dangerous if it is taken to the extreme.

The chorus, "I'm not a good tool / 'Cause you love to be cruel," which could be directly addressed to God, also implies that religion is not the answer for the "I." By using the word "tool," it is suggested that there is a certain amount of manipulation involved, and it raises the age-old question, is God benign (Patrick, *Amalgamut*)? The God that is present (or missing, as it were) in these lyrics is certainly not benign. It is not the *do ut des* relationship of mutual dependence that the ancient Greeks shared with their gods at one point, but rather a relationship with a god that uses human beings as tools (History). He is not only given sacrifices; he takes them and punishes human beings for their sins. The cruelty can apply in different ways. Is it the cruelty of the god of the people who carried out the terrorist acts, or the cruelty of the god who let such tragedies befall "his" people—the victims of terrorism and violence who were punished regardless of faith? If the latter is the case, it explains why the "I" has no faith in God. Surely, a god who would allow so many people to suffer cannot be benign. From that point of view, it is paradoxical that people seek help from a god who let 9/11, the Columbine shooting, and other tragedies take place. It is difficult to have faith in a God that lets people get so desperate that they will commit horrible acts of violence as a result. However, the first two lines of the song do propose that human beings are to blame for tragedies as well as the "missing" God is. "Hey God told us that we made a very big sin / You don't know where to begin" suggests that humans have sinned so much that they don't know which sin to repent (Patrick, *Amalgamut*). We expect God to help us when we need it, but to most of us, he does not matter much the rest of the time. Whether this is hypocrisy or not can be discussed, but it is certainly a consequence of human self-sufficiency. Still, now and again we have to realize that we cannot solve a given problem by ourselves. We all approach our problems in different ways, and we all react differently when we have to acknowledge that those problems may not have a solution. For some people, religion is the answer and for others it is not.

It is in the human nature to struggle for survival. Most of us have friends, relatives, or others to turn to for help when we cannot cope on our own, but sometimes, no one is willing to listen. In such cases, the reactions can sometimes be extreme. Suicides and violence attract attention, but when someone chooses one or both as a last resort, it is generally too late to start listening. We do not always want to hear, but we have to accept that other people have opinions that differ from our own, and that those opinions are valid too. Many cultures pride themselves on offering freedom for the people. Freedom to choose and freedom of speech, but what good is that freedom if no one is there to share it and no one is listening?

The Amalgamut as a whole is an album that deals with several current issues in the honest and to-the-point way that is one of Richard Patrick's trademarks. At Fil*ter*'s official website, he explains the somewhat peculiar title of the album:

> I called the record the *Amalgamut* because I took a trip across the country and started to realize that everything in America is somewhat different, but very similar at the same time. What I'm trying to say is, America is truly becoming the land that is a melting pot, and within this melting pot there is an immense amount of diversity.
>
> Be an individual in this country and realize that since the Revolutionary War, the Civil War, World War I, World War II, the Korean War, the Vietnam War, Desert Storm, and the War on Terror, thousands and thousands and thousands, maybe millions of men, have died for that freedom. This record is about going out there and being free, because the ideology of freedom isn't just in America, it's in England, it's in France, it's in Italy, it's in Germany, it's in Japan, it's in Canada, it's in Australia, and it's in many other countries. So please go out there and live your lives and remember that you're all free and that we're all Amalgamuts. (Patrick, *Rich Words*).

Knowing the background on which the song was written helps us understand it and interpret it. The above quotation is interesting with reference to "The Missing" for several reasons, one of them being the mention of terror and how the "ideology of freedom" is a basic human right in many countries. Religions do indeed interfere with people's freedom in more than one way. A person who lives fully by and believes fully in the words of any kind of ideology cannot be free, because ideologies in general do not allow freethinkers.

The music for "The Missing" deserves a mention too. Separating lyrics from the music is like separating poetry from its form, rhymes, and meter. Sounds and rhythm are essential. Traditionally, poetry was accompanied by music, and the repetitions, rhymes, and meter were tools to help the artist remember the words in societies that did not yet have a written language. Incidentally, such songs often served a religious purpose. Still, in our day, those tools are important because music speaks to us in a way that the written word on its own cannot. Somehow, good music appeals to our emotions. The music for this song is very fitting for the lyrics. It has a solemn feel to it that goes very well with the seriousness of the lyrics, as does the almost grandiose sound of the chorus. In this way, the music supports and substantiates the words of the lyrics to create a unity which is very giving to someone who is willing to listen and appreciate.

Earlier *Filter* songs have dealt with the subject of religion, but "The Missing" is much more mature than such songs as "Dose" and "Under" from their first album, *Short Bus* (Filter). Albeit these songs, with their feelings of youthful anger and their attacks on people trying to impose their views on others, "The Missing" outweighs them when it comes to thoughtfulness, and it is a more complete song in a number of ways. One might say that "The Missing" holds a more evolved version of the message in "Dose" and "Under." The anger is still there, but it is controlled and used in a creative and constructive way, which makes the message valid on another level.

Finally, a question remains. What or who is "The Missing"? It could have any number of meanings. Does it refer to God's absence or a more general lack of solutions or places to turn at times of crises? Is it a lament for everything and everyone that was lost? In the end, it is up to the listener to decide. We may be influenced by other people's ideas, but what truly matters to most human beings are their own opinions. After all, no one can really tell a free person what to believe.

Works Cited

Filter. Short Bus. Burbank, California: Reprise Records. 1995.

"History: Ancient Greece." *World Wide Virtual Library.* September 1993. April 2003. <www.westernculture.com/ancientgreeks.html>.

Patrick, Richard. "*The Amalgamut.*" *Rich Words.* 2002. April 2003. <www.officialfilter .com>.

Patrick, Richard. "The Missing." *The Amalgamut.* Burbank, California: Reprise Records. 2002.

Practicum

How does Marianne's model fulfill the criteria for a successful interpretive essay? Write a brief evaluation. Refer to specific examples from the text of her essay to support your evaluation. Share your responses with your classmates. Do you find that you agree with your classmates? Disagree?

Reflection in Action

When you began this chapter, what was your understanding of the relationship between art and life? Did you view art as an imitation of life? Did you believe that life could be affected by art? What was your understanding of the way meaning is communicated through artifacts?

Has your understanding of artistic representation changed? If your answer is yes, then how has it changed?

In your own words, explain the relationship between art and life, life and art.

Do you believe that art is an important and necessary part of life? Can artistic representations have a positive impact on our lives?

Expanding Your Vision: A Multimedia Assignment Option

Critical Inquiry: Digging Deeper

Interpretations of meaning are created and presented through many different mediums. Experience is often represented as a story, poem, song, or painting. Then the meaning communicated in that artifact is interpreted and represented in the form of another artifact. A story becomes a made-for-television movie. A poem becomes a song. A song becomes a music video. Art is transformed and meaning is signified in many different forms.

Take a moment and brainstorm a list of such artistic representations. Can you think of a story that has been interpreted and represented through another artifact? A song? A painting?

After you have come up with a list of artistic representations, freewrite and describe the original artifact and then describe the artistic representation of that artifact. What is your understanding of the meaning communicated by the original text? What is your understanding of the meaning communicated by the artistic representation? How is that meaning signified? Does the meaning change in the representation?

Share and discuss your examples with the class.

MULTIMEDIA ASSIGNMENT   Visi-Quest Eight: Expanding Your Vision by Creating a HYPERconTEXTualization Web Poem Project

An Overview

Use hyperlinks to create an interpretation of a song lyric by connecting words and/or phrases in the song with images collected from the Internet and your own files. The combination of words/phrases and linked images should communicate your understanding of the meaning of a song.

Step One: Reading to Understand

1. Select a song lyric to work with from your event casebook.

2. As usual, read the lyrics once without taking any notes, just to get familiar with it. Then work through the lyrics: Description + Association + Context.

Step Two: Creating an Interpretation

1. Once you have completed your Description + Association + Context, conduct a thirty-minute free-write. As you explore your thoughts about the lyrics, consider the following:
    ◦ What does this lyric say to you?
    ◦ What do you want your audience to understand about this song?
    ◦ What kinds of images will help you create that understanding for your audience?
2. With your purpose in mind (the interpretation you hope to communicate to your audience), go back through the lyrics and highlight the words and phrases that most clearly contribute to the meaning you wish to express. Depending on the length of your song, select at least five to eight words and/or phrases you would like to illustrate with visual images (you may illustrate as much of the original text as you would like).
3. Before going on, pause for a moment and brainstorm a list of possible keywords to use as you search the Internet for appropriate images and links.

Step Three: Gather Images and Links

1. Before you begin collecting images for your Web poem, create a master file in which to store those images.
    ◦ Open Microsoft Word.
    ◦ From the toolbar at the top of your screen, click **File.**
    ◦ In the dropdown menu, click **Save As.**
    ◦ A small window will appear. In the field beside **Save In,** click the arrow and a menu will drop. Select **3 _ Floppy (A:)** (to save on your floppy diskette).
    ◦ In the toolbar at the top of the window, locate the symbol for New Folder (usually the fifth symbol on the bar, a file with a starburst in the upper righthand corner). Click on the symbol.
    ◦ Another small window will appear. In the field beside **Name,** type WEB POEM PROJECT.
    ◦ Click the **Save** button.
2. Minimize Word and open your Web browser.

Note

There are many different search engines you might use on the Internet, but in our experience, Google has proven to be the most comprehensive.

3. In the address bar, type http://www.google.com and click **Go.**
4. Once you are on the Google home page, notice the main search bar and the tabs above it. For text-based links (and some images), use the Web search. For a more focused search for images, use the Images search function.

5. Type the keywords from your brainstorming list into the search bar and begin looking for text-based Web pages with images and/or isolated images that will illustrate various aspects of your song (the meaning communicated by specific words and phrases). This search may take some time; don't settle for the first pages you find.

Note

Your links will not only represent the words or phrases in the song, but they will work together (like the words, stanzas, and music in a song) to produce a particular effect, to communicate a specific meaning—your understanding of the message communicated by the song.

6. When you find an image that you would like to use, capture the image and save it on your disc in your WEB POEM folder.

Capturing an Image from a Text-Based Web Page

- Place your cursor on the image and right-click the mouse.
- In the dropdown menu, click **Save Picture As.**
- A small window will appear. In the field beside **Save In,** click the arrow, and a menu will drop. Select **3 _ Floppy (A:)** (to save on your floppy diskette).
- Double-click on the project folder.
- At the bottom on the window in the field beside **File Name,** type the name of your image.
- Click the **Save** button.
- Your image is now saved locally on your diskette.

Capturing an Image from a Google Image Search

- When you find an image you would like to use, click on the image. A new Web page will come up in your browser.
- At the top of the page, you will find a small picture of your image; at the bottom of the page, you will find the image in its original context (the Web page on which it is located).
- Click on the image at the top of the screen and it will open into a new Web page with an enlarged image of the photograph.
- Place your cursor on the image and right-click the mouse.
- In the dropdown menu, click **Save Picture As.**
- A small window will appear. In the field beside **Save In,** click the arrow, and a menu will drop. Select **3 _ Floppy (A:)** (to save on your floppy diskette).
- Double-click on the project folder.
- At the bottom on the window in the field beside **File Name,** type the name of your image.
- Click the **Save** button.

7. Take some notes and gather documentation information before you leave the Web site where the image is located. Below the URL on your Word document, write down the full name of the author or sponsor of the Web site, the title of the page, the full title of the Web site, the date the site was created or the date of last update, the date you visited the page, and the URL.

Note

It is absolutely imperative that you gather bibliographic information as you collect your images. Images, just like text sources, are intellectual property belonging to someone else, and the source of these images must be credited in your work in order to avoid *plagiarism.*

Once you have collected enough images and text-links to illustrate your interpretation, you are ready to move on.

Step Four: Creating Your Web Poem

1. Open a new document in Word and save this as your home page:
   - From the toolbar at the top of your screen, click **File.**
   - In the dropdown menu, click **Save As.**
   - A small window will appear. In the field beside **Save In,** click the arrow, and a menu will drop. Select **3 _ Floppy (A:)** (to save on your floppy diskette).
   - Double-click on the project folder.
   - In the field beside **File Name** type HOME PAGE.
   - Click the **Save** button.
2. Type the full text of your song in this new document. Play around with fonts (styles, sizes, and colors) and customize the "look" of your lyrics. I recommend double-spacing the lines and using at least a 14-point font. You might also select a background color for your page.

   Setting a Background for Your Page

   - In the toolbar at the top of your page, click **Format.**
   - In the dropdown menu, select **Background.**
   - A small side-menu will pop up. You may select a color from the palate on that menu, or you may select **More Colors** or **Fill Effects** to customize your background style.
   - If you select **More Colors,** a new window will emerge, and you will find a larger palate of colors from which to choose. Simply click on the color of your choice and select **OK.**
   - If you select **Fill Effects,** you will have choices of **Gradient** colors, **Textures, Patterns,** or the option of setting a **Picture** as your background. Make your selection and click **OK.**

Note

Your background should complement the rest of your page. Be careful not to choose a color that is too bold or a pattern or picture that is too "busy" and distracting. If you make a selection and decide that you want to change it, simply click on Edit on the toolbar at the top of your screen and select Undo. This will remove your background color, and you can make another choice.

Creating Hyperlinks between Words/Phrases and Images

   - Drag your cursor across the first word or phrase you would like to create a link for and highlight it.

○ At the toolbar at the top of your screen, click **Insert.** A menu will drop down. From that menu, select **Hyperlink.**

○ A small window will emerge titled **Insert Hyperlink.**

○ Click on **Recent Files.**

○ On the right side of the window under the field labeled **Browse For,** select **File.**

○ A new window will emerge titled **Link to File.**

○ Beside the field **Look In,** click on the arrow and select **3 _ Floppy (A:).**

○ Double-click on your project folder.

○ Select the image you wish to link, and click **OK.**

○ You will return to the screen **Insert Hyperlink.** Click **OK.**

Voila: The word or phrase you highlighted in your poem is now a hyperlink (usually indicated by the color blue and a line underscoring the word or phrase).

3. Before moving on, test the link you created. Press the **Ctrl** button on your keyboard and click on the word or phrase in your poem. The linked image should open on a new page.

4. Close that page and return to your Word document. Complete your links.

Note

If you make a mistake and link a word or phrase to the wrong image, or if you decide to change links, simply repeat the process above. Highlight the word or phrase, click Insert, Hyperlink, and follow the steps outlined above to make a new link. The old link will be replaced by your new selection.

---

5. When you have made hyperlinks between all of your selected words and phrases and the Web pages you located, it is time to save your document as a Web page:

○ In the toolbar at the top of your document screen, click **File.**

○ A menu will drop down. Click **Save As.**

○ A small window will pop up. Beside the field **Save In,** select **3 _ Floppy (A:).**

○ At the bottom of the small window beside **Save As Type,** click the arrow and select **Web Page.**

○ Click the **Save** button on the right of the screen. Your document should now be saved on your floppy disk as a Web page.

6. Before moving on, in a separate document, create a works cited page for your Web poem project that documents each image used in your poem as well as the poem itself. Save your works cited page in your project folder and create a link for it at the bottom of your home page.

Step Five: Testing Your Web Poem

1. Now you need to open the Web poem in your browser for a test drive:
    ◦ Close your document and open your Web browser.
    ◦ In the tool bar at the top of the screen, click **File.** In the dropdown menu, click **Open.**
    ◦ A small window will pop up. Click the button labeled **Browse.**
    ◦ **Look In** Drive (A:).
    ◦ Double-click on your project folder.
    ◦ Click on your Web poem file home page.
    ◦ Click **Open.** Your Web poem should open into your Web browser.
2. Test each of your links by clicking on the appropriate words or phrases.

Note

Student models of the Web poem assignment are located on the companion Web site for this textbook.

Reflection

Write a brief commentary for your audience in which you explain your overall interpretation of the lyrics, your selection of words and phrases, how the linked images illustrate those words and phrases, how they work together to create your interpretation of the song. Overall, what did you gain from this project in terms of understanding the song and communicating an interpretation?

Criteria for a Successful Web Poem

For this assignment, create a multimedia representation of your understanding of the meaning communicated by a particular artifact. A successful Web poem meets the following criteria:

- ◦ It is constructed according to the directions outlined in the Visi-Quest assignment.
- ◦ It advances one interpretation.
- ◦ It provides engaging visual images linked to specific words or phrases in the lyric to illustrate your understanding of the meaning of the lyric.
- ◦ The components (background, color scheme, etc.) are visually appealing.
- ◦ All hyperlinks are functional.

○ It provides correct MLA style documentation of all visual images used to illustrate the poem in the form of a works cited page.

In the Spotlight: A Student Model Web Poem

The Authors: Western Eyes—Quoc Luu and Christina Lall

Quoc Luu is a computer science major, and Christina Lall is a psychology major. Both students attended the University of North Carolina–Charlotte in the spring of 2003 when they completed this project.

Author's Etcetera

Christina had this to say about her Web poem project:

> I absolutely loved working on the Web poem! It allowed me to be creative in ways I've never explored before! I've never dissected a song like that before, never looked so closely at what a singer was trying to say. And I've never really thought much about Marilyn Manson, but this song (that was so controversial in the media) had so many layers of meaning, it was fantastic. I think most people miss the point of this song. I hope our Web poem helps to make at least part of what Manson was trying to say clear.

Web Poem: Interpretation of Marilyn Manson's "The Fight Song"

This is a screen shot of the first page of the Web poem (you must scroll down to view the rest of the lyrics). The background is a lithograph of the Shroud of Turin.

The banner that runs across the top of the page is a black background with orange lettering. It says "The Fight Song," which is the title of the lyrics displayed below. In all, there are seven hyperlinks between words or phrases in the lyrics and visual images selected to represent an interpretation of the meaning communicated by the song.

The visual images paired with the specific words and phrases work together to create the claim: "Marilyn Manson's 'The Fight Song' gives voice to the anger experienced by many misunderstood, ignored, and neglected teens. While it explains their sometimes violent and antisocial behavior, it also serves as a mantra to encourage those teens not to give up, but to fight, fight, fight."

Clicking on the hyperlinks brings up various screens containing photographic images that illustrate both the meaning of highlighted phrase and the overall claim of the Web poem.

Another screen was linked to the phrase *"doesn't give a shit."* The photograph on this screen depicts graffiti written on a soiled wall. When viewed in full color, the background is a mottled brown and white, and the word "apathy" is spray-painted in dark brown. The photo represents the hyperlinked phrase, and it also contributes to the overall claim expressed through the Web poem.

At the bottom of the Web poem, Quoc and Christina included footnotes to explain their interpretation of the lyrics. Words throughout the song are coupled with reference numbers that lead the audience to these footnotes and a link to the works cited page for this project (see p. 277).

Practicum

How does the Visi-Quest Eight by Western Eyes fulfill the criteria for this assignment? Review the criteria listed for this assignment and make an evaluation. Offer specific examples from the model to illustrate your critique. Then share your ideas with your classmates. Do you find that you and your classmates agree? Do you disagree? Why, or why not? How does this process of reading and evaluating a model assignment help you to successfully meet the requirements for this assignment yourself?

PART FOUR

The Journey So Far

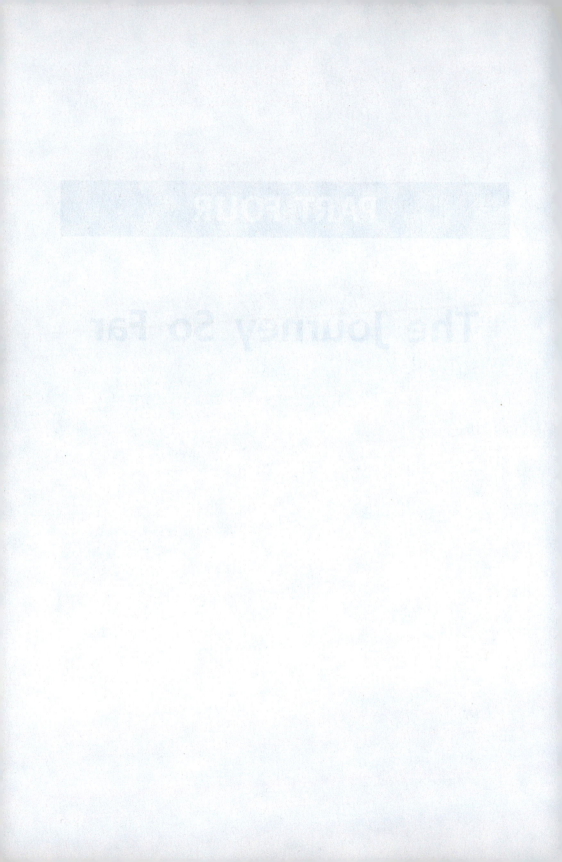

PART FOUR

The Journey So Far

9

Reflection in Presentation: Capstone Project

Begin with a *Question*: What Have I Learned and How Have I Grown?

> We come to terms as well as we can with our lifelong exposure to the world, and we use whatever devices we may need to survive. But eventually, of course, our knowledge depends upon the living relationship between what we see going on and ourselves. If exposure is essential, still more so is the reflection. Insight doesn't happen often on the click of the moment like a lucky snapshot, but comes in its own time and more slowly from nowhere but within. The sharpest recognition is surely that which is charged with sympathy as well as shock—it is a form of human vision.
>
> —*Eudora Welty*

When you began this class, you set forth on a journey, a *Quest,* along with your classmates and your instructor. Your destination: critical and civic literacy. You worked hard, you played some, and you became a community. It has been many weeks since that journey began, and it is just about time for you to move on to a new path in a new direction. But first, it is important that you take a moment to slow down, to look back and reflect on your experiences, growth, and change over the past few weeks.

You began this class by taking a long, hard look at the world around you in general and at one event in particular. You ventured into many new areas of thought along the way, and your voice has become a part of the conversation on some important social issues. You have learned and practiced many critical-thinking strategies, and in many ways, you have *become* critically and civically literate. It has been an intense experience. Now, as the Quest comes to a close, it is almost like you are coming home again before moving on, and in coming home, you will turn within. You are going to unpack your bags, rest, restore your strength, and talk about your journey.

Coming home in terms of this class means that you will turn inward and read what is going on inside of you. You will remember where you began this semester, and review the path your journey has taken. How have you changed? What has this journey meant to you? What have you learned about yourself and the world around you?

Mirror, Mirror on the Wall

Remember Grimm's fairytales? I am thinking of the one with the wicked step-mother—the story of Snow White. The wicked stepmother was the Queen, and the Queen was obsessed with her beauty. She spent a great deal of time primping, look-ing into her magic mirror, and asking, *Mirror, mirror on the wall, who is the fairest one of all?*

The mirror never lied. When the Queen was the most beautiful woman in the land, the mirror said so. When Snow White had grown more beautiful than the Queen, the mirror said so, even though the Queen didn't like that answer very much (and lots of mayhem ensued). The mirror spoke the truth.

In reflection, we find truth. The kind of reflection I am talking about is not sur-face—the mirror you use does not hang on a wall. The mirror is your mind, and you will turn that mirror in to look within yourself—to read the changes you have expe-rienced as you made your journey through this class.

Read Yourself Like a Book

Your definition of reading has changed a lot over the past few weeks. You probably began the semester thinking of reading in terms of words printed on a page. Now you know that you can read anything and everything. You can read a conversation, a photograph, a song, a painting, a look; you can read an event, a Web site, opinions, media coverage, and an issue as it unfolds over time. You now know that reading in-cludes all forms of experience, that it is the process of actively examining a source of information, whatever form that source may take, in order to gain understanding.

By reading the world around you, you broadened and enhanced your experience and understanding of life. Everything around you became bigger and richer, and your place in this world became more purposeful and meaningful. You learned to look at each new experience with a new understanding of the components that make up those experiences. You learned to recognize that each moment, each event, has meaning.

In much the same way, you can read yourself and your experiences. You can look back over the journey you have taken, each step along the way, then you can look within, and you can gain a new understanding of those experiences and find a greater meaning.

What Does This Mean to Me?

When the Queen asked her magic mirror who was the fairest in the land, she did not like the response she got once Snow White had blossomed into a lovely young woman. The Queen had always been the most beautiful (on the outside, anyway), and she did not like this change—not one bit. The Queen believed things were always going to stay the same, that she would forever be the most beautiful (or that the mirror would simply tell her so regardless of the truth). But as we all know, change happens—*especially when someone speaks the truth.* And change is not always easy. Speaking the truth is not always easy. *Recognizing* the truth is not always easy. Sometimes the truth hurts, and reflection is painful. Sometimes it is wonderful, and what you see staring back at you is absolutely breathtaking. Most often, it is a combination—some of the reflection is beautiful, some is not so beautiful. There is almost always something that seems unfinished, something in need of work.

The type of reflection you are about to engage in will not be easy: it may be a combination of beauty and discomfort, but it is necessary. Without looking back, we cannot move forward. There is no real learning without looking back, without reflection. You think you have learned a lot this semester? You are in for a big surprise. *This* is where your real learning begins.

Your reflection involves a review of your journey—where it began, your expectations as you began the journey, each step you took along the way, and where you find yourself now. Then you will look to the future and think about how to apply all you have learned to the next phase of your journey. In looking back, you will find meaning in all you have experienced, meaning that is unique to you. And you will tell the story of your journey—not in the form of a fairytale but in the form of a unique narrative known as a *portfolio.*

My, How You've Grown!

Actually, reflection is nothing new to you. After each major assignment, you were asked to pause and think about your experiences as you completed the assignment before moving on. Those writing activities were a particular kind of reflection known as *reflection in action.* A reflection in action involves looking back over a limited experience and examining the process of that experience for meaning. The kind of reflection you are about to practice is known as *reflection in presentation.* This type of reflection is more detailed and encompasses a broader experience, but it is similar to the other kind of reflection in that you are looking back over an experience (your experience throughout a semester rather than one assignment) and examining the process of that experience for meaning.

Your earlier reflections served as conclusions for one phase of the Quest before you moved onto the next. After completing each Quest, you were asked to gather all of the process work you completed for that particular assignment and to examine your expectations and knowledge as you began the assignment, each step you took as you completed the assignment, and the finished product. You were asked to think about how the process changed you, how you grew as a writer, a thinker, and a learner in very specific ways.

This new reflection serves as a conclusion of this phase of your journey before you move out into the world and on to greater adventures. You will be asked to gather and assemble in some organized fashion all of the process work you completed for each assignment this semester. You will be asked to examine your expectations and knowledge as you began your Quest, then you will examine each step you made throughout the semester. Finally, you will assemble all of your materials into one complete, finished product, and you will be asked to think and write about how this process has changed you, how you have grown as a writer, a thinker, and a learner.

This portfolio is a presentation of your journey this semester. It illustrates the tale of your experiences. Your final reflection is your opportunity to discover and then tell your audience what this journey has meant to you. It's your chance to say, *This is my journey. I made this journey with my classmates and my instructor, my friends, and my family, but the experience was mine, uniquely mine. And here is my story. This is what it means to me.*

The Story of Your Journey So Far: Creating a Portfolio

From the beginning of this class, from the moment you began your Pre-Quest, through each and every Quest that followed, you have been making a paper (or digital) trail and keeping a record of your journey—your process and progress. You have become a packrat out of necessity. You have saved every scribble, every sentence, every question, and every piece of correspondence, every photocopy, every note, draft, and revision. Hopefully, you have developed some sort of organizational strategy along the way, and all of the work you saved is fairly orderly (if not, you have truly got your work cut out for you with this next project).

Undoubtedly, there have been times when you wondered: Why? Why do I have to save *everything*? And I am sure there have been many times when you wanted to toss it all in the wastebasket and forget about it. But there was a method to this pack rat madness.

A Journey Unfolding

As you completed each Quest this semester, there were many practical reasons for saving your work. The biggest reason is that everything you did this semester was connected in some way. One Quest grew out of the assignment that came before it and then built onto that assignment and grew into another project. Nothing was isolated or superfluous—every piece of work was related and formed an interconnected web of learning and growth. The same is true for this final Quest—your portfolio. All of the work you have created this semester will come together in this last assignment as you complete your journey through this class.

This class has always been about the journey. The connectedness of each assignment should have driven home the point that *all* learning is connected. We are constantly building and rebuilding the framework through which we view the world. This has never been about crossing some finish line. In fact, there is no finish line. In terms of this class, you may have completed the requirements, but you are still learning and growing. You always will be. Yet, it is important as we make this journey to recognize milestones, markers of our achievements. We do this in many ways in our lives—by celebrating birthdays, anniversaries, and other special events. This collection of your work, this portfolio you are about to create, is a marker of your achievements during your journey this semester. It is a celebration.

On a Personal Level

Your portfolio is a celebration, an illustration of your hard work and determination. Left in pieces, each individual paper or project tells only part of the story of your journey through this course. To get the whole story, you have to look at the whole picture. A portfolio creates the whole picture by bringing all of your work together in one collection.

This collection of your work will surprise you, challenge you, inspire you, and puzzle you. You may be surprised by how much you have grown and changed. You may be challenged by the volume of work you produced and the task you now face of organizing it. You may be inspired to continue growing and changing by all you have learned. And you may be puzzled by questions with which you are left about your issue or any other topic you explored—questions that, for whatever reasons, remain unanswered.

This enormous paper trail, this collection of work, is *your story,* the story of your journey through this course. It lays before you in pieces, ready to be assembled into a final product, a tale to be shared with others. The final product will become your final Quest for this class. Your portfolio may take many different forms, and we discuss the possibilities in just a moment. It may be shaped by requirements established by your instructor, or it may be shaped by the content of your work and the strengths and weaknesses of your journey. Whatever the final form, this portfolio will serve as a showcase for your efforts, growth, and change; it will be a celebration of your development this semester. Your presentation of this portfolio signifies the completion of this part of your journey and all it has meant to you.

Measuring Growth and Change

Portfolios are more than just trophies or markers of achievement; they are, in and of themselves, fabulous learning tools and tools for measuring and assessing growth and change. *You* learn by creating the portfolio, and *your audience learns about you* by studying the finished product.

Because this is a college classroom, your portfolio will become a tool for your instructor to assess your growth and change as a writer, thinker, and learner. By studying your portfolio, your instructor will be able to experience your journey through this class. Beginning with your first Quest, he or she will follow the same path you took as you moved through each assignment. Your portfolio is evidence of your development of critical and civic literacy skills. Looking at this body of work, your instructor can identify patterns of growth and change, problems encountered, problems solved, and other problems yet to be addressed.

Your instructor will provide you with the specific criteria to be used when evaluating your portfolio, but undoubtedly he or she will expect your portfolio to be complete, creative, organized, and easy to read; to be an example of your best efforts; and to be focused and reflective. Your *reflective introduction* will help to establish a focus for your portfolio. It will, in a sense, teach your audience how to read your portfolio by highlighting the aspects of your journey that are significant to you.

Tools for Success: Collection, Selection, and Reflection

Your final Quest, the creation of your portfolio, is about to begin. How much of your work is actually included in the portfolio and what shape that work takes is largely up to your instructor. Some instructors require that you include every single piece of work completed during a course, some instructors ask you to include only certain pieces of work, some ask only for final revisions.

Your presentation of this portfolio signifies the completion of this part of your journey and all it has meant to you. It truly is your showcase. Keep that in mind as you assemble your portfolio. That is your driving purpose.

It is interesting how, even now, it always comes back to purpose and audience. As you prepare to complete this final Quest, as you have many times in the recent past, you have to once again ask yourself:

- ○ Who is your audience?
- ○ What do you want your reader to understand about your journey?
- ○ How will you best communicate that understanding to your audience?

As you put together your portfolio, there are many things to consider. Your portfolio is and does many things. It is a *collection* of the body of work you completed throughout this class. Within that collection, your portfolio showcases a *selection* of your best work. Finally, this portfolio serves as a *reflection* of what you learned and how you grew as you completed your journey. Here are some guidelines for you to follow as you make decisions to complete this final Quest.

Collection

- ○ **Sort your papers according to Quest.** As you prepare your portfolio, it will help to speed up the process if you sort your paperwork according to Quest. Make one pile for Quest One, another for Quest Two, and so on. This will help you to locate specific assignments as you assemble the portfolio and mark things off on your checklist.

○ **Use a checklist.** As you organize your collection of materials, your instructor may provide you with a checklist to follow (a list of assignments that you must include in the portfolio). If he or she does not provide a checklist, make one of your own. Go back through the assignment sheet for each Quest and make a list of every requirement. Then, as you locate each piece of work, mark it off your list and place the assignment in your folder or binder.

○ **Be sure each piece of work is clearly labeled.** As you mark off assignments on your checklist, make sure that each individual assignment is clearly labeled as to which Quest it belongs to and which step of the Quest it fulfilled. For example, an article located while researching the history of your issue should be labeled at the top of the first page, "Background Research, Quest Three." Or a first draft of your argument essay should be clearly labeled "Draft 1, Quest Six."

○ **Clearly divide each section.** Once you have organized all of your assignments according to each Quest, assemble the final collection in a large, three-ring binder. Use dividers to clearly separate each section of the portfolio (to clearly mark or distinguish the whole of Quest One from the whole of Quest Two). Label the divider.

The actual organization of your portfolio may be handled in several different ways. (Note: Your instructor may have a preference for one organizational pattern over another. The following information is an overview; you should, of course, follow the specific guidelines established by your instructor.)

○ **Chronological Organization.** For this type of portfolio, no one piece of work is showcased, but the entire journey is the focus. Your work is organized according to the order in which it was produced throughout the semester (i.e., the first assignment appears first in the portfolio, followed by the second assignment, the third, and so on). For instance, with a chronological organization, your Quest One would be placed first in your binder. Quest Two would follow Quest One, beginning with the invention work, followed by the planning, drafting, and so on. This organizational pattern would continue until you have included all of your Quests in your binder.

○ **Organization to Showcase Your Best Work.** A showcase portfolio begins with a section dedicated to whatever you consider to be your best work. This work might be from any stage of the process of any Quest. You might include your invention work for Quest Two because you think you did an especially thorough job of exploring your cultural inventory; then you might include your research from Quest Four because you are proud of the quality of the sources you discovered, a first draft for Quest Five because it demonstrates the development of your analytical skills, or your final revision of Quest Eight because it is an example of the culmination of all of your hard work throughout the semester. Following the showcased work, you would then organize the remainder of your portfolio chronologically.

> **Note**
>
> Another way to showcase is to organize the portfolio chronologically and then simply tag your best pieces to call attention to them, probably using some sort of Post-It note or a more creative attention-getter.

○ **Last First; First Last.** This sort of portfolio begins with a section devoted to the final versions of each Quest. Within this section, the final revision of each Quest is organized chronologically. This type of organization places an emphasis on the final product—the spit-and-polished work that represents the very best you are capable of producing. Following the final versions, the remainder of the process work is organized chronologically.

Selection

If your instructor requires that you include a section in your portfolio in which you showcase examples of your best work, your first task is to decide on your criteria for "best." (Again, this criteria may come from your instructor.) Here are some suggestions to help you decide what to include and what *not* to include:

○ **Favorite vs. Best.** I cannot tell you how many times I have heard students say, "I really enjoyed working on this assignment. It was my favorite, so I think it deserves an A." Your favorite assignment is not necessarily an example of your best work. The fact that you enjoyed the process (though enjoyment is a wonderful thing) does not mean that the work you produced is necessarily top quality. Nor is your best work the assignment most easily completed. In fact, sometimes your best work is the end result of the most difficult process—a process rife with errors, corrections, and struggles.

○ **Most Improved.** Providing examples of improvement is a wonderful idea for a showcase. Not only does it illustrate improvement and development in a general sense, but also it shows that you recognize your own improvement and development. This is an important critical-thinking skill. The ability to identify your strengths and weaknesses, to note moments of growth and change, indicates that you are aware of your own learning process and that you will be able to apply what you have learned to other situations.

○ **Most Meaningful Process.** You might decide to showcase a Quest with the most meaningful process. Again, remember that meaningful does not necessarily equal fun. Showcasing the process of a Quest that was most challenging to you in some way and then showing how you dealt with that challenge, or showcasing a process that was most thought-provoking, or most useful in terms of later Quests—these are all important examples of a meaningful process experience that would demonstrate your learning and growth.

- **High-Quality Final Product.** The most common showcase includes the final versions of each Quest. These final versions are the end results of a process that included a great deal of vision and re-vision. They are examples of growth and change. Remember, whether a part of a showcase or not, your final versions must be clearly focused, organized, adequately developed, and virtually error-free.

Reflection

In terms of a portfolio, *reflection* refers to the introductory piece that you will create in which you look back over your experiences of the past semester and call attention to what you have learned and how you have grown, and it refers to the portfolio as a whole. By creating your portfolio and the reflective introduction, you are making meaning of your experiences this semester, and you are communicating that meaning to your audience. In a sense, you are teaching your audience how to read your portfolio by calling attention to particular aspects of your journey.

Begin your reflection by deciding what about your journey you want to highlight, and then decide on an appropriate format. Whatever format you decide upon, remember that the content of your reflection will establish a focus for reading the remainder of your portfolio. If you say in your reflection that you learned a lot about voice, your reader will be looking in your portfolio for evidence of voice. If you say you learned a lot about research and thinking critically about sources, your reader will look for evidence of that in the portfolio. This essay will be the piece that pulls it all together. It should be created with great purpose. Your reflection moves beyond the introduction and refers to the portfolio as a whole. Ask yourself, What do I want to call attention to? How do I want my audience to read my journey? What do I want the focus to be?

You will probably be on your own with this reflection—no required process work to be shared with your classmates. So, this assignment is your ultimate test, in a way. It is time for you to show all you know about writing as a process. Though you may not be required to include process work for this assignment in your portfolio, you should utilize process. Complete some sort of invention work, make a draft, share with a peer, get comments, and then make at least one revision.

When you complete your reflection and place it in your three-ring binder, your portfolio should look and feel like it is complete. It should capture the spirit of your journey through this class.

Reflection Walk-Through

Before you begin this final Quest, let's take a look at some reflections written by students just like you who made this journey with me as their instructor. Though many of our experiences were common and shared, each reflection is unique and answers the question, *What have I learned and how have I grown?*

The last few weeks of the semester in my English classes in fall 2002, emotions were running high for everyone because we had been through so much in such a short period of time. Everyone had worked hard, we had learned a great deal, and, without a doubt, we had grown and changed in some amazing ways. In one respect, everyone was ready for a break, ready to move on. But moving on also meant leaving behind many of the people and experiences that had come to be quite important to us all, and we were not so eager to do that. Not just yet.

So, when I made the assignment for this portfolio, there was a collective sigh in the classroom. Some of that sigh was relief—the last Quest! Everyone knew: We made it! One more hoop to jump through, and then we could relax for a while. There was a sense of accomplishment waiting just around the corner, and that was a positive thing. But a part of that sigh was also sadness in knowing we were about to leave behind an experience that was good and important. There was a little bit of dread in that sigh, as well. We knew that in looking back, we were about to revisit many different kinds of emotions, and we were faced with an enormous task: How *do* you organize and sum up such an intense experience in a portfolio and capture the power and truth of that experience?

Reflection is itself a powerful experience—maybe the most powerful and gratifying learning experience available to us. The following reflections were a conclusion, a closing of one chapter in each student's life. They reflect the journey for the individual.

You will see in these reflections how certain aspects of the journey were more important for one individual than for another. Some were most moved by the idea of critical literacy and finding a voice, some were most moved by civic literacy, by becoming involved and by the potential to make a change. Some were most moved by the research and what they learned about the issue—the knowledge they gained.

Now, in their own words, here is the story of the journey as experienced by three of my former students.

Student Reflection in the Form of an Interview

The Author: Daniel Kreutzer

Daniel completed English 1103 in Fall 2002. He plans to major in business administration with a concentration in finance from a public college in North Carolina.

Author's Etcetera

Daniel had this to share about his final Quest:

> The whole reflection process was actually pretty rewarding. I was satisfied with the outcome, and finishing the reflection helped to end the class with a feeling of having summarized the whole semester in my mind. The thing I learned from writing the reflection and

putting together the portfolio is that I worked hard over the semester, and writing the reflection helped me to see that I needed to take something away from the class other than just a letter grade. The reflection was a good way to conclude my freshman experience. I was able to come up with my own thoughts and ideas in a format I had picked. What I attempted to do in the reflection was to get an honest and close look at me as a person to understand what I had accomplished and gained from my semester in English 1103. I attempted to add some humor to lighten the mood a bit.

An Interview with Daniel Kreutzer

Hi, my name is Charlie Rosendale, and I am a reporter for the *Quest Journal*. I recently sat down with Daniel Kreutzer at his home in Charlotte, North Carolina, where he attends the University of North Carolina at Charlotte. Days ago, Daniel completed work for a required English class, and I had the opportunity to talk to him about his experience. The following is the actual transcript of our conversation.

Quest Journal: So, you enrolled in English 1103 this past semester, is that right?

Daniel Kreutzer: Yes. That is correct, Charlie.

QJ: What exactly was the purpose of the class?

DK: Well, Charlie, aside from fulfilling a general education requirement, at first I thought this class would be about the mechanics of writing. You know, the basic grammar stuff like periods, exclamation points, and commas—the basic boring stuff we all learned in fourth grade but maybe with a college twist? That's what I thought. But after the very first day, my outlook on this class completely changed.

QJ: Wow! On the very first day! How did your outlook change, Daniel?

DK: Well, I'll tell you, Charlie. My professor introduced the class to the idea of *critical and civic literacy.* She said *critical literacy* was about examining the world around you with a critical eye, and *civic literacy* was about getting involved in that world. As soon as she introduced us to this new idea, I knew we weren't going to concentrate on question marks and prepositional phrases, though that sort of thing is important, of course. That first day I knew: I was on a quest to find my voice and to learn how to express myself.

QJ: Fantastic.

DK: Yes, that's true. Do you know how many people do not *want* you to have a voice in this world? Lots of people. Most high schools don't teach you how to think, much less how to have a voice in this world—they teach you "facts." Which is not necessarily a bad thing, but there's a big difference between memorizing a fact and thinking about an issue and speaking out about what you think. And we've all got something to say! But there are people who do not want to give us the opportunity to speak. I mean, an average citizen can't go on most television stations with their own opinions, and newspapers edit the content of our letters to the editor—we're constantly being censored or silenced by the powers-that-be.

QJ: So thinking for yourself is something your professor taught you?

DK: Hang on there a minute! I am a fairly smart guy with my own opinions. I would not say that my professor taught me how or what to think—that wasn't what this class was all about. But she made me *more aware* of the opportunities I have to form an opinion on every subject and to speak out on my opinion. But it's more than just speaking out. I learned that I must examine my beliefs and have evidence to support my opinions. I started the semester by studying the Columbine shootings, and I investigated the cause of that event. There seemed to be a couple of causes that most people blamed for the shootings. I found that the cause or issue someone blamed seemed to be connected to his or her beliefs about life in some fundamental way.

QJ: So, you focused on possible causes for the shooting, and then what?

DK: Well, I began to investigate the issue related to that possible cause. I looked at how the issue was connected to the country and ourselves.

QJ: How do you think this process benefited you?

DK: I began to realize that *everything* is connected, and we're all connected, too—no matter how far away an event seems from us and our everyday lives. I realized that all of the issues have places where they overlap and converge, and no one thing is to blame for an event like Columbine. I also saw a small piece of the history on my issue, and I learned other people's views on the subject.

QJ: So you learned to see the big picture, so to speak? Was there anything that challenged you while attempting to see the big picture?

DK: Charlie, I'm glad you asked me that. As a matter of fact, there were aspects of the class I found challenging. The most challenging thing—aside from getting up for class in the morning? Just kidding (laughing)! No, but seriously, the most challenging thing was learning to read the world around me and talk back to it. I mean, how do you talk back to a book or television news program? Basically, I think we do it by thinking, by coming up with our own outlook on a subject, and by living our lives so that we reflect our beliefs.

QJ: Any puzzling things crop up during your English class?

DK: Well, it puzzled me that so many people take for granted that what they're told is 100% true. Before I began this semester, I took things for granted, too. I used to listen to a news program and automatically assume it was "the truth" and factual and beyond questioning. Now, I find myself being skeptical about almost everything. Not in a bad way, but in a way that pushes me to think and look a little deeper into what I'm being told and what I'm seeing in the world around me. That is something I lost during my class: blind acceptance. About a week ago, I rented the movie *Wag the Dog*. This is a flick about a president who covers up a sexual misdoing by creating a fake war using the media. As I sat there watching it, I was actually getting angry. I started thinking: *My goodness, they could be doing this right now, and we'd never know—we'd never question it! Who do they think they are?!* I do not think I would have had that realization before taking this English class.

QJ: How did you make it through this class? I mean, what was your inspiration?

DK: Well, I think I was mostly inspired by the command to claim your education rather than receive it. We talked about that at the beginning of the semester, and it really helped me to make it through my first semester of college without becoming too stressed out with grades or the workload. Anytime I started to feel overwhelmed, I just remembered, *I'm here to claim my education*. Words to live by, I'm telling you!

QJ: How do you think you have changed over the past semester?

DK: Wow. That is a great question. Well, at the beginning of the semester, I was a guy who would do anything anyone suggested, then complain about it afterwards. As this semester progressed, I realized that to survive in the world today, I would need my own voice. I can no longer be double-minded and change my beliefs based on the situation I find myself in. My voice must be strong—and it must be completely mine. As the semester draws to a close, I now assert myself more. I'm not afraid to say what I think. I used to be afraid to say what I thought, because I had nothing to back up what I was thinking. Now I have found that if I just stop and think about a subject, I am able to prove or defend my opinions because I read the world around me and I read my own ideas, too. I don't take anything for granted anymore.

QJ: Well, it certainly sounds as if you have learned a lot. Where do you go from here, Daniel? How will you use what you learned to your benefit?

DK: Hmmm, I suppose I will apply what I learned in English to my everyday life. When I hear an opinion voiced, I will think about it and respond with my own opinion. I will also pay more attention to the history of a subject. I will understand that I am not just another creature in the general population, but I am one of a kind and my opinions matter just as much as anyone else's. While I am learning to voice my opinions, I remember the words of G. K. Chesterton, who said, "If anything is worth doing, it is worth doing badly." I may not be the greatest writer or speaker, but as I struggle to voice my opinions and research issues, I become better. I can start out doing something badly, but I will become better just by *doing* it. I'll keep trying because it is worth it, and I have something to say that's worth saying well. Period. Or maybe exclamation point!

QJ: Thank you, Daniel, for your time.

DK: Thank you, Charlie.

Student Reflection in the Form of a Collage

The Author: Jessica Jarvis

Jessica is from Saluda, North Carolina. At the time she completed this Quest, she was 19 years old and majoring in communications.

> **Author's Etcetera**
>
> Jessica shared this about her final Quest:
>
> As for the reflection, I found it surprisingly easy to write. I wanted to take a creative approach, so I made the collage first. After I finished with it, the writing was easy because I had put a lot of thought into the layout and content of the collage. The words came very easily. It was also a very big relief to finish the portfolio off with it. I liked the assignment because it forced me to think about what I really wanted to accomplish in college and helped me make goals for myself in the future.

As the Quest Turns: One Road Ends
as Another Begins

After reflecting on the past few months, I realize how different the outcome would have been had I not taken the time to acknowledge what brought me to Charlotte, North Carolina, to this moment in my life. This process of acknowledgment—the instigator of my great revelations—began with the creation of "My Declaration of Education." That assignment really forced me to think about why I am here, what I plan to do with my time at UNC Charlotte, and what my goals are for the future. I have chosen to represent this process visually in the form of a collage. Why a visual representation? Well, as the song says, *I once was blind, but now I **see.*** But because if there's one thing I have learned this semester, you may not see things and understand them exactly as I do, please allow me to explain.

My collage is divided into four sections: My expectations for my future, the new environment I have found myself in, the expectations others have for me, and my goals for the next few years.

THE FUTURE	
EXPECTATIONS	THE NEW PLACE
WHERE I AM NOW	

The Future

The background is a road, which represents the journey that lies ahead of me. At the beginning of the road is **TODAY,** and at the end of the road is **TOMORROW.** Also at the beginning of the road is the question, **WHERE ARE YOU GOING?** That's the question all college students are faced with, and it is the question I faced head-on as I began this semester. The words **GET READY** represent the fact that I am in college to prepare for my future. During my college career, I might face a **FORK IN THE ROAD** (or two or three), but no matter what I face, no matter what choices I make, I will learn from every moment, I will keep searching for the path that is meant for me, and I will **TAKE IT!**

Expectations

If there's one thing I've discovered so far, it's that so many people are putting pressure on me to succeed. My parents are always encouraging me to stay **ON TARGET** and to always give **100%.** I know they are right, but no one's expectations are as important as mine. This is why "My Declaration of Education" was so important to me. I knew that my parents would have high expectations for me, but I never knew how stressful those expectations would prove to be. If I didn't understand my own reasons for being here, I might not be able to face that stress and all of my responsibilities. I now understand that it's not **MAKE ME WORK FOR YOU** that drives me to succeed, it's make it work for me! My time at this university is when I will really figure out **WHAT I'M MADE OF.**

The New Place

I remember thinking when I first arrived in Charlotte, *wow.* I was so excited about living in the big **CITY.** But that excitement soon changed to one surprise after another—some good, some not so good. I never knew how much of a culture shock this move would be. I had no idea what a **COUNTRY GIRL** I am at heart—and that "country girl" is exactly how other people would perceive me. What a shock.

Another big culture shock that I am still learning how to deal with is, I have to share everything! Living in the dorm, **MY STUFF** is not just mine anymore. Another shock is living **ON A BUDGET** (money really *doesn't* grow on trees!). It's hard to deal with all of these responsibilities when (sometimes) all I really want to do is have fun with my **FRIENDS.** But I love this city and all it has to offer. There is so much to do here! How can anyone ever be bored? Of course, at some point I realized that I'm not *just* here to **PARTY.** It's not all about playtime. I'm here to earn my education. But every moment in this city is an education.

The biggest thing I have to remember about my new life [is that] this city holds a lot of opportunities, so I must never forget to **DREAM.** No longer do I have to deal with boundaries and living in a world of black and white. I can feel free to **FANTASIZE IN COLOR!** And the possibilities are endless.

Where I Am Now

I've looked at the past, I've tried to predict the future, and I've worried about other people and their plans for my life. The important thing for me to do is realize where I am now, the **NEW** position I hold in my life. **I AM NOT A TREND.** I am not a statistic for someone else to analyze, a number in a long line of generation X, Y, or Z. I am me. I have entered into **THE AGE OF INDIVIDUALITY,** and all I can do is take each day and each moment and each new experience with a **SMILE.** It's true that I have to work hard and apply myself, but above all I must remember to enjoy each moment for what it is. After all, how can I **GROW** without a little bit of sunshine?

Student Reflection in the Form of a Letter

The Author: Kim Michels

Kim hopes to graduate from college to become a successful person in the world, one day making a difference, whether it be ending youth violence or banning guns.

Author's Etcetera

Kim shared these final thoughts about her portfolio:

> This journey helped me view life a little differently. Now I know that there is not just one solution to a problem such as youth violence. The debates can go on forever. But we, as citizens, should not give up, because all violence does affect us in some way.
>
> This reflection was a relief for me. It brought my journey (quest) to an end and helped me see which way I want to go in college/life. There are certain strategies to writing which make it easier, and putting a portfolio together helped me see these steps a little more clearly. The portfolio also taught me that each step needs your full devotion in order to write that great paper.

Dear Ms. Stallings and Future Quest Seekers

I am sad to say that this semester has gone by surprisingly fast, but I am happy to say that it has been a great journey! This course has been the most relaxed, knowledge-filled, and interesting experience I have ever had during my years of formal education, and I must say that I learned more in these few weeks than in four years of high school!

At the beginning of the semester, we began our Quest by looking closely at a few important historical documents. History has not been my subject of choice in the past, but when I read the Declaration of Independence, the Declaration of Sentiments and Resolutions, and Claiming an Education, I was intrigued. Looking past the funny way they wrote way-back-when, it became clear that these historical documents provide meaningful rights and freedoms we all enjoy. Seeing them in this new way, it was like a window opened up for me. I had a new understanding and appreciation for history and for education. Like I wrote in my own Declaration of Education, "Education shall provide me with an ethical and intellectual contract between the teacher and student." You and I, Ms. Stallings, most certainly accomplished that. You helped me see what education is really about, and you even provided steps and strategies along the way that I can use in my "real life."

After you helped us realize where education could lead us, I looked at a major event: Columbine. Once again, sorrow, sadness, anger, confusion, tears, and guilt all rose to the surface as I revisited that event. Tragedies like this occur every day in our country—and around the world. People hear the news, ponder why something like that could happen, and then the tragedy becomes a faded memory buried in the back of our minds. I questioned: Why do so many people turn away from a tragic event like Columbine? And I think I understand the answer to that question now. It's simple, really. We are afraid because we know there are no simple solutions to preventing violence in America.

After studying this event, I looked at some major issues that are blamed for youth violence. I looked at music, movies, and other forms of media; I looked at parental, community, and personal responsibility; and I looked at video games, cliques, and guns. It was an amazing journey. And the topic I chose to focus on was guns.

After I researched the background on my event, I discovered that the same problems have been occurring and reoccurring for many years. These same issues have existed for a long time. Then I looked at the way these issues exist in society today.

Through my research, I found many articles that presented multiple perspectives on my issue—gun control. I read everything I could get my hands on as I attempted to become an expert on all perspectives on guns—from the tightest gun control laws to salons where gun lovers hang out, drink, dance, and—of course—shoot. However, no matter how much I tried to understand the gun culture, I came back to my strong opinion that a ban on guns will help reduce youth violence in America.

I learned so much through my research, and so much of what I learned frightens me. For instance, I'll never forget that an average of 35,000 Americans die each year as a result of gun violence. Or that so many firearms are sold each year, yet private gun show dealers are not expected to conduct any research on the people they sell to. What that means is a lot of guns end up in troubled hands, causing unnecessary deaths. In fact, I learned that most of the guns used in crimes—like the Columbine shooting—are purchased or obtained illegally at gun shows or through private dealers. I can't help but wonder, if our country made it nearly impossible to obtain firearms, wouldn't it be much harder for depressed, innocent teenagers who feel as if they have no other way out to follow through with their plans? Just as teen killer Andy Williams said in an interview, when asked if he would have committed his crime without access to his father's gun, he said, *"No, if I hadn't had the gun, there wouldn't have been a crime."*

You have just read a portion of my opinion towards guns and youth violence, and this only represents a fraction of what I learned this semester. My portfolio tells more of the story, but my story doesn't end here—neither does the problem of youth violence and guns. This semester has taught me that knowledge never ends. Knowledge itself is a never-ending story, but we can always keep digging for answers or clues to find a solution to end youth violence or any other problem. My own Quest for answers won't end here. I'll keep looking.

I am sick of hearing about shootings and murders. I want some answers! I want to see a change! Obviously, the things done in the past are not working, and we need to try something different. That is why we are here. This quest taught me how news and current events, no matter how far away they are, pertain to each and every one of us. Along with my peers, I learned to investigate events, research issues, and make claims of fact, value, and policy. I found and used my voice, and joined the conversation that was already in progress. In all of my searching, I found some answers along the way—and some new questions, too. All in all, the biggest lessons I have learned from this quest are: I know where I stand in life. I know my voice matters. I understand that life is a journey, and I now understand how connected *my* journey is with everyone else's.

I'm ready for the next step.

Practicum

In this walk-through, you have studied three different responses to the same assignment. How were these responses similar? How were they different? Of the three, which did you find most effective, and why?

Take a moment to compare and contrast the strengths and weaknesses you noted in each reflection. Share your response with your classmates. Do you and your classmates agree? Disagree?

How will these three examples help you as you begin to write your own final reflection and construct your portfolio?

WRITING ASSIGNMENT   Quest Nine, Part One: Making Choices and Assembling Your Portfolio

Following the process outlined in "Tools for Success," assemble your portfolio. Begin by organizing your materials according to Quest; then make a checklist. Confirm that each required assignment is present and accounted for. As you move through your checklist, clearly label each piece of work. Then decide on an organizational strategy for your portfolio and arrange each piece according to that strategy.

If your strategy involves some sort of showcasing, take the time to select the pieces that will appear in the showcase. Divide each section of your portfolio and clearly label the divider. Decide what the focus of your portfolio should be. Then move on to the last formal assignment: your reflective introduction.

Quest Nine, Part Two: Create a Reflective Introduction to Your Portfolio

As an introduction to your portfolio, write a reflective essay that explores and discusses where you began your semester (your goals and expectations, both academic and personal), how the semester progressed (high points, low points, the good, the bad, the ugly), and where you feel you are now as the semester comes to a close.

Consider these questions: What did you gain this semester? What did you lose? What surprised you? What challenged you? What inspired you? What puzzled you? And where do you go from here?

Your reflective introduction may take any form you wish. Be as straight-up academic as you would like to be, or be wildly creative. Write a letter addressed to your reader, a guidebook for future Quest students, write a short story, a poem, or an essay with an introduction, a body, and a conclusion. Use visuals. Use technology. Use whatever you like! The choice is yours. BUT, whatever format you chose, be sure to *fully explore* the journey you have embarked on over the course of the past semester. Refer to specifics—in your life, in class, in your work. Be descriptive and detailed. *Remember: This reflection sets the focus for your entire portfolio.*

Criteria for a Successful Portfolio and Reflective Introduction

For this assignment, create a portfolio and a reflective introduction for that portfolio. Some criteria for a successful Post-Quest follow.

Portfolio

- ○ A successful portfolio is complete (containing all required materials). Each piece of the portfolio is clearly labeled.
- ○ A successful portfolio is neatly organized, either chronologically, in a showcase format, or last work first/first work last.
- ○ A successful portfolio showcases some aspect of the collection, either favorite assignments, best assignments, most improved assignments, or most meaningful assignments.

Reflective Introduction

- ○ A successful reflective introduction is focused and establishes a focus for reading the remainder of the portfolio.
- ○ A successful reflective introduction is adequately developed with appropriate and specific examples from the portfolio. Examples and explanations demonstrate a thoughtful engagement.
- ○ A successful reflective introduction is organized in a logical pattern with a clear introduction and an engaging conclusion.
- ○ A successful reflective introduction is error-free.

Practicum

How do each of the models included in this chapter fulfill the criteria for a successful reflective introduction for a portfolio? Write a brief evaluation. Refer to specific examples from the text of each model to support your evaluation. Share your responses with your classmates. Do you find that you and your classmates agree? Disagree?

Reflection in Action

What did completing this portfolio mean for you? What did the process teach you? What did you learn? Why was it an important final step? What would you do differently throughout the semester to make this part of the process easier and more successful?

Expanding Your Vision: A Multimedia Assignment Option

Critical Inquiry: Digging Deeper

Chances are if you are familiar with portfolios at all, you are most familiar with the standard hard copy printed on paper and bound in some sort of folder or notebook. Presentation of a body of work in a book or booklet format allows for experience and creativity to be expressed in very particular ways.

Making the transformation from a print document to an interactive electronic document is a unique challenge. Take a moment and list the similarities between a print-based portfolio and an electronic portfolio (in content, organization, and appearance). What elements are most important to retain when making the transition from print to electronic media?

Then list the ways in which a print-based portfolio and an electronic portfolio might be different. What options do you have electronically that you do not have with a print document?

MULTIMEDIA ASSIGNMENT   Visi-Quest Nine: Expanding Your Vision by Creating an Electronic Portfolio

Following the directions below, create an electronic portfolio of your work for this class. This portfolio will be saved on a diskette and will contain all of your work created this semester.

Step One

In your word processing program, create a folder and label it ELECTRONIC PORTFOLIO.

Step Two

Move all of the files for your Quests and course work to that folder. Be sure each file is clearly labeled (for example, Pre-Quest Invention, Pre-Quest Draft, Pre-Quest Revision, Quest One Invention).

Step Three

Create a file to serve as a table of contents for your portfolio. List each individual piece of work in your table of contents in the order in which you would like it to be read.

Step Four

Create a hyperlink to each file.

Creating a Hyperlink

Your word processing program allows hypertext links to be made so that you can navigate around a document or open other files. Microsoft Word uses **Hyperlink,** a command under the **Insert** menu.

This is a very simple process.

1. Click on **Insert,** then click on **Hyperlink.** A window will pop up containing the files on your computer.
2. Select "A:" drive and select the folder ELECTRONIC PORTFOLIO.

(continued)

3. Within that folder, select the file you would like to create a link for in the table of contents. A link for that file will appear in your table of contents.
4. Repeat this process for each document you want to include in your electronic portfolio until everything in the table of contents has a hyperlink.

SAVE YOUR WORK REGULARLY!

Once you have created links for all of your work, create a label for your diskette that includes your name, the course name and number, your instructor's name, and the date. Your electronic portfolio is complete and ready to be shared.

Note

You may decide to add some sort of multimedia work to your electronic portfolio, such as a PowerPoint presentation as your reflective introduction. You may also get creative with colors and fonts to add a little personality to your portfolio. Because you do not have to worry about the costs of printing or the limitations of print media, there are a number of possibilities for creative expression that you might explore.

Criteria for a Successful Electronic Portfolio

For this assignment, create an electronic portfolio and a reflective introduction for that portfolio. Some criteria for a successful Post-Quest Visi-Quest include the following.

Electronic Portfolio

- A successful electronic portfolio is complete (containing all required materials). Each piece of the portfolio is clearly labeled.
- A successful electronic portfolio is organized, either chronologically, in a showcase format, or last work first/first work last. All hyperlinks are fully functional and easily navigated.
- A successful electronic portfolio showcases some aspect of the collection, either favorite assignments, best assignments, most improved assignments, or most meaningful assignments.

In the Spotlight: A Student Model Electronic Portfolio

The Author: Meghal Bhatt

Born in Mumai, India and raised just outside of Toronto, Canada, Meghal was enrolled in English 1102 during the spring of 2003. His major is Mechanical Engineering.

Following are several screenshots of Meghal's electronic portfolio. The complete portfolio may be viewed online at the companion Web site for this textbook.

Meghal began his electronic portfolio with a reflective introduction that continued through the presentation of each Quest. His original design was an aqua blue background, black font, and dark blue tabs with white lettering. It was attractive, engaging, and easily navigated.

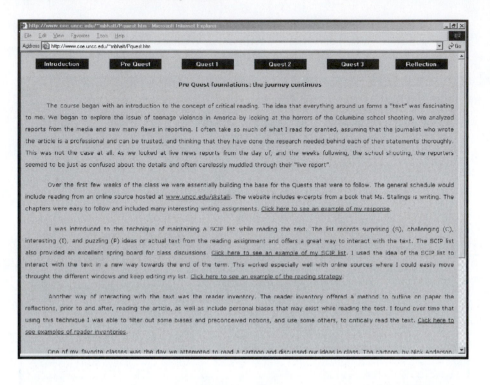

Here is an example of the way in which Meghal continued his reflective narrative as an introduction to each piece of the portfolio.

Reflection

The journey that began over four months ago will conclude in the official capacity on Monday, 5 May 2003, when I hand in my portfolio for to Prof. Stallings and post this website up on the net. In many ways this course has been both an intellectual and personal challenge. It challenged me to consider points of views that would never normally occur to me.

I am a creature of habit, and opinions tend to establish themselves in my minds as fact in very short order if I am not careful. Once established I select only evidence that supports my view point or my understanding of the situation. Subconsciously, and sometimes knowingly, I filter out the information that doesn't agree with my preconceived notions and ideas.

This course has taught me to look at the bigger picture objectively from various angles. To seek motivation from my own ideas and at the same time to appreciate others that exist. To engage in not just the official conversation, but to have my voice heard. To recognize not only new and different view points that exist, but also to persuade others to conform to my own.

In many ways this really is just the beginning of the journey. As an introductory course in writing this course has prepared me to effectively use reading strategies, organizational methodologies and refined my writing style to convey my ideas effectively and convincingly. I have used these writing strategies just recently to write what I consider a particularly impressive report on the Al-Aqsa Intifada for my history class. Using the techniques of gathering sources, evaluating their credibility, critically reading and interacting with the text, employing research registers and creating paper trails, and finally organizing my ideas around a claim and reasoning have held me in good stead towards completing the report.

What's more is that I have met some great people and made friends over the course of this term in the class. People who share an interest in talking about important current and social issues. People who come from different countries, cultures, backgrounds and experiences, who have all

Meghal concluded his electronic portfolio with a final reflection.

Practicum

How does Meghal's electronic portfolio fulfill the criteria for this assignment? Review the criteria listed for this assignment and make an evaluation. Offer specific examples from the model to illustrate your critique. Then share your ideas with your classmates. Do you find that you and your classmates agree? Do you disagree? Why, or why not? How does this process of reading and evaluating a model assignment help you to successfully meet the requirements for this assignment yourself?

PART FIVE

Event Casebooks

EVENT CASEBOOK ONE

The Youth Violence Pandemic

Focus on the Columbine High School Massacre

Initial Reports

News Report Local

The Author: Mike Anton

As soon as word of the shooting reached their offices, the *Rocky Mountain News*, Denver's oldest newspaper publication, dispatched reporters to the scene unfolding at Columbine High School. At that time, Mike Anton was one of the staff writers for *RMN*.

Based on his performance during that crisis and the following article (among others), Mike was awarded second place for Non-Deadline Writer of the Year (1999 In-House Winners). He is now working for the *Los Angeles Times*.

The following article was published April 20, 1999.

School War Zone

Up to 25 people were reported killed and more than a dozen wounded today when gunmen dressed in black overcoats and masks opened fire inside Columbine High School in Littleton.

Two gunmen killed themselves after a four-hour-plus standoff with police. A third person was led away in handcuffs by police.

The bloodiest school shooting in American history began about 11:40 a.m. and ended shortly before 4 p.m.

President Clinton asked Americans to pray.

Witnesses said the gunmen, reportedly students, fired randomly and set off explosives, laughing as they went. A Jefferson County SWAT team exchanged shots with the gunmen who were holed up inside the school.

"We saw three people get shot," one student said, her voice breaking. "They were just shooting. They didn't care who they shot. They were just shooting. We didn't think it was real and then we saw blood."

The wounded were taken to Swedish Hospital, St. Anthony's Central, Denver Health Medical Center and Littleton Hospital. The extent of the injuries was unclear. One girl taken to Swedish was said to have nine gunshot wounds in her chest.

"We are hearing we may see 20–25 victims" at four hospitals, said Stephanie Denning, spokeswoman for Denver Health Medical Center.

One teacher was reported to be among the victims.

Authorities said some victims were still inside the school as of 2:15 p.m. About 30 students were reported hiding in the choir room. Between 15 and 20 students were rescued by a SWAT team who led them out a window.

Seconds after the shooting began, hundreds of students and teachers poured out of the school while others sought refuge inside, hiding under desks and locking themselves in bathrooms.

"We hid in the counseling office," said Annie Ford, a Columbine senior. "I was peeking out the window and saw everybody sprinting, crying, crawling on the floor. People jumped the fence to get to Clement Park. I couldn't find any of my friends. There were a lot of people who saw the guy but they were hysterical and couldn't talk."

Said another student: "We were all under the table and the girl across the table from me was shot in the head right there."

The quiet neighborhood surrounding the school exploded into chaos, with paramedics tending to victims and police surrounding the grounds. Terrified parents rushed to the school, looking for their children. Students sought refuge in nearby houses.

"I was upstairs in the tech lab when I heard what I thought was hammering. I wondered: Who's hammering during class?" said Kevin Tucker, a teacher at Columbine. "I looked out and saw some students running past, and they said there'd been some shots fired. I shoved the kids back into the classroom and heard more shots."

Sophomore Amanda Stair, 15, was in the library when the shooting started. She also heard what sounded like grenades going off.

"We hid under different tables," Stair said. "Two guys in black trench coats walked in. They said get up or they would shoot us. I heard a lot of shots and one guy put his gun down on the desk I was under."

The library reeked of gunpowder, and when the fire alarm went off, one of the gunman shot the alarm.

Students were crying and screaming. The gunmen said they shouldn't, Stair said. "Don't worry," they said. "You're going to be dead in a few minutes."

Instead, the gunmen walked from the library and into the school cafeteria. As Stair and others ran from the library, they heard more shooting.

Sophomore Jenny Matthews, 16, and her friend Brian Anderson were walking the halls when they heard shots. Anderson was startled but thought he recognized one boy with a gun, Matthews said.

Anderson thought it was a paint gun. As he approached, the gunman turned and shot Anderson twice in the chest, Matthews said.

"Oh, my God, I've been shot," Anderson cried.

She then ran with other students and teachers down the hall. One teacher yelled for the kids to get out of the building. Then the teacher stopped to call police.

A gunman shot her twice in the head, said Matthews, who was in tears outside the school.

She also got some relief. As she watched Anderson wheeled into an ambulance [outside the] school he waved to her.

"He seemed like he was doing OK," she said.

Shortly before 1 p.m., a second volley of shots rang out. Officers explained they were shooting to keep the gunmen down as deputies made their way into the building.

About 1:45 p.m. Jefferson County sheriff's deputies surrounded three young men in dark clothing a few blocks from the school and trained guns on them. The three men raised their hands and were taken into custody.

It was not immediately known if the suspects were connected with the violence at Columbine.

Recent school shootings in Pearl, Miss., Jonesboro, Ark., West Paducah, Ky., and Springfield, Ore., led to calls for tighter security.

"This kind of thing is always in the back of your mind, but you never think it can happen," Tucker said. "I guess it can happen anywhere."

News Report National

The Author: Tom Kenworthy

Tom Kenworthy, previously a reporter in the *Washington Post*'s Denver bureau, covered the Columbine incident for *The Post* in 1999.

Up to 25 Die in Colorado School Shooting

(Editor's note: Steve Davis, spokesman for the Jefferson County Sheriff's Department, at a 5:30 a.m. EDT press conference Wednesday, revised the number of casualties to at least 15 and possibly 16 dead, including the shooters, and at least 23 hospitalized with wounds.)

LITTLETON, Colo., April 20–Two heavily armed young men stormed a suburban Denver high school at midday today and, in a shooting rampage on a scale unprecedented in an American school, killed as many as 25 students and faculty members.

The gunmen, whom police and fellow students described as disaffected outcasts, were found dead this afternoon in the library of Columbine High School after what police described as their "suicide mission." A third young man, described as a friend, was taken into custody but not charged. At least 20 other students were wounded.

Approaching the school from a nearby soccer field about 11:30 a.m., just as the first lunch hour began, the gunmen opened fire, moving into the cafeteria and then through the school, shooting apparently at random as hundreds of students fled in panic and hundreds of others took shelter in classrooms and libraries.

"We heard gunshots and 200 to 300 people ran into the neighborhoods," said Paul Freeman, a freshman who was in the cafeteria. "I was running and I heard everyone scream, 'He's in here,'" Freeman said. "Girls were crying and stuff."

The killings brought the country face to face once again with the tragic spectacle of seemingly senseless murder in the schools, renewing a horrific chain that since 1997 has included two killed at a school in Pearl, Miss.; three at a school in West

Paducah, Ky.; five at a school in Jonesboro, Ark.; and two at a school in Springfield, Ore. Measured by the number killed, the shooting today was the worst by far.

After hunching in terror in their hiding spots, many of the students were rescued hours after the gunmen opened fire by SWAT teams from four local police forces. Authorities and students who fled the school said the gunmen also carried explosives, which they detonated in several spots inside the building. One girl was seriously wounded by shrapnel.

The suspects were not immediately identified as hundreds of police officers continued to sweep the 2,000-student high school for more victims and survivors. They were described as members of a group known as the "Trench Coat Mafia."

The small group, said Columbine senior Zach Piercy, was composed mostly of seniors who wore black clothing and black trench coats to school and sounded dooms-day warnings about the Year 2000 and the end of the millennium. Some of their class-mates described them as white supremacists absorbed by Gothic fantasies.

Students who escaped from the rampage said the gunmen appeared to target athletes, who frequently teased the dozen or so members. "A lot of the wounded kids were wearing sports clothes like football jerseys and hats," Piercy said.

Jefferson County Sheriff John P. Stone told reporters late this afternoon that as many as 25 people were killed in the shooting rampage, which lasted for more than an hour after deputies first responded to the school. By early evening, SWAT team members and bomb squad units were still methodically sweeping the sprawling brick school for additional victims and survivors hiding in classrooms.

"It appears to be a suicide mission," said Stone, one of hundreds of police officers from Denver and suburban police forces who crowded the area throughout the afternoon.

Officers were executing search warrants of the suspects' homes, said Stone, and had found at least one explosive device at one of their houses.

Bomb disposal squads worked into the evening to disarm two explosive devices found in two vehicles in the student parking lot, as well as other explosives near or on the bodies of the two gunmen in the school library, said Steve Davis, a spokesman for the Jefferson County sheriff's department.

Davis said as many as 10 of the dead were found in the library. Additional bodies were found in the cafeteria and in hallways. Davis said 20 wounded victims were taken to area hospitals.

Jefferson County Commissioner Rick Sheehan said Columbine High School officials were aware of a group of students he described as "rambunctious," but he said they were unable to keep close enough track of the group to know in advance of the shooting rampage. "There's no way we have the kind of manpower to keep an eye on that," Sheehan said.

When asked whether he had been aware of the so-called Trench Coat Mafia, Sheehan said, "Not by any stretch of the imagination were we aware of any individuals this crazed or chaotic in their thinking."

Wounded students lay inside the school for several hours as frantic police officers tried to reach them. One bloodied student, his right arm limp, dangled from a second-floor window before being rescued.

Students described scenes of almost unfathomable horror as the gunmen moved through the school, shooting indiscriminately and setting off what appeared to be explosives. Frantic students hid in labs and classrooms, some calling parents with cellular phones to assure them they were safe and in hiding. Hundreds of panicked parents descended on the school in this community of 35,000 southwest of Denver, anxiously awaiting word of their sons and daughters.

"This is a wonderful neighborhood and a wonderful school," said Scott Cornwell, who waited behind a police tape for word of his son Matt, an 18-year-old senior who was pinned down in the school's choir room and had called, whispering that he was all right. "You just don't think it will happen here."

President Clinton, who last year hosted a White House conference on the issue of school violence after similar incidents, appeared in the briefing room tonight to urge that Americans "do more . . . to recognize the early warning signals" of troubled children with the capacity for violence.

Clinton said that he was reluctant to call the trend toward high school shootings an "epidemic" but that "there are a lot of kids out there who have weapons . . . and who build up these grievances." He pledged the assistance of the federal government in helping Colorado authorities respond to the incident.

Gov. Bill Owens, who said he has a 16-year-old daughter in high school, told reporters near the elementary school where many of the fleeing students were taken: "We can't imagine what the parents are going through today."

Owens condemned a "culture of violence" that he said gave rise to such tragedies, and added, "These are children who don't have the same moral background as the rest of us . . . It's just something you can't explain."

When asked whether stricter gun controls were needed, Owens replied, "I'm not going to get into this. There are kids still in the school, and we'll talk about that later."

The shooting came as the Colorado State Legislature is close to enacting new gun legislation liberalizing the state rules for carrying concealed handguns and just two weeks before the National Rifle Association's annual convention is held in Denver.

Students who saw the gunmen said the two were wearing the trademark fatigues and black trench coats of the millennium group. A third, apparently the friend, wore a T-shirt.

Piercy said it was mostly athletes who mocked and teased the members of the group, who in addition to their black clothing often painted their faces in "weird" psychedelic patterns.

As hundreds of heavily armed police officers, FBI and federal Bureau of Alcohol, Tobacco and Firearms agents arrived on the scene, accompanied by dozens of ambulances and other rescue vehicles, frantic parents were directed to a nearby elementary school to await word of their sons and daughters. In the late afternoon, an armored personnel carrier operated by the Colorado National Guard arrived on the back of a tractor-trailer and was dispatched to the front of the school to help remove the wounded.

But scores of others came to the school where they tearfully waited behind yellow police tape as the chilling reality of what had happened became known.

Elaine Brookfield came to await word of her son Brandon, a Spanish teacher at Columbine. "I'm just furious this can happen to good productive people, that they can get hurt and killed by thugs," she said. "I'd just like to beat the [expletive] out of whoever did this."

Chris Wisher, a 16-year-old sophomore, was outside the school with a friend when he saw the gunmen approach across a soccer field. "I heard what I thought was fireworks," said Wisher, but his puzzlement quickly turned to panic as he realized the gunmen were firing live ammunition directly at him from a distance of about 100 yards.

"They were just shooting randomly," said Wisher. "We felt shots going by us, and we fell to the ground."

Wisher said he recognized one of the shooters as a student member of the Trench Coat Mafia. "They all hang out together and don't have many friends. They got made fun of a lot. They looked like troublemakers."

Jason Greer, a 16-year-old sophomore, said he heard shots immediately after he walked into the cafeteria for lunch. Fleeing, he said he saw "one person laying face down when I left, as I was ducking through a doorway."

Stone, the Jefferson County sheriff, said officers found some explosives inside and outside the school but could not identify them. The two dead suspects found in the library "possibly" died of self-inflicted wounds, he said.

Asked for a possible motive, Stone said: "I wish I had an answer."

Multimedia Sources

Editorial Cartoon

The Author: Nick Anderson

Nick Anderson has worked as a cartoonist for the *Louisville Courier-Journal* (Kentucky) since 1995. His cartoons have appeared in the *New York Times,* the *Washington Post,* and *Newsweek.* In 2001, he won first place for editorial cartooning in the Best of Gannett competition. Below is the cartoon he produced for the April 23, 1999, edition of the *Courier-Journal.* It is titled, "Trench Coat Mafia."

Author's Etcetera

Here is a copy of an email exchange with Nick Anderson regarding one group analysis of his cartoon:

Kim,

I've gone through the email and posted my reply to each point below.

Nick

From: "Kim Stallings"
To: "Nick Anderson"
Subject: UNCC requests your opinion and help—analysis of your cartoon of 4/23/99
Date: Tue, 24 Sep, 2002, 5:09 PM

Hi, Nick:

Kim Stallings (UNC Charlotte), again. I contacted you a few months ago regarding your cartoon published 4/23/99—Trench Coat Mafia. I am using the cartoon in my textbook, QUEST. (I did receive your reply and have used the biographical information from your website—thank you!)

I am doing a "test-run" with the textbook this semester with several classes of freshmen. Today we (my students and I) analyzed your cartoon and came up with an incredible analysis. And we began to wonder:

○ Did we "get" the message you intended for us to get?
○ Did we read more into the cartoon than you intended?
○ And what did we miss?

So . . . we decided to write you. If you have a moment, it would be fantastic to hear from you. Could you take a look at the list we generated in response to your cartoon—and our subsequent analysis—and let us know what you think?

Thank you SO MUCH for your time.

What we identified as significant/meaningful (in no particular order):

○ all figures appear to be male
○ YES.
○ viewed from the back/rear
○ NO. . .IT COULD BE EITHER. . .THEY'RE SILHOUETTES.
○ shadow figures—no individual characteristics
○ RIGHT.
○ dark = fear, unknown
○ RIGHT.
○ shadow = something else is casting a shadow
○ NO. SILHOUETTES.
○ Media Violence and Guns are taller than the other figures
○ NO. MADE THE FIGURES RANDOM HEIGHTS.
○ figures have short hair, big ears, long necks, cuffed jeans, trench coats, earrings, big noses—caricatures of socially outcast individuals
○ CORRECT.
○ MV and G are holding the guns
○ CORRECT.
○ Social Isolation is on the outside of the group
○ NOT INTENDED.

(continued)

- posturing—Social Isolation looking down at Adult Neglect (indicating responsibility of AN in creating SI)
- OVER-ANALYSIS. NOT INTENDED.
- MV and G seem to be moving/active—turned towards Community Denial—looking down on CD
- OVER-ANALYSIS. NOT INTENDED.
- CD is looking straight ahead—ignoring all others
- OVER-ANALYSIS. NOT INTENDED.
- shoes pointed toward CD—CD turned in pigeon toed
- OVER-ANALYSIS. NOT INTENDED.
- labels are "seared" into the shadows . . .
- FAIR INTERPRETATION.
- Title—Trench Coat Mafia—but the TCM is made up of social ills
- TITLE IS INTENDED TO BE IRONIC. MY IDEA OF THE "REAL" TRENCH COAT MAFIA.

What we think these images mean/the message:
We (society) have identified/singled out Trench Coat Mafia as responsible for the incident, but the TCM is made up of all of the societal ills/scapegoats (Social Isolation, Adult Neglect, Media Violence, Community Denial, Guns). The most obviously responsible—providing "weapons"—are MV and G—but Community Denial is the real problem.

VERY GOOD ANALYSIS OF THE MESSAGE, ALTHOUGH I DIDN'T INTEND TO MAKE COMMUNITY DENIAL OR ANY OF THE SOCIAL ILLS PARAMOUNT. . . I INTENDED TO COMMUNICATE THAT THEY ALL CONSPIRE TO A GREATER OR LESSER DEGREE TO CREATE PATHOLOGIES LIKE THOSE MANIFESTED AT COLUMBINE.

We look forward to your response. THANK YOU!

Kim Stallings and UNCC English 1103-007 (Lisa, Amanda M., Carmen, Kelsey, Cassandra, Erin, Jessica, Kristen, Leah, Greg, Melissa, Summer, Amanda S., Kim, Jennifer, Danielle, Renee, Sara, Denish, Daniel, Julie, Michael)

Photograph

In a survey conducted by students around the country, of the more than 2,500 people asked what visual image stands out the most in their memory regarding the Columbine High School shooting, many recalled the haunting video still of Eric Harris and Dylan Klebold in the school cafeteria.

The following is a video still captured by the security surveillance cameras inside Columbine High School on April 20, 1999.

Public Speech

The Author: President Bill Clinton

President William Jefferson Clinton graduated from Georgetown University and in 1968 won a Rhodes Scholarship to Oxford University. He received a law degree from Yale University in 1973 and entered politics in Arkansas. Clinton was elected Arkansas Attorney General in 1976 and won the governorship in 1978. After losing a bid for a second term, he regained the office four years later and served until he was elected to serve as United States President in 1992. He held the office of the President for two consecutive terms.

The following is the text of a speech by President Bill Clinton on May 20, 1999, before the community of Columbine High School in Littleton, Colorado. It is published in the *Weekly Compilation of Presidential Documents, 5/24/99.*

Remarks to the Community of Columbine High School in Littleton, Colorado

The President. Thank you very much. Do that cheer for me one more time.

Audience members. We are—Columbine! We are—Columbine! We are—Columbine!

The President. Thank you.

Dr. Hammond; Mr. DeAngelis; President DeStefano and the State legislators, county commissioners; Attorney General Salazar; especially Governor Owens, thank you for being here. To all the officials who are here; most especially to the students of Columbine and the students who are here from Chatfield and Dakota Ridge. And Heather Dinkel, thank you for standing up here in front of this big crowd and making a fine talk. Weren't you proud of her? She did a good job representing you today. [Applause]

I want to say a special word of thanks to the families who met with Hillary and me before we came over here, for telling us the stories and showing us the booklets commemorating the lives of their very special children. I also want to thank the fine young people who still are hospitalized with whom I spoke by telephone yesterday—two of them, Patrick Ireland and Sean Graves, are here today. They left the hospital to be here.

I know there are some other people here who are also still injured who have come. I thank all of you for coming. This has been a long, hard month for all of you, and as Hillary said, it's been a hard month for America.

You heard her say that part of our job in these last 6 years, more than we ever could have imagined when we moved to Washington after the election in 1992, has been to be with grieving people, after the Oklahoma City building was blown up and the Embassies were blown up and our airmen were killed in the bombing in Saudi Arabia and so many other occasions—and last year several times—after violence in schools. But something profound has happened to your country because of this. I want you all to understand that. I'm not even sure I can explain it to you.

One of the incidents of school killing last year occurred in my home State. It's a small State. I was Governor there 12 years. I knew the people involved; it was heart-breaking. One of the mothers of one of the children who was killed still works with us for safer schools and safer childhoods. And all America grieved. But I think they thought, "Oh, this is terrible, I wish somebody would do something about this."

But somehow, when this happened here—maybe because of the scope of it, and I think mostly because of you, how you reacted, all of you, the relief workers, the law enforcement people, the family members who were brave enough to speak there was a different reaction. People thought, "This has happened in my neighborhood; what can I do?" I say that because you have a unique chance—a chance—to make sure that the children of Columbine are never forgotten.

But first, you have to deal with you and your lives. You're all left with searing memories and scars and unanswered questions. There has to be healing. There has to be answers. And for those things that will not heal or cannot be answered, you have to learn to go on with your lives.

I hope you have been comforted by the caring not only of your neighbors but of your country and people from all around the world. All America has looked and listened with shared grief and enormous affection and admiration for you. We have been learning, along with you, a lot about ourselves and our responsibilities as parents and citizens.

When America looks at Jefferson County, many of us see a community not very different from our own. We know if this can happen here, it can happen anywhere. And we see with admiration the fundamentally strong values and character of the people here, from the students to the school officials, to the community leaders, to the parents.

I think most Americans have looked at you and thought, among other things, that—God forbid—if something like this should ever happen to us, I hope we would behave as well. I hope we would also hold on to our faith as well.

I am impressed that you are moving forward. Most of the children have returned to school, even returned to sports and other activities. I am proud of all of you who are, in your own way, going back to living your lives, looking toward the future, to commencement or college or a summer job or just getting back to the ordinary business of life, which takes an extraordinary effort now. But I have to say, I think what's impressed me most is the way, in the midst of this, you have held on to your faith.

One of the greatest moments of grief in my life occurred 15 years ago, when Hillary and I had to go to the memorial service for a young man who was a senior at Yale University, a Rhodes Scholar, on the football team, the editor of the newspaper, the leader of his class academically. This young man happened to come from an African-American family in our hometown and a poor family at that. His father was a minister in a very small church. And we had the service in the high school auditorium.

His father was lame, and he walked with a pronounced limp. And he gave his son's eulogy, walking down in front of us with his limp, saying, "His mother and I do not understand this, but we believe in a God too kind ever to be cruel, too wise ever to do wrong, so we know we will come to understand it by and by."

In the Scriptures, Saint Paul says that all of us in this life see through a glass darkly. So we must walk by faith, not by sight. We cannot lean on our own wisdom. None of this can be fully, satisfactorily explained to any of you. But you cannot lose your faith.

The only other thing I really want to say to you is that throughout all your grief and mourning and even in your cheers and your renewal and your determination to get on with your life and get this school back together and show people what you are, there is something else you can do, and something I believe that you should do for yourselves and your friends, to make sure they will be remembered. Every special one of them.

Your tragedy, though it is unique in its magnitude, is, as you know so well, not an isolated event. Hillary mentioned there was another school shooting in Atlanta today. Thankfully, the injuries to the students don't seem to be life threatening. But there were several last year which did claim lives.

We know somehow that what happened to you has pierced the soul of America. And it gives you a chance to be heard in a way no one else can be heard, by the President and by ordinary people in every community in this country. You can help us to build a better future for all our children: a future where hatred and distrust no longer distort the mind or harden the heart; a future where what we have in common is far more important than what divides us; a future where parents and children are more fully involved in each other's lives, in which they share hopes and dreams, love and respect, a strong sense of right and wrong; a future where students respect each other even if they all belong to different groups, or come from different faiths or races or backgrounds; a future where schools and houses of worship and communities are literally connected to all our children; a future where society guards our children better against violent influences and weapons that can break the dam of decency and humanity in the most vulnerable of children.

One thing I would like to share with you that I personally believe very much: These dark forces that take over people and make them murder are the extreme manifestation of fear and rage with which every human being has to do combat. The older you get, the more you'll know that a great deal of life is the struggle against every person's own smallness and fear and anger and a continuing effort not to blame other people for our own shortcomings or our fears.

We cannot do what we need to do in America unless every person is committed to doing something better and different in every walk of life, beginning with parents and students and going all the way to the White House. For the struggle to be human is something that must be a daily source of joy to you, so you can get rid of your fears and let go of your rage and minimize the chance that something like this will happen again.

Because of what you have endured, you can help us build that kind of future, as virtually no one else can. You can reach across all the political and religious and racial and cultural lines that divide us. You have already touched our hearts. You have provoked Hillary and me and the Vice President and Mrs. Gore to reach out across America to launch a national grassroots campaign against violence directed against young people. You can be a part of that.

You can give us a culture of values instead of a culture of violence. You can help us to keep guns out of the wrong hands. You can help us to make sure kids who are in trouble—and there will always be some—are identified early and reached and helped. You can help us do this.

Two days from now, you're going to have your commencement. It will be bitter-sweet. It will certainly be different for those of you who are graduating than you thought it was going to be when you were freshmen. But as I understand it, there will be some compensations. Even your archrivals at Chatfield will be cheering you on. When you hear those people cheer for you, I want you to hear the voice of America, because America will be cheering you on. And remember that a commencement is not an end. It is a beginning.

You've got to help us here. Take care of yourselves and your families first. Take care of the school next. But remember, you can help America heal, and in so doing you will speed the process of healing for yourselves.

This is a very great country. It is embodied in this very great community, in this very great school, with these wonderful teachers and children and parents. But the problem which came to the awful conclusion you faced here is a demon we have to do more to fight. And what I want to tell you is, we can—together.

I close here with this story. My wife and I and our daughter have been blessed to know many magnificent people because the American people gave us a chance to serve in the White House. But I think the person who's had the biggest influence on me is the man who is about to retire as the President of South Africa, Nelson Mandela.

He is 80 years old, he served 27 years in prison. For 14 years he never had a bed to sleep on. He spent most of his years breaking rocks every day. And he told me once about his experience. And I asked him: "How did you let go of your hatred? How did you learn to influence other people? How did you embrace all the differences in, literally, the centuries of oppression and discord in your country and let a lot of it go away? How did you get over that in prison? Didn't you really hate them?"

And he said, "I did hate them for quite a long while. After all, look what they took from me—27 years of my life. I was abused physically and emotionally. They separated me from my wife, and it eventually destroyed my marriage. They took me away from my children, and I could not even see them grow up. And I was full of hatred and anger." And he said, "One day I was breaking rocks, and I realized they had taken so much. And they could take everything from me except my mind and my heart. Those things I would have to give away. I decided not to give them away."

I see here today that you have decided not to give your mind and your heart away. I ask you now to share it with all your fellow Americans.

We love you, and we need you.

Thank you, and God bless you.

Web site

The URL: www.safeyouth.org/scripts/teens.asp

The National Youth Violence Prevention Resource Center provides a wide variety of information on youth violence prevention, sponsored by the Centers for Disease Control and Prevention and other federal agencies.

The following screenshot and informational page, published in 2002, are located on the organization's Web site.

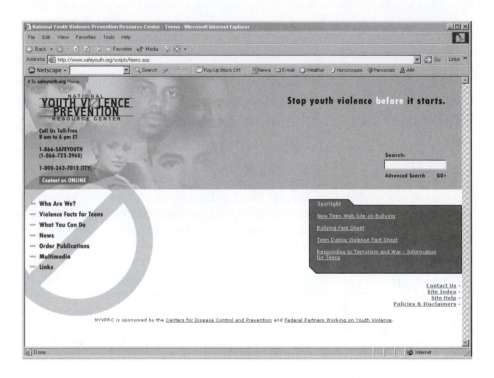

Facts for Teens: School Violence

Introduction

In the last few years, a great deal of media attention has been focused on school shootings. This has led many teens to become concerned about their own safety, wondering whether such tragic violence could happen in their schools.

However, in terms of risk for homicide, schools are about the safest place for teens—safer than their homes or their neighborhoods—and violent deaths at schools or school events are extremely rare.

Less than 1% of the murders of children and teens in the United States are school-related, and there is no evidence that school-related homicides are on the rise. You are much more likely to be struck by lightning than to be killed at your school. In the 1998–99 school year, a total of 34 children and teens were murdered on school property, at a school event, or on their way to and from school.[1]

This is not to suggest that school violence is not a serious problem in the United States.

Although incidents like the one in Littleton, Colorado, tend to get all the attention, if you've ever been ruthlessly teased, laughed at, shoved around, or bullied at school, you know there's more to violence in school than mass shootings.

In fact, school violence includes a range of activities, including bullying, threatening remarks, physical fights, assaults with or without weapons, and gang violence.

How serious of a problem is school violence?

In a 1999 national survey of high school students.[2]

- 7% of students (and 11% of male students) said they had carried a weapon to school in the last month;
- 8% of students said they had been threatened or injured with a weapon such as a gun, knife, or club on school property in the past year;
- 14% said that they had been involved in a physical fight on school property in the past year; and
- 5% said they had missed at least one day of school in the last month because they felt unsafe at school or when traveling to or from school.

Additionally, students tell us that bullying continues to be a serious problem, particularly in middle schools. In 1999, about 10% of students in grades 6 and 7 reported being bullied, compared with about 5% of students in grades 8 and 9 and about 2% in grades 10 through 12.[3]

In some important ways, however, schools are becoming safer.

In the last few years, violent crimes at school have declined, and fewer students are carrying weapons to school or getting into fights. Between 1993 and 1999, the number of students reporting carrying a weapon to school in the previous month dropped by over 40%. The number of students who reported being involved in a physical fight on school property during the past year dropped by over 12%.[4]

As a result, many students are beginning to feel safer. Between 1995 and 1999, the number of students who avoided one or more places at school out of fear for their safety decreased by over 40%.[5] Students were also much less likely to fear being attacked or harmed at school or while traveling to and from school.[6]

It is important to remember, however, that some schools are much safer than others. For a few schools, serious violent crime continues to be a very real problem.

What You Can Do

Start with yourself.

Make a commitment not to contribute to violence in any way. Do not bully, tease, or spread negative gossip about others. Respect others and value differences. Try to broaden your social circle to include others who are different from you.

Learn about ways to resolve arguments and fights without violence, and encourage your friends to do the same. Many schools, churches, and after-school programs offer training in conflict resolution skills.

Do not carry a gun.

Teens sometimes carry guns because they are afraid, but carrying a gun will not make you safer.

Guns often escalate conflicts and increase the chances that you will be seriously harmed. You also run the risk that the gun may be turned on you or that an innocent person will be hurt. And, you may do something in a moment of fear or anger that you will regret for the rest of your life.

Finally, it is illegal for a teen to carry a handgun, and it can lead to criminal charges and arrest.

How can you protect yourself without a gun?

If someone is threatening you and you feel that you are in serious danger, do not take matters into your own hands. Find an adult you can trust and discuss your fears, or contact school administrators or the police. Take precautions for your safety, such as avoiding being alone and staying with a group of friends if possible.

If you know someone is carrying a gun or planning to harm someone else—report him or her. Most of us have learned from an early age that it is wrong to tattle, but in some instances it is the most courageous thing you can do. Tell a trusted adult, such as a teacher, guidance counselor, principal or parent. If you are afraid and believe that telling will put you in danger or lead to retaliation, find a way to anonymously contact the authorities.

Take the initiative to make your school safer.

Join an existing group that is promoting non-violence at your school, or launch your own effort. Several of the online resources listed at the end of this document can help you get started. You might want to consider some of the following ideas.[7]

- ○ Start a conflict resolution program to teach students to handle conflict peacefully.
- ○ Start a drama troupe to develop productions with non-violence themes, such as peaceful conflict resolution, respect for diversity, and tolerance.
- ○ Launch a school crime watch program.
- ○ Plan a non-violence rally or dance, and encourage other students to make a commitment to avoiding conflicts.
- ○ Start a "peace pledge" campaign, in which students promise to settle disagreements without violence, to reject weapons, and to work toward a safe school for all.
- ○ Set up an anonymous hot line so students can share their concerns if they feel threatened or know of someone who may become violent.
- ○ Set up a forum for students to talk about how school violence is affecting their lives and to brainstorm about possible solutions.

Helpful Links

ERIC/CASS Bullying in Schools Virtual Library. http://ericcass .uncg.edu/virtuallib/bullying/bullyingbook.html
   If you or a friend is being bullied, this site provides links to numerous resources with information about bullying, including strategies for preventing bullying and tips for youth about how to respond to bullies.

Combating Fear and Restoring Safety in Schools. www.ojjdp.ncjrs.org/
jjbulletin/9804/contents.html

This bulletin, from the Office of Juvenile Justice and Delinquency Prevention examines the climate of violence that threatens our schools and describes steps that concerned citizens are taking to restore security and calm.

Indicators of School Crime and Safety, 2000. www.ojp.usdoj.gov/
bjs/abstract/iscs00.htm

A joint effort by the Bureau of Justice Statistics and National Center for Education Statistics, the report provides the most current detailed statistical information to inform the Nation on the nature of crime in schools.

2000 Annual Report on School Safety. www.ed.gov/offices/OESE/
SDFS/annrept00.pdf

The joint Report, prepared by the U.S. Department of Education and the U.S. Department of Justice, examines data on homicides and suicides at school, injuries at school, crimes against students, crimes against teachers, weapons at school, the consequences of bringing firearms to school, and student perceptions of school safety. The Report highlights effective programs, and lists resources for more information about school safety and crime issues.

Youth In Action Bulletins. www.ojjdp.ncjrs.org/pubs/youthinactionsum.html

These Bulletins developed by the Office of Juvenile Justice and Delinquency Prevention provide guidance for teen leaders who are developing their own crime prevention efforts. Relevant titles include:

- **Arts and Performances for Prevention.** www.ncjrs.org/html/
ojjdp/youthbulletin/9912_1/contents.html

    This Bulletin shows how you can use arts and performances to convey a non-violence message and provides step-by-step instructions to help you get started and to keep you going.

- **Stand Up and Start a Youth Crime Watch.** www.ncjrs.org/pdffiles/
94601.pdf

    This Bulletin provides information for students on how to start a school crime watch. A school crime watch helps youth watch out for each other to make the entire school area safer and more enjoyable. The school crime watch is a student-led effort that helps youth take a share of responsibility for their school community.

- **Want to Resolve a Dispute? Try Mediation.** www.ncjrs.org/html/
ojjdp/youthbulletin/2000_03_1/contents.html

    This Bulletin shows how you can start and carry out a youth mediation program in your school or community that will help prevent violence.

References

1. Reported in 2000 Annual Report on School Safety, pp 9–11. SOURCE: *The School-Associated Violent Deaths Study.* Centers for Disease Control and Prevention, the U.S. Department of Education, and the U.S. Department of Justice.

2. Centers for Disease Control and Prevention. *Youth risk behavior surveillance–United States 1999*. In: CDC Surveillance Summaries, June 9, 2000. *MMWR* 2000;49(No. SS-5), pp. 7–8.
3. Reported in *Indicators of School Crime and Safety, 2000*, p. 13. SOURCE: U.S. Department of Justice, Bureau of Justice Statistics, School Crime Supplement to the National Crime Victimization Survey, January–June, 1999.
4. Calculated from data reported in Fact Sheet: Youth Risk Behavior Trends, 1991–1999, Centers for Disease Control and Prevention.
5. Calculated from data reported in *Indicators of School Crime and Safety, 2000*, p. 32. SOURCE: U.S. Department of Justice, Bureau of Justice Statistics, School Crime Supplement to the National Crime Victimization Survey, January–June, 1995, and 1999.
6. Reported in *Indicators of School Crime and Safety, 2000*, pp. 30–31. SOURCE: U.S. Department of Justice, Bureau of Justice Statistics, School Crime Supplement to the National Crime Victimization Survey, January–June, 1995, and 1999.
7. For more information about these ideas and further suggestions, visit the following websites:
   * *Youth In Action Bulletins*. Office of Juvenile Justice and Delinquency Prevention, Department of Justice
   * *Girl Power! And Violence Prevention*. Department of Health and Human Services.

Magazine Article

The Author: Marilyn Manson

Brian Warner, better known as Marilyn Manson, has been the focus of negative press since the release of his first album, *Antichrist Superstar*. Immediately following the Columbine High School shooting, Manson's music was attacked as an indirect cause of the shooting—even though the killers supposedly were not Manson fans. In the following article, published in *Rolling Stone* magazine on June 24, 1999, Manson directly addresses those accusations.

Columbine: Whose Fault Is It?

It is sad to think that the first few people on earth needed no books, movies, games or music to inspire cold-blooded murder. The day that Cain bashed his brother Abel's brains in, the only motivation he needed was his own human disposition to violence. Whether you interpret the Bible as literature or as the final word of whatever God may be, Christianity has given us an image of death and sexuality that we have based our culture around. A half-naked dead man hangs in most homes and around our necks, and we have just taken that for granted all our lives. Is it a symbol of hope or hopelessness? The world's most famous murder-suicide was also the birth of the death icon—the blueprint for celebrity. Unfortunately, for all of their inspiring morality, nowhere in the Gospels is intelligence praised as a virtue.

A lot of people forget or never realize that I started my band as a criticism of these very issues of despair and hypocrisy. The name Marilyn Manson has never celebrated the sad fact that America puts killers on the cover of *Time* magazine, giving them as much notoriety as our favorite movie stars. From Jesse James to Charles Manson, the media, since their inception, have turned criminals into folk heroes. They just created two new ones when they plastered Dylan Klebold and Eric Harris' pictures on the front of every newspaper. Don't be surprised if every kid who gets pushed around has two new idols.

We applaud the creation of a bomb whose sole purpose is to destroy all of mankind, and we grow up watching our president's brains splattered all over Texas. Times have not become more violent. They have just become more televised. Does anyone think the Civil War was the least bit civil? If television had existed, you could be sure they would have been there to cover it, or maybe even participate in it, like their violent car chase of Princess Di. Disgusting vultures looking for corpses, exploiting, filming and serving it up for our hungry appetites in a gluttonous display of endless human stupidity.

When it comes down to who's to blame for the high school murders in Littleton, Colorado, throw a rock and you'll hit someone who's guilty. We're the people who sit back and tolerate children owning guns, and we're the ones who tune in and watch the up-to-the-minute details of what they do with them. I think it's terrible when anyone dies, especially if it is someone you know and love. But what is more offensive is that when these tragedies happen, most people don't really care any more than they would about the season finale of *Friends* or The Real World. I was dumbfounded as I watched the media snake right in, not missing a teardrop, interviewing the parents of dead children, televising the funerals. Then came the witch hunt.

Man's greatest fear is chaos. It was unthinkable that these kids did not have a simple black-and-white reason for their actions. And so a scapegoat was needed. I remember hearing the initial reports from Littleton, that Harris and Klebold were wearing makeup and were dressed like Marilyn Manson, whom they obviously must worship, since they were dressed in black. Of course, speculation snowballed into making me the poster boy for everything that is bad in the world. These two idiots weren't wearing makeup, and they weren't dressed like me or like goths. Since Middle America has not heard of the music they did listen to (KMFDM and Rammstein, among others), the media picked something they thought was similar.

Responsible journalists have reported with less publicity that Harris and Klebold were not Marilyn Manson fans—that they even disliked my music. Even if they were fans, that gives them no excuse, nor does it mean that music is to blame. Did we look for James Huberty's inspiration when he gunned down people at McDonald's? What did Timothy McVeigh like to watch? What about David Koresh, Jim Jones? Do you think entertainment inspired Kip Kinkel, or should we blame the fact that his father bought him the guns he used in the Springfield, Oregon, murders? What inspires Bill Clinton to blow people up in Kosovo? Was it something that Monica Lewinsky said to him? Isn't killing just killing, regardless if it's in Vietnam or Jonesboro, Arkansas? Why do we justify one, just because it seems to be for the right reasons? Should there ever be a right reason? If a kid is old enough to drive a car or buy a gun, isn't he old enough to be held personally responsible for what he does with his car or gun? Or if he's a teenager, should someone else be blamed because he isn't as enlightened as an eighteen-year-old?

America loves to find an icon to hang its guilt on. But, admittedly, I have assumed the role of Antichrist; I am the Nineties voice of individuality, and people tend to associate anyone who looks and behaves differently with illegal or immoral activity. Deep down, most adults hate people who go against the grain. It's comical that people are naive enough to have forgotten Elvis, Jim Morrison and Ozzy so quickly. All of them were subjected to the same age-old arguments, scrutiny and prejudice. I wrote a song called "Lunchbox," and some journalists have interpreted it as a song about guns. Ironically, the song is about being picked on and fighting back with my Kiss lunch box, which I used as a weapon on the playground. In 1979, metal lunch boxes were banned because they were considered dangerous weapons in the hands of delinquents. I also wrote a song called "Get Your Gunn." The title is spelled with two n's because the song was a reaction to the murder of Dr. David Gunn, who was killed in Florida by pro-life activists while I was living there. That was the ultimate hypocrisy I witnessed growing up: that these people killed someone in the name of being "prolife." The somewhat positive messages of these songs are usually the ones that sensationalists misinterpret as promoting the very things I am decrying.

Right now, everyone is thinking of how they can prevent things like Littleton. How do you prevent AIDS, world war, depression, car crashes? We live in a free country, but with that freedom there is a burden of personal responsibility. Rather than teaching a child what is moral and immoral, right and wrong, we first and foremost can establish what the laws that govern us are. You can always escape hell by not believing in it, but you cannot escape death and you cannot escape prison.

It is no wonder that kids are growing up more cynical; they have a lot of information in front of them. In the past, there was always the idea that you could turn and run and start something better. But now America has become one big mall, and because of the Internet and all of the technology we have, there's nowhere to run. People are the same everywhere. Sometimes music, movies and books are the only things that let us feel like someone else feels like we do. I've always tried to let people know it's OK, or better, if you don't fit into the program. Use your imagination—if some geek from Ohio can become something, why can't anyone else with the willpower and creativity?

I chose not to jump into the media frenzy and defend myself, though I was begged to be on every single TV show in existence. I didn't want to contribute to these fame-seeking journalists and opportunists looking to fill their churches or to get elected because of their self-righteous finger-pointing. They want to blame entertainment? Isn't religion the first real entertainment? People dress up in costumes, sing songs and dedicate themselves in eternal fandom. Everyone will agree that nothing was more entertaining than Clinton shooting off his prick and then his bombs in true political form. And the news—that's obvious. So is entertainment to blame? I'd like media commentators to ask themselves, because their coverage of the event was some of the most gruesome entertainment any of us have seen. I think that the National Rifle Association is far too powerful to take on, so most people choose Doom, *The Basketball Diaries* or yours truly. This kind of controversy does not help me sell records or tickets, and I wouldn't want it to. I'm a controversial artist, one who dares to have an opinion and bothers to create music and videos that challenge people's ideas in a world that is watered-down and hollow. In my work I examine the America we live in, and I've always tried to show people that the devil we blame our atrocities on is really just each one of us. So don't expect the end of the world to come one day out of the blue—it's been happening every day for a long time.

Online Article

The URL: http://www.natcath.com

According to the National Catholic Reporter Web site, the National Catholic Reporter Publishing Company reports, comments, and reflects on the church and society. It strives for excellence in its publications, supporting a full, honest and open exchange of ideas. It works out of a Roman Catholic tradition and an ecumenical spirit. It emphasizes solidarity with the oppressed and respect for all. It understands that peace, justice, and integrity of environment are not only goals but also avenues of life.

National Catholic Reporter is an independent newsweekly that is frequently the first to report on serious issues important to thinking Catholics and the first place to find open, honest, and ongoing discussion of those issues. *NCR* makes a commitment to in-depth reporting of global peace and justice issues and consistently wins national and international awards for "Best Investigative Reporting" and "General Excellence" from the Catholic Press Association.

Founded in 1964, NCR has earned a reputation for fearless, balanced writing on a wide range of topics: spirituality, human rights, living the faith, social justice, catholic trends, and liturgical developments. Regular special features include book and movie reviews, exclusive articles by noted writers, and listings for retreats, renewal programs, and educational opportunities.

The following article was published on May 28, 1999.

Teen Violence: Does Violent Media Make Violent Kids?

By Teresa Malcolm
NCR Staff

As shocking episodes of youth violence unfold in one all-American community after another—Pearl, Miss.; Paducah, Ky.; Littleton, Colo.; and now Conyers, Ga.—grief and incomprehension fuel a demand for answers, an explanation of how young people from seemingly good homes and average backgrounds could commit such astonishingly brutal deeds.

Video games, TV shows and movies, music and Web sites that celebrate violence figure high on the list of the usual suspects.

By any measure, these forms of popular culture have an enormous impact on shaping the imaginations of young people. Yet for some who study the situation in times of calm as well as crisis, the predictable thrust and parry of media critics and defenders that follow the latest tragedy often raises all the wrong questions.

Suspicions of direct cause-and-effect are important. Did scenes of a student shooting his classmates in the movie "The Basketball Diaries," for example, push a given child to walk into school and start shooting? However, experts say such thinking may obscure the more pervasive social effects of violent programming.

The "Mean World" Syndrome

"The impact may not be on potential perpetrators, but on the rest of the population, who begin to believe that violence is inevitable, that crime is everywhere and that they must be afraid," said Sr. Elizabeth Thoman, a member of the Sisters of the Humility of Mary and executive director of the Center for Media Literacy in Los Angeles, Calif.

Thoman's center produces media literacy programs for schools across the country.

She said the public fear generated by media violence—the "mean world" syndrome—shows up in all sorts of socially toxic ways, from a diminished sense of community to "tough on crime" legislation, from barred doors to the death penalty.

Perspectives such as Thoman's, however, have been largely shunted to the sidelines in the aftermath of Littleton and now Conyers, Ga., where six students were injured May 20 when a sophomore opened fire.

In the wake of the Littleton shootings, most commentators directly implicated movies, music, video games and the Internet in the actions of Eric Harris and Dylan Klebold. The killings became the focal point of a Senate committee hearing on violent media.

President Clinton convened a summit and promised an ongoing national campaign against youth violence, while Vice President Al Gore announced a new agreement with on-line providers to restrict violent material, changes that would "honor the lives of those who were killed."

While politicians declared there was a clear consensus on the detrimental effects of media violence on youth, executives of entertainment industries cautiously deflected criticism: It takes an already disturbed young person to move from watching a violent movie or playing a "first-person shooter" video game to killing real people, they said.

Independent media critics such as Thoman say that what is needed is something deeper and more systematic, including grassroots education for both children and adults, leading them to question their own media choices and making them aware of the ways they can be manipulated in a pervasive media culture. Parishes and schools are ideal places to begin this education, they say.

The U.S. bishops have addressed the issue in the form of a 1998 document, "Renewing the Mind of the Media," which is now being developed into a 12-minute video.

Henry Herx, head of the bishops' Office of Film and Broadcasting, said that parents may have a "certain lack of imagination" about how much media has changed since their childhood.

"When they were kids, they were watching rather stylized violence," Herx said. "They weren't involved with the kind of up-front, intense depiction of violence and sexuality that I think really does shake young people."

Thoman, however, faults "Renewing the Mind of the Media" for dealing with the issues of sex and violence in the same document. It focuses heavily on the problem of pornography and uses the same "three levels of concern" of hard-core, soft-core and frivolous portrayals for both sexuality and violence.

"There is a pleasure factor to sexuality, where there is no pleasure factor to violence," Thoman said. "When you lump those things together, it's hard to separate what is legitimately pleasurable in human sexuality from the problematic aspects of violence. . . . We shouldn't feel positively about violence."

"Renewing the Mind of the Media" calls on government to "reassert regulatory functions" over the media in the public interest. It suggests writing letters to media outlets and setting up discussion groups in dioceses, parishes and Catholic education, as well as dialogues with media and business leaders.

A recent update of a 1993 document from the U.S. Catholic Conference's Committee, "Family Guide for Using Media," also outlines ways for parents to examine the values being promoted in the media in light of Catholic teaching and asks them to look at ways the media manipulates or shows bias.

With large corporations controlling much of the media, "the ordinary person feels powerless," said Sr. Mary Ann Walsh, spokesperson for the U.S. bishops. "Sure I can turn my television off, but is there some way of saying that these are public airwaves?"

Walsh said churches are in a position to mobilize public opinion, particularly as an interfaith effort. "The Catholic, Protestant, Jewish and Muslim communities have to form coalitions" to combat any mistaken idea that only splinter groups object to media exploitation, Walsh said.

What a Young Father Views

Thoman said the question of what parents are watching is overlooked in the debate that springs up periodically about the effects of media violence on youth. Of particular importance, she said, are young fathers. "How does a young man who has grown up with action movies and video games suddenly change his viewing habits when he has a 2-year-old boy?" she asked.

While he may think that he grew up watching violence and turned out OK, he needs to question if the violence in the media and the culture is the same today. "Does entertainment satisfy him without shocking him? Does he go for ever more adrenaline-rushing images?"

Thoman said that boys' high schools, particularly those run by religious orders of men, need to address the role of media literacy and the development of masculine images in a media culture, beyond simply telling boys and young men not to watch such entertainment.

According to Thoman, one of the most successful examples of local efforts to cope with the impact of the media can be found in Bemidji, Minn., where the elementary school of St. Philip's Parish has been "taking the bull by the horns and really seeing media as a ministry."

Building on the media literacy lessons taught at every grade level in the school, the students of the St. Philip's theater group helped write and produce a humorous video—"The No-Skills Family Watches TV"—that has been widely distributed in the area as a teaching tool.

The video, with all the roles played by students, opens in a board room, where advertisers and producers discuss how they will get the viewer to stay to the commercial—by using "jolts" like kisses, humor and violence. "Quicken the pace with a car crash—shoot the driver—naked people in the back seat!" one character exclaims.

The wise, long-suffering cat of the "No-Skills" family offers commentary as the humans gather, entranced, in front of the television. A "Manipulation Control Center" monitors the viewers through binoculars, delivering jolts to get them to the commercials. The ads are clever parodies with fake products and celebrity endorsements, like the basketball player who shills "Hypie Anti-Gravity Shoes": "You can have it all—power, money, friends and status. Don't waste one more moment being pathetic."

According to Sandra Pascoe Robinson, media literacy educator at St. Philip's, the humor has been an important tool to break through people's defensiveness. "I have found that talking about media awareness is such an emotionally charged topic," she said. Laughing about the "No-Skills Family" provides a springboard for conversation. "There's a knee-jerk reaction—'I don't have a problem, and don't ask me to turn off the TV.' But as soon as the humor is there, the guards are down and we can talk," she said.

First-Graders as Critics

Robinson has found the most receptive audiences in very young children. Even children in older grades already have their viewing patterns established, she said. "I'm finding the first-graders to be incredibly astute at looking at their shows and critiquing them," Robinson said.

Robinson noted how the children at St. Philip's have carried their newfound media skills into their homes. They are encouraged to see critiquing the media as a way of taking care of their younger brothers and sisters—"to see this as a collective responsibility," she said.

The children are also bringing the message back to their parents. "There are some parents struggling with their own issues with media, and this is part of the very emotional response I get at times," Robinson said. She said one mother told of how her elementary school-age daughter challenged her father's preference for action films, leading to dialogue about the violence in the movies he was bringing home.

Many parents are naive about what messages their children are receiving, said Robinson, a mother of three children in their late teens and early 20s. "All TV, all movies are educational," she said. "What are they learning? If you step back and look critically, some of the messages are very frightening. . . . Violence is entertaining, sex is no big deal, the more things I have, the happier I'll be—those are the three big messages I see."

Robinson recalled a lesson she gave to a third-grade class at another parochial school. When she brought up video games, "two boys way in the back jumped up and machine-gunned the class," she said. "The response was strong and automatic and violent. That was part of their favorite video game."

She questioned media leaders who say that the violent entertainment they produce has no effect. "In that half-hour program there are 25 commercials—because media is an effective way to sell things," she said. "So how can they say they're not selling violence as entertainment, as fun, as funny?"

In late April, the Center for Media Literacy launched a Web site funded by grants from religious communities and devoted to the topic of violence and the media (www.medialit.org/Violence/indexviol.htm). The center was "literally in the midst of uploading pages" when the story from Littleton broke, Thoman said. The stories of the killers' media influences—music, video games and the Internet—began to hit the newscasts, and the latest round of public debate fired up again.

Thoman has not seen the nature of that debate change much since 1993, when the center launched a campaign on media violence. "After the Littleton experience, we still hear the same questions—does watching violence cause violence?" she said.

Meanwhile, news coverage of Littleton has provided ample opportunities to view the media packaging the center seeks to demystify. "Within hours of Littleton, we heard about the 'teen rampage' or the 'Rocky Mountain tragedy,' " Thoman said. "Every station found a way to package this thing with music and drama."

With techniques familiar from the Gulf War to Kosovo, "it's more than just reporting the news, it's reporting the news in a way that's entertaining, so you'll be there when the commercials are on," she said.

Transcript from NewsHour with Jim Lehrer (PBS)

The Correspondent: Elizabeth Farnsworth
The Speakers: Gerald Tirrozi, James Garbarino, and Franklin Zimring

An accomplished journalist, writer, and producer-director, Elizabeth Farnsworth joined the NewsHour as a contributing correspondent in 1984 and became chief correspondent and principal substitute anchor in 1995. She became a senior correspondent in October 1999 to concentrate primarily on covering foreign affairs and the arts from the NewsHour office in San Francisco.

Farnsworth graduated magna cum laude from Middlebury College in 1965, earned her master's in Latin American history from Stanford University in 1966, and lived in Peru and Chile for extended periods. She is married, has two children, and lives in Berkeley, California.

The following broadcast on April 21, 1999.

Littleton, CO

Elizabeth Farnsworth: And joining me now is Gerald Tirozzi, Executive Director of the National Association of Secondary School Principals and a former Assistant Secretary at the US Department of Education. James Garbarino, Professor at Cornell University and Co-Director of its Family Life Development Center; he is the author of *Lost Boys: Why Our Sons Turn Violent and How We Can Save Them.* Franklin Zimring, Professor of Law at the University of California at Berkeley; his new book is *American Youth Violence,* And Dr.

Joan Kinlan, child and adolescent psychiatrist and former head of the Psychiatry Unit for Incarcerated Children in Washington, DC.

James Garbarino, before we get in to more generally the whole issue of violence in schools, let's look at this one very specifically and in particular let's take off from what the DA just said about looking for warning signs. From what you've heard about this case, were there warning signs that would have raised a real red flag for you?

James Garbarino: Well, I think probably there were. But as you pointed out, one of the problems we face is that a lot of kids show a lot of warning signs. You know, the proportion of kids in our country who are disturbed enough to need professional mental health services has roughly doubled in the last 25 years from about 10 percent to about 20 percent. But I think these—you know—these boys and their attraction to the dark side of our culture coupled with the fact that they did seem to have a grievance against their peers certainly should have had more caring probably, not just from their peers, but from adults. And it's very clear that most school systems around the country really just aren't the mental health services that troubled kids need and the spiritual services that they need. I think that's a very important part of all of this, the kind of spiritual emptiness that so many kids feel. And when they feel it, when things go bad in their lives, there's nothing to fall back on and also there's no limits to their behavior.

Elizabeth Farnsworth: Dr. Joan Kinlan, do you agree with that? Is that what you see, the kind of emptiness?

Dr. Joan Kinlan: I do. I think that Dr. Garbarino is really talking about the spiritual emptiness that often is present in these kids and often these kids, too, have come from homes in which there's violence, especially domestic violence. Of course, this then is magnified by any kind of TV violence, and often they've had some kind of difficulty themselves, like learning disabilities or emotional problems. But really they haven't developed the coping skills because certainly all kids have losses, abandonments, rejections but they don't have the inner resilience to really cope effectively and not resort to aggression.

Elizabeth Farnsworth: Did you see in what you've heard so far, would you have seen warning signs that that should have been dealt with in this situation?

Dr. Joan Kinlan: I think that there are many troubled youths in our schools. And I think it's very hard to say which one is going to be the one that's going to do something really terribly violent, like these two particular youngsters did, and I think what we need to do is to have a more caring atmosphere, certainly schools in which there's an authoritative principal who is caring and nurturing to his teachers, is able to set up an atmosphere in the entire school in which this atmosphere prevails; clearly strict attention to rules but also having a nurturing side. And I think that that really helps in our school system.

Elizabeth Farnsworth: Gerald Tirozzi, what do you see in this case that particularly hit you and stood out?

Gerald Tirozzi: Well———

Elizabeth Farnsworth: Aside from the horror of it. I mean, with the specifics of this case.

Gerald Tirozzi: We, I think it sends a lot of clear messages that, you know, regardless of how careful we want to be in our schools across America and in fairness, a youngster has I guess it's one in one millionth of a chance to be killed in a school building but it points out this can happen anywhere. I mean, this is a great community, Littleton, Colorado. You would not expect this to happen there. I think it speaks—to me, it speaks loud—it speaks volumes to the image that many of our youngsters—most of our youngsters are bombarded with images of violence in our society, television, movies, more recently even the Internet is becoming a player. And also, candidly, I think it speaks to the need of this country to come to grips with the issue of gun control. And I think what the President has put forth is an ambitious agenda and I think Congress has to take that very, very seriously and expand the Brady bill.

Elizabeth Farnsworth: Mr. Zimring, how do you see this event in relation to the other events in Arkansas, and Oregon and elsewhere?

Franklin Zimring: Well, this one involves, first of all, much older shooters. It does take place in the school and they're still students but they're 18 and 17.

Elizabeth Farnsworth: The others were as young as 11.

Franklin Zimring: As young as 11. And 13 and 11-year-olds have homicide risks and rates which are one twentieth those of 17-year-olds and 18-year-olds. It's also an extraordinarily premeditated thing. These are troubled kids and grandiose and all the rest of this, but they're also premeditated and armed in ways which are a real contrast with the episodic school shootings that we saw last year. This is almost a mix between Oklahoma City and the school shootings. And I think there's another very important contrast. When you listen to the state's attorney, what the system knew of those kids just doesn't predict serious violence. Their juvenile justice involvement was for property crime; it was the kind of thing typically kids get involved in; they did well in diversion. Everything that the school and system knew about them doesn't point a finger to particular danger. My guess is, however, that unless these are incredibly closed-mouthed kids, what other kids knew in the immediate foreground to this kind of behavior probably was more indicative that there were trouble brewing. And I think that one of the techniques that schools have got to work on when they're talking about these problems, is opening up so that friends and significant peer structures when something like this is brewing will feel trusting enough and threatened enough by this kind of talk so that there is a little bit of specific intervention. I think that everything that every adult knew in Littleton, when you combine it all, wouldn't have given us any indication that this was happening.

Elizabeth Farnsworth: Well, Mr. Tirozzi, isn't that something that has been recommended, in fact sent out by the Department of Justice and Education to all high schools to have some kind of a procedure whereby students can warn if they're hearing this from fellow students, that they may be violent?

Gerald Tirozzi: Yes. That did go out. It was an excellent guide, and it was distributed across the country but, in fairness, it takes leadership at the local school level on the part of the superintendent and the principal to make certain those guidelines are being used wisely. But there are two very important guidelines in that brochure. One states do no harm, which means, you know, you have to be very careful that you don't stereotype students or children because certain characteristics are coming to the forefront. In fairness, having been a principal, teacher and school superintendent myself, you know, what a youngster displays in one day doesn't tell you automatically that he or she is going to commit a violent act the next. And so we have to really do this on balance in schools, and it's very difficult for schools to do alone. I would hope parents can see some of these signs, that communities should see these signs. And, to me, it speaks to the issues of communities and schools really, really working closely together with families. We have to do this together. It's no one's unique responsibility.

Elizabeth Farnsworth: Mr. Garbarino, there are some elements in common among these shootings, though, are there not—even those these boys were older young boys, obsession in almost all cases with some aspect of popular culture which was violent, whether films, or video games or music and other things in common—do you think that that's true?

James Garbarino: Well, I think it is. You know, no one case has all the elements but there certainly are a lot of very common elements, as I say, the preoccupation with the dark side, this disconnection, and the righteousness of their rage. I think the comparison to Oklahoma City is a very good one that this is more like a terrorist attack. But when you look closely and inside at the other cases, you can see that element as well, that attack on the most important psychological structures that they feel are oppressing them, what they feel subjectively. I should also point out that—you know—we only hear about the cases that break apart like this. But just a month and a half ago in a small town in Pennsylvania, a 15-year-old boy was making these kind of threats; three students told the principal that night and the next day when the boy showed up, he was detained and it turned out he had a rifle in the bushes and was planning one of these assaults. So let's understand that people are responding, albeit imperfectly.

Elizabeth Farnsworth: And, Mr. Garbarino, if I were to say why, ask the question that the President posed and I think most of our viewers are posing, what would your answer be? We've gotten into this a little already, but tell me.

James Garbarino: Well, I would say that, you know, there is a sort of epidemic abroad in the land. It has its roots in various elements of American culture. But some kids are more susceptible than others. It's as if they were talking about air pollution in a big city. We know that everyone is affected, but some kids are more affected than others. The asthmatic kids are more affected. I tend to view these kids as being kind of psychological asthmatics; that they're the ones who succumb to all the poisons in our culture because of their individual experience, because they get involved in peer groups where they reinforce each other. You know, remember Truman Capote's book *In Cold Blood* about two men who killed a whole family. Capote concluded neither man by himself would have committed those crimes but put together there was a kind of evil chemistry between them. And that, I think, is an important element in at least some of these cases.

Elizabeth Farnsworth: Dr. Kinlan, how would you answer the question why, beyond what you said earlier?

Dr. Joan Kinlan: I think that it's been talked about a little bit more. I think that there's been a real difference in our society right now. It's a culture of more violence—American—it has the highest number of homicides per person and highest number of guns than any other industrialized place. In addition, I think there's been a real change in the family. The family is not really there as much for kids. Often we have both parents working, there's not as much supervision. And we certainly know that with poor supervision that there's a greater degree of crimes. The American Academy of Pediatrics has pointed out that 1.2 million latchkey kids go home unsupervised to homes where there are guns. And that's of concern. And kids who then may have difficulty with controlling their impulses then have an aggressive vehicle to use.

Elizabeth Farnsworth: And, Mr. Zimring, how would you answer that question?

Franklin Zimring: Well, I think that to the extent that adolescence is an epidemic of poor impulse control there's nothing in recent generations that isolates or explains that. I think that's a characteristic of 20th century adolescence. So I think we don't want to look there. To a certain extent, I guess I'm terribly skeptical of looking to the broadest possible explanations for this particular shooting in Littleton, Colorado. There are obviously dangerous elements in American culture, but I think very much like Oklahoma City, which is now five years old and hasn't been repeated, I think that my own tendency is to look more sort of to ways in which we can prevent loss, prevent harm, get wind of these things, if possible, when they are brewing and intervene in a non-harmful way, and not immediately jump to the conclusion that we have to look—to say that in essence the entire of a society is implicated every time that something very tragic happens amongst us.

Elizabeth Farnsworth: Mr. Tirozzi, what has been learned from the experience of the other high schools who have been coping, the schools that have had killings in other places like Arkansas and Mississippi, what have they learned about what happens next?

Gerald Tirozzi: Well, it has varied from community to community, but essentially they've worked very hard to pick up the pieces. It's a very hard and difficult memory to overcome. But based on conversations I've actually had with the individual principals, I think with the help of mental health specialists who have gone in and really worked with students and faculty, they've begun to build a solid foundation. And some have really tried to make the effort as business as usual so the youngsters get a sense that school can go on. It's been very difficult but my sense based on my conversations with them, it's really beginning to move along.

Elizabeth Farnsworth: And what about the safety aspects? What did they change?

Gerald Tirozzi: Well, in several of the schools they have police officers or they've advanced security guards. And that's very, very important. But do I want to remind folks across the country, you look at your average middle or senior high school, you're probably talking 75 to 150 exterior doors on these buildings. And it's almost impossible—I mean—to protect every door and put enough guards in buildings. I think the real answer—as one of your commentators said a moment ago—I think is really looking at the whole issue of prevention, front loading the process instead of always back loading the process. We put a lot of dollars into security and metal detectors; we put very little into prevention. And that's where society has to get its act together.

Elizabeth Farnsworth: And just statistically for the parents who are wondering when they send their child to schools tomorrow, schools are still, in general, a pretty safe place for kids?

Gerald Tirozzi: Absolutely. As I said earlier, an expert just reported the other day the chances of a youngster being murdered in school are one in one million, you know, which—schools are safe places but, in fairness, these incidents can happen anywhere at any time.

Elizabeth Farnsworth: All right. Well, thank you all four very much.

Scholarly Publication

The Author: Marshall Croddy, PhD

Marshall Croddy, PhD, a lawyer, is director of program materials development for the Constitutional Rights Foundation and the author of numerous educational publications and texts in the areas of law and civics. The following essay was published in *Social Education* in 1997.

Violence Redux: A Brief Legal and Historical Perspective on Youth Violence

- To a busy urban street comes the staccato clap of automatic weapons fire. From a passing car, someone fires at a rival gang member, but misses and kills a young girl instead. The press features stories about a "mad dog" killer. Weeks later the young suspect too is dead, murdered by rivals.
- On an empty field late at night, the sounds of yelling and cursing can be heard. Two young men struggle in a drunken brawl after a weekend party. One falls to the ground mortally wounded with a skull fracture. The other is arrested for murder.

20th Century U.S. Homicide Rates

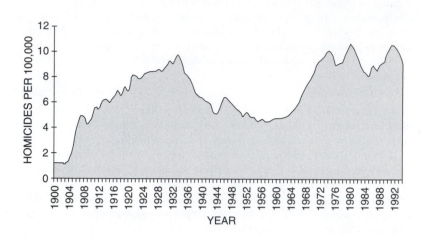

- Two young college men, 18 and 19 years old and of upper middle class backgrounds, kidnap a 14-year-old boy for ransom and brutally kill him. They are eventually captured and tried for their senseless crime.

Stories such as these confront us on a daily basis. But these particular stories are yesterday's news. The first took place in the early 1930s on the streets of New York; the second occurred in Springfield, Illinois, in 1837: and the third is based on the 1924 Leopold and Loeb murder case. They serve to illustrate a sad truth about America's past and present: violence perpetrated by and against young people has always been part of the American experience. And, in spite of overall reductions in violent crime rates over the past few years the juvenile violent crime rate is still depressingly high.[1]

Violence and Youth

If one watches the local television news, it is easy to get the impression that violence in America is not only a bigger problem than in the past, but that it has reached crisis proportions. Yet many indicators show that violent crime in America is actually decreasing. For example, the National Crime Victimization Survey (NCVS) shows that the percentage of households experiencing some kind of violent crime has generally declined since 1975. According to the Uniform Police Report (UCR), the murder rate has also dropped in recent years.

Polls have demonstrated that people's perceptions about crime and violence do not necessarily reflect real trends. For example, in the mid-1990s, polls started indicating a greater public concern over crime and violence, when the actual rates had leveled off and were declining.

Experts offer various explanations. According to some, concerns over violent crime are somewhat constant, but at various times get overshadowed by other issues. Others suggest that recent concerns over violent crime are based less on personal experience or actual crime rates, and more on perceptions fueled by the media, which tend to highlight violent and dramatic crimes.

Many older people tend to think that today's youth are more likely to break the law than young people in the past, and are more violent than ever. How accurate is this perception? In 1970, youth 18 and under accounted for 26 percent of all arrests, while by the early 1990s, this figure had actually dropped to 16 percent. However, beginning in the mid-to-late 1980s, experts began noticing a nationwide increase in the rates of violent crimes against youth, especially those 12 to 15 years old. More disturbing, these trends occurred while the population of teenagers was on the decline.

Beginning in 1985 the national rate of youth arrests for violent crime increased in every year except 1992, 1994 and 1995. Also, beginning in 1985, there was a disturbing increase in the adolescent murder rate—although it too started to decline in the early 1990s. In 1995, the arrest rate for violent crime by 10- to 17-year-olds was 622 per 100,000, down from a peak of 655 per 100,000 in 1990. These rates are not too different from overall rates for violent crime, which in 1995 were 515 per 100,000.[2]

Perhaps the most important consideration about youth crime is how to head it off. Delbert S. Elliott a researcher in the field of youth violence, notes that according to self-report studies, the highest rates of participation in violent acts are at ages 16 to 17. On the other hand, if a young person does not get involved with violence before the age of 20, he or she is unlikely to do so. And, while 80 percent of young offenders stop being violent by the age of 21, the remaining 20 percent commit a high percentage of violent crimes.

Even more importantly, teenagers are often the targets of violence. On average, teens are much more likely to be victims of violence than are adults or senior citizens, with African American males in the age range of 16 to 19 being especially vulnerable.[3]

The Gang Problem

One of the chief risks for youth in regard to violence is being drawn into a gang. The problem is not new. Historically—and while not unknown in rural areas—gangs involving juveniles have always been a significant factor in large urban areas. As early as 1791, children's gangs were noted in Philadelphia. During the mid-19th century, well-organized adult gangs and their youthful cohorts became a serious problem in New York and other cities on the eastern seaboard. As the urban population swelled from the twin influences of industrialization and immigration, job seekers from the countryside and from abroad who could not find work often fell in with what would now be recognized as youth street gangs.[4]

In one memorable affray in 1903, hundreds of young men from three different predominantly Irish gangs—the Eastmans, the Five Pointers and the Gophers—waged an hour long gun battle on New York's East Side. Only after police arrived in massive force did the fighting end, leaving three dead and seven wounded on the streets. The incident, only one in a series that terrorized the East Side for many years, was sufficiently deadly and notorious that Tammany politicians themselves were forced to get involved to negotiate a peace among the warning factions.[5]

The New York street gangs thrived and evolved throughout the early decades of the 20th century. Young men living in crowded and decaying tenements sought refuge and companionship on the streets. There, from very early ages, they formed cliques with other like-situated youth, bonding together for protection, friendship, and mischief making. Many were products of families cut off from the social stability of the old communities from which they came, some stressed by cultural and language alienation as well as poverty. The pocket communities where they lived—the Lower East Side, parts of Brooklyn, the Bowery—were also economically and socially stressed, reducing the reach of social control.

During Prohibition, these cliques proved a potent recruiting ground for older gangs cashing in on the artificial scarcity and high demand economics of alcohol. The result was a murderous war for territory and vice control by gangsters in cities from New York to Chicago.[6] Such crime bosses as Charles "Lucky" Luciano, Al Capone, and Benjamin "Bugsy" Siegel all emerged from the street gang milieu, along with hundreds of less famous figures. Of course, the vast majority of youth from these and similar backgrounds did not become violent criminals but rather productive members of society.

A survey of modern research suggests that many of the same factors that spurred the development of violent gangs in the early decades of this century are at work today:

> When communities are weakened by demographic and economic shifts that concentrate poverty and destabilize their institutions, conventional processes of socialization and control fail. When intergenerational relationships break down or are distorted by such developments, the likelihood that gangs will flourish and compete with one another, often with deadly consequences, is enhanced.[7]

Of course, the object of competition between gangs today is profit from illegal drugs rather than outlawed alcohol. It is also arguable that today's gang violence is more widespread, more deadly, and more random than in the past—though even now it would be hard to imagine a melee like some that took place in New York at the turn of the century.

But youth gangs continue to thrive in areas of poverty and social destabilization. Today, black and Chicano gangs operate in communities cut off from the mainstream economy and blighted by the erosion of the old manufacturing base. White skinhead groups bond together in hate on the false assumption that other ethnic groups are responsible for a lack of perceived opportunity in their own rust belt and rural environments.[8] Asian youths and others whose families seek to cope in a societal milieu different from their own traditions form part of the mix.

As the above examples suggest, there is little evidence from national self-report studies for any difference in predisposition to violence by race, or presumably ethnicity, once social class is taken into account.[9] And, as in the past, only a tiny minority of youth become chronic offenders; unfortunately, it is chronic offenders who account for about two-thirds of all violent offenses.[10]

Solutions to America's problems with violence in general, and youth gangs in particular, have proven illusory. Youth violence is after all a multifaceted and multicausal problem. Research points to a variety of interactive factors affecting individuals that can give rise to violence, including psychosocial development, neurological and hormonal differences, and social processes.[11] Such factors defy simple solutions, and as with cancer, there are no magic bullets.

Risk Factors and Their Association with Behavior Problems in Adolescents

	Adolescent Problem Behavior				
Risk Factors	Substance Abuse	Delinquency	Teen Pregnancy	School Drop-Out	Violence
Community					
Availability of Drugs	x				
Availability of Firearms		x			x
Community Laws and Norms Favorable Toward Drug Use, Firearms, and Crime	x	x			x
Media Portrayals of Violence					x
Transitions and Mobility	x	x		x	x
Low Neighborhood Attachment and Community Disorganization	x	x			x
Extreme Economic Deprivation	x	x	x	x	x
Family					
Family History of Problem Behavior	x	x	x	x	x
Family Management Problems	x	x	x	x	x
Family Conflict	x	x	x	x	x
Favorable Parental Attitudes and Involvement in the Problem Behavior	x	x			x
School					
Early and Persistent Attitudes and Involvement in the Problem Behavior	x	x	x	x	x
Academic Failure Beginning in Elementary School	x	x	x	x	x
Lack of Commitment to School	x	x	x	x	x
Individual/Peer					
Alienation and Rebelliousness	x	x		x	
Friends Who Engage in a Problem Behavior	x	x	x	x	x
Favorable Attitudes Toward the Problem Behavior	x	x	x	x	
Early Initiation of the Problem Behavior	x	x	x	x	x
Constitutional Factors	x	x			x

Addressing social factors is particularly difficult and controversial. How does society solve the problems of poverty, family dysfunction and child abuse, alcohol and drug addiction, racial discrimination, and American culture's fascination with violence? Proposed or tried solutions today face prickly political debates over governmental versus individual responsibility, welfare versus workfare, and the federal versus state role in dealing with juvenile crime and violence.

But it is the historical and ongoing debates over rehabilitation versus punishment, and when children should be treated like adults, that have had the most effect on how we deal with juvenile offenders.

Common Law and Juvenile Crime

The origins of these debates can be traced to our English jurisprudential roots. In the Middle Ages, a period characterized by much shorter lifespans, children were expected to work by the age of 5 or 6. By ages 12 to 14, youths were often married, and few people lived past 40 years old. It was the common belief that anyone old enough to commit a crime was old enough to be punished for it, often in the same harsh manner as adults. In two notable cases from the early law of England, a 13-year-old girl was burned to death for killing her mistress, and an 8-year-old boy was hanged.[12]

By the 16th and 17th centuries, these attitudes began to soften. It was also during this period that the common law developed the notion of *parens patriae,* that is, that the monarch was the parent of the country and should intervene to protect children if necessary.

During the 18th century, another concept evolved that is with us today: the idea of intent. Before a person could be punished for a crime, he or she not only had to commit a forbidden act that resulted in harm, but also had to intend to commit that act. The concept of intent raised a troubling issue in regard to children. At what age were they able to form intent? The common law relied on Christian beliefs, which held that at age 7, children reached the "age of reason" and could tell right from wrong, thus making them capable of forming criminal intent.

By the late 18th century, English common law judges routinely dismissed criminal cases against children under 7, and put the burden on the prosecution to prove that children between 7 and 14 were capable of forming criminal intent. In this, prosecutors were often successful. In a 1796 case, for example, the prosecution successfully argued that a 10-year-old defendant had formed the requisite criminal intent in a murder case because the boy had hidden the victim's body and thus demonstrated that he knew he had been wrong to kill.

If tried and convicted, children were treated in the same manner as adults. This could mean a long term in adult prison or jail, flogging, and, especially, hanging—a real possibility given the long list of capital offenses. In actual practice, the courts showed leniency toward the youngest offenders. For example, between 1801 and 1836, while English courts sentenced 103 children under 8 to death, none were actually executed.

In America throughout the 19th century, the age of criminal culpability gradually increased. Today, though states vary, the early teens are generally established as the basic age after which one can be held accountable for criminal acts.[13] For example, in California, children under the age of 14—in the absence of clear proof that at the time of committing the charge against them they knew of its wrongfulness—are not capable of committing crimes.[14]

Separate Justice for Juveniles

Unfortunately, throughout the first decades of the 19th century, children who were convicted of crimes ended up in the same prisons with adults. Through contacts with older criminals, young offenders often learned how to perfect their criminal lifestyles and were often abused by the older inmates.

By the 1820s, American reformers—especially in the cities—began calling for alternatives to adult punishment, and for ways to care for the increasing numbers of street waifs. In 1824, using *parens patriae* as an underlying rationale, New York City established the nation's first reform school (called a House of Refuge) for abandoned, deprived, and criminal children. Its program of religion, education, and hard work was copied in most urban areas, and became the model for how America treated juvenile offenders well into the 20th century.

Unfortunately, the system had significant drawbacks. Usually, the institutions were run by private organizations on a profit motive, the labor of the young inmates being the primary capital. Often, moral development and education got sacrificed for greater productivity, and children spent less and less time in classroom and chapel, and more time in the workshops. Some institutions became notoriously corrupt, and conditions deteriorated. Moreover, the system of mixing offender populations with deprived and abandoned young people had predictable results. Reform schools, like the adult prisons before them, soon developed the reputations of being "universities of crime."

Trying to address this problem, turn-of-the-century Progressives fueled the creation of a new juvenile justice system that would lead to the one we know today. The spark of reform was lit when the Chicago Reform School burned down in the Great Fire of 1871. It had been so corrupted by vice and crime that many judges had refused to send any but the most hardened juvenile offenders there, preferring instead to sentence most youth to adult jails, which offered a safer environment.

After the fire, the city government refused to provide the funds to rebuild it. The Chicago Women's Club developed a school for young people in the regular jails, and helped establish a city police station for women and children arrestees so they would not have to mix with adult male criminals. In the process, they began the movement for a completely new juvenile justice system.

In 1899, their work bore fruit when Illinois opened its first juvenile court, the flagship of an entirely separate system of justice for juveniles. Rather than punish young people as criminals, it was designed to treat and rehabilitate them. Rather than mixing children with hardened offenders, it would create institutions to meet the specific needs of offenders and of abused or neglected children. Fundamentally, the Progressives believed that criminality among those of tender years was a product of social and family causes, and that delinquency should be treated more like a disease than a crime. Within 25 years, all states but Maine and Wyoming had passed laws based on the Illinois model.

Contemporary Views of Juvenile Justice

Until the mid-1970s, both the assumptions behind and the presumed effectiveness of the juvenile justice system went largely unchallenged. Then the public mood shifted. A perception arose that juvenile delinquency was getting worse, and that the system was coddling young criminals. This outlook may have been fueled by high rates of recidivism, as well as by statutory anomalies that allowed juveniles to serve much less time for violent crimes, even murder, than would adult felons.

A "get tough" mood swept the country, which translated into legislative action largely designed to increase juvenile sentences and try more juveniles as adults. From 1978 to 1988, these changes increased the lock-up rate for juveniles by nearly 50 percent. Today, many authorities on juvenile justice note a virtual abandonment of rehabilitation as the primary emphasis in the system, and a much greater focus on punishment and incapacitation.[15]

In addition, many states began lowering the age at which young people can be tried as adults, particularly when the juvenile is accused of a violent crime. In New York, all persons 16 and over charged with criminal offenses are processed as adults. Forty-eight states now have laws permitting juveniles to be *waived* to the adult system. Vermont allows a waiver at the youngest age: 10 years old. In an eerie reminder of the way things once were an increasing number of teenagers are being convicted and serving hard time.[16]

It is questionable whether such practices will significantly reduce the rates of juvenile violent crime over the long run. By 1991—and in the face of "get tough" policies—juvenile homicides, forcible rapes, and aggravated assaults rose to the highest levels in American history (then declining in most years afterward). Experts offer a variety of explanations. Some argue that juvenile offenders—often incarcerated in overcrowded, and sometimes gang-ridden, facilities—come out more likely to commit violent crimes than when they went in.[17]

Others suggest that the threat of incarceration does little to deter those juveniles most likely to commit violent crimes. They see the psychological and social pressures to be violent as overriding the operation of rational choice. They also suggest that incarceration, particularly with regard to gang members, has become almost an accepted part of the lifestyle.

Still others argue that rates for violent crime—and, indeed, crime in general—are resistant to any kind of intervention, and are simply tied to demographics. According to this theory, the greater the percentage of males between the ages of 15 to 25 in the population, the more likely it is that crime rates will go up.

The question of whether society is justified in emphasizing youth violence has also been raised. In a 1996 book. *Scapegoat Generation: America's War on Adolescents,* researcher Mike Males cited the decline in violent youth crime, particularly in Los Angeles and California. He also provided statistics suggesting that other age groups and types of people are just as violent. Though controversial, Males argued that the perception of a generation of violent youth has been used by the media to "demonize" young people.[18] He concluded in an interview: "We do not stereotype adult groups that way. Young people deserve the same fairness."

The problems with the juvenile justice system have led to a new round of calls for reform. Proposals include earlier intervention, providing alternatives to incarceration for the vast majority of offenders, and spending more money for probation, counseling, and education programs.[19]

A number of these ideas are reflected in a new comprehensive strategy for dealing with serious, violent and chronic juvenile crime, offered by the Office of Juvenile Justice and Delinquency Prevention. It outlines several principles for addressing the problem:

- Strengthening families, including the use of family surrogates, if necessary
- Supporting core social institutions that affect young people, including schools
- Promoting delinquency prevention efforts in both the public and private sector
- Intervening immediately and effectively when delinquent behavior occurs
- Identifying and controlling the small group of serious, violent, and chronic juvenile offenders who have committed felony offenses or have failed to respond to intervention and non-secure treatment and rehabilitation at the community level.[20]

This plan seemingly seeks a middle ground, in that its elements address both the research on the causes of violent delinquency and the need to promote public safety by incapacitating the most dangerous offenders. President Clinton's proposed 1997 youth crime bill incorporates several of these strategies by increasing penalties for gang-related violence while also launching new prevention programs.[21]

Not everyone supports the Administration's "reform" approach. The new Republican-sponsored House Bill, titled the Juvenile Crime Control Act of 1997, offers $1.5 billion in block grants to states that adopt tougher measures when trying juveniles in their jurisdictions. States would have to assure that juveniles of 15 years or above who commit serious violent crimes would be tried as adults; that penalties for repeat juvenile offenders would be increased; that juveniles who commit second crimes would have their records made public: and that parents who fail to supervise convicted juveniles would be subject to court sanction. In addition, the legislation would allow convicted juveniles in some cases to be sentenced to adult prisons.[22]

It remains to be seen whether in an era of shrinking government, new approaches or the "get tough" philosophy will prevail. In truth, both will probably entail greater expenditures of public money into the underfunded juvenile justice system. In either case, it is likely that the debate will continue as it has throughout our history.

Notes

1. Office of Juvenile Justice and Delinquency Prevention. *Comprehensive Strategy for Serious, Violent and Chronic Juvenile Offenders. Program Summary* (D.C.: U.S. Department of Justice, 1994), 1–5.
2. U.S. Department of Justice. Office of Justice Programs, *Criminal Justice Statistics Online,* Table 43 (1995).
3. *Ibid.*

4. Marshall L. Croddy et al. *Criminal Justice in America* (Los Angeles: Constitutional Rights Foundation, 1994).
5. Herbert Asbury, *The Gangs of New York* (New York Knopf. 1928), 279–282.
6. *See,* for example, Robert Lacey, *Little Man* (New York: Little Brown, 1991) and Laurence Bergreen. *Capone* (New York: Simon & Schuster, 1994).
7. Albert J. Reiss, Jr., and Jeliery A. Roth (eds). "Perspectives on Violence," *Understanding and Preventing Violence* (D.C.: National Research Council, 1993), 145.
8. Robert K. Jackson and Wesley D. McBride, *Understanding Street Gangs* (Sacramento, 1985).
9. Delbert S. Elliott, *Youth Violence: An Overview* (Boulder, CO: Institute of Behavioral Science. 1994), 4.
10. Office of Juvenile Justice and Delinquency Prevention, 5.
11. Reiss and Roth, 102.
12. M. Cherif Bassiouni, *Criminal Law and Its Processes* (Springfield: Charles C. Thomas, 1969), 87.
13. *Ibid.*
14. *California Penal Code,* Part 1, Title 1 Section 26 (1983).
15. Ron Harris, "A Nation's Children in Lockup," *Los Angeles Times* (8/22/93): A1.
16. Croddy, 217.
17. Harris, A20.
18. Mike Males, *Scapegoat Generation: America's War on Adolescents* (Monroe, ME: Common Courage Press, 1996).
19. Edward Humes, "Lessons in Juvenile Injustice," *Los Angeles Daily Journal* (6/12/96): 6.
20. Office of Juvenile Justice and Delinquency Prevention, 9.
21. James Risen, "U.S. Violent Crime Drops Record 7%" *Los Angeles Times* (6/2/97): A1.
22. Jerry Gray, "Bill to Combat Juvenile Crime Passes House," *The New York Times* (5/9/97): A1.

Scholarly Article

The Author: Kevin J. H. Dettmar, PhD

Kevin J. H. Dettmar is a professor and chairman of the English department at Southern Illinois University at Carbondale. He received his BA in English and psychology from the University of California, Davis (1981), a postgraduate diploma in Anglo-Irish literature from Trinity College, Dublin (1982), and a PhD in British literature from UCLA (1990). Before coming to SIUC, he taught for a year as a visiting assistant professor at Loyola Marymount University in Los Angeles, and for eight years at Clemson University (South Carolina), where he also served as associate chair of the Department of English for three years and as associate dean of the College of Architecture, Arts & Humanities for a semester. He came to SIUC as professor and chair of the Department of English in August 1999.

Professor Dettmar's scholarly area is twentieth-century British and American literature and culture—especially the intersections of literary and cultural texts. He is the author of *The Illicit Joyce of Postmodernism: Reading Against the Grain* (Univ. of Wisconsin Press, 1996), and editor or co-editor of *Rereading the New: A Backward Glance at Modernism* (Univ. of Michigan Press, 1992); *Marketing Modernisms: Self-Promotion, Canonization, and Rereading* (Univ. of Michigan Press, 1996); and *Reading Rock & Roll: Authenticity, Appropriation, Aesthetics* (Columbia Univ. Press, 1999). He is also a member of the editorial team that assembled the new *Longman Anthology of British Literature* (1998). Professor Dettmar has published a wide range of essays on topics, including Kathy Acker, Samuel Beckett, James Joyce, W. B. Yeats, James Clarence Mangan, William Gass, *The Simpsons,* and cellos in alternative rock, and is an occasional contributor on popular culture topics to the Chronicle of Higher Education.

The following article appeared in the *Chronicle of Higher Education* in June 2000.

Ironic Literacy: Grasping the Dark Images of Rock and Roll

Few weeks ago, my 14-year-old daughter, Audrey, came upstairs to tell me that a Columbine High School junior, a basketball star named Greg Barnes, had hanged himself. When his father found him, Blink-182's "Adam's Song" was playing in the background. Currently in heavy rotation on the modern-rock stations, it is a song in which the singer/speaker contemplates suicide.

My daughter learned of the suicide—nearly a week after the fact—because it was the topic of conversation on the morning show carried by her favorite pop-music radio station. One of the hosts had seen something about the suicide on CNN the previous night, and was outraged that the song had been getting airplay. (The station on which Audrey heard the news doesn't play the song, though it has played other Blink-182 songs.) A lively conversation took place on the air, with telephone callers, and on the "Graffiti Wall" of the show's site on the World Wide Web. Though some callers tried to argue that no one commits suicide because of what he might have heard in a song, a large number agreed with the host's opinion that if a song doesn't express something positive, it shouldn't be played on the radio.

Although a majority of participants in the show's online colloquy voiced their opposition to formal censorship, many expressed a desire for a kind of point-of-purchase censorship, suggesting, for instance, that the parental-advisory label found on a CD like Blink-182's *Enema of the State* be turned into a purchase restriction, similar to the PG-13 and R ratings for films. Many listeners spoke in favor of parental supervision, including a teenager who wrote on the show's Web site: "The parents should be well informed of the music that their children listen to. They should take everyone of their kid's CDs or tapes and listen to them, and then decide what to do. My parents do it and I think everyone else's should. My parents has took [sic] away my Eminem CD, my Dr. Dre CD, my Kid Rock CD, and also my Limp Bizkit CD."

Perhaps it's an occupational hazard, but, as an English teacher, I can't help seeing in all this not the issue of censorship, but a parable about the hazards of reading poorly, and about the dangers of a populace just marginally literate when it comes to understanding irony—particularly as it is used in rock music.

Greg Barnes's death followed by just two weeks the one-year anniversary of the mass shooting at Columbine High School. Rock 'n' roll was at the scene of that crime as well, at least by implication: In the wake of the shooting, investigators discovered that the killers, Eric Harris and Dylan Klebold, had listened obsessively to the "goth" music of Marilyn Manson, Rammstein, and KMFDM. A kind of ad-hoc cause-and-effect argument was advanced in some quarters that the music's dark messages were in some way responsible for the boys' dark acts. Harris, for instance, had posted the lyrics to KMFDM's "Son of a Gun" on his Web site:

> Shockwave Massive attack Atomic blast Son of a gun is back.

There are certainly sentiments here to give one pause—especially a journalist hot on the scent of a story. But the story that the song actually tells, while hardly sophisticated, is more complicated than those lines suggest, for the "son of a gun" is later called a "sh——for brains." Thus the song, while on the surface appearing to glamorize violence, attempts on another level to question the very values its hero identifies with.

That narrative strategy—giving voice to views with which one disagrees as a way to expose that position's flaws—is called irony. Rock 'n' roll has deployed irony as a narrative strategy from its earliest days. But rock's irony has become increasingly sophisticated and understated over time, and with its increasing textual density has come an increased risk that a certain kind of fan will miss the point of a song entirely.

Truth be told, rock 'n' roll has never done a good job of presenting the case against suicide, with or without irony. The locus classicus is David Bowie's "Rock 'N' Roll Suicide," the closing track on *The Rise and Fall of Ziggy Stardust* and the *Spiders from Mars*. Yet, while the anguish in Bowie's voice on that track is, by the end of the song, almost unbearable, the argument, finally, is quite mundane:

> Oh no love! you're not alone
> You're watching yourself but you're too unfair
> You got your head all tangled up but if I could only make you care

"Jumper," a recent hit song by Third Eye Blind, is another good example of the limitations of the genre:

> I wish you would step back from that ledge, my friend
> You could cut ties with all the lies
> That you've been living in

Even one of the most beautifully elegiac albums of the past decade, Neil Young's *Sleeps With Angels*, finally falls short, as Young tries to imagine going back in time and persuading Nirvana's front man, Kurt Cobain, not to take his own life:

> When you get weak, and you need to test your will
> When life's complete, but there's something missing still

Distracting you from this must be the one you love
Must be the one whose magic touch can change your mind.

Cobain's wife, Courtney Love, no doubt believed herself to be providing just that kind of support when Cobain took his life. Surely resisting suicide involves more than just being distracted from life's emptiness.

A recent spoken-word piece by Bobby Gaylor called, very simply, "Suicide," takes a less simplistic view. Although it's essentially a novelty record, it touched a number of people with its irreverent, sometimes vulgar, take on the subject. As the music comes up, Gaylor begins his perverse "pep talk":

Animals don't have a choice.
If they're not happy with their place in the world . . . , too bad.
They have to live the life they've been given.
Humans, on the other hand, don't have to.
We have a choice.
If you don't like your place in the world you can get off anytime you want.
Suicide. That's right.

For the first two minutes, the piece maintains that air of cold indifference. In the second section, Gaylor begins to think out loud of all the reasons that suicide might be a good thing, both for the one who ends his life and for those he leaves behind:

"Now, I'm not saying 'Kill yourself.' But if you're gonna be an idiot and do it anyway, it's no sweat off of my back. There's a lot of good that could come from it. A little bit of bad thrown in."

The good part for the narrator: "A job will open . . . An apartment will become available . . . There'll be more air for me." The good part for the person considering suicide: "You'll never get AIDS . . . You won't have to worry about calories ever . . . No more Barry Manilow . . . For a few years anyway."

The third and final section, however, slides imperceptibly into the small, everyday joys—and the huge, life-changing ones—that the deceased will never experience: "You'll . . . miss McDonald's French Fries . . . Bugs Bunny . . . The amazing electrifying feeling that surges through your body when you kiss someone for the first time."

In the end, Gaylor jeers at the would-be suicide the way a Manhattan cab driver might: "Hey, you were born—Finish what was started."

"Suicide" is so broadly ironic that it borders on satire—no reasonably intelligent person who listens through to the end could remain in doubt about the song's intentions. In an interview on the Virgin Megastore Web site, Gaylor explained his motivation for the song:

I wrote it for a friend who was suicidal, and that's how it all began. I didn't know what to say, you just keep harping on about the usual "think about your family, and all the people that love you, man. Your friends, I mean, you'd be letting them down. We all love you" and it's like, they kind of know that already, and they've already gone beyond that. So I sat down going "ok, I'm a creative son of a b——h. I should be able to write something here that can get his attention." So I did.

Listeners who have logged on to the guest book on Gaylor's site, while acknowledging that sometimes "people get pi——d and don't listen to the whole thing," overwhelmingly approve of the song and its strategy. A counselor hoped that teenagers would listen to the song's message. A fan heard the single on the radio and couldn't wait for the CD to come out so he could bring it to his church youth group. One note was posted by the father of a 13-year-old girl who hanged herself two years ago: "I just wish that Jodie would have heard your recording. I hope it helps others. . . ."

Blink-182's "Adam's Song" attempts a much riskier ironic strategy than Gaylor's "Suicide." The singer, Mark Hoppus, in the voice of a character named Adam, speaks of his despair from the position of one clinging precariously to life. Suicide seems to him like the logical answer. My students and I spent some time discussing the song recently in my graduate seminar on irony in the public sphere. They decided that the song attempts to "say no" to suicide by dramatizing the illogical thought processes of the fictional Adam, and that it suggests, by the song's close, reasons to hold on to life. Hoppus said in an interview that the message of the song is: "Whatever your personal demons are, find the strength to fight them, and realize that there are better things ahead."

His intention would seem to be similar to Gaylor's, and yet "Adam's Song" is in the news because it supplied the background music for a suicide. It's important to note, though, that Greg Barnes's suicide, for all its tragedy, was largely ignored by the major news media until the possible link to rock 'n' roll became public knowledge.

One of the most egregious examples of misreading in the context of rock occurred when Kurt Cobain ended his life, on April 5, 1994. His suicide note contained a quotation from the Neil Young song "My My, Hey Hey (Out of the Blue)": "I don't have the passion anymore and so remember, its better to burn out than to fade away."

While I have no interest in either correcting the reading or questioning the motives of a dead man, it must be said that Cobain, whether intentionally or not, gets Young's point badly wrong. Young wrote "My My, Hey Hey" about one of the most outlandish stage creations of the rock era: Johnny Rotten, the character that the singer John Lydon created to front the Sex Pistols ("The king is gone but he's not forgotten / This is the story of Johnny Rotten").

In context, the lines "It's better to burn out / Than to fade away," in the song's opening stanza, refer to Lydon's decision to kill off Johnny Rotten after the Sex Pistols' disastrous U.S. tour in January 1978. The king is dead, but John Lydon is alive and kicking; he went on after the Pistols' demise to found the band Public Image Ltd.

Young's song is a tribute to Lydon's "public image"; to quote it as a justification of suicide requires either an ignorance of its larger context—an ignorance that's difficult to ascribe to an avid punk-rock fan like Cobain—or an active forgetting by someone bent on destroying himself.

Something of this dense textual history finds its way into Blink-182's "Adam's Song." In media reports of the recent Columbine suicide, it's the opening and closing lines of the song's first verse that are always quoted. For instance, the day after the news broke, an article in the the *Denver Post*—headlined "Song Only Clue to Student's Despair"—suggested that "the only clue as to why Columbine High basketball star Greg Barnes cut short such a promising young life may lie in lyrics found playing over and over in his garage. . . . 'Adam's Song,' by the group Blink 182, was playing when Greg's parents found the body. . . . The lyrics include the phrases, 'I never thought I'd die alone' and 'I'm too depressed to go on. You'll be sorry when I'm gone.' "

Between those lines, however, is a knowing echo of the Nirvana song "Come As You Are." Adam, contemplating suicide, suggests that he has obeyed Cobain's instructions ("Take your time / Hurry up / The choice is yours / Don't be late") in all but one telling detail:

> I took my time, I hurried up
> The choice was mine I didn't think enough.

"Come As You Are," like almost all of Nirvana's music, is frequently read in the wake of Cobain's suicide as a cry for help:

> And I swear
> That I don't have a gun
> No I don't have a gun.

The grim truth is that Cobain did have a gun, and on the day he died he put its muzzle in his mouth. Hence, as Adam thinks about taking his own life, he seems to see Cobain as a role model who has gone there before him. But by the end of the song, Adam's crisis has passed. That small but important detail seems to have eluded the journalists writing about the Columbine suicide.

> I never conquered, rarely came
> But tomorrow holds such better days
> Days when I can still feel alive
> When I can't wait to get outside.

We'll probably never know whether Greg Barnes failed to hear the song through to the end, or whether, because of his own pain, he wasn't able to hear the entirety of what the song was saying. Some of those writing on the Graffiti Wall of the radio show that my daughter heard testified that "Adam's Song" had helped them out of their own suicidal depressions.

Songs, like any other text, can always be appropriated for inappropriate ends—by both rock's insiders and its outsiders, by despondent teens and slipshod media pundits. Sarah McLachlan, for instance, recently demanded that her song "I Will Remember You" be removed from a graphic video showing the bloody aftermath of the Columbine High School massacre being sold by the Jefferson County Sheriff's Department. But to the degree that songs like "Adam's Song" and "My My, Hey Hey" (and fiction like *American Psycho,* or television programs like *South Park*) are used to justify the very behaviors they seek to condemn—through irony—we as cultural educators have much to answer for.

To Clone or Not to Clone

Initial Reports

News Report National

The Author: Scott Allen

Scott Allen is a staff writer for the *Boston Globe*. The following article was published on February 13, 2004.

U.S. Researchers Lose Edge in Stem Cell Work

For American biologists, accustomed to being research leaders in so many areas, the announcement this week that South Koreans were the first to successfully clone a human embryo was humbling—and a call to arms.

Many researchers see embryonic stem cells, which can develop into any type of cell in the body and could help treat a variety of diseases, as one of the most promising and challenging fields in science. But since the August 2001 decision by the Bush administration to restrict funding for the work that can be done using those cells, American scientists have watched momentum in this field shift to other countries with rules that are more clearly defined and more financial support from their governments.

This time, the South Korean researchers beat them in the race to extract the prized stem cells from a cloned embryo. But even before Wednesday's announcement, important work already was being done in Britain, Israel, Singapore, and China, all of which have less-restrictive funding policies than the United States. And even though private groups such as the Juvenile Diabetes Research Foundation have begun awarding grants to scientists, they acknowledge that there are limits to what can be achieved without the massive assistance of US government funding.

"The cost is that the best and the brightest will not be able to do this research," said Dr. Irving Weissman, professor at Stanford University who is in many ways the father of the field of stem cell research. "You are going to start picking up Nature and Science and all the great [research] journals, and you are going to read about how South Koreans and Chinese and Singaporeans are making advances that the rest of us can't even study."

When President Bush made his 2001 announcement that federal funds would not be available for research on new lines of embryonic stem cells, many scientists objected. At least one leading researcher left his job in California for the greater freedom of England, where the government supports more types of stem cell research. And there was wide debate on the ways in which the restrictions would hold back science.

In the following years, scientists say, the results have become clearer: The problem is not only one of money, but also in the culture of science. The Korean experiment was funded with private money and also would have been legal in the United States. More broadly, since federal funding drives most biology research in the United States, scientists have little incentive to develop new cells that they cannot get federal grants to work with. They also have little incentive to turn their careers in such an uncertain direction.

"It has a chilling effect," said Dr. James Bradner, 31, a researcher at the Dana-Farber Cancer Institute and Harvard University who studies adult stem cells. Bradner said he and others starting out in their research careers believe it is risky—perhaps career suicide—to study embryonic stem cells. "I had to give real thought to whether it made sense to learn this trade in the United States."

But Dr. James Battey, chairman of the National Institutes of Health committee that oversees funding for stem cell research, said any envy of experiments in South Korea and other countries is misplaced. Although experiments such as the Korean one could not have been performed with federal money in the United States, Battey said the NIH has awarded grants related to stem cell work worth about $60 million since 2002, including support for 28 research projects.

"We need to step back and look at the whole area of regenerative medicine," Battey said. "Right now, most of what needs to be done is at the very basic stages, and American scientists are in as good a position as any in the world to approach those basic science questions."

He acknowledged that only about 15 genetically unique lines of embryonic stem cells are available for federal funding, far fewer than the 60-plus that Bush cited when he limited federal funding to stem cell lines that had been extracted from embryos before the summer of 2001. But Battey predicted the number of available cell lines would continue to grow as previously unavailable lines mature, while the amount of red tape for getting federal funding is decreasing.

Research into adult stem cells, which are not as flexible as embryonic stem cells, remains a promising and vibrant area in the United States, agreed Dr. Leonard Zon of Children's Hospital in Boston, president of the International Society for Stem Cell Research.

"There's not going to be a brain drain" because of the South Korean breakthrough, Zon said. "But it's a shame that we can't do these kind of experiments."

But Dr. Rudolf Jaenisch, a leading cloning specialist at the Massachusetts Institute of Technology, said the government is repeating with embryonic stem cells the mistakes of decades earlier, when it restricted the use of government funds for re-search into in-vitro fertilization—a technology that is now commonplace. In the United States, he said, the research went ahead anyway, but behind the veil of private companies with powerful commercial interests and little incentive to be open about their methods, he said.

As scientists begin to consider how to wage a political battle to change federal law, two of the scientists behind the South Korean announcement held a news conference in Seattle, pleading with all nations to pass laws that will make it illegal to use their technology to attempt to clone a baby.

The scientists, Woo Suk Hwang and Dr. Shin Yong Moon, said they would wel-come scientists from other countries into their laboratories to share their techniques.

They also provided more details about the work itself, in which they created a sin-gle stem cell line by cloning a cell from an anonymous volunteer. They said they would make the stem cell lines available to other scientists and would not commer-cialize their work.

At the news conference, the scientists said they had attempted but failed to clone cells from male donors. That raised questions about the viability of the process because the team has shown that it can clone only the cells of women, using their own egg cells.

Jose Cibelli, the paper's only American coauthor, said he was struck by the dif-ferences between doing this type of research in the United States and in Korea. Be-fore he moved to Michigan State University, Cibelli worked at Advanced Cell Technology in Worcester, the company that published the first paper claiming to have cloned human cells.

At ACT, about five researchers were on the team, he said. When he visited the South Korean lab on the outskirts of Seoul, he said, he was impressed to find 50 re-searchers working on cloning and regenerative medicine. Cibelli, a professor of ani-mal biotechnology, also noted that Hwang's team had 12 times more eggs to work with than ACT, and far more public and private support for their long-term goals. ACT relied wholly on private funding.

"The glory is for the Korean group," Cibelli said.

News Report—TIME Magazine

The Author: Michael D. Lemonick, et al.

Michael D. Lemonick and a team of staff writers composed the following article. It was published on February 23, 2004.

How a Team Cloned Human Cells to Fight Disease—and Why That's Revolutionary

Back when it was no more than a cheesy science-fiction plot device, human cloning seemed like something that would eventually be revealed to a horrified world full-blown and fully grown—a monstrous carnival apparition ("The Amazing Cloned Boy!") out of a medical freak show.

It hasn't quite turned out that way. Cloning has been emerging gradually, over the past decade, in small increments. Each advance has been startling enough, prompting ethical debates, cautionary references to Aldous Huxley's brave new world and calls for restrictive legislation. But there have been so many milestones, starting even before the birth of Dolly the sheep in 1996, that each one seems a little less startling than the one before. Sometimes an advance is so subtle that it sounds just like the breakthrough that made headlines the year before.

That's how a report in the journal *Science* sounded last week—at least at first blush. Woo Suk Hwang and Dr. Shin Yong Moon, from Korea's Seoul National University, announced that they had created more than 200 embryos by cloning mature human cells and had grown 30 of them to the blastocyst stage of development, each more than 100 cells strong. This isn't the first time cloned human embryos have been produced: in 2001 the Massachusetts biotech firm Advanced Cell Technology made several. They all died quickly, but in a sense the first cloned human cells are actually old news.

Still, two things make the Korean experiment more than a little noteworthy. The first is simply that their embryos didn't die. That's a very big deal; many experts were convinced that human clones would be impossibly fragile. Second, the scientists extracted embryonic stem cells from the blastocysts and coaxed some of them into a self-perpetuating colony.

That could ultimately prove to be an even bigger deal. Embryonic stem cells are the unspecialized raw material that give rise to every cell type in the body—in fact, some of Moon and Hwang's stem cells evidently turned into bone, muscle and immature brain cells. If scientists can learn to control their development, stem cells could in theory supply replacement tissues to treat any ailment involving cell damage—and there are plenty, including heart disease, diabetes, spinal-cord injury, Parkinson's and Alzheimer's. "Our goal," said Hwang during a press conference at a meeting of the American Association for the Advancement of Science in Seattle last week, "is not to clone humans, but to understand the causes of diseases."

That disclaimer didn't satisfy critics. Indeed, the Korean breakthrough adds fuel to two different ethical debates at once. The first—whether cloning for reproduction should be allowed—is pretty well settled. Only a handful of loose-cannon scientists and members of the Raelian sect, who believe humans were created by aliens, openly favor human cloning. It is explicitly banned in many countries, including Korea.

But the debate over stem-cell research, whether those cells come from cloning or from conventional in-vitro fertilization, is far from over, at least in the U.S. Right-to-life and religious groups, including the Roman Catholic Church, believe that human life begins at conception and thus that harvesting stem cells is tantamount to murder. With views like that on one side and high-profile advocates like Christopher Reeve and Michael J. Fox touting the benefits of therapeutic cloning on the other, the Bush Administration has tried to split the difference. In August 2001 the President declared that the U.S. government would fund stem-cell research—but only using stem-cell lines that had already been isolated.

Only a dozen or so such lines have proved useful, which most American scientists consider far too few to work with. They can still tap a much more limited pool of private funding, but a bill introduced in the Senate last year would have hamstrung them further by banning human cloning even for therapeutic purposes. If that law had passed and the Koreans had done their work in the U.S., said Donald Kennedy, editor in chief of *Science* and a participant in last week's press conference, "they would have been jailed."

By rejecting a watered-down bill that would have banned reproductive cloning only, conservatives have ensured that the U.S is, bizarrely, one of few developed countries that doesn't forbid human cloning. Responsible scientists wouldn't try it, but an unethical researcher could read the *Science* paper and attempt to use the technique to bring a clone to term. "I'm afraid that some nitwit is going to try," says Larry Goldstein, a cellular and molecular biologist at the University of California at San Diego. But given the high rate of spontaneous abortions and genetic defects seen in other species, it's not likely to work. The *Science* paper is a recipe for cloning, said Kennedy, "only in the sense that 'catch a turtle' is the recipe for turtle soup." Said Hwang: "In my humble opinion, it's not so easy to mimic our technology."

Several factors helped the Koreans succeed where others had failed. To start with, they had a large supply of eggs. The researchers lined up 16 female volunteers who found the project through its website. To avoid any taint of coercion, the women weren't paid. They were fully informed about the research and its risks, however, and given several opportunities to change their mind. In the end, the 16 women furnished 242 eggs—many more than in any previous cloning attempt.

The scientists' basic strategy was the same as in most post-Dolly cloning experiments: remove the nucleus of the egg, with its single set of chromosomes, and replace it with the nucleus of a mature cell, containing two sets (in this case, the mature nuclei came from cumulus cells, which surround eggs during development). With a quantity of eggs that a commentary in *Science* calls "whopping," the scientists were able to experiment with different techniques to find which worked best—varying the time between inserting the new nucleus and zapping it with electricity to trigger cell division, for example, or testing different growth media.

The Korean team believes that two other factors may have helped them succeed. While most cloners suck out an egg's nucleus with a tiny pipette, Moon and Hwang made a pinhole in the cell wall and used a tiny glass needle to apply pressure and squeeze the nucleus out. "It's more gentle with the egg and allows you to remove only the DNA and leave some of the major components of the egg still inside," says Jose Cibelli, a professor of animal biotechnology at Michigan State University and a co-author of the *Science* paper. "Actually, it's pure speculation, but we can't come up with anything else, so we think that may be important." Technicians also honed their skills until they could transfer a nucleus in less than a minute, a much better time than most labs and one less likely to allow deterioration.

What makes the achievement even more significant is that it gives doctors a way to create stem cells bearing a patient's own DNA. Tissues grown from those cells could replace diseased tissue in the patient without any risk of rejection.

It could be years, however, before such replacement actually happens. "This is an important step forward," says Goldstein, "but it's just one obstacle out of the way." The Korean technique has only worked in women so far, perhaps because they alone have cumulus cells, which seem especially amenable to cloning. It should work in men too, but first, researchers will have to isolate the male equivalent of cumulus cells. Moreover, scientists are still learning how to coax stem cells into becoming particular types of tissue, and for many diseases they don't even know what kind of cells they need to end up with. "With juvenile diabetes," says Goldstein, "I think we have a sense of what cells we want to make. With ALS [Lou Gehrig's disease] we have less of a sense."

Some researchers say all the talk about replacement tissue overlooks a more immediate benefit of stem cells: if you cloned them from someone with a genetic disorder, you could perform all kinds of experiments zeroing in on the DNA that is causing the problem. "If you had that," says Dr. Irv Weissman, director of Stanford's Institute for Cancer/Stem Cell Biology and Medicine, "this would be a transforming technology as important as recombinant DNA."

The way things stand, all the benefits of stem cells will probably be developed—as this latest breakthrough was—outside the U.S. "I'm not really surprised it came from Korea," says Goldstein, citing the researchers' skill and experience. "I'm disappointed it didn't happen first in the U.S. But given the absolute stranglehold that federal policy has put on this field, that doesn't surprise me either."

Even with sensible laws, of course, there's always a chance that cloning technology will be misused. Plenty of useful technologies are abused every day, says Dr. William Gibbons, professor of obstetrics and gynecology at Eastern Virginia Medical School—including automobiles and antibiotics. "It doesn't mean that these are inherently bad," he says. The trick is to legislate against the misuse, not against the technology.

Multimedia Sources

Editorial Cartoon

The Author: Nick Anderson

Since joining the *Louisville Courier-Journal* in January 1991, a month after graduating from Ohio State, Anderson's cartoons have been published in *Newsweek*, the *New York Times*, the *Washington Post*, *USA Today*, and the *Chicago Tribune*.

At Ohio State, Anderson majored in political science and was editorial cartoonist for the university newspaper. In 1989, he won the Charles M. Schulz Award for best college cartoonist in the United States, Canada, and Mexico. He interned one summer with the *Courier-Journal*. After graduation, the newspaper created a position for him as associate editorial cartoonist and illustrator. He was promoted to chief editorial cartoonist in September 1995.

In 1996, he began syndication with the Washington Post Writers Group. He won the John Fischetti award for editorial cartooning in 1999 and the Sigma Delta Chi Mark of Excellence Award in 2001.

The following cartoon was published on March 17, 2000.

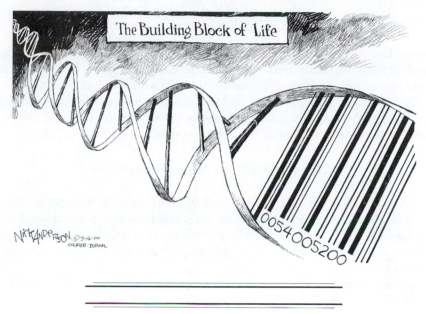

Editorial Cartoon

The Author: Joe Heller

Joseph Heller has been the editorial cartoonist for the *Green Bay Press Gazette* since 1985. He received his B.A. in fine arts from the University of Wisconsin–Milwaukee. The following cartoon was published in 2000.

Article about a Web site

The Source: Reuters Ltd.

Reuters Ltd. is a global information company providing information for professionals in financial, media, and corporate markets. Established in 1851, Reuters has been a major force in reporting the news around the world for over a century.

The following article, published on April 30, 2004, reported on the controversy surrounding a Web site promotion for the major motion picture "Godsend." You can view this website at the following URL: http://www.godsendinstitute.org.

Movie Website Stirs Cloning Controversy

LOS ANGELES, California (Reuters)—A Web site meant to promote upcoming film drama *Godsend* is stirring controversy among people who oppose human cloning and want the site shut down because they think the site is real, the film's makers say.

One problem is that the site, www.godsendinstitute.org, doesn't make mention of the movie.

Instead, it promotes what purports to be a fertility clinic run by Dr. Richard Wells, who is billed as being "the top genetic engineering researcher" in the United States and a man who bears an uncanny resemblance to actor Robert De Niro, who stars in the movie.

"Almost everyone who goes to the site thinks it's real, but by the time they leave, most have figured it's fiction. Some even applaud it," said Tom Ortenberg, president of film releasing for Lions Gate Entertainment Corp.

But some Web surfers have begun petitions to close the site because, they claim, it is insensitive to people who have lost a loved one or family member and might actually be seeking to have that person cloned, which is the topic of the film.

"The work being done by the Godsend Institute . . . is out of control and needs to be stopped," wrote one poster at the Web site petitionstop.com.

Ortenberg said Lions Gate is getting several hundred phone calls a day to the fake clinic's toll-free number, but none have been from people who had a death in the family and were looking for help.

Movie marketing on the Web goes back years. Perhaps the best example of a "hoax" campaign is the one for $140 million domestic box office hit, *The Blair Witch Project,* in 1999.

That movie earned legions of fans based on its Web site that led people to believe that the Blair Witch and the three kids who went into a forest to find her truly existed.

But in recent years, Ortenberg said, movie promotion on the Internet has grown increasingly bland. "For Internet-based movie marketing to be effective as users mature and as consumers get more savvy, the campaigns need to be more interactive and more interesting," he said.

Independent companies like Lions Gate use the Web to market movies because it is less expensive than traditional media and there is a high degree of correlation between Web surfers and movie goers.

Ortenberg calls the *Godsend* site "a million dollar idea" built for only about $10,000. He said it has generated millions of hits and hundreds of thousands of unique users.

Godsend debuts nationwide in theaters on Friday, April 30 [2004]. Greg Kinnear and Rebecca Romijn-Stamos star as a married couple who lose their son and attempt to bring him back to life by having Wells (that's really De Niro) create a clone.

Quest Note: The site does, in fact, reveal that it is a movie-based publicity stunt. At the bottom of the home page there is a link: Disclaimer.

Magazine Article

The Author: Leon Kass

Leon R. Kass, M.D., is professor in social thought at the University of Chicago, Hertog fellow at the American Enterprise Institute, and chairman of the President's Council on Bioethics. Excerpted from *Life, Liberty and the Defense of Dignity,* published by Encounter Books, San Francisco, October 2002, this article appeared in *American Spectator.*

The Age of Genetic Technology Arrives

As one contemplates the current and projected state of genetic knowledge and technology, one is astonished by how far we have come in the less than fifty years since Watson and Crick first announced the structure of DNA. True, soon after that discovery, scientists began seriously to discuss the futuristic prospects of gene therapy for genetic disease and of genetic engineering more generally. But no one then imagined how rapidly genetic technology would emerge. The Human Genome Project, disclosing the DNA sequences of all thirty thousand human genes, is all but completed. And even without comprehensive genomic knowledge, biotech business is booming. According to a recent report by the research director for GlaxoSmith-Kline, enough sequencing data are already available to keep his researchers busy for the next twenty years, developing early-detection screening techniques, rationally designed vaccines, genetically engineered changes in malignant tumors leading to enhanced immune response, and, ultimately, precise gene therapy for specific genetic diseases. The age of genetic technology has arrived.

Genetic technology comes into existence as part of the large humanitarian project to cure disease, prolong life, and alleviate suffering. As such, it occupies the moral high ground of compassionate healing. Who would not welcome personal genetic profiling that would enable doctors to customize the most effective and safest drug treatments for individuals with hypertension or rheumatoid arthritis? Who would not welcome genetic therapy to correct the defects that lead to sickle cell anemia,

Huntington's disease, and breast cancer, or to protect against the immune deficiency caused by the AIDS virus?

And yet genetic technology has also aroused considerable public concern, for it strikes most people as different from other biomedical technologies. Even people duly impressed by the astonishing genetic achievements of the last decades and eager for the medical benefits are nonetheless ambivalent about these new developments. For they sense that genetic technology, while in some respects continuous with the traditional medical project of compassionate healing, also represents something radically new and disquieting. Often hard-pressed to articulate the precise basis of their disquiet, they talk rather in general terms about the dangers of eugenics or the fear of "tampering with human genes" or, for that matter, "playing God."

Enthusiasts for genetic technology, made confident by their expertise and by their growing prestige and power, are often impatient with the public's disquiet. Much of it they attribute to ignorance of science: "If the public only knew what we know, it would see things our way and give up its irrational fears." For the rest, they blame outmoded moral and religious notions, ideas that scientists insist no longer hold water and only serve to obstruct scientific progress.

In my own view, the scientists' attempt to cast the debate as a battle of beneficial and knowledgeable cleverness versus ignorant and superstitious anxiety should be resisted. For the public is right to be ambivalent about genetic technology, and no amount of instruction in molecular biology and genetics should allay its—our—legitimate human concerns. Rightly understood, these worries are, in fact, in touch with the deepest matters of our humanity and dignity, and we ignore them at our peril.

I will not dispute here which of the prophesied technologies will in fact prove feasible or how soon.[A] To be sure, as a practical matter we must address the particular ethical issues raised by each new technical power as it comes into existence. But the moral meaning of the entire enterprise does not depend on the precise details regarding what and when. I shall proceed by raising a series of questions, the first of which is an attempt to say how genetic technology is different.

Is Genetic Technology Special?

What is different about genetic technology? At first glance, not much. Isolating a disease-inducing aberrant gene looks fairly continuous with isolating a disease-inducing intracellular virus. Supplying diabetics with normal genes for producing insulin has the same medical goal as supplying them with insulin for injection.

Nevertheless, despite these obvious similarities, genetic technology is also decisively different. When fully developed, it will wield two powers not shared by ordinary medical practice. Medicine treats only existing individuals, and it treats them only remedially, seeking to correct deviations from a more or less stable norm of health. By contrast, genetic engineering will, first of all, deliberately make changes that are transmissible into succeeding generations and may even alter in advance specific future individuals through direct "germ-line" or embryo interventions. Secondly, genetic engineering may be able, through so-called genetic enhancement, to create new human capacities and, hence, new norms of health and fitness.[B]

For the present, it is true, genetic technology is hailed primarily for its ability better to diagnose and treat disease in existing individuals. Confined to such practices, it would raise few questions (beyond the usual ones of safety and efficacy). Even intrauterine gene therapy for existing fetuses with diagnosable genetic disease could be seen as an extension of the growing field of fetal medicine.

But there is no reason to believe that the use of gene-altering powers can be so confined, either in logic or in practice. For one thing, "germ-line" gene therapy and manipulation, affecting not merely the unborn but also the unconceived,[C] is surely in our future. The practice has numerous justifications, beginning with the desire to reverse the unintended dysgenic effects of modern medical success. Thanks to medicine, for example, individuals who would have died from diabetes now live long enough to transmit their disease-producing genes. Why, it has been argued, should we not reverse these unfortunate changes by deliberate intervention? More generally, why should we not effect precise genetic alteration in disease-carrying sperm or eggs or early embryos, in order to prevent in advance the emergence of disease that otherwise will later require expensive and burdensome treatment? In short, even before we have had more than trivial experience with gene therapy for existing individuals—none of it successful-sober people have called for overturning the current (self-imposed) taboo on germ-line modification. The line between somatic and germ-line modification cannot hold.

Despite the naive hopes of many, neither will we be able to defend the boundary between therapy and genetic enhancement. Will we reject novel additions to the human genome that enable us to produce, internally, vitamins or amino acids we now must get in our diet? Will we decline to make alterations in the immune system that will increase its efficacy or make it impervious to HIV? When genetic profiling becomes able to disclose the genetic contributions to height or memory or intelligence, will we deny prospective parents the right to enhance the potential of their children?[D] Finally, should we discover—as no doubt we will—the genetic switches that control our biological clock and that very likely influence also the maximum human life expectant, will we opt to keep our hands off the rate of aging or our natural human life span? Not a chance.

We thus face a paradox. On the one hand, genetic technology really is different. It can and will go to work directly and deliberately on our basic, heritable, life-shaping capacities at their biological roots. It can take us beyond existing norms of health and healing—perhaps even alter fundamental features of human nature. On the other hand, precisely because the goals it will serve, at least to begin with, will be continuous with those of modern high-interventionist medicine, we will find its promise familiar and irresistible.

This paradox itself contributes to public disquiet: rightly perceiving a powerful difference in genetic technology, we also sense that we are powerless to establish, on the basis of that difference, clear limits to its use. The genetic genie, first unbottled to treat disease, will go its own way, whether we like it or not.

How Much Genetic Self-Knowledge Is Good for Us?

Quite apart from worries about genetic engineering, gaining genetic knowledge is itself a legitimate cause of anxiety, not least because of one of its most touted benefits—the genetic profiling of individuals. There has been much discussion about how knowledge of someone's genetic defects, if leaked to outsiders, could be damaging in terms of landing a job or gaining health or life insurance, and legislative measures have been enacted to guard against such hazards. Little attention has been paid, however, to the implications of genetic knowledge for the person himself. Yet the deepest problem connected with learning your own genetic sins and unhealthy predispositions is neither the threat to confidentiality nor the risk of "genetic discrimination" in employment or insurance, important though these practical problems may be.[E] It is, rather, the various hazards and deformations in living your life that will attach to knowing in advance your likely or possible medical future. To be sure, in some cases such foreknowledge will be welcome, if it can lead to easy measures to prevent or treat the impending disorder, and if the disorder in question does not powerfully affect self-image or self-command. But will and should we welcome knowledge that we carry a predisposition to Alzheimer's disease or schizophrenia, or genes that will definitely produce, at an unknown future time, a serious but untreatable disease?

Still harder will it be for most people to live easily and wisely with less certain information—say, where multigenic traits are involved. The recent case of a father who insisted that ovariectomy and mastectomy be performed on his ten-year-old daughter because she happened to carry the BRCA-1 gene for breast cancer dramatically shows the toxic effect of genetic knowledge.

Less dramatic but more profound is the threat to human freedom and spontaneity, a subject explored twenty-five years ago by the philosopher Hans Jonas, one of our wisest commentators on technology and the human prospect. As Jonas observed, "Knowledge of the future, especially one's own, has always been excepted [from the injunction to 'Know thyself'] and the attempt to gain it by whatever means (astrology is one) disparaged—as futile superstition by the enlightened, but as sin by theologians." Everyone remembers that Prometheus was the philanthropic god who gave fire and the arts to humans. But it is often forgotten that he gave them also the greater gift of "blind hopes"—"to cease seeing doom before their eyes"—precisely because he knew that ignorance of one's own future fate was indispensable to aspiration and achievement. I suspect that many people, taking their bearings from life lived open-endedly rather than from preventive medicine practiced rationally, would prefer ignorance of the future to the scientific astrology of knowing their genetic profile. In a free society, that would be their right.

Or would it? This leads us to the third question.

What About Freedom?

Even people who might otherwise welcome the growth of genetic knowledge and technology are worried about the coming power of geneticists, genetic engineers and, in particular, governmental authorities armed with genetic technology.[F] Precisely because we have been taught by these very scientists that genes hold the secret of life, and that our genotype is our essence if not quite our destiny, we are made nervous by those whose expert knowledge and technique touch our very being. Even apart from any particular abuses and misuses of power, friends of human freedom have deep cause for concern.

C. S. Lewis, no friend of ignorance, put the matter sharply in *The Abolition of Man:*

> If any one age really attains, by eugenics and scientific education, the power to make its descendants what it pleases, all men who live after it are the patients of that power. . . . But even within this master generation (itself an infinitesimal minority of the species) the power will be exercised by a minority smaller still. Man's conquest of Nature, if the dreams of some scientific planners are realized, means the rule of a few hundreds of men over billions upon billions of men.

Most genetic technologists will hardly recognize themselves in this portrait. Though they concede that abuses or misuses of power may occur, especially in tyrannical regimes, they see themselves not as predestinators but as facilitators, merely providing increased knowledge and technique that people can freely choose to use in making decisions about their health or reproductive choices. Genetic power, they tell us, serves not to limit freedom, but to increase it.

But as we can see from the already existing practices of genetic screening and prenatal diagnosis, this claim is at best self-deceptive, at worst disingenuous. The choice to develop and practice genetic screening and the choices of which genes to target for testing have been made not by the public but by scientists—and not on liberty-enhancing but on eugenic grounds. In many cases, practitioners of prenatal diagnosis refuse to do fetal genetic screening in the absence of a prior commitment from the pregnant woman to abort any afflicted fetus. In other situations, pregnant women who still wish not to know prenatal facts must withstand strong medical pressures for testing.

In addition, economic pressures to contain health-care costs will almost certainly constrain free choice. Refusal to provide insurance coverage for this or that genetic disease may eventually work to compel genetic abortion or intervention. State-mandated screening already occurs for PKU (phenylketonuria) and other diseases, and full-blown genetic screening programs loom large on the horizon. Once these arrive, there will likely be an upsurge of economic pressure to limit reproductive freedom. All this will be done, of course, in the name of the well-being of children.

Already in 1971, geneticist Bentley Glass, in his presidential address to the American Association for the Advancement of Science, enunciated "the right of every child to be born with a sound physical and mental constitution, based on a sound genotype." Looking ahead to the reproductive and genetic technologies that are today rapidly arriving, Glass proclaimed: "No parents will in that future time have a right to burden society with a malformed or a mentally incompetent child." It remains to be seen to what extent such prophecies will be realized. But they surely provide sufficient and reasonable grounds for being concerned about restrictions on human freedom, even in the absence of overt coercion, and even in liberal polities like our own.

What About Human Dignity?

Here, rather than in the more-discussed fears about freedom, lie our deepest concerns, and rightly so. For threats to human dignity can—and probably will—arise even with the free, humane, and "enlightened" use of these technologies. Genetic technology, the practices it will engender, and above all the scientific teachings about human life on which it rests are not, as many would have it, morally and humanly neutral. Regardless of how they are practiced or taught, they are pregnant with their own moral meanings and will necessarily bring with them changes in our practices, our institutions, our norms, our beliefs, and our self-conception. It is, I submit, these challenges to our dignity and humanity that are at the bottom of our anxiety over genetic science and technology. Let me touch briefly on four aspects of this most serious matter.

"Playing God"

Paradoxically, worries about dehumanization are sometimes expressed in the fear of superhumanization, that is, that man will be "playing God." This complaint is too facilely dismissed by scientists and non-believers. The concern has meaning, God or no God.

Never mind the exaggeration that lurks in this conceit of man's playing God. (Even at his most powerful, after all, man is capable only of playing God.) Never mind the implicit innuendo that nobody has given to others this creative and judgmental authority, or the implicit retort that there is theological warrant for acting as God's co-creator in overcoming the ills and suffering of the world. Consider only that if scientists are seen in this godlike role of creator, judge, and savior, the rest of us must stand before them as supplicating, tainted creatures. Despite the hyperbolic speech, that is worry enough.

Practitioners of prenatal diagnosis, working today with but a fraction of the information soon to be available from the Human Genome Project, already screen for a long list of genetic diseases and abnormalities, from Down syndrome to dwarfism. Possession of any one of these defects, they believe, renders a prospective child unworthy of life. Persons who happen still to be born with these conditions, having somehow escaped the spreading net of detection and eugenic abortion, are increasingly regarded as "mistakes" as inferior human beings who should not have been born.[G] Not long ago, at my own university, a physician making rounds with medical students stood over the bed of an intelligent, otherwise normal ten-year-old boy with spina bifida. "Were he to have been conceived today" the physician casually informed his entourage, "he would have been aborted." Determining who shall live and who shall die—on the basis of genetic merit—is a godlike power already wielded by genetic medicine. This power will only grow.

Manufacture & Commodification

But, one might reply, genetic technology also holds out the promise of redemption, of a cure for these life-crippling and life-forfeiting disorders. Very well. But in order truly to practice their salvific power, genetic technologists will have to increase greatly their manipulations and interventions, well beyond merely screening and weeding out. True, in some cases genetic testing and risk management aimed at prevention may actually cut down on the need for high-tech interventions aimed at cure. But in many other cases, ever-greater genetic scrutiny will lead necessarily to ever more extensive manipulation. And, to produce Bentley Glass's healthy and well-endowed babies, let alone babies with the benefits of genetic enhancement, a new scientific obstetrics will be necessary, one that will come very close to turning human procreation into manufacture.

This process was already crudely begun with in vitro fertilization. It is now taking giant steps forward with the ability to screen in vitro embryos before implantation (so-called pre-implantation genetic diagnosis). And it will come to maturity with interventions such as cloning and, eventually, with precise genetic engineering. Just follow the logic and the aspirations of current practice: the road we are traveling leads all the way to the world of designer babies—reached not by dictatorial fiat, but by the march of benevolent humanitarianism, and cheered on by an ambivalent citizenry that also dreads becoming merely the last of man's manmade things.

Make no mistake: the price to be paid for producing optimum or even only genetically sound babies will be the transfer of procreation from the home to the laboratory. Such an arrangement will be profoundly dehumanizing, no matter how genetically good or healthy the resultant children. And let us not forget the powerful economic interests that will surely operate in this area; with their advent, the commodification of nascent human life will be unstoppable.

Standards, Norms, & Goals

According to Genesis, God, in His creating, looked at His creatures and saw that they were good—intact, complete, well-working wholes, true to the spoken idea that guided their creation. What standards will guide the genetic engineers?

For the time being, one might answer, the norm of health. But even before the genetic enhancers join the party, the standard of health is being deconstructed. Are you healthy if, although you show no symptoms, you carry genes that will definitely produce Huntington's disease? What if you carry, say, 40 percent of the genetic markers thought to be linked to the appearance of Alzheimer's disease? And what will "healthy" and "normal" mean when we discover your genetic propensities for alcoholism, drug abuse, pederasty, or violence?[H] The idea of health progressively becomes at once both imperial and vague: medicalization of what have hitherto been mental or moral matters paradoxically brings with it the disappearance of any clear standard of health itself.

Once genetic enhancement comes on the scene, standards of health, wholeness, or fitness will be needed more than ever, but just then is when all pretense of standards will go out the window. "Enhancement" is, of course, a euphemism for "improvement" and the idea of improvement necessarily implies a good, a better, and perhaps even a best. If, however, we can no longer look to our previously unalterable human nature for a standard or norm of what is good or better, how will anyone know what constitutes an improvement? It will not do to assert that we can extrapolate from what we like about ourselves. Because memory is good, can we say how much more memory would be better? If sexual desire is good, how much more would be better? Life is good, but how much extension of the life span would be good for us? Only simplistic thinkers believe they can easily answer such questions.[I]

More modest enhancers, like more modest genetic therapists and technologists, eschew grandiose goals. They are valetudinarians, not eugenicists. They pursue not some faraway positive good, but the positive elimination of evils: diseases, pain, suffering, the likelihood of death. But let us not be deceived. Hidden in all this avoidance of evil is nothing less than the quasi-messianic goal of a painless, suffering-free and, finally, immortal existence. Only the presence of such a goal justifies the sweeping-aside of any opposition to the relentless march of medical science. Only such a goal gives trumping moral power to the principle "cure disease, relieve suffering."

"Cloning human beings is unethical and dehumanizing, you say? Never mind: it will help us treat infertility, avoid genetic disease, and provide perfect materials for organ replacement" Such, indeed, was the tenor of the June 1997 report of the National Bioethics Advisory Commission, Cloning Human Beings. Notwithstanding its call for a temporary ban on the practice, the only moral objection the commission could agree upon was that cloning "is not safe to use in humans at this time," because the technique has yet to be perfected.[J] Even this elite ethical body, in other words, was unable to muster any other moral argument sufficient to cause us to forgo the possible health benefits of cloning.[K]

The same argument will also justify creating and growing human embryos for experimentation, revising the definition of death to increase the supply of organs for transplantation, growing human body parts in the peritoneal cavities of animals, perfusing newly dead bodies as factories for useful biological substances, or reprogramming the human body and mind with genetic or neurobiological engineering. Who can sustain an objection if these practices will help us live longer and with less overt suffering?

It turns out that even the more modest biogenetic engineers, whether they know it or not, are in the immortality business, proceeding on the basis of a quasi-religious faith that all innovation is by definition progress, no matter what is sacrificed to attain it.

The Tragedy of Success

What the enthusiasts do not see is that their utopian project will not eliminate suffering but merely shift it around. Forgetting that contentment requires that our desires do not outpace our powers, they have not noticed that the enormous medical progress of the last half-century has not left the present generation satisfied. Indeed, we are already witnessing a certain measure of public discontent as a paradoxical result of rising expectations in the health care field: although their actual health has improved substantially in recent decades, people's satisfaction with their current health status has remained the same or declined. But that is hardly the highest cost of success in the medical/humanitarian project.

As Aldous Huxley made clear in his prophetic Brave New World, the road chosen and driven by compassionate humaneness paved by biotechnology, if traveled to the end, leads not to human fulfillment but to human debasement. Perfected bodies are achieved at the price of flattened souls. What Tolstoy called "real life"—life in its immediacy, vividness, and rootedness—has been replaced by an utterly mediated, sterile, and disconnected existence. In one word: dehumanization, the inevitable result of making the essence of human nature the final object of the conquest of nature for the relief of man's estate. Like Midas, bioengineered man will be cursed to acquire precisely what he wished for, only to discover—painfully and too late—that what he wished for is not exactly what he wanted. Or, worse than Midas, he may be so dehumanized he will not even recognize that in aspiring to be perfect, he is no longer even truly human. To paraphrase Bertrand Russell, technological humanitarianism is like a warm bath that heats up so imperceptibly you don't know when to scream.

The main point here is not the rightness or wrongness of this or that imagined scenario; all this is, admittedly, highly speculative. I surely have no way of knowing whether my worst fears will be realized, but you surely have no way of knowing they will not. The point is rather the plausibility, even the wisdom, of thinking about genetic technology like the entire technological venture, under the ancient and profound idea of tragedy in which success and failure are inseparably grown together like the concave and the convex. What I am suggesting is that genetic technology's way of approaching human life, a way spurred on by the utopian promises and perfectionist aims of modern thought and its scientific crusaders, may well turn out to be inevitable, heroic, and doomed. If this suggestion holds water, then the question regarding genetic technology is not "triumph OR tragedy," because the answer is "both together."

In the nineteenth and early twentieth century, the challenge came in the form of Darwinism and its seeming opposition to biblical religion, a battle initiated not so much by the scientists as by the beleaguered defenders of orthodoxy. In our own time, the challenge comes from molecular biology, behavioral genetics, and evolutionary psychology, fueled by their practitioners' overconfident belief in the sufficiency of their reductionist explanations of all vital and human phenomena. Never mind "created in the image of God"; what elevated humanistic view of human life or human goodness is defensible against the belief, asserted by most public and prophetic voices of biology, that man is just a collection of molecules, an accident on the stage of evolution, a freakish speck of mind in a mindless universe, fundamentally no different from other living—or even nonliving—things? What chance have our treasured ideas of freedom and dignity against the reductive notion of "the selfish gene" (or, for that matter, of "genes for altruism"), the belief that DNA is the essence of life, or the teaching that all human behavior and our rich inner life are rendered intelligible only in terms of their contributions to species survival and reproductive success?

These transformations are, in fact, welcomed by many of our leading scientists and intellectuals. In 1997 the luminaries of the International Academy of Humanism—including biologists Crick, Dawkins, and Wilson, and humanists Isaiah Berlin, W. V. Quine, and Kurt Vonnegut—issued a statement in defense of cloning research in higher mammals and human beings. Their reasons were revealing:

> Views of human nature rooted in humanity's tribal past ought not to be our pri-
> mary criterion for making moral decisions about cloning. . . . The potential ben-
> efits of cloning may be so immense that it would be a tragedy if ancient theological
> scruples should lead to a Luddite rejection of cloning.

In order to justify ongoing research, these intellectuals were willing to shed not only traditional religious views, but any view of human distinctiveness and special dignity, their own included. They failed to see that the scientific view of man they celebrated does more than insult our vanity. It undermines our self-conception as free, thought-ful, and responsible beings, worthy of respect because we alone among the animals have minds and hearts that aim far higher than the mere perpetuation of our genes.

The problem may lie not so much with the scientific findings themselves, but with the shallow philosophy that recognizes no other truths but these and with the arrogant pronouncements of the bioprophets. For example, in a letter to the editor complaining about a review of his book *How the Mind Works*, the well-known evolutionary psy-chologist and popularizer Stephen Pinker rails against any appeal to the human soul:

> Unfortunately for that theory, brain science has shown that the mind is what the
> brain does. The supposedly immaterial soul can be bisected with a knife, altered
> by chemicals, turned on or off by electricity, and extinguished by a sharp blow or
> a lack of oxygen. Centuries ago it was unwise to ground morality on the dogma
> that the earth sat at the center of the universe. It is just as unwise today to ground
> it on dogmas about souls endowed by God.

One hardly knows whether to be more impressed by the height of Pinker's arro-gance or by the depth of his shallowness. But he speaks with the authority of science, and few are able and willing to dispute him on his own grounds.

There is, of course, nothing novel about reductionism, materialism, and deter-minism of the kind displayed here; these are doctrines with which Socrates contended long ago. What is new is that, as philosophies, they seem (to many people) to be vin-dicated by scientific advance. Here, in consequence, is perhaps the most pernicious re-sult of our technological progress, more dehumanizing than any actual manipulation or technique, present or future: the erosion, perhaps the final erosion, of the idea of man as noble, dignified, precious, or godlike, and its replacement with a view of man, no less than of nature, as mere raw material for manipulation and homogenization.

Hence our peculiar moral crisis. We are in turbulent seas without a landmark pre-cisely because we adhere more and more to a view of human life that both gives us enormous power and, at the same time, denies every possibility of nonarbitrary stan-dards for guiding its use. Though well equipped, we know not who we are or where we are going. We triumph over nature's unpredictability only to subject ourselves, tragically, to the still greater unpredictability of our capricious wills and our fickle opinions. Engineering the engineer as well as the engine, we race our train we know not where. That we do not recognize our predicament is itself a tribute to the depth of our infatuation with scientific progress and our naive faith in the sufficiency of our humanitarian impulses.

Does this mean that I am therefore in favor of ignorance, suffering, and death? Of killing the goose of genetic technology even before she lays her golden eggs? Surely not. But unless we mobilize the courage to look foursquare at the full human meaning of our new enterprise in biogenetic technology and engineering, we are doomed to become its creatures if not its slaves. Important though it is to set a moral boundary here, devise a regulation there, hoping to decrease the damage caused by this or that little rivulet, it is even more important to be sober about the true nature and meaning of the flood itself.

That our exuberant new biologists and their technological minions might be persuaded of this is, to say the least, highly unlikely. For all their ingenuity, they do not even seek the wisdom that just might yield the kind of knowledge that keeps human life human. But it is not too late for the rest of us to become aware of the dangers—not just to privacy or insurability, but to our very humanity. So aware, we might be better able to defend the increasingly beleaguered vestiges and principles of our human dignity, even as we continue to reap the considerable benefits that genetic technology will inevitably provide.

Notes

[A] I will also not dispute here the scientists' reductive understanding of life and their treatment of rich vital activities solely in terms of the interactions of genes. I do, however, touch on the moral significance of such reductionism toward the end of this essay.

[B] Some commentators, in disagreement with these arguments, insist that genetic technology differs only in degree from previous human practices that have existed for millennia. For example, they see no difference between the "social engineering" of education, which works on the next generation through speech or symbolic deed, and biological engineering, which inscribes its effects, directly and irreversibly, into the human constitution. Or they claim to see no difference between the indirect genetic effects of human mate selection and deliberate, direct genetic engineering to produce offspring with precise biological capacities. Such critics, I fear, have already bought into a reductionist view of human life and the relation between the generations. And they ignore the fact that most people choose their mates for reasons different from stud farming.

[C] Correction of a genetically abnormal egg or sperm (that is, of the "germ cells"), however worthy an activity, stretches the meaning of "therapy" beyond all normal uses. Just who is the "patient" being "treated"? The potential child-to-be that might be formed out of such egg or sperm is, at the time of the treatment, at best no more than a hope and a hypothesis. There is no medical analogue for treatment of non-existent patients.

[D] To be sure, not all attempts at enhancement will require genetic alterations. We have already witnessed efforts to boost height with supplementary growth hormone or athletic performance with steroids or "blood doping:" Nevertheless, the largest possible changes in what is "normally" human are likely to come about only with the help of genetic alterations or the joining of machines (for example, computers) to human beings.

[E] I find it odd that it is these issues that have been put forward as the special ethical problems associated with genetic technology and the Human Genome Project. Issues of privacy and risks of discrimination related to medical conditions are entirely independent of whether the medical condition is genetic in origin. Only if a special stigma were attached to having an inherited disease—for example, only if having thalassemia or sickle cell anemia were more shameful than having gonorrhea or lung cancer—would the genetic character of a disease create special or additional reasons for protecting against breaches of confidentiality or discrimination in the workplace.

[F] Until the events of September 11 and the anthrax scare that followed, they did not worry enough. It is remarkable that most bioethical discussions of genetic technology had naively neglected its potential usefulness in creating biological weapons, such as, to begin with, antibiotic-resistant plague bacteria, or later, aerosols containing cancer-inducing or mind-scrambling viral vectors. The most outstanding molecular geneticist were especially naive in this area. When American molecular biologists convened the 1975 Asilomar Conference on recombinant DNA research, which called for a voluntary moratorium on experiments until the biohazards could be evaluated, they invited Soviet biologists to the meeting who said virtually nothing but who photographed every slide that was shown.

[G] One of the most worrisome but least appreciated aspects of the godlike power of the new genetics is its tendency to "redefine" a human being in terms of his genes. Once a person is decisively characterized by his genotype, it is but a short step to justifying death solely for genetic sins.

[H] Many scientists suspect that we have different inherited propensities for these and other behavioral troubles, though it is almost certain that there is no single "gene for x" that is responsible.

[I] This strikes me as the deepest problem with positive eugenics: less the threat of coercion, more the presumption of thinking we are wise enough to engineer "improvements" in the human species.

[J] This is, of course, not an objection to cloning itself but only to hazards tied to the technique used to produce the replicated children.

[K] I forbear mentioning what is rapidly becoming another trumping argument: increasing the profits of my biotech company and its shareholders, an argument often presented in more public-spirited dress: if we don't do it, other countries will, and we will lose our competitive edge in biotechnology.

Web site

The Source: http://humancloning.org

The Human Cloning Foundation started with five board members—a lawyer, a bioethicist, an Internet expert, an activist, and a physician. It now has two board members who choose not to be public with their names. It's a nonprofit organization incorporated in the state of Georgia. The following screenshot is of the Web site's home page, followed by an article published on that site. The article was written by Gregory E. Pence, professor in the Department of Philosophy and School of Medicine at the University of Alabama, Birmingham.

The Top Ten Myths about Human Cloning

1. **Cloning Xeroxes a person.** Cloning merely re-creates the genes of the ancestor, not what he has learned or experienced. Technically, it re-creates the genotype, not the phenotype. (Even at that, only 99% of those genes get re-created because 1% of such a child's genes would come from those in the egg—mitochondrial DNA). Conventional wisdom holds that about half of who we are comes from our genes, the other half, from the environment.

Cloning cannot re-create what in us came from the environment; it also cannot re-create memories. The false belief that cloning re-creates a person stems in part from the common, current false belief in simplistic, genetic reductionism, i.e., that a person really is just determined by his genes. No reputable geneticist or psychologist believes this.

2. **Human cloning is replication or making children into commodities.** Opponents of cloning often use these words to beg the question, to assume that children created by parents by a new method would not be loved. Similar things were said about "test tube" babies, who turned out to be some of the most-wanted, most-loved babies ever created in human history.

Indeed, the opposite is true: evolution has created us with sex drives such that, if we do not carefully use contraception, children occur. Because children get created this way without being wanted, sexual reproduction is more likely to create unwanted, and hence possibly unloved, children than human cloning.

Lawyers opposing cloning have a special reason for using these pejorative words. If cloning is just a new form of human reproduction, then it is Constitutionally protected from interference by the state. Several Supreme Court decisions declare that all forms of human reproduction, including the right not to reproduce, cannot be abridged by government.

Use of words such as "replication" and "commodification" also assumes artificial wombs or commercial motives; about these fallacies, see below.

3. **Human cloning reduces biological diversity.** Population genetics says otherwise. Six billion people now exist, soon to be eight billion, and most of them reproduce. Cloning requires in vitro fertilization, which is expensive and inefficient, with only a 20% success rate. Since 1978, at most a half million babies have been produced this way, or at most, one out of 12,000 babies.

Over decades and with such great numbers, populations follow the Law of Regression to the Mean. This means that, even if someone tried to create a superior race by cloning, it would fail, because cloned people would have children with non-cloned people, and resulting genetic hybrids would soon be normalized.

Cloning is simply a tool. It could be used with the motive of creating uniformity (but would fail, because of above), or it could be used for the opposite reason, to try to increase diversity (which would also fail, for the same reason).

4. **People created by cloning would be less ensouled than normal humans, or would be subhuman.** A human who had the same number of chromosomes as a child created sexually, who was gestated by a woman, and who talked, felt, and

spoke as any other human, would ethically be human and a person. It is by now a principle of ethics that the origins of a person, be it from mixed-race parents, unmarried parents, in vitro fertilization, or a gay male couple hiring a surrogate mother, do not affect the personhood of the child born.

The same would be true of a child created by cloning (who, of course, has to be gestated for nine months by a woman).

Every deviation from normal reproduction has always been faced with this fear. Children greeted by sperm donation, in vitro fertilization, and surrogate motherhood were predicted to be less-than-human, but were not.

A variation predicts that while, in fact, they will not be less-than-human, people will treat them this way and hence, such children will be harmed. This objection reifies prejudice and makes it an ethical justification, which it is wrong to do. The correct response to prejudice is to expose it for what it is, combat it with reason and with evidence, not validate it as an ethical reason.

5. **People created by cloning could be used for spare organs for normal humans.** Nothing could be done to a person created by cloning that right now could not be done to your brother or to a person's twin. The U. S. Constitution strongly implies that once a human fetus is outside the womb and alive, he has rights. Decisions backing this up give him rights to inherit property, rights not to suffer discrimination because of disability, and rights to U. S. citizenship.

A variation of this myth assumes that a dictator could make cloned humans into special SWAT teams or suicidal bombers. But nothing about originating people this way gives anyone any special power over the resulting humans, who would have free will. Besides, if a dictator wants to create such assassins, he need not wait for cloning but can take orphans and try to indoctrinate them now in isolated camps.

6. **All people created from the same genotype would be raised in batches and share secret empathy or communication.** Pure science fiction. If I wanted to recreate the genotype of my funny Uncle Harry, why would my wife want to gestate 5 or 6 other babies at the same time? Indeed, we now know that the womb cannot support more than 2 to 3 fetuses without creating a likely disability in one. Guidelines now call for no more than two embryos to be introduced by in vitro fertilization, which of course is required to use cloning.

Such assumptions about cloned humans being created in batches are linked to nightmarish science fiction scenarios where humane society has been destroyed and where industrialized machines have taken over human reproduction. But this is just someone's nightmare, not facts upon which to base state and federal laws.

7. **Scientists who work on human cloning are evil or motivated by bad motives.** The stuff of Hollywood and scary writers. Scientists are just people. Most of them have kids of their own and care a lot for kids. No one wants to bring a handicapped child into the world. Movies and novels never portray life scientists with sympathy. This anti-science prejudice started with Mary Shelley's *Frankenstein* and continues with nefarious scientists working for the government on *The X Files*.

People who call themselves scientists and grandstand for television, such as Richard Seed and Brigette Boisselier of the Raelians, are not real scientists but people who use the aura of science to gain attention. Real scientists don't spend all their time flying around the world to be on TV but stay at home in their clinics doing their work.

8. **Babies created by cloning could be grown in artificial wombs.** Nope, sorry. Medicine has been trying for fifty years to create an artificial womb, but has never come close to succeeding. Indeed, controversial experiments in 1973 on live-born fetuses in studying artificial wombs effectively shut down such research.

Finally, if anything like such wombs existed, we could save premature babies who haven't developed lung function, but unfortunately, we still can't—premature babies who can't breathe at all die. Thus, any human baby still needs a human woman to gestate him for at least six months, and to be healthy, nine months. This puts the lie to many science fiction stories and to many predictions about cloning and industrial reproduction.

9. **Only selfish people want to create a child by cloning.** First, this assumes that ordinary people don't create children for selfish reasons, such as a desire to have someone take care of them in old age, a desire to see part of themselves continue after death, and/or the desire to leave their estate to someone. Many people are hypocritical or deceived about why they came to have children. Very few people just decide that they want to bring more joy into the world, and hence create a child to raise and support for life as an end-in-himself. Let's be honest here. Second, a couple using cloning need not create a copy of one of them. As said above, Uncle Harry could be a prime candidate.

On the other hand, if a couple chooses a famous person, critics accuse them of creating designer babies. Either way, they can't win: if they re-create one of their genotypes, they are narcissistic; if they choose someone else's genes, they're guilty of creating designer babies.

In general, why should a couple using cloning have a higher justification required of them than a couple using sexual reproduction? If we ask: what counts as a good reason for creating a child, then why should cloning have any special test that is not required for sexual reproduction? Indeed, and more generally, what right does government have to require, or judge, any couple's reasons for having a child, even if they are seen by others to be selfish?

Couples desiring to use cloning should not bear an undue burden of justification.

10. **Human cloning is inherently evil: it can only be used for bad purposes by bad people.** No, it's just a tool, just another way to create a family. A long legacy in science fiction novels and movies make the word "cloning" so fraught with bad connotations that it can hardly be used in any discussion that purports to be impartial. It is like discussing equal rights for women by starting to discuss whether "the chicks" would fare better with equal rights. To most people, "cloning" implies selfish parents, crazy scientists, and out-of-control technology, so a fair discussion using this word isn't possible. Perhaps the phrase, "somatic cell nuclear transplantation" is better, even if it's a scientific mouthful. So if we shouldn't call a person created by cloning, a "clone," what should we call him? Answer: a person.

Magazine Article

The Author: Neil Munro

National Journal Group is a leading publisher of magazines, newsletters, books, and directories for people who have a professional interest in politics, policy, and government. Based in Washington, D.C., National Journal Group is committed to providing publications and services that are nonpartisan, reliable, and of the highest quality. Neil Munro is a staff writer for the *Journal*. The following article was published March 6, 2004.

Cloning as Economic Development

Facing fresh competition from overseas scientists, including most recently the South Koreans who cloned human embryos last year, advocates of cloning in the U.S. increasingly are highlighting the boosts the technology could give to the American research community, and to economic development.

In January, for example, the New Jersey Legislature narrowly approved a law making it a crime to use cloning to create a live person. But the same law allows cloning of human embryos for research purposes. The legislation "will encourage collaboration, investment, and the building of centers that, at least in part, use human-embryo stem cells," said Ira Black, who is a scientist at the University of Medicine and Dentistry of New Jersey and helped craft the law.

In February, Gov. James McGreevey requested $6.5 million in state funds to create a new stem-cell research center, saying it "will put New Jersey at the forefront of medical and pharmaceutical research in the nation."

In California, a group made up of scientists and parents of sick children is promoting a proposed ballot initiative that would steer almost $3 billion into the field over the next 10 years. The campaign's Web site argues that the research could cure millions of sick Californians, save billions of dollars in health care costs, and "create projects and jobs that will generate millions of dollars in new tax revenues for our state."

What's spurring this focus on research and economic benefits is the difficulty so far of developing successful therapies that use cloned and transplanted stem cells. The lack of therapies has discouraged investors and forced many U.S. cloning companies to slash their research staffs or even shut their doors, said Robert Lanza, a scientist at Advanced Cell Technologies, a cloning-research company in Worcester, Mass.

Advocates of human cloning say stem cells from cloned embryos could one day be grown into organs or tissues for transplant into human patients. But so far, such stem cells have proven difficult to manage, said Lanza. "They have a mind of their own . . . [and can] become a hodgepodge of cells," including heart cells and neurons, where another kind of cell is desired. The quality standards for transplanted cells "have to be foolproof . . . you don't want to put heart cells in a patient and have them grow into a tooth," he said. And perfecting the methods will take time. "Venture capitalists want a product in a year or two," Lanza said, but realistically they'll have to wait "five to 10 years at least," before a therapy is available using stem-cell transplants.

However, cloning done for research purposes, as opposed to that done for stem-cell transplant, can generate short-term revenue for cloning companies, Lanza said. "What has been overlooked here . . . is that this is going to help us in drug discovery," said Lanza.

The growing costs of drug development underscore the business case for cloning for research. Pharmaceutical companies argue that the cost of developing a new drug—including the costs of testing and marketing, and the money sunk into prospective drugs that ultimately fail—can range between $500 million and $800 million. Much of the risky early development is farmed out to universities and small biotech companies.

In drug research, scientists search for interesting biological processes, such as a protein that slows a type of cancer, or a chemical trigger that prompts a cell to produce insulin. To find those biological processes, and also to test likely drugs, university and company researchers already use many types of cells, creatures, and animals, which they dub "tools" or "models." These test models include endlessly copied human and animal cells, as well as naturally produced E. coli bacteria, mice, rats, dogs, and monkeys and other primates. Scientists have also developed many genetically modified mice, called "knockout mice," that simulate human patients with cancer, arthritis, obesity, diabetes, and other ailments. The creation and sale of these various creatures is a $1 billion-a-year business.

Cloning could improve the efficiency of medical research by enabling scientists at diverse locations to work on a standard set of cloned cells or test models. This would help them share ideas, tips, data, and patents. It would allow "an efficient, expeditious approach at the basic level . . . [and allow] nearly an incalculable savings in time," said Black. Already, scientists have cloned mice, rabbits, and cats for experiments.

Cloning of humans goes a step further, and could also allow researchers to peer into the earliest stages of human development so as to understand the subsequent emergence of diseases, or perhaps attractive genetic attributes. If human cloning were made routine, for example, groups of scientists could identify a person with a particular attribute, such as an inclination toward breast cancer, hair loss, or unusual endurance, and then clone an embryo from that person to study the emergence of the particular attribute.

Understanding the unfolding of human traits is "the Holy Grail of developmental biology," said Kenneth Breslauer, dean of the life sciences department at Rutgers University. "It is the key of knowledge to unlocking the most basic understanding of how whole complex organisms evolve," he said.

New Jersey's new stem-cell program, perhaps not surprisingly, will be run by Rutgers and the University of Medicine and Dentistry of New Jersey, respectively Breslauer's and Black's employers.

But the promise of cloning humans for research purposes comes with its own set of business and ethics problems.

For example, advocates of cloning for research face scientific rivals who argue that stem cells drawn from human adults, not from cloned human embryos, can serve as a noncontroversial alternative model for drug development and testing. Moreover, research groups in other states and countries are offering their own solutions—new and better mice, computer modeling, and tiny, cell-sized machines are a few examples—and all the groups are pitching their methods to investors and the media in the hope of winning support. This competition occurs within and between universities, states, and nations. For example, Minnesota has subsidized the development of research on stem cells from adult humans at its state university, and the governments of Singapore and Australia are jointly funding a human-cloning company, ES Cell International, run by a U.K. scientist.

Faced with such competition, scientists watch each other's work closely: "We want to know whether different embryonic stem cells confer different advantages," said Black, who works with stem cells from human embryos as well as those from adult animals.

Another problem with cloning for research purposes is that no obvious scientific or business case exists for limiting the maturation of embryos. "The more stages of development you can study, the better understanding you have," said Stuart Newman, a scientist at New York Medical College. But ethically, many reasons may exist for halting the growth of a cloned human embryo. Some "people say gestate for a week, or two weeks . . . but the technological imperative and the business imperative just roll over any arbitrary boundary that people would like to set," Newman said.

Under the new law in New Jersey, for example, cloned human embryos can legally be placed in women for subsequent growth, but cannot result in birth. The draft California ballot initiative says that cloned human embryos would only be allowed "initially" to develop up to 12 days.

Improved technology, meanwhile, is allowing longer gestation of human embryos outside the womb. In New York state, a research team has developed an artificial womb that can nurture embryos to the point when they can help in the study of infertility and in basic-science experiments. "This model would provide new avenues for testing new drugs, bypassing human subjects completely and substantially lowering costs involved with drug testing," and could also grow tissue for possible transplants, according to Hung-Ching Liu, the team's lead scientist. Liu works at a private fertility clinic and at Cornell University's medical college.

Another approach to the creation of better test models is the creation of chimeras, which are creatures that combine human and animal tissues and cells. For example, AIDS researchers have long used special mice that carry a slice of human thymus taken from aborted fetuses. One of the scientists who developed this type of mouse was Irving Weissman, who combines careers as a businessman, a research director at Stanford University, and an advocate for cloning research. He's one of the scientists who launched the California ballot initiative; he also founded a company, Stemcells Inc., that created a strain of mouse models whose brains include some human brain cells. Using human stem cells to build better animal models "is certainly the hope," said Black, but "I don't think anyone is quite realistically thinking of chimeric monkeys."

Certainly, scientists discuss which ethical boundaries they should not cross. "Even we have discussions over what is ethical," said Lanza. "People will be giving that more thought, and will be more creative in using these technologies in this regard."

Breslauer, of Rutgers, said, "There will always be a push and pull in the science community, of people who are not as comfortable with a new approach for either scientific reasons, or their legitimate feel for ethics or morality . . . we already have this discourse going on."

But "making half-animal, half-human chimeras is morally unacceptable," said Art Caplan, a pro-cloning professor of ethics at the University of Pennsylvania. "The imagery is so powerful that whatever comes out of those models would be destroyed."

Not so, said Ruth Faden, a bioethicist at Johns Hopkins University, where researchers use a patented method to extract stem cells from aborted fetuses. "The big worry is the blurring between humans and nonhumans in such a way that new creatures would challenge us as to whether they would be treated like humans." But "any number of policies could head that off," she added. However, she also questioned whether advantageous research could really be curbed: "Show me an instance in which we have successfully prohibited a profitable avenue of science."

Companies and scientists are under great pressure to use the best models they can, Newman said. "Without very strict regulations, the cruelest things imaginable will be done to animals and quasi-humans, if it is a way of getting drugs to market," he said.

To head off such developments, Newman has sought to patent chimeras, principally because he wants to prevent the use of such models to develop and test ways to genetically modify humans. He filed the patent application in partnership with Andy Kimbrell, director of the Washington-based International Center for Technology Assessment. In a related action, Kimbrell's group has also allied with the American Anti-Vivisection Society to file a lawsuit challenging a patent held by the University of Texas System for a method of irradiating a beagle, then infecting the dog with a lethal mold to test anti-fungal compounds.

Another possibility is that companies could bypass domestic regulations governing test models if they chose to outsource their research to countries without such regulations. Thus the debate will also be shaped, Caplan said, by the desire to keep jobs at home.

Regardless of these ethical debates, said Lanza, the scientific and business "results will speak for themselves. . . . In the end, [what counts] is what works."

Web site

The Source: http://www.ornl.gov/sci/techresources/Human_Genome/home.shtml

Begun formally in 1990, the U.S. Human Genome Project is a 13-year effort coordinated by the U.S. Department of Energy and the National Institutes of Health. The project originally was planned to last 15 years, but rapid technological advances accelerated the expected completion date to 2003.

The screenshot on page 384 is the home page for the project. Below is an Introduction to Human Genome Research published on the site.

Human Genome Research: An Introduction

The U.S. Human Genome Project (HGP), composed of the DOE and NIH Human Genome Programs, is the national coordinated effort to characterize all human genetic material by determining the complete sequence of the DNA in the human genome. The HGP's ultimate goal has been to discover all the more than 30,000

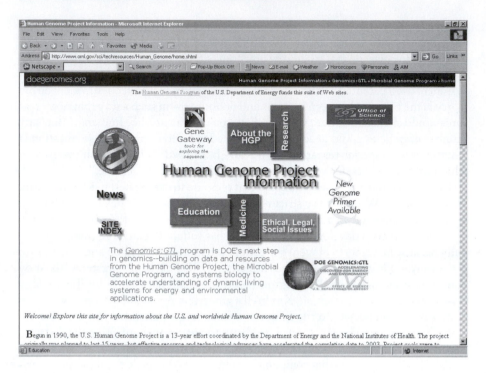

human genes and render them accessible for further biological study. To facilitate the future interpretation of human gene function, parallel studies have been carried out on selected model organisms. View timeline and history for background information on the project.

The HGP will meet an ambitious schedule to complete the full sequence in 2003, two years ahead of previous projections. Technology available shortly after the start of the HGP in 1990 could have been used to attain HGP objectives, but the cost and time required would have been unacceptable. Because of this, a major emphasis of the project's early years was to optimize existing methods and develop new technologies to increase DNA mapping and sequencing efficiency by 10- to 20-fold. The genome was sequenced with technologies and methods that evolved over the past 10 years.

In the course of completing the sequence, an interim "working draft" of the human sequence was produced and published in *Nature* (15 February, 2001) simultaneously with a companion publication of the human sequence generated by Celera Genomics Corporation (*Science*, 16 February, 2001). Other goals have involved further improving sequencing technologies; studying human genome sequence variation, both at the level of single nucleotides (single nucleotide polymorphisms, or SNPs) and entire chromosomal segments, referred to as haplotypes; sequencing the mouse, rat, frog, pufferfish, and sea squirt genomes; and sequencing of additional microbial genomes. All this supports ongoing efforts in comparative genomics, the most powerful way to elucidate the roles of the many related genes observed in the genomes of these model organisms. The DOE Human Genome Program also has developed high-throughput approaches to identify cis-regulatory sequences in the human and other genomes, based on shared nonprotein-coding sequences in the genomes of such evolutionarily diverse organisms as the sea squirt (*Ciona intestinalis*), the pufferfish (*Fugu rupribes*), and the frog (*Xenopus tropicalis*). Additional longstanding elements of the DOE Human Genome Program have included studies of the ethical, legal, and social implications (ELSI) of genome research; bioinformatics and computational biology; training genome scientists; and encouraging cross-disciplinary interest in genome research by scientists in disciplines such as physics, engineering, and computation.

The DOE Human Genome Program has supported research projects at universities, the DOE Joint Genome Institute, DOE-owned national laboratories, and other research organizations. As part of the international Human Genome Project, vital and very active genome research also has been pursued by researchers and science-funding agencies outside the United States.

Information obtained as part of the HGP will dramatically change almost all biological and medical research and dwarf the catalog of current genetic knowledge. Both the methods and data developed through the project are likely to benefit investigations of many other genomes, including a large number of commercially important plants and animals. In a related project to sequence the genomes of environmentally and industrially interesting microbes, in 1994 DOE initiated the Microbial Genome Program. For this reason, in addition to the DOE and NIH programs, genome research is being carried out at agencies such as the U.S. Department of Agriculture, the National Science Foundation, and the private sector.

Presidential Speech

The Speaker: George W. Bush

The following is a transcript of a speech given by President George W. Bush on April 10, 2002.

President Bush Calls on Senate to Back Human Cloning Ban

Remarks by the President on Human Cloning Legislation
The East Room
1:18 P.M. EDT
THE PRESIDENT: Well, thank you all so very much for coming to the White House. It's my honor to welcome you to the people's house.

I particularly want to honor three folks who I had the honor of meeting earlier: Joni Tada, Jim Kelly and Steve McDonald. I want to thank you for your courage, I want to thank you for your wisdom, I want to thank you for your extraordinary perseverance and faith. They have triumphed in the face of physical disability and share a deep commitment to medicine that is practiced ethically and humanely.

All of us here today believe in the promise of modern medicine. We're hopeful about where science may take us. And we're also here because we believe in the principles of ethical medicine.

As we seek to improve human life, we must always preserve human dignity. (Applause.) And therefore, we must prevent human cloning by stopping it before it starts. (Applause.)

I want to welcome Tommy Thompson, who is the Secretary of Health and Human Services, a man who is doing a fine job for America. (Applause.) I want to thank members from the United States Congress, members from both political parties who are here. I particularly want to thank Senator Brownback and Senator Landrieu for sponsoring a bill about which I'm going to speak. (Applause.)

As well, we've got Senator Frist and Senator Bond and Senator Hutchinson and Senator Santorum and Congressman Weldon, Stupak, and eventually Smith and Kerns. They just don't realize—(applause)—thank you all for coming—they seem to have forgotten we start things on time here in the White House. (Laughter.)

We live in a time of tremendous medical progress. A little more than a year ago, scientists first cracked the human genetic code—one of the most important advances in scientific history. Already, scientists are developing new diagnostic tools so that each of us can know our risk of disease and act to prevent them.

One day soon, precise therapies will be custom made for our own genetic makeup. We're on the threshold of historic breakthroughs against AIDS and Alzheimer's disease and cancer and diabetes and heart disease and Parkinson's disease. And that's incredibly positive.

Our age may be known to history as the age of genetic medicine, a time when many of the most feared illnesses were overcome.

Our age must also be defined by the care and restraint and responsibility with which we take up these new scientific powers.

Advances in biomedical technology must never come at the expense of human conscience. (Applause.) As we seek what is possible, we must always ask what is right, and we must not forget that even the most noble ends do not justify any means. (Applause.)

Science has set before us decisions of immense consequence. We can pursue medical research with a clear sense of moral purpose or we can travel without an ethical compass into a world we could live to regret. Science now presses forward the issue of human cloning. How we answer the question of human cloning will place us on one path or the other.

Human cloning is the laboratory production of individuals who are genetically identical to another human being. Cloning is achieved by putting the genetic material from a donor into a woman's egg, which has had its nucleus removed. As a result, the new or cloned embryo is an identical copy of only the donor. Human cloning has moved from science fiction into science.

One biotech company has already began producing embryonic human clones for research purposes. Chinese scientists have derived stem cells from cloned embryos created by combining human DNA and rabbit eggs. Others have announced plans to produce cloned children, despite the fact that laboratory cloning of animals has lead to spontaneous abortions and terrible, terrible abnormalities.

Human cloning is deeply troubling to me, and to most Americans. Life is a creation, not a commodity. (Applause.) Our children are gifts to be loved and protected, not products to be designed and manufactured. Allowing cloning would be taking a significant step toward a society in which human beings are grown for spare body parts, and children are engineered to custom specifications; and that's not acceptable.

In the current debate over human cloning, two terms are being used: reproductive cloning and research cloning. Reproductive cloning involves creating a cloned embryo and implanting it into a woman with the goal of creating a child. Fortunately, nearly every American agrees that this practice should be banned. Research cloning, on the other hand, involves the creation of cloned human embryos which are then destroyed to derive stem cells.

I believe all human cloning is wrong, and both forms of cloning ought to be banned, for the following reasons. First, anything other than a total ban on human cloning would be unethical. Research cloning would contradict the most fundamental principle of medical ethics, that no human life should be exploited or extinguished for the benefit of another. (Applause.)

Yet a law permitting research cloning, while forbidding the birth of a cloned child, would require the destruction of nascent human life. Secondly, anything other than a total ban on human cloning would be virtually impossible to enforce. Cloned human embryos created for research would be widely available in laboratories and embryo farms. Once cloned embryos were available, implantation would take place. Even the tightest regulations and strict policing would not prevent or detect the birth of cloned babies.

Third, the benefits of research cloning are highly speculative. Advocates of research cloning argue that stem cells obtained from cloned embryos would be injected into a genetically identical individual without risk of tissue rejection. But there is evidence, based on animal studies, that cells derived from cloned embryos may indeed be rejected.

Yet even if research cloning were medically effective, every person who wanted to benefit would need an embryonic clone of his or her own, to provide the designer tissues. This would create a massive national market for eggs and egg donors, and exploitation of women's bodies that we cannot and must not allow. (Applause.)

I stand firm in my opposition to human cloning. And at the same time, we will pursue other promising and ethical ways to relieve suffering through biotechnology. This year for the first time, federal dollars will go towards supporting human embryonic stem cell research consistent with the ethical guidelines I announced last August.

The National Institutes of Health is also funding a broad range of animal and human adult stem cell research. Adult stem cells which do not require the destruction of human embryos and which yield tissues which can be transplanted without rejection are more versatile that originally thought.

We're making progress. We're learning more about them. And therapies developed from adult stem cells are already helping suffering people.

I support increasing the research budget of the NIH, and I ask Congress to join me in that support. And at the same time, I strongly support a comprehensive law against all human cloning. And I endorse the bill—wholeheartedly endorse the bill—sponsored by Senator Brownback and Senator Mary Landrieu. (Applause.)

This carefully drafted bill would ban all human cloning in the United States, including the cloning of embryos for research. It is nearly identical to the bipartisan legislation that last year passed the House of Representatives by more than a 100-vote margin. It has wide support across the political spectrum, liberals and conservatives support it, religious people and nonreligious people support it. Those who are pro-choice and those who are pro-life support the bill.

This is a diverse coalition, united by a commitment to prevent the cloning and exploitation of human beings. (Applause.) It would be a mistake for the United States Senate to allow any kind of human cloning to come out of that chamber. (Applause.)

I'm an incurable optimist about the future of our country. I know we can achieve great things. We can make the world more peaceful, we can become a more compassionate nation. We can push the limits of medical science. I truly believe that we're going to bring hope and healing to countless lives across the country. And as we do, I will insist that we always maintain the highest of ethical standards.

Thank you all for coming. (Applause.) God bless.

Scholarly Publication

The Authors: William P. Cheshire Jr., Edmund D. Pellegrino, Linda K. Bevington, C. Ben Mitchell, Nancy L. Jones, Kevin T. FitzGerald, C. Everett Koop, and John F. Kilner

Mayo Clinic is a charitable, not-for-profit organization based in Rochester, Minnesota. Its mission is to provide the best care to every patient, every day, through integrated clinical practice, education, and research. It is governed by a 31-member board of trustees composed of public members and Mayo physicians and administrators.

The following article was published in August 2003.

Stem Cell Research: Why Medicine Should Reject Human Cloning

Speculation that the world's first human clone may have been born,[1,2] combined with reports that human embryos have been cloned for research purposes[3,4] calls for careful public and professional scrutiny of the critically important matter of human cloning.

Human cloning is the asexual production of a human being whose genetic makeup is nearly identical to that of a currently or previously existing individual.[5,6] Whereas the deliberations of international, national, and state regulatory bodies have in most cases, favored the prohibition of what has been called *reproductive* cloning—in which a cloned human embryo is created with the intent that a human clone will be born—they have differed considerably what has been termed *research* cloning. Research cloning involves the creation of a cloned human embryo for the purpose of scientific investigation of early human development or for medical research aimed at developing treatments for disease. Because embryonic stem cells are pluripotent, having the capacity to differentiate into the full range of human tissues, some believe that these cells hold the potential to revolutionize medicine by providing a source of replacement tissue that might one day restore the health of persons suffering from a variety of debilitating conditions.[7] Transplanted embryonic stem cells derived from a patient's clone may be compatible (as would adult-derived stem cells from the patient) with that patient's immune system and hence, in principle, be resistant to immune rejection.

Our contention is that human cloning should not be permitted, whether for research or reproductive purposes. While we enthusiastically affirm the importance of medical research and ardently support the goal of healing people, we believe that the harms human cloning would bring to medicine would exceed the anticipated benefits.

Reproductive Cloning

An overwhelming majority of scientists, health care professionals, policy makers, bioethicists, theologians, and the general public have indicated their opposition to the birth of cloned human beings.[6,8,9] The following concerns have been advanced.

Human cloning would be hazardous to the gestating clone and the surrogate mother. The current state of nonhuman animal cloning technology is so rudimentary that the procedure has resulted in a staggeringly high occurrence of severe physical and genetic defects and premature aging is cloned offspring.[10,11] Embryologists estimate that a single successful human cloning might come at the cost of hundreds of failed attempts.[8] Even if issues of safety were overcome, which is unlikely apart from unethical human experimentation, compelling ethical objections remain.

Human cloning would signify an egregious disrespect for personal autonomy. In forcing on the human clone a selected identity bound to certain, perhaps unfulfilled, expectations placed on the genetic original, cloning would frame that person's life and limit that person's autonomy permanently. Cloning would also encumber that person with profound emotional burdens. The cloned individual would not be born with the special privilege of having a unique genetic identity, but rather would always live in the shadow of the other person whom he or she was intended to duplicate genetically. The social stigma of being known as a clone, combined with confused parentage and expectations of measuring up to the achievements of the genetic original or of "replacing" a deceased loved one, could result in unimaginable psychological turmoil.[6] If cloning became common practice, its deviation from the traditional design and accompanying moral responsibilities of the human family might well disrupt social stability.

Moreover, cloning brings to mind images of assembly-line manufacture more suited for the making of replaceable appliances than unique human beings. Deeply held public intuition thus regards the prospect of human cloning to be a repugnant departure from the intimate and richly meaningful process of natural procreation. Unlike other reproductive technologies that assist procreation, cloning seeks to produce a human being with a particular genetic code. It is not technology that we oppose, but rather the misuse of technology that enables some people to exert nearly absolute control over the genetic makeup of others. This substitution of human genetic replication for procreation would constitute a serious affront to human dignity.[12] If cloning proceeds along its current path of development, it will foster a grave devaluation of humanity. Whether cloning were to become a widespread or an occasional practice, its acceptance would shift societal attitudes away from appreciating people as distinct individuals and toward a new way of sizing up people as useful or attractive commodities of technology assembled to satisfy others' expectations.

Some will defend human cloning as a right of reproductive liberty that ought never be restricted. However, there exists no inalienable right to engage in human cloning as a means of realizing one's desire for a child, regardless of the particular motivation behind such a desire.[13] Furthermore, although reproduction is a private matter, development and implementation of genetic technology on which reproductive decisions will be based are matters of definite public interest. No reason has been advanced that is weighty enough to justify overlooking the considerable hazards described herein and resorting to cloning as a means of human reproduction. The disturbing dangers of human cloning to public health and well-being should be of concern to physicians in particular because the menacing key to this Pandora's box is a medical procedure.

Implications of a Partial Ban

Proposals to ban human cloning for purposes of reproduction have attracted broad support. However, enacting a ban solely on reproductive cloning, while simultaneously permitting research cloning, would almost certainly fail to achieve its stated objective. For the following reasons, we contend that a partial ban could well result in instances of both types of cloning, leading to a society that most Americans would deem undesirable.[14]

Unenforceability

First, a partial ban would be unenforceable. If a ban on reproductive cloning only were adopted, enforcement would necessarily entail the legally mandated destruction of human embryos created for research cloning. Such required destruction would not only constitute a form of clear discrimination against a class of human beings based on the means of conception but also would likely be objected to or wholly disregarded by many, particularly by those who desire to implant the embryos. Because the legality of terminating the lives of unborn human beings by abortion is frequently defended as a matter of personal choice, it is difficult to imagine that most Americans would welcome a governmental policy that mandated the destruction of embryonic human life and the punishment of those who defied the law (either by knowingly implanting a cloned human embryo or by giving birth to a human clone.)[15,16] Such acts of defiance would be viewed by many as the private exercise of a reproductive option entitled to certain protections, effectively circumventing a partial ban. Although we do not believe that people have a right (rooted in reproductive liberty) to *create* human beings via cloning, we nevertheless maintain that parents should never be forced to destroy their offspring, *once created,* regardless of their method of origin.

Currently, the parents of embryos created via in vitro fertilization (IVF), for example, are given a great measure of decision-making power regarding the fate of their embryos. Some fertility clinics exceed clinical policy requirements in their efforts to determine parents' wishes regarding stored embryos, and all clinics are obligated to honor decisions both for and against implantation.[17] Our autonomy-steeped culture would surely have difficulty accepting a policy that would deny people the same choice simply because their embryos were created through cloning.

Regardless of their legality, both IVF and reproductive cloning are technologies that lie within the realm of reproduction. Because of the private context of reproduction and the underregulation of the US fertility industry, prohibiting the implantation of cloned human embryos would be a formidable task met with considerable resistance, regardless of whether reproductive cloning is legally permissible. Of importance, although public consensus favors a law prohibiting the reproductive cloning of human beings, continued legislative stalemate on proposals to adopt a comprehensive cloning ban prohibiting both research and reproductive cloning might mean that even reproductive cloning would remain legal.

If cloned human embryos were created in the laboratory for research purposes only, the mandate that they not be implanted or otherwise allowed to progress toward birth would prove extremely difficult to uphold. Therefore, the birth of cloned human beings—the very thing that a ban on reproductive cloning should prevent—would likely result.

Compassionate Transgressions

Second, if cloned human embryos were available for research, appeals to compassion within the privacy of the physician-patient relationship would likely lead to their implantation. Consider the following hypothetical scenarios.

A cloned human embryo is created with the intent of producing tissue needed to save the life of a seriously ill child. Before the tissue can be obtained, the ill child dies. Her grieving parents, distraught over their tragic loss, request that the embryo be implanted so that they may have another child who is a near genetic duplicate of the daughter whom they so desperately miss.

A man agrees to be cloned with the intent of donating the resultant embryo to research. Subsequent to creation of the cloned embryo, he learns that both he and his wife are infertile. Realizing that their prospect for having a genetically related child suddenly appears to be compromised, the man changes his mind and requests that his clone be implanted in his wife instead of donated to research.

In such cases, it would be difficult for many physicians to deny the wishes of those desiring to implant a cloned embryo.

Ineffective Detection

Third, violations of a partial ban would often go unnoticed. If laboratory creation of cloned human embryos was permitted but implantation of such embryos was banned, it would be infeasible to monitor the fate of each and every cloned embryo. The somatic cell nuclear transfer procedure typically results in the creation of multiple embryos. To prevent a single embryo from being implanted within the private context of the physician-patient relationship would surely prove to be impossible. Moreover, policies that would require genetic testing of every neonate at birth to ensure that he or she is not a clone (and that would penalize the parties responsible for implanting a cloned embryo) would likely be regarded as a violation of privacy. Even if such testing were allowed, it would fail to ensure that reproductive cloning had not oc-curred because the baby could be a clone of an unknown or unrevealed person, rather than being a near genetic duplicate of one of the parents.

As a result, threats to levy fines or inflict other punishments would not always deter those wishing to engage in technology they perceived to be undetectable. Poli-cies that prohibit, and penalize those who request or assist in, the implantation of cloned human embryos would therefore ultimately fail to prevent reproductive cloning once cloned human embryos were produced for research purposes.

Facilitation via Technological Advance.

Fourth, a policy that prohibited cloning for reproduction while permitting cloning for research would actually facilitate the means to achieving the activity it intended to pre-vent. To permit research cloning as a legitimate activity of science would undoubt-edly result in an increased number of human clone births.

Ongoing embryological research is poised to overcome many of the remaining technical obstacles to human cloning. Some experts estimate that the successful and efficient production of healthy cloned human embryos, suitable for implantation might be months or at most a few years away.[18,19] If this methodology is perfected and IVF practitioners are trained in its use, the implantation of cloned human embryos would no longer be the distant prospect of a few laboratories in possession of spe-cialized resources but could become a simple and brief procedure within reach of most fertility clinics that perform intracytoplasmic sperm injection or other labor-intensive forms of fertilization.

If the goal is to avoid instances of human reproductive cloning, as advocates of a partial ban fervently assert, then a law designed to prevent a requisite activity oc-curring over a period of months or years should be regarded as preferable to a law for-bidding the implantation of cloned human embryos that could be accomplished in only minutes. Many existing US laws offer precedents. For example, to prevent pri-vate citizens from developing nuclear weapons, current laws ban the unlicensed pos-session of plutonium and enriched uranium.[20] It would be foolhardy to distribute plutonium widely and then expect people not to engage in the production and use of nuclear weaponry because it is easier to withhold the means to produce a weapon than it is to prevent its production and use.

Even persons who do not find research cloning to be morally objectionable may nevertheless oppose cultivating the industry due to the inevitability that cloned human beings would be born if the development of technology for research cloning were not banned.[21]

Evasive Language

Fifth, a partial ban would eliminate only the language of reproductive cloning. To speak of a distinction between "reproductive" cloning and "research" cloning is to ne-glect an important commonality between both forms of cloning. Regardless of in-tent, both generate in the same manner a human embryo. Therefore, both methods of human cloning are reproductive in that they give rise to new individual human lives.[22] A partial ban clearly understood would not truly be a ban against cloning but against the implantation—and hence the survival—of human clones.

The choice of language applied to cloning should recognize that, on biologic grounds alone, the human embryo is a living human organism. Structurally, the embryo is genetically complete. What is necessary for continued growth is suitable nurture and environment, 2 conditions that live human beings need as much in their adult stage as in their embryonic stage. Metabolically, at every cell division the embryo copies the complete human genome with nearly perfect fidelity and, in transcribing his or her genetic code, has begun the journey toward actualization of all the functional capacities that uniquely typify a being of the species *Homo sapiens.*

Some well-intentioned thinkers will defend research cloning and human embryo research in general on the grounds that, rather than being fully present at conception, human worth develops gradually as the nervous system reaches a stage of maturation when certain functional capacities are demonstrable. We consider such a gradualist view to be an inadequate account of the value of human life. To suppose that human life consists only in functional capacities is to mistake the *detection* of life for its *existence.* Life ontologically precedes biologic function, and one must first *be* a human being to develop and possess human capacities. Similarly, although some have argued that the embryo fertilized in vitro must enter the womb to count as human, we maintain that the moral status of a human being is independent of age or geographical location.

A gradualist view can also run counter to the widely accepted belief that diminished or less developed capacities may obligate increased care or protection. Some of the very people who would gain from the alleged benefits of research cloning are themselves in a state of functional decline due to degenerative disease. If one accepts the gradualist criterion that moral worth depends on one's stage of development or function, then, by the same logic, individuals who are ill or disabled (eg, those with Alzheimer disease, Parkinson disease, or spinal cord injury) would have an uncertain claim to full human worth because of their loss of function. From the gradualist perspective, the widely held belief in human equality grounded in a common basis for dignity vanishes.

Because material traits alone are an unsatisfactory guide to assessing human moral status, no empirical description of a human being, no matter how exact, can fully grasp the magnificent complexity of the individual within. Drawing from their experience in responding to human frailty and suffering, physicians understand this well. The practice of medicine teaches that the meaning of human joy cannot be fully explained by a map of molecules in motion, or the tears of human suffering by the trickling of neurotransmitters. Thus, human dignity, which medicine recognizes as being irreducible to mere physical characteristics, cannot be denied on material grounds to a portion of the biologic life span. To discount the emergence of human dignity at the very beginning of life—when life, although just barely measurable yet has distinctly begun—would be a serious error. Language that undermines the humanity of early human life inevitably exposes other vulnerable classes of humanity to the risk of similar devaluation. Regrettably, medicine has witnessed throughout history the tragic consequences that ensue when a certain subgroup of human beings is denied the full status of humanity for the purpose of research or economic gain.

Summary

A ban on human cloning for both research and reproductive purposes would be the most effective and ethically responsible safeguard against the birth of human beings via cloning. Once human embryos were developed to the stage at which stem cells are present, a primary objective of research cloning, they would also be suitable for implantation.[23] Then, as we have illustrated, the birth of cloned human embryos would be only a short step away; once a cloned human embryo was implanted in a woman's body, no responsible public policy would mandate the termination of pregnancy.

Advocates of a less than comprehensive ban may respond to the preceding arguments by pointing out that all legal bans function imperfectly. Although it is of course true that no law functions perfectly (eg, people continue to murder even though homicide is illegal), a society serious about prohibiting a certain act should adopt laws that will reduce, to the greatest extent possible, the likelihood of that act occurring. Although a comprehensive ban on human cloning may indeed fail to prevent all instances of reproductive cloning, prohibiting not only the implantation but also the creation of cloned human embryos would prove to be a far more effective mechanism for securing a society free from reproductive cloning. A comprehensive cloning ban is also the only policy consistent with the priority medicine should place on the value of human life.

Legal and Ethical Precedent

Historically, extracorporeal human embryos have been afforded certain protections[24] that have received broad support. For example, many present-day proponents of embryo and stem cell research dependent on the destruction of already existing human embryos created during IVF procedures recoil at the prospect of deliberate creation and sacrifice of human embryos.[25] A substantial proportion of the public is also opposed to the creation and destruction of cloned human embryos for research purposes.[26,27]

Policy Timeline

In 1994, the National Institutes of Health proposed that the federal government begin funding research in which human embryos were created for destructive experimentation. This proposal was greeted with nearly universal condemnation from the public, various professional communities, and the major news media.[28,29] President William J. Clinton appropriately chose not to grant federal funding for the creation of embryos for research, and Congress went one step further in passing an amendment prohibiting funding for all research harmful to human embryos.[24] When opposition to this amendment has been voiced by members of Congress, bipartisan support for its prohibition against creating human embryos for destructive research has remained undiminished.[30]

The National Bioethics Advisory Commission's report on cloning human beings,[5] the National Institutes of Health guidelines for embryonic stem cell research,[31] and the Stem Cell Research Act of 2001[32] all explicitly proscribed the special creation of embryos for research purposes. More recently, the President's Council on bioethics unanimously rejected human cloning for purposes of reproduction, while pronouncing a majority recommendation for a moratorium on human cloning for biomedical research.[6]

Ethical Tradition

In addition to constituting a break with US legal tradition and much of public sentiment, research cloning violates existing ethical guidelines designed to protect human subjects.

The Nuremberg Code (1945) stipulates that, "No experiment should be conducted where there is an *a priori* reason to believe that death or disabling injury will occur...."[33] This fundamental principle of nonmaleficence is reflected also in the Declaration of Helsinki (1964, latest revision 2000), the Belmont Report (1979), and the Council of Europe's Convention on Human Rights and Biomedicine (1996), which represent the accumulated wisdom of a half century of reflection on the grave consequences of conscripting nonconsenting human beings for destructive research. Of importance, these moral codes do not exempt human beings at the beginning or end of life as somehow not being under the protection due all human subjects. To the contrary, these codes demand even greater degrees of protection for the most vulnerable of human subjects, eg, children. We maintain that cloned human embryos, as human beings, likewise are vulnerable human subjects and are worthy of such protections.[34,35]

Although a strong lobby to legalize research cloning has been formed by certain scientists, biotechnology firms, and patient advocacy groups, the fact remains that the prospect of creating and destroying human embryos for research purposes has, for valid reasons, been consistently opposed in both the legal and the ethical arenas. It is incumbent on advocates of research cloning who wish to overturn well-established ethical standards to make and defend a sufficient and compelling case. No convincing case has been presented that provides substantive arguments for rejecting the existing set of governing principles that has been carefully formulated and deeply etched into the prevailing ethos of our culture.

A policy allowing research cloning would therefore run counter to US jurisprudence regarding the treatment of human embryos and to the intent of ethical codes designed to protect human subjects in research. Of note, a noncomprehensive ban permitting research cloning would establish, for the first time in US history, a class of human beings created for the sole purpose of experiments that will destroy them and whom ironically it is a crime *not* to destroy. In recognition of this fact, and of research cloning's inherent potential for reproductive applications, the burden of proof must lie on those who wish to justify such a momentous break with legal and ethical precedent. We assert that no such justification has been offered, as defended in the subsequent section.

Appeals to Medical Benefit

In justifying a policy promoting the creation and subsequent destruction of cloned human embryos, advocates of research cloning have frequently turned to the rationale of utility. Utilitarianism in its classic form advocates acting in whatever ways will result in the "greatest good for the greatest number." (Although other forms such as rule utilitarianism have emerged in ethical theory, they are not nearly as influential in public discussion.) Proponents who invoke a utilitarian rationale for research cloning maintain that the lives of nascent human beings should be regarded as having less value than the anticipated health benefits for others and the increased medical knowledge that research cloning would allegedly offer.

Some scientists and biotechnology companies seeking to close in on medical breakthroughs, as well as some patients who hope that such advances will result in a treatment or cure for their particular affliction, have been among the most vocal advocates of research cloning, and the pressure they apply to those who seek to prohibit such a practice is immense.[36–39] Although the goal of medical breakthroughs is laudable and the hopes of patients are certainly understandable, the praiseworthy endeavor to alleviate human suffering does not justify the use of all possible means.

We affirm the importance of weighing consequences as an empirically grounded method for deciding many difficult issues in medical science, but we also recognize that utilitarianism as an ethical theory is incomplete. It has distinct flaws, which even its most sophisticated articulations are incapable of resolving. This is because utilitarian philosophies attempt to sever ethical reasoning from any prior commitment to moral norms other than maximizing utility. Immaterial realities that on independent grounds we know to be valid—such as love, justice, and human dignity—have no validity per se (ie, apart from their consequences in particular situations).

The utility defense of human cloning fails because utilitarianism alone is incompetent to give due regard to human life, which in so many ways (as the practice of medicine reminds us) transcends calculation. Just as there is more to right and wrong than the utilitarian calculus, so there is more to humanity, even wondrous embryonic humanity, than empirical measurements can apprehend. Therefore, human life and death decisions should not be left solely to the impersonal assessment of utilitarian analysis. The skillful surgeon knows to operate with the greatest care near vital structures, and there are some things that the scalpel of utilitarian logic should never be allowed to cut.

In summary, we find appeals to utility, even the utility of medical benefit, to be an insufficient defense of research cloning. In further support of this contention, we offer the following arguments.

Utilitarian Justifications Are Self-defeating

The utilitarian rationale for research cloning is self-defeating. According to utilitarian theory, inflicting some harm in the pursuit of benefit is justifiable only if there is no other less harmful way to secure that benefit. Research cloning fails to meet this criterion because an increasing body of evidence suggests that stem cell research from nonembryonic sources (as well as other methods of tissue repair or regeneration) may hold equal or even greater promise for treating human infirmities.[40–46]

How much utility research cloning would afford is simply unknown. With human embryonic stem cell research still in its infancy and published research on stem cells obtained from cloned human embryos lacking, the claim that the utility of such experimentation justifies a practice long held to be unethical and illegal is extremely weak. Although a few advances to date suggest that such research might yield various therapies in a number of years,[7,47] embryonic stem cell research has been fraught with so many obstacles[48,49] that currently not a single therapy has clearly benefited a patient.[50]

Utility justifications must establish that any harms resulting from a certain practice will be outweighed by the resultant benefits. Furthermore, as utilitarian philosophy has traditionally acknowledged, distant or uncertain benefits should be given less weight than present or certain harms.[51] Research cloning would undoubtedly inflict substantial harms without the certainty of near-term benefit. Human embryos sacrificed for their stem cells would immediately suffer definite harm in that the harvesting of these cells would necessitate their death. By contrast, the speculative benefits of research cloning would likely not occur until decades later, if ever. As such, multitudes of human embryos would likely need to be destroyed before a single patient could benefit from this research.

In the broadest sense, utilitarian justifications of research cloning are self-defeating because they are unduly persuaded by potential good consequences that appear at first glance. However, attempts to justify research cloning must also consider the full range of bad consequences that may not be as immediately apparent but are just as real. For example, women donating their eggs for use in the cloning process would be required to take superovulatory drugs and receive numerous hormone treatments before undergoing the invasive extraction procedure. Such a procedure carries rare yet serious health risks, including ovarian rupture, severe pelvic pain, bleeding into the abdominal cavity, acute respiratory distress, pulmonary embolism, possible increased risk of ovarian cysts and cancers, and potentially infertility.[52–56] Thomas Okarma, president, CEO, and director of Geron Corporation, Menlo Park, Calif, has no ethical qualms about destroying embryos for research but now believes that the potential of research cloning for medical benefit is "vanishingly small"; estimates are that treatment of a single patient via research cloning would require "thousands of [human] eggs on an assembly line."[57] Others have calculated similarly overwhelming estimates.[58] As a result, certain groups of women, such as those economically disadvantaged, would be at great risk of exploitation, a danger of biomedical research that existing ethical codes are designed to prevent.

In addition, if cloned embryos created for the purpose of research were instead implanted into a woman (which we have argued is a highly likely prospect), the probable deformities in, and even death of, the cloned children[8] would constitute great harm for them and result in unspeakable grief for their parents and families.

Moreover, some experimental evidence suggests that embryonic stem cells (especially those obtained from cloned embryos) might actually constitute harm to patients who receive therapies derived from such cells.[40,59,60] Of note, some ethically questionable acts previously justified in the name of utility, for example, transplantation of embryonic cells and fetal tissue into patients, have actually resulted in grave harm, rather than therapeutic benefit.[61,62] For the preceding reasons, an increasing number of scientists doubt that research cloning will ever yield the balance of benefit over harm that some anticipate.[40,63]

Such doubt is buttressed by 2 further observations. First, even if research cloning were to yield the promised cornucopia of medical therapies, some patients who are morally opposed to the destruction of embryonic human life would likely refuse these treatments, unless they are willing to abandon their moral convictions. Thus, conscientious abstention would diminish the utility of this technology. Other patients, desperate for treatment, might compromise their principles using their own form of utilitarian reasoning but at the cost of a troubled conscience. Second, the allocation of funding and other resources to human cloning and other human embryonic technologies would divert previous resources from the development of morally noncontroversial technologies. Because Americans are so divided on this important issue, the most prudential policies will be those that avoid conflict in society by rejecting contentious human cloning agendas and embracing the promising avenues of stem cell research from nonembryonic sources and other therapies that do not depend on the destruction of human embryos. Moreover, supporting research on the development of therapies acceptable to patients with moral convictions opposed to research cloning would benefit both patients and researchers alike because such research programs would be less liable to become entangled in public controversy.

To assert that the utility of research cloning justifies the certain destruction of cloned human embryos created for this purpose is to make a claim that is highly dubious even on utilitarian grounds. Utilitarian calculation, if done correctly, argues against pursuing research cloning. Invoked as a justification for research cloning, it is self-defeating.

Utilitarian Justifications Are Dangerous

Not only is the utilitarian claim to produce the most beneficial outcome inaccurate in the case of research cloning, the attempt to do so is itself unacceptably dangerous.[14] As long as a favorable balance of good over bad consequences ensues for society as a whole, utilitarian logic allows for literally any harm to be inflicted on an individual or a minority group regardless of whether doing so is widely regarded as unethical or even evil.

For example, scientists would acquire some extremely valuable information about the body's response to ionizing radiation by injecting radioactive plutonium into a group of people and then studying them over time. Although a few people might suffer harm, an untold number of persons at risk for occupational exposure to radiation might receive great benefit from the knowledge gained. However, conducting an experiment of this type would definitely be unethical. Lest anyone think that such an experiment would be inconceivable in the United States, it is worth noting that this very protocol was carried out, in the absence of informed consent, at the Los Alamos Scientific Laboratory, New Mexico, in the late 1940s.[64] History provides numerous other examples of unethical medical research, including the experiments conducted at Tuskegee, Ala, at the Willowbrook State School, Staten Island, NY, and during some foreign totalitarian regimes. All these research protocols were defended at the time by utilitarian reasoning but were later recognized to have been unethical. In each case, it became clear that the potential for obtaining benefits from the research, regardless of how important such benefits may have been or who would have gained from them, did not render the research justifiable.

The Purpose of Medicine

The physician, out of concern for the patient who desires a child or a stem cell transplant, may initially be attracted to the argument that a ban on human cloning should allow certain exceptions based on compassion. Of note, however, a medical procedure is not judged to be good simply because a patient may desire it. What the patient perceives as his or her own good must be brought into proper relationship with other levels of good—what is good for the patient, for humanity, and for the cloned human being. Otherwise, an act motivated by unrestrained compassion may become harmful.

Although emotionally compelling, compassion is by itself an insufficient guide to ethical behavior. Rather, wisdom looks both to compassion and to understanding. Compassion is not to be a moral law unto itself but most be subject to moral analysis, based on sound reasons, and carried out with forethought of consequences.

If human cloning for biomedical research were to become a reality, physicians would be called on to perform the procedures to extract oocytes from healthy women for the purpose of generating cloned embryos. Physicians would face the temptation to implant some of those embryos as treatment for infertility (with possible risk to their careers if a partial ban on cloning were enacted). If it proves impossible to grow replacement organs from embryonic stem cells in vitro, physicians could be called on to implant into women cloned embryos to be grown to the fetal stage and later terminated to serve as transplant donors. Physicians, in prescribing drugs, vaccines, or cellular therapies developed from research on cloned embryos or their stem cells, would occasionally incur complicity with the prerequisite destruction of early human life. Physicians would inherit the strange tasks of counseling patients about the option of receiving treatments derived from clones of themselves and of informing patients morally opposed to receiving such treatments that more expensive noncloning alternatives might not be covered by their insurance plans.

Considered realistically, human cloning fails to qualify as a healing act. The physician's integrity as a healer requires that he or she always act to preserve life, and never by means of human death. The intention to heal can in no way justify the act of terminating the life of another human being. Accordingly, physicians consider nonmaleficence.[65] Such ordering of ethical priorities in medicine has long placed the profession of medicine on higher moral ground than that reachable by pragmatic rationalizations. This is why Hippocrates' prime maxim, "First, do no harm,"[66] has endured since antiquity as a guiding principle among physicians who, by honoring it, have earned their patients' trust.

To rewrite medical ethics to permit human cloning would ensnare physicians in a perilous compromise of professional standards. To acquiesce to human embryonic cloning would be to disregard, to an unprecedented degree, the value of new human life. Human cloning would also represent a decided step toward the devaluing of humanity universally because justifications of human cloning research disturbingly imagine a category of dismissible human life. Such a designation is utterly foreign to the Hippocratic ethic, which respects human beings at all stages of life.

Although the potential for eventual health benefits from research cloning has been vigorously advanced, its violation of human dignity by treating nascent human life as no more valuable than an expendable means to others' ends falls short of the purpose for which medicine exists. The medical good aims not only to improve physiologic function and to secure the good as perceived by the patient but also strives to safeguard and promote the higher good for the patient.[67] This higher good includes the preservation of the dignity of humans as humans, for which the physician is obligated to guard the welfare of the most vulnerable of human beings, including the cloned human embryo.

Conclusion

Human cloning, for whatever purpose, represents an abuse of scientific freedom, not its realization. This new technology should adhere to the standard that science should always serve humanity, never that a segment of humanity would be created to serve science. As history has conspicuously recorded, no program sacrificing those at the margins of humanity to science has ever stood the test of time. Ethical reflection always reaches, in due course, the conclusion that the least of human beings deserve the care and concern that the medical profession presumes is due all human beings. Whether the ethical cinder of human cloning will lodge in the eye of society's conscience is an issue still within the reach of sensible preventive intervention.

For the sake of their patients, as well as the future of humanity, we urge health care professionals to oppose all forms of human cloning. In keeping with the Hippocratic ethic, we recommend that biomedical research on non-embryonic stem cells be pursued and funded aggressively. We also commend legislation and policies at all levels that will protect people from the unfavorable outcomes of human cloning, both now and for generations to come. Only a ban prohibiting both research and reproductive cloning will offer such protection.

We thank Mr. Russell C. DiSilvestro for his critical review of the submitted manuscript.

References

1. Mayer PW (Associated Press). Doc says clone will be born soon. CBS News Web site. November 27, 2002. Available at: http://www.cbsnews.com/stories/2002/12/27/tech/main534440.shtml. Accessibility verified June 19, 2003.
2. Ritter M. Company claims birth of human clone; experts are skeptical. The Augusta Chronicle Web site. December 27, 2002. Available at: http://www.augusta

chronicle.com/stories/122802/tec_clone1.shtml. Accessibility verified June 19, 2003.

3. Cibelli JB, Lanza RP, West MD, Ezzell C. The first human cloned embryo. *Sci Am.* 2002;286:44–51.

4. Cibelli JB, Klessling AA, Cunniff K, Richards C, Lanza RP, West MD. Rapid communication: somatic cell nuclear transfer in humans; pronuclear and early embryonic development. *E-biomed J Regenerative Med.* 2001;2:25–31.

5. *Cloning Human Beings: Report and Recommendations of the National Bioethics Advisory Commission.* Rockville, Md: The President's Council on Bioethics; June 1997:17–18.

6. Kass LR. *Human Cloning and Human Dignity: The Report of the President's Council on Bioethics.* New York, NY: PublicAffairs, 2002.

7. Committee on the Biological and Biomedical Applications of Stem Cell Research. Board on Life Sciences, National Research Council, Board on Neuroscience and Behavioral Health, Institute of Medicine. *Stem Cells and the Future of Regenerative Medicine.* Washington, DC: National Academy Press, 2001.

8. Jaenisch R, Wilmer I. Developmental biology: don't clone humans! *Science.* 2001;291:2552.

9. "Cloning" humans is a turn off to most Americans: embryonic cloning for research is also opposed [Gallup poll analyses]. May 16, 2002.

10. Westphal SP. Cloned monkey embryos are a "gallery of horrors." *New Scientist.* December 12, 2001.

11. Wilmut I. Are there any normal cloned mammals? *Nat Med.* 2002;8:215–216.

12. Cheshire WP. Toward a common language of human dignity. *Ethics Med.* 2002;18(2):7–10.

13. Forsythe CD. Human cloning and the constitution. *Valparaiso Univ Law Rev.* 1998;32:469–542.

14. Kilner JF. Human cloning. In: Kilner JF, Cunningham PC, Hager WD, eds. *The Reproduction Revolution: A Christian Appraisal of Sexuality, Reproductive Technologies, and the Family.* Grand Rapids, Mich: WB Eerdmans Publishing Co., 2000:124–139.

15. Kass LR. Preventing a brave new world: why we should ban human cloning now. *New Repub.* 2001;224:30–39.

16. Andrews LB. *The Clone Age: Adventures in the New World of Reproductive Technology.* New York, NY: Henry Holt & Co., 1999:74.

17. Disposition of abandoned embryos: ASRM Ethics Committee report. Birmingham, Ala: American Society of Reproductive Medicine, 1997.

18. Boiani M, Eckardt S, Schöler HR, McLaughlin KJ. Oct4 distribution and level in mouse clones: consequences for pluripotency. *Genes Dev.* 2002;16:1209–1219.

19. Solter D. Cloning v. clowning. *Genes Dev.* 2002:16:1163–1166.

20. Atomic Energy Act, 42 USC §2077 and 42 USC §2014(us) (1954).

21. Associated Press. Sen. Smith changes stance on stem cells. Northwest News Channel 8 Web site. May 6, 2002.

22. Langman J. *Medical Embryology.* 4th ed. Baltimore, Md: Williams & Wilkins, 1981:1.

23. Smith WJ. Cloning and Congress: no ban is better than a phony ban. *The Weekly Standard.* July 1, 2002.

24. Consolidated Appropriations Act §510, Pub L No. 108-7 (2003).

25. Krauthammer C. Research cloning? No. *Washington Post.* May 10, 2002:A37.
26. Poll on American support of human cloning. Washington, DC: Stop Human Cloning: April 22, 2002.
27. Cloning opposed, stem cell research narrowly supported: public makes distinctions on genetic research. Washington, DC: The Pew Research Center for the People & the Press and The Pew Forum on Religion & Public Life; April 9, 2002. Available at: http://www.pewtrusts.com/pdf/vf_pew_research_religion_cloning.pdf. Accessibility verified July 11, 2003.
28. Embryos: drawing the line [editorial]. *Washington Post.* October 2, 1994;sect C:6.
29. Embryo research is inhuman [editorial]. *Chicago Sun-Times.* October 10, 1994:25.
30. Lowey N. 142 Congressional Record at H7343. July 11, 1996. Quoted in: Americans oppose cloning human embryos for research. Available at: www.nrlc.org/Killing_Embryos/factsheetcloning.html. Accessibility verified July 1, 2003.
31. National Institutes of Health. National Institutes of Health Guidelines for Research Using Human Pluripotent Stem Cells. *65 Federal Register* 51976-51981 (2000).
32. *Amendment to the Stem Cell Research Act of 2001: Referred to the Committee on Health, Education, Labor, and Pensions,* 107th Cong. 1st Sess (April 5, 2001) (statement of Arlen Specter, senator).
33. Annas GJ, Grodin MA, eds. *The Nazi Doctors and the Nuremberg Code: Human Rights in Human Experimentation.* New York, NY: Oxford University Press, 1992:2.
34. Smith T. *Ethics in Medical Research: A Handbook of Good Practice.* Cambridge, England: Cambridge University Press, 1999:278.
35. Ramsey Colloqaium. The inhuman use of human beings: a statement on embryo research. *First Things.* 1995;49:17–21.
36. Ezzell C. Stem cell showstopper? *Sci Am.* 2001;285:27.
37. Solter D, Gearhardt J. Putting stem cells to work. *Science.* 1999;283:1468–1470.
38. Lanza RP, Cibelli JB, West MD. Human therapeutic cloning. *Nat Med.* 1999;5:975–977.
39. Lanza RP, Cibelli JB, West MD. Prospects for the use of nuclear transfer in human transplantation. *Nat Biotechnol.* 1999;17:1171–1174.
40. Treating disease with adult stem cells and embryonic stem cells: adult stem cells more promising, more successful. Available at: www.stemcellresearch.org/facts/quotes2.htm. Accessibility verified June 27, 2003.
41. Lillge W. The case for adult stem cell research. *21st Century Science & Technology Magazine.* Winter 2001–2002.
42. Orlic D, Kujstura J, Chimenti S, et al. Bone marrow cells regenerate infarcted myocardium. *Nature.* 2001;410:701–705.
43. Verfaillie CM. Adult stem cells: assessing the case for pluripotency. *Trends Cell Biol.* 2002;12:502–508.
44. Jiang Y, Varssen B, Leavik T, Blackstad M, Reyes M, Verfaillie CM. Multipotent progenitor cells can be isolated from potential marine bone marrow, muscle, and brain. *Exp Hematol.* 2002;30:896–904.
45. Lu D, Sanberg PR, Mahmood A, et al. Intravenous administration of human umbilical cord blood reduces neurological deficit in the rat after traumatic brain injury. *Cell Transplant.* 2002;11:275–281.
46. Chen J, Sanberg PR, Li Y, et al. Intravenous administration of human umbilical cord blood reduces behavioral deficits after stroke in rats. *Stroke.* 2001;32: 2682–2688.

47. US Department of Health and Human Services, National Institutes of Health. *Stem Cells: Scientific Progress and Future Research Directions.* Available at: http://www.nih .gov/news/stemcell/scireport.htm. Accessibility verified June 27, 2003.

48. Vogel G. Cell biology: stem cells: new excitement, persistent questions. *Science.* 2000;290:1672–1674.

49. Embryonic stem cell research: a reality check. March 2002. Available at: www .stemcellresearch.org/facts/quotes3.htm. Accessibility verified July 10, 2003.

50. University of Wisconsin–Madison. Clinical application still years away. Available at: www.news.wisc.edu/packages/stem_cells/index.html?get-patients. Accessibility verified June 27, 2003.

51. Sidgwick H. *The Methods of Ethics,* 6th ed. New York, NY: Macmillan Co. 1901.

52. International Center for Technology Assessment. Six reasons why progressives should not support the Harkin-Specter bill (S. 1893) on human cloning. Available at: www.cloninginformation.org/info/icta-why_oppose_harkin-specter.htm. Accessibility verified June 27, 2003.

53. Norsigian J. Statement before the US Senate Health, Education, Labor and Pensions Committee. March 5, 2002.

54. Andrews L, Nelkin D. *Body Bazaar: The Market for Human Tissue in the Biotechnology Age.* New York, NY: Crown Publishers, 2001.

55. Venn A, Watson L, Bruinsma F, Giles G, Healy D. Risk of cancer after use of fertility drugs with *in-vitro* fertilization. *Lancet.* 1999;354:1586–1590.

56. Delvigne A, Rozenberg S. Epidemiology and prevention of ovarian hyperstimulation syndrome (OHSS): a review. *Hum Reprod Update.* 2002;8:559–577.

57. Gellone D. Clone profit? Unlikely. *LA Times.* May 10, 2002. Business section.

58. Smith WJ. Practical council: important stuff from the Kass Commission. *National Review Online.* August 13, 2002.

59. Odorico JS, Kaufman DS, Thomson JA. Multilineage differentiation from human embryonic stem cell lines. *Stem Cells.* 2001;19:193–204.

60. Scientific problems with using embryonic stem cells. November 2001. Available at: www.stemcellresearch.org/facts/escproblems.htm. Accessibility verified July 10, 2003.

61. Folkerth RD, Durso R. Survival and proliferation of nonneural tissues; with obstruction of cerebral ventricles, in a parkinsonian patient treated with fetal allografts. *Neurology.* 1996;46:1219–1225.

62. Freed CR, Greene PE, Breeze RE, et al. Transplantation of embryonic dopamine neurons for severe Parkinson's disease. *N Engl J Med.* 2001;344:710–719.

63. Aldhouse P. Can they rebuild us? *Nature.* 2001;410:622–625.

64. *Advisory Committee on Human Radiation Experiments—Final Report.* Washington, DC: US Government Printing Office. GPO Stock No. 061-000-00-848-9.

65. Beauchamp TL, Childress JF. *Principles of Biomedical Ethics,* 4th ed. New York, NY: Oxford University Press: 1994:189–258, 271–287.

66. Hippocrates. *Epidemics.* Book I, sect XI.

67. Pellegrino ED. The internal morality of clinical medicine: a paradigm for the ethics of the helping and healing professions. *J Med Philos.* 2001;26:559–579.

Essay

The Author: Stephen S. Hall

The Hastings Center is an independent, nonpartisan, and nonprofit bioethics research institute founded in 1969 to explore fundamental and emerging questions in health care, biotechnology, and the environment.

The Center's research projects are diverse; recent topics range from genetic paternity testing to newborn screening to palliative care. The work is carried out by interdisciplinary teams that convene at the Center's home, overlooking the Hudson River, to frame and examine issues that inform professional practice, public conversation, and social policy. The *Hastings Center Report* brings the best scholarship and commentary in bioethics to readers worldwide.

Stephen S. Hall is a contributing writer at the *New York Times Magazine.* His pieces have also appeared in the *New York Times* Book Review, the *Atlantic Monthly, Smithsonian, Technology Review, Science,* and other periodicals. He is the author of three critically acclaimed books about contemporary science.

The following essay appeared in the *Hastings Center Report* in the May/June 2003 edition.

Eve Redux: The Public Confusion over Cloning

As any well-informed newspaper reader knows by now, the white-robed prophet Rael (neé Claude Varilhon) is a soft-spoken, French-born, Canadian-based apostle of cloning technology who claims to have been conceived by a human mother and a space alien. The former race car driver also claims to have had two encounters with aliens in the 1970s and to have boarded their spaceship. He believes that humans were created by cloning techniques developed by alien civilizations, and he has established a sect called the Raelians to promote human reproductive cloning, to the point of forming a private company called Clonaid. Rael considers himself a half-brother to Jesus Christ and requests that visitors address him as "Your Holiness."

In the calculus of most working journalists, the combination of UFO-ology, prophetic megalomania, and alien conception would ordinarily land Rael and his followers on the gentle, lowland slopes of any credibility curve. And yet a steady stream of writers—sometimes from prominent publications—have made the pilgrimage to "U.F.O.-land" in Valcourt, Quebec, to interview Rael (apparently some even agreed to submit questions in advance and call him "Your Holiness"). For its loony entertainment value, Rael and his be-robed colleagues make for an irresistible human interest story, but that also helps explain why Raelian claims to have created a cloned human child named "Eve" received such widespread and frenzied attention in the press in December 2002. Although the sect did not provide a shred of scientific evidence to back up its claim, the news prompted a familiar, even reflexive cultural reaction: social conservatives fulminated, the president reiterated his absolute opposition to all forms of cloning, and respectable scientists were left shaking their heads.

In a larger sense, that reaction helps explain why the national debate on cloning and stem cell research has so often spun off the road and into a ditch of techno-social voyeurism, ideological rhetoric, and political histrionics. While reporting for my book *Merchants of Immortality,* I've been a front-row observer to many events in this debate, and I've been struck by several recurrent themes; overreaction by both the press and politicians to sensational (and often unsubstantiated) claims, the absence of critical judgment in assessing these claims, the role of private entities (whether biotech companies or sects) in setting the tempo and terms of the public debate with their announcements, and a devaluation of science in the overall discourse. The public, and policymakers, have been poorly served by the quality of this important bioethical discussion.

A key moment in this debate occurred in August 2001, at a workshop on cloning sponsored by the National Academy of Sciences, because it revealed an illuminating gap between the rigorous, devil-in-the-details ethos of science and the rather more superficial world of public perception. Rudolf Jaenisch, a biologist at the Whitehead Institute, described derailed molecular studies that identified a series of glitches embedded in the DNA of cloned mice. These so-called "epigenetic" flaws—aberrations in the regulation or expression of genes but not in the genetic sequence of the genes themselves—could trigger arrested development or serious post-natal dysfunction. After Jaenisch laid out the data, a member of the National Academy panel directed a question at Brigitte Boisselier, the head scientist of Clonaid, who had previously described the Raelians' intent to clone human babies. What, she was asked, was Clonaid doing to identify the sort of epigenetic flaws that Jaenisch's group had described in the scientific literature?

Boisselier dipped her head politely, smiled reassuringly, and announced in an eerily lilting voice that Clonaid scientists had already developed molecular assays to test for ten such epigenetic flaws in human embryos. The claim was absurd. I was sitting in the audience that day, and almost fell out of my chair. Developing reliable molecular probes for such potential genetic aberrations would tax the ingenuity and resources of any top-flight laboratory, probably for years. Several members of the NAS panel of experts reacted with an unusually public display of scorn to Boisselier's claim, rolling their eyes or shaking their heads in disgust. "Ludicrous," grunted Alan Trounson, an Australian in vitro fertilization expert.

Yet the preposterousness of Boisselier's claim is, for most lay readers, probably lost in the fog of scientific minutiae, and that is the haze into which much of the substance of this debate has disappeared. I had expected Trounson's bluntly dismissive tone to permeate news accounts of the National Academy forum the following day, but I was surprised. While the accounts were skeptical, they were politely so, and more attention was focused on the intent of the would-be cloners than on a clear-eyed assessment of their chances of success. And so it hardly came as a surprise that when Brigitte Boisselier held a press conference on 27 December 2002, to announce the birth of the world's first human clone, the press greeted the news in similar fashion; it dutifully reported the claim, but it remained perhaps a little too polite and a little slow to contextualize and critically assess the scientific claims. The claim, however dubious, made front-page news around the world, and served

as a global infomercial for Raelian philosophy. "Some media experts say we got between $600 million and $700 million worth of coverage," Rael later boasted, "and
I did nothing," Neither, apparently, did the Raelian cloners. By January 2003. Rael
was also conceding to some interviewers that he couldn't deny the baby clone was
a hoax.

In one sense, the purported birth of "Eve," the first human clone, was an aberra-
tion: within days of the initial claim, the event had the odor of a hoax—as it should
have had to anyone with passing familiarity with either the technical vicissitudes of
cloning ("somatic cell nuclear transfer," to use the technical term) or the savvy self-
marketing of the Raelians. But in another sense, the short, nasty, and brutal life of this
unconfirmable story is emblematic of precisely the types of events that have con-
vulsed the national debate about cloning and, earlier, embryonic stem cells over the
past few years. Each such revelation triggers a drearily familiar set-piece: lawmakers
threaten legislation, social conservatives express moral outrage, scientists run for
cover, and the public is left feeling fearful and confused.

The public debate on cloning, as on embryonic stem cells, has repeatedly been
driven by these extra-scientific (not to say extraterrestrial) announcements mediated by the press. These events undoubtedly qualify as news, and yet at the same
time do not qualify as science—if we understand the latter to be a rigorously executed, socially responsible, and peer-reviewed published piece of experimentation
that, pending reproducibility, at least has the whiff of truth about it. If the ethical
implications of this research are too important to be left to scientists alone, as many
observers have correctly asserted, it is also true that the scientific details of this research are too important to be misunderstood, misrepresented, or dismissed by non-
scientists—that includes not only members of the media, but also politicians,
ideologues, entrepreneurs, bioethicists, and even the scientists who sometimes imply
too strenuously that therapeutic cloning and seem cell therapy will surely cure human
disease. The first casualty in a heated political debate about science is complexity,
and modern biological science is nothing if not a monument to complexity.

When I was a young aspiring writer living in Rome, I was asked by a prominent
business newspaper to cover financial news, a topic about which I had no training and
no knowledge. The request came on a Friday. Over the weekend, I purchased a copy
of "Teach Yourself Economics." On Monday, I began filing dispatches.

I mention this because on any given story, especially on technical topics like stem
cells and cloning, news coverage will reflect a broad spectrum of expertise and in-
experience, and this becomes a factor in the public life of a technological idea. In
point of fact, the Eve announcement received judicious and skeptical treatment
in major newspapers, which reported the "news" (as indeed is their mission to do)
but kept this dubious claim off the front page. Nonetheless, a certain politesse operates in objective journalism that renders critical assessment subservient to even-
handedness. I would argue that critical judgment—not technical understanding, not
explanatory skill, not even literary talent—is the single most important quality for
anyone who aspires to write about science and technology; it is also, by far, the most

difficult skill to acquire. The absence of critical judgment, the demands of competition, and the unremitting pressure of deadlines helps create the kind of media
epiphenomena that characterized the cloning of Eve and the earlier announcement
of the creation of cloned human embryos by the Massachusetts company Advanced
Cell Technology.

Critical judgment becomes especially important in this arena because so much
information is obscured by a proprietary fog; "news" is often released without prior
peer-review publication, and always with an eye toward maximum publicity. Much
of cloning and stem cell research is conducted by the private sector or with private
funding outside the purview of the NIH: there is no federal pressure or moral sua-
sion to be candid with the public. Indeed, when bioethicists who advise private companies refuse to discuss ongoing research, as has happened in my experience, they
promote (however reluctantly) the privatization of a national debase that requires
absolute transparency.

In the last year or so, several bioethicists I respect have intimated that science
writers too often function as mindless cheerleaders of technological innovation, that
they are camp followers who plunge headlong in the direction of Progress while leaving their moral compasses at home. Speaking only for myself, I do not see my role as
that of a cheerleader, but I plead guilty to a fascination with serious intellectual inquiry, aided by powerful technologies, to attain new knowledge, new understanding, and new plateaus of appreciation for the natural world in which we live. In fact,
over the years I've managed to offend many of my secular humanist friends (my
background is in English literature) by suggesting that science represents the last
avant garde in contemporary society. By that I mean not only a loosely institutionalized quest for the new, but a kind of New that has the power to force society to rethink
some of its most basic premises. Many of the bioethical debates we are now having
attest to the power of the changes wrought, or promised, by contemporary biology,
and in fact were anticipated many decades ago by the American philosopher John
Dewey. In his 1922 book *Human Nature and Conduct,* John Dewey wrote, "situations
into which change and the unexpected enter are a challenge to intelligence to create
new principles. Morals must be a growing science if it is to be a science at all, not
merely because all truth has not yet been appropriated by the mind of man, but because life is a moving affair in which old moral truth ceases to apply." To the extent
that science, too, is a moving affair, it constantly challenges the traditional notion
that moral wisdom is fixed and absolute.

Setting aside for a moment the suspicion that so much indignant ink, legislative
breast-beating and ideological emotion about Eve may have been expended on a non-
event, there were very good scientific reasons to suspect the Raelian claim was a hoax.
Indeed, the scientific odds against a successful human clone—and by success, I mean
the creation of a viable, genetically intact embryo that develops into a normal, healthy
child—are overwhelming. The success rate in animal cloning experiments varies
from species to species, but has always been very low, on the order of 3 or 4 per cent.
In primates—the animals closest to humans on the phylogenetic ladder—hundreds
of cloning experiments have failed to produce a single viable embryo, much less a

live birth. Anyone who has sat through a recitation of this dismal data at a scientific meeting (and I have) becomes an instant agnostic about the prospects for a healthy human clone any time soon.

An equally distressing media circus occurred in November 2001, when researchers at ACT, including Jose Cibelli, announced they had created "the first human cloned embryo." The disconnect between the scientific and cultural appraisal of this experiment underscores the problem of critical judgment. While Harold Varmus, former director of the NIH, and Harvard biologist Douglas Melton were writing that the experiment "showed little experimental progress and advanced no new ideas," the editor of *Scientific American*, which published an "exclusive" account of the work, was telling reporters the ACT research represented "one of the major landmarks of biotechnology achievement in the past decade."

This shear between public and professional perception brings us closer to the underlying structural flaw of the entire debate. The National Institutes of Health has been relegated, by politics and long-standing social divisions, to a diminished role in supporting, monitoring, and shaping stem cell and cloning research (a role to which is has been consigned in reproductive medicine for more than twenty-five years). As a result, this area of science and technology has been driven by private enterprise rather than public accountability, lurid rhetoric rather than the rigor of scientific fact.

The private sector development of in vitro fertilization in the United States grew directly out of the failure of the government to act in the 1970s on recommendations by a pioneering bioethics panel, the National Commission for the Protection of Human Subjects of Biomedical and Behavioral Research, which concluded that fetal and embryo research was a legitimate area of scientific inquiry worthy of federal funding but that such research required the consideration and approval of an Ethics Advisory Board. As many readers of the *Hastings Center Reports* no doubt recall, the Ethics Advisory Board's recommendation to support research in reproductive medicine was never implemented, and that goes a long way toward explaining why we're having the same old disagreements today, focused though they are on a newer technology. Although the EAB considered, and ultimately approved, federal funds for in vitro fertilization research (including the study of embryos created by IVF that might ultimately be sacrificed). Patricia Harris, then secretary of HEW, refused to grant final approval, and then allowed the charter of the ethics board to expire—even though federal regulations required in approval for certain types of research to proceed. The practical effect of this limbo has been that reproductive medicine, including research on infertility and fertilization technology, was ceded to the private sector, and very few researchers in reproductive medicine sought funding from the NIH. That appears to be the evolving case with embryonic stem cells as well. A highly placed NIH official recently confided to me that the agency has been surprised that so few researchers have applied for seem cell funding.

Although the privatization of research has its roots in the 1970s, history has repeated itself more recently. Corporate funding for human embryonic stem cell research grew directly our of the Clinton administration's famous repudiation of the

NIH's 1994 Human Embryo Research Panel report, which advocated federal funding for a broad spectrum of embryo research, including the creation of embryos for research purposes. The flight to private funding sources accelerated when Congress in 1996 passed a ban on federal funding for any form of embryo research a ban enacted without public debate by conservative Republicans in the House of Representatives.

This decades-long ability of politics to trump expert scientific judgment has shaped the rhetorical environment in which our current discussions take place. Scientific fact and judgment have increasingly been estranged from the conversation. Much of the "debate" over embryonic stem cell research, for example, hinged on assertions that adult stem cell research promises the same clinical benefits without any of the same ethical vexations. Those assertions are at their core scientifically based, with profound medical implications for all Americans, and yet you would be hard-pressed to find more than a handful of scientists who subscribe to that argument.

One of those scientists, David Prentice of Indiana State University, advised senators, testified in Congress, and was quoted in countless media reports, yet he had not published a single peer-reviewed research article on stern cells and in fact had been turned down for an NIH grant for stem cell-related work. As Thomas Murray has suggested, the opponents of embryonic stem cell research may have learned a tactic from the tobacco industry: that of creating the appearance of a scientific controversy or disagreement when in reality there was none. In a 2001 report on stern cell research, the NIH reflected the judgment of the overwhelming majority of scientists in suggesting that it is too early in the scientific story to choose one technology over the other.

This same devaluation of scientific knowledge has long been a feature of the cloning debate. Reproductive cloning (to create children) is widely and legitimately opposed, not least because of safety issues, but it has become rhetorically coupled to therapeutic, or research, cloning (which seeks to create short-lived embryos from which embryonic stem cells can be harvested, for both research and perhaps therapeutic applications). Opponents of cloning argue that research cloning will inevitably lead to reproductive cloning, and that the instrumentalization of nascent human life is a moral line that should never be crossed. But these important moral concerns hinge on scientific distinctions that are either misunderstood or largely ignored.

Representative David Weldon, who has sponsored several bills in the House of Representatives to ban all forms of human cloning (including cloning for research), asserted during a House debate in July 2001. "The biological fact is, and I say this as a scientist and as a physician, that [cloned embryos] are indistinguishable from a human embryo that has been created by sexual fertilization." In terms of genetic integrity and life potential, at the very least, this is demonstrably incorrect. A "natural" embryo has, at best, a 28 per cent chance of resulting in a human life, and perhaps as little as 14 per cent—much less potential than many people are aware. But a cloned embryo has, according to current knowledge, even less potential. Part of the reason is that the vast majority of cloned embryos appear to be genetically flawed. Research by Rudolf Jaenisch's lab has documented that many genes in the cloned embryo are dysfunctional, probably due to incomplete reprogramming.

These scientific facts about the minimal "nascence" of nascent life should inform our thinking about the moral significance of embryos as they cross successive developmental thresholds, which in turn should inform discussions about the ethical acceptibility of this research. For the most part, they have not:

Ironically, the rise of in vitro fertilization has resulted in the creation of hundreds of thousands of human embryos that, if not strictly for research purposes, are destined to be discarded as a by-product of medical utility. By some estimates, American fertility clinics created as many as 600,000 embryos between 1991 and 2001, and most were destroyed—a price society appears willing to pay to treat infertility. It is hard to argue that creating cloned human embryos for research purposes, with their even more limited potential for life and their considerable potential to relieve human suffering represents a significantly different moral threshold.

That moral paradox brings me to a final observation. I've been struck, and a little disappointed, by how much the current debate has been driven by the promise of medical utility rather than by the value of basic knowledge. Although the possible human medical benefits of embryonic stem cells and therapeutic cloning are not difficult to surmise, equal value lies in basic research on human development—a compelling biological mystery that has fascinated humanity's keenest minds since Aristotle. While some have made the argument that to instrumentalize this nascent human life is an affront to human dignity. I see it differently to refrain from plumbing the mystery of human life, on the only planet known to possess any life at all, when we have the ethical infrastructure to do it both wisely and well, seems to mark a retreat from the way we have pursued knowledge for many centuries. When anatomists first began to conduct human dissections during the dawn of the Renaissance, it provoked great moral anguish and a sense of violation that, at some level, must have seemed like an affront to human dignity. But then as now, the preservation of an abstract notion of human dignity may have as a material cost the willful preservation of human ignorance and a perverse perpetuation of human suffering.

Until we bring more rigor and less emotion to our discussion of these new technologies, our public policy will again and again become hostage to homes, publicity stunts, and rhetorical excess. Late in March 2003, Brigitte Boisselier and Rael were back in the news, popping up in Sao Paulo, Brazil, to announce that Clonaid had successfully created five human clones. As before, they did not produce any scientific evidence to support the claim, and as before, the press dutifully passed along the news. Why Sao Paulo? As the Reuters account noted. Boisselier and Rael "were in Brazil to present Rael's book on cloning."

Scholarly Publication

The Author: Seymour W. Itzkoff

Mankind Quarterly is a professional and scholarly journal that deals with both physical and cultural anthropology, including related subjects such as psychology, demography, genetics, linguistics, and mythology. It is published by the Institute for the Study of Man.

Seymour W. Itzkoff has been a professor at Smith College since 1965. He is a true renaissance man, trained in music, education, and the philosophy of science. Itzkoff is the author of a book on Ernst Cassirer, another on Emanuel Feuermann (a virtuoso cellist), several books on education theory, a four-book series on the evolution of intelligence, and three (as of 1995) additional books on group intelligence and its national and international implications.

The following article was published in Fall 2003.

Intervening with Mother Nature:
The Ethics of Human Cloning

The author examines reactionary ethical objections to research in medical genetics with particular regard to human reproduction, and selects the debate over the ethics of human cloning as occupying a central position for further analysis.

Key Words: Medical genetics: human reproduction; germ-line intervention; genetic disease; intelligence; human cloning eugenics.

Leon R. Kass, Chairman of the President's Council on Bioethics, has stated that "Cloning not only carries high risks of bodily harm for the cloned child, but it also threatens the dignity of human procreation, giving one generation unprecedented genetic control over the next. It is the first step toward a eugenic world in which children become objects of manipulation and products of will.[1]

As a scientific experiment in bio-cloning may not work. Kass may be right. The bodily harm may be too great to yield a viable and functioning human being. We do not know, but we will try, despite the objections of officialdom. What is just as important as this most recent meddling with Mother Nature is that, if successful, human clones will constitute a truly remarkable, if not a revolutionary break with our reproductive sexual heritage.

Before we cry out with revulsion, our churches, synagogues, mosques, echoing lamentations of the power brokers and the religious conservatives fear less the poisonous smog of the internal combustion engine or the deafening cacophony of the "boom box" need to see what is behind the Current panic. Is it a real concern for human welfare or is it the politics of reaction?

We humans have tampered with nature ever since we experimented with the fermenting of grapes, or plunged a stuck pig into a blazing fire. Edward Jenner in the late century intuited the solution to the scourge of smallpox. Inoculate a related weak strain, cowpox, to prevent a truly horrifying plagues of small pox. Jenner's scientific insight empowered us, in the medical sciences as elsewhere in technology and engineering, to shape nature so that it might serve the good of the human species.

Certainly, "giving one generation genetic control over the next" is an ambiguous phrase. For, in inoculating children against disease we will [see] the softening of the randomness of disease and death in terms of the demographic profile of the next generation. As such, we exercise a measure of control over the genetic nature of subsequent generations.

---

[1]Kass, Leon. "How One Clone Leads to Another." *The New York Times*, 1/24/03.

During the twentieth century, two world wars and countless genocidal events selectively affected the most talented and productive minorities in the world, eliminating by the millions their genetic profiles from the generations that would follow.
The twentieth-century contribution to the future of the species was the destruction
worldwide of approximately 200 millions of our most talented, intelligent, productive humans.[2]

By the actions of human will, politically nihilistic and barbarous, we have reshaped
the genetic nature of future human generations throughout the planet.

The unprecedented nature of genetic transmission through cloning might be revolutionary both in technology and in character. The future impact of a successful
cloning methodology is difficult to foretell, were there to be large-scale adoption of
such asexual reproduction. It could be a widely accepted international methodology
for the conscious improvement of the species, i.e., eugenics. Else, an elitist preoccupation of the few. What we do know is that disease, war, genocide, even the subsi-
dization of life at the edge, the medically salvaged, genetic carriers of disabilities have
long become clear interventions with nature that allow the present generation to
shape the genetic nature of the future. Cloning Humans?

The debate within the scientific community focuses on the use of experimentally-
created (cloned) and normally conceived embryos in their first few days of existence
from which we might harvest colonies of stems cells, the root structures out of which
so many other organs are formed. The pro-cloning argument is that these stem cells
represent the key to the advancement of medicine. A wide variety of possible cures
now becomes possible, from the creation of new organs without fear of their being internally rejected, to the rehabilitation of people with differing neurological disabilities. Indeed, the future is so open-ended concerning the possibilities for the use of
these cells that a vast new area of rehabilitative medicine might thereby be born.

These techniques have already been shown to have produced cloned animals that
are designed for certain uses, such as cows, for their specialized milk production.
Most recently, a mule was cloned. Despite Western Europeans' aversion to the new
and their attempts to boycott genetically modified crops, these latter are being widely
planted. The planting of such crops, which are immune to disease, insect resistant,
is exponentially expanding in Asia, thus threatening to put an end to starvation.[3]
The international revulsion in the U.S. is also great. President George Bush in 2002
banned government financing of embryo research. Clearly, ideology reigns.

The possibility of creating cloned humans identical with the parent cells has mobilized officialdom, philosophers/ethicists, and theologians, from around the world.
They rightly fear that banning cloning in the United States and in much of the West
will not be enough. Other, dissenting and developed nations might not see cloning
as a priori negative. In China, Israel, Russia, Japan, nations with the medical and
technological wherewithal to attempt to clone a human being, the issue is still open.
Once the cat is out of the bag officially, for instance, successful human clones, we

---

[2]Rummel, R. J. 1994. Death by Government, New Brunswick, N.J.: Transaction.
[3]Barboza, D. 2003. "Development of Biotech Crops Is Booming in Asia," *The New York Times*,
2/21/03.

will be forced to follow suit, else take up the rear in medical research. But even if these potentially-dissident nations put a halt to such work in their government-sponsored labs, there are many free lancers ready to fill the breach.

Even in the U.S., where the House of Representatives, religious and so-called "ethicist" organizations have declared the attempt to clone a human as immoral—but not in the Senate—it could be accomplished. Should cloning be banned?

Most opposition to human cloning now focuses on the research build up to the creation of stem cells by the joining of the sexual cells of normal humans either within the body as a result of sexual congress, or in vitro, as a result of external test tube insemination of the egg cell by donated sperm. Many of these "created" embryos are the remains of the multiple embryos produced by couples in their attempts to effect normal pregnancies and birth. They are usually frozen, to be brought back later for genetic analysis and implantation in the female for a normal pregnancy. Many of these embryos become "extras." One implantation becomes successful, and the numerous embryos produced are rejected for full-term births. These extras are then volunteered for medical or stem cell research.

The anti-cloning argument proceeds from the view that the process of creating a plenitude of embryos for stem cell research is the first stage of widespread human cloning. It would become a separate process from the actual sexual union of egg and sperm for purpose of producing a normal birth. The view is that such work approaches the borders of inhuman experimentation, a tampering with one of the most fundamental biosocial acts, our fundamental sexual identity, and the creation of the next generation. The opponents, political, theological, ethical, view the normal sexual relations involved in creating a child as the closest to a divine act as we can get (Onan, son of Judah, Genesis 38:9.). Such a violation of our individual and our species' "godly" nature cannot be permitted. What is next on the horizon, they ask, *eugenics?*

The Moral/Religious Dimension

The Catholic Church has long wrestled with the issue of artificial birth control, coming down on the side of abstinence when the moral needs of the family, the health of the mother, economic stability requires that no new children enter the family circle. The Church strenuously objects to abortion as a birth control means. Cloning is seen as an extreme and horrific immoral procedure. Other religions are more pluralistic in their response to the issue of cloning. Perhaps they and we are overwhelmed by existing techniques of birth control, in vitro fertilization, all the varied methods of shopping for the "right" combination of female eggs and male sperm to accomplish the acts of conception through birth.

In a world empty of humans, when wars inevitably led to the destruction, even genocide, of small tribal and national units, the Biblical injunction to procreate with its extreme hostility toward homosexuality and celibacy, anything that threatened the demographic survival of the ethnic group, had a thread of reality in its concerns. As with all such religious injunctions, the carriers of the message from God were always humans, laws of God usually promulgated on the basis of important contextual human needs.

Certainly, lessening the "dignity of human procreation through cloning, giving one generation unprecedented genetic control over the next" (Leon Kass, see above), is a fear opined in the context of a number of existing determinations of the nature and fate of the next generation by the present. For example, cannot it be said that the next generation's well being is undermined when individuals have far more children than the social environment can absorb, thus reshaping the genetic structure of subsequent generations, by duress: possible oblivion: starvation, disease, sterility? David Heyd has asked us to fix in our minds the ubiquitous truth that parents choose to have children for their own, not the children's benefit. This is a fundamental power exercised by the current generation over the next. The real question, then, directs itself to the method of genetic control exercised by one generation over the next. This is what Kass must object to, not the ubiquitous fact of control.[4]

What shocks today is the newly-developed technique of implanting the nucleus of an adult cell or "somatic" cell into a human egg cell from which the nucleus has been removed, thus creating a one-celled embryo. This embryo is subsequently grown in a Petri dish for five more days, thence assigned for either the harvesting of embryonic stem cells for research, else implanted in a human female's uterus for development and birth. Both the harvesting of such embryos and the prior act of cloning to produce such an embryo are at the heart of the momentary moral and religious fear.

The U.S. President's Council on Bioethics: ". . . the production of cloned embryos for any purpose is a significant leap in transforming procreation into a form of manufacture."[5] Presumably, "form of manufacture" means that the pre-selection of the genetic material to be united with the female egg is identical to the genetic makeup of the pre-selected parental somatic cell. One notes that the development of techniques to overcome fertility often result in multiple births, many identical in genetic makeup. These could likewise, without excessive verbal legerdemain, be considered *artificially* created, sic: manufactured genetic entitles. Again, could not the commonality of in vitro fertilization of donated semen or eggs, even artificial insemination of female(s) by semen donors also be defined as the *manufacture* of humans?

The question then focuses on techniques that take place with normal within-the-body inseminations, else sexual and asexual external techniques in reproduction. Perhaps the moral dilemma centers on the supposed sanctity of sexual reproduction, inside or outside the body. Yet, one hears few moral objections to reproductive technologies that since the 1970s have produced almost a million children, worldwide. These involve the above-noted "test tube" in vitro fertilization, sperm injected into egg cells (intercytoplasmic sperm injection), human embryos grown on cows and monkeys, component DNA from the eggs of two females, thus a child with genetic

---

[4]Heyd, D. 1992. Genethics; Moral Issues in the Creation of People, Berkeley, CA: University of California Press.
[5]Kass, Leon, op. cit.

material from three parents. All these new techniques in part, to ameliorate the sterility of potential parents has caused the major birth defect rate to grow from 4 percent in normal sexual reproduction to 9 percent through these infertility technologies. Yet the U.S. government here engages in little regulation.[6]

Except for the Catholic Church's opposition to any tampering with the reproductive powers of sexuality, except abstinence, in practice rejected by Catholics in all developed nations. Catholic Spain and Italy being the great exemplifications of the use of artificial birth control by members of the educated Western community, no clear religious or moral ground exists for saying "desist." The Old Testament, the source of the religious guidance and injunctions concerning human sexual behavior for the three major Western religions, advocates unlimited procreation, prohibits *coitus interruptus,* abortion, masturbation, homosexual behavior, all actions that have been seriously modified in their status as moral and religious transgressions by most modern religious. At the same time the Old Testament did sanctify the genocide of women and children, as well as male members of antagonistic ethnicities. It also promoted slavery, and polygyny.

Slippery-Slope Medicine

Here we confront the issue of correct interpersonal and social behavior. From a broader moral concern than strictly theological sanction, there are many who strongly reject the practice of creating an embryo and, after six days, or later, willfully ending its nascent life. The moral concern over such an act transcends particularistic religious sanction, for which there is little historical clarification. It is rooted in a definition of life. The issue has first addressed itself to abortion, where the Supreme Court (Roe v. Wade, 1972) required the states to permit abortion for the first trimester, to regulate it during the second trimester. The controversy now focuses on so-called partial-birth abortion (Stenberg v. Carhart, 2000). Here the Supreme Court ruled that Nebraska's banning of partial birth abortions was too broad. A ban here, during the third trimester, with an allowance for reasons of health, would have sufficed. On September 28, 2000, the U.S. Food and Drug Administration approved the use of RU-486, a pill that induces abortions during the first trimester.

Presumably the question of governmental legislative and legal intrusion in certain morally sensitive areas of public policy with regard to the "livingness" of embryos and fetuses during the first two trimesters of life is settled. In early 2003, the U.S. Senate was still entangled in defining whether a fetus, even in the second trimester, was a child that would "fully experience the pain" of an abortion.[7]

Constitutionally and ethically, up to the third trimester, choice over "life or death" resides in the privacy of the bearer of the fetus, her family and medical advisors. As we have pointed out above, most infertility technologies exercise this choice in creating a functioning embryo that is to be or not to be brought to term.

---

[6]Skloot, R. L. 2003. "The Other Baby Experiment." *The New York Times,* 2/22/03.
[7]*The Washington Post,* Editorial, 3/10/03.

Thus, it is fair to say that the destruction of an embryo or fetus during pregnancy is an action within the law, and thus of established moral validation. It is inconceivable, a *reductio ad absurdum,* to postulate a federal law that permits certain behavior and then prevents the "moral" sanctioning of such behavior. Similarly validated is the creation of embryos by fertile couples to be genetically screened. The decision to bring to term or not, for those with reproductive or other problems, is likewise sanctioned within the law. These embryos could be frozen for subsequent genetic analysis and implantation. Surplus embryos could be contributed to scientific research and eventually destroyed.

The artificial creation of an asexual embryo, either for reproductive or stem cell research, has become the core of the most recent controversy over morality in this dramatic scientific and technological surge in bio-genetics. Stanford University's institute for stem cell research recently drew the ire of the President's Council on Bioethics because of its attempt to create embryos through somatic cell nuclear transfer (SCNT), now the most efficient manner of producing these living organisms for stem cell research.[8]

Opponents of this growing technique for producing stem cells, research that could eventually teach us much about the origins of disease, tissue rejection. organ repair and replacement, fear the slippery slope. By contrast, they hope that the use of adult cells can eventually lead to the production of stem cells, and thus avoid this revolution in the creation of "new life."

The President's Council on Bioethics declared that: ". . . the production of cloned embryos for any purpose is a significant leap in transforming procreation into a form of manufacture . . . saying yes to cloned embryos, even for research, means saying yes, at least in principle, to an ever-expanding genetic mastery of one generation over the next. Once cloned embryos exist in laboratories, the eugenic revolution will have begun. . . . Science already permits us to screen human embryos in vitro for thousands of human genes. These include . . . not just sex, height, or skin color, but even intelligence, temperament or sexual orientation."[9]

In the area of socially-regulated moral behavior, the people and its government have a legal right to prohibit or sanction such behavior. The fact that the in vitro or in utero analysis of embryos for possible genetic defects takes place legally, thence allowable abortion or technological fertility and birth, emphasizes that a non-cloning aspect of the eugenics revolution is well under way. Another ubiquitous example is ultrasound technology. As utilized in China alone, it reduces the number of females born to China's 1.3 billion population by 1.7 million per year. In India, and elsewhere throughout the world, millions of females have been aborted after screening by ultrasound machines.[10]

---

[8]Parens, E. 2003. "Clear Thinking on Cloning," *The Washington Post,* 2/1/03.
[9]Kass, op cit.
[10]Rothblatt, M. 1997. UnZipped Genes: Taking Charge of Baby Making in the New Millennium, Philadelphia: Temple University Press.

That the eugenics revolution is not a mere phrase is a fear that some may say has been exploited by the Cystic Fibrosis Foundation. Their *raison d'etre* may disappear with genetic screening. They oppose genetic testing, without which children, parents, and society bear the responsibility for the medical burden of this devastating genetic condition.[11]

This struggle for scientific knowledge amidst the power interests favoring the status quo, especially when focused on the discoveries involved in our genome, often involve deeply rooted political and ideological self-interest. Given the accepted view that approximately 50 percent of male homosexuality admits of a genetic origin, would the future discovery of a genetic location for male homosexuality allow parents to make a choice to abort or not? And would there not be deep protests by the political community representing homosexuals to defeat such free analysis and consequent decision-making?

An example of the positive moral impact on an ethnic community subject to genetic/eugenic research and applications are European (Ashkenazi) Jews, the main carriers of the genes for Tay-Sachs disease, a merciless neurological disorder that kills the vast majority of afflicted children by age five. By genetic screening of adults at risk, or women in pregnancy, thus eligible for an abortion, the incidence of the disease since the late 1970s has diminished by 95 percent in the Jewish population. Now researchers are directing their work at a constellation of other genetically-transmitted conditions that affect Ashkenazi Jews and others, such as Cystic Fibrosis, Canavan, and Goucher.[12]

The moral question is how far our knowledge of the genetic nature of humans, both disabilities and advantages (intelligence, health), should extend into practice. The line between knowing and doing is a fine one. It is easier simply to prohibit the search for new knowledge before it gets to the stage of policy application. Thus, the inevitable moral slippery slope to the acceptance of a wide new range of biological/genetic "knowing and doing" becomes the center of a great national debate.

The Politics of Cloning

Concerning the issue of the power of one generation over the genetic nature of succeeding generations as discussed above, Kass and the President's Council subscribe to a spurious concern. The truth about human progress, horrific and benign, is that the act of creation usually takes place first; then comes the reconsideration of the wisdom of its use and practice. The mere moral objection to innovation because of the

---

[11]Marshall, E. I. 1996. The Human Genome Project: Cracking the Code within Us, New York: Franklin Watts, Kristof, N. 2003. "The New Eugenics" *The New York Times,* 7/04/03.

[12]Kolata, G. 2003. "Using Genetic Tests Ashkenazi Jews Vanquish a Disease," *The New York Times,* 2/18/03; Goddard, I. 2003. "Genetic Testing Offered," *South Florida Sun-Sentinel,* 2/21/03.

radical nature involved in the progressive technological jump usually does not block its application. If only we had foreseen the polluting and congestive impact of the internal combustion engine, seemingly benign and enthusiastically endorsed when introduced, would we have so easily acquiesced?

It is reactionary and ideological to foreclose progress in science and society merely on the suspicion of negative outcomes. One cannot predict the future. If the outcomes of human cloning are negative, were they to result in incessant failure or pathological results, then legislative action to regulate and limit human cloning would be justified on rational/evidential grounds. Hysteria and moral obfuscation would not. At this point, it is clear that the beginning stages of this biotechnology will reveal much failure. The products of failed experiments will not be allowed to enter the world. However, suppose after several years of failure, positive results occur, a normal healthy child. We would be well advised to inquire of this functioning productive human, ". . . are you worthy of your creation?"

Picture the aging parents of a child killed in an accident. They wish to recreate the child through cloning. Would we refuse them? A young husband dies suddenly. His wife wants a memory of their love in the form of a child cloned from his tissue[.] Could we say "no"? A different kind of experiment might be the cloning of a truly great mind. Several female proxies could be used, at the least to study the results of different intra-uterine and extra-uterine environments in the nurturing of the genetic potentialities of genius in human achievement. There is more to the historical implications of asexual human reproduction (cloning), than the mere venality of wealthy individuals striving for genetic immortality.[13]

The preemptive strike that so-called ethicists and politicians wish to achieve against stem-cell research that creates six-day-old embryos, not to say human cloning, has a deeper opposition. This again derives from the so-called slippery-slope argument, "the eugenics revolution." Eugenics has always spoken to the enhancement of the human species, by the possibility of eliminating such genetic conditions as Down's Syndrome, Tay-Sachs, as well as a host of tragic human disabilities that are increasingly controllable through the aegis of our exploding knowledge of the structure of the human genome.

The presumptive morality ideologues are certainly not against such human interventions. Kass focuses on one eminent danger involved in human genetic screening, and presumably the choice humans might make in creating a child: ". . . intelligence, temperament, or sexual orientation". These are ideological code words that center especially on intelligence and sexual orientation. Consider, a world of political activism without the highly intelligent, creative homosexual community, eliminated for all intents and purposes by the previous generation of parental choosers over the genetic destiny of their own family life, and, implicitly, the world's. Imagine hearing impaired activists fighting cochlear implants or genetic screening so that the community of deaf and hearing-impaired persons might re-

---

[13]Silver, L. M. 1997. Remaking Eden: Cloning and Beyond in a Brave New World, New York: Avon.

main a politically potent group, or simply to ensure that there will be hearing-impaired people in future generations.

Note that it is genetically-rooted intelligence that lies at the heart of the opposition to the advancement of our knowledge of the human genome and the application of this knowledge to new therapies and procedures. The battleground is littered with unconsidered and unapplied evidence that human behavior is overwhelmingly shaped by our genetic intelligence, both quantitatively and qualitatively. Several important studies are pertinent here; L. M. Terman and M. H. Oden's longitudinal studies of high I.Q. children (1920–1945) revealed the educational and vocational success of the tested individuals. These studies, along with the Minnesota Twin Study, the results of which Thomas Bouchard started to present in 1988, clearly showed how closely linked intelligence and I.Q. are to the civilizational accomplishments of individuals, their social groups, even their nationalities and races.[14]

This research has proved anathema to various neo-Marxian political groups that view such accomplishments as accidental familial, sociological, and historical events that are unrelated to our biogenetic nature. According to the so-called left/liberal view, our human social natures are created by our environment, i.e., the political controllers. Here lies the *raison d'etre* for the genocide of talented minorities during the twentieth century. It started with the early-twentieth-century destruction of the Christian Armenians in Turkey, included the Jews, continued under Stalin and Mao. It contained an underlying demonology that the successful populations achieved their positions through illegitimate political if not criminal practices, not through education and ability.

The theme is the same today in the West, where the failures of various ethnic, religious and national groups to compete with high-ability minorities and nations has become a political weapon aimed at human achievement. The ideological fear concerns ongoing scientific research into the deepening mystery of the nature/nurture interaction. By not merely mapping the genome but by identifying intelligent humans on the basis of specific gene complexes, even before birth, eugenics could be seen as a triumphant addition to the search for the good of humankind. The already failed environmentalist view of the primarily social origins of intelligence variability would be seen by all but the most unreachable as incontrovertibly wrong.

As it is, science is closing in on the genetic formulation of intelligence. Years ago, intelligence was seen as a blending of many genetic elements. The reason for this view lay in the many psychosocial elements that researchers used in their definition of intelligent behavior. More recently, partially through the above analysis of Thomas

---

[14]Terman, L. M. 1925. Genetic Studies of Genius, Vol. I, Mental and Physical Traits of a Thousand Gifted Children. Stanford, CA: Stanford University Press; Terman, L. M., & Oden, M. H. 1948. The Gifted Child Grows Up: Twenty-Five Year Follow Up. Stanford, CA: Stanford University Press; Bonchard, T. J. 1993. "The Genetic Architecture of Human Intelligence," in P. A. Vernon, Ed., Biological Approaches to the Study of Human Intelligence, Norwood, N.J.: Ablex.

Bouchard, but also of Robert Plomin (U.S.-Great Britain), and Volkmar Weiss (Germany), "general intelligence—I.Q." is interpreted as a product of only a few major genes out of our human total of 22,000.[15] This change in perspective has been developed through a mathematical analysis of intra-familial I.Q. variability. These acknowledged large differences between full siblings preclude a blending model, and argue for the "right" major gene(s) complexes falling into one familial slot rather than the other.

We are gradually penetrating this mystery. More and more correlations are being made between brain size and intelligence, neurological synaptic electrical variance, and, most recently, brain scan studies correlated with I.Q. tests. Dr. Jeremy Gray, of Washington University, St. Louis, the lead author of a recently-reported study, argued that brain activity as imaged in the scans showed that high-I.Q. persons taking an I.Q. test showed enhanced neurological activity in the lateral pre-frontal cortex, an area important for good working memory, planning, and goal directed activity.[16] Commentators unanimously agreed that "standard intelligence tests do measure something important" (Dr. John Duncan, deputy director. Medical Research Councils Brain Sciences Unit, Cambridge England). Further, "the idea that performance on a task that's supposed to tap into general intelligence can predict real differences in activity in the brain lends support for the idea that there is a general intelligence" (I.Q.) (Dr. Earl Miller, Professor of Neuroscience, Picower Center for Learning and Memory, Mass. Institute of Technology).[17]

The cloning of humans and the stem cell production issue are indeed the tip of the iceberg, the slippery slope, or any other metaphor that points to the growing impact of scientific research that could undercut the twentieth-century ideological opposition to viewing human behavior as biologically/genetically determined. Let us suppose that we will soon identify the specific genes in our chromosomes that are linked with certain quantitative levels of intelligence and others that have qualitative valences, positive as well as negative, that might be predictive of violence, drug addiction, sexual pathologies? Would not such discoveries spill over into the legislative as well as the personal choice realm?

Let us assume that the quantitative analysis of general intelligence linked to biochemical gene structure begins to be predictive of educational achievement, the ability to think about causes, real or paranormal. Suppose we could attribute failed social, educational, moral behavior not to the depredations of "society" but to an individual's genetic makeup. From such a position, we could move to the macrosociological impact. What are the links of an individual's genetic makeup to societies that cannot raise themselves economically, govern themselves democratically, rule out hallucinatory religious obeisance, or generate a political program of scientific, evidential, decision-making. When this day arrives, we will realize a com-

---

[15]Plomin, R., et al. 1997. Behavioral Genetics. New York: Freeman: Weiss. V. 1992. "Major Genes of General Intelligence," Personality and Individual Differences 13:1115–1134.

[16]Gray, J. R. 2003. In Nature Neurosciences, March.

[17]Goode, E. 2003. "Brain Scans Reflect Problem-Solving Skill," The New York Times 2/17/03.

pletely different intellectual ordering of our national and international dynamics. We may be forced, unless ideology interdicts, to come to a wholly different understanding of the causes of our contemporary and historical dilemmas, political, economic, and social.

This would be a Copernican turn in our understanding. But for many true believers of the contemporary mythos, these are fighting ideas. Cloning is the controversial trip wire that allows for this recent ideological mobilization.

EVENT CASEBOOK THREE

What Price, Freedom?

Focus on
Homeland Security
and The Patriot Act

Initial Reports

News Report—National, Local

The Source: ABC News

ABCNEWS.com, established May 15, 1997, is one of the fastest-growing news sites on the Internet. With editorial and technical resources from ABC News and The Walt Disney Internet Group, ABCNEWS.com consistently provides users with up-to-the-minute, engaging, informative, and interactive coverage of a range of issues and events. ABCNEWS.com, as one of the world's leading Internet news organizations, brings the same high standards and dedication to journalism as ABC News has historically brought to radio and television news.

The following article was published October 26, 2001.

Anti-Terror Bill Becomes Law

It will give law enforcement and intelligence officials important new tools," he said at a ceremony in the East Room of the White House.

Bush said the USA Patriot Act of 2001, as it is officially known, will allow government agencies to keep up with a new, highly-sophisticated enemy.

Key provisions of the legislation allow investigators to use roving wiretaps, following a suspect rather than a particular phone. It also gives the government the power to detain immigrants for up to seven days if they're suspected of involvement with terrorists, up from two days.

The bill calls for tripling the number of immigration and border patrol agents along the 3,000-mile border with Canada.

The new measure also provides new tools to fight money laundering by terrorists, allow government agencies to better share information about suspects and more easily track their communications, and increase penalties for terrorism-related crimes.

"Current statutes deal more severely with drug traffickers than terrorists," Bush said. "That changes today."

Strong Bipartisan Support

The Senate voted 98–1 to approve the measure on Thursday [Oct. 25, 2001], with only Sen. Russ Feingold, D-Wis., in opposition., and Mary Landrieu, D-La., did not vote. The legislation cleared the House, 357–66, on Wednesday [Oct. 24, 2001].

Congressional concern about constitutional rights and civil liberties forced the Bush administration to scale back its demands. For that reason, many of the new powers given the government under this measure would expire in four years unless extended by Congress. That concession was not enough to win over Feingold.

Sen. Orrin Hatch, R-Utah, promised Congress would make sure the government does not abuse its new powers, which he says could have helped prevent the Sept. 11 attacks.

"If these tools had been in law, I believe we would have caught these perpetrators," Hatch said.

Putting New Powers to Work

Attorney General John Ashcroft told a U.S. Conference of Mayors meeting on Thursday [Oct. 25, 2001] that his troops would waste no time putting the new tools to use in the hunt for terrorists.

Justice Department officials say they are ready to go with new advice and guidance to federal prosecutors and agents the minute the president signs the bill. One official said the most immediately useful provisions are those that expand the ability to read addresses on e-mails, and to share information between criminal investigators and intelligence agencies.

The Patriot Act

Following are some of the new powers and provision of the Patriot Act:

- ○ Wiretaps: Law enforcement can now apply for roving wiretaps on terrorism suspects, letting them monitor any phone the person uses. Currently, officials must obtain permission for each individual phone line they monitor.
- ○ Increased Penalties: Increased penalties and specific crime statues for mass transportation crimes, conspiracy and possession of biological weapons. The Patriot Act also makes it a crime to knowingly harbor terrorists.
- ○ New powers for the Treasury Department to pressure foreign countries and banks to provide information on depositors. U.S. banks will be barred from doing business with unregulated off-shore banks. E-mail: Law enforcement can subpoena e-mail addresses of e-mails sent and received by suspects.
- ○ Sharing Information: Agreements to enhance data sharing between the FBI, State Department, Immigration and Naturalization Service, CIA and other governmental agencies potentially involved or confronted with counterterrorism duties. Makes it easier to share grand jury and wiretap information between agencies.
- ○ Border Security: The law triples the number of border patrol agents along the Canadian border and authorizes $50 million for improvements of border security.

○ Detention of Aliens: The law allows authorities to detain illegal aliens who are certified as terrorism suspects for up to seven days before charging them with criminal or immigration violations.

Public Speech

The Speaker: President George W. Bush

George W. Bush is the forty-third President of the United States. He was sworn into office January 20, 2001. He received a bachelor's degree from Yale University in 1968, and then served as an F-102 fighter pilot in the Texas Air National Guard. President Bush received a Master of Business Administration from Harvard Business School in 1975. After graduating, he moved back to Midland and began a career in the energy business. After working on his father's successful 1988 presidential campaign, he assembled the group of partners that purchased the Texas Rangers baseball franchise in 1989. He served as managing general partner of the Texas Rangers until he was elected Governor. President Bush served for six years as the forty-sixth Governor of the State of Texas; he was the first Governor in Texas history to be elected to consecutive four-year terms.

The following is a transcript of a speech given by President Bush on October 26, 2001, before signing into law the antiterrorism bill—The Patriot Act.

George W. Bush Signs the Antiterrorism Bill

Speaker: George W. Bush, President of the United States

Bush: Be seated please.

(Applause)

Good morning, and welcome to the White House. Today, we take an essential step in defeating terrorism while protecting the constitutional rights of all Americans.

With my signature, this law will give intelligence and law enforcement officials important new tools to fight a present danger. I commend the House and Senate for the hard work they put into this legislation.

Members of Congress and their staffs spent long nights and weekends to get this important bill to my desk. I appreciate their efforts and bipartisanship in passing this new law.

I want to thank the vice president and his staff for working hard to make sure this law was passed.

I want to thank the secretary of state and the secretary of treasury for being here, both of whom lead important parts of our war against terrorism.

I want to thank Attorney General John Ashcroft for spending a lot of time on the Hill to make the case for a balanced piece of legislation.

I want to thank the director of the FBI and the director of the CIA for waging an incredibly important part on the two-front war: one overseas and a front here at home.

And I want to thank Governor Tom Ridge for his leadership.

Bush: I want to thank the members of Congress who are here on the stage, the leaders on this impressive effort: Senator Hatch and Senator Leahy and Senator Sarbanes and Senator Gramm and Senator Reid. I also want to thank Representatives Porter Goss, LaFalce, Oxley and Sensenbrenner for their hard work. And I want to welcome the men and women of law enforcement here at the White House with us today as well.

The changes effective today will help counter a threat like no other our nation has ever faced. We've seen the enemy in the murder of thousands of innocent unsuspecting people. They recognize no barrier of morality; they have no conscience. The terrorists cannot be reasoned with; witness the recent anthrax attacks through our Postal Service.

Our country is grateful for the courage the Postal Service has shown during these difficult times. We mourn the loss of the lives of Thomas Morris and Joseph Cursine postal workers who died in the line of duty, and our prayers go to their loved ones.

I want to assure postal workers that our government is testing more than 200 postal facilities along the entire eastern corridor that may have been impacted. And we will move quickly to treat and protect workers where positive exposures are found.

Bush: But one thing is for certain, these terrorists must be pursued, they must be defeated, and they must be brought to justice.

(Applause)

And that is the purpose of this legislation.

Since the 11th of September, the men and women of our intelligence and law enforcement agencies have been relentless in their response to new and sudden challenges.

We have seen the horrors terrorists can inflict.

We may never know what horrors our country was spared by the diligent and determined work of our police forces, FBI, ATF agents, federal marshals, custom officers, Secret Service, intelligence professionals and local law enforcement officials. Under the most trying conditions, they are serving this country with excellence and often with bravery. They deserve our full support and every means of help that we can provide.

We're dealing with terrorists who operate by highly sophisticated methods and technologies, some of which were not even available when our existing laws were written.

Bush: The bill before me takes account of the new realities and dangers posed by modern terrorists. It will help law enforcement to identify, to dismantle, to disrupt and to punish terrorists before they strike.

For example, this legislation gives law enforcement officials better tools to put an end to financial counterfeiting, smuggling and money laundering.

Secondly, it provides—gives intelligence operations and criminal investigations the chance to operate not on separate tracks but to share vital information so necessary to disrupt a terrorist attack before it occurs.

As of today, we're changing the laws governing information sharing.

And as importantly, we're changing the culture of our various agencies that fight terrorism.

Countering and investigating terrorist activity is the number one priority for both law enforcement and intelligence agencies.

Surveillance of communications is another essential tool to pursue and stop terrorists. Existing law was written in the era of rotary telephones. This new law that I sign today will allow surveillance of all communications used by terrorists, including e-mails, the Internet and cell phones.

Bush: As of today, we'll be able to better meet the technological challenges posed by this proliferation of communications technology. Investigations are often slowed by a limit on the reach of federal search warrants. Law enforcement agencies have to get a new warrant for each new district they investigate, even when they're after the same suspect. Under this new law, warrants are valid across all districts and across all states.

And finally, the new legislation greatly enhances the penalties that will fall on terrorists or anyone who helps them. Current statutes deal more severely with drug traffickers than with terrorists. That changes today.

We are enacting new and harsh penalties for possession of biological weapons. We're making it easier to seize the assets of groups and individuals involved in terrorism. The government will have wider latitude in deporting known terrorists and their supporters. The statute of limitations on terrorist acts will be lengthened as will prison sentences for terrorists.

This bill was carefully drafted and considered.

Bush: Led by the members of Congress on this stage and those seated in the audience, it was crafted with skill and care, determination and the spirit of bipartisanship for which the entire nation is grateful.

This bill met with an overwhelming—overwhelming—agreement in Congress, because it upholds and respects the civil liberties guaranteed by our Constitution. This legislation is essential not only to pursuing and punishing terrorists, but also preventing more atrocities in the hands of the evil ones.

This government will enforce this law with all the urgency of a nation at war. The elected branches of our government and both political parties are united in our resolve to find and stop and punish those who would do harm to the American people.

It is now my honor to sign into law the U.S.A. Patriot Act of 2001.

(Applause)

―――――――――――――――――

―――――――――――――――――

Multimedia Sources

Editorial Cartoon

The Artist: Don Wright

A cartoonist for the *Palm Beach Post,* Don Wright offers wisdom and hard-hitting commentary that explore the issues of the day. He is a five-time recipient of the Overseas Press Club Award for his cartoons on foreign affairs and is a two-time Reuben Award winner.

...THIS NEW, MODERN DESIGN BROUGHT TO YOU BY THE PATRIOT ACT.

Editorial Cartoon

The Author: Mike Keefe

Mike Keefe has been the editorial cartoonist for *The Denver Post* since 1975. He is also a weekly contributor to *USA Today* and a regular on America Online. Nationally syndicated, his cartoons have appeared in *Time, Newsweek, Business Week, US News and World Report, The New York Times, The Washington Post,* and in over 200 newspapers across the country.

He has won top awards for his cartoons and served as a juror for the 1997 Pulitzer Prizes in Journalism.

The following cartoon was published in *The Denver Post* on May 26, 2005.

Transcript from NewsHour with Jim Lehrer (PBS)

The Correspondent: Margaret Warner

PBS, headquartered in Alexandria, Virginia, is a private, nonprofit media enterprise owned and operated by the nation's 349 public television stations. A trusted community resource, PBS uses the power of noncommercial television, the Internet, and other media to enrich the lives of all Americans through quality programs and education services that inform, inspire, and delight. Available to 99 percent of American homes with televisions and to an increasing number of digital multimedia households, PBS serves nearly 100 million people each week.

The following is a transcript from the August 19, 2003, edition of *Online NewsHour with Jim Lehrer.*

Considering the Patriot Act

Margaret Warner: Today's speech by Attorney General John Ashcroft was billed as the first in a cross-country campaign that will take him to more than a dozen cities over the month. At every stop, he'll be making the case that the USA Patriot Act, passed in the immediate aftermath of 9/11, has protected Americans from another catastrophic terrorist attack.

This week alone, he'll address law enforcement audiences in Philadelphia, Cleveland, Detroit, and Des Moines. The attorney general's road trip comes amidst a growing backlash against the law. Some 140 communities and three states have passed resolutions condemning it as an infringement on civil liberties. Ashcroft spoke today at the American Enterprise Institute in Washington.

Ashcroft's Defense of the Patriot Act

John Ashcroft: This morning's attack confirms the worldwide terrorist threat is real. It is imminent. Our enemies continue to pursue ways to murder the innocent and the peaceful. They seek to kill us abroad and at home.

But we will not be deterred from our responsibility to preserve American life and liberty, nor our duty to build a safer and more secure world. In the long winter of 1941, Winston Churchill appealed to the United States for help in defending freedom from Nazism with the phrase, "give us the tools, and we will finish the job."

In the days after September 11, we appealed to the Congress for help in defending freedom from terrorism with the same refrain. "Give us the tools, and we will finish the job." Congress responded by passing the USA Patriot Act by an overwhelming margin. And while our job is not yet finished, we have used the tools provided in the Patriot Act to fulfill our first responsibility to protect the American people.

The Patriot Act opened opportunity for information sharing. To abandon this tool would disconnect the dots, risk American lives, sacrifice liberty, and reject September 11's lessons.

Almost two years after Americans died at the Pentagon, we know that cooperation works. The Patriot Act creates teamwork at every level of law enforcement and intelligence. To block cooperation against terrorists would be to make our nation more vulnerable to attack. It would reject the teachings of September 11.

Almost two years after Americans and the citizens of more than 80 other nations died at the World Trade Center, we know that prevention works. The Patriot Act gives us the technological tools to anticipate, adapt, and outthink our terrorist enemy. To abandon these tools would senselessly imperil American lives and American liberty, and it would ignore the lessons of September 11.

The cause we have chosen is just. The course we have chosen is constitutional. We did not seek this struggle, but we embrace this cause.

Providence, which has bestowed on America the responsibility to lead the world in liberty, has also handed America a great trust: To provide security that ensures liberty. We accept this trust, not with anger or arrogance, but with belief—belief that liberty is the greatest gift of our creator; belief that such liberty is the universal endowment of all humanity; belief that as long as there is an America, liberty must not, will not, shall not perish from the earth. Thank you very much. God bless you and God Bless America.

The Man Behind the Policy

Margaret Warner: Now for a closer look at the man at the helm of the Justice Department and the act that has stirred such controversy, we're joined by Viet Dinh, the former assistant attorney general for the Office of Legal Policy at the Justice Department. He helped draft the Patriot Act; and he now teaches at the Georgetown University Law Center. And Laura Murphy, director of the Washington National Office of the American Civil Liberties Union. The ACLU has filed suit against the Justice Department over one provision of the Patriot Act. Welcome to you both.

John Ashcroft, clearly the president's point man on the war on terror here at home, what's been his impact, Viet Dinh? That is, to what degree has he personally shaped the response, the whole way this administration has responded domestically to the war on terror?

Viet Dinh: I think totally and from the beginning, on September 11 the president called a meeting of his National Security Council for obvious reasons. At the end of that meeting, the president pulled the attorney general aside and said, "John, you make sure this does not happen again."

The attorney general then set out a course of vision and a course of leadership that defined our work at the Department of Justice to ensure that preventing and disrupting terrorist activity is the overriding goal of the Department of Justice.

It started with a top-to-bottom review of the tools we had at our disposal which ended up in the near unanimous passage of the USA Patriot Act; it continued with the reorganization of the FBI in order to improve communication and coordination; it continued with the transfer of the Immigration Services over the homeland security and the assistance with the Department of Homeland Security to make that transition seamless, and it continues to this day whereby over 300 persons have been charged in terrorism-related investigations. Over 130 persons have been convicted.

But overwhelmingly I think the number-one statistic that illustrates the success thus far of the campaign is a non-statistic. Nothing has happened in the last 24 months. And every single day that nothing happens, that all is well in America, everybody's bored on their drive home, is a momentous achievement for law enforcement, for the Department of Justice, for all the state and local partners and for John Ashcroft personally.

Margaret Warner: Do you see John Ashcroft's personal stamp on all of this even if you don't agree with the way Viet Dinh characterized it? Do you see his stamp, his sign on this?

Laura Murphy: Well, I think he's deeply, personally invested in the fate of legislation and Executive Branch activities that focus on the prosecution of terrorists, but I don't think he's as knowledgeable about the policies that he's implemented as he should be.

When he was before the House Judiciary Committee on June 5, he really could not articulate answers to some of the specific questions that many of the House Democratic and Republican members asked him. He wasn't clear on Section 215 of the Patriot Act, which allows the government to seize library records, for example. He was not entirely accurate in his response about the use of "sneak and peek" warrants, which allows the government to come into your home, search your belongings, remove belongings without telling you.

So I think he's deeply invested in this. He wants it to be a political success, but I don't think he is looking out for the Constitution and the Bill of Rights as carefully as he should, and I think when we are fearful and we act in fear and act in haste, we lose sight of our values. He's also there to protect American values.

I think he pressured the Congress to pass the USA Patriot Act. They went too far too fast. And now he's in the position of back pedaling and trying to explain why the act is necessary when an overriding majority of the House of Representatives voted to repeal the "sneak and peek" provisions of the USA Patriot Act in an astounding vote about a month ago. So I think he's in trouble.

Margaret Warner: Why is . . . pick up on that point. Why is he going on this road show now, Viet Dinh? It because, in fact, Congress has knocked down a couple of these provisions or refused to fund them and because he is hearing more criticism of it?

Viet Dinh: First of all, Congress has not withheld funding. The other amendment happened in the middle of the night. The very next day when the Department of Justice actually discovered I think that sounder heads and more reasoned debate will prevail here.

Margaret Warner: And let me just explain that amendment. That was the amendment that would have denied funding to the so-called "sneak and peek" provisions, which allows searches without telling people.

Viet Dinh: Not without. It's a delay notice provision that pre-existed the USA Patriot Act but then again your point is a very good one. And I disagree somewhat with Laura's characterization that this is a purely defensive or counteroffensive move.

I think that the purpose of the trip as is evident on the audiences he's choosing, the locales that he is visiting, is twofold: One is to speak to the men and women who do the actual groundwork in this war against terror: The prosecutors, the state and local police officers, the FBI agents, to tell them that their work is worthy of thanks and of praise and not of criticism or disparagement, and also to explain the USA Patriot Act and the related activities of the Department of Justice to the American public, to disabuse that public of the misinformation, the misconceptions and the misunderstanding that unfortunately has pervaded in the last summer or so.

And I do think that the attorney general is correct in his citation of the public support for the activities on men and women in law enforcement to protect the security of America and the safety of American people.

What he needs to do is go to the people, speak to them directly and to answer their concerns, to listen to their constructive criticism, where applicable, and to tell them exactly what government is doing and what it is not doing.

Opposition to the Patriot Act

Margaret Warner: Your organization has been critical of this campaign that he's embarking on.

Laura Murphy: Absolutely. I think the attorney general is on the ropes. Over 151 local communities have passed resolutions denouncing provisions of the Patriot Act. Three states have passed resolutions denouncing the provisions of the Patriot Act, Hawaii, Vermont, and Alaska.

In Alaska they told their law enforcement officials to refrain from enforcing provisions of the Patriot Act that violated constitutional rights such as investigating people without probable cause that a crime has been committed.

So this is . . . the population is in an uproar. It is not limited to the ACLU. We're talking about Grover Norquist of the Americans for Tax Reform and David Keene from the American Conservative Union and the Free Congress Foundation joining forces with the ACLU, making identical claims that this act goes too far in abridging our basic freedoms.

Viet Dinh: Let me just—one note of correction because I think there is a misstatement both in Laura's comment and the opening segment about the level of local and state opposition to the USA Patriot Act. If one actually reads these resolutions and these enactments, there's nothing disagreeable about them. They are merely statements of principle of saying that the Constitution. . . .

Laura Murphy: That's not correct.

Viet Dinh: That the Constitution is sacred and that the states and locals will not do anything in abridgment of the Constitution. Where the federal government, be it in the USA Patriot Act or elsewhere, asks state and local officials to violate the Constitution, of course they shouldn't do it.

But to this day, not a single provision of the USA Patriot Act has been overturned by a court. Indeed Laura's and the ACLU's challenge last week or two weeks ago was the first time that any provision was actually challenged.

Laura Murphy: I say read the Alaska resolution, read the Detroit City Council resolution, read the Baltimore resolution, where they have the force of law. Some are resolutions and some are legally binding on police departments not to cooperate with these anti-civil liberty provisions of the Patriot Act.

Margaret Warner: Let me ask you this, though, is Attorney General Ashcroft right when he says so far that the courts have primarily sided with the Justice Department on the various challenges?

Laura Murphy: The jury is out because we just brought the first challenge to the Patriot Act two-and-a-half weeks ago. The case has not been adjudicated so it remains to be seen whether or not. . . .

Margaret Warner: There have been a number of challenges on all kinds of things.

Laura Murphy: They haven't been directly to the Patriot Act. Some have dealt with the Foreign Intelligence Surveillance Court and in other areas.

But again it takes a while for a challenge to work its way through the judicial process. He cannot state factually that the courts have reviewed all of the provisions of the Patriot Act and upheld them. That has yet to be seen.

Margaret Warner: All right. Let me ask you both about the key assertion in his remarks. And I assume he's going to be saying this around the country, which is something you essentially said right at the end of your opening comment: without these stronger powers, the

Justice Department and the U.S. Government would not have been able to withstand another catastrophic attack and the fact that there hasn't been one is evidence that they're working and should not be rolled back. Sum up the gist of that argument.

Has the Patriot Act Prevented More Attacks?

Viet Dinh: In 1982 when the IRA attempted to assassinate Margaret Thatcher but unsuccessfully for obvious reasons, it released a very simple statement. It said today we were unlucky but remember we only have to get lucky once. You have to get lucky every day. And that sums up the essence of the counterterrorism mission.

We can never say that any one act, any one legislation was instrumental in preventing another terrorist or catastrophic attack or preserving the peace for the last two years. The Department of Justice did say to Congress that the peace over the last two years, the success in the campaign thus far, would have been very difficult if not impossibly so without the USA Patriot Act.

Margaret Warner: All right. Let me get your views on that. Would you concede that perhaps these strengthened powers have enabled the U.S. Government to do more certainly than they could have pre-9/11?

Laura Murphy: Well, there are provisions of the USA Patriot Act that are non-controversial. For example, giving more border patrol agents to the northern border—hiring more translators.

Margaret Warner: Some of the things he talked about sharing information from intelligence to law enforcement.

Laura Murphy: I think the way he presented it was very misleading. The CIA could always share information with the FBI when they found indication of criminal activity.

So the idea that it was the law and not the inbred bureaucracy of the CIA and the FBI that prevented information-sharing from going on, what they wanted to do was weaken the threshold for conducting intelligence investigations and get around the criminal statutes. So the information-sharing discussion that the attorney general had I think was very, very misleading.

But let me say, in sum, it is as if I say I have an elephant gun in my office and there are no elephants in my office, therefore, the gun has been successful. We cannot protect the American people by military might and increased law enforcement powers alone. We also have to protect our values, and the attorney general is not being as mindful as he should be and is repeating the mistakes of history in sacrificing some of our civil liberties in the war on terrorism.

Margaret Warner: Let me ask you a final question to respond to her main point which is that last point that in the post 9/11 fever perhaps some civil liberties were trampled on. There were some excesses. Do you think that's the case?

Viet Dinh: The Inspector General of the Department of Justice had issued several reports about those allegations. And I think that to the extent that those allegations are credible and are well founded they are very regrettable. I do think that the attorney general is seeking to protect the liberty of America by providing the security for America.

The ACLU and the members of its coalition opposed the 1996 anti-terrorism act. It believes that we were ready prior to September 11. And the question is now are we ready for the next terrorist attack? I sincerely hope that we are and I sincerely hope that our government officials are always evaluating and reevaluating what they do to strike that balance true.

Margaret Warner: Very interesting and spirited discussion. Laura Murphy and Viet Dinh, thank you both.

Laura Murphy: Thank you.

Viet Dinh: Thank you so much

Web site

The Source: http://www.dhs.gov/dhspublic/

The Department of Homeland Security (DHS), established after the terrorist attacks of September 11, 2001, has three primary missions: prevent terrorist attacks within the United States, reduce America's vulnerability to terrorism, and minimize the damage from potential attacks and natural disasters.

The following is a screenshot of the home page for Homeland Security, followed by a brief overview of the DHS "Strategic Plan." The full text is available in PDF format at the following URL: http://www.dhs.gov/interweb/assetlibrary/DHS_StratPlan_FINAL_spread.pdf

The DHS Strategic Plan: Securing Our Homeland

The National Strategy for Homeland Security and the Homeland Security Act of 2002 served to mobilize and organize our nation to secure the homeland from terrorist attacks. This exceedingly complex mission requires a focused effort from our entire society if we are to be successful. To this end, one primary reason for the establishment of the Department of Homeland Security was to provide the unifying core for the vast national network of organizations and institutions involved in efforts to secure our nation. In order to better do this and to provide guidance to the 180,000 DHS men and women who work every day on this important task, the Department developed its own high-level strategic plan. The vision and mission statements, strategic goals and objectives provide the framework guiding the actions that make up the daily operations of the department.

Vision

Preserving our freedoms, protecting America . . . we secure our homeland.

Mission

We will lead the unified national effort to secure America. We will prevent and deter terrorist attacks and protect against and respond to threats and hazards to the nation. We will ensure safe and secure borders, welcome lawful immigrants and visitors, and promote the free-flow of commerce.

Strategic Goals

Awareness—Identify and understand threats, assess vulnerabilities, determine potential impacts and disseminate timely information to our homeland security partners and the American public.

Prevention—Detect, deter and mitigate threats to our homeland.

Protection—Safeguard our people and their freedoms, critical infrastructure, property and the economy of our Nation from acts of terrorism, natural disasters, or other emergencies.

Response—Lead, manage and coordinate the national response to acts of terrorism, natural disasters, or other emergencies.

Recovery—Lead national, state, local and private sector efforts to restore services and rebuild communities after acts of terrorism, natural disasters, or other emergencies.

Service—Serve the public effectively by facilitating lawful trade, travel and immigration.

Organizational Excellence—Value our most important resource, our people. Create a culture that promotes a common identity, innovation, mutual respect, accountability and teamwork to achieve efficiencies, effectiveness, and operational synergies.

News Article

The Author: Angie Cannon

U.S. News & World Report came into existence through a journalistic merger. In 1933, journalist David Lawrence published the first issue of a weekly newspaper called the *United States News*. Six years later, he launched a magazine called *World Report*. When the two weeklies merged in 1948, *U.S. News & World Report* was born.

From 1962 to 1984, *U.S. News* was employee-owned. In 1984, publisher and real estate developer Mortimer B. Zuckerman bought the company. Mr. Zuckerman is also chairman and co-publisher of the *New York Daily News*. A graduate of Harvard Law School, Mr. Zuckerman is a former associate professor at the Harvard Graduate School of Business, where he taught for nine years.

U.S. News began its Internet ventures in 1993, with a two-year stint as a content provider to the CompuServe Information Service. U.S. News Online (www .usnews.com), the magazine's Web site, went online November 6, 1995. All articles from the print edition of *U.S. News* also appear on U.S. News Online.

Angie Cannon is a staff writer for *U.S. News*. The following article was published on May 12, 2003.

Taking Liberties

Are tough new responses to terrorism upsetting the balance between legal rights and national security?

Zacarias Moussaoui, the only person charged in an American court with conspiring in the September 11 terrorist attacks, calls the federal judge hearing his case the "death judge." His own lawyers, whom he has rejected, are "death lawyers." And Attorney General John Ashcroft? He's a "natural-born liar."

Moussaoui is, to put it mildly, hardly a sympathetic defendant. But the case of the French citizen often dubbed the "20th hijacker" is not only drawing lots of media attention but raising a host of vexing new legal questions as well.

The Moussaoui case represents just one in a panoply of tough new legal responses to the terrorism threat that are changing the balance between an individual's constitutional rights and the government's need to protect national security. The Bush administration is planning military tribunals for foreign terrorism suspects and detaining as "material witnesses"—without charges—individuals it suspects of links to terrorism. Increasingly, liberals and conservatives alike are questioning whether such measures go too far. Is the war on terrorism, they ask, compromising civil liberties?

Moussaoui's case could provide some answers to the question. After a closed hearing this week, U.S. District Judge Leonie Brinkema must rule by May 15 on a critical issue: Should a defendant charged with terrorism-related crimes be allowed to question a witness thought to have information useful to his defense if the witness is a member of a terrorist organization? Or can the government, as it asserts, block such questioning on national security grounds? A compromise over Moussaoui's due-process rights could keep his trial on track for the fall. Failing that, the government may send his case to a military tribunal, where he would have fewer rights than in federal court.

The precedent that would be set by that scenario troubles civil libertarians, already alarmed by what they see as a Justice Department too ready to cast aside individual rights in its pursuit of terrorists. "We tend to overreact in times of war and then we apologize for it afterward," says George Washington University law Prof. Stephen Saltzburg.

Every week seems to bring fresh examples of the shifting balance between fighting terrorism and upholding personal freedoms. Last month, for example, Ashcroft decided that broad groups of illegal immigrants can be locked up indefinitely if immigration officials say their release would jeopardize national security. Yet just a few weeks earlier, a Denver judge had released two Pakistanis being held while the FBI investigated them for possible terrorism ties. The government, the judge said, failed to show the suspects were dangerous. In some other cases, defense attorneys maintain, prosecutors are securing guilty pleas by implying that the alternative could be to declare a suspect an enemy combatant—thus throwing him into a legal black hole.

Americans are willing to accept some curbs on civil liberties as the cost of fighting terrorism, polls show. But there are signs of uneasiness. More than 90 communities—mostly liberal college towns such as Boulder, Colo., Berkeley, Calif., and Ann Arbor, Mich.—have passed symbolic resolutions urging the feds to respect people's civil rights in the terrorism war. In a similar vein, some librarians are destroying patrons' records rather than risk having to disclose them to federal agents as required under the U.S.A. Patriot Act. In a recent speech, Supreme Court Justice Stephen Breyer, a Clinton appointee, urged lawyers to question the government's tactics, such as the lack of access to counsel for some detainees.

Such worries are not voiced solely by liberals. At an American Civil Liberties Union forum last month, David Keene, head of the American Conservative Union, urged policymakers to "tread lightly when it comes to rights guaranteed by the U.S. Constitution." And Wisconsin Republican Rep. James Sensenbrenner, the chairman of the House Judiciary Committee, recently joined his Democratic counterpart, John Conyers of Michigan, in asking the Justice Department to answer some 100 questions about its tactics, including how many religious sites federal authorities have entered without disclosing their identities and how many people have been detained as material witnesses.

No charges. Authorities are increasingly using the 1984 material witness statute to circumvent limitations on holding individuals without charges. But the tactic is highly debated—and not always productive. The Washington Post last fall counted at least 44 people arrested as material witnesses in terrorism cases. The paper found that 20 were released without ever being asked to appear before a grand jury. Only two were ever indicted on terrorism-related charges.

Today's civil liberties debate has plenty of historical echoes. Since the nation's founding, Americans have relied on the basic legal protections spelled out in the Bill of Rights, including trial by jury, protection from unreasonable searches, the right to counsel, the right to confront accusers, and the right to obtain favorable witnesses. But during past wartimes, civil liberties have been curbed dramatically. President Lincoln suspended habeas corpus (which allows a suspect to challenge the legal grounds for his detention) during the Civil War, for instance, while President Roosevelt interned Japanese-Americans during World War II.

Some scholars question making too much of the parallel between those events and today's war on terrorism. "The Bush administration has done nothing like that," says Cass Sunstein, a liberal constitutional law professor at the University of Chicago. "This isn't to say that there are no legitimate criticisms. But by historical standards, it's been a pretty cautious response." Today's culture, he suggests, has become much more protective of civil liberties since the expanded definition of constitutional protections that followed the civil rights revolution of the 1960s.

The administration's legal tactics have certainly drawn plenty of fire. But the Justice Department and its defenders argue that dramatic steps are needed because the threat is grave. "The very protections in the Constitution recognize that they may vary by circumstances," says William Barr, the former attorney general during the first Bush administration. "And here where you are dealing with extraordinary threats that could take tens of thousands of lives, a rule of reason has to prevail."

The complex details of several terrorism cases show how little agreement there is on what legal rights it is reasonable to give suspects. In the Moussaoui trial, the Justice Department argues that Moussaoui should be denied the access he seeks to Ramzi Binalshibh, an alleged planner of the 9/11 attacks being held and questioned by U.S. officials. Moussaoui says Binalshibh's testimony would show that he was not involved in the 9/11 attacks. But the government argues that permitting Moussaoui's defense team access to Binalshibh "will undoubtedly become terrorist defendants' favorite trump card" to compromise prosecutions or hobble interrogations of al Qaeda leaders.

Another closely watched case raises important questions about whether a U.S. citizen may be detained without access to legal counsel. Jose Padilla, 31, a former Chicago gang member arrested at O'Hare International Airport in May 2002, was initially detained as a material witness. One month later, President Bush designated him an enemy combatant, and he was transferred to a naval brig in Charleston, S.C. The government said that Padilla was part of a plot to detonate a radioactive "dirty bomb" in the United States. In the year since, Padilla has not been charged or allowed to see a lawyer.

U.S. District Judge Michael Mukasey in New York has ruled that the president has the power to jail U.S. citizens captured on U.S. soil as enemy combatants, but he also has twice ruled that Padilla should be allowed to meet with a lawyer. The government is appealing; Justice Department lawyer Paul Clement recently argued that granting Padilla access to a lawyer "could irreparably compromise the military's efforts to obtain intelligence from Padilla."

Gag order. A third case is raising questions about whether the government is misusing the material witness statute. Maher "Mike" Hawash, 39, is a software engineer, a naturalized American of Palestinian descent, who has an American wife and three children. By all accounts, he was leading a middle-class American life. But on

March 20, FBI agents picked him up in the parking lot of Intel Corp., in Hillsboro, Ore., on his way to work. For five weeks he was held in solitary confinement in a small cell as a material witness to a terrorism investigation. Agents searched his house for hours, taking computers and financial records. He did have access to a lawyer, but the judge imposed a gag order on attorneys and also barred the public from hearings. "It's Alice in Wonderland meets Franz Kafka," says Steven McGeady, a former Intel vice president, who is leading a support effort for Hawash.

Finally, last week, Hawash was charged with conspiracy to wage war against the United States and conspiracy to provide material support to al Qaeda, a charge that has become a key tool in the government's pursuit of possible terrorists. The government's complaint says that Hawash traveled to China with several other Portland residents, who already have been charged, in an attempt to enter Afghanistan and fight against U.S. forces after September 11. Shortly before he left the United States in October 2001, the complaint says, he transferred the title to his house to his wife and signed a power of attorney giving her authority to act on his behalf. Hawash returned to the United States after he was unsuccessful in entering Afghanistan, prosecutors say.

But Hawash's relatives say he told them his China travels had to do with his personal software business, according to the complaint. To complicate matters, a former Intel colleague told the *Wall Street Journal* that Hawash had told others that he traveled to the West Bank around that time. But all the government's evidence, says McGeady, is "weak and amounts to guilt by association."

Hawash originally was held under the material witness law, which permits the government to detain someone whose testimony is "material in a criminal proceeding." The law was intended to be used when a person is likely to flee the country to avoid testifying. Critics say the Justice Department is using it as a way to detain people indefinitely while searching for evidence against them.

Whatever the outcome of the Moussaoui, Padilla, and Hawash cases, critics say that since 9/11 there have been many other instances of newly aggressive tactics by the Justice Department. In the wartime atmosphere often cited by defenders of antiterrorism measures, "there is always a danger of saying 'we can tolerate this' and 'we can tolerate that,' " says law professor Saltzburg. "It's when you put those all together that you get a climate that frightens people."

Transcript

The Author: James X. Dempsey

Jim Dempsey joined the Center for Democracy and Technology at the beginning of 1997. He became executive director in 2003. In addition to day-to-day management responsibilities, he works on privacy and electronic surveillance issues and heads CDT's international project, the Global Internet Policy Initiative (GIPI).

Prior to joining CDT, Mr. Dempsey was deputy director of the Center for National Security Studies. From 1995 to 1996, Mr. Dempsey also served as special counsel to the National Security Archive, a nongovernmental organization that uses the Freedom of Information Act to gain the declassification of documents on the U.S. foreign policy.

From 1985 to 1994, Mr. Dempsey was assistant counsel to the House Judiciary Subcommittee on Civil and Constitutional Rights. His primary areas of responsibility for the Subcommittee were oversight of the Federal Bureau of Investigation, privacy and civil liberties. He worked on issues at the intersection of national security and constitutional rights, including terrorism, counterintelligence, and electronic surveillance as well as crime issues, including the federal death penalty, remedies for racial bias in death sentencing, information privacy, and police brutality. Mr. Dempsey has traveled extensively outside the United States to speak on civil liberties issues and consult with government officials and human rights organizations.

From 1980 to 1984, Mr. Dempsey was an associate with the Washington, D.C., law firm of Arnold & Porter, where he practiced in areas of government and commercial contracts, energy law, and antitrust. He also maintained an extensive pro bono representation of death row inmates in federal habeas proceedings. He clerked for the Hon. Robert Braucher of the Massachusetts Supreme Judicial Court.

Mr. Dempsey is author of several articles on Internet policy, including *Communications Privacy in the Digital Age: Revitalizing the Federal Wiretap Laws to Enhance Privacy,* and co-author of the book *Terrorism and the Constitution: Sacrificing Civil Liberties in the Name of National Security* (2002) (with Prof. David Cole of Georgetown law school).

The following is a transcript of Mr. Dempsey's testimony before Congress on May 20, 2003.

Terrorism Investigations and the Constitution

Statement of James X. Dempsey Executive Director, Center for Democracy & Technology
Footnote before the Committee on the House Judiciary Subcommittee on the Constitution

May 20, 2003

Mr. Chairman, Mr. Nadler, Members of the Subcommittee, thank you for the opportunity to testify today at this important hearing. We commend Chairman Sensen-Brenner and Mr. Conyers and you, Chairman Chabot and Mr. Nadler, for the oversight you are conducting of the effectiveness of the nation's counter-terrorism laws and their implications for civil liberties. The Center for Democracy and Technology urges you to continue this process, and we look forward to being of assistance to you however we can. In my testimony today, I make specific suggestions for further avenues of oversight.

I. Summary

The main points I wish to make today are these: The threat terrorism poses to our nation is imminent and grave. The government must be provided with strong legal authorities to prevent terrorism to the greatest extent possible and to punish it when it occurs. These authorities must include the ability to infiltrate organizations, collect information from public and private sources, and carry out wiretaps and other forms of electronic surveillance. These legal powers, however, must be subject to checks and balances; they must be exercised with a focus on potential violence, guided by the particularized suspicion principle of the Fourth Amendment, and subject to Executive, legislative and judicial controls. Yet the checks and balances, weak in some key respects before 9/11, have been seriously eroded by the PATRIOT Act and Executive Branch actions. Prior to 9/11, the government had awesome powers but failed to use them well. Those failures had little if anything to do with the rules established to protect privacy. The changes in the PATRIOT Act were hastily enacted—mistakes were made that Congress should rectify, by reasserting standards and checks and balances and by practicing ongoing, nonpartisan, detailed oversight, starting with close scrutiny of the government's claims that the PATRIOT Act changes have been vital to recent successes.

In response to the specific question posed by the title of this hearing, my central point is that, both before 9/11 and now, the government had and still has authority to go anywhere and collect any information to prevent terrorist attacks. Before 9/11, the exercise of that authority domestically was controlled and focused—the government had to have some minimal basis to suspect that some criminal conduct was being planned or that there was some minimal connection with a foreign terrorist group. Under the changes that have been made since 9/11, the FBI is authorized by the Attorney General to go looking for information about individuals with no reason to believe they are engaged in, or planning, or connected to any wrongdoing. Before 9/11, mosques and political events were not off-limits and the FBI did go into religious and political gatherings to collect information—where it had some minimal reason for believing that there was some connection between that mosque or political meeting and terrorism. Now, FBI agents can apparently wander down the street and visit mosques or political meetings like anyone else—on a whim. Before 9/11, the FBI was not prohibited from use of commercial databases. But under the PATRIOT Act and other laws, the FBI may have the authority to scoop up entire databases of information, including data on persons suspected of no wrongdoing. Our laws are totally inadequate to deal with the reality of decentralized commercial databases and the new techniques of data mining.

Both before 9/11 and today, the only question has ever been one of standards, checks and balances and procedures. With the changes adopted since 9/11, domestic law enforcement and intelligence agencies have fewer standards to guide them and are subject to less oversight and accountability to check up on their performance. The result, I fear, is unfocused investigative activity that is bad for security and bad for civil liberties.

I will concentrate today on the surveillance issues that I understand are the Subcommittee's main interest, but for purposes of context, I must briefly mention that some of the greatest abuses of civil liberties since 9/11 do not flow from the PATRIOT Act and have not been the subject of Congressional authorization or scrutiny, including:

- secret arrests of hundreds and maybe more than 1,000 people;
- the detention of many of those for days, weeks or even longer without charges, even though Congress had set a 7-day limit even for non-citizens detained as suspected terrorists;
- abuse of the material witness statute to hold people without charges;
- the blanket closing of deportation hearings;
- the indefinite detention of two American citizens in military prisons without criminal charges;
- selective targeting of immigrants for enforcement based on their religion.

II. US v. Miller *and the Dragnet Approach of Section 215 and National Security Letters*

In the 1970s, the Supreme Court issued a series of momentous decisions holding that citizens lose their constitutional rights in information provided to third parties in the course of commercial transactions. *United States v. Miller,* 425 U.S. 435 (1976), held that there is no constitutional privacy interest in the records held by banks showing who has paid you money, to whom you have paid money, amounts, dates, etc. *Smith v. Maryland,* 442 U.S. 735 (1979), held that telephone users have no constitutional privacy interest in the transactional information that shows who is calling them, whom they are calling, when, how often and for how long. Fast forward through the digital revolution, and the "business records" exception has become a gaping hole in the Fourth Amendment. Under current law, you have no constitutional privacy right in any of the data you generate as you go about your daily life, using credit cards, building access cards, or Easy Passes, making travel plans, or buying things. Taken together, the transactional data generated every time you dial your telephone, write a check, send an email, or go to the doctor can provide a full picture of your life, your work, your interests and your associations, but it is, under current law, constitutionally unprotected.

The PATRIOT Act exploited this situation, granting broad authorities beyond anything contemplated in *US v. Miller* or *Smith v. Maryland.* Section 215 of the Act amended the Foreign Intelligence Surveillance Act to authorize the government to obtain a court order from the FISA court or designated magistrates to seize "any tangible things (including books, records, papers, documents, and other items)" that an FBI agent claims are "sought for" an authorized investigation "to protect against international terrorism or clandestine intelligence activities." The subject of the order need not be suspected of any criminal wrongdoing whatsoever; indeed, if the statute is read literally, the order need not name any particular person but may encompass entire collections of data related to many individuals.

Section 505 of the PATRIOT Act similarly expanded the government's power to obtain telephone and email transactional records, credit reports and financial data with the use of a document called the National Security Letter (NSL), which is issued by FBI officials without judicial approval. Footnote Sections 507 and 508 granted authority to the Attorney General or his designee to obtain a court record for disclosure of education records.

In the past, the government could obtain a person's records from a bank, credit bureau, telephone company, hospital, or library in the course of a criminal investigation. In addition, prior to the PATRIOT Act, in international terrorism investigations, the FBI had the power to compel disclosure of credit, financial and communications records with National Security Letters and travel records under the predecessor of Section 215. However, Congress had set a straightforward and relatively low standard that required some factual predicate and particularized focus: the government had to have reason to believe that the records being sought pertained to an "agent of a foreign power"—an intelligence officer, for example, or a member of an international terrorist organization. Reason to believe is a very low standard, much lower than probable cause.

The PATRIOT Act eliminated both the "agent of a foreign power" standard and the reason to believe standard, giving the FBI access with National Security Letters to specific categories of records in intelligence investigations with no factual basis to believe that the records pertained to a possible terrorist. And Section 215 created a massive catch-all provision that gave the FBI the ability to compel anyone to disclose any record or tangible thing that the FBI claims is "sought in connection with" an investigation of international terrorism or "clandestine intelligence activities," even if the record does not pertain to a suspected spy or international terrorist.

The implications of this change are enormous. Previously, the FBI could get the credit card records of anyone suspected of being a foreign agent. Under the PATRIOT Act, broadly read, the FBI can get the entire database of the credit card company. Under prior law, the FBI could get library borrowing records only with a subpoena in a criminal investigation, and generally had to ask for the records of a specific patron. Under the PATRIOT Act, broadly read, the FBI can go into a public library and ask for the records on everybody who ever used the library, or who used it on a certain day, or who checked out certain kinds of books. It can do the same at any bank, telephone company, hotel or motel, hospital, or university—merely upon the claim that the information is "sought for" an investigation to protect against international terrorism or clandestine intelligence activities.

How these provisions are actually being applied is the subject of great uncertainty, at least as far as one can tell from the public discussion to date. The DOJ and the FBI could be much more forthcoming, for example, about what they are doing in libraries. Up to now, the ambiguous statements of FBI officials have only fanned suspicion and distrust.

Congress should closely inquire into the DOJ's interpretation of Section 215 and the National Security Letter authorities. The DOJ and FBI have never actually said how they are interpreting Section 215 and the new NSL authorities. The further questions submitted by Chairman Sensenbrenner on April 1, 2003, are a good start, but the Committee should also ask: Is the DOJ interpreting and using Section 215 and the NSL authorities to obtain access to entire databases, i.e., without naming individuals to whom the records pertain? If not, why shouldn't the statute be revised to clarify the particularized suspicion standard?

I have heard it argued that these changes merely conform the intelligence standard to the criminal standard, since investigators in criminal cases can obtain anything with a subpoena issued on a relevance standard. First of all, the standard in Section 215 and two of the three NSL statutes is less than relevance—it is "sought for." Second, a criminal case is at least cabined by the criminal code—something is relevant only if it relates to the commission of a crime. But on the intelligence side, the government need not be investigating crimes—at least for non-U.S. persons, it can investigate purely legal activities by those suspected of being agents of foreign powers. The standard for opening an investigation is far less than probable cause, and once an investigation is opened, under the PATRIOT Act changes, an agent can get anything from anyone by say "I am seeking this in connection with an open investigation."

Moreover, there are other crucial protections applicable to criminal subpoenas that are not available under Section 215 and the NSLs. For one, third party recipients of criminal subpoenas can notify the record subject, either immediately or after a required delay. Section 215 and the NSLs prohibit the recipient of a disclosure order from ever telling the record subject, which means that the person whose privacy has been invaded never has a chance to rectify any mistake or seek redress for any abuse. Secondly, the protections of the criminal justice system provide an opportunity for persons to assert their rights and protect their privacy, but those adversarial processes are not available in intelligence investigations that do not end up in criminal charges.

I look forward to the day when *Smith v. Maryland* and *US v. Miller* are placed in the same category as the discredited Olmstead decision of 1928—decisions based on an unduly cramped understanding of privacy, unsuited to changing technology. *Kyllo v. United States,* 533 U.S. 27 (2001), the case requiring a warrant for infra-red searches of homes, showed that the Supreme Court is sensitive to ensuring that changes in technology do not render privacy. Meanwhile, Congress should statutorily reestablish the requirement of particularized suspicion and require some factual showing on the part of government officials seeking access to records.

III. The Need for Close Congressional Scrutiny of the Effectiveness and Privacy Implications of Data Mining and Establishment of Guidelines for Any Application of the Technology

One important avenue of oversight for this Committee is how the FBI intends to use the technique known as data mining, which purports to be able to find evidence of possible terrorist preparations by scanning billions of everyday transactions, potentially including a vast array of information about Americans' personal lives such as medical information, travel records and credit card and financial data. The FBI's Trilogy project includes plans for data mining. According to an undated FBI presentation obtained by the Electronic Privacy Information Center, the FBI's use of "public source" information (including proprietary commercial databases) has grown 9,600% since 1992.

Two kinds of questions must be asked about data mining. First, is the technique likely to be effective? Secondly, assuming it can be shown to be effective, what should be the rules governing it? This week, the Defense Department will be releasing a report on the Total Information Awareness ("TIA") project at the Pentagon's Defense Advanced Research Projects Agency ("DARPA"), which hopefully will illuminate some of these issues. Among the questions to be asked specifically of the FBI is how the PATRIOT Act authorities discussed above and the changes in the FBI guidelines discussed below might relate to its data mining plans.

Current laws place few constraints on the government's ability to access information for terrorism-related data mining. Under existing law, the government can ask for, purchase or demand access to most private sector data. Unaddressed are a host of questions: Who should approve the patterns that are the basis for scans of private databases and under what standard? What should be the legal rules limiting disclosure to the government of the identity of those whose data fits a pattern? When the government draws conclusions based on pattern analysis, how should those conclusions be interpreted? How should they be disseminated and when can they be acted upon?

Adapting the Privacy Act to government uses of commercial databases is one way to look at setting guidelines for data mining. But some of the principles are simply inapplicable and others need to have greater emphasis. For example, perhaps one of the most important elements of guidelines for data mining would be rules on the interpretation and dissemination of hits and on how information generated by computerized scans can be used. Can it be used to conduct a more intensive search of someone seeking to board an airplane, to keep a person off an airplane, to deny a person access to a government building, to deny a person a job? What due process rights should be afforded when adverse actions are taken against individuals based on some pattern identified by a computer program? Can ongoing audits and evaluation mechanisms assess the effectiveness of particular applications of the technology and prevent abuse?

All of these questions must be answered before moving forward with implementation. Congress should limit the implementation of data mining until effectiveness has been shown and guidelines on collection, use, disclosure and retention have been adopted following appropriate consultation and comment.

IV. The FBI Guidelines: Impact on Civil Liberties
   and Security—The Need for Congressional Oversight
   and Re-establishment of Meaningful Limits

On May 30, 2002, Attorney General John Ashcroft issued revised Guidelines on General Crimes, Racketeering Enterprise and Terrorism Enterprise Investigations ("Domestic Guidelines"). The Attorney General claimed that the changes were necessary to free the FBI from unnecessary constraints in the fight against international terrorism. Yet the guidelines the Attorney General changed were not applicable to international terrorism. And the types of things the Attorney General said he wanted to permit—visiting mosques, surfing the Net—were never prohibited under the old guidelines.

The FBI is subject to two sets of guidelines, a classified set for foreign intelligence and international terrorism investigations ("International Terrorism Guidelines"), and an unclassified set on general crimes, racketeering and domestic terrorism. Last year, the Attorney General changed the Domestic Guidelines. He has not yet changed the International Guidelines, which relate to investigations of Osama bin Laden and Al Qaeda. (The Department of Justice may be reviewing the International Guidelines. This Committee should find out what is going on and insist on being fully consulted.) The International Terrorism Guidelines in some ways give the FBI even more latitude than the domestic guidelines. The irony is that the FBI's failed investigations of the Osama bin Laden group were conducted under those looser guidelines, reinforcing the conclusion that the problem before 9/11 was not the limits imposed by law or policy but the failure of the FBI to use the authority and information it already had.

The Role of Congress

In the 1960s, the FBI conducted wide-ranging investigations and neutralization efforts against non-violent activity across the political spectrum. While there were acts of violence being carried out on America's streets, the FBI's COINTELPRO program and related efforts focused on politics. The exercise was essentially worthless from a security standpoint: it produced no advanced warning of any violent activity. By the mid-70s, there was a reaction against this approach, within the Justice Department, the FBI itself, the Congress and the public at large. Internal and external investigations of the abuses led to the adoption of guidelines by Attorney General Edward Levi, which set standards for FBI "domestic security" investigations.

The initial issuance and subsequent major revisions of the FBI Guidelines were undertaken in conjunction with Congressional consultation and oversight. In effect, the Guidelines had a "quasi-legislative" status. Indeed, the Guidelines were adopted in lieu of legislation. A major debate in the 1970s was over the framing of a statutory charter for the FBI. (The CIA has a legislative charter; the FBI does not.) After Attorney General Levi issued the guidelines, Congress dropped the push for a legislative charter, based on two grounds: (i) Executive Branch claims that the guidelines embodied all the protections that would be included in a charter but did so with greater detail, providing just the right mix of guidance and flexibility to the FBI, and (ii) the understanding that Guideline changes would be subject to prior Congressional review and public input. Every subsequent Attorney General (except Attorney General Ashcroft) consulted with this Committee on guidelines changes. When Attorney General William French Smith undertook major revisions of the guidelines at the beginning of the Reagan Administration, the effort was accompanied by over a year of consultation, public debate, and Congressional hearings. Never before has an Attorney General undertaken major revisions to the FBI Guidelines without any prior consultation with the relevant Committees of Congress.

Major Concerns with the Changes

A major change brought about by the Ashcroft Guidelines is that they authorize investigative activity in the absence of any indication of criminal conduct. The central feature of the Levi/Smith/Thornburgh guidelines was the criminal standard: the FBI could initiate a full domestic counter-terrorism investigation when facts and circumstances reasonably indicated that two or more people were engaged in an enterprise for the purpose of furthering political goals through violence. FBI agents could conduct quite intrusive preliminary investigations on an even lower standard. The old guidelines allowed FBI agents to go into any mosque or religious or political meeting if there was reason to believe that criminal conduct was being discussed or planned there, and, in fact, over the years the FBI conducted terrorism investigations against a number of religious organizations and figures, ranging from the white supremacist Christian Identity Movement to the African-American Church of Yahweh. Separate guidelines even allowed undercover operations of religious and political groups, subject to close supervision.

Under the Levi/Smith/Thornburgh guidelines, once an investigation or even a preliminary inquiry was opened, the FBI could use any and all public source information (including the Internet) to collect personally identifiable information relevant to the investigation. In fact, an investigation could consist solely of the collection of newspaper articles and Internet material and the indexing of that information by name. The evidence could in fact consist largely or exclusively of information about the exercise of First Amendment rights. The only requirement was that there first had to be some minimal reason to believe that something illegal was being planned.

Now, the FBI is cut loose from that standard, with no indication as to how it should prioritize its efforts or avoid chilling First Amendment rights.

Visiting Religious and Political Meetings The new guidelines purport to give the FBI authority to attend public meetings of a religious or political nature, without any scintilla of suspicion of criminal or terrorist activity. The problem is compounded by poor guidance on what can be recorded and the lack of time limits on the retention of data acquired.

In the past, under the Domestic Guidelines, the FBI was guided by the criminal nexus—in deciding what mosques to go to and what political meetings to record, it had to have some reason to believe that terrorism might be discussed. Under the new guidelines, even before opening a preliminary inquiry, the FBI can go to mosques and political meetings. How will it decide which ones to go to? We fear it will be on the basis of politics, religion, or ethnicity.

Should FBI Agents Surf the Net Like Teenagers? According to justifications issued by the DOJ with the new guidelines, FBI agents previously could not conduct online searches under the term "anthrax," even after the initial appearance of the anthrax letters. That is absurd—there was an ongoing investigation. Anyhow, no privacy rights or civil liberties are implicated in searches—before or after the appearance of the anthrax letter—for words like "anthrax." That is not what the guidelines were about. The question is whether the FBI can make searches for "Palestinian rights" or other terms with a political, ethnic or religious significance, as the starting point for an investigation. The change either authorizes politically guided investigations or it authorizes fishing expeditions.

Pursuing Investigations That Turn Up Nothing Finally, the revisions decreased the internal supervision and coordination at various stages of investigation, in particular expanding the scope and duration of preliminary inquiries (by definition, these are cases that are opened on less than reasonable indication of criminal or terrorist conduct), encouraging the use of more intrusive techniques with no sense of prioritization and allowing intrusive investigations to go on for periods without producing results and without internal review or any outside or independent scrutiny.

Preliminary inquiries can use all techniques except two: mail openings and wiretaps. This means that the FBI can use informants, Internet searches, undercover operations, and physical and photographic surveillance. Under the old guidelines, if 90 days of investigation turned up no indication of criminal activity, the investigation could be continued only with HQ approval. Under the new guidelines, preliminary inquiries can continue 1 year without HQ approval. This means that the FBI can conduct an investigation, using highly intrusive techniques, for one year (and longer with HQ approval) even if the investigation is turning up no reasonable indication of criminal activity.

Broadening the FBI's surveillance authority threatens civil liberties and wastes resources while increasing the risk of intelligence failures. The salient identifiable cause of the September 11 intelligence failure was the inability of the FBI and other agencies to use the information they already had. The guidelines are likely to compound that defect, thereby producing no improvement in security.

Congressional Oversight Is Necessary

Consistent Congressional oversight is vital to protect our security and our civil liberties. Attorney General Ashcroft changed the FBI Guidelines with the stroke of a pen without prior notice or consultation with Congress. This is not only unprecedented, but does not bode well for Congressional oversight over FBI activity to ensure both protection of constitutional rights and success in the fight against terrorism.

In responding to the issues raised by the guideline changes, we recommend the following steps:

- Require through appropriations language prior notice and meaningful consultation before future guideline changes can take effect, including changes in the International Guidelines.
- Require the adoption, following Congressional consultation and comment, of Guidelines for collection, use, disclosure and retention of public event information. Such guidelines should include a provision specifying that no information regarding the First Amendment activities of a US person or group composed substantially of US persons can be disseminated outside the FBI except as part of a report indicating that such person or group is planning or engaged in criminal activity.
- Provide resources and authority to the General Accounting Office and the DOJ Inspector General to collect and analyze information on implementation of the antiterrorism guidelines and to submit to Congress public and classified reports on their impact on an open society, free speech, and privacy and benefits and costs to national security.

V. Rectifying Flaws in the Surveillance Laws

We should not loose sight of the fact that before the PATRIOT Act there were concerns that the checks and balances in the surveillance laws were insufficient. As a result of the digital revolution more information is more readily available to government investigators than ever before. The judges have not aggressively regulated electronic surveillance. Last year, only one government application for electronic surveillance was turned down. For each of the prior three years (1999–2001), not a single judge anywhere in the country, state or federal, turned down a single request for surveillance in any case, criminal or intelligence. The minimization requirement has been judicially eviscerated. The Congress could start by taking up the helpful changes to surveillance law developed and passed by the House Judiciary Committee in the 106th Congress, under H.R. 5018, including:

- ○ Heightened protections for access to wireless location information, requiring a judge to find probable cause to believe that a crime has been or is being committed. Today tens of millions of Americans are carrying (or driving) mobile devices that could be used to create a detailed dossier of their movements over time—with little clarity over how that information could be accessed and without an appropriate legal standard for doing so.
- ○ A meaningful standard for use of expanded pen registers and trap and trace capabilities, requiring a judge to at least find that specific and particularly facts reasonably indicate criminal activity and that the information to be collected is relevant to the investigation of such conduct.
- ○ Addition of electronic communications to the Title III exclusionary rule in 18 USC S.2515 and add a similar rule to the section 2703 authority and the pen register and trap and trace authority. This would prohibit the use in any court or administrative proceeding of email or other Internet communications intercepted or seized in violation of the privacy standards in the law.
- ○ Require high-level Justice Department approval for applications to intercept electronic communications, as is currently required for interceptions of wire and oral communications.
- ○ Require statistical reports for S.2703 disclosures, similar to those required by Title III.

Beyond these changes, there are issues raised by the PATRIOT Act that need to be addressed:

Require more extensive public reporting on the use of FISA, to allow better public oversight.

Make the use of FISA evidence in criminal cases subject to the Classified Information Procedures Act.

Limit the use of secret searches.

Conclusion

We need limits on government surveillance and guidelines for the use of information not merely to protect individual rights but to focus government activity on those planning violence. The criminal standard and the principle of particularized suspicion keep the government from being diverted into investigations guided by politics, religion or ethnicity. Legal standards should focus on perpetrators of crime, avoid indulging in guilt by association, maintain procedures designed to identify the guilty and exonerate the innocent, insist on limits on surveillance authority, and bar political spying.

Scholarly Article

The Author: Andrew C. McCarthy

National Review Online is one of the top Web journals for news and analysis. NRO has established itself as the site of choice for hundreds of thousands who seek a unique, unbiased view on politics and culture. Like its print parent, *National Review* magazine, NRO has filled an important role by providing America (and the world) with an alternative source of biting, witty, and well-written news and commentary.

Andrew C. McCarthy, a former chief assistant U.S. attorney who led the 1995 terrorism prosecution against Sheik Omar Abdel Rahman and eleven others, is a regular *National Review* contributor.

The following article was published on June 14, 2004.

The Patriot Act Without Tears: Understanding a Mythologized Law

It was mid-August 2001, the last desperate days before the 9/11 terrorist attacks. Desperate, that is, for an alert agent of the FBI's Foreign Counterintelligence Division (FCI); much of the rest of America, and certainly much of the rest of its government, blithely carried on, content to assume, despite the number and increasing ferocity of terrorist attacks dating back nearly nine years, that national security was little more than an everyday criminal-justice issue.

Since 1995, a "wall" had been erected, presumptively barring communications between FCI agents and their counterparts in law enforcement—the FBI's criminal agents and the assistant U.S. attorneys who collectively, after a string of successful prosecutions through the 1990s, had become the government's best resource for information about the threat of militant Islam. This wall was not required by law; it was imposed as policy. Justice Department lawyers, elevating litigation risk over national security, designed it to forestall accusations that the federal government had used its intelligence-eavesdropping authority to build criminal cases.

This FCI agent collided, head-on, with the wall; and strewn in the wreckage was the last, best hope of stopping 9/11. Putting disconnected clues together, the agent had deduced that two Qaeda operatives, Khalid al-Midhar and Nawaf al-Hazmi, had probably gotten into the U.S. Alarmed, he pleaded with the FBI's criminal division to help him hunt down the terrorists—but they refused: For agents to fuse their information and efforts would be a transgression against the wall. The prescient agent rued that, one day soon, people would die in the face of this paralyzing roadblock. Al-Midhar and al-Hazmi remained undetected until they plunged Flight 77 into the Pentagon on 9/11.

Facing Reality

By October 2001, the world had changed—and the USA Patriot Act was passed. So patent was the need for this law that it racked up massive support: 357–66 in the House, 98–1 in the Senate. In the nearly three years since, however, it has been distorted beyond recognition by a coalition of anti-Bush leftists and libertarian extremists, such that it is now perhaps the most broadly maligned—and misunderstood—piece of meaningful legislation in U.S. history. If our nation is serious about national security, the Patriot Act must be made permanent; instead, it could soon be gone—and the disastrous "intelligence wall" rebuilt.

Contrary to widespread calumny, Patriot is not an assault on the Bill of Rights. It is, basically, an overhaul of the government's antiquated counter-terror arsenal, which had been haplessly fighting a 21st-century war with 20th-century weapons. Indeed, Patriot's only obvious flaw is its cloying acronym, short for "The Uniting and Strengthening America by Providing Appropriate Tools to Intercept and Obstruct Terrorism Act of 2001." But once you get past the title, Patriot is all substance, and crucial to national security.

The most essential improvement wrought by Patriot has been the dismantling of the intelligence wall. The bill expressly amended the government's national-security eavesdropping-and-search authority (under the Foreign Intelligence Surveillance Act or FISA) to clarify that intelligence agents, criminal investigators, and prosecutors not only may but should be pooling information and connecting dots. This is common sense: Along the way toward mass murder, terrorists inevitably commit numerous ordinary crimes, everything from identity theft to immigration fraud to bombing. One could not surveil them as agents of a foreign power (as FISA permits) without necessarily uncovering such crimes, and this, far from being a problem, is a bonus since these lay the groundwork for prosecutions that can both stop terrorists before they strike and pressure them to turn state's evidence.

Yet, as has been detailed in a decisive 2002 opinion by the Foreign Intelligence Surveillance Court of Review, FISA had for decades been misinterpreted by the government and the courts, which, owing to their obsession over the "rights" of enemy operatives, erroneously presumed that national-security intelligence was somehow separate and severable from criminal evidence. This false dichotomy culminated in the wall built by the Clinton Justice Department (and substantially maintained by Bush's DOJ), with awful consequences.

Tearing down the wall—as well as repealing legislation that had barred criminal investigators from sharing with intelligence agents the fruits of grand-jury proceedings and criminal wiretaps—has paid instant dividends. For example, while the wall once caused intelligence and criminal agents in Buffalo to believe they could not be in the same room together during briefings to discuss their parallel investigations of an apparent sleeper cell in Lackawanna, N.Y., the Patriot Act allowed the criminal investigators to learn that a theretofore anonymous letter to one of their subjects had, as intelligence agents knew, been penned by a Qaeda operative. This and other fact-sharing broke an investigative logjam, revealing a history of paramilitary training at al-Qaeda's Afghan proving grounds, and directly resulted in guilty pleas and lengthy sentences for six men who had provided material support to the terror network.

In a similar way, in 2002 law-enforcement agents in Oregon learned through an informant that Jeffrey Battle was actively scoping out Jewish schools and synagogues for a terrorist attack. It later emerged that Battle was among a group that set out to train with al-Qaeda in Afghanistan (they never made it). Battle was plainly a time bomb, but his confederates had not yet been fully revealed—and there naturally was fear that if Battle were arrested and removed from the scene the investigators would lose their best hope of identifying other terrorists. Because the wall was down, the criminal investigators had the confidence to delay the arrest and continue the investigation, knowing the intelligence agents using FISA were now free to share what they were learning. As a result, not only Battle but six others, collectively known as the "Portland 7," were identified, convicted on terrorism-support charges, and sentenced to between three and 18 years in prison.

Thanks to Patriot's removal of the blinders, action—sometimes long overdue—has been taken against many other accused and convicted terrorists. Criminal investigators won access to a historic trove of intelligence demonstrating that Prof. Sami al-Arian had been using his University of South Florida redoubt as an annex of the deadly Palestinian Islamic Jihad group responsible for over 100 murders, including that of Alisa Flatow, a young American woman killed in an Israeli bus bombing. The sharing provisions also ensured the convictions of nine other defendants in Virginia, on charges ranging from support of the Qaeda-affiliated Lashkar-e-Taiba to conspiracy to levy war against the U.S.; the conviction in Chicago of bin Laden intimate Enaam Arnaout for using his Benevolence International Foundation as a conduit to fund terrorist cells in Bosnia and Chechnya, and of Khaled Abdel-Latif Dumeisi for working in the U.S. for Saddam Hussein's brutal Iraqi Intelligence Service; the indictment of a University of Idaho graduate student, Sami Omar al-Hussayen, for using his computer skills to support the recruiting and fundraising of Hamas and Chechnyan terror groups; the indictment in Brooklyn of two Yemeni nationals who bragged about having raised millions of dollars for bin Laden; and the smashing of a drugs-for-weapons plot in San Diego that solicited Stinger anti-aircraft missiles for the Taliban in exchange for heroin and hashish. Moreover, while much information provided by criminal investigators to the intelligence community must remain classified, the Justice Department also credits the sharing provisions with the revocation of visas for suspected terrorists, tracking and choking off of terrorist funding channels, and identifying of terrorists operating overseas.

21st-Century Tactics

Besides paving the way for agents to pool critical information, Patriot has been invaluable in modernizing investigative tools to ensure that more information is actually captured. While the critics' persistent caviling misleadingly suggests that these tools are a novel assault on privacy rights, for the most part they merely extend to national-security intelligence investigations the same methods that have long been available to law-enforcement agents probing the vast array of federal crimes, including those as comparatively innocuous as health-care fraud.

Among the best examples is the so-called "roving" (or multipoint) wiretap. As the telephony revolution unfolded, criminals naturally took advantage, avoiding wiretap surveillance by the simple tactic of constantly switching phones—which became especially easy to do once cellphones became ubiquitous. Congress reacted nearly 20 years ago with a law that authorized criminal agents to obtain wiretaps that, rather than aim at a specific telephone, targeted *persons,* thus allowing monitoring to continue without significant delay as criminals ditched one phone for the next. Inexplicably, this same authority was not available to intelligence agents investigating terrorists under FISA. Patriot rectifies this anomaly.

On the law-enforcement side, Patriot expands the substance of the wiretap statute to account for the realities of terrorism. Most Americans would probably be surprised to learn that while the relatively trivial offense of gambling, for example, was a lawful predicate for a criminal wiretap investigation, chemical-weapons offenses, the use of weapons of mass destruction, the killing of Americans abroad, terrorist financing, and computer fraud were not. Thanks to Patriot, that is no longer the case.

Analogously, Patriot revamped other telecommunications-related techniques. Prior law, for example, had been written in the bygone era when cable service meant television programming. Owing to privacy concerns about viewing habits, which the government rarely has a legitimate reason to probe, federal law made access to cable-usage records practically impossible—creating in service providers a fear of being sued by customers if they complied with government information requests. Now, of course, millions of cable subscribers—including no small number of terrorists—use the service not only for entertainment viewing but for e-mail services.

While e-mail-usage records from dial-up providers have long been available by subpoena, court order, or search warrant (depending on the sensitivity of the information sought), cable providers for years delayed complying with such processes, arguing that their services fell under the restrictive umbrella of prior cable law. This was not only a potentially disastrous state of affairs in terrorism cases, where delay can cost lives, but in many other contexts as well—including one reported case in which a cable company declined to comply with an order to disclose the name of a suspected pedophile who was distributing child pornography on the Internet even as he bragged online about sexually abusing a young girl. (Investigators, forced to pursue other leads, needed two extra weeks to identify and apprehend the suspect.) Recognizing that it made no sense to have radically different standards for acquiring the same information, Patriot made cable e-mail available on the same terms as dial-up.

Patriot also closed other gaping e-mail loopholes. Under prior law, for example, investigators trying to identify the source of incriminating e-mail were severely handicapped in that their readiest tool, the grand-jury subpoems, could be used only to compel the service provider to produce customers' names, addresses, and lengths of service—information often of little value in ferreting out wrongdoers who routinely use false names and temporary e-mail addresses. Patriot solved this problem by empowering grand juries to compel payment information, which can be used to trace the bank and credit-card records by which investigators ultimately establish identity. This not only makes it possible to identify potential terrorists far more quickly—and thus, it is hoped, before they can strike—but also to thwart other criminals who must be apprehended with all due speed. Such subpoenas, for example, have been employed repeatedly to identify and arrest molesters who were actively abusing children. The Justice Department reports that, only a few weeks ago, the new authority prevented a Columbine-like attack by allowing agents to identify a suspect, and obtain his confession, before the attack could take place.

Further, Patriot clarified such investigative matters as the methods for lawful access by investigators to stored e-mail held by third parties (such as AOL and other service providers). And it cured the incongruity that allowed agents to access voice messages stored in a suspect's own home answering machine by a simple search warrant but anomalously forced them to obtain a far more cumbersome wiretap order if the messages were in the form of voicemail stored with a third-party provider.

A Library of Red Herrings

One Patriot reform that has been irresponsibly maligned is Section 21.5 of the act, which merely extends to national-security investigations conducted under FISA the same authority to subpoena business records that criminal investigators have exercised unremarkably for years. Indeed, even under Section 215, intelligence agents remain at a comparative disadvantage since they must get the approval of a FISA court before compelling records production while prosecutors in criminal cases simply issue grand-jury subpoenas. Nonetheless, this commonsense provision came under blistering, disingenuous assault last year when the ACLU and others raised the red herring of library records—which are not even mentioned in the statute. In 2002, for example, the *Hartford Courant* was compelled to retract in full a story that falsely accused the FBI of installing software on computers in the Hartford Public Library to monitor the public's use of the Internet. (In fact, the FBI had obtained a court-ordered search warrant to copy the hard drive of a single computer that had been used criminally to hack into a business computer system in California.)

In 2003, the ACLU issued a warning that Section 215 would allow federal "thought police" to "target us for what we choose to read or what Websites we visit." In reality, Section 215 (unlike criminal-grand-jury subpoems authority) expressly contains safeguards protecting First Amendment rights, and further provides that the attorney general must, twice a year, "fully inform" Congress about how the provision has been implemented. As of September 2003, the provision had not been used a single time—neither for library records nor, indeed, for records of any kind.

Unlike reading habits, financing—the lifeblood of terrorist networks—actually is a Patriot target. The act has significantly crimped the ability of overseas terrorists to use foreign banks and nominees to avoid seizures of their funds, it cracked down on the so-called "hawalas" (that is, unlicensed money-transmitting businesses) that have been used to funnel millions of dollars to terror groups, it extended the reach of civil money-laundering penalties—which loom large in the minds of financial institutions—against those who engage in transactions involving the proceeds of crime. And it further choked the funding channels by making currency smuggling itself (rather than the mere failure to file a report about the movement of currency) a crime, an initiative that bolsters the legal basis for seizing all, rather than a portion, of the smuggled funds. These and other Patriot finance provisions have enabled the government to obtain over 20 convictions to date and freeze over $130 million in assets worldwide.

Mention should also be made of another Patriot improvement that has been speciously challenged: the codification of uniform procedures for so-called sneak-and-peek warrants, which allow agents to conduct a search without seizing items, and delay notification to the person whose premises have been searched—thus ensuring that an investigation can proceed and agents can continue identifying other conspirators. Such warrants have been used for many years, and delayed notification has been a commonplace—just as it is in other areas, such as wiretap law, where alerting the subject would prematurely end the investigation.

Sneak-and-peek delayed notification, however, evolved through federal case law rather than by statute, and consequently there was a jumble of varying requirements depending on which federal circuit the investigation happened to be in. All Patriot did in this regard was impose a uniform national standard that permits delay if notification could cause endangerment to life, facilitation of flight, destruction of evidence, intimidation of witnesses, or similar substantial jeopardizing of investigations. Yet critics drummed up outrage by portraying sneak-and-peek as if it were a novel encroachment on privacy rather than a well-established tool that requires prior court approval. So effective was this campaign that the House of Representatives responded by voting to deny funding for the delayed-notification warrants. Inability to delay notification, of course, would defeat the purpose of using sneak-and-peek in the first place. The Senate has not seemed inclined to follow suit, but that so prudent a provision could become the subject of controversy illustrates how effectively the opposition has discredited the Patriot Act.

Palpably, the Patriot Act, far from imperiling the Constitution, went a long way toward shoring up the perilous state of national security that existed on the morning of 9/11. That is why it is so excruciating to note that, despite all we have been through, we will be transported right back to that precarious state if Congress fails to reauthorize Patriot. Because of intense lobbying by civil-liberties groups instinctively hostile to anything that makes government stronger—even in the areas of national defense, where we need it to be strong if we are to have liberties at all—Patriot's sponsors had to agree, to secure passage, that the act would effectively be experimental. That is, the information sharing, improved investigative techniques, and several other provisions were not permanently enacted into law but are scheduled to "sunset" on December 31, 2005. Dismayingly, far from grasping the eminent sense in making these improvements permanent, the alliance of Democratic Bush-bashers and crusading Republican libertarians is actually pushing a number of proposals to *extend* the sunset provision to parts of Patriot that were not originally covered.

At a time when the 9/11 Commission's public hearings highlight intelligence lapses and investigative backwardness—and when al-Qaeda publicly threatens larger-than-ever attacks while continuing to fight our forces and allies on the battlefield and in murderous attacks throughout the world—it is remarkable that elected officials would have *any* priority other than making the Patriot Act permanent.

Article

The Author: Julian Sanchez

Julian Sanchez is the Assistant Editor for *Reason* magazine. The following article was published in *Reason* magazine in April 2004.

PATRIOT Spawn

When a draft of the Domestic Security Enhancement Act, nicknamed PATRIOT II, was leaked last year, public outrage scuppered the proposal. But since then key provisions of the bill have been introduced piecemeal, in what many civil libertarians see as an attempt to fly below the public's radar.

In December, as Americans were glued to coverage of Saddam Hussein's capture, President Bush took the unusual step of signing a bill on a Saturday. The new law, the Intelligence Authorization Act for Fiscal Year 2004, expanded the definition of "financial institutions" covered by the PATRIOT Act. Law enforcement agencies may now obtain records without a court order not only from banks but from insurers, travel agencies, stockbrokers, real estate agencies, car dealerships, casinos, jewelers, pawnshops, the U.S. Postal Service, and any other business "whose cash transactions have a high degree of usefulness in criminal, tax, or regulatory matters."

Other components of PATRIOT II remain in the legislative pipeline. The Clear Law Enforcement for Criminal Alien Removal Act, which has attracted more than 100 House co-sponsors, would turn local law enforcement officials into deputy immigration cops. The Terrorist Penalties Enhancement Act would impose the death penalty for acts of domestic terrorism that result in a person's death. H.R. 3037, introduced by Rep. Tom Feeny (R-Fla.), would empower the attorney general to issue secret administrative subpoenas not subject to judicial oversight. (These are similar to the existing "national security letters," but have a wider scope.) Sen. Jon Kyl

(R-Ariz.) has introduced a bill to provide for mandatory pretrial detention of those accused of certain terrorism-related crimes.

American Civil Liberties Union Legislative Counsel Charles Mitchell believes the fragmentation of PATRIOT II is troubling because "it's always easier to get people to give up a little than a lot. They say, 'We already have these powers; we're just tweaking them.' But when you add up the tweaks, you've got a dramatic expansion of power."

Scholarly Article

The Author: Mark S. Hamm

Mark S. Hamm is a professor in the Department of Criminology, Indiana State University. The following is a chapter in the book *Cultural Criminology Unleashed,* edited by Jeff Ferrell, Keith Hayward, Wayne Morrison, and Mike Presdee.

The USA Patriot Act and the Politics of Fear

The terrorist attacks of 11 September left Americans with a myriad of powerful emotions—anxiety, fear, sorrow, despair, and incandescent rage. Among these emotions, scholars argue that *fear* represents the common baseline for comprehending the complex aftermath of 9/11.[1] That fear was caused by extraordinary images of indiscriminate violence—planes crashing into buildings, skyscrapers in flames, men and women leaping to their deaths, and landmark structures collapsing to the ground as panicked crowds ran for safety amid a whirlwind of dust and debris. This vivid imagery demonstrated that the point of terrorism is fear. And fear, in turn, would define the very fabric of subsequent responses.

Apocalypse and Public Policy

"The shocking imagery of 9/11 redefined the scope of events," argues Michael Barkun, "transforming spectators into survivors." We all became survivors on 9/11, writes Barkun, survivors of nothing less than "a world-destroying power."[2] Indeed, the very name given to the World Trade Center site—Ground Zero—came from the lexicon of nuclear weapons, themselves associated with the capacity to destroy civilization. The emotional aspects of 11 September were therefore directly associated with its political aspects via a long-standing American fascination with Christian apocalyptic speculation. The 9/11 attacks led to a marked increase in church attendance and a spectacular rise in sales for books with apocalyptic themes published in the United States.[3] According to a 2001 Time/CNN poll, roughly 30 percent of Americans believed that the attacks were predicted in the Bible. Another 35 percent thought about the implications of the daily news for the end of the world, and 60 percent believed that the future will unfold in accordance with the Book of Revelation.[4]

These visions were reinforced by the nineteen hijackers, and their leader—Osama bin Laden—whose messianic pronouncements claimed that the attacks were prophesied in Muslim apocalyptic literature which predicts a disintegration of Islam followed by epic events that will lead to a worldwide resurgence of the Islamic faith.[5] The U.S. response to 9/11 was also specifically apocalyptic in belief and intent. From his very first speeches following the attacks, President George W. Bush nationalized our fear by launching America on a "crusade" of "infinite justice" against "evil-doers" who had committed "barbarism." To fight this evil, Bush was willing to take on extremist elements of the Muslim world, in almost a Biblical sense. "We will rid the world of evil-doers," he said on 14 September, 2001. "Either you are with us or against us. You're either evil or you're good."[6] The war on terrorism was therefore presented to the world as a mandate from God. "I know many Americans feel fear today," the President acknowledged when he began the war on 7 October.[7] "To answer these attacks and rid the world of evil," he said, "we will export death and violence to the four corners of the earth in defense of this great nation."[8]

Anthrax and the USA Patriot Act

While 9/11 was known for its agonizing imagery, the anthrax attacks were marked by silence. Beginning on 4 October, 2001, 23 cases of cutaneous anthrax were reported in the United States, resulting in five deaths. It hardly mattered that there was no evidence linking al Qaeda to the attacks, for in terms of popular opinion the anthrax outbreak became part of the 9/11 narrative, thus amplifying the nation's fear. Nowhere was this more evident than on Capitol Hill.

On 15 October, an intern in South Dakota Senator Tom Daschle's office cut open a taped business envelope, letting out a puff of airy white powder that entered the ventilation system of the Hart Senate Office Building. As the airborne anthrax wafted through the building, chaos erupted in government buildings across Washington. Mail deliveries were suspended, bundles of mail and packages were quarantined, meetings were postponed, tours were canceled, and military specialists were dispatched to search for biological and chemical agents. Soon anthrax spores were turning up in other Capitol office buildings, prompting discussions about shutting down the government.[9] Against this turbulent backdrop Congress enacted one of the most sweeping criminal justice reforms in American history.

On 26 October, 2001, President Bush signed the USA Patriot Act into law. The short-term objective of the Act was to enhance the authority of the Federal Bureau of Investigation's (FBI) "PENTBOMB" case. PENTBOMB focused on identifying the terrorists who hijacked the planes on 9/11 and anyone who aided them. The Act's long-term objective was to avert subsequent terrorist attacks in the United States and against U.S. interests abroad.[10]

But much had already been accomplished prior to passage of the Act. The day after 9/11, President Bush had directed the FBI to develop a "scorecard" on the investigation as a way to measure its progress.[11] In response, PENTBOMB investigators began compiling a watch list of potential hijackers and other individuals who might be planning future attacks. By 22 September, the watch list had grown to a staggering 331. That meant that there were 331 suspected al Qaeda operatives in the United States—15 times the number of terrorists who had hijacked the planes on 9/11. "I was floored," Bush later recalled to Bob Woodward. "And [given the trauma of 9/11] the idea of saying, there's 331 al Qaeda-type killers lurking, to the point where they made a list . . . just wasn't necessary."[12] This executive decision, meant to shield Americans from the fear of terrorism, created a model of intense secrecy that would characterize the Patriot Act. Ironically, while the Act was intended to curb the fears of 9/11, it would actually reproduce those fears in its own execution.

The USA Patriot Act—an acronym for United and Strengthening America by Providing Appropriate Tools Required to Intercept and Obstruct Terrorism—gives far-reaching new powers to both the FBI and international intelligence agencies, based on revisions of fifteen different statutes. It also eliminates the checks and balances that previously gave courts the opportunity to ensure that these powers were not abused.

Among its provisions, the 342-page Act grants the Justice Department the authority to: (1) share foreign intelligence surveillance information, (2) increase penalties for money laundering, (3) seize foreign assets in U.S.-based accounts of foreign banks if there is probable cause that the funds were obtained illegally, and (4) place stricter controls on immigration, including the authority to detain non-citizens without a hearing, and to deport immigrants without any evidence that they have committed a crime. For U.S. citizens and non-citizens alike, the Act also grants Justice the authority to: (5) tap telephones, e-mail messages, and personal computer hard drives (including roving wiretaps), without a legal probable cause, (6) request private and personal business and bank records, without a court hearing, and (7) solicit a patron's list of library books. The Act also allows the Justice Department to: (8) investigate a person who is not suspected of a crime and/or is not the target of a terrorist investigation, (9) secretly conduct "sneak-and-peek" searches without a warrant, (10) withhold the names and other information about individuals arrested and detained, (11) hold closed hearings, and (12) monitor jailhouse conversations between attorneys and clients. Finally, the Act (13) creates a new definition of domestic terrorism, (14) gives government the power to designate domestic groups, including religious and political groups, as "terrorist organizations," and (15) expands the authority of the President to designate individuals as "enemy combatants."

According to the Justice Department, these expanded powers are necessary because "the threat presented by terrorists who carried out the September 11 attacks required a different kind of law enforcement approach. . . . The Department needed to disrupt such persons from carrying out further attacks by turning its focus to *prevention*, rather than investigation and prosecution."[13]

The Controversy

Controversy surrounding the Patriot Act began almost immediately and it centered on three issues, all of which turned on the matter of government secrecy. First, the media started to report allegations of mistreatment among the terrorist suspects who had been rounded up and detained because their names had appeared on the FBI watch list. (Once the number of detainees reached 1,200, officials stopped keeping statistics.) Through their attorneys, these "special interest" detainees, as they were known (nearly all Muslim or Arab men who were not U.S. citizens), alleged that they were not informed of the charges against them for extended periods of time; were frequently denied contact with attorneys; remained in detention even though they had no involvement in terrorism; or were physically abused and mistreated in other ways while incarcerated.[14] Attorneys also argued that the Justice Department subjected detainees to arbitrary detention; violated due process by holding closed proceedings against them; trampled basic free speech rights—including the public's right to know "what their government is up to"—by refusing to release the names of detainees; and ran roughshod over the presumption of innocence by presuming that the detainees were guilty of terrorist activities. The attorneys concluded that the Justice Department shielded itself from scrutiny by keeping from the public information that is crucial to understanding the extent to which the Patriot Act had been enacted in accordance with U.S. law and international human rights law.[15]

Many of these charges were confirmed in June 2003 when the Justice Department's inspector general released a blistering report that found "significant problems" in the post-9/11 detention of suspected terrorists. Many detainees were classified as terrorism suspects on scant evidence, or no evidence at all. Others were detained for months without charge. There was a "pattern of physical and verbal abuse" and detainees were routinely denied bail and access to lawyers. The report said that the Justice Department had "poorly handled" its policies and practices. Although the report generated headlines around the world that spoke of "unduly harsh conditions" imposed by American officials, Attorney General John Ashcroft dismissed these charges by saying that the Justice Department made "no apologies" for how it went about protecting the American public from further acts of terrorism.[16]

Such hubris hardly ever goes unnoticed and Ashcroft's pugnacity created a unique opportunity for lawmakers and government officials to reflect candidly on what took place behind the scenes during passage of the Patriot Act, leading to the second major controversy. Although the Patriot Act passed 357–66 in the House of Representatives and 98–1 in the Senate, these figures belie the politics of fear that gripped Congress during the anthrax attacks. Conservative Representative Don Young (R-Alaska), a member of the Homeland Security Committee, admitted to reporters that the Patriot Act was "the worst act we ever passed. Everybody voted for it, but it was stupid, it was what you call 'emotional voting.' "[17] Then Representative Bob Barr (R-Georgia) declared it the "most massive violation of civil liberties in our history."[18] A Congressional observer estimated that "fewer than five percent of the people who voted for the bill ever read it."[19] Representative Ron Paul (R-Texas) explained why. "The bill was not made available to members of Congress," he said, "[it] wasn't even printed before the vote."[20] Even Rand Beers, the Bush administration's senior counter-terrorism policy advisor, weighed in with a criticism. The Patriot Act, he said, was "making us less secure, not more secure. As an insider, I saw the things that weren't being done."[21]

Resistance

The third issue also generated wide interest, though it received only marginal attention from the media. This issue, too, arose from fear—a fear that the Patriot Act threatened fundamental civil liberties. The most dramatic response to this was a collective resistance of local governments to the federal law. As of this writing (July 2003), 133 communities in 25 states have passed resolutions condemning the Act.[22] These have included big cities like Philadelphia, Detroit, Baltimore, and San Francisco, and small towns like Dillon, Montana, Reading, Pennsylvania, Takoma Park, Maryland, and Ithaca, New York. Statewide resolutions have been passed in Alaska, Hawaii, and Vermont. In all, nearly 12 million Americans live in communities that have passed anti–Patriot Act resolutions.[23]

These resolutions assert that the Act contradicts and undermines constitutionally protected rights without making the United States more secure from terrorism. Although these resolutions are largely symbolic, since federal law trumps any local ordinance, they nevertheless speak volumes about the extent to which the extended law enforcement powers have undercut public support for the war on terrorism. In Carrboro, North Carolina, city police are required to stand in the way of any unreasonable searches and seizures conducted by the FBI under authority of the Patriot Act. Police in Detroit are authorized to decline federal requests that are considered "fishing expeditions," such as compiling a list of mosque attendees. And in the tiny town of Arcata, California, enforcing the Patriot Act is actually a crime punishable by a fine.

Other opponents have made the more serious charge that the antiterrorism laws are being misapplied to advance agendas that have nothing to do with preventing another attack on America. Of primary concern is the revised intelligence-gathering powers of the FBI. Since 9/11, the agency has reportedly collected intelligence on environmental and anti-globalization groups in the U.S., even though these groups have not engaged in terrorism.[24] The greatest threat to freedom in the United States, then, is posed not by terrorists themselves but by the government's own response. No less a publication than the *New York Times* reported that one of the nation's leading scholars of international law suggested at a meeting of diplomats that President Bush's advisors were planning to use the authority of the Patriot Act to suspend the elections of 2004.[25] In other words, the erosion of civil liberties under the Bush administration constitutes an early stage of the kind of fascism that Hitler brought to Germany. In this nightmare, John Ashcroft is the reincarnation of Hermann Goering.

Cultural Conflict

These denunciations served to legitimize the belief that people can and should organize themselves politically to repeal the new antiterrorism initiative. Many of these local efforts combined politics with culture to produce a colorful collective resistance. Here in Bloomington, Indiana, for instance, the anti–Patriot Act resolution was presented to the City Council in a four-hour meeting that included speeches from scholars, human rights activists, Vietnam veterans, artists, and common citizens. These presentations ranged from legal and sociological analyses of the Patriot Act to poems, songs, and personal testimonies of fear. The name John Ashcroft was mentioned pejoratively in nearly every presentation—sometimes accompanied by tambourines, guitars, burning incense and sage. The emotional highpoint came with the testimony of a librarian—known to all as a peaceful young woman—who had recently been approached by two severe FBI agents and told to turn over the borrowing records of several Muslim students from Indiana University. She did not comply and was threatened with arrest.

Such local efforts were part of a wider cultural resistance that occurred as more and more Americans became aware of the Patriot Act's implications for civil liberties. Rocker John Mellencamp released a remake of the traditional American ballad, "To Washington," with references to the president who "had made things worse." Mellencamp then issued a highly controversial open letter to America, declaring, "We have been lied to and terrorized by our own government and it is time to take action." Neil Young released a song critical of the Patriot Act, while such divergent rock, punk, country, and hip hop artists as Merle Haggard, Eddie Vedder, Green Day, Willie Nelson, Jay-Z, Steve Earle, and the Dixie Chicks used their voices to take aim at the Patriot Act, U.S. policy on Iraq, and the Bush administration's assault on the environment. The crowning moment of this artistic tirade occurred at New York's Shea Stadium on 4 October, 2003, when America's working-class poet laureate, Bruce Springsteen, was joined by legendary troubadour Bob Dylan for a glorious romp of "Highway 61 Revisited." Springsteen then told the crowd of 50,000 adoring fans, "Shout a little louder if you want the president impeached!"[26]

The Response

This assault forced the government to launch its own lobbying efforts to calm the public's fear of the Patriot Act. First, the White House assured Americans that any encroachments on civil liberties would affect only foreign nationals.[27] Then President Bush enthusiastically praised Attorney General Ashcroft for doing a "fabulous job" in the war on terrorism.[28] Ashcroft addressed his critics with these words:

> For those who scare peace-loving people with phantoms of lost liberty, my message is this: your tactics only aid terrorists, for they erode our national unity and diminish our resolve. They give ammunition to America's enemies, and pause to America's friends. They encourage people of goodwill to remain silent in the face of evil.[29]

In subsequent Congressional testimony, Ashcroft claimed that the Patriot Act had made it possible to increase surveillance powers, thereby uncovering the status of al Qaeda cells in the United States and abroad. According to the Attorney General, this led to critical intelligence about al Qaeda safe houses, financing, recruitment, training camps, weapons caches, and locations in the U.S. being scouted for potential attacks by al Qaeda. In summarizing these successes, Ashcroft declared that *"more than 3,000* foot soldiers of terror have been incapacitated . . . and *hundreds* of suspected terrorists have been identified and tracked throughout the U.S."[30]

As for the anti–Patriot Act resolutions, the Attorney General proclaimed: "We do not stand for abuse."[31] "The guarding of freedom that God grants is the noble charge of the Department of Justice," he told reporters, adding: "The terrorists who attacked the United States have exploited God's gift." And the Patriot Act, he said, would be used "to guarantee God's gift."[32]

Far from being an impediment to freedom, then, the Bush Administration considers the Patriot Act a valuable tool. Indeed, it is considered a *God-given* tool that has enhanced its ability to investigate and thwart terrorist attacks. "Let me state this as clearly as possible," said the Attorney General. "Our ability to prevent another catastrophic attack on American soil would be more difficult, if not impossible, without the Patriot Act. It has been the key weapon used across America in successful counter-terrorist operations to protect innocent Americans from the deadly plans of terrorists."[33]

Terrorism Research in a Time of War

Strangely silent in this controversy has been a group whose professional training most prepares them to comment on the ramifications of criminal justice policy: academic criminologists. Such an analysis would consider two essential questions: (1) To what extent are the policy outputs of the Justice Department consistent with the original objectives of the Patriot Act? and (2) What effects, in turn, do these outcomes have on subsequent legislative decisions?[34] What follows is a brief attempt to address these problems, along with several challenges facing scholars during a time of war. The USA Patriot Act has one, and only one, clearly stated output. "Our *single* objective," said the Attorney General, "is to prevent terrorist attacks by taking suspected terrorists off the street."[35] The objective of the Act is not to investigate or prosecute terrorist acts, but to prevent them by bringing suspected terrorists under state control.

To the extent that this objective is achieved, it has important implications for subsequent legislative actions. The Patriot Act carries a "sunset" provision to expire on 31 December, 2005. (Some surveillance provisions do not expire.) Should the Act achieve its stated objective, then Congress will presumably renew it. Should it fail, then presumably the Act will be either revised or terminated. There is presumably only one failure scenario: The FBI fails to prevent another terrorist attack on America.

At least four methodological issues obtain from this sum-zero game, each with its own set of implications for criminological research. First and foremost is an issue of logic: Any evaluation of the Patriot Act requires disproof of a negative, which is notoriously difficult. If there are no future attacks on the United States by al Qaeda or other terrorist groups, then it may be assumed that the Act has achieved its objective. But if there are no attacks, how do we know that they were actually "prevented" by the Patriot Act? How do we know whether the absence of terrorism was related in part to the Act (and if so, what parts worked?), or whether the Act was unrelated to the absence of terrorism? And, at what point can we be assured that terrorism does not *in fact* exist?

Implications for Research

The objective of the Patriot Act reflects a particularly Western slant on a problem framed by the legal institution responsible for its prevention. Yet terrorism is a dynamic phenomenon that is increasingly framed by non-Western sensibilities—most notably, the idea of *jihad*, or international holy war. Certainty about this worldwide *jihad* may not come for a long time. A major lesson of 9/11 is that al Qaeda works on its own time line, often coming back to targets it might not have destroyed the first time around. The 9/11 attacks were the result of eight years of elaborate planning, religious indoctrination, and paramilitary training that began after the 1993 attack on the World Trade Center.[36]

Because terrorism occurs within a distinctive context of social, political and cultural factors, changes in any one these factors (e.g., increased public awareness) can explain an absence of terrorism. By ignoring these possible changes, the Patriot Act suffers from its own parochialism and isolation. Consistent with the Bush administration's global war on terrorism, the Patriot Act deals with the symptoms rather than the root causes of terror and extremism. As Turk notes, terrorism cannot be stopped solely by a public policy. It can only be ended by "removing the deprivations . . . that create the environment in which people's fears and hopelessness make terrorism appear to be their only option."[37] In this case, those fears are lodged in Muslim grievances. Moreover, there is no way to develop a comparative understanding of the *granularity* of the Justice Department's institutional performance—whether through aggregate quantitative analysis or through ethnographic and historical work—with other nation-states whose post-9/11 counter-terrorism achievements (e.g., Pakistan) have taught us that complex problems require nuanced solutions. These solutions involve not only law enforcement and intelligence capabilities, but also cross-cultural fluency and diplomatic skill.

The second methodological problem involves the Bush administration's doctrine of secrecy. President Bush has taken the firm position that the government's actions in the war on terrorism will remain "secret even in success."[38] Indeed, FBI Director Robert Mueller is on record saying that "terrorist attacks have been prevented" since 9/11 but these successes "don't become public."[39] Yet Attorney General Ashcroft *has* released aggregate numbers on the war's success by stating that more than 3,000 "foot soldiers of terror" have been incapacitated, "hundreds" more have been identified and tracked, thereby interrupting their "deadly plans" of terror. But how can these figures be verified when the press, legislators, advocacy groups, social scientists, and law academics are denied independent access to basic information about these terrorists or their plots? Even the names of terrorist suspects are withheld from the public.

Implications

These conditions fail to meet even the most rudimentary standard for policy-oriented research on terrorism. Analysts therefore have little way of assessing whether the administration's actions under the Patriot Act are actually preventing terrorism. They also have no way of evaluating whether the provisions of the Act are being applied in accordance with the law, nor do they have a way of evaluating whether the fundamental values and principles of America's constitutional republic are being compromised in the process.

The third problem relates to the credibility of official statements about the Patriot Act's effectiveness. Take, for example, the Attorney General's claim that hundreds of terrorists have been identified and tracked across the United States via the Patriot Act, leading to the successful disruption of numerous plots. Publicly available information paints a very different picture:

- The Justice Department's own inspector general examined the files of 762 of the 1,200 "special interest" detainees arrested following 11 September. None of them was ever linked to 9/11 or any other terrorist plot.[40]
- Under the Patriot Act, the Justice Department has conducted a massive counter-terrorism sweep to deport some 13,000 Muslim men. Of that group, more than 3,000 have been arrested under the premise that they pose a "security threat" to the United States. Yet the Justice Department has acknowledged that the majority of these men were involved in offenses such as violating immigration rules, using fake identity documents, and various civic infractions.[41] There is no evidence that any of them were involved in plotting terrorist attacks against the United States.
- Since 9/11, approximately 680 men from more than forty countries have been detained indefinitely at the U.S. naval base at Guantanamo Bay, Cuba. The vast majority of these "enemy combatants" are suspected al Qaeda fighters who were captured on the battlefields of Afghanistan; thus the actions leading to their incapacitation are unrelated to the Patriot Act.[42] And while the FBI has used the Act's provisions to interrogate some of these enemy combatants, to date terrorism charges have been brought against only one of them.
- The Patriot Act has contributed little to what the administration considers its most important successes in the war on terrorism. These include the arrests of Abu Zubaydah, a Qaeda planner and recruiter; Khalid Sheikh Mohammed, the Qaeda chief of operations; Jose Padilla, the former Chicago gang member turned al Qaeda operative who allegedly planned to attack a U.S. city with a crude radioactive bomb; Zacarias Moussaoui, reportedly the 20th hijacker of 9/11; Richard Reid, who tried to set off a shoe bomb on a trans-Atlantic flight; and John Walker Lindh, the so-called "American Taliban." None of these suspects were incapacitated under the Patriot Act.
- There has only been one major terrorism trial since 9/11. This case involved two Arab immigrants from Dearborn, Michigan, convicted in June 2003 for plotting to attack U.S. airports, military bases, and landmarks. Yet these immigrants were arrested on 17 September, 2001—before the Patriot Act was implemented.[43]
- There *are* cases in which the Patriot Act has been used to arrest suspected terrorists in the United States. In each case, though, suspects have been arrested for conspiring to provide "material support and resources" to al Qaeda. None have

been accused of preparing, planning, or committing acts of terrorism. These cases include Minnesota resident Illyas Ali and two Pakistani accomplices, currently incarcerated in a Hong Kong prison for trying to sell drugs to raise money for al Qaeda; James Ujama, convicted of running a Qaeda training camp in Bly, Oregon; six young Yemeni men from Lackawanna, New York, convicted of training at an al Qaeda camp in Afghanistan; and five residents of Portland, Oregon, convicted of making an unsuccessful attempt to visit a bin Laden camp.[44]

○ Under the Patriot Act, only one known al Qaeda member has been charged with plotting a terrorist attack against America. Iyman Faris—a 34-year-old Kashmiri resident of Columbus, Ohio, who suffers from mental illness—was taken into custody by the FBI in 2003 for planning to destroy the Brooklyn Bridge in New York City shortly after 9/11. Accounts vary as to why his plan was aborted, yet the plot *was not* prevented by the Patriot Act.[45]

Implications

The disjunction between official claims-making and publicly available information creates a reliability problem. Because the problem of reliability is a basic one in social science—especially in criminology—researchers have developed a number of techniques for dealing with it. Yet each technique requires a baseline accounting of fact (e.g., police records) which is prohibited under the Patriot Act. This problem is exacerbated by the numerous classifications used to define individuals affected by U.S. counter-terrorism policy in the post-9/11 era. What terrorism researcher can keep track of so many disembodied "special interest" detainees, "security threats," "enemy combatants," "terrorist suspects," and "American Taliban" catalogued in U.S. military stockades, jails, prisons, and foreign lock-ups?

Finally, any analysis of the Patriot Act will face a serious time series problem. Earlier I listed fifteen provisions of the Act as it was originally implemented in October, 2001. (Again, this is only a partial listing.) Since then, the Attorney General has instituted more than a dozen Executive orders changing various rules of the Act. These have dealt mainly with surveillance and matters related to the interrogation of material witnesses. Justice Department attorneys have drafted a blueprint for the Domestic Enhancement Security Act (Patriot Act II), which contains additional provisions for expanding arrest and deportation authority.

Implications

Although there is a time-series design for examining such a fluid implementation problem,[46] the solution requires data. And, once again, there is little reliable data afforded under the Patriot Act. As such, any systematic analysis of the Act must be viewed as the social scientific equivalent of nailing jello to a wall.

Conclusions

Using selected statistics for a political purpose is one of the oldest tricks in the book. A classic example occurred in the mid 1960s when the Federal Bureau of Narcotics (FBN) reported a 66 percent drop in federal prosecutions for drug offenses from 1925 to 1966. The FBN concluded, therefore, that narcotics prohibition was a successful policy, thereby guaranteeing increased budgets and the development of new technologies of power targeted on vulnerable populations of urban blacks and foreign nationals. Against the FBN figures, criminologist Alfred Lindesmith contrasted non-federal prosecutions (state and municipal), showing that prosecutions had actually *increased* by more than 500 percent for the period in question, thereby raising doubts about the nation's drug policy. Lindesmith concluded that the official data were "worthless . . . they are nevertheless popularly accepted because the Bureau is in a position to repeat them endlessly in the mass media."[47]

The same can be said of the Patriot Act. Not only are official claims about the Act uncritically reported in the media, oftentimes the media function as a public relations organ for the Justice Department. In its coverage of the Attorney General's 2003 Congressional testimony, for example, the Associated Press reported: "The USA Patriot Act has stopped more than 3,000 'foot soldiers' of terror, Ashcroft said."[48] Ashcroft did not say that. Publicly available information indicates that some 3,000 al Qaeda fighters have been incapacitated in the *global war* on terrorism, largely through the efforts of intelligence agencies in Pakistan, Jordan, Spain, Germany, and France. The Patriot Act played no role whatsoever in this effort.

Nevertheless, the Justice Department has used the Act to justify substantial spending increases. For 2003, the Department's budget request was $30.2 billion, representing a 13 percent increase over its 2002 request.[49] Even though counter-terrorism is the Department's top priority, its post-9/11 requests have included increases in more than sixty programs that do not directly involve that priority (e.g., cybercrime, prisons, drug enforcement). As it turns out, the Attorney General has failed to endorse FBI requests for counter-terrorism field agents, intelligence analysts, Arabic translators, and domestic preparedness.[50]

The Justice Department's budget increases are therefore based less on the pragmatics of combating terrorism than they are on institutionalizing the politics of fear. In dozens of press conferences, the Attorney General and the FBI Director have failed to comment on the details of the Patriot Act and how the law will affect ordinary Americans. Instead, they have repeatedly played on the fears of Americans and their inability to assess terrorism threats. Return to the case of Jose Padilla for a moment.

On 8 June, 2002, Ashcroft revealed in a dramatic announcement via satellite from Moscow, "We have disrupted an unfolding terrorist plot to attack the United States by exploding a radioactive dirty bomb."[51] President Bush deemed Padilla so grave a threat to national security that he ordered him held incommunicado until the war on terrorism was over. A day later, the administration began to back pedal. Assistant Secretary of Defense Paul Wolfowitz told reporters that there was not an actual plot "beyond some fairly loose talk,"[52] while other sources reported that Ashcroft had been chastised by the White House for overplaying the Padilla arrest. But the damage had already been done. By exaggerating the "dirty bomb" threat, Ashcroft ignited public anxiety and ill reasoning, setting off a buying frenzy for duct tape and survival supplies. This is not an isolated incident, but part of a pattern of Justice Department warnings about impending doom. Director Mueller has repeatedly proclaimed on national television, "We can *expect* more terrorist acts in the United States."[53]

The Justice Department asserts that critics fail to understand the seriousness of the terrorism threat, and misconstrue how the Patriot Act is used to prevent another attack. But given the administration's doctrine of secrecy, it is effectively asking the public to be taken on faith. Add to this the results of emerging research showing that Justice Department prosecutions of terrorism-related cases since 9/11 have produced few significant results,[54] plus the methodological problems presented in this essay, and we arrive at a situation where there is virtually no way for researchers to verify Ashcroft's contention that progress is being made in the war on terrorism. This situation has occurred not through oversight but by design. That is, the Patriot Act carries no requirement for the Justice Department to report to Congress about how the policy has been employed and no requirement for reporting to the federal courts. The veil of secrecy, invoked in the name of national security, has effectively prevented public scrutiny of the government's "key weapon" in the fight against terrorism.

Yet Congress has the responsibility to do *precisely* that as it goes about the business of deciding whether the sun should set on the Patriot Act at the end of 2005. So, in this vein, I will end with a modest proposal.

A Test

The most contentious part of the Patriot Act is the increased ability of the federal government to conduct surveillance on anyone without a search warrant. This provision is contained in Section 213 of the Act (Authority for Delaying Notice of the Execution of a Warrant). Also known as the "sneak-and-peek" provision, Section 213 allows law enforcement to avoid giving prior warning when searches of personal property are conducted. Before the Patriot Act, the government was required to obtain a warrant and give notice to the person whose property was to be searched. The Patriot Act took away the right of every American fully to be protected under the Fourth Amendment against unreasonable searches and seizures.

Congress can examine the extent to which this provision has *in fact* prevented acts of terrorism against the United States. If the provision has failed to achieve the Patriot Act's primary objective—or worse yet, it has been misused to round up and incarcerate innocent people—then Congress faces a different kind of problem, namely: How can the abrogation of freedoms be justified when there is no proof that security is enhanced in the trade-off?

There is, however, an even more important test for the provision: Would it have made any difference in stopping the 11 September attacks? The starting point for this test is the widely cited fact that 9/11 was the result of a massive intelligence failure caused by a legal wall prohibiting the sharing of information between law enforcement and intelligence communities. The Act was designed to tear down the wall and there is little public anguish over this section of the policy. Yet when combined with new surveillance provisions, it increases the likelihood of creating an intelligence overload.

For instance, the FBI now has the authority to investigate religious and political groups to determine their possible ties to terrorist organizations, leading to the surveillance of mosques and the Muslims who attend them. The FBI is now allowed to tap their telephones, monitor their e-mails, confiscate their business records, and secretly search their homes and businesses without having to show evidence of a crime. The FBI can then share that information with the CIA, and the CIA can share it with foreign intelligence agencies. Used often enough, this strategy can create more data than intelligence systems can effectively manage. And to what end?

In general, terrorists keep a low profile and do not advocate publicly for social change. The 9/11 hijackers evidenced no public or religious activism during their time in the United States. Instead, they were busy penetrating airline security. In July 2001, a Phoenix FBI agent sent a memo to Washington headquarters recommending that the Bureau investigate the possibility that Islamic radicals were receiving training at U.S. flight schools. The agent determined that several Middle Eastern flight students were linked to bin Laden's terrorist network. Yet counterterrorism specialists did not discover the Phoenix memo until after 11 September. It had been buried in an intelligence overload.[55]

In the final analysis, popular support for the war on terrorism will turn on evidence made available to the public. That evidence will be based on intelligence. To the extent that Congress is able to extract this intelligence from its administrative sources, it will be able to open up a national debate that may inspire confidence in the government's approach to counter-terrorism. Such a strategy may brake the currents and crosscurrents of fear caused by 9/11. In so doing, the government might well avoid Samuel Taylor Coleridge's dire warning, "In politics, what begins in fear usually ends up in folly."[56]

Notes

1. Barkun 2003; Berry 2001; Louis 2002.
2. Barkun 2003:17.
3. Benjamin and Simon 2002.
4. *Ibid.*
5. B. Lewis 2003.
6. Bush 2001.
7. Quoted in Woodward 2002:209.
8. *Ibid.*:49.
9. Thompson 2003.
10. U.S. Department of Justice 2003. Hereafter referred to as DoJ.
11. Woodward 2002.
12. *Ibid.*:117.
13. DoJ:13.
14. DoJ.
15. Human Rights Watch 2002.
16. Lichtblau 2003a.
17. Quoted in Tapper 2003.
18. Quoted in Hentoff 2003a.
19. Quoted in Tapper 2003.
20. Quoted in O'Meara 2001.

21. Quoted in Krugman 2003.
22. Clymer 2003.
23. Wenzel 2003.
24. Dreyfuss 2003.
25. Traub 2003.
26. Cave 2003.
27. Hentoff 2003b.
28. *Ibid.*
29. Ashcroft, 2001.
30. Ashcroft 2003. Emphasis added.
31. *Ibid.*
32. Fox News 2002.
33. Ashcroft 2003.
34. Mazmanian and Sabatier 1983.
35. Ashcroft 2001.
36. Benjamin and Simon 2002.
37. Turk 2002:349.
38. Quoted in Woodward 2002:108.
39. Mueller 2003.
40. DoJ.
41. Dreyfuss 2003.
42. N. Lewis 2003.
43. Hakim 2003.
44. Arena 2002; Associated Press 2002.
45. Lichtblau 2003b.
46. Campbell and Stanley 1966.
47. Lindesmith 1965:119.
48. Holland 2003.
49. Ashcroft 2002.
50. Clymer 2003; White House Press release 2003.
51. Quoted in Lee 2003.
52. Quoted on CBS News 2002.
53. For example, Mueller 2003.
54. Burnham and Long 2003. Since 11 Sept., 2001, about 6,400 people were referred by investigators for criminal charges involving terrorism, but fewer than one-third actually were charged and only 879 were convicted. The median prison sentence was only 14 days.
55. Benjamin and Simon 2002.
56. Quoted in Glassner 1999:xxviii.

EVENT CASEBOOK FOUR

The Process and Progress of Equality

Focus on Global Women's Rights

Initial Reports

News Report—National

The Author: From Staff and Wire Reports

Since it first began publication over a century ago, the *Washington Post* has grown into one of the most recognized news organizations in the world. The following article was published on June 5, 2000.

Global Struggle for Women's Rights Spotlighted at New York Meeting

A handful of nations have not only failed to make significant progress on women's rights, they are trying to undo progress that has been made, rights activists and officials said during a symposium in New York sponsored by Rutgers University's Center for Global Women's Leadership.

States such as Algeria, Libya, Iran, Pakistan, Afghanistan and the Vatican were criticized on those grounds during the symposium Sunday in New York.

"They do not change their legislation," said Pierre Sane, secretary-general of Amnesty International. "They do not change their discriminatory practices that exist, they do not bring an end to violence against women. They do not hold states' agencies accountable when they commit human rights violations."

The symposium drew from around the world women campaigning for an end to domestic violence, genital circumcision, bride burning and other abuses of women's rights.

"Women have a lot to say about how to advance women's rights, and governments need to learn from that, listen to the movement and respond," said Charlotte Bunch of the Rutgers center.

Lack of Political Will Blamed

The symposium came just as world leaders gathered for a special session of the U.N. General Assembly to discuss progress made since the Fourth World Conference on Women in Beijing in 1995 laid out a platform on female equality.

Theo-Ben Giurab, president of the U.N. General Assembly, said the global drive toward female equality has not progressed as far as it should have. "If there had been political will, we would have gone a long way toward meeting the goals and objectives set in Beijing," he said.

Mary Robinson, U.N. High Commissioner for Human Rights, says recalcitrant countries may yet reverse what progress women have made there. "The few that don't want progress are very effective, and that's a problem," she said. "A problem because the gains made are still fragile."

Those who support the plan outlined in the 150-page platform drafted at the 1995 Beijing conference should start pressuring governments to send a message "that we're not regrouping, or retrenching, or going backwards," Robinson said.

The Beijing platform runs the gamut from promoting women's inheritance rights to calling on governments to provide equal education and employment and demanding that business and government put women in top decision-making posts.

Sane said Algeria, Libya, Iran, Pakistan and the Vatican were playing "a very destructive role" in negotiations on a final forward-looking document to be issued from this week's U.N. conference. Other delegates included Sudan on the list.

"We need to fight," Sane said. "We know that in previous world conferences, advances have been made because of the pressure."

U.N. officials say women have nevertheless made gains worldwide in areas such as education and health. But the biggest achievement, many leaders say, has been a strengthening of the global women's movement and a greater sense of female empowerment.

"Women themselves have organized and mobilized, so it's not only waiting for the state to deliver or the international community, but the women through this empowerment have taken their future into their own hands," said Sunila Abeysekera, executive director of the organization Inform.

Correspondent Deborah Feyerick and the Associated Press contributed to this report.

News Report—Report/Newsmagazine (Alberta Edition)

The Author: Paul Bunner

The following article was published on July 3, 2000.

Religious Conservatives Celebrate a Rare Win over the Anti-Family Clique at the UN

An improbable alliance of First World conservative Catholics and Third World Muslims scored a rare victory at the United Nations in New York in mid-June. Delegates from the Vatican, Poland, Slovakia and Latin America joined with representatives of Arab and African regimes like Libya, Algeria and Sudan to defeat the powerful European Union-JUSCANZ coalition (Canada, Japan, the United States, Australia and New Zealand) in their attempt to advance "the sexual and reproductive rights of women." This is defined by the feminist-dominated Western bloc as unfettered access to abortion, exalted status for lesbians, and diminution of parental authority over children.

Toronto lawyer Gwen Landolt attended the Beijing+5 conference (so named because it was a follow-up to the 1995 UN gathering in Beijing which established a global women's rights agenda) on behalf of REAL Women of Canada. She had no qualms about teaming up with one small group of repressive, anti-Christian countries to defeat an infinitely larger coalition which in its own way is also repressive and anti-Christian. "The UN is a world apart," says Mrs. Landolt. Of the 1,700 non-governmental organizations officially recognized by the UN, only 15 are pro-life and pro-family, she explains. And of the 3,000 lobbyists at the New York meeting, only 30 deviated from the pro-abortion, pro-homosexual orthodoxy that dominated the discussions.

The startling defeat of that orthodoxy occurred only because the administrators of the conference insisted on adherence to the traditional UN definition of consensus. Every vote on every resolution needed virtually unanimous consent. The UN has not followed its own consensus rules at most of its recent conferences, says Mrs. Landolt, citing the creation of the International Criminal Court as one recent UN invention achieved without consensus. This has allowed the rich, western delegations to "bully" representatives from developing countries and impose their agenda.

It remains to be seen whether the consensus rule at Beijing+5 represents a permanent return to form for the UN. In the meantime, its dominant feminist clique is trying to discredit and marginalize pro-family UN lobbyists like Mrs. Landolt and conservative Christian organizations like the U.S.-based Human Life International. One such effort was a report on "Right-Wing Anti-Feminist Groups at the United Nations," produced by an academic at the University of Quebec in Montreal. The $98,000 study was paid for by the Social Sciences and Humanities Research Council of Canada, the same federal government agency that recently made headlines for giving $50,000 to a University of British Columbia professor to conduct a three-year study on the history of strippers in Vancouver.

The report documents alleged "violence and intimidation" practised by conservative groups at UN meetings, a phrase that describes carrying Bibles, and wearing buttons emblazoned with words such as "Motherhood" and "Family." It also profiles and criticizes conservative leaders like Mrs. Landolt, who is said to have "demonstrated racism when she called black representatives of the National Action Committee on the Status of Women 'donkeys' " in a *National Post* interview. In fact, Mrs. Landolt was referring to all NAC members, not just black ones.

The smear was typical of "these radical women," shrugs Mrs. Landolt. "If you don't agree with their views, they want to decapitate you."

Multimedia Sources

Editorial Cartoon

The Author: Ann Telnaes

Born in Sweden, Ann Telnaes attended the California Institute of the Arts and graduated with a Bachelor of Fine Arts degree, specializing in character animation. Before beginning her career as an editorial cartoonist, Ann worked for several years at Walt Disney Imagineering as a designer. She has also been an animator for various studios in London, Los Angeles, New York, and Taiwan.

Ann's editorial cartoons have been exhibited in Washington, D.C., and Paris, France, and have appeared in such prestigious publications as the *Washington Post,* the *Boston Globe, Minneapolis Star Tribune, Le Monde, Courrier International,* the *Chicago Tribune, Los Angeles Times, Newsday,* the *New York Times,* and *Austin American Statesman.* Among other awards, she received the Pulitzer Prize for Editorial Cartooning in 2001.

The following cartoon was published in 2001.

Editorial Cartoon

The Author: Ann Telnaes

The following cartoon was published in June 1998.

Transcript

The Speaker: Regan E. Ralph

Regan E. Ralph, JD, was appointed vice president and director of health and reproductive rights at the National Women's Law Center in 2001. Prior to joining the center, Ralph was executive director of the women's rights program at Human Rights
Watch. She received her law degree from Yale Law School and remains an adjunct professor of women's studies at Georgetown University.

The following is testimony before the Senate Committee on Foreign Relations
given by Regan Ralph in February 2000.

Testimony before the Senate Committee on Foreign Relations
Subcommittee on Near Eastern and South Asian Affairs

February 22, 2000

My name is Regan Ralph, and I am the Executive Director of the Women's Rights
Division of Human Rights Watch. It is a pleasure to be here today, and I appreciate
the attention this committee is devoting to the growing human rights problem of
trafficking in persons.

Trafficking in persons—the illegal and highly profitable transport and sale of
human beings for the purpose of exploiting their labor—is a slavery-like practice
that must be eliminated. Human Rights Watch has been involved in documenting and
monitoring this serious human rights violation for many years. We have reported on
the trafficking of women and girls from Bangladesh to Pakistan (*Double Jeopardy*),
from Burma to Thailand (*Modern Form of Slavery*), and from Nepal to India (*Rape*

for Profit). We have also conducted extensive research regarding other incidences of trafficking, including the trafficking of women from Thailand to Japan and from Eastern Europe and the former Soviet Union to Bosnia. Reports resulting from these investigations are forthcoming.

The number of persons trafficked each year is impossible to determine, but it is clearly a large-scale problem, with estimates ranging from hundreds of thousands to millions of victims worldwide. The State Department estimates that each year, 50,000 to 100,000 women and children are trafficked into the United States alone, approximately half of whom are trafficked into bonded sweatshop labor or domestic servitude. Trafficking is also a truly global phenomenon. The International Organization for Migration has reported on cases of trafficking in Southeast Asia, East Asia, South Asia, the Middle East, Western Europe, Eastern Europe, South America, Central America, and North America. And press reports in the past year have included accounts of persons trafficked into the United States from a wide variety of countries. In August 1999, a trafficking ring was broken up in Atlanta, Georgia, that authorities believe was responsible for transporting up to 1,000 women from several Asian countries into the United States and forcing them to work in brothels across the country. Four months later, a man pleaded guilty to keeping five Latvian women in involuntary servitude in Chicago. He had recruited the women from Latvia with promises of $60,000-a-year wages. But when they arrived, he pocketed most of their earnings and forced them to work by confiscating their passports, keeping them under constant surveillance, and threatening to kill them and have their families murdered if they disobeyed him.

Trafficking Patterns

In Human Rights Watch's documentation of trafficking in women, we have found that while the problem varies according to the context, certain consistent patterns emerge. Furthermore, while our research has focused on the trafficking of women and children into the sex industry, reporting from numerous credible sources shows similar patterns in the trafficking of women, men, and children into forced marriage, bonded sweatshop labor, and other kinds of work. In all cases, the coercive tactics of traffickers, including deception, fraud, intimidation, isolation, threat and use of physical force, and/or debt bondage, are at the core of the problem and must be at the center of any effort to address it.

In a typical case, a woman is recruited with promises of a good job in another country or province, and lacking better options at home, she agrees to migrate. There are also cases in which women are lured with false marriage offers or vacation invitations, in which children are bartered by their parents for a cash advance and/or promises of future earnings, or in which victims are abducted outright. Next an agent makes arrangements for the woman's travel and job placement, obtaining the necessary travel documentation, contacting employers or job brokers, and hiring an escort to accompany the woman on her trip. Once the arrangements have been made, the woman is escorted to her destination and delivered to an employer or to another intermediary who brokers her employment. The woman has no control over the nature or place of work, or the terms or conditions of her employment. Many women learn they have been deceived about the nature of the work they will do, most have been lied to about the financial arrangements and conditions of their employment, and all find themselves in coercive and abusive situations from which escape is both difficult and dangerous.

The most common form of coercion Human Rights Watch has documented is debt bondage. Women are told that they must work without wages until they have re-paid the purchase price advanced by their employers, an amount far exceeding the cost of their travel expenses. Even for those women who knew they would be in debt, this amount is invariably higher than they expected and is routinely augmented with arbitrary fines and dishonest account keeping. Employers also maintain their power to "resell" indebted women into renewed levels of debt. In some cases, women find that their debts only increase and can never be fully repaid. Other women are even-tually released from debt, but only after months or years of coercive and abusive labor. To prevent escape, employers take full advantage of the women's vulnerable position as migrants: they do not speak the local language, are unfamiliar with their surroundings, and fear arrest and mistreatment by local law enforcement authori-ties. These factors are compounded by a range of coercive tactics, including constant surveillance, isolation, threats of retaliation against the woman and/or her family members at home, and confiscation of passports and other documentation.

Government efforts to combat trafficking in persons have been entirely inade-quate. In many cases, corrupt officials in countries of origin and destination actively facilitate trafficking abuses by providing false documents to trafficking agents, turn-ing a blind eye to immigration violations, and accepting bribes from trafficked women's employers to ignore abuses. We have even documented numerous cases in which po-lice patronized brothels where trafficked women worked, despite their awareness of the coercive conditions of employment. And in every case we have documented, of-ficials' indifference to the human rights violations involved in trafficking has allowed this practice to persist with impunity. Trafficked women may be freed from their em-ployers in police raids, but they are given no access to services or redress and instead face further mistreatment at the hands of authorities. Even when confronted with clear evidence of trafficking and forced labor, officials focus on violations of their im-migration regulations and anti-prostitution laws, rather than on violations of the traf-ficking victims' human rights. Thus the women are targeted as undocumented migrants and/or prostitutes, and the traffickers either escape entirely, or else face minor penalties for their involvement in illegal migration or businesses of prostitution.

These policies and practices are not only inappropriate, they are ineffective. By making the victims of trafficking the target of law enforcement efforts, governments only exacerbate victims' vulnerability to abuse and deter them from turning to law enforcement officials for assistance. By allowing traffickers to engage in slavery-like practices without penalty, governments allow the abuses to continue with impunity.

Trafficking in Women: Case Studies

Drawing on Human Rights Watch research, I will provide a few specific examples that illustrate the pattern outlined above. I will then offer recommendations for measures the U.S. government can take to combat this modern form of slavery and provide re-dress for its victims.

Thailand to Japan

From 1994 to 1999, Human Rights Watch carried out an extensive investigation of the trafficking of women from Thailand into Japan's sex industry. We will be publishing a report on trafficking into Japan later this year. We interviewed numerous trafficking victims directly, and received information regarding many more cases from local advocates and shelter staff in Japan and Thailand. Our findings indicate that thousands of Thai women are trafficked into forced labor in Japan each year, their rights violated with impunity as the Japanese and Thai governments fail to respond adequately to the problem.

Statements by the Thai and Japanese governments have made clear that they are well aware of these abuses. However, this has not been translated into effective measures to provide women with the means to protect themselves from abuse or to seek redress for violations. When Japanese authorities raid establishments that employ trafficked women, the women are arrested, detained in immigration facilities, and summarily deported with a five-year ban on reentering the country. This punitive treatment is applied regardless of the conditions under which the women migrated and worked in Japan, and even when there is clear evidence of trafficking and/or forced labor. Trafficking victims have no opportunity to seek compensation or redress, and no resources are provided to ensure their access to medical care and other critical services. Moreover, their traffickers and employers face little fear of punishment. If arrested at all, they are charged only with minor offenses for violations of immigration, prostitution, or entertainment business regulations.

The Thai government has adopted laws and policies aimed to combat trafficking in Thai women and assist victims in returning home. However, law enforcement efforts have so far proved ineffective, and women's vulnerability to trafficking persists. Many women continue to lack viable employment opportunities at home, and, at the same time, have no information about how to protect their rights overseas. In addition, the government has adopted overly broad policies aimed to prevent "potential" trafficking victims from traveling abroad. For example, the passport applications of women and girls ages fourteen to thirty-six are subjected to special scrutiny, and if investigators suspect that a woman may be going abroad for commercial sexual purposes, her application is rejected. This policy, however well-intended, trades one human rights problem for another by discriminating against women seeking to travel and limiting their freedom of movement. It also makes women who want to migrate even more dependent on the services of trafficking agents, because it is difficult for women to obtain travel documents by themselves. Finally, the Thai government makes no effort to assist trafficked women in seeking redress.

The women we interviewed described the shock, horror and, often, powerlessness they felt when they discovered that contrary to their promises of lucrative jobs, they were saddled with enormous "debts" and would not receive any wages until these amounts were repaid. This would require months—or even years—of unpaid work under highly coercive and abusive conditions. Those who had been promised jobs in factories or restaurants faced an additional blow when they learned from their employers or coworkers that their debt had to be repaid through sex work.

The women had been recruited for work in Japan by friends, relatives, or other acquaintances, who told them about high-paying overseas employment opportunities. The recruiters introduced them to agents who handled their travel arrangements and hired escorts to accompany the women to Japan. In some cases, the women became suspicious about their job offers during—or even before—their travel overseas, but once their agent had initiated the arrangements, they were closely supervised and felt they could not safely change their minds. Upon their arrival in Japan, the women were delivered to brokers who sold them into debt bondage in the sex industry. Most worked as bar "hostesses," entertaining customers at the bar and accompanying customers to nearby hotels to provide sexual services. While in debt, they could not refuse any customers or customers' requests without their employers' permission, and they often endured violence and other abusive treatment at the hands of both customers and employers. The women were also subjected to excessive work hours and dangerous health risks—including the risk of contracting HIV and other sexually transmitted diseases.

Excerpts from a few of their stories provide an idea of the slavery-like conditions they endured. In Thailand, Lee[1] had an alcoholic and abusive husband and three young children she was struggling to feed. When a recruiter offered to find her a job as a sex worker in Japan, she agreed. She told us, "I knew there would be some debt for the airplane ticket and all, but I was never told how much." She found out after she arrived in Japan and was taken to a room by a broker to be sold. In her words, "There were lots of women and people came to choose women and buy them. I was bought on the third day, and told that my price"—and therefore her debt—"was 380 bai [approximately US$30,000]. After three or four days of working at the bar, I realized how much 380 bai was. The other girls said to me, 'That's a lot of debt and you're old. You'll never pay it off.' Then I prayed that it would only take six or seven months to pay it off, and I went with all of the clients I could."

Human Rights Watch also interviewed a woman who was promised a job in a Thai restaurant in Japan, but instead was taken to a bar where the other Thai "hostesses" told her she would have to work as a prostitute. She recalled, "They told me there was no way out and I would just have to accept my fate. I knew then what had happened to me. That first night I had to take several men, and after that I had to have at least one client every night."

Another woman we interviewed was released from debt after eight months of grueling, unpaid labor. According to Khai, "I had calculated that I must have paid it back long ago, but the [bar manager] kept lying to me and said she didn't have the same records as I did. During these eight months, I had to take every client that wanted me and had to work everyday, even during my menstruation." Despite the terrible and coercive conditions, including physically abusive clients, Khai did not try to escape. Her manager had threatened to resell her and double her debt if she "made any trouble," and forbade her from going outside without supervision. The manager had also confiscated her passport, and, Khai explained, "Without my documents I was sure I would be arrested and jailed by the police."

Eastern Europe and the Former Soviet Union to Bosnia

In March 1999, Human Rights Watch traveled to Bosnia to document the incidence of trafficking in women from Eastern Europe and the former Soviet Union. We interviewed trafficking victims, local and international officials, and local advocates. We also looked through police and court records and went to Ukraine to interview staff from La Strada, an NGO which has assisted many women returning from Bosnia. Our research indicated that since the end of the war in Bosnia and Herzegovina, thousands of women had been trafficked into Bosnia for forced prostitution.

At the time of our investigation, Bosnia was under the authority of a combination of local and international agencies. Our conversations with local police, representatives from the Joint Commission Observers, and members of the International Police Task Force indicated that all of these officials were well aware of the trafficking problem. They knew that foreign women were working in slave-like conditions across Bosnia, unable to leave the brothels. Nonetheless, little was done to prevent the trafficking of women into forced prostitution, or to provide redress or protection for victims. We even found evidence that some officials were actively complicit in these abuses, participating in the trafficking and forced employment of the women and/or patronizing the brothels.

The women had traveled from Belarus, Moldova, Ukraine, Romania, and Hungary, lured by promises of legal work and safe passage. When the women arrived in Bosnia, brothel owners seized their passports and subjected them to slavery-like practices. They were treated like chattel, often resold from brothel owner to brothel owner, and the promises of good incomes turned out to be lies: instead of being able to remit money home to their families and children, the women found themselves forced to work without wages. As Vika told Human Rights Watch, "They tricked me. Everything was fine at first. But when we wanted to leave, the owner sold us for 1500 DM [approximately US$900]. The new owner told us that we had to work off three more months. He said he would sell us to another man." Most of the women had agreed to jobs in the sex industry, but when brothel owners refused to pay them, some women refused to work, incurring violent punishment. According to one woman interviewed by Human Rights Watch, "Every time I refused to work, they beat me."

When authorities encountered trafficked women during brothel raids, they treated them like criminals, compounding the human rights abuses they had endured at the hands of their traffickers. The women were arrested, fined for their illegal immigration status and their illegal work as prostitutes, and then deported. And in early 1999, "deportation" in the Bosnian context—a country without an immigration law—translated into being dumped across a border. From the Federation, women found themselves dumped in Republika Srpska. And vice versa. This pseudo-deportation scheme only facilitated the trafficking cycle. Women dumped across the internal borders could be quickly picked up and re-sold.

Burma to Thailand

Trafficking in persons is not a new phenomenon, and research conducted by Human Rights Watch in the early 1990s revealed similar patterns of human rights abuses, as well as similar levels of indifference—and even outright complicity—on the part of law enforcement officials.

More than six years ago, Human Rights Watch reported on the trafficking in Burmese women and girls into brothels in Thailand. We interviewed thirty trafficking victims in Thailand, and obtained many additional interview transcripts from a local NGO. Nyi Nyi's case was typical: She was recruited from Burma at age seventeen by a friend who had worked in Thailand. She had no idea what type of work she would do, but she agreed to go. When she met the agent, he gave her 15,000 baht (approximately US$600), which she gave to her sister. Then the agent sent Nyi Nyi to a brothel in northern Thailand, in a truck driven by a police officer. When Nyi Nyi arrived, she learned that the 15,000 baht from the agent was a "debt," which she would have to repay through prostitution. Nyi Nyi could not speak Thai, did not know where she was in Bangkok, and was always afraid of being arrested by the police. She never dared to talk to anyone, and she was relieved that the police who came to the brothel as customers never chose her. After about a year of working almost every day, she was told that she had repaid her debt, but did not have enough money to pay for a return trip to Burma. So she continued to work, and a short time later she was arrested during a brothel raid. The police initially promised that she would be taken back to Burma in a few days, but instead Nyi Nyi was sent to a reformatory for prostitutes, where she was confined for the next six months.

Nepal to India

In 1995, Human Rights Watch released another report on trafficking in persons, this one based on interviews with women and girls who had been trafficked from Nepal to India. Some were tricked by fraudulent marriage offers, others were sold by relatives, and a few were abducted. All ended up in the hands of trafficking agents who brought them to brothels and sold them into debt bondage. One of the women we interviewed explained that her husband had left her, and when a neighbor told her about an Indian man who wanted to marry her, she agreed. A meeting was arranged, but instead of eloping, her "fiancé" drugged her and took her to a brothel in India. At the brothel, she was told that she had to work to pay off her purchase price of Rs.20,000 (approximately US$666). Each day she was forced to sit in a room in the brothel with the other women, and when a customer chose her, she could not refuse; those who tried were beaten and verbally abused. After working for ten years, serving nine or ten customers a day, she was still in "debt." She told us, "Nobody was allowed to leave after four years like people say they are." Finally she met a Nepali man at the brothel, and with his help, she managed to escape.

U.S. Policy—Recommendations

Human Rights Watch commends the U.S. government for prioritizing trafficking in persons as a domestic and foreign policy concern. Senator Paul Wellstone has played a key role in mobilizing government efforts to combat trafficking in persons in a way that promotes and protects the rights of women and particularly trafficking victims. His leadership led to new legislation requiring the Department of State to increase and improve its reporting on trafficking in its annual *Country Reports on Human Rights Practices*. We hope that additional attention to this issue will help to close the gaps in the U.S. State Department's reporting on this subject. The report on Japan released last year, for example, alluded to the mistreatment of illegal workers, but trafficking and debt bondage were not mentioned, and the report asserted that "there are presently no known cases of forced or bonded labor" in Japan.

In 1998, President Clinton identified trafficking in women and girls as a "fundamental human rights violation," and tasked the President's Interagency Council on Women with the challenging task of developing and coordinating government policy on this issue. Currently, the U.S. government is involved in several important initiatives. These include participation in the negotiation of a protocol on trafficking supplementing the Convention against Transnational Organized Crime; implementation of foreign aid programs designed to prevent trafficking, assist victims, and prosecute traffickers; and consideration of legislation in the U.S. Congress against trafficking in persons.

As it participates in efforts to design and implement multilateral approaches to combating trafficking in persons, Human Rights Watch urges the U.S. government to promote human rights, and especially women's human rights, as the cornerstone of such efforts. This is of crucial importance in the negotiations for a protocol against trafficking in persons supplementing the United Nations Convention against Transnational Organized Crime. The final shape of this protocol will have significant implications for the effectiveness of multinational efforts to prevent and prosecute trafficking abuses, as well as for the protection and redress available to trafficking victims.

The United States is also involved in a number of other important discussions that will strongly influence the ways in which governments respond to trafficking in persons. In March of this year, the United States is co-hosting the Asian Regional Initiative Against Trafficking in Women and Children (ARIAT) in Manila, where Asian and Pacific nations will discuss national action plans and develop a regional strategy. At the G8 summit in Okinawa in July, the Group of Eight will have the opportunity to continue their discussions about joint efforts to combat trafficking in persons. Last month, Human Rights Watch sent an observer to a symposium on trafficking in persons in Tokyo that the Japanese Ministry of Foreign Affairs sponsored in preparation for the G8 discussions. We hope that President Clinton, in his public and private remarks at the Okinawa summit, will stigmatize governments that are complicit in trafficking or tolerate trafficking. He should also use this opportunity revisit the plan of action to combat trafficking in persons adopted by the G8 Ministerial Meeting in Moscow last October, encouraging governments to enact domestic legislation necessary for the effective investigation and prosecution of those involved in trafficking and pressing for the inclusion of concrete measures to protect the rights of all trafficking victims.

The United States should take advantage of all channels and opportunities to promote a human rights approach to trafficking based on the following recommendations:

- Defining "trafficking" to encompass trafficking into all forms of forced labor and servitude—in any occupation or labor sector—including trafficking into forced marriage. The definition should also be limited to situations involving coercion, in recognition of men and women's ability to make voluntary decisions about their migration and employment, with coercion understood to include a full range of abusive tactics used to extract work or service.
- Actively investigating, prosecuting, and punishing those involved in the trafficking of persons in countries of origin and destination, and imposing penalties appropriate for the grave nature of the abuses they have committed. Particular attention should be paid to evidence of collaboration by government officials in the facilitation of trafficking abuses.
- Exempting trafficking victims from prosecution for any immigration violations or other offenses that have occurred as a result of their being trafficked.
- Ensuring that trafficking victims have the opportunity to seek remedies and redress for the human rights violations they have suffered, including compensation for damages, unpaid wages, and restitution. This requires guaranteeing victims' access to legal assistance, interpretation services, and information regarding their rights, and allowing all trafficked persons to remain in the country during the duration of any proceedings related to legal claims they have filed.
- Taking strong precautions to ensure the physical safety of trafficked persons. This includes witness protection measures for those who cooperate with law enforcement efforts and asylum opportunities for those who fear retaliation in their countries of origin. Countries of origin, transit, and destination must also cooperate to ensure the safe repatriation of trafficked persons, working together with non-governmental organizations to facilitate their return home.
- Protecting women's rights and addressing the inequality in status and opportunity that makes women vulnerable to trafficking and other abuses. States should support policies and programs that promote equal access to education and employment for women and girls. They should also provide women with information about their rights as workers and how to protect these rights overseas. Programs should be designed and implemented with the cooperation of local non-governmental organizations.

There is increasing evidence that trafficking is on the rise in the United States as well. To effectively respond to the trafficking of persons into this country, we urge the U.S. government to enact domestic legislation that incorporates the standards outlined above. We welcome recent indications that law enforcement officials are increasingly charging traffickers with offenses appropriate to the serious nature of their crimes, but much remains to be done to improve the protections and services available to trafficked persons. Such measures are crucial for upholding the rights of victims and for encouraging them to cooperate in the investigation and prosecution of traffickers. In particular, we hope that such legislation will address this issue by:

- Banning all forms of involuntary servitude and debt bondage as forced labor. U.S. statutory proscriptions on peonage and involuntary servitude have been narrowly interpreted to include only those situations in which victims are made to work through force of law or actual or threatened physical force. This excludes many of the slavery-like practices that Human Rights Watch has found common in cases of trafficking, in which labor is extracted through non-physical means such as debt bondage, blackmail, fraud, deceit, isolation, and/or psychological pressure.
- Providing victims of trafficking with access to legal assistance, translation services, shelter, and health services, and ensuring that all trafficked persons are allowed to remain in the United States throughout the duration of any civil or criminal proceedings against their abusers.
- Preventing the further victimization of trafficked persons by guaranteeing their immunity from prosecution for immigration violations or other crimes related to their having been trafficked, and taking adequate measures to ensure the protection of their physical safety. Such measures should include opportunities for all trafficking victims who fear retaliation upon return to their home country to apply for permanent settlement on that basis.

Trafficking in persons is a profound human rights abuse, and women are particularly vulnerable to this practice due to the persistent inequalities they face in status and opportunity. It is time for governments to take this problem seriously. Concrete steps are needed to prevent trafficking, punish traffickers and the corrupt officials who facilitate their crimes, and provide protection and redress for victims. This is a crucial moment in the fight against trafficking, with efforts underway in domestic, regional, and international fora to define appropriate state actions. It is imperative that the United States take advantage of this moment to demonstrate its leadership on this critical human rights issue.

Notes

1. All names of traffficking victims have been changed.

Web site

The Source: http://www.unifem.org

UNIFEM was created in 1976, in response to a call from women's organizations attending the 1975 U.N. First World Conference on Women in Mexico City. Today, UNIFEM works in over 100 countries and has 14 Regional Programme Directors and a growing network of affiliated gender advisors and specialists in Africa, the Arab States, Asia and the Pacific, Central and Eastern Europe and the Commonwealth of Independent States, Latin America, and the Caribbean.

The following is a screenshot of the Web site's home page and text that describes the organization's mission.

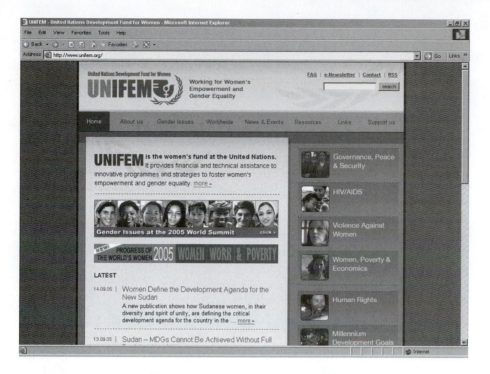

Progress for Women Is Progress for All

UNIFEM is the women's fund at the United Nations. Established in 1976, it provides financial and technical assistance to innovative approaches aimed at fostering women's empowerment and gender equality. Today the organization's work touches the lives of women and girls in more than 100 countries. UNIFEM also helps make the voices of women heard at the United Nations—to highlight critical issues and advocate for the implementation of existing commitments made to women.

Placing the realization of women's human rights and security at the centre of all of its efforts, UNIFEM focuses its activities on four strategic goals:

○ Reducing women's poverty and exclusion;
○ Ending violence against women;
○ Reversing the spread of HIV/AIDS among women and girls;
○ Supporting women's leadership in governance and post-conflict reconstruction.

To pursue these goals, UNIFEM is active in all regions and at different levels. It works with countries to formulate and implement laws and policies to eliminate gender discrimination and promote gender equality in such areas as land and inheritance rights, decent work for women and ending violence against women.

UNIFEM also aims to transform institutions to make them more accountable to gender equality and women's rights, to strengthen the capacity and voice of women's rights advocates, and to change harmful and discriminatory practices in society.

> Women want a world free from hatred, violence and poverty, a world of equal opportunities and rights, a world that is prosperous and secure for all.
>
> —*Noeleen Heyzer, Executive Director, UNIFEM*

Two international agreements frame UNIFEM's work: the Beijing Platform for Action resulting from the Fourth World Conference on Women in 1995, and the Convention on the Elimination of All Forms of Discrimination Against Women (CEDAW), known as the women's bill of rights. The spirit of these agreements has been affirmed by the Millennium Declaration and the eight Millennium Development Goals for 2015, combating poverty, hunger, disease, illiteracy and gender inequality, and building partnerships for development. In addition, Security Council resolution 1325 on women, peace and security is a crucial reference for UNIFEM's work in support of women in conflict and post-conflict situations.

Reducing Women's Poverty and Exclusion

While globalization offers new opportunities, it has also intensified economic insecurity for many poor women. As capital moves freely across borders, these women are increasingly concentrated in insecure, unsafe and badly paid work in the informal economy or forced to join the growing "undocumented" migrant labour stream.

UNIFEM works to enhance women's economic security by strengthening their rights to land and inheritance, increasing their access to decent work, and empowering women migrant workers in both sending and receiving countries. In Jordan, a country of destination for migrant workers, UNIFEM has worked with the Government to formulate a minimum standard contract for migrant women that is being used to monitor working conditions. Also in Jordan, UNIFEM's partnership with CISCO Systems helped shape gender-sensitive training programmes that have increased women's access to job opportunities presented by information technology. The initiative will be replicated in several Arab countries.

Women have recognized that if you want to see how governments are implementing their commitments to women, follow the money. In over 30 countries UNIFEM supports national and local initiatives to include gender perspectives in budgeting processes, and to collect and use sex-disaggregated data in public policy formulation.

Ending Violence Against Women

Violence against women is the most pervasive human rights violation—whether women are subjected to domestic violence, trafficked across borders, or the victims of systematic rape in conflict zones. Studies have shown that as many as one out of three women worldwide will be beaten, coerced into sex or otherwise abused in her lifetime.

Despite great progress in laws and policies to address gender-based violence, there is a large implementation gap. Through its Trust Fund to End Violence Against Women, UNIFEM supports innovative strategies to bridge this gap—working across multiple levels and sectors simultaneously, strengthening community ownership and including men as partners. In Eastern and Southern Africa, for example, men from all walks of life spread the message against violence through music, dance and drama in rural and urban communities. In Tanzania, the Women's Judges Association received a grant to train judges and magistrates on jurisprudence and equality. And in China, a Trust Fund grant helped expand the network of support stations for domestic violence cases.

Reversing the Spread of HIV/AIDS Among Women and Girls

HIV/AIDS increasingly has a young woman's face. Today, over 60 per cent of 15–24 year olds living with HIV/AIDS are women.

UNIFEM focuses on enhancing HIV/AIDS policies and translating them into effective strategies on the ground. The fund works with National AIDS Councils and Ministries to devise national programmes and policies that ensure women's equal access to prevention, care and treatment. In Brazil, support was rendered to an organization of Afro-Brazilian women to monitor access to HIV/AIDS-related public services.

UNIFEM also assists HIV-positive women who are advocating for a future in which they can live without stigma and violence, have easy access to drugs and continue to live healthy and meaningful lives. Support to the Positive Women's Network in India, for example, has resulted in their issues being taken up by the National Commission of Women. In addition, UNIFEM has formed a partnership with the Indian Railways—the third largest employer in the world—to reach employees with critical information on gender and HIV/AIDS through peer educators.

Supporting Women's Leadership in Governance and Post-Conflict Reconstruction

Women remain vastly under-represented in national or local assemblies, accounting for a worldwide average of some 15 per cent of seats in national parliaments. When it comes to negotiating peace and facilitating reconstruction after wars, women's exclusion is even more pronounced—despite the fact that they are particularly affected and can be part of the solution.

In post-conflict situations, when electoral processes, new constitutions and legislative structures are being created, it is critical for women to be involved. UNIFEM has actively supported women in electoral and constitutional processes in a number of countries. In Afghanistan, for example, where in December 2003 the Loya Jirga enshrined equality between men and women in the nation's new Constitution. This achievement required broad-based alliances and ongoing advocacy. A UNIFEM-facilitated Gender and Law Working Group—comprised of the Office of the State Minister for Women, the Ministry of Women's Affairs (MOWA), Supreme Court judges and women's NGOs—reviewed the draft Constitution and advocated for the recognition of women as full citizens.

Newspaper Article

The Author: Ellen Goodman

Ellen Goodman, a member of the Washington Post Writers Group, is the author of Pulitzer Prize commentary appearing in more than 450 newspapers. One of those rare writers and thinkers who senses emerging shifts in our public and private lives, Goodman alters perceptions of confounding issues.

A 1963 cum laude graduate of Radcliffe College, Goodman returned to Harvard in 1973–74 as a Nieman Fellow, where she studied the dynamics of social change. Her column was syndicated by the Washington Post Writers Group in 1976. In 1980, Goodman was awarded the Pulitzer Prize for Distinguished Commentary. Her work has won many other awards, including the American Society of Newspaper Editors Distinguished Writing Award in 1980. She received the Hubert H. Humphrey Civil Rights Award from the Leadership Conference on Civil Rights in 1988. In 1993, at its Seventh Annual Exceptional Merit Media Award Ceremony, the National Women's Political Caucus gave her the President's Award. In 1994, the Women's Research & Education Institute presented her with their American Woman Award.

The following article was published on June 26, 2004.

A Forty-Year Search for Equality

BOSTON—And now for a small story from the Latter-Day Annals of Working Womanhood.

Fresh out of college in 1963, I got my first job at _Newsweek_ magazine. In those days, women were hired as researchers and men were hired as writers . . . and that was that.

It was, as we used to say, a good job _for a woman_. If we groused about working _for_ the men we studied _with_ in college, we did it privately. It was the way things were.

I don't share my garden-variety piece of personal history as a lament or gripe. Woe isn't me. Nor am I one to regale the younger generation with memories of the bad old days when I walked four miles in the snow to school. They already know that women were treated as second-class citizens.

But what they don't know, I have found, is that this was _legal_.

It was legal to have segregated ads that read "male wanted" and "female wanted." It was legal to fire a flight attendant if she got married. It was legal to get rid of a teacher when she became pregnant.

If a boss paid a woman less because she was a woman, he was unapologetic. If he didn't want to hire a woman for a "man's job," he just didn't.

We sometimes forget that the lives of men and women didn't just passively evolve. But on July 2 we'll celebrate the 40th anniversary of a powerful engine of this social change, the Civil Rights Act of 1964.

One unexpected word was tucked into Title VII of that landmark legislation banning racial segregation and discrimination: sex.

Legend has it that Rep. Howard W. Smith, a Virginian and head of the House Rules Committee, introduced sex as a joke. He was trying to ridicule the idea that you could legislate social behavior.

But the segregationist was just half of an odd couple. The other half were feminists. The National Women's Party had been trying to get such a law long before they brought it to Smith. After he introduced the sex discrimination amendment to ripples of laughter, Rep. Martha Griffiths of Michigan, one of only nine women in Congress, argued for it fiercely.

Omitting sex, she said, would protect only African American males from discrimination. And if blacks were protected, the only unprotected class left would be white women.

When President Johnson signed the bill, it became illegal for the first time to discriminate in employment on the grounds of sex. What had seemed to many a "natural" way of treating men and women differently because of their roles in the family and society became what the courts now call "invidious."

"This is the act that put meaning into the word discrimination," says historian Alice Kessler-Harris, who remembers when she was forced to sign a paper promising to tell her employer if she became pregnant. "Title VII legitimized a women's search for equality in the workforce."

This 40-year "search" has seen enormous success stories. In the first Title VII case, the Supreme Court ruled that it was illegal to refuse to hire a woman because she had small children. Under pressure, newspapers stopped segregating their employment pages. Women tiptoed into some "male jobs" and took hold in others.

Today's working women sometimes wonder whether we've won the booby prize— the right to be treated like men. We haven't yet figured out the next phase, how to get support for family and work.

But there are still plenty of reminders that the bad old days are not so old. They may be alive and well and living in your workplace.

Just last Tuesday a federal court allowed a class-action suit on behalf of 1.6 million women employees of Wal-Mart. The plaintiffs' statistics and anecdotes could fill a volume in another generation's Annals of Working Womanhood.

When a single mother discovered that her male counterpart made $23,000 more, her Wal-Mart boss replied, "he has a wife and two children to support." When a woman wanted to sell hardware, she was sent to sell baby clothes. And another woman looking for a promotion confronted a store manager who said, "Men are here to make a career and women aren't."

"What we see with Wal-Mart and other cases," says Marcia Greenberg of the National Women's Law Center, "is an everyday struggle to make sure the promise of the law really becomes a reality."

When the old feminists lobbied the old segregationist to include sex, Smith said mischievously and maybe maliciously, "I don't think it can do any harm . . . maybe it can do some good."

He was joking. But they were left smiling.

Public Awareness Campaign

The Source: http://www.mdgender.net

The mdgender.net is a collaborative effort of the U.N. Inter-Agency Network on Women and Gender Equality, the OECD/DAC Network on Gender Equality, and the Multilateral Development Bank Working Group on Gender.

The following is an example of the group's outreach program.

Gender Equality & the Millennium Development Goals

The Millennium Development Goals (MDGs) set out a powerful agenda for a global partnership to fight poverty, offering a shared vision of a better world by the year 2015.

They aim to cut extreme poverty by half, ensure every child has the chance to go to school and live a long and healthy life, and bring discrimination against women to an end.

The risks of dying as a result of childbirth are to be dramatically reduced, deadly diseases brought under control, the environment better managed, and the benefits of progress more equally shared by all the nations of the world.

Together, the aspirations set out in the eight MDGs and their associated targets and indicators represent a powerful framework for action, drawing on the Millennium Declaration, agreed by 189 countries at the UN in September 2000.

No Progress Without Gender Equality

The third goal challenges discrimination against women, and seeks to ensure that girls as well as boys have the chance to go to school. Indicators linked to this goal also aim to measure progress towards ensuring that more women become literate, have more voice and representation in public policy and decision making, and have improved job prospects.

But the issue of gender equality is not limited to a single goal—it applies to all of them. Without progress towards gender equality and the empowerment of women, none of the MDGs will be achieved.

Women disproportionately suffer the burden of poverty, are the primary agents of child welfare, are the victims of widespread and persistent discrimination in all areas of life, and put their lives at risk every time they become pregnant. They are increasingly susceptible to HIV/AIDS and other major diseases, play an indispensable role in the management of natural resources, and have the right to gain as much as men from the benefits brought by globalisation.

The Millennium Development Goals and Targets

1. Eradicate extreme poverty and hunger
   - Halve, between 1990 and 2015, the proportion of people whose income is less than one dollar a day.
   - Halve, between 1990 and 2015, the proportion of people who suffer from hunger
2. Achieve universal primary education
   - Ensure that, by 2015, children everywhere, boys and girls alike, will be able to complete a full course of primary schooling
3. Promote gender equality and empower women
   - Eliminate gender disparity in primary and secondary education, preferably by 2005, and in all levels of education no later than 2015
4. Reduce child mortality
   - Reduce by two-thirds, between 1990 and 2015, the under-five mortality rate
5. Improve maternal health
   - Reduce by three quarters, between 1990 and 2015, the maternal mortality ratio
6. Combat HIV/AIDS, malaria and other diseases
   - Have halted by 2015 and begun to reverse the spread of HIV/AIDS
   - Have halted by 2015 and begun to reverse the incidence of malaria and other major diseases
7. Ensure environmental sustainability
   - Integrate the principles of sustainable development into country policies and programmes and reverse the loss of environmental resources
8. Develop a global partnership for development
   - Develop further all open, rule based, predictable, non-discriminatory trading and financial system
   - Address the special needs of the least developed countries
   - Address the special needs of landlocked countries and small island developing States
   - Deal comprehensively with the debt problems of developing countries through national and international measures in order to make debt sustainable in the long term

Recognising women's contributions and realising and protecting their rights thus impacts across all eight of the MDGs. Failure to address these concerns will lead to failure in achieving the MDGs themselves. Upholding the rights of women brings widespread benefits to everyone. And the links in respect of the MDGs are broad, not narrow.

A Win for Women is a Win for All

Getting more girls through school not only impacts directly on their own welfare. Research has shown that women with only a few years of primary education have better economic prospects, have fewer and healthier children, and are more likely in turn to ensure their own children go to school. The benefits to families and society of these gains are enormous—and the impacts on poverty reduction immediate and direct.

These synergies are characteristic of the MDGs themselves. Progress in one area will often support progress in others. Furthermore, achieving the goals requires more than a set of narrow, sector specific actions.

Reducing income poverty is not just dependent on a better investment climate and more vibrant markets, it also depends on the availability of a healthy and well-educated workforce, and open information flows supporting creativity and entrepreneurship. Improvements to health are as dependent on better housing and environmental conditions and a better-educated population as they are on improved medical and clinical services. To fully benefit from globalisation, countries have to ensure that women as well as men are empowered to take advantage of the opportunities it offers.

Empowering and investing in women can not be done in a piecemeal fashion, nor can it be limited to instrumental actions aimed at achieving specific goals, valuable though these can be in the immediate term. Sustainable progress requires a broader framework of action, of the kind set out at the 4th World Conference on Women in 1995, underpinned by the commitment of 171 countries to the 1978 Convention on the Elimination of All Forms of Discrimination Against Women (CEDAW).

Broad Actions, Specific Gains

The chart below illustrates how broad-based actions in support of gender equality and women's empowerment can lead to the kinds of development gains directly relevant to the achievement of the MDGs.

Broad-based and concerted actions aimed at bringing women's interests directly into policy formulation and public spending decisions, creating more economic opportunities, reforming public services with women in mind, bringing about legal and other reforms to support their empowerment, and increasing their security and social protection, can all bring developmental benefits valuable in their own right. But these are also directly relevant, and indispensable, to the achievement of the MDGs themselves. A win for women is truly a win for all.

Gender Equality & Delivering the MDGs

Selected Actions Promoting Gender Equality

- Women's participation promoted in national Poverty Reduction Strategies (PRSs)
- Actions taken to promote greater involvement by women in public life
- Wider use made of sex-disaggregated data for planning, monitoring and impact assessment
- Gender budget initatives used to inform public policy and allocation of resources
- Reforms of legal systems and land and inheritance laws favouring greater security and protection for women
- Legal and social programmes, including for sexual and reproduction health and rights, give women and girls greater protection from violence and sexual harassment
- Promotion of social change supporting greater autonomy for women and more equitable sharing of burdens in the domestic economy

- Needs and rights of girls and women given greater priority in reforming and improving public services
- Girls and women enabled to gain greater access to technical training and information and communication technologies

Development Impacts

- Women's interests and rights better reflected in public policy and investment
- Women's economic empowerment leads to increased incomes for the poor
- Child nutrition improved
- More schooling opportunities for girls and boys
- Improved literacy rates among women
- Risk factors for infant and child mortality reduced
- Risk factors for maternal mortality reduced
- Girls and women empowered to protect themselves from HIV/AIDS and other infectious diseases
- Women have greater control over management of natural and other resources
- Women have more skills and opportunities to benefit from globalisation.

The Millennium Development Goals

1. Eradicate extreme poverty and hunger
2. Achieve universal primary education
3. Promote gender equality and empower women
4. Reduce child mortality
5. Improve maternal health
6. Combat HIV/AIDS, malaria and other diseases
7. Ensure environmental sustainability
8. Develop a global partnership for development

This leaflet is the result of a collaborative effort by *UNDP, UNIFEM, UNFPA, The World Bank, and the OECD/DAC Network on Gender Equality.* For more information visit www.mdgendernet.org. July 2003.

Presidential Speech

The Speaker: President and Mrs. George W. Bush

Laura Bush was born on November 4, 1946, in Midland, Texas, to Harold and Jenna Welch. Inspired by her second-grade teacher, she earned a bachelor of science degree in education from Southern Methodist University in 1968. She then taught in public schools in Dallas and Houston. In 1973, she earned a master of library science degree from the University of Texas at Austin and worked as a public school librarian in Austin. In 1977, she met and married George Walker Bush. They are the parents of twin daughters, Barbara and Jenna, who are named for their grandmothers. The following is the transcript from a speech delivered on March 12, 2004.

President, Mrs. Bush Mark Progress in Global Women's Human Rights

Remarks by the First Lady and the President on Efforts to Globally Promote Women's
Human Rights

Mrs. Bush: Welcome to the White House. Thank you all very much for coming today; I'm
so glad you're here. And a special thanks to Dr. Khuzai, Ambassador Ssempala, Sharon
Cohn, and Mrs. Jawad. Thank you all for joining us.

The Ambassador from Afghanistan and Mrs. Jawad were here recently to see the film,
"Osama." If you haven't seen it yet, I hope you'll have a chance to see it; I want to encourage you to see it. It's the story of a young Afghan girl who pretends to be a boy so she
can go to work and support her mother. And it's a sobering reminder of what life was like
under the Taliban. And it's a reminder of why all of us are committed to helping all women
gain equal rights.

President Bush and I often like to tell stories about this room that we're in. Many historic happenings, of course, have happened here in this room, and also some amusing ones.
When President Adams and his wife, Abigail, lived here, there was no glass in the windows,
and this drafty room provided the perfect place for the Adams to hang their laundry.
(Laughter.) Although, Abigail Adams, like many women during her time—and since, I
might add—handled the domestic duties, she believed that women should have an active
role in developing our young nation.

As her husband helped to establish our democracy, she wrote to him and said, "In the
new code of laws, I desire you would remember the ladies and be more generous and favorable to them than your ancestors." Abigail Adams is one of the many women who helped
establish the vitality of our nation. Others, like Elizabeth Cady Stanton and Susan B. Anthony, led the determined struggle to gain suffrage for women. And, today, their actions continue to inspire women around the world.

Earlier this week, millions of women celebrated International Women's Day and the
many accomplishments of women worldwide. As they gathered, they honored generations
of mothers, grandmothers and great grandmothers who sacrificed so that all of us can live
better lives.

The struggle for women's rights is a story of ordinary women doing extraordinary things.
And today, the women of Afghanistan are writing a new chapter in their history. Afghan
women who were once virtual prisoners in their homes, unable to go to school or to work,
are helping rebuild their country. Several women helped draft and review the country's
new constitution, which reserves seats in parliament for women. In more than 2000 villages, women lead local councils. And this year, all Afghan women will have the opportunity to vote in the presidential election.

Women are registering to vote in greater numbers, even though they're threatened by
terrorists as they try to register. They're bravely defying these threats, walking for miles to
register and holding their voter cards like passports to freedom.

Many women are working again and some are even running their own businesses
through micro-enterprise programs. In Herat, female credit officers now have more clients
than their male counterparts. Many women are learning to read and write, and they're becoming the greatest advocates for their daughters' right to education.

In two weeks, nearly 5 million Afghan children, including more than 2 million girls,
will begin a new school year. Just three years ago, 90 percent of girls were forbidden to go
to school. Today, at the Sultana Razia School, girls talk about their future and about rebuilding their country. One little girl said, "I want to become a lawyer because I want to
bring justice and freedom to Afghanistan, especially for women."

I'm proud to be a part of America's efforts to advance the rights of Afghan women and girls. Beginning this fall, the United States will reestablish the American school in Kabul for Afghan children and for children of international families. I'm also working with our government and the private sector to develop a teacher training institute that will help prepare more women teachers for Afghan schools. The women of Afghanistan are gaining greater rights, and their solidarity is an inspiration for women worldwide, especially to the women of Iraq.

Earlier this week, during the signing of Iraq's interim constitution, Iraqi women marched together and many spoke publicly after decades of oppression. In al-Fardous Square, more than 200 women marched for greater rights, chanting, "Yes for equality, yes, for freedom." They were supported and applauded by a group of Iraqi men. One man smiled and said that, "This is the first time women have demonstrated freely in Iraq."

Iraqi women are working with the United States State Department to develop democracy programs that educate women about their rights. Women's self-help and vocational centers are springing up across Iraq, from Karbala to Kirkuk. Our commitment to the women of Iraq is part of a broader effort to support women across the Middle East, from girls' literacy programs in Yemen, to microcredit initiatives for women entrepreneurs in Jordan, to legal workshops in Bahrain.

We're making progress toward greater rights for women in the Middle East and around the world. But still, too many women face violence and prejudice. Many continue to live in fear, imprisoned in their homes. And in brothels, young girls are held against their will and used as sex slaves.

For a stable world, we must dedicate ourselves to protecting women's rights in all countries. Farahnaz Nazir, founder of the Afghanistan Women's Association, said, "Society is like a bird. It has two wings. And a bird cannot fly if one wing is broken." Without women, the goals of democracy and peace cannot be achieved. Women's rights are human rights, and the work of advancing human rights is the responsibility of all humanity.

President Bush is firmly committed to the empowerment in education and health of women around the world. The President knows that women are vital to democracy and important for the development of all countries. And he has three very strong women at home who won't let him forget it. (Laughter and applause.)

Ladies and gentlemen, please welcome my husband, President George Bush. (Applause.)

The President: Thank you all very much. It takes me 45 seconds to walk to work, and sometimes I get introduced by my wife. (Laughter.) It's a heck of a job. Thanks, Laura.

Laura is—you know, one of the interesting moments in our family came when she gave a radio address. She used the President's time to give a radio address, to speak to the women of Afghanistan. And it made a big difference in people's lives. And it was from that moment forward that she, personally, has dedicated time to make sure that people who have been enslaved are free, particularly women. And I'm proud of Laura's leadership. (Applause.)

In the last two-and-a-half years, we have seen remarkable and hopeful development in world history. Just think about it: More than 50 million men, women and children have been liberated from two of the most brutal tyrannies on earth—50 million people are free. All these people are now learning the blessings of freedom.

And for 25 million women and girls, liberation has a special significance. Some of these girls are attending school for the first time. It's hard for people in America to imagine. A lot of young girls now get to go to school. Some of the women are preparing to vote in free elections for the very first time.

The public whippings by Taliban officials have ended. The systematic use of rape by Saddam's regime to dishonor families has ended. He sits in the prison cell.

The advance of freedom in the greater Middle East has given new rights and new hopes to women. And America will do its part to continue the spread of liberty.

I want to thank a man who is working hard to continue the spread of liberty, and that's the Secretary of State, Colin Powell. (Applause.) I appreciate three members of my Cabinet who are here: Secretary Gayle Norton, Secretary Ann Veneman, and Secretary Elaine Chao. I put together, in all due humility, the greatest Cabinet ever. (Laughter and applause.) And one of the reasons why is these three ladies have agreed to serve. (Applause.) The President has got to get pretty good advice—I mean, really good advice, frankly, from people other than his wife. (Laughter.) I get great foreign policy advice from Condoleezza Rice, who is with us today. (Applause.)

I want to thank other members of my administration who are here for this very important occasion to end what has been a very important dialogue. Deputy Secretary of Defense Paul Wolfowitz is with us; Andrew Natsios, who runs USAID; Paula Dobriansky, of the Department of State. I want to thank you for going to Afghanistan recently with Joyce Rumsfeld, Secretary Rumsfeld's better half, who also went to Afghanistan recently to spread the word that America will stay the course; that when we say something we mean it and that we say we're going to—(applause.)

I just named a distinguished American to be a U.S. delegate to the U.N. Commission on the Status of Women, my sister, Dorothy. Thank you for being here, Doro. (Applause.) And I took the recommendation of Vice President Cheney for another member of the same delegation. He suggested that America would be well served by his eldest daughter, Liz. And he's right. Good to see you, Liz. (Applause.)

I want to thank Rend Al-Rahim, who is with us today. Rend, thank you for coming. She's the senior Iraqi representative to the United States. That is a forerunner to ambassadorial status, I guess. Certainly I'm not speaking for what is going to be the sovereign government of Iraq. She's good at what she does, I'm telling you. (Applause.)

There's a lot of ambassadors who are here. I want to thank you all for coming. It's good to see you. I appreciate you taking time to be here. This is an important conference. The message of the United States, about freedom and liberty in the Middle East, is a serious message. And I thank the governments for being here to listen and to help us advance this vital cause for what's good for the world. And so thanks for coming. There's a lot of countries represented here, particularly Middle Eastern countries.

As I told you, Joyce went to—and Paula went to Afghanistan. There are other members of the U.S. Afghan Women's Council that went to Kabul. I want to thank you all for going. I hear it's—one of the travelers, Karen Hughes, reported back, and Margaret did, as well— Margaret Spellings, who is my Domestic Policy Advisor. They said it's unbelievable what's taking place there. The country is transitioning from despair to hope. And it's easy to see now. It's changing, and changing for the better. The people of Afghanistan have just got to know that we'll stand with them for however long it takes to be free.

I appreciate the Iraqi women who attended the Commission on the Status of Women in New York this week. I want to thank you all for coming. I appreciate you being here.

I want to thank my friend, Dr. Raja Khuzai, who's with us today. This is the third time we have met. The first time we met, she walked into the Oval Office—let's see, was it the first time? It was the first time. The door opened up. She said, "My liberator," and burst out in tears—(laughter)—and so did I. (Applause.)

Dr. Khuzai also was there to have Thanksgiving dinner with our troops. And it turned out to be me, as well. Of course, I didn't tell her I was coming. (Laughter.) But I appreciate that, and now she's here again. I want to thank you, Doctor, for your hard work on the writing of the basic law for your people. You have stood fast, you have stood strong. Like me, you've got liberty etched in your heart, and you're not going to yield. And you are doing a great job and we're proud to have you back. Thanks for coming. (Applause.)

Ambassador Ssempala is with us, as well, from Uganda. It's great to see you again, Ambassador. Thanks. She made our trip to Uganda so special that time. She paved the way for what was a special trip. I'm going to talk a little bit about HIV/AIDS. I want to thank you and your country's leadership in that important issue. (Applause.)

Shamim Jawad is with us—Ambassador Said Jawad's better half. I want to thank you very much for being here, Shamim. Thanks for coming. I appreciate your coming. (Applause.)

The Director of the Anti-Trafficking Operations for International Justice Mission is Sharon Cohn. She's with us. Let me tell what that means: that means she's working to end sex slavery. She is a noble soul who cares deeply about the plight of every woman. And I'm honored that you're up here, Sharon. I want to thank you very much for your strong commitment. This government stands with you, and our country stands with you. We abhor—we abhor—the practice of sex slavery, and we will do all we can to help you. (Applause.)

Support for human rights is the cornerstone of American foreign policy. As a matter of national conviction, we believe that every person in every culture is meant by God to live in freedom. As a matter of national interest, we know that the spread of liberty and hope is essential to the defeat of despair and bitterness and terror. The policy of the American government is to stand for the non-negotiable demands of human dignity—the rule of law, the limits on the power of the state, free speech, freedom of worship, equal justice, respect for women, religious and ethnic tolerance, and protections for private property. That is what we believe and we're not going to change.

We have transformed this belief in human rights into action. Last year, our government devoted nearly $75 million to combat the worldwide trafficking in human beings. It's a brutal trade, inhumane trade, by sick people that targets many women and girls. I spoke out against this practice at the United Nations. I called upon the world to join us. This country is determined to fight and end this modern form of slavery.

HIV/AIDS has orphaned millions of children worldwide. In some African countries, nearly 60 percent of adults carrying the virus are women. In 2002, we created the Mother and Child HIV Prevention Initiative to prevent viral transmission of the virus between generations. It's an important initiative by this government, but it wasn't enough.

Last year, I announced an emergency plan for AIDS relief, a $15 billion commitment over five years to fight this deadly disease. This country is determined to turn the tide against this modern plague. When we see disease and suffering, we will not turn our back.

The economic empowerment of women is one effective way to improve lives and to protect rights. Each year for the past five years, the United States government has provided an average of $155 million in small loans, micro-loans. About 70 percent of those benefit women. It turns out the world is learning what we know in America: The best entrepreneurs in the country are women. In America, most new small businesses are started by women. With the right help, that will be the case around the world, as well.

We're determined to help women to find the independence and dignity that comes from ownership. These are necessary responses to urgent problems. Yet, in the end, the rights of women and all human beings can be assured only within the framework of freedom and democracy. If people aren't free, it is likely that women will be suppressed.

Human rights are defined by a constitution; they're defended by an impartial rule of law; they're secured in a pluralistic society. The advance of women's rights and the advance of liberty are ultimately inseparable. America stands with the world's oppressed peoples. We've got to speak clearly for freedom, and we will, in places like Cuba or North Korea or Zimbabwe or Burma.

We stand with courageous reformers. Aung San Suu Kyi is a courageous reformer and a remarkable woman who remains under house arrest for her efforts to bring democracy to her nation. Earlier today, the Libyan government released Fathi Jahmi. She's a local government official who was imprisoned in 2002 for advocating free speech and democracy. It's an encouraging step toward reform in Libya. You probably have heard, Libya is beginning to change her attitude about a lot of things. We hope that more such steps will follow in Libya, and around the world.

The advance of freedom cannot be held back forever. And America is working to hasten the day when freedom comes to every single nation. We understand a free world is more likely to be a peaceful world.

When Iran's Shirin Ebadi accepted the Nobel for peace—Nobel Prize for Peace last year, here's what she said: "If the 21st century wishes to free itself from the cycle of violence and acts of terror and war, and avoid repetition of the experience of the 20th century, there is no other way except by understanding and putting into practice every human right for all mankind, irrespective of race and gender, faith, nationality, or social status."

That's a powerful statement coming from Iran. No wonder she won the Nobel Prize. She's a proud Iranian. She is a devout Muslim. She believes that democracy is consistent with Islamic teachings. And we share in this belief. That's what we believe in America. A religion that demands individual moral accountability and encourages the encounter of the individual with God is fully compatible with the rights and responsibilities of self-government. Promotion of democracy in the greater Middle East is important. It's a priority of ours. And it will be a long and difficult road. But we're on the way.

Three years ago, the nation of Afghanistan was the primary training ground for al Qaeda. You heard Laura talk about the movie, "Osama." See it. It'll help enrich the words I'm about to say: The Taliban were incredibly barbaric. It's hard for the American mind to understand "barbaric." Watch the movie. Women were forbidden from appearing in public unescorted. That's barbaric. Women were prohibited from holding jobs. It's impossible for young girls to get an education. That's barbaric. It's not right.

Today, the Taliban regime is gone, thank goodness. Girls are back in class. The amazing accomplishment, though, is that Afghanistan has a new constitution that guarantees full participation by women. The constitution is a milestone in Afghanistan's history. It's really a milestone in world history, when you think about it. All Afghan citizens, regardless of gender, now have equal rights before the law.

The new lower house of parliament will guarantee places for women. Women voters in Afghanistan, as Laura said, are registering at a faster rate than men for the June election. What's new? (Laughter.) Afghanistan still has challenges ahead, no doubt about it. But now the women of that country, instead of living in silence and fear, are a part of the future of the country. They're a part of a hopeful tomorrow.

Iraq has a different history, and yet a different set of challenges. Only one year ago—only one year after being liberated from an incredibly ruthless person and a ruthless regime, Iraqi women are playing an essential part in rebuilding the nation. They're part of the future of the country.

Every woman in Iraq is better off because the rape rooms and torture chambers of Saddam Hussein are forever closed. He is a barbaric person. He violated people in such a brutal way that some never thought that the spirit of Iraq could arise again. We never felt that way here in this administration. We felt that people innately love freedom and if just given a chance, if given an opportunity, they will rise to the challenge.

Three women now serve on the Iraqi Governing Council—you just heard me praise one. The historic document that was written recently guarantees the basic rights of all

Iraqis, men and women, including freedoms of worship, expression and association. The document protects unions and political parties and outlaws discrimination based on gender, ethnic class and religion. It's an amazing document that's been written.

Iraqi women are already using their new political powers to guard against extremism and intolerance in any form, whether it be religious or secular. The women leaders of Afghanistan and Iraq have shown incredible courage. When you think about what life was like months ago for many women, the fact that they have risen up is a testament to their souls, to their very being, their bravery. Some have paid for their new freedoms with their lives but, in so doing, their sons and daughters will be forever grateful. These leaders have sent a message throughout the Middle East and throughout the world: every man and woman in every culture was born to live in freedom.

The momentum of liberty is building in the Middle East. Just think about what's taken place recently. In 2002, Bahrain elected its own parliament for the first time in nearly three decades. Liberty is marching. Oman has extended the vote to all adult citizens. On Monday, the Sultan appointed the nation's first female cabinet minister. We're making progress on the road to freedom. Qatar has a new constitution. Yemen has a multiparty political system. Kuwait has a directly elected national assembly. Jordan held historic elections last summer. Times are changing.

America is taking the side of those reformers who are committed to democratic change. It is our calling to do so. It is our duty to do so. I proposed doubling the budget for the National Endowment for Democracy to $80 million. We will focus its new work on bringing free elections and free markets and free speech and free labor unions to the Middle East.

By radio and television, we're broadcasting the message of tolerance and truth in Arabic and Persian to tens of millions of people. And our Middle East Partnership Initiative supports economic and political and educational reform throughout the region. We're building women's centers in Afghanistan and Iraq that will offer job training and provide loans for small businesses and teach women about their rights as citizens and human beings. We're active. We're strong in the pursuit of freedom. We just don't talk a good game in America, we act.

In Afghanistan, the U.S.-Afghan Women's Council is developing projects to improve the education of women, and to train the leaders of tomorrow. You heard Laura talk about her deep desire to help train women to become teachers, not only in the cities, but in the rural parts of Afghanistan. We'll succeed. We'll follow through on that initiative. We're pursuing a forward strategy of freedom—that's how I like to describe it, a forward strategy of freedom in the Middle East. And I believe there's no doubt that if America stays the course and we call upon others to stay the course, liberty will arrive and the world will be better off.

The momentum of freedom in the Middle East is beginning to benefit women. That's what's important for this conference. A free society is a society in which women will benefit.

I want to remind you of what King Mohammed of Morocco said when he proposed a series of laws to protect women and their families. It's a remarkable statement. It's like he's put the stake in the ground for women's rights.

He said, "How can society achieve progress while women, who represent half the nation, see their rights violated and suffer as a result of injustice and violence and marginalization, notwithstanding the dignity and justice granted to them by our glorious religion." It's a strong statement of freedom. He's right. America stands with His Majesty and others who share that basic belief. The future of Muslim nations will be better off for all with the full participation of women.

These are extraordinary times, historic times. We've seen the fall of brutal tyrants. We're seeing the rise of democracy in the Middle East. We're seeing women take their rightful place in societies that were once incredibly oppressive and closed. We're seeing the power and appeal of liberty in every single culture. And we're proud once again—this nation is proud—to advance the cause of human rights and human freedom.

I want to thank you all for serving the cause. The cause is just, the cause is right, and the cause is good. May God bless. (Applause.)

Government Document

The Author: The United Nations, Main Committee

The United Nations was established on October 24, 1945, by 51 countries committed to preserving peace through international cooperation and collective security. Today, nearly every nation in the world belongs to the United Nations: membership totals 191 countries. The United Nations is not a world government and it does not make laws. It does, however, provide the means to help resolve international conflicts and formulate policies on matters affecting all of us. At the United Nations, all the Member States—large and small, rich and poor, with differing political views and social systems—have a voice and a vote in this process.

The following declaration was made on September 8, 2000, and adopted by the General Assembly [*without reference to a Main Committee (A/55/L.2)*] 55/2.

United Nations Millennium Declaration

I. Values and Principles

1. We, heads of State and Government, have gathered at United Nations Headquarters in New York from 6 to 8 September 2000, at the dawn of a new millennium, to reaffirm our faith in the Organization and its Charter as indispensable foundations of a more peaceful, prosperous and just world.

2. We recognize that, in addition to our separate responsibilities to our individual societies, we have a collective responsibility to uphold the principles of human dignity, equality and equity at the global level. As leaders we have a duty therefore to all the world's people, especially the most vulnerable and, in particular, the children of the world, to whom the future belongs.

3. We reaffirm our commitment to the purposes and principles of the Charter of the United Nations, which have proved timeless and universal. Indeed, their relevance and capacity to inspire have increased, as nations and peoples have become increasingly interconnected and interdependent.

4. We are determined to establish a just and lasting peace all over the world in accordance with the purposes and principles of the Charter. We rededicate ourselves to support all efforts to uphold the sovereign equality of all States, respect for their territorial integrity and political independence, resolution of disputes by peaceful means and in conformity with the principles of justice and international law, the right to self-determination of peoples which remain under

colonial domination and foreign occupation, non-interference in the internal affairs of States, respect for human rights and fundamental freedoms, respect for the equal rights of all without distinction as to race, sex, language or religion and international cooperation in solving international problems of an economic, social, cultural or humanitarian character.

5. We believe that the central challenge we face today is to ensure that globalization becomes a positive force for all the world's people. For while globalization offers great opportunities, at present its benefits are very unevenly shared, while its costs are unevenly distributed. We recognize that developing countries and countries with economies in transition face special difficulties in responding to this central challenge. Thus, only through broad and sustained efforts to create a shared future, based upon our common humanity in all its diversity, can globalization be made fully inclusive and equitable. These efforts must include policies and measures, at the global level, which correspond to the needs of developing countries and economies in transition and are formulated and implemented with their effective participation.

6. We consider certain fundamental values to be essential to international relations in the twenty-first century. These include:

   ○ **Freedom.** Men and women have the right to live their lives and raise their children in dignity, free from hunger and from the fear of violence, oppression or injustice. Democratic and participatory governance based on the will of the people best assures these rights.

   ○ **Equality.** No individual and no nation must be denied the opportunity to benefit from development. The equal rights and opportunities of women and men must be assured.

   ○ **Solidarity.** Global challenges must be managed in a way that distributes the costs and burdens fairly in accordance with basic principles of equity and social justice. Those who suffer or who benefit least deserve help from those who benefit most.

   ○ **Tolerance.** Human beings must respect one another, in all their diversity of belief, culture and language. Differences within and between societies should be neither feared nor repressed, but cherished as a precious asset of humanity. A culture of peace and dialogue among all civilizations should be actively promoted.

   ○ **Respect for nature.** Prudence must be shown in the management of all living species and natural resources, in accordance with the precepts of sustainable development. Only in this way can the immeasurable riches provided to us by nature be preserved and passed on to our descendants. The current unsustainable patterns of production and consumption must be changed in the interest of our future welfare and that of our descendants.

   ○ **Shared responsibility.** Responsibility for managing worldwide economic and social development, as well as threats to international peace and security, must be shared among the nations of the world and should be exercised multilaterally. As the most universal and most representative organization in the world, the United Nations must play the central role.

7. In order to translate these shared values into actions, we have identified key objectives to which we assign special significance.

II. Peace, Security and Disarmament

8. We will spare no effort to free our peoples from the scourge of war, whether within or between States, which has claimed more than 5 million lives in the past decade. We will also seek to eliminate the dangers posed by weapons of mass destruction.

9. We resolve therefore:

   - To strengthen respect for the rule of law in international as in national affairs and, in particular, to ensure compliance by Member States with the decisions of the International Court of Justice, in compliance with the Charter of the United Nations, in cases to which they are parties.
   - To make the United Nations more effective in maintaining peace and security by giving it the resources and tools it needs for conflict prevention, peaceful resolution of disputes, peacekeeping, post-conflict peace-building and reconstruction. In this context, we take note of the report of the Panel on United Nations Peace Operations and request the General Assembly to consider its recommendations expeditiously.
   - To strengthen cooperation between the United Nations and regional organizations, in accordance with the provisions of Chapter VIII of the Charter.
   - To ensure the implementation, by States Parties, of treaties in areas such as arms control and disarmament and of international humanitarian law and human rights law, and call upon all States to consider signing and ratifying the Rome Statute of the International Criminal Court.
   - To take concerted action against international terrorism, and to accede as soon as possible to all the relevant international conventions.
   - To redouble our efforts to implement our commitment to counter the world drug problem.
   - To intensify our efforts to fight transnational crime in all its dimensions, including trafficking as well as smuggling in human beings and money laundering.
   - To minimize the adverse effects of United Nations economic sanctions on innocent populations, to subject such sanctions regimes to regular reviews and to eliminate the adverse effects of sanctions on third parties.
   - To strive for the elimination of weapons of mass destruction, particularly nuclear weapons, and to keep all options open for achieving this aim, including the possibility of convening an international conference to identify ways of eliminating nuclear dangers.
   - To take concerted action to end illicit traffic in small arms and light weapons, especially by making arms transfers more transparent and supporting regional disarmament measures, taking account of all the recommendations of the forthcoming United Nations Conference on Illicit Trade in Small Arms and Light Weapons.

- To call on all States to consider acceding to the Convention on the Prohibition of the Use, Stockpiling, Production and Transfer of Anti-personnel Mines and on Their Destruction, as well as the amended mines protocol to the Convention on conventional weapons.

10. We urge Member States to observe the Olympic Truce, individually and collectively, now and in the future, and to support the International Olympic Committee in its efforts to promote peace and human understanding through sport and the Olympic Ideal.

III. Development and Poverty Eradication

11. We will spare no effort to free our fellow men, women and children from the abject and dehumanizing conditions of extreme poverty, to which more than a billion of them are currently subjected. We are committed to making the right to development a reality for everyone and to freeing the entire human race from want.

12. We resolve therefore to create an environment—at the national and global levels alike—which is conducive to development and to the elimination of poverty.

13. Success in meeting these objectives depends, *inter alia*, on good governance within each country. It also depends on good governance at the international level and on transparency in the financial, monetary and trading systems. We are committed to an open, equitable, rule-based, predictable and non-discriminatory multilateral trading and financial system.

14. We are concerned about the obstacles developing countries face in mobilizing the resources needed to finance their sustained development. We will therefore make every effort to ensure the success of the High-level International and Intergovernmental Event on Financing for Development, to be held in 2001.

15. We also undertake to address the special needs of the least developed countries. In this context, we welcome the Third United Nations Conference on the Least Developed Countries to be held in May 2001 and will endeavour to ensure its success. We call on the industrialized countries:
    - To adopt, preferably by the time of that Conference, a policy of duty- and quota-free access for essentially all exports from the least developed countries;
    - To implement the enhanced programme of debt relief for the heavily indebted poor countries without further delay and to agree to cancel all official bilateral debts of those countries in return for their making demonstrable commitments to poverty reduction; and
    - To grant more generous development assistance, especially to countries that are genuinely making an effort to apply their resources to poverty reduction.

16. We are also determined to deal comprehensively and effectively with the debt problems of low- and middle-income developing countries, through various national and international measures designed to make their debt sustainable in the long term.

17. We also resolve to address the special needs of small island developing States, by implementing the Barbados Programme of Action and the outcome of the

twenty-second special session of the General Assembly rapidly and in full. We urge the international community to ensure that, in the development of a vulnerability index, the special needs of small island developing States are taken into account.

18. We recognize the special needs and problems of the landlocked developing countries, and urge both bilateral and multilateral donors to increase financial and technical assistance to this group of countries to meet their special development needs and to help them overcome the impediments of geography by improving their transit transport systems.

19. We resolve further:
    ◦ To halve, by the year 2015, the proportion of the world's people whose income is less than one dollar a day and the proportion of people who suffer from hunger and, by the same date, to halve the proportion of people who are unable to reach or to afford safe drinking water.
    ◦ To ensure that, by the same date, children everywhere, boys and girls alike, will be able to complete a full course of primary schooling and that girls and boys will have equal access to all levels of education.
    ◦ By the same date, to have reduced maternal mortality by three quarters, and under-five child mortality by two thirds, of their current rates.
    ◦ To have, by then, halted, and begun to reverse, the spread of HIV/AIDS, the scourge of malaria and other major diseases that afflict humanity.
    ◦ To provide special assistance to children orphaned by HIV/AIDS.
    ◦ By 2020, to have achieved a significant improvement in the lives of at least 100 million slum dwellers as proposed in the "Cities Without Slums" initiative.

20. We also resolve:
    ◦ To promote gender equality and the empowerment of women as effective ways to combat poverty, hunger and disease and to stimulate development that is truly sustainable.
    ◦ To develop and implement strategies that give young people everywhere a real chance to find decent and productive work.
    ◦ To encourage the pharmaceutical industry to make essential drugs more widely available and affordable by all who need them in developing countries.
    ◦ To develop strong partnerships with the private sector and with civil society organizations in pursuit of development and poverty eradication.
    ◦ To ensure that the benefits of new technologies, especially information and communication technologies, in conformity with recommendations contained in the ECOSOC 2000 Ministerial Declaration, are available to all.

IV. Protecting Our Common Environment

21. We must spare no effort to free all of humanity, and above all our children and grandchildren, from the threat of living on a planet irredeemably spoilt by human activities, and whose resources would no longer be sufficient for their needs.

22. We reaffirm our support for the principles of sustainable development, including those set out in Agenda 21, agreed upon at the United Nations Conference on Environment and Development.

23. We resolve therefore to adopt in all our environmental actions a new ethic of conservation and stewardship and, as first steps, we resolve:
    - To make every effort to ensure the entry into force of the Kyoto Protocol, preferably by the tenth anniversary of the United Nations Conference on Environment and Development in 2002, and to embark on the required reduction in emissions of greenhouse gases.
    - To intensify our collective efforts for the management, conservation and sustainable development of all types of forests.
    - To press for the full implementation of the Convention on Biological Diversity and the Convention to Combat Desertification in those Countries Experiencing Serious Drought and/or Desertification, particularly in Africa.
    - To stop the unsustainable exploitation of water resources by developing water management strategies at the regional, national and local levels, which promote both equitable access and adequate supplies.
    - To intensify cooperation to reduce the number and effects of natural and man-made disasters.
    - To ensure free access to information on the human genome sequence.

V. Human Rights, Democracy and Good Governance

24. We will spare no effort to promote democracy and strengthen the rule of law, as well as respect for all internationally recognized human rights and fundamental freedoms, including the right to development.
25. We resolve therefore:
    - To respect fully and uphold the Universal Declaration of Human Rights.
    - To strive for the full protection and promotion in all our countries of civil, political, economic, social and cultural rights for all.
    - To strengthen the capacity of all our countries to implement the principles and practices of democracy and respect for human rights, including minority rights.
    - To combat all forms of violence against women and to implement the Convention on the Elimination of All Forms of Discrimination against Women.
    - To take measures to ensure respect for and protection of the human rights of migrants, migrant workers and their families, to eliminate the increasing acts of racism and xenophobia in many societies and to promote greater harmony and tolerance in all societies.
    - To work collectively for more inclusive political processes, allowing genuine participation by all citizens in all our countries.
    - To ensure the freedom of the media to perform their essential role and the right of the public to have access to information.

VI. Protecting the Vulnerable

26. We will spare no effort to ensure that children and all civilian populations that suffer disproportionately the consequences of natural disasters, genocide,

armed conflicts and other humanitarian emergencies are given every assistance and protection so that they can resume normal life as soon as possible.

We resolve therefore:

- To expand and strengthen the protection of civilians in complex emergencies, in conformity with international humanitarian law.
- To strengthen international cooperation, including burden sharing in, and the coordination of humanitarian assistance to, countries hosting refugees and to help all refugees and displaced persons to return voluntarily to their homes, in safety and dignity and to be smoothly reintegrated into their societies.
- To encourage the ratification and full implementation of the Convention on the Rights of the Child and its optional protocols on the involvement of children in armed conflict and on the sale of children, child prostitution and child pornography.

VII. Meeting the Special Needs of Africa

27. We will support the consolidation of democracy in Africa and assist Africans in their struggle for lasting peace, poverty eradication and sustainable development, thereby bringing Africa into the mainstream of the world economy.
28. We resolve therefore:
    - To give full support to the political and institutional structures of emerging democracies in Africa.
    - To encourage and sustain regional and subregional mechanisms for preventing conflict and promoting political stability, and to ensure a reliable flow of resources for peacekeeping operations on the continent.
    - To take special measures to address the challenges of poverty eradication and sustainable development in Africa, including debt cancellation, improved market access, enhanced Official Development Assistance and increased flows of Foreign Direct Investment, as well as transfers of technology.
    - To help Africa build up its capacity to tackle the spread of the HIV/AIDS pandemic and other infectious diseases.

VIII. Strengthening the United Nations

29. We will spare no effort to make the United Nations a more effective instrument for pursuing all of these priorities: the fight for development for all the peoples of the world, the fight against poverty, ignorance and disease; the fight against injustice; the fight against violence, terror and crime; and the fight against the degradation and destruction of our common home.
30. We resolve therefore:
    - To reaffirm the central position of the General Assembly as the chief deliberative, policy-making and representative organ of the United Nations, and to enable it to play that role effectively.
    - To intensify our efforts to achieve a comprehensive reform of the Security Council in all its aspects.

- To strengthen further the Economic and Social Council, building on its recent achievements, to help it fulfil the role ascribed to it in the Charter.
- To strengthen the International Court of Justice, in order to ensure justice and the rule of law in international affairs.
- To encourage regular consultations and coordination among the principal organs of the United Nations in pursuit of their functions.
- To ensure that the Organization is provided on a timely and predictable basis with the resources it needs to carry out its mandates.
- To urge the Secretariat to make the best use of those resources, in accordance with clear rules and procedures agreed by the General Assembly, in the interests of all Member States, by adopting the best management practices and technologies available and by concentrating on those tasks that reflect the agreed priorities of Member States.
- To promote adherence to the Convention on the Safety of United Nations and Associated Personnel.
- To ensure greater policy coherence and better cooperation between the United Nations, its agencies, the Bretton Woods Institutions and the World Trade Organization, as well as other multilateral bodies, with a view to achieving a fully coordinated approach to the problems of peace and development.
- To strengthen further cooperation between the United Nations and national parliaments through their world organization, the Inter-Parliamentary Union, in various fields, including peace and security, economic and social development, international law and human rights and democracy and gender issues.
- To give greater opportunities to the private sector, non-governmental organizations and civil society, in general, to contribute to the realization of the Organization's goals and programmes.

31. We request the General Assembly to review on a regular basis the progress made in implementing the provisions of this Declaration, and ask the Secretary-General to issue periodic reports for consideration by the General Assembly and as a basis for further action.

32. We solemnly reaffirm, on this historic occasion, that the United Nations is the indispensable common house of the entire human family, through which we will seek to realize our universal aspirations for peace, cooperation and development. We therefore pledge our unstinting support for these common objectives and our determination to achieve them.

―――――――――――――

―――――――――――――

Online Article

The Author: Ana Elena Obando

Founded in 1997, WHRnet aims to provide reliable, comprehensive, and timely information and analyses on women's human rights in English, Spanish, and French. WHRnet updates readers on women's human rights issues and policy developments globally and provides information and analyses that support advocacy actions. A team of regionally based content specialists provides regular news, interviews, perspectives, alert and campaign information, and Web highlights.

The site provides an introduction to women's human rights issues worldwide; an overview of U.N. Regional Human Rights Systems; a research tool that serves as a gateway to the best available online resources relevant to women's human rights advocacy; and a comprehensive collection of related links.

Ana Elena Obando, of Costa Rica, represents the Inter-American Coalition of Activist Women. The following was published in February 2004 on http://www .whrnet.org/docs/issue-genderviolence.html.

How Effective Is a Human Rights Framework in Addressing Gender-based Violence?

The Legal and the Political

When the United Nations adopted the Universal Declaration of Human Rights in 1948, establishing that "All human beings are born free and equal in dignity and rights" and "Everyone is entitled to all the rights and freedoms set forth in this Declaration, without distinction of any kind, such as race, colour, sex, language, religion, political or other opinion, national or social origin, property, birth or other status . . . ," the international community didn't imagine that 40 years later women would demand, in their condition as human beings, the eradication of all forms gender-based violence against them—including violence against women occurring in the so called "domestic" or private sphere.

Despite the strides made since then there still remains a lot to be accomplished before the right to a life without violence becomes the reality for women around the world. On Saturday, February 14, 2004, V-Day and Amnesty International organized a march to commemorate the hundreds of young women who were murdered with impunity in the last decade in Ciudad Juarez and Chihuahua, Mexico. In spite of constant pressures and denunciations from the victims' families as well as local, national and international nongovernmental organizations to resolve these crimes, Mexican authorities still have not initiated the appropriate actions to investigate them.

Even after the visit of the Inter-American Commission on Human Rights' Special Rapporteur on the Rights of Women to Ciudad Juarez and her report on the situation of women in this region, the authorities still insist on treating these crimes in an isolated fashion, denying the existence of common characteristics in the disappearances and murders of hundreds of women based on their gender, ethnic, age and socio-economic condition.

The cases in Ciudad Juarez and Chihuahua are just one painful example of what happens to women on a daily basis in every region of the world. They serve as a testimony of the existing gap between the human rights discourse and its imperfect implementation. In a world where the human rights framework did in reality translate into justice and equality for women, impunity would not be a constant axis cutting across the different forms of violence against women.

From past experience we know that we cannot depend on a singular strategy such as the legal system or the human rights framework to end one of the most extreme manifestations of power inequality between women and men. We need to be ready to move on to other strategies. This does not mean abandoning the rights discourse nor its framework altogether, but rather critically analyzing the mechanisms which after all have arisen from a context of patriarchal domination. Similarly, we need to consider the impact of the more recent phenomenon of neoliberalism and how this factors in the application of the human rights framework.

We are now in a situation where the universality of human rights is being confronted and challenged by the market logic. States and governments that should be first and foremost guaranteeing human rights are instead responding to other external political and economic interests framed in the discourse of neoliberalism which often tends to be antithetical to the concerns and needs of women. Militarization politics, repression, impunity and other forms of human rights violations are mechanisms of social disintegration and political intimidation, the purpose of which is to concentrate social, political and economic power of the corporate elite.

Just as men use violence against women to retain their gender privileges and States exert military violence to affirm their hegemonic place in the world, corporations use economic violence to maintain and accumulate their powers. In other words, the values and attitudes behind violence in the private sphere are the same that can lead to armed conflict or to people's impoverishment.

Conceptualizing the human rights framework as a paradigm that will solve everything as opposed to one indicator of how these mechanisms operate, only serves to divert our efforts to finding more radical solutions. This is because legal advances can only influence social change if they are accompanied by, among other things, the strengthening of Feminist Social Welfare States and the building of a movement that positions itself as one more political actor, with the capacity to negotiate and make agreements with itself and with other legitimate actors.

It is important to re-evaluate the human rights framework to determine how far it has helped advance the struggle against gender based violence, its strengths and limitations in making a contribution to positive change, and determine where the women's movements can focus their efforts in the future. This is more urgent than ever in the present context where the market logic of the capitalist patriarchy underlying neoliberal globalization is undermining and imposing limitations on the institutions responsible for guaranteeing human rights.

Violence Advances, and So Do Human Rights

The three World Conferences on Women's rights held in Mexico City (1975), Copenhagen (1980) and Nairobi (1985), their parallel NGO forums, the Conferences in the 90s and the organizing that took place for these events are all key in understanding the conformation of the international women's movement, the dimensions of its political agency and the legal and political advances that women around the world now enjoy. The issue of violence against women was the entry point which allowed the women's movement to become familiar with and start using the United Nations system, as well as to expand and reconceptualize human rights theory and practice.

The governments' responsibility for the eradication of violence against women was already recognized in the Nairobi Forward-looking Strategies for the Advancement of Women. But perhaps the most significant advancement for the protection of women's human rights was the adoption, in November 1979, of the Convention on the Elimination of All Forms of Discrimination against Women (CEDAW). The first international human rights treaty based on women's experiences and needs, CEDAW deals specifically with women's rights. CEDAW defines the concept of discrimination against women in a broad manner and prohibits discrimination regardless of the perpetrator—individuals, organizations or enterprises.

Although the Convention failed to include the right to be free from violence, in 1992 the Committee on the Elimination of Discrimination against Women issued its General Recommendation No. 19 requesting States to include in their progress reports information on violence against women and on measures introduced to deal with it. The Recommendation affirms that States which are parties to the Convention should take appropriate and effective measures to overcome all forms of gender-based violence, whether by public or private act.

Other treaties such as the American Convention on Human Rights, and specifically the opinion issued by the Inter-American Court of Human Rights in the Velasquez Rodriguez case, establish a framework for the responsibility of States in affirmative duties to protect citizens against violations committed by State or private agents. A State can therefore be held accountable for not implementing appropriate measures to prevent such violations or not responding according to the treaty requirements.

In 1993, the Vienna World Conference on Human Rights recognized that *the human rights of women and of the girl-child are an inalienable, integral and indivisible part of universal human rights,* and moreover that violence against women is a violation of the fundamental principles of international human rights and humanitarian law. The Conference called for the incorporation of a gender perspective in both the human rights mechanisms and at the international, regional and national levels in order to eliminate violence against women.

In December 1993, the UN General Assembly approved the Declaration on the Elimination of Violence against Women. This instrument expresses the political consensus concerning the States' obligations to prevent gender-based violence and redress the wrongs caused to those women who are subjected to it. Although it didn't clarify the content of the category of violence against women nor did it define the range of the States' obligations, the definition of violence at least specifies the contexts where it may occur. The Declaration also reinforces the commitments contained in the Vienna Declaration by not allowing States to justify human rights violations under the pretext of cultural, religious or historical circumstances.

In 1994, the UN Human Rights Commission adopted a resolution to mainstream gender at all levels of human rights and to implement programmatic activities at the international, regional and national levels. In the same year, the Commission designated Radhika Coomaraswamy as the first Special Rapporteur on Violence against Women and its Causes and Consequences. Her mandate allows her to receive complaints and initiate investigations on violence against women in all countries parties to the United Nations.

Also in 1994 the Organization of American States (OAS) approved the Inter-American Convention on the Prevention, Punishment and Eradication of Violence against Women ("Convention of Belém do Pará"). According to this convention, the Inter-American Commission of Women (ICW) is responsible for adopting positive measures to advance the Convention's implementation. In addition, any person or group of persons, or any nongovernmental entity legally recognized in one or more member States of the OAS, may lodge petitions with the Inter-American Commission on Human Rights (IACHR) containing denunciations or complaints about violence against women. One such case considered by the IACHR in April 2001 was that of Maria da Penha Maia Fernandes, in which the State of Brazil was held accountable for its tolerance and omission with respect to violence against women. The IACHR declared that ". . . tolerance by the State organs is not limited to this case; rather, it is a pattern. The condoning of this situation by the entire system only serves to perpetuate the psychological, social and historical roots and factors that sustain and encourage violence against women" (par. 55) and that ". . . society sees no evidence of willingness by the State, as the representative of the society, to take effective action to sanction such acts" (par. 56). [Inter-American Commission on Human Rights, Case 12.051, Maria da Penha Maia Fernandes, Report No. 54/01 of April 16, 2001].

In 1994, the IACHR established its Special Rapporteurship on the Rights of Women. The mandate of this rapporteus is to analyze and report on the extent to which the law and practices of member States affect the rights of women and comply with the broad obligations of equality and nondiscrimination set forth in the American Declaration of the Rights and Duties of Man and the American Convention on Human Rights.

The Programme of Action of the International Conference on Population and Development (Cairo, 1994) recognized that reproductive rights are human rights, and that gender-based violence is an obstacle to women's health, to their education and participation in development. It also called States to implement the Declaration on the Elimination of Violence against Women and CEDAW.

Although rape had been cited explicitly by the UN Human Rights Commission as a form of torture since 1992, it wasn't until 1995 that the IACHR, dedicated a section in its "Report on the Situation of Human Rights in Haiti" to the issue of sexual violence perpetrated against women under an illegal regime. For the first time it declared that rape "represents not only inhumane treatment that infringes upon physical and moral integrity under Article 5 of the [American] Convention [on Human Rights], but also a form of torture in the sense of Article 5(2) of that instrument."

The Declaration and Platform for Action of the Fourth World Conference on Women (Beijing, 1995) dedicated a whole section to the issue of violence against women, recognizing that its eradication is essential for equality, development and world peace. The Platform also explicitly recognized that "the human rights of women include their right to have control over and decide freely and responsibly on matters related to their sexuality, including sexual and reproductive health, free of coercion, discrimination and violence" (par. 96).

In 1996, the UN Commission on the Status of Women considered the proposal to create an Optional Protocol to CEDAW, a mechanism which was approved in 1999 and entered into force in 2000. The Protocol contains two communication and investigation procedures which allow women to challenge a State's discriminatory policies and practices.

Also in 1996, the International Criminal Tribunal for the Former Yugoslavia issued its first accusation judging rape and other types of sexual violence as war crimes and crimes against humanity, including torture and slavery. Likewise, the International Criminal Tribunal for Rwanda judged rape as genocide. Previously, rape in the context of war was seen as natural and inevitable, and legally it was regarded as a moral offense, not the grave crime it is now considered.

In 1998, during the 42nd Session of the UN Commission on the Status of Women, a resolution was approved to demand that governments modify definitions and legal patterns in order to ensure that these include the defense of all women and girls affected by armed conflicts. In particular, the resolution explicitly stated that systematic rape and sexual slavery in the context of armed conflict constituted war crimes. Governments were further called on to formulate multidisciplinary national plans, programs and coordinated strategies aimed at eradicating all forms of violence against women and girls. Moreover they were required to define objectives and compliance timelines for implementation and other procedures to reinforce the law at the local level.

Also in 1998, the creation of the International Criminal Court was agreed upon and the ICC entered into force in 2001. For the first time ever, the Rome Statute of the ICC codified at the international level that rape constitutes a war crime or a crime against humanity and not merely a crime against personal dignity. Forced pregnancy, enforced sterilization, sexual slavery, enforced prostitution and any other form of sexual violence of comparable gravity were also included under crimes against humanity (Article 7). The Statute contemplates "a fair representation of female and male judges"; investigation and prosecution of gender-based crimes against women; the victims' rights to protection and to participate in some stages of the process, and their right to redress, compensation and rehabilitation; the establishment of experts on sexual violence within the Office of the Prosecutor as well as a Victims and Witnesses Unit within the Registry, with gender-sensitive specialists responsible for their protection. The Statute's implementation in the internal penal legislations of each signatory country is of utmost importance, since it contains very progressive substantive and procedural gender norms.

Despite the other difficulties of the Beijing + 5 conference, it is fair to mention that for the first time honor crimes were included prominently in the discourse; language was strengthened concerning dowry-related deaths and violence; governments were called on to introduce legislation on marital rape, and racially-motivated crimes as well as acid attacks were included as forms of violence. Finally, governments were required to launch a campaign of zero tolerance towards violence against women.

Feminists from all regions of the world have taken on the task of translating the international advances, frequently of documents which are not legally binding, into legal norms and governmental policies. In Latin America and the Caribbean, for example, 15 countries have passed laws against domestic violence in the last decade. However, most of these laws do not have a more progressive gender-specific language (with the exception of the Dominican Republic), but rather include all family members as potential victims of domestic violence.

The first example of this type of law against domestic violence took place in Puerto Rico in 1989, when the first legal instrument was passed, called Law No. 54 for the Prevention of and Intervention against Domestic Violence. This legislation was a landmark for the classification and sanction of the crimes of mistreatment through threats, restriction of freedom and marital sexual assault, as well as for the establishment of protective orders for victims of domestic violence.

Costa Rica, Puerto Rico, Argentina, Paraguay and Uruguay have introduced the concept of sexual harassment in their legislations, whether through the Labor Code or in laws that deal specifically with sexual harassment. And even though the private nature of these acts makes it difficult to prove them in court, the law recognized and transformed, under its framework, an everyday experience of abuse which previously had been considered merely an "office romance," "domestic affair" or similarly disparaged.

The creation of women's institutes, ministries, departments and advocacy offices are other advances resulting from the organizing of an international movement against gender-based violence.

The extralegal, *strictu sensu* actions which have taken place since the 90s are countless. The International Criminal Tribunals, the tribunals challenging sexual slavery by the military and the processes held in Vienna and Beijing to document and make visible women's human rights violations all help to sensitize public opinion to gender-based violence. Furthermore, they help in establishing the responsibilities of the States, international bodies and civil society. Also contributing to this are the various denunciation and visualization campaigns; the creation of networks and NGOs specialized in prevention, care and visualization of violence at the international and regional levels; tripartite commissions; emergency hotlines; investigations and diagnoses; the elaboration of indicators and the series of policies formulated in several countries stemming from governments' commitments—all of these demonstrate the sizable work and organizing of a movement whose political agency has translated into multiple advancements in several spheres and in the appropriation of a framework which could be the base for a true human rights culture.

Strengths and Limitations of the Human Rights Framework

Feminists know that the Law, one of the main institutions of the patriarchy, does not operate in a neutral, ahistorical fashion, or independently from the underlying power relations in society. If we look at the advances achieved so far, in general terms it could be said that these have served to make visible women's experiences, concerns and needs, and sometimes to reveal their unequal position within the different structures of oppression.

The ways in which international law is used to encourage changes in a country's policies and legislations are a determining factor in evaluating the effectiveness and limitations of the human rights framework.

1. The first strength of the human rights framework is that is **legitimizes** and **officially recognizes** the **experiences of violence** suffered by women. This helps to transform the experience from mere "individual" and "isolated" problem to a human rights violation which governments have the obligation to respond to. Governments must abstain from perpetrating such violations, sanction them and report to the various Committees. One limitation of the framework is that the implementation of human rights ultimately depends on the will of the State, which is responsible for facilitating its exercise.

The cases of Ciudad Juarez and Chihuahua are one example of this assertion. According to Lydia Alpízar, the "Stop Impunity" campaign used the human rights framework to pressure government authorities, raise public awareness, mobilize support, underscore the responsibility of the Mexican government and show that the State's inaction is a demonstration of sexism and discrimination. At the same time, the limitation of the framework was revealed, given the lack of political will and due diligence from the State to prevent, investigate and sanction the crimes committed.

Amnesty International's report, "Intolerable Killings: Ten years of Abductions and Murders in Ciudad Juarez and Chihuahua" (AMR 41/026/2003), deals with the Mexican authorities' failure to take action to investigate the feminicides that have occurred. It exposes the failure of the authorities to treat the cases within a given pattern, denying family members a proper response and an effective judicial remedy. Through concrete cases, the report provides an analysis of the State's lack of will and its blatant indifference, negligence, unjustifiable delays and inability to prevent, investigate and sanction the murders. It also exposes the obligations acquired by the State of Mexico through international human rights standards, and provides a series of conclusions and recommendations which, according to Amnesty International, need to be fully and effectively carried out.

Violence against women, as demonstrated by these cases, not only constitutes a form of discrimination; it also violates the rights to life, to physical integrity, liberty, security and judicial protection enshrined in the International Covenant on Civil and Political Rights, the American Convention on Human Rights and the Convention on the Elimination of All Forms of Discrimination against Women (CEDAW), among others. These international standards reaffirm the State's obligation to discover the truth and provide justice and redress to the victims, even when their rights have been violated by private parties.

Furthermore, under the Inter-American Convention on the Prevention, Punishment and Eradication of Violence against Women ("Convention of Belém do Pará"), the State participates in responsibility at the international level when it fails to apply due diligence to prevent, investigate and impose penalties for violence against women perpetrated by private actors.

According to the report by the Inter-American Commission on Human Rights' Special Rapporteur on the Rights of Women, the vast majority of the murders in Ciudad Juarez are still unpunished; only in approximately 20 per cent of these cases have there been prosecutions and sentences. On the other hand, almost at the same time the number of murders began to increase, some of the officials in charge of investigating them and of prosecuting the perpetrators started using a discourse which definitely blamed the victims for the crimes. According to public statements from certain high-level authorities, the victims wore miniskirts, went out dancing, were "loose" or prostitutes. There have been reports that the response from the competent authorities to members of the victims' families ranged from indifference to hostility.

Moreover, while the murders committed in Ciudad Juarez increasingly attract international attention and have been condemned by many in that city and in all of Mexico (including the President and First Lady, the Congressional Gender and Equity Commissions, the UN High Commissioner for Human Rights, the UN Special Rapporteurs on Extrajudicial, Summary or Arbitrary Executions and on the Independence of Judges and Lawyers, the Executive Director of the United Nations Fund for Women) but this political condemnation has not been sufficient to revert impunity.

Moreover, with the neoliberal model which is leading societies towards the reduction of their social safety nets, there emerges an institutional pattern, promoted by different types of States, for the discriminatory treatment of women. This pattern means that not even the more well-to-do States are guaranteeing women's rights. And although the problem goes beyond political will—given the complexity of the interrelation of religious, State and corporate powers—this leads one to wonder which institutions feminism should support or help build so that the protection of women's human rights are not left at the mercy of political, economic or religious will or of a sexist administration of justice. How do we ensure that these become part of a mechanism that at the same time operates with the participation of the various social groups. This question is open for debate.

2. The second strength of the human rights framework has been to apply the **principle of indivisibility of human rights** in order to break the existing hierarchy between civil and political rights and economic, social, and cultural rights. This is significant because to ensure women's right to be free from violence requires that the State guarantee the eradication of social and economic conditions which maintain and perpetuate women's subordination.

However, in reality civil and political rights continue to receive more importance than economic, social and cultural rights within international law and in governmental budgets. This continues despite the fact that governments are obliged to allocate resources to ensure all the above rights. Moreover, many countries, for example those in Latin America, have compromised their ability to secure economic, social and cultural rights of their population by signing on to a series of free market agreements with the United States. The fatal effects of this free trade model have already been witnessed in Mexico, with signing on to NAFTA a decade ago.

It is important to discuss how a holistic and inclusive development model would function in practice under the feminist principles of equality, empowerment, sustainability, solidarity, cooperation and productivity. And what the role of the State and of civil society would be vis-à-vis the human rights framework.

Still, a differentiation must be made between the use of the framework by women, which has had very positive results as illustrated below, and the actions by the State to guarantee rights to its citizens, something that opens a whole new issue for analysis.

For example, based on her work with refugee women, June Munala explains that people are generally aware of their rights and basic needs. This is the reason why it is easy to speak about female genital mutilation (FGM) in the context of the human rights of women and girls, since this issue is closely linked to women's social and economic disempowerment. In her opinion, the principle of indivisibility of human rights is a starting point to tackle the numerous factors behind this practice. In order for communities to see FGM as a human rights violation, she redefines it as a multiple violation—to the right to health, to nondiscrimination, to life, to be free from torture, to freedom, personal security and privacy.

Moreover, Carrie Cuthbert and other authors who have worked on domestic violence explain how the human rights framework has helped them demonstrate the links between violations; for example, the economic problems facing mothers after a divorce and the multiple forms of discrimination that battered women experience. They have used the human rights principles and standards in the courts in order to connect the economic difficulties related with the high cost of litigation in family courts, the problems of obtaining child support and other issues dealing concretely with children's economic rights.

3. The third strength of the human rights framework has been to **challenge,** particularly in light of violence against women, the **false public/private dichotomy of international law.** This has implications at the level of State responsibility, and beyond this should lead us to analyze structural inequality and dichotomic thought. This questioning also demystifies violence as something natural and converts it into a political phenomenon.

However, the limitation is that, in practice, the public/private dichotomy still gives more value to public actions and therefore responds more actively to forms of State violence and to the repression of actors within the public/political sphere. This is why violence against women by private actors is not as present in human rights caselaw and doctrine. It is also the reason why national justice systems frequently don't grant it the seriousness and importance such crimes warrant.

The standard of due diligence to prevent and respond to violence perpetrated by non-State actors was clearly illustrated in the cases of Velasquez Rodriguez and Maria da Penha Maia Fernandes cited above. Using the first case, feminist activists have established parallels between domestic violence and torture to introduce certain grave forms of violence against women in the definition of torture when the State has failed to exercise due diligence. Hence the importance that the women's rights advocates keep insisting, particularly at the local level, that international standards be implemented by national justice systems.

4. The fourth strength of the human rights framework has been to help **challenge the traditional concept of human rights and "humanity"** to such degree that today we could assert that there can't be human rights without women's rights. The framework's limitation is that sexism, racism, classism and homophobia are still present in human rights interpretation and practice. Those who choose to use the framework should bear in mind that it has failed to incorporate the diverse experiences of gays, lesbians, transgender people, indigenous people, afro-descendants and other groups who are yet to be treated as "human beings" and on whom the framework's impact is therefore unequal. As long as the human concept fails to integrate all dif-

ferences in practice, its meaning will continue to be partial and, consequently, the exercise of the rights of numerous people will be limited by subhuman categories.

Human stereotypes are currently exacerbated especially by the media, which reinforces the hierarchy of the human paradigm. We still face the challenge of creating a culture based on the ethics of human rights, the axis of which should be an inclusive humanity. We need to continue making inroads in the traditional mass media in a creative way and at the same time resist the temptation of overusing legal strategies.

The successful dimensions of the human rights framework have generated, within the movement, a strong tendency to legalize women's problems. When it comes to strategies, usually the proposal is to formulate a new national legislation or invest human and economic resources in lobbying for an international document. Often the legislation passed ends up not being legally binding and does not improve women's condition of subordination.

Frequently new laws or litigation on rights under the patriarchy will not change the hierarchical social structure or the structural oppression, since both are systematically reproduced by the major economic, political and cultural institutions. One strong critique within the women's movements is that many activists stopped setting their own independent agendas and were absorbed by the priorities of the UN system or by the work around the human rights framework. This has served to omit analysis and debate about multiple oppressions and domination structures.

This is why the question still is: How can we fight against the different social, political and economic structures of oppression, retain those rights already achieved and use the human rights discourse to help generate social change?

I think we must use the new technologies available to open debates on new paradigms, visions and ethics which will help us build a feminist proposal of what is necessary and possible.

5. Another strength and collateral effect of the use of the human rights framework has been the **opening of political spaces within the legal framework.** This has been done in order to define, for instance, concepts such as women's sexual and reproductive health free from coercion and violence, or to be able to speak about discriminations against the rights of lesbians, gays, bisexuals and transgender people as human rights violations.

Before feminists took on the theory and practice of human rights, violations to these rights had no dimensions of gender, class, race, sexual orientation, ethnicity, age, culture, economic status, etc. In other words, the multiple oppressions and violations which combine in individuals due to their diverse conditions were not made visible. Today this is done by feminism, but not by governments.

Perhaps the principle of universality from an approach of diversity, which to this day is not understood nor applied by governments or human rights officials, should be analyzed in connection with the neoliberal mechanism which excludes individuals, groups and social categories. This is particularly necessary since the so-called principle of universality is being reduced to serve elites and therefore threatening to turn rights into one more monopoly of those who concentrate the goods, powers and resources of the world.

Numerous governments still offer up cultural relativism as the only source of moral validity before the principle of universality. Despite the existence of principles and standards and the moral and political legitimacy of international law, women are still victims of multiple violations which prevent them, in the name of culture, traditional customs or religious extremisms, from enjoying their full human rights and liberties.

One interesting position is that of activists such as Ayesha Imam from Nigeria, who states that the human rights concept does not exclude international law nor is it the property of international human rights organizations. According to her, human rights can also be found in Muslim, customary and secular laws. Therefore, she doesn't deem it necessary to always refer to international instruments when speaking of human rights, because she can find them in religious or secular discourses. However, it seems that when there's little space for the universal validity of human rights standards, this may have profound consequences for women's rights. This is because many cultures or religious practices reduce women's social, economic and political status, thus perpetuating their subordination.

Uché U. Ewelukwa, in response to progressive interpretations feminists have made of Sharia law in Nigeria (for example, in Amina Lawal's case), thinks that these should recognize that Sharia legislation violates constitutional standards and international human rights principles. She believes that the human rights framework is an instrument which may be used by local groups because it provides a legal base and moral legitimacy to press governments that have publicly acquired commitments before the international community. Moreover, unlike the Sharia framework, that of human rights allows for transcultural, transnational and transreligious moral judgments in situations where life is being seriously threatened. The characteristics which Uché attributes to the framework could serve as a guide to nurture the human rights culture respecting differences among countries, social groups and people.

6. The human rights framework has also been strengthened by the incorporation of new language in UN documents. This includes the diverse forms of gender-based violence against women and many other terms so far unknown or not translated to other languages, **providing a feminist vocabulary** which is more inclusive in terms of the rights discourse.

The gender perspective, for instance, is a key concept which has permeated the UN system's documents. There is, however, a reductionist trend concerning the scope of this perspective, as well as numerous distortions. The feminist philosophical and political-theoretical content of a gender perspective, according to Marcela Lagarde, has been distorted by technical uses and, frequently due to institutional obligation, women and men become familiar with it in a superficial and diminished way.

Some human rights bodies within the UN system, which haven't mainstreamed gender, have attempted to pass on their responsibilities to other institutions specializing in women's rights because they consider that these are less important and, after all, women have "particular" rights. Those "specialized" institutions also have fewer resources than others. The same logic may be applied to governments that place "women's issues" in the hands of ministries created to this effect which are equally lacking in budget.

Conclusions

One could write an entire book about the effects the human rights framework has had on the women's movement. It has facilitated opportunities for working jointly to promote common political actions, learning to resolve differences, agreeing upon common objectives, educating governments and the general public, mobilizing and lobbying, using the new technologies to maintain the networks created, documenting cases, going from invisibility to the social problematization of violence and instigating the demand for concrete accountability mechanisms—to name a few—all of which are part of the feminist movement's political capital.

The issue of violence against women is still characterized by two important aspects: the theme of impunity and the implementation of human rights mechanisms. The latter should ultimately be part of a new vision that incorporates, along with the human rights framework, the connections to the issues and to the institutions working for peace, economic justice and security.

The status of women of all regions and the diverse violations to their human rights, which were previously hidden and silenced, have all surfaced, linking local movements to a global women's movement that continues to grow. It is time to close the cycle of victimization and violence, and open one of empowerment. We need to encourage women to recognize themselves as subjects with rights, who have the capacity to confront a justice system which is highly sexist, racist, classist and homophobic.

The experience of the movement for women's rights demonstrates not only its community possibilities but also the limitations of a political strategy focused on those rights. The demands for rights are not the answer to social change; at the same time the human rights framework cannot be abandoned, since it is one more instrument in the fight against patriarchy if used creatively. It is through the human rights framework that women can articulate new and different social and political worlds. This is possible if we analyze and use rights in connection with other social, political, economic and cultural relations that occur in our societies and as long as we know how to identify the conditions that allow us to multiply the strengths of the human rights framework.

The human rights framework is one aspect of the daily lives of women, one dimension of their social relationships and multiple identities. Human rights have meanings which link women to each other and may, at the same time, oppress or empower them. Basing the human rights culture on the ethic of respect, interdependency, and egalitarian human relationships could be a key in deconstructing the mechanisms that threaten to put an end to our planet.

Additional Resources

Facts and Figures

- At least 60 million girls who would otherwise be expected to be alive are "missing" from various populations, mostly in Asia, as a result of sex-selective abortions, infanticide or neglect. (UN Study on the Status of Women, Year 2000)
- Globally, at least one in three women and girls has been beaten, coerced into sex, or otherwise abused in her lifetime by a member of her family; for the

majority of women the abuse is repeated over months or years. (*Women in the World Atlas*, 2003)

- In a recent survey by the Kenyan Women Rights Awareness Program, 70% of the men and women interviewed said they knew neighbors who beat their wives. Nearly 60% said women were to blame for the beatings. Just 51% said the men should be punished. (*The New York Times*, 10/31/97)
- Four million women and girls are trafficked annually. (United Nations)
- An estimated one million children, mostly girls, enter the sex trade each year. (UNICEF)
- In Bangladesh, 47% of adult women report physical assault by a male partner. (UNFPA)
- In a study of 475 people in prostitution from five countries (South Africa, Thailand, Turkey, USA, and Zambia):
  - 62% reported having been raped in prostitution.
  - 73% reported having experienced physical assault in prostitution.
  - 92% stated that they wanted to escape prostitution immediately.
  (Melissa Farley, Isin Baral, Merab Kiremire, Ufuk Sezgin, "Prostitution in Five Countries: Violence and Posttraumatic Stress Disorder." 1998, *Feminism & Psychology* 8 (4): 405–426)
- In Pakistan, 80% of women say that they have experienced physical abuse by a male intimate. (*Women in the World Atlas*, 2003)
- So-called "honour killings" take the lives of thousands of young women every year, mainly in North Africa, Western Asia and parts of South Asia. In 1999, more than 1000 women in Pakistan were victims of honour crimes. (UNFPA)
- In South Africa, it is estimated that a woman is raped every 83 seconds: only 20 of these cases are ever reported to the police. (Vetten: 1996, Tribune: 1991)
- More than 90 million African women and girls are victims of female circumcision or other forms of genital mutilation. (Heise: 1994)
- In Uganda, HIV infection rate is six times higher in young girls than in boys, with a difference in rates that starts even at nine years of age and reaching a peak between the ages of 12 and 19 years. This is due to the fact that older men, convinced that young girls are HIV-free, seek them out for sexual exploitation. (Uganda Ministry of Health)
- Canadian data on solved crimes indicate that 52% of all female homicide victims in 2001 were killed by someone with whom they had an intimate relationship at one point in time, either through marriage or dating—compared to 8% of male victims. (Canadian Centre for Justice Statistics, Statistics Canada)
- In Brazil, 72% of women murdered where killed by a relative or friend. (*Women in the World Atlas*, 2003)
- In Zimbabwe, domestic violence accounts for more than 60% of murder cases that go through the high court in Harare. (Zimbabwe Women's Resource Centre and Network—ZWRCN)
- A 1998 study in Zaria, Nigeria, found that 16% of female patients seeking treatment for sexually transmitted infections were children under the age of 5. (UNFPA).

- According to the World Health Organization, between 12% and 25% of women around the world have experienced sexual violence at some time in their lives.
- Laws in many countries, such as India, Papua New Guinea and Malaysia, have explicit exceptions for marital rape. Laws in countries such as Uruguay and Ethiopia allow rapists to marry their victims in order to escape punishment.
- In situations of armed conflict and civil war, an increasing use of rape as a war weapon has been observed in approximately 100 countries.
- In some countries, women and girls are attacked with acid as a result of family disputes for rejecting sexual relations or marriage. A growing number of such acid burns have been reported in Bangladesh, Nigeria and Cambodia. Survivors are permanently disfigured and/or blinded.
- The World Health Organization estimates that violence is the leading cause of death for women between the ages of 15 and 44, more than cancer, traffic accidents and malaria combined.

Scholarly Article

The Author: Amnesty International

Amnesty International is a worldwide movement of people who campaign for internationally recognized human rights. In pursuit of their vision, Amnesty International undertakes research and action focused on preventing and ending grave abuses of rights to physical and mental integrity, freedom of conscience and expression, and freedom from discrimination, within the context of its work to promote all human rights.

The following was published in 1997 in *Female Genital Mutilation: A Human Rights Information Packet.*

What Is Female Genital Mutilation?

The Different Types of Mutilation

Female genital mutilation (FGM) is the term used to refer to the removal of part, or all, of the female genitalia. The most severe form is infibulation, also known as pharaonic circumcision. An estimated 15% of all mutilations in Africa are infibulations. The procedure consists of clitoridectomy (where all, or part of, the clitoris is removed), excision (removal of all, or part of, the labia minora), and cutting of the labia majora to create raw surfaces, which are then stitched or held together in order to form a cover over the vagina when they heal. A small hole is left to allow urine and menstrual blood to escape. In some less conventional forms of infibulation, less tissue is removed and a larger opening is left.

The vast majority (85%) of genital mutilations performed in Africa consist of clitoridectomy or excision. The least radical procedure consists of the removal of the clitoral hood.

In some traditions a ceremony is held, but no mutilation of the genitals occurs. The ritual may include holding a knife next to the genitals, pricking the clitoris, cutting some pubic hair, or light scarification in the genital or upper thigh area.

The Procedures Followed

The type of mutilation practised, the age at which it is carried out, and the way in which it is done varies according to a variety of factors, including the woman or girl's ethnic group, what country they are living in, whether in a rural or urban area and their socio-economic provenance.

The procedure is carried out at a variety of ages, ranging from shortly after birth to some time during the first pregnancy, but most commonly occurs between the ages of four and eight. According to the World Health Organization, the average age is falling. This indicates that the practice is decreasingly associated with initiation into adulthood, and this is believed to be particularly the case in urban areas.

Some girls undergo genital mutilation alone, but mutilation is more often undergone as a group of, for example, sisters, other close female relatives or neighbours. Where FGM is carried out as part of an initiation ceremony, as is the case in societies in eastern, central and western Africa, it is more likely to be carried out on all the girls in the community who belong to a particular age group.

The procedure may be carried out in the girl's home, or the home of a relative or neighbour, in a health centre, or, especially if associated with initiation, at a specially designated site, such as a particular tree or river. The person performing the mutilation may be an older woman, a traditional midwife or healer, a barber, or a qualified midwife or doctor.

Girls undergoing the procedure have varying degrees of knowledge about what will happen to them. Sometimes the event is associated with festivities and gifts. Girls are exhorted to be brave. Where the mutilation is part of an initiation rite, the festivities may be major events for the community. Usually only women are allowed to be present.

Sometimes a trained midwife will be available to give a local anaesthetic. In some cultures, girls will be told to sit beforehand in cold water, to numb the area and reduce the likelihood of bleeding. More commonly, however, no steps are taken to reduce the pain. The girl is immobilized, held, usually by older women, with her legs open. Mutilation may be carried out using broken glass, a tin lid, scissors, a razor blade or some other cutting instrument. When infibulation takes place, thorns or stitches may be used to hold the two sides of the labia majora together, and the legs may be bound together for up to 40 days. Antiseptic powder may be applied, or, more usually, pastes—containing herbs, milk, eggs, ashes or dung—which are believed to facilitate healing. The girl may be taken to a specially designated place to recover where, if the mutilation has been carried out as part of an initiation ceremony, traditional teaching is imparted. For the very rich, the mutilation procedure may be performed by a qualified doctor in hospital under local or general anaesthetic.

Geographical Distribution of Female Genital Mutilation

An estimated 135 million of the world's girls and women have undergone genital mutilation, and two million girls a year are at risk of mutilation—approximately 6,000 per day. It is practised extensively in Africa and is common in some countries in the Middle East. It also occurs, mainly among immigrant communities, in parts of Asia and the Pacific, North and Latin America and Europe.

FGM is reportedly practised in more than 28 African countries (see FGM in Africa: Information by Country (ACT 77/07/97)). There are no figures to indicate how common FGM is in Asia. It has been reported among Muslim populations in Indonesia, Sri Lanka and Malaysia, although very little is known about the practice in these countries. In India, a small Muslim sect, the Daudi Bohra, practise clitoridectomy.

In the Middle East, FGM is practised in Egypt, Oman, Yemen and the United Arab Emirates.

There have been reports of FGM among certain indigenous groups in central and south America, but little information is available.

In industrialized countries, genital mutilation occurs predominantly among immigrants from countries where mutilation is practised. It has been reported in Australia, Canada, Denmark, France, Italy, the Netherlands, Sweden, the UK and USA. Girls or girl infants living in industrialized countries are sometimes operated on illegally by doctors from their own community who are resident there. More frequently, traditional practitioners are brought into the country or girls are sent abroad to be mutilated. No figures are available on how common the practise is among the populations of industrialized countries.

The Physical and Psychological Effects of Female Genital Mutilation

Physical Effects

The effects of genital mutilation can lead to death. At the time the mutilation is carried out, pain, shock, haemorrhage and damage to the organs surrounding the clitoris and labia can occur. Afterwards urine may be retained and serious infection develop. Use of the same instrument on several girls without sterilization can cause the spread of HIV.

More commonly, the chronic infections, intermittent bleeding, abscesses and small benign tumours of the nerve which can result from clitoridectomy and excision cause discomfort and extreme pain.

Infibulation can have even more serious long-term effects: chronic urinary tract infections, stones in the bladder and urethra, kidney damage, reproductive tract infections resulting from obstructed menstrual flow, pelvic infections, infertility, excessive scar tissue, keloids (raised, irregularly shaped, progressively enlarging scars) and dermoid cysts.

First sexual intercourse can only take place after gradual and painful dilation of the opening left after mutilation. In some cases, cutting is necessary before intercourse can take place. In one study carried out in Sudan, 15% of women interviewed reported that cutting was necessary before penetration could be achieved. Some new wives are seriously damaged by unskilful cutting carried out by their husbands. A possible additional problem resulting from all types of female genital mutilation is that lasting damage to the genital area can increase the risk of HIV transmission during intercourse.

During childbirth, existing scar tissue on excised women may tear. Infibulated women, whose genitals have been tightly closed, have to be cut to allow the baby to emerge. If no attendant is present to do this, perineal tears or obstructed labour can occur. After giving birth, women are often reinfibulated to make them "tight" for their husbands. The constant cutting and restitching of a women's genitals with each birth can result in tough scar tissue in the genital area.

The secrecy surrounding FGM, and the protection of those who carry it out, make collecting data about complications resulting from mutilation difficult. When problems do occur these are rarely attributed to the person who performed the mutilation. They are more likely to be blamed on the girl's alleged "promiscuity" or the fact that sacrifices or rituals were not carried out properly by the parents. Most information is collected retrospectively, often a long time after the event. This means that one has to rely on the accuracy of the woman's memory, her own assessment of the severity of any resulting complications, and her perception of whether any health problems were associated with mutilation.

Some data on the short and long-term medical effects of FGM, including those associated with pregnancy, have been collected in hospital or clinic-based studies, and this has been useful in acquiring a knowledge of the range of health problems that can result. However, the incidence of these problems, and of deaths as a result of mutilation, cannot be reliably estimated. Supporters of the practice claim that major complications and problems are rare, while opponents of the practice claim that they are frequent.

Effects on Sexuality

Genital mutilation can make first intercourse an ordeal for women. It can be extremely painful, and even dangerous, if the woman has to be cut open; for some women, intercourse remains painful. Even where this is not the case, the importance of the clitoris in experiencing sexual pleasure and orgasm suggests that mutilation involving partial or complete clitoridectomy would adversely affect sexual fulfilment. Clinical considerations and the majority of studies on women's enjoyment of sex suggest that genital mutilation does impair a women's enjoyment. However, one study found that 90% of the infibulated women interviewed reported experiencing orgasm. The mechanisms involved in sexual enjoyment and orgasm are still not fully understood, but it is thought that compensatory processes, some of them psychological, may mitigate some of the effects of removal of the clitoris and other sensitive parts of the genitals.

Psychological Effects

The psychological effects of FGM are more difficult to investigate scientifically than the physical ones. A small number of clinical cases of psychological illness related to genital mutilation have been reported. Despite the lack of scientific evidence, personal accounts of mutilation reveal feelings of anxiety, terror, humiliation and betrayal, all of which would be likely to have long-term negative effects. Some experts suggest that the shock and trauma of the operation may contribute to the behaviour described as "calmer" and "docile", considered positive in societies that practise female genital mutilation.

Festivities, presents and special attention at the time of mutilation may mitigate some of the trauma experienced, but the most important psychological effect on a woman who has survived is the feeling that she is acceptable to her society, having up-held the traditions of her culture and made herself eligible for marriage, often the only role available to her. It is possible that a woman who did not undergo genital mu-tilation could suffer psychological problems as a result of rejection by the society. Where the FGM-practising community is in a minority, women are thought to be particularly vulnerable to psychological problems, caught as they are between the social norms of their own community and those of the majority culture.

Why FGM Is Practised

Cultural Identity

Custom and tradition are by far the most frequently cited reasons for FGM. Along with other physical or behavioural characteristics, FGM defines who is in the group. This is most obvious where mutilation is carried out as part of the initiation into adulthood.

Jomo Kenyatta, the late President of Kenya, argued that FGM was inherent in the initiation which is in itself an essential part of being Kikuyu, to such an extent that "abolition . . . will destroy the tribal system". A study in Sierra Leone reported a similar feeling about the social and political cohesion promoted by the Bundo and Sande secret societies, who carry out initiation mutilations and teaching.

Many people in FGM-practising societies, especially traditional rural communi-ties, regard FGM as so normal that they cannot imagine a woman who has not un-dergone mutilation. Others are quoted as saying that only outsiders or foreigners are not genitally mutilated. A girl cannot be considered an adult in a FGM-practising so-ciety unless she has undergone FGM.

Gender Identity

FGM is often deemed necessary in order for a girl to be considered a complete woman, and the practice marks the divergence of the sexes in terms of their future roles in life and marriage.

The removal of the clitoris and labia, viewed by some as the "male parts" of a woman's body, is thought to enhance the girl's femininity, often synonymous with docility and obedience.

It is possible that the trauma of mutilation may have this effect on a girl's person-ality. If mutilation is part of an initiation rite, then it is accompanied by explicit teach-ing about the woman's role in her society.

Control of Women's Sexuality and Reproductive Functions

In many societies, an important reason given for FGM is the belief that it reduces a woman's desire for sex, therefore reducing the chance of sex outside marriage. The ability of unmutilated women to be faithful through their own choice is doubted. In many FGM-practising societies, it is extremely difficult, if not impossible, for a woman to marry if she has not undergone mutilation. In the case of infibulation, a woman is "sewn up" and "opened" only for her husband. Societies that practise infibulation are strongly patriarchal. Preventing women from indulging in "illegitimate" sex, and protecting them from unwilling sexual relations, are vital because the honour of the whole family is seen to be dependent on it. Infibulation does not, however, provide a guarantee against "illegitimate" sex, as a woman can be "opened" and "closed" again.

In some cultures, enhancement of the man's sexual pleasure is a reason cited for mutilation. Anecdotal accounts, however, suggest that men prefer unmutilated women as sexual partners.

Beliefs about Hygiene, Aesthetics and Health

Cleanliness and hygiene feature consistently as justifications for FGM. Popular terms for mutilation are synonymous with purification (*tahara* in Egypt, *tahur* in Sudan), or cleansing (*sili-ji* among the Bambarra, an ethnic group in Mali). In some FGM-practising societies, unmutilated women are regarded as unclean and are not allowed to handle food and water.

Connected with this is the perception in FGM-practising communities that women's unmutilated genitals are ugly and bulky. In some cultures, there is a belief that a woman's genitals can grow and become unwieldy, hanging down between her legs, unless the clitoris is excised. Some groups believe that a woman's clitoris is dangerous and that if it touches a man's penis he will die. Others believe that if the baby's head touches the clitoris during childbirth, the baby will die.

Ideas about the health benefits of FGM are not unique to Africa. In 19th Century England, there were debates as to whether clitoridectomy could cure women of "illnesses" such as hysteria and "excessive" masturbation. Clitoridectomy continued to be practised for these reasons until well into this century in the USA. However, health benefits are not the most frequently cited reason for mutilation in societies where it is still practised; where they are, it is more likely to be because mutilation is part of an initiation where women are taught to be strong and uncomplaining about illness. Some societies where FGM is practised believe that it enhances fertility, the more extreme believing that an unmutilated woman cannot conceive. In some cultures it is believed that clitoridectomy makes childbirth safer.

Religion

FGM predates Islam and is not practised by the majority of Muslims, but has acquired a religious dimension. Where it is practised by Muslims, religion is frequently cited as a reason. Many of those who oppose mutilation deny that there is any link between the practise and religion, but Islamic leaders are not unanimous on the subject. The Qur'an does not contain any call for FGM, but a few hadith (sayings attributed to the Prophet Muhammad) refer to it. In one case, in answer to a question put to him by 'Um 'Attiyah (a practitioner of FGM), the Prophet is quoted as saying "reduce but do not destroy". Mutilation has persisted among some converts to Christianity. Christian missionaries have tried to discourage the practice, but found it to be too deep rooted. In some cases, in order to keep converts, they have ignored and even condoned the practice.

FGM was practised by the minority Ethiopian Jewish community (Beta Israel), formerly known as Falasha, a derogatory term, most of whom now live in Israel, but

Testimony

"I was genitally mutilated at the age of ten. I was told by my late grandmother that they were taking me down to the river to perform a certain ceremony, and afterwards I would be given a lot of food to eat. As an innocent child, I was led like a sheep to be slaughtered.

Once I entered the secret bush, I was taken to a very dark room and undressed. I was blindfolded and stripped naked. I was then carried by two strong women to the site for the operation. I was forced to lie flat on my back by four strong women, two holding tight to each leg. Another woman sat on my chest to prevent my upper body from moving. A piece of cloth was forced in my mouth to stop me screaming. I was then shaved.

When the operation began, I put up a big fight. The pain was terrible and unbearable. During this fight, I was badly cut and lost blood. All those who took part in the operation were half-drunk with alcohol. Others were dancing and singing, and worst of all, had stripped naked.

I was genitally mutilated with a blunt penknife.

After the operation, no one was allowed to aid me to walk. The stuff they put on my wound stank and was painful. These were terrible times for me. Each time I wanted to urinate, I was forced to stand upright. The urine would spread over the wound and would cause fresh pain all over again. Sometimes I had to force myself not to urinate for fear of the terrible pain. I was not given any anaesthetic in the operation to reduce my pain, nor any antibiotics to fight against infection. Afterwards, I haemorrhaged and became anaemic. This was attributed to witchcraft. I suffered for a long time from acute vaginal infections."

Hannah Koroma, Sierra Leone

it is not known if the practise has persisted following their emigration to Israel. The remainder of the FGM-practising community follow traditional Animist religions.

References

1. Lightfoot-Klein, H., *"The Sexual Experience and Marital Adjustment of Genitally Circumcised and Infibulated Females in the Sudan"*, The Journal of Sex Research, 26 (3), pp. 375–392, 1989.
2. Lightfoot-Klein, H., *Prisoners of Ritual: An Odyssey into Female Genital Circumcision in Africa*, Haworth Press, New York, 1989.
3. Baasher, T.A., *"Psychological Aspects of Female Circumcision"* Traditional Practices Affecting the Health of Women and Children, Report of a seminar, 10–15 February, 1979, WHO-EMRO Technical Publication 2, WHO, Alexandria, Egypt, 1979, pp. 71–105.
4. Assaad, M.B., *"Female Circumcision in Egypt: Social Implications, Current Research and Prospects for Change"*, Studies in Family Planning, 11:1, 1980, pp. 3–16.

5. Kenyatta, J., *Facing Mount Kenya: The Tribal Life of the Kikuyu,* Secker and Warburg, London, 1938.

6. Assaad, M.B., ibid.

7. Katumba, R., *"Kenyan Elders Defend Circumcision"*, Development Forum, September, 1990, p. 17.

EVENT CASEBOOK FIVE

Five-Second Delay

Focus on Television, Freedom of Expression, and Standards of Decency after Super Bowl 2004

Initial Reports

News Report—National

The Source: CNN.com

CNN.com is among the world's leaders in online news and information delivery. Staffed twenty-four hours, seven days a week by a dedicated staff in CNN's world headquarters in Atlanta, Georgia, and in bureaus worldwide, CNN.com relies heavily on CNN's global team of almost 4,000 news professionals. CNN.com features the latest multimedia technologies, from live video streaming to audio packages to searchable archives of news features and background information. The site is updated continuously throughout the day.

The following article was published online on February 2, 2004.

Apologetic Jackson says "Costume Reveal" Went Awry

FCC to Investigate Incident at End of Halftime Show

Singer Janet Jackson apologized Monday to anyone who was offended when her right breast was exposed during the halftime show Sunday at the Super Bowl.

"The decision to have a costume reveal at the end of my halftime show performance was made after final rehearsals," Jackson said in a statement.

"MTV was completely unaware of it. It was not my intention that it go as far as it did. I apologize to anyone offended—including the audience, MTV, CBS and the NFL."

MTV produced the halftime show, which was broadcast by CBS. Both had issued their own apologies.

On Monday, Federal Communications Commission Chairman Michael Powell ordered an investigation of the incident.

An estimated 140 million people were watching the show when at the end, pop star Justin Timberlake popped off part of Jackson's corset, exposing her breast. Powell told CNN he was not convinced the incident was an accident.

"Clearly somebody had knowledge of it. Clearly it was something that was planned by someone," he said. "She probably got what she was looking for."

Jackson spokesman Stephen Huvane said the incident "was a malfunction of the wardrobe; it was not intentional. . . . He was supposed to pull away the bustier and leave the red-lace bra."

Huvane said an unauthorized copy of Jackson's single "Just a Little While" has appeared on the Internet, so Virgin Records decided to release it Monday. The song is from the album *Damita Jo*, set to be released March 30.

MTV posted this tease on its Web site last week: "Janet Jackson's Super Bowl show promises shocking moments."

Powell said he was watching the game Sunday evening with his two children and found the incident "outrageous."

"I knew immediately it would cause great outrage among the American people, which it did," he said, citing "thousands" of complaints received by Monday morning. "We have a very angry public on our hands."

Powell said MTV and the CBS network's more than 200 affiliates and company-owned stations could be fined $27,500 apiece.

"I think it's all of their problem," he said. "The law allows you to reach many of the different parties." He said he would like to see the enforcement penalties strengthened to 10 times their current amount.

"We all as a society have a responsibility as to what the images and messages our children hear when they're likely to be watching television," he said.

"I don't think that's being moralistic, and I don't think that's government trying to tell people how to run their businesses. I don't think you need to be a lawyer to understand the basic concepts of common decency here."

Powell said he "expressed my great displeasure" over the incident in a telephone call Monday with CBS President and CEO Mel Karmazin, who "promised to cooperate" with the investigation.

Although Karmazin expressed "a great deal of regret," Powell said those sentiments would not deter the investigation.

The stock price of Viacom, the parent of CBS, rose more than 1 percent Monday.

"CBS deeply regrets the incident that occurred during the Super Bowl halftime show," the network said in a statement. "We attended all rehearsals throughout the week, and there was no indication that any such thing would happen.

"The moment did not conform to CBS broadcast standards, and we would like to apologize to anyone who was offended."

A statement from MTV said the tearing of Jackson's costume "was unrehearsed, unplanned, completely unintentional and was inconsistent with assurances we had about the content of the performance.

"MTV regrets this incident occurred, and we apologize to anyone who was offended by it."

Despite its apology, MTV did not hesitate to promote the incident after the fact. A Web page headline said: "Janet Jackson Got Nasty at the MTV-Produced Super Bowl Halftime Show."

Continuing, the Web page said, "Jaws across the country hit the carpet at exactly the same time. You know what we're talking about . . . Janet Jackson, Justin Timberlake and a kinky finale that rocked the Super Bowl to its core."

Not everyone was buying the apologies.

"They can apologize all they want, but this was wrong, and heads are going to fall," said New York-based media strategist Robbie Vorhaus, who once worked for CBS.

Performing together in a routine that had included a number of bump-and-grind moves, Timberlake reached across Jackson, flicking off the molded right cup of the bustier, leaving her breast bare except for a starburst-shaped decoration held in place by a nipple piercing.

Timberlake issued his own apology. "I am sorry if anyone was offended by the wardrobe malfunction during the halftime performance at the Super Bowl," he said. "It was not intentional and is regrettable."

The White House also weighed in on the issue. "Our view is that it's important for families to be able to expect a high standard when it comes to programming," White House spokesman Scott McClellan said.

NFL Commissioner Paul Tagliabue joined the chorus. "The show was offensive, inappropriate and embarrassing to us and our fans. We will change our policy, our people and our processes for managing the halftime entertainment in the future in order to deal far more effectively with the quality of this aspect of the Super Bowl."

AOL, owned by CNN parent company Time Warner, attempted to distance itself from the dispute.

"While AOL was the sponsor of the Super Bowl Halftime Show, we did not produce it. In deference to our membership and the fans, AOL and AOL.com will not be presenting the halftime show online as originally planned."

News Article—International

The Source: The Australian

The Australian is the country's only national broadsheet newspaper. The editorial values focus on leading and shaping public opinion on the issues that affect Australia. Led by a team of highly credible and experienced journalists, editorial themes cover economic, political, and social issues.

The following article was published on February 7, 2004.

America Beats Breasts, Rends Garments over TV Boob

Wardrobe malfunction emerged as a memorable phrase, together with WMD—weapon of mass distraction—as the world pondered the meaning of the exposure of Janet Jackson's right breast during a half-time performance at the US Super Bowl, the country's most-watched televised sporting event. Jackson and Justin Timberlake bumped and ground their way through Girls Gone Wild until he tore open her bodice to reveal a bosom adorned with a "nipple-brooch." The nation was electrified, the "money shot" became the most searched image in Internet history, and the event's organisers, characterising American prudishness, were offended. "Wardrobe malfunction" was Timberlake's expression: he was expecting a red bodice under the jacket. "She's a 37-year-old singer who's using a hot young star to keep her career alive," his spokesman said. The media judged the worldwide TV audience more important than the straight-man's identity. "Years from now, or, more correctly, tomorrow, nobody will remember who won," The *San Francisco Chronicle*'s Tim Goodman wrote. "They will remember it only as the day 90 million or so Americans saw Janet Jackson's breast. Boy, wouldn't it be nice to release an album right about now?" Jackson 'fessed up, exonerating the show's producers, MTV, its broadcasters, CBS and the National Football League, but Marvin Kalb wrote in London's *Financial Times:* "rarely has hypocrisy lurked so transparently behind every expression of 'shock.'" CBS dumped Jackson as a Grammy Awards presenter and announced a five-second delay to that telecast in case others misbehaved. New York's *Daily News* reported Federal Communications Commission chairman, Michael Powell, mourned that a "celebration" had been "tainted by a classless, crass and deplorable stunt" and launched an investigation. "Celebration of what?" the *Daily News*'s Mike Lupica asked, noting the ads for male potency pills shown during the telecast. "The whole event—except for the football game—is a monument to excess. She just got into the game."

The ripples spread, people recalled Bono saying "f——" at the 2003 Golden Globes and Madonna tongue-kissing Britney Spears on MTV. A debate about standards on TV ensued. NBC dropped a breast shot from an episode of medical drama *ER* and Oscars organisers also opted for a five-second delay. But real analysis was left for non-Americans. While the headline on Kalb's FT piece read "America's hypocrisy laid bare,'" the *Times*'s Joan Smith was kinder, noting "the contradictions of a culture obsessed with women's breasts." The *Economist* rejected the idea that secular Britons were no longer shockable, "while Americans have clung to their religion and associated puritanism," citing the Internet hit-rate as indicative of demand. The attitudes were more likely a by-product of the US media structure. While the British market was a free-for-all of unbridled, smutty competition, even at the high end, US newspapers enjoyed local monopolies and could afford "a loftier attitude."

And they "set the tone for TV and the regulators' attitudes."

Multimedia Sources

Editorial Cartoon

The Author: Jim McCloskey

Jim McCloskey has worked as an editorial cartoonist for the *News Leader* in Staunton, Virginia, since 1989. He also serves on the editorial board of the newspaper and has worked in advertising sales. His cartoons have been honored with many awards, including the "Best of Gannett 2001" and the "Best of Gannet 2002." In 2002,

McCloskey's first book, *Drawing Flak,* was published. The volume contains 150 of the artist's favorite cartoons.

The following cartoon was published in 2004 following the Super Bowl.

Editorial Cartoon

The Author: Brian Fairrington

Brian Fairrington is a nationally syndicated cartoonist for the *Arizona Republic,* as well as one of the top illustrators in Arizona.

The following cartoon was published nationally in February of 2004.

Transcript

The Speakers: James Carville, Paul Begala, Robert Novak, and Tucker Carlson

Broadcast in front of a live audience and featuring daily political guests, *Crossfire* examines the political and social issues impacting the United States.

The following transcript is from the February 11, 2004, broadcast.

Super Bowl Fallout Continues

(Begin videotape)

Announcer: Crossfire. On the left, James Carville and Paul Begala; on the right, Robert Novak and Tucker Carlson.

In the Crossfire: Janet Jackson's Super Bowl exposure gets U.S. lawmakers' attention.

Unidentified Male: Never let it be said that I wasn't part of political piling on. That's why I'm here today. This is a big issue.

Announcer: Does the Super Bowl halftime show prove that TV needs better taste or more government regulation?

Unidentified Male: We received 200,000 complaints on the Super Bowl incident alone.

Unidentified Female: I guess because I don't watch MTV, it was shocking.

Announcer: Today on *Crossfire*.

(End videotape)

Announcer: Live from the George Washington University, Paul Begala and Tucker Carlson.

(Applause)

Paul Begala, Co-host: Hello, everybody, and welcome to *Crossfire.*

Janet Jackson's breast was a rather touchy subject on Capitol Hill this morning. Members of the House and the Senate and the Federal Communications Commission all agreed that they were shocked, shocked, about what had happened at the Super Bowl.

Carlson: At hearings on not one, but both sides of Capitol Hill today, lawmakers developed wardrobe malfunctions, profane language, and sex in the media—they denounced them, not developed them—all of which are regular features of *Crossfire,* needless to say.

However, the incident drawing most of the attention, indeed, creating a rare display of bipartisan unity, was the Janet Jackson–Justin Timberlake portion of the Super Bowl halftime show. Now, no doubt you're familiar with that. But what should we as a nation of couch potatoes do about it exactly?

Well, exposing themselves to the *Crossfire* today are radio show host Doug Tracht, better known to his nationally syndicated audience as the Greaseman, along with Pat Trueman of the Family Research Council.

(Applause)

Begala: Gentlemen, thank you for joining us.

Doug Tracht, Radio Talk Show Host: Thank you.

Begala: Mr. Trueman, you know, when I was raised to believe that the Republican Party was the party of Lincoln, who freed the slaves, Eisenhower, who liberated the war from—the world from fascism, Reagan, who opposed the evil empire of Soviet communism, I look around today and here's what Republicans stand against.

They don't—they are interested in investigating Bill Clinton's wiener, Janet Jackson's boob, and whether two gay guys make out in Massachusetts. That's a little sad and a little sick, isn't it?

(Cheering and applause)

Patrick Trueman, Senior Adviser, Family Research Council: So, is your point that the Jackson family ought to be teaching my kids about sex? Because I disagree with that.

You know, we have a right in our own home to control what comes into that home. And because I can't always sit there with my kids with four televisions in the house, the United States Congress has passed a law prohibiting indecent material. The Supreme Court has upheld it. The FCC is supposed to enforce it. They haven't been doing it. But Janet Jackson . . .

Begala: So it does take a village. It takes a government to raise a family. This is the new conservative position.

Trueman: Look, this is not a promo for Hillary Clinton here.

But this is simply a statement that it's not too much to expect entertainers today, during a time when kids are in the audience, to rely on something other than indecent material and sex, with someone exposing themselves, to entertain the public.

(Applause)

Carlson: OK, Mr. Tract, Mr. Greaseman, let's put this to what I think of as the Spike Lee test, Spike Lee, famous director, creator of the movie *She's Gotta Have It.* If Spike Lee thinks it's over the top, it's probably too much.

Here's what he says about the Janet Jackson performance: "What's going to be next? It's getting crazy. And it's down to money, money and fame. Somehow, the whole value system has been upended."

It's not about artistic expression, is it? As Spike Lee suggests, it's about making money, isn't it?

Tracht: It always is about making money.

But I think, in this instance, geez, it just shows what a humorless nation we are at this point. Rather than have the FCC investigate obscenity, I think we should have the FBI investigating as to what happened to the talent on that show, the chaotic screaming, yelling and whooping.

(Laughter)

(Applause)

Carlson: Well, I agree. I mean, I think we're probably in agreement, then. There are nice ways to display breasts on television. But there are also sort of boring, vulgar ways to do it. And this

(Crosstalk)

Tracht: But don't you think—I mean, I was watching the Super Bowl. It went by in such a flash. As I put another Dorito in my yap, I thought, did I—no, it couldn't have, and then went on.

It wasn't until this brouhaha. And I've seen Janet Jackson's rather nice and succulent appendage many times . . .

(Laughter)

Tracht: . . . since they showed it over and over. It's on the Internet, every time you turn around. I think, if just let it go by and then, maybe in retrospect, we could all say, you know what? Maybe it wasn't the right venue. It was the Super Bowl. Maybe it shouldn't have been MTV. Maybe we should have gotten Dwight Yoakam out there or some more mainstream entertainment.

Everybody could have said, whoops, sorry, we made a mistake. But, instead, this pounding, this grinding, someone's gotta give a pound of flesh. Can't we just have a couple of chuckles and move on? Are we so consumed with this?

Begala: And, in fact, Mr. Trueman, it seems to me that some of our friends on the right— I'm curious as to whether you fall into this category—are very, very concerned, of course, about sex, but a lot less concerned when there's money at stake.

For example, there's a story on the AP. "One father who watched the Super Bowl game with his 12-year-old son said the Jackson dance passed without comment," just as Doug suggested. "But he was caught short when the boy turned to his father and asked, 'Dad, what's erectile dysfunction?' "

Apparently, it's this disease that hits Republican men. I don't really know much about it myself.

(Laughter)

Carlson: Like you haven't struggled with that your whole life. Come on, Paul.

(Crosstalk)

Begala: What in the world—why are you all whining about a half a second of a booby exposed, when we have commercial after commercial about this other stuff?

Trueman: Let's join together and try to do something about the commercials, if you're so upset.

But it wasn't just that one- or two-second display of Janet Jackson's breast. There was simulated sex. There was simulated S&M material. And, really, what happened here is this. The FCC last year said that the F-word—I won't use it on the program—I don't use it at all—was fine on network television, so long as it was an expletive, not a verb. And that set the public off. That set Congress off.

It even got the attention of Michael Powell, who's always opposed to any enforcement of indecency regulations on television. So, when the—when that came, then the Super Bowl comes, and you get 20 minutes of real disgusting material, not just the breast. Then, the public is upset. And that's why you have Congress finally doing something about getting the FCC to enforce indecency law, simply because kids are in the audience.

If you want to see breasts, there's plenty of places to do it. If you want to see simulated sex, there's plenty of places

(Crosstalk)

Begala: Don't go past that.

(Crosstalk)

Trueman: Not on network television.

Carlson: OK. Now, Doug, I want to put this in some context. I want to show you two quick clips. One is from Bono at the Golden Globes last year. The next is Nicole Richie at the Billboard Music Awards. You may have seen them.

Here they are.

(Begin video clip)

Bono, U2: That is really, really (expletive deleted) brilliant.

Nicole Richie, Actress: Have you ever tried to get cow (expletive deleted) out a Prada purse? It's not so (expletive deleted) simple.

(End video clip)

Carlson: So my question is, Doug, A, why are there so many award shows? And, B . . .

(Laughter)

(Applause)

Carlson: Is it—is it—I mean, that's totally—that doesn't add anything. That's just—that's just, look at me. This is—these are fading celebrities attempting to get publicity. It's pathetic, isn't it?

Tracht: I agree.

I think the art to communication, if you're going to be adult and spicy, is to do it in a way that little kids and old grandma watching wouldn't be offended. I think, just to throw out profanity for profanity's sake, as they did on those particular shows, shows a lack of ability with the English language and a lack of ability to impress any other way than to shock, which is endemic throughout our broadcast industry now.

(Applause)

Begala: Mr. Trueman, let me suggest, the guy who's got the real answer to this is not Michael Powell, who wants to be everybody's nanny. It's his boss, George W. Bush. A man I don't often praise has exactly the right solution.

Let me quote our president on February 14, 2000. He said: "Put the off button on." Now, in his own Forrest Gumpian way, that's a very wise statement.

(Laughter)

Begala: Isn't it up to moms and dads, not nanny-state, to decide what their children watch? Isn't President Bush right?

Trueman: Obviously—obviously, you don't have kids or you don't have older kids, because . . .

Begala: Well, I have an off button that I know how to work.

(Crosstalk)

Trueman: Well, I can't—I can't walk around the house with my 12-year-old and my 10-year-old and my 15-year-old.

Begala: So you want the government to raise your children for you.

Trueman: And it's just—it's a simple thing to say, just don't put this stuff. Don't use the F-word. Don't use nudity on network television.

You know, you can get that on cable. You can—if you want to buy your kids *Playboy* magazine, that's your business. But you know what? Janet Jackson doesn't have a right to come into my living room and get

(Crosstalk)

Begala: But turn it off. I turned off that halftime show when I saw Kid Rock when desecrating the American flag, because I'm an engaged parent.

(Crosstalk)

Begala: So don't go whining to me. You want the government to be a parent for you, right?

Tracht: Apparently, if you are a parent, your kids aren't—what are they, 3, 4? You don't have much to watch them. But if your kids—as I have, a 15-, a 10-, and a 12-year-old, they're around the house. They're looking at this stuff. And it's not too much to expect that, on network television, that my house is not invaded with this kind of material.

Begala: Pat Trueman gets the last word.

(Applause)

Begala: I thank you very much for joining us from the Family Research Council. Doug Tracht, radio's Greaseman, thank you very much.

(Crosstalk)

Tracht: Thank you.

Begala: Thank you very much, Mr. Trueman.

Web site

The Source: http://www.firstamendmentcenter.org

The First Amendment Center works to preserve and protect First Amendment freedoms through information and education. The center serves as a forum for the study and exploration of free-expression issues, including freedom of speech, of the press, and of religion, and the right to assemble and petition the government.

The First Amendment Center, with offices at Vanderbilt University in Nashville, Tennessee, and Arlington, Virginia, is an operating program of the Freedom Forum and is associated with the Newseum. Its affiliation with Vanderbilt University is through the Vanderbilt Institute for Public Policy Studies.

A 1978 graduate of the University of Illinois College of Law, Kenneth A. Paulson is senior vice president for the Freedom Forum and executive director of the First

Amendment Center. In his role at the First Amendment Center, Paulson draws on his background as both a journalist and lawyer to promote greater understanding of the First Amendment. His column on the First Amendment appears in newspapers nationwide and online at the Freedom Forum's news and online at http://www .firstamendmentcenter.org.

The following article was published on February 6, 2004.

Flashpoint: Janet Jackson and Government Regulation of TV: Inside the First Amendment

Free speech? It wasn't Janet Jackson's speech that broke free at the Super Bowl.

Viewers outraged by Jackson's breast-baring, Nelly's crotch-grabbing and Kid Rock's irreverent draping of the American flag may be a little mystified by all the talk of free expression and limits on how the Federal Communications Commission can respond.

After all, these images were broadcast into our homes on CBS affiliate stations, all operating under licenses issued by the federal government. Doesn't that give the government the clout to impose some standards?

The answer is yes—and no. Despite FCC Chairman Michael Powell's assertions of outrage, there's relatively little the government can do. Years of deregulation and the enormous political clout derived from media mergers have defanged the FCC. Yes, fines can be imposed on the stations, but that's just another operating expense for major media.

Janet Jackson's exposure also lays bare the unique nature of America's broadcasters—media companies that are licensed by the government, but also enjoy First Amendment protection.

The government can regulate indecent programming—essentially references to "sexual or excretory activities or organs"—between 6 a.m. and 10 p.m., when children are most likely to be watching or listening. Beyond that, the government generally has to keep its hands off programming unless it meets the very narrow legal definition of obscenity.

That leaves broadcast media with considerable content latitude, inevitably leading to some distasteful and unpalatable programming and the occasional Janet Jackson firestorm.

Yet the system is fundamentally sound. In a nation in which our most immediate and powerful medium is television, we can't turn content regulation over to a handful of political appointees in Washington. Nor can we deny the importance of protecting programs with mature themes and content.

The kind of outrage generated by the Jackson incident inevitably leads to calls for greater regulation. One bill in Congress would increase the current maximum penalty of $27,500 tenfold. Public pressure on Congress has increased dramatically, and hearings on indecent programming continue on Capitol Hill.

The answer can't be found in legislation or regulation. Even if Congress and the FCC were able to impose greater limits on the content of broadcast television, they wouldn't be able to address the far more provocative landscape of cable television.

Courts have long distinguished between broadcast programs—distributed free of charge over the airwaves—and cable programs—delivered by private companies only to paying subscribers. The government and the FCC have no more control over what is delivered via your cable system than they do over the magazines sent to your mailbox.

Of course, the distinction between broadcast and cable programs is blurred in a nation in which both services are largely delivered by either cable or satellite. Parents concerned about their kids seeing potentially disturbing programs are not going to be mollified by an explanation of delivery systems.

In the end, the solution is not a government regulatory scheme. It's a mistake to undermine free expression because of the crassness of a Super Bowl halftime show. The real answer lies with:

- **An unbundling of channels by America's cable television systems.** Cable systems now essentially give subscribers a "take it or leave it" package, bundling family programming with more-mature channels some would rather not have in their households. An à la carte system would allow parents to tailor television delivery to their standards.
- **The use of technology.** Every television set in America is equipped with a V-chip system that permits parents to block programming through the rating system. It's a flawed and underused system, but is nonetheless a tool for parents.

In addition, most television owners can program their sets to skip over certain channels entirely, avoiding unpleasant surprises while channel surfing.
○ **Free speech.** Those who are concerned about indecent programming shouldn't write to Congress. They should be writing to cable companies, networks, program producers and sponsors. In America, the real pressure is on the pocketbook.

Underlying all of this is a business reality. Broadcasters and cable programmers alike are producing more violent, sexual and provocative content because it attracts viewers. The First Amendment makes possible the marketplace of ideas, but doesn't require us to buy.

Magazine Article

The Author: Robert Corn-Revere

Consumers' Research is a magazine dedicated to providing consumers with the information they want. This magazine covers the issues that affect pocketbooks and choices in the marketplace.

Robert Corn-Revere is a communications law specialist at the Washington, D.C., law firm of Hogan & Hartson. He also teaches at the Communications Law Institute at Catholic University.

The following article is excerpted from his testimony before the U.S. House of Representatives Committee on Energy and Commerce, Subcommittee on Telecommunications and the Internet, January 28, 2004. It was published in February 2004.

Indecency, Television and the First Amendment

The Federal Communications Commission and the enforcement of its indecency rules have received a great deal of attention lately. Much of it—though by no means all—centers on a recent staff decision declining to impose a penalty on broadcast of one particular expletive during a live broadcast of the Golden Globe Awards last January, That decision currently is under review by the full Commission, and Chairman Powell has stated publicly that he intends for the agency to overrule the Bureau order. According to press reports, the Chairman proposed a rule "that would nearly guarantee an FCC fine if [the profanity is] uttered between 6 a.m. and 10 p.m. on radio and broadcast television."

Much of the adverse reaction to the staff Golden Globes Order centers on its observation that the word "'f**king' may be crude and offensive, but, in the context presented here," may not be actionably indecent when used "as an adjective or expletive to emphasize an exclamation." In a less discussed part of the Order, however, the Bureau also found that "fleeting and isolated remarks of this nature do not warrant Commission action," a proposition for which there is ample precedent. In fact, the initial FCC orders that preceded Supreme Court review in *FCC v. Pacifica Foundation* stressed that it would be inequitable to hold a licensee responsible for indecent language when "public events likely to produce offensive speech are covered live, and there is no opportunity for journalistic editing." But whether or not the Golden Globes Order is defensible on other grounds, it may be fairly safe to assume given the present climate that the days of the Bureau decision are numbered.

The official responses spawned by the current controversy would seem to ensure this outcome. Both the House of Representatives and the Senate introduced resolutions condemning the Golden Globes Order, and have urged the FCC generally to take a more activist role in indecency enforcement.

Chairman Powell has endorsed the imposition of vastly higher fines, and has called for a 10-fold increase in forfeiture levels in order to create more of a deterrent effect on broadcast programmers. These actions have come after the Commission announced its intention to impose a number of significant fines under existing rules, and the agency has threatened to revoke the licenses of broadcasters who commit "serious violations" of the indecency policy.

Any Change in the FCC's Indecency Policy Requires a Comprehensive Constitutional Review of the Rules

Whatever course the FCC and Congress may take in this area, neither body can avoid the need for thorough constitutional scrutiny of its actions. As Chairman (then Commissioner) Powell has said, "as government pushes the limits of its authority to regulate the content of speech, the more its actions should be constitutionally scrutinized, not less." He previously has stressed that "any responsible government official who has taken an oath to support and defend the Constitution must squarely address this important question."

With respect to regulating broadcast content, Chairman Powell has criticized as a "willful denial of reality" the Commission's failure to re-examine the "demonstrably faulty premises for broadcast regulation," including the claim "that broadcasting is uniquely intrusive as a basis for restricting speech." Of this rationale he has said, "[t]he TV set attached to rabbit ears is no more an intruder into the home than cable, DBS, or newspapers for that matter. Most Americans are willing to bring TVs into their living rooms with no illusion as to what they will get when they turn them on." The Chairman has explained that "[t]echnology has evaporated any meaningful distinctions among distribution [media], making it unsustainable for the courts to segregate broadcasting from other [media] for First Amendment purposes. It is just fantastic to maintain that the First Amendment changes as you click through the channels on your television set."

Yet the FCC's reluctance to address these basic issues led Commissioner Powell to observe that "the government has been engaged for too long in willful denial in order to subvert the Constitution so that it can impose its speech preferences on the public—exactly the sort of infringement of individual freedom the Constitution was masterfully designed to prevent." The government has a constitutional obligation to address these significant First Amendment issues to the extent it modifies or reaffirms its indecency enforcement policy. The same constitutional duty applies regardless whether Congress or the FCC takes the lead in this area. The Commission's existing approach to indecency enforcement is fraught with constitutional difficulties, and any effort to increase enforcement efforts, raise the level of fines, or to specify a per se indecency rule will make these problems even more pressing.

FCC v. Pacifica Foundation *Does Not Provide Unlimited Authority to Define and Punish Broadcast Indecency*

Senate Resolution 283, adopted [in December] by unanimous consent, urges the FCC to "vigorously and expeditiously enforc[e] its own United States Supreme Court-approved standard for indecency in broadcast media, as established in the declaratory order In the Matter of a Citizen's Complaint Against Pacifica Foundation Station WBAI (FM)." But in this regard, it is important not to read too much into the Pacifica precedent. The Supreme Court's 5–4 decision in that case did not give the FCC carte blanche authority to decide what broadcasts are indecent or to impose unlimited penalties.

The ability to regulate so-called "indecent" speech is a limited constitutional exception, not the general rule. The Supreme Court has invalidated efforts to restrict indecency in print, on film, in the mails, in the public forum, on cable television and on the Internet. The Pacifica Court applied a somewhat different standard for broadcasting, but that decision cannot be read too broadly. Pacifica was a fragmented (5–4) decision that did not approve a particular standard or uphold a substantive penalty against the licensee. The Supreme Court subsequently has acknowledged that the FCC's definition of indecency was not endorsed by a majority of the Justices, and it repeatedly has described Pacifica as an "emphatically narrow holding."

Accordingly, it is not prudent simply to assume that policies approved in the past remain valid now or in the future. The Supreme Court has long held that "because the broadcast industry is dynamic in terms of technological change[,] solutions adequate a decade ago are not necessarily so now, and those acceptable today may well be outmoded ten years hence." The Commission recently reaffirmed this principle in its omnibus broadcast ownership proceeding, noting that current regulations failed to account for vast changes in the media landscape.

To begin with, it is far less plausible for the FCC to justify indecency regulations on the premise that "the broadcast media have established a uniquely pervasive presence in the lives of all Americans." As the Commission most recently concluded, "the modern media marketplace is far different than just a decade ago." It found that traditional media "have greatly evolved," and "new modes of media have transformed the landscape, providing more choice, greater flexibility, and more control than at any other time in history." It also must be noted that society has changed as well, and has grown far more tolerant of the wide range of content that is available. In 1951 a Houston television station caused a public outcry when it planned to air a bedding commercial showing a husband and wife in a double bed, and that same decade the Everly Brothers' song "Wake Up, Little Susie" was banned in Boston. We do not live in the same culture as when Rob and Laura Petrie on the *Dick Van Dyke Show* had to sleep in separate beds, yet the FCC's indecency rules are based on a history of indecency enforcement dating back to 1927.

The law also has evolved since the Supreme Court considered the FCC's broadcast indecency rules. The Court has since confirmed that "indecent" speech is fully protected by the First Amendment and is not subject to diminished scrutiny as "low value" speech, as three Justices who joined the *Pacifica* plurality opinion had suggested. Rather, it stressed that "[t]he history of the law of free expression is one of vindication in cases involving speech that many citizens find shabby, offensive, or even ugly," and that the government cannot assume that it has greater latitude to regulate because of its belief that "the speech is not very important." Additionally, since *Pacifica*, the Court has invalidated government-imposed indecency restrictions on cable television channels despite its finding that "[c]able television broadcasting, including access channel broadcasting, is as 'accessible to children' as over-the-air broadcasting, if not more so." More importantly, in *Reno v. ACLU*, the Court for the first time subjected the indecency definition (in the Internet context) to rigorous scrutiny and found it to be seriously deficient.

Throughout this period, the FCC has shown a marked inability to clarify and apply its own standard. After a decade in which the FCC applied its policy only to the seven specific words in the George Carlin monologue (the so-called "seven dirty words"), it switched to enforcing a "generic" indecency policy. In 1994, the Commission settled an enforcement action (in part to avoid having to respond to a First Amendment defense in court) and committed to providing "industry guidance" as to the meaning of the indecency standard within six months of the settlement agreement. It took another six and one-half years for the Commission to fulfill this condition by issuing a policy statement in 2001 purporting to offer interpretive guidance on the indecency standard. Yet despite this belated attempt at clarification, the Commission itself has been unable to interpret its own standard.

The Indecency Standard Provides Less Constitutional Protection Than Does the Test for Obscenity

The unfortunate history of obscenity law and the change that occurred after courts imposed the discipline of the First Amendment on this area of the law should have been instructive in the development of an indecency standard since such speech is supposed to be constitutionally protected. However, the test for indecency prohibits the transmission (at a time of day when children are likely to be in the audience) of "language or material that, in context, depicts or describes, in terms patently offensive as measured by contemporary community standards for the broadcast medium, sexual or excretory activities or organs." The indecency standard applies to selected passages, not to works as a whole; it is based not on the average person in a community, but upon children; and literary or artistic merit does not bar liability.

The Indecency Standard Does Not Require Review of the Work as a Whole

The FCC has never required an examination of the work "as a whole," or that the material appeal to the prurient interest. Quite to the contrary, the Commission has expressly rejected claims that it "is required [to] take into account the work as a whole." Accordingly, the FCC has found a violation of the law where less than five percent of a program was devoted to sexually-oriented material. The Commission concluded that it could impose a fine "[w]hether or not the context of the entire [program] dwelt on sexual themes." Similarly, if the FCC reverses the staff Golden Globes Order, it will have decided that a single word uttered in the course of a three-hour live telecast is sufficient to render the program indecent.

The focus of indecency enforcement on selected passages and not the work as a whole is a significant constitutional defect. Because of this, the Supreme Court found that the indecency standard when applied to the Internet "unquestionably silences some speakers whose messages would be entitled to constitutional protection."

The Indecency Standard May Restrict Material That Has Serious Literary, Artistic, Political or Scientific Values

The FCC has stated that the merit of a work is not a complete defense to an indecency complaint, but is only "one of many variables that make up a work's 'context.'" In many instances, "the programming's very merit will be inseparable from its seminal 'offensiveness.'" The FCC has even acknowledged that, because serious merit does not save material from an indecency finding, there is a "broad range of sexually-oriented material that has been or could be considered indecent" that does "not [include] obscene speech." Thus, the Commission has expressly declined to hold that "if a work has merit it is per se not indecent," and that material may be found indecent for broadcast even where the information is presented "in the news" and is presented "in a serious, newsworthy manner." In this regard, it is sobering to realize that a federal district court held that the videotape "Abortion in America: The Real Story," transmitted as part of a political advertisement by a bona fide candidate for public office, was indecent.

In striking down the Communications Decency Act's indecency standard as applied to the Internet, the *Reno* Court found the absence of a "societal value" requirement "particularly important." It noted that requiring the inclusion of a work's merit "allows appellate courts to impose some limitations and regularity on the definition by setting, as a matter of law, a national floor for socially redeeming value." No such requirement is contained in the indecency standard. As a result, the Court concluded that application of the indecency standard threatened to restrict "discussions of prison rape or safe sexual practices, artistic images that include nude subjects, and arguably the card catalogue of the Carnegie Library." The FCC has been baffled by such questions.

The Indecency Standard Lacks Strong Procedural Safeguards

As a general matter, the First Amendment requires the government to use "sensitive tools" to "separate legitimate from illegitimate speech." Strict procedural requirements govern any administrative procedure that has the effect of denying or delaying the dissemination of speech to the public. In particular, the First Amendment commands that any delay be minimal, and that the speaker have access to prompt judicial review. Where ongoing government regulation of speech is involved, the government's obligation to provide due process is heightened. In every case where the government seeks to limit speech, the constitutional presumption runs against the government, which must justify the restriction.

The FCC's regime of enforcing the indecency rules is inconsistent with these basic principles. For example, the Commission has begun to issue letters of inquiry that indicate "a complaint has been filed" and demand detailed responses from licensees but do not indicate the identity of the complainants. Indeed, the Commission does not require its anonymous complainants to submit a tape or transcript of allegedly offending broadcasts, and has indicated that when a complaint is received it is the licensee's obligation to prove that the transmission in question was not indecent. As the Chief of the FCC's Enforcement Bureau said at a conference of the National Association of Broadcasters' state leadership, "[i]f the station can't refute information in the complaint, we'll assume the complainant got it right."

Finally, once the Commission, in its sole discretion, decides that a particular broadcast is indecent, the process to review that decision is anything but prompt. For the licensee, challenging an indecency determination generally requires refusing to pay a proposed forfeiture and enduring an enforcement proceeding before it may raise a defense in court, assuming the government initiates a collection action. During this time, the Commission may withhold its approval of other matters the licensee has pending before the agency. For this reason, no licensee has been able to hold out long enough to test the validity of an FCC indecency determination.

Judicial Scrutiny of the Indecency Standard in Other Contexts Underscores its Constitutional Problems

Recent decisions of the Supreme Court and of lower courts confirm that the indecency standard cannot survive rigorous constitutional review. Although these decisions did not examine the indecency regime in the context of broadcasting, their analysis undermines the key premises of the same standard the FCC historically has used to enforce its broadcast rules.

Reno v. ACLU represents the first time the Supreme Court subjected the indecency test to rigorous First Amendment review and in doing so it found the standard to be seriously deficient. Writing for a near-unanimous Court, Justice Stevens concluded that the indecency restrictions of the Communications Decency Act were invalid because of vagueness and overbreadth. This finding is especially meaningful since Justice Stevens also wrote the *Pacifica* decision.

Since then, virtually every court that has ruled on similar laws has held that they are unconstitutional. The question, then, is whether First Amendment protections for broadcasting are so attenuated as to permit the government to apply a standard that the courts have now found to be patently defective.

The primary rationale for such different treatment, cited both by the Supreme Court and now touted by the Commission, is that more intensive content regulation has been permitted for broadcasting historically. The Court in *Pacifica* described the "pervasive presence" of broadcasting and relied on the fact that broadcast licensees have been barred by federal law from transmitting "obscene, indecent or profane language" ever since the Radio Act of 1927. The Commission continues to point to "special justifications" for the different treatment, including "the history of extensive government regulation of the broadcast medium," spectrum scarcity, and the "invasive nature" of broadcasting. Given the changes in the media landscape most recently catalogued by the FCC in various proceedings, the principal remaining "special justification" is the history of content regulation by the FCC. But this is a tenuous basis upon which to perpetuate a constitutionally deficient standard.

FCC Enforcement Experience Confirms the Imprecision of the Indecency Standard

FCC decisions under the indecency standard provide scant guidance either for those who must enforce or comply with the law. Since there is no body of court decisions interpreting or applying the indecency standard in particular cases, licensees must look to the Commission for guidance. But the FCC's rulings provide no real assistance, because most are unavailable, thus constituting a body of secret law. The vast majority of indecency decisions are unpublished, informal letter rulings that are stored in individual complaint files at the FCC. In this regard, the dismissals would be most helpful to understanding the Commission's application of the standard, but these decisions, with a few exceptions, are not made public. Even where the Commission reaches the merits of an indecency complaint, its decision typically consists of conclusory statements regarding its determination that a particular broadcast is indecent.

The FCC's inability to describe how the factors it uses would apply in a given case highlights the absence of precision in the indecency standard itself. Administrative procedures that the Commission believed would mitigate the inherent uncertainty of the standard have proven to be an utter failure. The FCC in the past has asserted that, if individual rulings fail to "remove uncertainty" in this "complicated area of law," it may use its power to issue declaratory rulings to clarify the indecency standard. In practice, however, the Commission has never granted such a request. (E.g., When Pacifica Radio sought to broadcast its annual Bloomsday reading from James Joyce's Ulysses, the Commission declined to issue a declaratory ruling that the material was not indecent despite a 60-year-old judicial precedent supporting the literary value of the book.)

There Are No Quick Fixes That Can Cure the Constitutional Dilemma Posed by the Indecency Standard

Given the inherent imprecision of the indecency standard, it is superficially tempting to remove uncertainty simply by specifying which words are forbidden on radio and television. The FCC followed this approach between 1978 and 1987 by focusing enforcement on the seven words contained in the George Carlin routine that led to *Pacifica*. However, the Commission concluded that the approach was unsatisfactory, and in mid-1987 announced that it would apply the indecency standard generically. Now, after 16 years of experience with the generic standard, people both inside and outside the FCC are advocating once again the adoption of specific prohibitions. As noted earlier, Chairman Powell reportedly has called for a per se ban on profanity between 6 a.m. and 10 p.m. (with a possible exception for political speech), and Congressman [Doug] Ose [R-Calif.] has introduced a new list of prohibited words.

Such a per se approach is unlikely to remove uncertainty in the way its proponents hope, and would raise a host of new constitutional questions. A per se approach would be easier to apply than the current indecency standard (at least initially), but would impose significant penalties on speech that unquestionably is protected by the First Amendment. For example, such a rule would impose significant penalties on any broadcaster who permitted readings from certain portions of the Bible.

It would also impose sanctions on broadcasters who transmitted one of the forbidden words during a newscast, or in the presentation of classic literature. Such an inflexible rule would thus invite close judicial scrutiny for restricting too much expression, including speech that has serious literary, artistic, or scientific merit.

Perhaps for that reason, Chairman Powell reportedly has suggested a possible exception to a per se rule for "political" speech. However, from a constitutional standpoint, it is difficult to justify such a carve-out without also including news, commentary, literature, or art. Moreover, assuming such a technical limitation is possible, it is difficult to predict how it would provide the type of limits that its proponents presumably intend. For example, if U-2's Bono had made a political statement during the Golden Globe presentation (e.g., "thanks for the trophy, and, by the way, f**k the war in Iraq"), the Commission would face the same interpretive problem that currently exists, given the weight of precedent in this area. In short, there are no easy answers in this area, whether one proposes a straight per se indecency rule; or one with one or more exceptions. Either way, Congress and the FCC will have the task of drawing and defending a line between speech that is protected and expression that can be punished.

Web site

The Source: http://www.fcc.gov

The Federal Communications Commission (FCC) is an independent United States government agency, directly responsible to Congress. The FCC was established by the Communications Act of 1934 and is charged with regulating interstate and international communications by radio, television, wire, satellite, and cable. The FCC's jurisdiction covers the fifty states, the District of Columbia, and U.S. possessions.

The following excerpt is from the FCC Web site and may be viewed in its entirety at this URL: http://www.fcc.gov/parents/content.html.

Obscenity, Indecency, and Profanity

It's Against the Law!

It is a violation of federal law to broadcast obscene programming at any time. It is also a violation of federal law to broadcast indecent programming during certain hours. Congress has given the Federal Communications Commission (FCC) the responsibility for administratively enforcing the law that governs these types of broadcasts. The Commission may revoke a station license, impose a monetary forfeiture, withhold or place conditions on the renewal of a broadcast license, or issue a warning, for the broadcast of obscene or indecent material. For more information about FCC indecency enforcement actions, see http://www.fcc.gov/eb/broadcast/opi.html.

Obscene Broadcasts Are Prohibited at All Times

Obscene speech is not protected by the First Amendment and cannot be broadcast at any time. To be obscene, material must meet a three-prong test:

- An average person, applying contemporary community standards, must find that the material, as a whole, appeals to the prurient interest;
- The material must depict or describe, in a patently offensive way, sexual conduct specifically defined by applicable law; and
- The material, taken as a whole, must lack serious literary, artistic, political, or scientific value.

Indecent Broadcast Restrictions

The FCC has defined broadcast indecency as "language or material that, in context, depicts or describes, in terms patently offensive as measured by contemporary community broadcast standards for the broadcast medium, sexual or excretory organs or activities." Indecent programming contains patently offensive sexual or excretory references that do not rise to the level of obscenity. Indecent programming may, however, be restricted in order to avoid its broadcast during times of the day when there is a reasonable risk that children may be in the audience.

Consistent with a federal statute and federal court decisions interpreting the indecency statute, the Commission adopted a rule pursuant to which broadcasts—both on television and radio—that fit within the indecency definition and that are aired between 6:00 a.m. and 10:00 p.m. are subject to indecency enforcement action.

Profane Broadcast Restrictions

Profane material is defined as including language that denotes certain of those personally reviling epithets naturally tending to provoke violent resentment or denoting language so grossly offensive to members of the public who actually hear it as to amount to a nuisance.

Like indecency, profane speech is prohibited on broadcast radio and television between 6:00 a.m. and 10:00 p.m.

First Amendment and Obscenity/Indecency

Expressions of views that do not involve a "clear and present danger of serious substantive evil" come under the protection of the Constitution, which guarantees freedom of speech and freedom of the press. The Communications Act prohibits the FCC from censoring broadcast material, in most cases, and from making any regulation that would interfere with freedom of speech. According to an FCC opinion on this subject, "the public interest is best served by permitting free expression of views." This principle ensures that the most diverse and opposing opinions will be expressed, even though some may be highly offensive. The Courts have said that indecent material is protected by the First Amendment to the Constitution and cannot be banned entirely. Nonetheless, the FCC has taken numerous enforcement actions against broadcast stations for violations of the restrictions on broadcast indecency.

Enforcement of Indecent Broadcast Restrictions

Enforcement actions in this area are based on documented complaints received from the public about indecent or obscene broadcasting. The FCC's staff reviews each complaint to determine whether it has sufficient information to suggest that there has been a violation of the obscenity or indecency laws. If it appears that a violation may have occurred, the staff will start an investigation by sending a letter of inquiry to the broadcast station.

If a complaint does not contain information sufficient to determine that a violation may have occurred, the complaint will be dismissed. In such a case, the complainant has the option of re-filing the complaint with additional information, filing a petition for reconsideration of the staff action, or filing an application for review (appeal) to the full Commission.

If the facts and information contained in the complaint suggest that a violation did not occur, then the complaint will be denied. In that situation, the complainant has the option of filing a petition for reconsideration of the staff action or an appeal to the full Commission.

Context

In making indecency determinations, context is key! The FCC staff must analyze what was actually said during the broadcast, the meaning of what was said, and the context in which it was stated.

How can I file a complaint about obscenity, indecency or profanity on the radio or television?

The Commission asks complainants to provide the following information:

1. the date and time of the alleged broadcast;
2. the call sign of the station involved; and
3. information regarding the details of what was actually said (or depicted) during the alleged indecent, profane or obscene broadcast.

With respect to item (3), in making indecency determinations, context is key! The Commission staff must have sufficient information regarding what was actually said during the alleged broadcast, the meaning of what was said and the context in which it was stated. There is flexibility in how a complainant may provide this information. For example, the complainant may provide a significant excerpt of the program describing what was actually said (or depicted) or a full or partial tape or transcript of the material. In whatever form the complainant provides the information, it must be sufficiently detailed such that the Commission can determine the words and language actually used during the broadcast and the context of those words or language.

Congressional Testimony

The Author: Brent Bozell, III

For 208 years, the Committee on Energy and Commerce, the oldest legislative standing committee in the U.S. House of Representatives, has served as the principal guide for the House in matters relating to the promotion of commerce and to the public's health and marketplace interests. The Subcommittee on Telecommunications and the Internet deals with interstate and foreign telecommunications including, but not limited to, all telecommunication and information transmission by broadcast, radio, wire, microwave, satellite, or other mode.

Founder and Chairman of the Board of the Media Research Center, Mr. Bozell runs the largest media watchdog organization in America. Established in 1987, the MRC produces several newsletters and books. The very popular *Notable Quotables* lists the most biased media quotes, and at year-end a panel of fifty opinion leaders selects the much-cited awards for the year's most biased reporting.

The following is a transcript of testimony Mr. Bozell delivered before the House Energy and Commerce Subcommittee on Telecommunications and the Internet on January 28, 2004.

Broadcast Industry

Chairman Upton and Members of the Committee, I appreciate the opportunity to appear before you to testify on this important issue.

I represent the Parents Television Council's 850,000 members, along with untold millions of parents who, like me, are disgusted, revolted, fed up, horrified—I don't know how to underscore this enough—by the raw sewage, ultra violence, graphic sex, and raunchy language that is flooding into our living rooms night and day.

A major responsibility of the FCC is to ensure that those who use the public airwaves adhere to standards of decency. Yet, looking at the FCC's track record on indecency enforcement, it becomes painfully apparent that the FCC could care less about community standards of decency or about protecting the innocence of young children.

In the past two years, the FCC has received literally hundreds of thousands of complaints of broadcast indecency from fed-up, angry, frustrated parents, yet the

FCC hasn't seen fit to agree with a single complaint. In fact, in the entire history of the FCC this agency has never—never—fined a single television station in the continental United States for broadcast indecency.

In the FCC's view, everything on broadcast TV is—and always has been—decent. This is ludicrous.

The FCC is a toothless lion and its non-actions are not only irresponsible, they're inexcusable. Either the FCC has no idea what it's doing, or it just doesn't care what the public thinks. There's no third explanation.

Indecencies and obscenities are now everywhere on broadcast TV. This past year, the Parents Television Council released a series of three Special Reports looking at the State of the Television Industry. Sex on TV has become increasingly explicit, with children exposed to more direct references to genitalia, prostitution, pornography, oral sex, kinky practices, masturbation, and depictions of nudity during prime time viewing hours—and yes, that includes the so-called "Family Hour"—than they would have been just a few short years ago. Foul language during the family viewing hour alone increased by 95% between 1998 and 2002.

Thanks to some envelope-pushing shows you can now hear words like "asshole" and "bullshit" on primetime broadcast TV. Live awards shows are pushing the boundaries of acceptable language for broadcast TV by "accidentally" allowing the "f" and "s" words to slip past network censors. The "f" word has been used on broadcast television four times in the last year alone.

The broadcast networks are laughing at the public because they know they can do or say whatever they want to over the broadcast airwaves and the FCC won't lift a finger to penalize them.

And it's not just the late night dramas that are pushing standards downward.

Consider the following, which aired on an NBC special this past May at 8:00—during the so-called Family Hour. In this scene, Dana Carvey appears as one of his old Saturday Night Live characters, "Church Lady," to talk to former child star Macaulay Culkin about his sleepovers with Michael Jackson.

Church Lady: "Did he ever dangle anything in front of you at the sleepovers?" Culkin: "Dangle what?" Church Lady: "Oh, I don't know. Say, his 'happy man loaf'? . . . When he moon-walked, he didn't moon you as he walked, did he? . . . How about your friends you took to the sleepovers. Did he ever get into Billy's jeans?" Second guest, Michael Imperioli: "I mean come on, you trying to tell me you're screwing your little jingle bells up against the King of Pop and his shalonz never rose up to salute you? Come on, man. Side by side on the Sealy Posturepedic, you never played 'hide the toast'? Give me a break." Church Lady: "Alrighty, well, I think it's time to 'Beat It.'"

What child needs to be exposed to this? Is pedophilia now a laughing matter? Would you want to have to explain to your youngster what "hide the toast" means? Nevertheless, this was broadcast over the public airwaves—the public's airwaves—right into the family home, "the one place," according to the Supreme Court, "where people ordinarily have the right not to be assaulted by uninvited and offensive sights and sounds."

My libertarian instinct makes me uncomfortable with the notion of coming before Congress to ask for your help, but I do so now, on behalf of tens of millions of parents, simply because it's time that Congress inserted itself to halt this growing problem. The Congress, pure and simple, needs to insist that the FCC do its job correctly.

What should the FCC be doing that it's not doing presently?

It begins with the need for the FCC to start monitoring what's on broadcast television. The FCC has a whopping $278 million + annual subsidy from the Congress, yet somehow can't find the time or the resources to monitor what's on broadcast television. (Parenthetically, let me point out that with a budget of approximately two percent of the FCC's, the Parents Television Council manages to do it.)

It shouldn't be up to the public to point out the violations on the airwaves. It should be up to the FCC to find them.

How disinterested is the FCC in its responsibility to monitor indecency on television? Even with that $278 million annual subsidy, the FCC apparently still can't afford to have a single person working full time on this issue. Not a one. That fact comes to us from the FCC directly.

Second, the FCC needs to start responding to complaints instead of playing games with the public. I have been promised personally by Chairman Powell that every complaint would get a response, and yet on a regular basis, thousands upon thousands of people filing complaints hear nothing. I refer you to our report, Dereliction of Duty, which documents how the FCC has sat on thousands of complaints going back almost two years.

While accepting an award during the December 2002 Billboard Music Awards on Fox, pop-star Cher said, "People have been telling me I'm on the way out every year, right? So f*ck 'em." How long should it have taken the FCC to decide if this was indecent? The answer is: quite a while, apparently. It's been over a year and the FCC has yet to act on it.

The FCC must also be told to stop playing games with the public when it comes to filing complaints. The Chairman of the FCC assured me personally that it was absolutely false that the FCC was requiring the public to attach a transcript of the actual show in question, something that is virtually impossible for a complainant to have handy at the moment. And yet if you look at the FCC website, that's exactly what it instructs the public to do.

The FCC must be told to stop playing games with numbers. The FCC reported that claimed that in the second quarter of 2003 it received only 351 complaints about broadcast indecency. That was preposterous, simply untrue. In that same period, PTC members alone filed over 8,000 complaints. The FCC in turn lumped all of them in one basket and called it one complaint.

The FCC must be told to stop blocking—yes, blocking—complaints, too! Recently we were told by many of our supporters that their e-mailed complaints were being returned as "undeliverable." When we looked into this we were told by a source within the FCC that they were being blocked deliberately.

Third, the FCC must be told to start enforcing the law by attaching meaningful fines to those who are violating the public trust with deliberate indecencies on broadcast television. The $27,000 maximum fine is a joke, and everyone knows it. It is most welcome news, Chairman Upton, that you are proposing that fine be increased tenfold and that the fines be increased up to $3 million for continued offenses. But the fact remains that all is for naught so long as the FCC refuses to levy fines when appropriate. The FCC must be told in no uncertain terms that it has the obligation to do that to protect the public airwaves. Moreover, Congress should insist that the FCC fine stations for each violation. If a shock-jock uses the "s" word ten times on his show, his station should receive ten fines, not one.

Finally, the FCC must get serious about revoking station licenses for those who refuse to abide by standards of decency. The use of the public airwaves is not an entitlement, a right. It is a privilege, and a privilege to be honored. Rather than giving networks more stations as a reward for their irresponsible behavior, perhaps the Congress ought to consider steps to reduce the number of stations allowed for those continuously spitting in the public's face.

I am a father of five who has spent twenty-five years trying to shield my children from offensive messages coming across the airwaves I own. God willing, I'll be a grandfather some day. Wouldn't it be wonderful if my grandchildren didn't have to endure such abuse? If the Congress takes the appropriate steps to force the FCC to do its job, the public trust will be protected and this assault on decency will come to an end. Only Congress can do that, too.

And if you do, an entire generation of grandparents, parents, and their children will thank you for it.

Congressional Testimony

The Author: Mel Karmazin, President and Chief Operating Officer of Viacom

Mel Karmazin became president and chief operating officer of Viacom in May 2000, upon the merger of Viacom and CBS. He had served as president and chief executive officer of CBS Corporation since January 1999. Mr. Karmazin serves on the Viacom Board of Directors and is responsible for overseeing all of Viacom's operations. Viacom is one of the world's largest entertainment and media companies, and a leader in the production, promotion, and distribution of entertainment, news, sports, music, and comedy. The company's properties include CBS, MTV, Nickelodeon, VH1, BET, Paramount Pictures, Viacom Outdoor, Infinity Broadcasting, UPN, Spike TV, TV Land, CMT: Country Music Television, Comedy Central, Showtime, Blockbuster, and Simon & Schuster. Mr. Karmazin is a graduate of Pace University.

The following testimony was given before the House Energy and Commerce Subcommittee on Telecommunications and the Internet on February 11, 2004.

Broadcast Decency Enforcement Act of 2004

Good morning Chairman Upton and Members of the Subcommittee. I am Mel Karmazin, President and Chief Operating Officer of Viacom.

Thank you for inviting me to appear before you today. The topic of this hearing is H.R. 3717, "The Broadcast Decency Enforcement Act of 2004." With such a subject naturally comes scrutiny of the state of television and radio in America today.

In a universe of television and radio programming that is informative, educational and entertaining, the incidences of indecency are infinitesimal. There are more than 1,700 television stations and nearly 13,500 radio stations nationwide, broadcasting a total of some 8 billion minutes each year. And yet, in any given year, programming that is found to be indecent typically represents a handful of incidents covering only a few hours of that time—even under the vaguest indecency definition that exists today.

This illustration is not meant to diminish the serious concerns and legitimate debate about indecency. Rather, it is an attempt to put into perspective the frequency, or more correctly, infrequency, of indecency and to shine a light on all the positive social contributions that we and other broadcasters make. In the interest of time, rather than enumerate all of our efforts, I will submit for the record in this hearing an impressive compendium of the localism, programming and diversity achievements of Viacom's broadcasting divisions. One example you will find discussed in that litany is our HIV/AIDS awareness campaign. Launched last year in partnership with the Kaiser Foundation, the campaign mobilizes the full range of Viacom's properties. In 2003, Viacom devoted $180 million in media value to messages on HIV/AIDS and produced 15 television programs on the topic, which reached more than 50 million people. And for 2004, Viacom has pledged $200 million in ad value to the campaign.

Largely unnoticed in the recent controversy was our decision to air a highly valuable spot on HIV/AIDS during the Super Bowl pre-game show. This message reached about 72 million people, and in the 48 hours following its airing, the campaign's website received 215,000 unique visits, allowing individuals to obtain important information on the disease. Equally unnoticed was MTV's launch during the Super Bowl half-time of its "Choose or Lose 2004" campaign with a timely message to young people about voter registration, a cause certain to resonate in these halls.

But a few regrettable moments in that same Super Bowl have since overshadowed our many good deeds and the quality programming that our company produces and delivers day-in and day-out. We had eagerly anticipated broadcasting the NFL championship game since 2001, when we last aired the event. Super Bowl XXXVIII was the fifteenth one that CBS has televised. In the months leading up to February 1, CBS Sports and engineers excitedly prepared to showcase in both analog and high definition what has become the centerpiece for a national day of celebration. At the same time, MTV made ready its plans for production of the game's half-time show, featuring some of the most popular recording artists in the music industry: Janet Jackson, Kid Rock, Justin Timberlake, P. Diddy and Nelly. This is the second time that MTV produced the half-time event—it also did so in 2001.

MTV's preparations for this year's half-time event included a full review, in tandem with CBS, of the script and lyrics and attendance at all rehearsals throughout the week before the Super Bowl so as to conform to broadcast standards. The script called for no untoward behavior. In rehearsals, Nelly did not reach for an area below his belt, and Jackson and Timberlake certainly did not practice the stunt they performed on air. Further, as Jackson has acknowledged in both written and televised statements, it was devised by her alone, without the knowledge or participation of anyone at CBS or MTV.

In addition to these preparations, CBS put in place for the broadcast of both MTV-produced segments on Sunday—the one-hour *TRL Total Request Live* at noon Eastern and the half-time show—a five-second delay device designed to eliminate inappropriate audio. With respect to video, the first line of defense, as is always the case at live entertainment and sporting events, was the cut-away camera, which moves the camera away from inappropriate graphic subjects. Given the history of broadcast television up until this Super Bowl, deleting troublesome video was never a concern, except, perhaps, for the occasional streaker dashing across a sports field.

Having taken these steps and with our delay and cut-away systems ready, we truly believed that we had thoroughly prepared and taken all precautions needed to deliver a sports and entertainment event that would be enjoyed and applauded by fans throughout America and around the world. We were wrong. Although we are proud of 99 percent of what people saw on CBS last Sunday during eight hours of Super Bowl sport, pageantry and music, we understand what a difference one percent can make. We apologized right after the incident. And I take this occasion to apologize again, to our viewers, to our affiliates, to both teams and the NFL, and to our advertisers for not having in place the technology needed to remove objectionable video before it reached our audience.

Some have publicly stated that they don't believe that we were duped by Jackson and Timberlake. Even with the facts before them, they never will. Yet, logically, there was nothing to gain for Viacom—not for ratings, not for advertising dollars, not for promotional value. Our reputation and the reputations of CBS and MTV are too valuable to risk by engaging in such stunts.

Others have said that we should have anticipated what would happen because of the talent involved. Yet, to our knowledge, neither Jackson nor Timberlake, seasoned performers in numerous live television events, had ever engaged in such an antic. The well-received half-time show MTV produced three years ago had also included performances by Timberlake and Nelly.

The unfortunate Super Bowl half-time episode instructs us that unacceptable conduct may occur at live entertainment events on broadcast television that the cut-away camera approach cannot cure. Artists are pushing new limits, and as they do, high definition digital technology is delivering their words and actions clearly and crisply and often on very large screens into America's homes. Personal video recorders, like TiVo, transform what once was a fleeting, did-that-really-happen television moment into a repeated performance. It was reported that TiVo subscribers hit rewind on the Jackson–Timberlake incident nearly three times more than they did on any other moment in the Super Bowl, even those nail-biting final seconds of the game. These TiVo-recorded images of fleeting television moments are then magnified and transported around the world almost instantaneously via the Internet. Of course, the enlarged still photos appearing on websites are not what a Super Bowl viewer saw. Our first-line defense of the cut-away camera did work to make the incident truly fleeting. And the cut-away camera did, a few moments later, manage to completely protect the home audience from viewing a streaker who had eluded heavy police security and darted across Reliant Stadium's field in front of 70,000 fans. We must be vigilant at the moment of broadcast to protect our own viewers, but we cannot be responsible for the images that are stilled, distorted and then disseminated via a medium over which we have no control. However, we do understand that our first line of defense has to be made more effective.

For the live Grammy Awards show this past Sunday, the CBS Television Network implemented an enhanced delay system for deletion of any inappropriate audio and video footage, had it been needed. Under this system, the broadcast of the live Grammy Awards event was delayed by a full five minutes. Developed by CBS engineers on short notice, at great cost, and under tremendous pressure, the system is groundbreaking—no other network has ever undertaken the task of creating a system that is capable of eliminating video from a live program. In fact, the system we used for the Grammys truly is an invention in process, and we are at the mercy of the technology and of our personnel on the scene. While we would like to commit to using this enhanced technology for all potentially problematic live network events, we are still studying how it works. But I pledge to you that the CBS Television Network will use it or something better whenever appropriate.

We do note a concern that anything more drastic could mean eliminating all live programming. That would not be a good outcome for viewers of broadcast television. Moreover, with an enhanced delay system in place, some celebrities in fact may believe they can do and say anything based on the assumption that the network will catch the inappropriate-for-broadcast behavior before it airs.

Our rigorous attempts to deal with inappropriate footage during live events leads to a discussion of Congressman Upton's bill, which seeks to increase fines ten-fold for violations of the FCC's indecency policies. The ultimate goal of any indecency law or rule should be to keep indecency from being broadcast to American listeners and viewers. Fines have a deterrent effect, for sure, and, if assessed judiciously, can also motivate broadcasters to take more precautions, which, in turn will minimize indecent broadcasts. But it is also important that, as the FCC levies fines, it exercise its discretion to adjust the amounts downward for behavior that is clearly not deliberate, that is, where the broadcaster has taken all reasonable precautions to comply with the indecency rules.

One other point I would like to make is that the enormous fines proposed under the legislation could devastate small broadcasters, who will have much less ability to pay and could be driven to bankruptcy. As a broadcaster, I urge you to consider the significant impact of the legislation on small station owners.

However, we firmly believe that instituting increased fines is putting the cart before the horse. There is a chronic problem that is not cured by increased fines, and that is the vagueness of the FCC's indecency standard. Before the FCC levies any fine, it must determine that a broadcaster has violated a rule. In the case of indecency, the rules are neither clear nor static. The precedent constantly changes, and the standard is not clearly articulated to broadcasters. For example, in two prominent decisions released shortly after the FCC published its long-awaited "Industry Guidance" on indecency in 2001, the FCC issued fines for Eminem and Sarah Jones performances found to be indecent. The FCC later reversed course, found the performances not to be indecent and rescinded the fines. More recently, the FCC's Enforcement Bureau, consistent with Commission precedent, found Bono's use of a particular word on a live awards show to be so fleeting and non-sexual as to be deemed not indecent. Now it is reported that the FCC intends to reverse course and find Bono's utterance to be indecent. These multiple course "corrections" in the context of adjudicatory proceedings typically involving a single party and taking months, or even years, of deliberation, illustrate the difficult task facing broadcasters as an industry in determining whether certain program material—especially in live broadcasts when they are under timing pressures—crosses the line. In short, broadcasters need a much better roadmap.

The FCC should undertake a full rule making proceeding in which all interested parties can participate so that the constitutional parameters of indecency enforcement can be made as intelligible as possible. The Commission has never held such a proceeding relating to indecency, nor has the FCC ever tried to establish a mechanism by which it can reliably ascertain the required contemporary community standard for the broadcast medium. Given the fast-paced nature of change in our society, such an updated standard is critically needed. Then the courts can decide whether the lines have been drawn in proper deference to the First Amendment.

Our request for clear guidelines from the FCC and the courts is in no way an abdication of our responsibility as broadcasters in setting our own internal guidelines. Therefore, I take this opportunity today to reaffirm and explain these long-standing commitments and practices, as well as to announce the institution of a new one, to our CBS and UPN viewers and to Infinity listeners.

First, we reaffirm our policy across the networks and our owned radio and television stations that certain expletives like those contained in the George Carlin monologue "Filthy Words" and which led to the Supreme Court's *Pacifica* decision should not be broadcast at any time of the day, including "safe harbor" periods—except in the rare instance where deleting such language would undermine classic creative content delivered in context. Several years ago, for example, CBS aired a live production of *On Golden Pond,* in which we allowed language we would not have otherwise permitted. We also note that other networks have taken the same approach when airing movies such as *Schindler's List* and *Saving Private Ryan.* When such exceptions are used, however, warnings to viewers about language are frequently interspersed within the programming. As has always been the case, appropriate action, up to and including termination, will be taken against any Viacom employee who violates this policy.

Second, it has been the practice for several years now, that all of our Infinity radio stations that produce their own potentially problematic live entertainment or news programming, or sporting events containing a live entertainment or interview element, have in place delay systems and the personnel to operate those devices in order to delete inappropriate expletives, as well as other unacceptable sexual descriptions or depictions within that programming. We will continue to use these systems and discipline Infinity employees who fail to vigilantly utilize them.

And third, starting this quarter, for the first time all of our owned and operated CBS and UPN televisions will purchase and install delay systems to be used under the same circumstances as described for the Infinity radio stations.

In conclusion, we hope that these policies and changes help reassure you and our viewers and listeners of our commitment to continue to deliver the high quality programming they expect and deserve from our company. On behalf of our entire organization let me again state that I regret the incident that occurred during the Super Bowl half-time show. Our country has the finest free broadcasting system in all the world, and Viacom is proud to be a part of that system.

Article

The Author: Lauren Gelman

FindLaw is the highest-trafficked legal Web site, providing the most comprehensive set of legal resources on the Internet for legal professionals, businesses, students, and individuals.

Lauren Gelman is the associate director of the Center for Internet and Society at Stanford Law School. She and law student Rob Courtney drafted reply comments filed by twenty-one technology companies in the FCC's Digital Broadcast Content Protection rulemaking.

The following article was published on March 18, 2004.

The Silver Lining of the Janet Jackson Incident: A Demonstration of Democracy-Enhancing Technology and the Need to Fight the "Broadcast Flag" Rule

I was at home watching the Super Bowl when I saw CBS broadcast—live, as it happened—the now-famous moment when during their performance, Justin Timberlake ripped off part of Janet Jackson's costume and, for a few seconds, exposed her breast. Like many viewers, I immediately hit pause, and the replay button on my TIVO (a few times) in order to confirm that the event was not a figment of my imagination.

Later, I learned that some more technically talented viewers had done more: They had grabbed a copy of the "clothing malfunction," exported it to their computers, and uploaded it to their weblogs. According to Scott Rafer, CEO of Feedster, thousands used his website to find and view the event.

What happened next was predictable: public outrage, an enraged and energized Congress, Capitol Hill testimony by repentant executives, and new legislation addressing indecency on television.

I'm no fan of increased regulation of speech, but the controversy had at least a small silver lining: It served as a demonstration of the power of innovation to promote the democratic process. In this case, the innovators were the entrepreneurial companies that harnessed the open nature of the Internet to enable users to easily capture, transfer, upload, post, and search for the TV clip.

Even those who missed the game could, because of these companies, easily watch and talk about the incident that was about to be a catalyst for major policy changes at the FCC. Their technologies thus enlarged the marketplace of ideas and influenced public debate.

Shouldn't government be doing all it can to support technologies and companies that enhance democracy like this? I believe the answer is yes.

But to the contrary, the Federal Communication Commission (FCC) is currently considering new technology regulations that would halt innovation in technologies that capture, manipulate and transfer digital television.

That, I believe, is a terrible mistake—and one that if it cannot be stopped, hopefully, can be subject to some degree of damage control.

The FCC's Proposed "Broadcast Flag" Rule

The proposed FCC rule is commonly referred to as the "broadcast flag" rule. It would require companies to incorporate FCC-approved technology that protects digital TV (DTV) content from copying, into devices that grab DTV out of the airwaves, or transmit it to other devices like computers.

The purported purpose of this scheme is to ensure protection of copyrighted images. In reality, however, it goes much further than that. Images that are only a few moments long, such as those of the Jackson incident, fall within copyright's "fair use" exception, which allows us to use content without prior approval by the creator.

Copying a small part of a larger work—whether it's a novel, a play, or a televised broadcast—traditionally has, and ought to, count as fair use. Yet the proposed "broadcast flag" rule allows content owners to prevent these uses.

If We Must Live with a "Broadcast Flag" Rule, It Ought to Be a Limited One

At this stage in the rulemaking, some kind of broadcast flag regulation is inevitable. But the issues of exactly how the FCC will approve certain technologies, and under what circumstances is extremely controversial, and still open to debate.

For example, an interpretation of the so-called "robustness requirement" standard—which that requires content to be completely protected against any determined attempt by an expert hacker to crack the technology—may preclude all software-based DTV players, whether open-source or proprietary, because of the inherent malleability of software.

Under other proposed standards, it is unclear whether companies could manufacture even those technologies that allow users fair uses of DTV. As noted above, the FCC has essentially ignored the crucial fair use issues.

The Innovations That Will Be Stymied by the "Broadcast Flag" Rule

We will doubtless lose fabulous innovations as a result of the "broadcast flag" rule. The Jackson clip was captured off of the current "analog" TV stream. But once digital television goes mainstream, creators can have direct access to a digital feed that will explode their ability to use and reuse broadcast content.

What will that mean in practice? Technology will support a wide variety of new uses of digital content, so that blog commentary on political programs will be enhanced by footage from ads and speeches, documentarians will be able to easily grab clips from TV, news websites will be able to integrate video into their text reporting, and parodies and reviews of TV shows will be able to incorporate content directly from their sources. Schoolchildren will be able to work on more sophisticated and multi-faceted projects, more easily. And frequent travelers will be able to time and space-shift television broadcasts onto a laptop to watch away from home.

The result will both benefit society, and empower individuals. For instance, an individual might create his or her own 9/11 memorial using a mixture of images and text.

The "broadcast flag" rule will put an end to all that.

There Is No Proven Harm From the Ability to Use and Reuse Broadcast Content

There is no question that the rule will destroy many positive uses of technology and dry up the well of innovation. For instance, no software is currently available to grab DTV waves out of the air and capture them on a television or computer—the current generation of DTV tuners rely on dedicated hardware. The FCC rule may ensure that no such software ever exists.

Yet the available evidence so far suggests there will be *no* harm. While it currently takes many, many hours to upload or download a TV show to the Internet, some people do it. Yet there is no rash of people trading TV shows in a manner that harms the industry, and no evidence that there ever will be, even if it becomes a speedier endeavor.

For now, people still come home and watch TV on their couch, and the networks are still in business. Neither CBS nor the National Football League lost any money because of the distribution of the Jackson clip. And on the plus side, our democratic process was enhanced. Millions of people had access to view for themselves content that was subject to a national debate—whether or not they were watching TV when the event occurred.

The FCC should not regulate in a manner that will freeze innovations that facilitate democracy and hurt both consumers and industry. Especially while the technology industry is trying to pull itself out of the dot-com bust, this is the last thing it—or the economy as a whole—needs.

Scholarly Article

The Author: Marjorie Heins

The Free Expression Policy Project (FEPP), founded in 2000, provides research and analysis on difficult censorship issues and seeks free, speech-friendly solutions to the concerns that drive censorship campaigns. In May 2004, FEPP became part of the Democracy Program at the Brennan Center for Justice at NYU School of Law.

Marjorie Heins, founder of FEPP, is a fellow in the Brennan Center for Justice at NYU School of Law Democracy Program. She is the author of *Not in Front of the*

Children: "Indecency," Censorship, and the Innocence of Youth, which won the American Library Association's Eli M. Oboler Award in 2002 for the best published work in the field of intellectual freedom. From 1991 to 1998, she directed the American Civil Liberties Union's Arts Censorship Project, where she was co-counsel in a number of Supreme Court cases, including *National Endowment for the Arts v. Finley* and *Reno v. ACLU* (the challenge to the 1996 Communications Decency Act). She is also the author of *Sex, Sin, and Blasphemy: A Guide to America's Censorship Wars* (1993, 1998), *Cutting the Mustard: Affirmative Action and the Nature of Excellence* (1988), "Three Questions About Television Ratings," in *The V-Chip Debate* (1998), and numerous other book chapters and articles about civil rights, civil liberties, and intellectual freedom. From 1998 to 2000, she was a fellow of the Open Society Institute, which supported the research for *Not in Front of the Children.* In the 1980s she was a staff attorney at the Civil Liberties Union of Massachusetts, a visiting professor at Boston College Law School, and chief of the Civil Rights Division of the Massachusetts Attorney General's office.

The following article was published on February 3, 2004.

What Is the Fuss About Janet Jackson's Breast?

The barrage of complaints about CBS-TV's broadcast of the Super Bowl on February 1 was, of course, about much more than the baring of Janet Jackson's right breast during the half-time concert. It was—at least so the pundits reported—about the "coarsening" of American popular culture: MTV suggestiveness, crotch-grabbing gestures by rock musicians, uninhibited use of Anglo-Saxon words on the formerly "family-friendly" television airwaves. The fact that this coarsening was manifested during a sports event watched by hundreds of millions of Americans, adults and minors alike, probably accounts for much of the public outrage.

But attacks on the Federal Communications Commission's ostensibly lax enforcement of its rule against "indecency" on the airwaves were much in the news for weeks before the Super Bowl flare-up. In January, Representative John Dingell, among others, pointedly asked NBC why it did not bleep the rock star Bono's repeated use of the word "fuck" to express his exuberance during the live broadcast of the 2003 Golden Globes Awards (as in: "this is really, really fucking brilliant"). Representative Doug Ose introduced legislation to ban the "seven dirty words" from the airwaves no matter what the context. Senator John McCain has scheduled hearings for February 11 on "Protecting Children From Violent and Indecent Programming."

It *is* curious, though, how mini-culture wars like this get started, particularly at a time when there are so many more pressing issues on the public-policy agenda (the quagmire in Iraq, the Bush Administration's dissembling over weapons of mass destruction, the economy, even the question whether Howard Dean's primal scream was nonpresidential enough to sink his primary hopes). Indeed, one can't help wondering whether, confronted by all these serious issues, the brouhaha over Ms. Jackson's breast was simply a welcome bit of comic relief. Of course, ironically, the mass media stokes and reinforces the attacks against it by publicizing the cries of outrage.

The FCC's power to censor indecency on broadcast television and radio (that is, whatever it considers "patently offensive" as measured by "contemporary community standards") is a First Amendment anomaly. Speech that the agency considers indecent or patently offensive at any particular time is fully protected by the First Amendment, and may have serious political, artistic, or educational value. Yet the federal government claims power to suppress it, and the Supreme Court has so far agreed.[1]

The agency's record of enforcement has been as variable as the political winds. Until 1987, enforcement was lax, as long as broadcasters avoided the notorious "seven dirty words" that had been condemned back in 1978 in the Supreme Court case of *FCC v. Pacifica*. Pressures from the religious right in 1987 triggered a change: now, the FCC announced a "generic" test for patent offensiveness that would embrace sexual innuendo and double entendre along with taboo words. Of the three broadcasts the commission cited in this 1987 decision, two came from noncommercial radio: a KPFK-Pacifica reading from a play about homosexuality and AIDS, and a punk rock song played on a student radio station. (The third was a Howard Stern show.)[2]

Given the massive dominance of commercial over noncommercial broadcasting, the FCC's history of condemning nonprofit, alternative radio suggests that political appointees to a federal agency are the last ones who should be deciding what speech Americans will be allowed to hear. In recent years, the FCC has continued to apply its subjective "patent offensiveness" standard to suppress non-mainstream, countercultural expression such as the song "Your Revolution," by feminist rap artist Sarah Jones.[3]

If federal officials aren't the best choice for deciding what Americans can see or hear, then how do we address widespread objections to breast-baring, crotch-grabbing, and other "Animal House" behavior on television? The first response is that punishments by the FCC are not exactly going to put all of the vulgar words and lusty thoughts that cram our culture back into Pandora's Box. Sexual explicitness in today's culture is a fact of life. Often, one can avoid it if one doesn't enjoy that sort of thing (though perhaps not on Super Bowl Sunday).

Parents cannot always block their children's eyes and ears, however; the best approach here has to be good media literacy education, sexuality education, and lots of independent alternatives to mass-market, lowest-common-denominator culture.[4]

On top of this, strengthening media ownership limits—rather than weakening them, as the FCC and Congress have been doing for the past two decades—could go far toward reducing the power of giant corporations like CBS/Viacom to decide what millions of Americans will get to hear, read, or watch (in this case, lots of raunchy entertainment and commercials, but *not* a political ad that criticized the Bush Administration, which CBS refused to air during the Super Bowl). While the government should not be in the business of censoring media content, it does have an important role to play in *structural* regulation of the media industry. Breaking up the oligopolies can expand the diversity of ideas, viewpoints, and cultural styles that are available in the mass media.[5]

But the connection between media conglomeration and low-grade entertainment like the Super Bowl half-time event is not one that mainstream journalism is generally willing to make. When I suggested it to one reporter recently, he replied that since he worked for a media conglomerate himself, that part of the interview was unlikely to make it into his story.

February 3, 2004

> "If the flap over Jackson's stray breast serves to point up America's ridiculous censorship rules, this tempest in a B-Cup may turn out to be worth all the uproar."
>
> —*Peter Howell,* Toronto Star, *Feb. 6, 2004*

Notes

1. See *More Than Seven Dirty Words,* http://www.fepproject.org/commentaries/rustytrombone.html; *The Strange Case of Sarah Jones,* http://www.fepproject.org/commentaries/sarahjones.html. The Supreme Court case upholding the FCC's power to censor "indecency" is *FCC v. Pacifica Foundation,* 438 U.S. 726 (1978).
2. Public Notice, *New Indecency Enforcement Standards To Be Applied to All Broadcast and Amateur Radio Licensees,* 2 FCC Rcd 2726 (1987); *Pacifica Foundation,* 2 FCC Rcd 2698 (1987); Regents of the University of California, 2 FCC Rcd 2703 (1987); *Infinity Broadcasting,* 2 FCC Rcd 2705 (1987); see Marjorie Heins, *Not in Front of the Children: "Indecency," Censorship, and the Innocence of Youth* (2001), pp. 109–13.
3. See *The Strange Case of Sarah Jones,* http://www.fepproject.org/commentaries/sarahjones.html; *"Your Revolution" is Not Indecent After All,* http://www.fepproject.org/news/sarahjones.html.
4. See *Media Literacy: An Alternative to Censorship,* http://www.fepproject.org/policyreports/medialiteracy.html; *White Paper to the National Research Council: Identifying What is Harmful or Inappropriate for Minors,* http://www.fepproject.org/whitePapers/NRCwhitePapers.html.
5. See *Media Democracy and the First Amendment,* http://www.fepproject.org/reviews/mediademoc.html.

EVENT CASEBOOK SIX

All's Fair in War?

Focus on Gulf War II and the Prisoner Abuse Controversy

Initial Reports

Newspaper Article—National Source

The Author: Joseph L. Galloway

Joseph L. Galloway is the senior military writer on staff for Knight Ridder Newspapers in their Washington Bureau. One of America's preeminent war correspondents with over four decades as a reporter and writer, he has a weekly column on military affairs syndicated nationally by Knight Ridder Tribune Syndicate, a partnership between Knight Ridder and the Chicago Tribune Group. He also served on assignment as a special consultant to General Colin Powell at the State Department.

On May 1, 1998, Galloway was decorated with a Bronze Star Medal with V for rescuing wounded soldiers under fire in the Ia Drang Valley in November 1965. His is the only medal of valor the U.S. Army awarded to a civilian for actions during the Vietnam War.

Galloway received the National Magazine Award in 1991 for a *U.S. News* cover article on the 25th anniversary of the Ia Drang Battles and the National News Media Award of the U.S. Veterans of Foreign Wars in 1992 for coverage of the Gulf War. In 2000, he received the President's Award for the Arts of the Vietnam Veterans Association of America. In 2001, he received the B.G. Robert L. Denig Award for Distinguished Service presented by the U.S. Marine Corps Combat Correspondents Association.

The following article was published in various Knight Ridder affiliates on May 3, 2004.

Seven Severely Reprimanded in Iraqi Prisoner Abuse Scandal

WASHINGTON—Seven Army officers and non-commissioned officers have been severely reprimanded for failing to prevent the abuse of Iraqi prisoners held in the Abu Ghraib prison in Baghdad, a senior Pentagon official said Monday.

The official, who spoke on condition that he not be identified, said six of the officers and non-commissioned officers received the most severe reprimands possible—an administrative action that will almost certainly finish their careers in the Army. A seventh received a somewhat milder reprimand.

The reprimands were the first disciplinary actions in the case. Pictures taken at the prison showed detainees stripped naked, forced to simulate sex acts and apparently threatened with electrocution.

The seven officers and sergeants who received the administrative punishments weren't accused of abuse. They were deemed responsible for failing to properly train, discipline and control the actions of the military police pulling guard duty in Abu Ghraib. The Pentagon didn't disclose their names.

Six other Army Reserve military police soldiers face court-martial trials on charges that they abused and tortured Iraqi prisoners held in Abu Ghraib, where Saddam Hussein once kept, tortured and killed thousands of prisoners.

The reprimands grew out of an investigation requested by Lt. Gen. Ricardo Sanchez, commander of American forces in Iraq, and conducted by Maj. Gen. Antonio M. Taguba. The investigation looked into the command climate that allowed the prisoner abuse to take place. The seven officers and NCOs will not face any further punishment.

The Pentagon official said the allegations of American MPs abusing and torturing Iraqis, who were in a special section of the prison where military intelligence agents were conducting interrogations, first came to light in January and have been under intensive investigation ever since.

He added that at least five investigations are underway or just concluding. They are the criminal investigation launched Jan. 14 with the seizure of evidence by Army Criminal Investigation Division agents; Taguba's chain of command investigation; an Army inspector general investigation and inspection of all American-operated detention facilities in Iraq; an assessment of military intelligence interrogation procedures ordered by the Army chief of intelligence, or G-2; and a special assessment of Army Reserve training procedures ordered by the commander of all Army Reserve forces.

"There are a lot of eyes on this problem," the official said. "This is about leadership, training and discipline. This is about something that violates all human dignity and will not be tolerated in our Army."

White House spokesman Scott McClellan told reporters traveling with President Bush on a Midwest campaign swing on Monday that Bush called Defense Secretary Donald H. Rumsfeld "to discuss the strong actions and steps that the military is taking to address matters in the prison system in Iraq and prevent prisoner abuse." He said Bush wanted "to make sure that appropriate action was being taken against those responsible for these shameful, appalling acts."

The commander of the Army Reserve 800th MP Brigade responsible for Abu Ghraib, Brig. Gen. Janis Karpinski, has hired a lawyer. She appeared on ABC's *Good Morning America* on Monday and declared that she knew nothing about the abuse while it was going on.

The Pentagon official said Karpinski's brigade, which includes the unit guarding the prisoners at Abu Ghraib, the 320th Military Police Battalion, has returned to the United States and has been demobilized. It was replaced by two active Army military police brigades, the 16th MP Brigade from Fort Bragg, N.C., and the 89th MP Brigade from Fort Hood, Texas.

Bryan G. Whitman, a spokesman for the Department of Defense, said, "While it is possible for a small number of individuals to tarnish us all, it also has to be remembered that it was another soldier who brought all this to light because he saw things he knew were wrong and reported them."

The ranking Democrat on the House Select Committee on Intelligence, Rep. Jane Harman, D-Calif., said she was writing Rumsfeld to request Taguba's report "and an immediate briefing on specific steps the military is taking to punish wrongdoers and prevent further acts of abuse at all military prisons."

Newspaper Article—International Source

The Author: Naseer Al-Nahr

In 1975, Saudi Research and Publishing Company (SRPC) launched the first Saudi English-language daily newspaper, *ArabNews*. For more than a quarter of a century, *ArabNews* has been breaking cultural barriers and unifying Arabs and non-Arabs alike in responding to their need for information. *ArabNews* has evolved successfully into the well-respected, leading paper it is today.

The following article was published in *ArabNews* on May 6, 2004.

Arabs Unimpressed by President Bush or Prisoner Abuse

BAGHDAD, 6 May 2004—US President George W. Bush stopped short of apologizing as he told a skeptical Arab world yesterday that the actions of soldiers who mistreated Iraqi prisoners "don't represent America" and pledged that "justice will be served." The Arabs were generally unimpressed as Bush called the abuse "abhorrent." "This is a serious matter, a matter that reflects badly on our country," Bush conceded in an interview with Al-Arabiya, a popular Arabic station. But he added: "This is a free country. We do not tolerate this kind of abuses."

Bush gave interviews to two Arabic television stations, hoping to limit damage from the prisoner-abuse scandal that has torn at the United States' already weakened image in the region. But his message was a hard sell, and many watching said Bush's words did little to change their opinions.

"Bush had a whole year to fulfill his promises regarding bringing freedom and democracy to Iraq," said Mouwaddaq Fadhil, a 55-year-old taxi driver in Baghdad. Al-Arabiya, popular throughout the Arab world, first aired most of the interview, unedited, in English with no subtitles. An hour later, it aired the full interview dubbed into Arabic. Bush also gave an interview to Al-Hurra. The people of Iraq "must understand that what took place in that prison does not represent the America that I know," Bush told Al-Hurra.

"The America I know is a compassionate country that believes in freedom. The America I know cares about every individual. The America I know has sent troops into Iraq to promote freedom, good honorable citizens that are helping Iraqis every day," he told Al-Hurra. Few people watch Al-Hurra, but the interview with Al-Arabiya was greeted by many with disgust.

"The apology will not change anything. It does not hold," said Abdel Gawad Ahmed, a lawyer in Cairo watching the interview at his union headquarters. "Is it an apology for the victims we see every day? Or for violating international conventions? Will this apology do me any good?"

Added Sari Mouwaffaq, a Baghdad mechanic: "Bush's statements today will not restore the dignity which the tortured detainees lost. Bush's apology, or his attempt to find excuses, has no value to us."

Bush did not specifically apologize for the mistreatment of prisoners at Abu Gharib prison near Baghdad. But, he said: "The actions of these few people do not reflect the hearts of the American people."

Bush told Al-Arabiya: "The practices that took place in that prison are abhorrent and they don't represent America. They represent the actions of a few people. . . . We will find the truth. We will fully investigate," Bush said. "The world will see the investigation and justice will be served."

Multimedia Sources

Editorial Cartoon

The Author: John Sherffius

Winner of the Scripps Howard Foundation National Journalism Award for Editorial Cartooning in 2002, popular cartoonist John Sherffius resigned from his position at *St. Louis Post Dispatch* in December 2003 after an editor ordered him to alter the content of a cartoon. John continues to create stirring political cartoons syndicated nationally, as well as sculptures (such as "The Daily Reader" for The People Project, http://www.thepeopleproject.com).

The following was published May 4, 2004 on Daryl Cagle's Pro-Cartoonist's Index.

Photograph

The Author: Jean-Marc Bouju

French photographer Jean-Marc Bouju of The Associated Press photographed the following on March 31, 2003. An international jury of the 47th annual World Press Photo contest selected the image as World Press Photo of the Year 2003.

An Iraqi man comforts his 4-year-old son at a regroupment center for POWs of the 101st Airborne Division near An Najaf, Iraq. The man was seized in An Najaf with his son and the U.S. military did not want to separate father and son.

Transcript from NewsHour with Jim Lehrer (PBS)

The Correspondent: Jim Lehrer

Jim Lehrer began his career in Dallas, first as a newspaperman and later as an achor on a local news program. He started working for PBS in 1972, and in 1975 started *The MacNeil/Lehrer Report* (later called *The MacNeil/Lehrer NewsHour*) with Robert MacNeil. In 1999, Lehrer was awarded the presidential National Humanities medal, and he is commonly one of the moderators during debates in the United States presidential elections.

He graduated from Victoria College in Texas and the University of Missouri. The following transcript is from a May 4, 2004, show published online.

Iraqi Prisoner Abuse

Kwame Holman: In closed meetings today, military officials heard strong reactions from members of Congress to the revelations of abuse of imprisoned Iraqis. It's been nearly a week since CBS' *60 Minutes II* broadcast photos depicting the abuse. They also were reproduced in this week's *New Yorker* magazine. The actions occurred at the Abu Ghraib Prison outside Baghdad late last year. A military investigation led to an internal Army report completed in March by Maj. Gen. Antonio Taguba.

So far, six soldiers have been charged, and at least six others, including the commanding officer at the prison, have been reprimanded. At the Pentagon this afternoon, Secretary of Defense Donald Rumsfeld said the military's first investigation was launched the day after the abuses were reported, a press release on the allegations was issued in mid-January, and six investigations either are completed or ongoing. Rumsfeld then fielded questions from the Pentagon press corps.

Charles Aldinger, Reuters: Mr. Secretary, this administration has said repeatedly that in removing Saddam Hussein, the United States has gotten rid of a man who has murdered and raped and pillaged and tortured people in his country. And now these photographs and stories show that in fact the U.S. military has done that to prisoners in Iraq. And you say that this has—I believe you said it's damaged U.S. attempts to establish trust in the country. I guess I'd ask you more broadly, is this a major setback for U.S. efforts in Iraq?

Donald Rumsfeld: Oh, I'm not one for instant history, Charlie. The fact is, this is an exception. The pattern and practice of the Saddam Hussein regime was to do exactly what you said, to murder and torture. And the killing fields are filled with mass graves. And equating the two, I think, is a fundamental misunderstanding of what took place. Yes?

Martha Raddatz, ABC News: General Myers said on Sunday that he had not seen the report. I don't believe you had seen the report even if—I don't know if you have now. Isn't this something you would have liked to have been flagged about?

Donald Rumsfeld: It's, I guess the way to put it is that the department has been aware of it since it was first noticed, and up the chain of command we're told that there were investigations into alleged abuses as long ago as last Jan. 16. It takes time for reports to be finished—correction: to be gathered. This is a very comprehensive report. I mean, the fact of the matter is that this is a serious problem. And it's something that the department is addressing.

The system works. The system works. There were some allegations of abuse in a detention facility in Iraq. It was reported in the chain of command. Immediately it was announced to the public. Immediately an investigation was initiated. Six separate investigations have been undertaken over a period of months since January.

Reporter: On Capitol Hill today, there was quite a bit of anger expressed at the fact that they're just finding out about this now. Shouldn't you have done a better job keeping Congress informed? At least they feel they should have been kept informed.

Donald Rumsfeld: Well, we informed the world on Jan. 16 that these investigations were underway. It seems to me that that is a perfectly proper thing to do. The investigations were announced. The world knew it. It was briefed to the press and the world.

Gen. Peter Pace: If I can just interject, the term "routine" is not a good term to use in this regard because this is anything but routine. It has been handled anything but routine. Immediately the commanders called all of the chain of command, to include to myself, General Myers, and—I'm not in the chain of command, excuse me, but I knew about it almost immediately—General Myers, the secretary. That information flow of suspected events and what individuals are doing about investigating it and what types of investigations were needed, that information was shared completely.

What is being done correctly—and we want to take care of an event that is—as bad as it is, we do not want to turn our justice system on its head in response to it. We want at each level for each commander to do his or her duty, which is to take the documentation that they have, read it thoroughly—and these things can be that thick—take the time, read it thoroughly, make the judgments that they must make, see whether or not there's some other facet of this that should be looked into at their level, make the decisions they're able to do, and pass it on up the chain.

Reporter: A number of times from the podium you've said U.S. troops do not torture individuals. Is this one of those rare exceptions here that torture took place?

Donald Rumsfeld: I think that—I'm not a lawyer. My impression is that what has been charged thus far is abuse, which I believe technically is different from torture. Just a minute. I don't know if the—it is correct to say what you just said, that torture has taken place, or that there's been a conviction for torture. And therefore I'm not going to address the "torture" word.

There's no question but that it has been my conviction that all of our rules, all of our procedures, all of our training is against abuse of people that are detained. You know that. I know that. I've been over it in detail. And the fact that it happens, notwithstanding the fact that it's against everything that they're taught, against everything that we believe, it's also against anything that any individual on their own ought to believe is right. And so there's, all I can say is what I've said.

Reporter: Mr. Secretary, have you yet read the Taguba report?

Donald Rumsfeld: It's—which—yeah. You're—I think you're talking about the executive summary. I've seen the executive summary.

Reporter: Have you read through it, sir?

Donald Rumsfeld: I've been through it—whether I have read every page, no. There's a lot of references and documentation to laws and conventions and procedures and requirements. But I have certainly read the conclusions and the other aspects of it.

Reporter: Just to follow up on Jamie's question, given the ramifications of not only what is in this report, the findings specifically, but the pictures, the photographs that you knew, as of a couple of weeks ago, were going to be broadcast, why did you not feel incumbent upon you at that time to ask for the findings, to take a look at the pictures beforehand, so you could perhaps be prepared to deal with some of the world reaction?

Donald Rumsfeld: I think I did inquire about the pictures and was told that we didn't have copies.

Reporter: Mr. Secretary, I did ask how you felt this episode has in fact damaged the U.S. efforts.

Donald Rumsfeld: I've answered that. I answered that earlier. I'm not in a position to make a judgment. Time will tell. Clearly we would wish it would not because it is an exceptional, isolated . . . we hope an isolated case. And our country is our country, and it is a wonderful country. And the American people are wonderful people, and our armed forces are wonderful people. And when one drops a plumb line through the totality of that, is it perfect? No. Are there things like this that happen? Yes. But over time, the people tend to find their way to fair, reasonable conclusions.

Kwame Holman: The Senate Intelligence Committee announced today it will hold a closed hearing on the abuse tomorrow afternoon.

Reaction from Lawmakers

Jim Lehrer: And to Margaret Warner.

Margaret Warner: For more on the congressional reaction we go to two members of the Senate Armed Services Committee who attended this morning's closed-door briefing by Pentagon officials: Sen. Carl Levin of Michigan, the ranking Democrat on the committee, and Sen. Jeff Sessions of Alabama. Welcome to you both.

Based on the briefing you all got this morning, Senator Levin, what's your conclusion about what went wrong? What explains those photographs we saw of American soldiers abusing Iraqi prisoners?

Sen. Carl Levin: Well, I'd say it's a failure at a number of levels—obviously, the troops themselves who participated, but also, anybody in command or supervision who tolerated it, who heard about it, who should have known about it. There's a major, massive failure here which allowed some despicable conduct to take place, and it's at a number of levels. We don't know exactly yet who is involved.

We know that there's been six troops, six soldiers who have been the subject of criminal investigations. Apparently three of them have already been referred for a court martial. Three of them are still under investigation. We've got a couple of officers, noncommissioned, and a couple of general officers who are under investigation, and who have, I think, already been disciplined to some extent. But this is just really the beginning of what is required here, which is a very thorough, a very intense, a very tough, and a very prompt investigation.

Margaret Warner: Senator Sessions, how detailed was this morning's briefing that you all got? For example, did they take questions or talk to you all about allegations that have been in the newspaper that not only active duty military, but in fact perhaps private contractors and military intelligence and perhaps even CIA people were involved? How much detail did you get?

Sen. Jeff Sessions: A lot of questions were asked about that, and a number of answers were received. Some answers were not complete at this time, and they said they would fill in the information later. It does appear to me that a number of people at the lower level were involved. How much the superior officers are responsible for not having the right supervision, not setting the right command leadership tone, we don't know yet. We'll look into that as we go.

Margaret Warner: So, in other words, were you told, essentially, that the military isn't sure yet, the investigators aren't sure yet how high up the responsibility goes?

Sen. Jeff Sessions: Well, we were told some of that. Some things we were told, they were not sure about. But I think it's pretty clear that at least a couple of contractors may have been involved. Interestingly, I authored a piece of legislation in 2000 that deals with the ability to prosecute employees of the Department of Defense, civilian employees, if they violate laws outside the country. So I think that statute, in fact, would cover the circumstances, and would allow for a prosecution of a contractor in a United States court if they violated any law.

Margaret Warner: And did that legislation pass? That is law?

Sen. Jeff Sessions: Yes, it did. It passed in 2000.

Evaluating the System of Reporting Abuses

Margaret Warner: Senator Levin, another issue that came up, according to Senator Kennedy, when he left the briefing, he said he thought that perhaps this was not an isolated incident. He said he feared that these allegations are "the beginning rather than the end." What impression did you get from the briefing in terms of whether this kind of abuse occurred in other facilities?

Sen. Carl Levin: The people who briefed us this morning didn't have any reference to this kind of abuse, but as to allegations of abuse of prisoners, there have been a number of those allegations over the last couple years. There have been many of them. They have been in various places in the investigative process. But this type of abuse, we were told by our briefers, was not similar to the other types, which we were informed about, at least numerically.

Margaret Warner: Senator Sessions, today at his press conference, Secretary Rumsfeld—and he was speaking now of the way the Department of Defense has handled it—he said "the system worked." And by that, he said he meant that once a single soldier complained in January, an investigation was immediately started. Other investigations have been started. How do you judge the way the Department of Defense has handled this?

Sen. Jeff Sessions: Well, I think fundamentally that's correct. A single soldier complained in early January. A general was put into looking into the allegations, and prepared a thorough report. Then unfortunately it broke before it had been properly announced to the public and explained to the Congress. That has caused some difficulties, no doubt. It would have been better had the defense department moved more promptly and carefully in deciding how to make this public. Ultimately, it was heading for that. So they did investigate it, and much of what we hear is a result of the investigation, the Department of Defense has conducted. People are being charged as a result of it already. And so, to that extent, I think it's fair to say this military does not tolerate this, and takes action to deal with it.

Margaret Warner: Senator Levin, your view on that, about whether the system worked?

Sen. Carl Levin: The system did not work in terms of the notice to the Congress of a very, very serious incident that's going to have an effect on America, our security, and on our troops for a long time to come. This report was finished sometime in February, we're now told. It was acted upon in early April, we're now told. We knew nothing about it until we saw it on a TV show. At the same day that Secretary Rumsfeld came up here to brief us on events in Iraq, he didn't even tell us that same day as to what was going to explode that evening, although he apparently knew all about it. So in terms of informing the public, this is just too secretive an administration on this issue, and on too many other issues.

Margaret Warner: Now, let me just remind you of what Secretary Rumsfeld said about that today, and General Pace said the same thing: That these investigations go up a chain of command, and that each successive level is supposed to read the whole report, deal with it at their level, and that there's a sort of methodical process. Are you saying that should have been leapfrogged at some point and come directly to your committee, and if so, what would you have done about it?

Sen. Carl Levin: What I'm saying is that the action was taken on April 3, I believe, apparently, we're told today, on the recommendations in this report, so that the actions had already been taken. And surely, we should have been informed about actions which were taken in an event which is this major an event, that could be this calamitous, that could have this kind of an impact on our relations in the world, how we're perceived in the world. We all hope that this is just a few soldiers.

We know there's contractors now that were apparently either involved or who knew about it, and it's stunning to me that we have contractors doing interrogation. That's something that we surely should have been informed about a long time before now. So I'm not at all satisfied. I hope the investigation has been thorough as far as the Army can go, but I don't think we can take that for granted. We have to have checks and balances, we've got to have oversight, and that's what hopefully the Armed Services Committee is going to do.

Margaret Warner: And general—Senator Sessions—excuse me, I almost made you a general—you share that view that at least once these charges had been filed and these actions had been taken, your committee should have been told?

Sen. Jeff Sessions: Well, I think so. I think the results of the confusion make clear that it would have been better had that occurred. I did want to say, though, really, the Defense Department moved on this. They charged people, and they followed up with a thorough investigation by a high-ranking officer. That's what we expect of them. They did not, I think, handle the public relations well, and it's made it more difficult for us than otherwise would have been the case.

The Roles of Contractors and Training

Margaret Warner: Senator Levin just referred to the fact—and you both have now—that contractors were involved, and he was kind of stunned that they were even involved in interrogations. One of the conclusions of the report by General Taguba, and it was discussed today at the Rumsfeld press conference, was that part of this was the result of just having inadequate military forces on the ground to do the job. You all have oversight of the military. What is your view of that, and what were you told this morning about that, about whether that was a significant factor?

Sen. Jeff Sessions: Well, let me say this: I think every soldier is taught the Geneva Conventions. They're taught how to treat a prisoner of war, even if they're not in the MPs, the military police. Apparently these soldiers were military police. Some of them had been correctional officers before. No matter how many were there, how did they have time to do this kind of thing? This is unacceptable by any American standards of law or the military law. So I think how many troops we had there or whether they were thoroughly trained in prisons is really beside the point. The question is, did they have enough supervision? Were they managed effectively? Certainly they made individual decisions that were just calamitous.

Margaret Warner: Senator Levin, your view on that issue, and what you heard this morning about whether there were adequate, trained military people to do this job?

Sen. Carl Levin: Well, I think that—I don't know about the training. We'll find that out during the investigation. It shouldn't take special training, frankly, for people not to behave this way. That should not be needed. This is just so basic. This kind of conduct, it seems to me, is so brutal, it's so bestial that it shouldn't take special training for anybody not to participate in that kind of conduct.

But in terms of using contractors for interrogation, it seems to me that is a fundamental mistake. This is a governmental function. It should be carried out by the Army, people that are responsible to us. General—Senator Sessions—I made him a general now, too—Senator Sessions indeed did get a law passed which I hope will be sustained in court, which goes to the issue of whether someone who is working for us can be held criminally accountable if they violate the law as a contractor, even though it's overseas. That was, I think, something which took a lot of foresight on Senator Sessions' part. But that does not answer the question of whether they should be engaged in this conduct to begin with. Whether or not we should be having private contractors doing interrogation for the government, I think is just fundamentally wrong. It shouldn't be privatized that way.

Sen. Jeff Sessions: I have a little different tact on that. We have a lot of former military people with military intelligence experience—former FBI agents, police officers—who can be contracted to handle these kind of interrogations, and are used to doing it in these circumstances. So I don't complain that they've used contractors. I think it could be very helpful, really. But it does indicate that we need good supervision and good management. No one can be left unsupervised in these kind of circumstances.

Margaret Warner: Senator Sessions and Senator Levin, thank you both.

Web site

The Source: http://www.hrw.org

Human Rights Watch is the largest human rights organization based in the United States. Human Rights Watch conducts fact-finding investigations into human rights abuses in all regions of the world, then publishes those findings in dozens of books and reports every year, generating extensive coverage in local and international media. This publicity helps to embarrass abusive governments in the eyes of their citizens and the world. Human Rights Watch then meets with government officials to urge changes in policy and practice—at the United Nations, the European Union, in Washington, and in capitals around the world.

Human Rights Watch believes that international standards of human rights apply to all people equally and that sharp vigilance and timely protest can prevent the tragedies of the twentieth century from recurring. At Human Rights Watch, the more than 150 dedicated professionals remain convinced that progress can be made when people of good will organize themselves to make it happen.

The following is a screenshot of the Human Rights Watch coverage of the Iraqi prisoner abuse. The full Web site may be accessed at the following URL: http://www.hrw.org/.

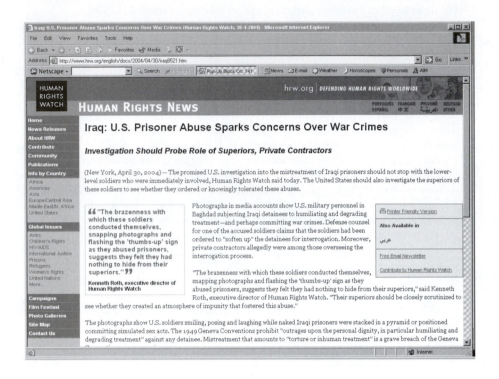

Iraq: U.S. Prisoner Abuse Sparks Concerns Over War Crimes

Investigation Should Probe Role of Superiors, Private Contractors

(New York, April 30, 2004)—The promised U.S. investigation into the mistreatment of Iraqi prisoners should not stop with the lower-level soldiers who were immediately involved, Human Rights Watch said today. The United States should also investigate the superiors of these soldiers to see whether they ordered or knowingly tolerated these abuses.

Photographs in media accounts show U.S. military personnel in Baghdad subjecting Iraqi detainees to humiliating and degrading treatment—and perhaps committing war crimes. Defense counsel for one of the accused soldiers claims that the soldiers had been ordered to "soften up" the detainees for interrogation. Moreover, private contractors allegedly were among those overseeing the interrogation process.

"The brazenness with which these soldiers conducted themselves, snapping photographs and flashing the 'thumbs-up' sign as they abused prisoners, suggests they felt they had nothing to hide from their superiors," said Kenneth Roth, executive director of Human Rights Watch. "Their superiors should be closely scrutinized to see whether they created an atmosphere of impunity that fostered this abuse."

The photographs show U.S. soldiers smiling, posing and laughing while naked Iraqi prisoners were stacked in a pyramid or positioned committing simulated sex acts. The 1949 Geneva Conventions prohibit "outrages upon the personal dignity, in particular humiliating and degrading treatment" against any detainee. Mistreatment that amounts to "torture or inhuman treatment" is a grave breach of the Geneva Conventions—or a war crime.

The record of the United States in addressing alleged mistreatment of detainees by its personnel in Iraq and Afghanistan causes serious concern. In Afghanistan, as Human Rights Watch has previously reported, the U.S. government has yet to provide information on its investigations into the officially declared "homicide" deaths more than two years ago of two detainees in U.S. custody at Bagram airbase. The United States has also not adequately responded to allegations of other abuses in U.S. detention in Afghanistan, including cases of beatings, severe sleep deprivation, and exposure of detainees to extreme cold.

In Iraq a U.S. army lieutenant colonel who admitted that in August he threatened to kill an Iraqi detainee, firing a shot next to the man's head during a violent interrogation, received a fine as a disciplinary measure, but was not subjected to a court martial. The U.S. army in January discharged three reservists for abusing detainees at a detention camp near Basra in southern Iraq.

"It's clear that the United States has not taken the issue of prisoner abuse seriously enough," said Roth. "These sordid photos from Iraq show that systematic changes in the treatment of prisoners are needed immediately. The investigations should be made public."

The alleged involvement of private contractors is another dimension of the problem that merits investigation. Human Rights Watch is concerned that these contractors operate in Iraq with virtual impunity—exempt by the terms of their engagement with the U.S. military from prosecution by Iraqi courts, outside the military chain of command and thus ineligible for court-martial, and not subject to prosecution by U.S. courts. Under the Geneva Conventions, the United States nonetheless remains responsible for the actions of those running the detention facilities, be they regular soldiers, reservists or private contractors.

"If the Pentagon seeks to use private contractors in military or intelligence roles, it must ensure that they are subject to legal restraints," said Roth. "Allowing private contractors to operate in a legal vacuum is an invitation to abuse."

Magazine Article

The Author: Sam Smith

Sam Smith is an award-winning writer, activist, and social critic, and editor of the *Progressive Review* since 2001. In 2001, he was nominated by the national alternative news syndicate, Alternet, for one of its New Media Heroes Award. The *Review* was also nominated for an Alternative Press Award.

Graduated from Harvard in 1959 with a major in anthropology, Smith was operations officer and navigator aboard a Coast Guard cutter and later executive officer of the Baltimore Coast Guard reserve unit.

The *Progressive Review* is one of the few alternative publications remaining of the hundreds started in the 1960s. It has had the longest running act on the off-Broadway of Washington journalism—the third generation of a publication that started in 1966 as the *Capitol East Gazette*. The *Gazette* served an inner-city neighborhood, covering such community issues as real estate speculation, freeway construction, public education, and city services. In 1969, the paper changed to a citywide focus under the name of the *DC Gazette,* and then again, in 1984, to the *Progressive Review.*

The following article was published on May 10, 2004.

Signs on the Road to Abu Ghraib

Like a drunk driver staring at the dead bodies in the wreckage, like a violent husband looking down at the lifeless body of his wife, America now has to face its consequences. The denials, the excuses, the concealment no longer work; blood washes away even the cleverest rhetoric.

The media, in its role as defense counsel to the powerful, wants us to believe it was just an anomaly, something that shouldn't have happened, usually doesn't, and—after the proper bureaucratic response—won't again. But that's just more denial, excuse, concealment. It is not deviance that has been revealed, but culture, values, habit. Abu Ghraib is just as much a part of America's story as the TV series *Friends.* It just has a different ending.

There were plenty of signs along the road to Abu Ghraib. Some were just hints, others flashed in large lighted letters from the overpass. But most of America ignored them on the way to becoming the psychotic parody of itself so brutally illustrated at Abu Ghraib.

What follows is a list of some of the things we might have noticed over the past two decades had we not been so enthralled by our delusions, distractions, and deviances. There is no attempt to weigh individual importance; they are all important for the reason Jane Jacobs notes in her new book: "A culture is unsalvageable if stabilizing forces themselves become ruined and irrelevant . . . . The collapse of one sustaining cultural institution enfeebles others, makes it more likely that others will give way . . . until finally the whole enfeebled, intractable contraption collapses." The dead branch precedes the dead trunk.

A good place to start, however, is with Margaret Thatcher, the woman who taught Ronald Reagan economics and helped launch in this country an unprecedented change in how we not only viewed money but everything else as well. I wrote about it in *Why Bother?:*

> Thatcher had a mean and narrow view of life; she didn't even accept the existence of community, declaring once that "there is no such thing as society. There

are individual men and women, and there are families." Thatcher wrapped herself in economic slogans that justified greed not only to accomplish economic ends but also to deal with gays and abortions and everything else she didn't like. In her paradigm, the free market and Victorian tyranny formed a civil union. By the time Reagan, Bush, and Clinton were through with the concept, they had created a gaping corporate exemption from common morality and decency. The market not only offered adequate justification for any act, it had replaced God as the highest source of law.

Until the Reagan-Bush-Clinton era it would have been next to impossible to find a culture that survived for long believing that the unfettered, rapacious flow of money and goods was the core of human existence. Elsewhere, to be sure, commerce had looked to bottom lines, but these had included those established by church, community, government, and tradition.

And as the market was attacking conventional moral assumptions and cultural values, post-modernism was launching a second front.

Giovanna Borradori has called post-modernism a "definitive farewell" to modern reason. Pauline Marie Rosenau wrote: "Post-modernists recognize an infinite number of interpretations (meanings) of any text are possible because, for the skeptical post-modernists, one can never say what one intends with language, [thus] ultimately all textual meaning, all interpretation is undecipherable. . . Many diverse meanings are possible for any symbol, gesture, word."

The semiotician Marshall Blonsky observed, "Character and consistency were once the most highly regarded virtue to ascribe to either friend or foe. We all strove to be perceived as consistent and in character, no matter how many shattering experiences had changed our lives or how many persons inhabited our bodies. Today, for the first time in modern times, a split or multiple personality has ceased to be an eccentric malady and becomes indispensable."

Together, brutal capitalism and post-modernism firebombed principles of cooperation, decency, individual ethical responsibility, community, and social democracy. In their place came simple brute power manifesting itself in whatever guise seemed most useful at the time. With hubris rather than horror, America celebrated the collapse of its own consensus of conscience.

Well before September 11, I wrote: "The American establishment—from corporate executive to media to politician—had reached a remarkable consensus that it no longer had to play by any rules but its own. There is a phrase for this in some Latin American countries: the culture of impunity. In such places it has led to death squads, to the live bodies of dissidents being thrown out of military helicopters, to routine false imprisonment and baroque financial fraud. We are not there yet but are certainly moving in the same direction.

"In a culture of impunity, rules serve the internal logic of the system rather than whatever values typically guide a country, such as those of its constitution, church or tradition. The culture of impunity encourages coups and cruelty, [and] at best practices only titular democracy. . . . A culture of impunity varies from ordinary political corruption in that the latter represents deviance from the culture while the former becomes the culture. Such a culture does not announce itself. It creeps up day by day, deal by deal, euphemism by euphemism. . . .

"In a culture of impunity, what replaces constitution, precedent, values, tradition, fairness, consensus, debate and all that sort of arcane stuff? Mainly greed. As Michael Douglas put it in Wall Street: 'Greed, for lack of a better word, is good. Greed is right. Greed works.' Of course, there has always been an overabundance of greed in America's political and economic system. But a number of things have changed. As activist attorney George LaRoche points out, 'Once, I think, we knew our greedy were greedy but they were obligated to justify their greed by reference to some of the other values in which all of us could participate. Thus, maybe "old Joe" was a crook but he was also a "pillar of the business community" or "a member of the Lodge" or a "good husband" and these things mattered. Now the pretense of justification is gone and greed is its own justification.' The result is a stunning lack of restraint. We find ourselves without heroism, without debate over right and wrong, with little but an endless narcissistic struggle by the powerful to get more money, more power, and more press than the next person. In the chase, anything goes and the only standard is whether you win, lose, or get caught." In the late 1920s, the French essayist Julien Benda wrote *The Treason of the Intellectuals*. Benda already saw a new class of intelligentsia that favored many of the same principles popular among today's leaders. Among them:

> The extolling of courage at the expense of other virtues. Placing the warrior, the aggressor, the "killer litigator," and the reckless higher in society than the wise, the just, and the sensible.
> The extolling of harshness and the scorn for human love—pity, charity, benevolence.
> A cult of success . . . the teaching which says that when a will is successful that fact alone gives it a moral value, whereas the will which fails is for that reason alone deserving of contempt.

But behind such enormous shifts in our common philosophy, more modest but important changes were taking place, things such as the misbegotten war on drugs which in many ways was the domestication of warfare, turning our guns from foreign enemies towards our own inner cities and more fatal to young black males than assignment to Vietnam had been to their parents. From the assault on constitutional rights, to the mistreatment of prisoners and increasing brutality, the war on drugs set the pattern with which the whole country would become familiar following September 11. The difference was that now the country's elite could not avoid what was happening. Liberals, shocked to learn of Abu Ghraib, had said not a mumbling word as their beloved Bill Clinton oversaw a doubling of the nation's prison population with all its attendant cruelties, many of which were precise precedents for what happened in Iraq.

We also instituted zero tolerance so students would learn early in life that in the new American state draconian punishment was only a mere slip-up away. And of what were we zero intolerant? Of students, the poor, those who prefer drugs less addictive or damaging than vodka or tobacco, the alienated, the unconventional, the mentally ill, and any other group that stood zero chance in such a culture.

We were not, however, totally without tolerance. For example, we tolerated television and movies and computer games that taught young people how to kill and maim. We were tolerant of anyone with enough zeroes after the dollar sign in their gross income. We tolerated the destruction of our national, state and local sovereignty by an international gang of lawyers and their corporate clients. We tolerated an extraordinary and growing maldistribution of wealth. The destruction of the environment, the commercialization of community and sport. And so forth.

There was, in fact, no ethical principle that guided us as we oscillated between cruel suppression and self-serving laissé faire. In its ad hoc nature, its absurd results, and the uniform vulnerability of the targets, zero tolerance reminded one of nothing so much as southern justice before the civil rights movement or the unequal ministration of the law in a police state. In many ways zero tolerance was just another way of saying we had legalized prejudice and hate as well as arbitrary and capricious power.

The bully on the playground and the abusive husband provided prototypes for zero tolerance because, like the abusive and bullying politician of today, they likewise exercised great power without reason or justice against a victim too weak to resist. And there were plenty of models. The *Christian Science Monitor* reported that "according to student rankings, says [Jaana Juvonen, a psychologist at the University of California], US schools are roughly on par with those in the Czech Republic as the least friendly in the Western world."

In more subtle changes, our media and intelligentsia rewrote the Constitution by claiming it was about balancing rights and responsibilities even though the latter word is never mentioned in the document. The alteration would be used to justify any assault on rights that came to mind. We jailed people for offenses that formerly would have been resulted in a fine. We handcuffed people for things that formerly would have only rated a summons. We hauled senior citizens to the station house for . . . having forgotten their drivers license.

Drivers licenses were used in other ways, including their revocation for consorting with prostitutes, operating a boat while drunk, violating the fish and game code, failing to pay child support, growing peyote, playing sound equipment on public transit, beating upon a vending or slot machine, dumping refuse on conservancy lands, or using a fake ID to purchase liquor.

Back in the 1990s, I compiled a list of some of the indications that our democracy was in deep trouble. Here are just some of the items listed under justice:

- Increased use of privatized prisons without adequate public supervision.
- Use of prison slave labor to serve corporate interests.
- Large increase in surprise raids on private homes.
- Mandatory sentencing that transfers discretionary judicial power from the courts to prosecutors.
- Use of racial profiling in searches and traffic stops.
- Great increase in use of paramilitary tactics and equipment by police departments.
- Greater use of abusive weaponry such as pepper spray, stun guns and gas.
- Greater use in prisons of torture and deprivation techniques such as lock-downs.

- Increased use of lock-ups and handcuffing for minor offenses such as traffic violations.
- Increased use of capital punishment.
- Increased use of military in traditionally civilian law enforcement roles.
- Increased use of "emergencies" to justify undemocratic actions.

Then in our politics, we elected as our two most recent presidents men whose personal manner included the lifelong abuse of power, but who received a pardon from half the nation—albeit a different half in each case—because politics now mattered infinitely more than decency or honor.

Those at the other end of the national pyramid did not fare so well. Those who merely dared to demonstrate their dissatisfaction through protest were jailed and mistreated in an unprecedented manner and those imprisoned for whatever reasons were increasingly brutalized, tortured, or left to rot. As Abu Graib was being exposed, the *New York Times* reported that the percentage of the imprisoned given life sentences had increased 83% in the past decade.

And how did we react to all this? Did Ted Koppel frown about it? Did Jim Lehrer express deep concern? Did CSPAN take us to prisons to show what was going on there while others were giving talks at the National Press Club? Did Harvard's Kennedy School of Government warn us about it?

No, instead we celebrated, fostered and impregnated our national character with brutality and barbaric behavior of all sorts. So powerful became our culture of violence, that a leading film practitioner of it was easily elected governor of our largest state despite his lack of political credentials. So indifferent did we become to our own constitution that we watched approvingly as police officers routinely ignored it on weekly cop shows.

Meanwhile, the military contributed more than its share as it brainwashed young men who couldn't otherwise survive under the rules of brutal capitalism, taught them how to kill, and then released them back to civilian society. One of them was named Timothy McVeigh.

Finally, when I think of all the changes that have occurred as we have moved towards the brutal, the bullying, and the barbaric in recent years, an image comes to mind so insignificant in every regard except as a metaphor. It used to be that when someone won something they smiled and cheered and waved their arms with delight. Today, with remarkable frequency, the victory is observed with raised tight fists beating hard into the wind and with a distorted grimace of triumph as though it were not a game that had been won or an honor received, but the death of a terrible foe. It is the look not of a hero but of a killer.

Web site

The Author: Rebecca Hagelin

Townhall.com is an interactive community on the Internet that brings Internet users, conservative public policy organizations, congressional staff, and political activists together under the broad umbrella of "conservative" thoughts, ideas, and actions. Townhall.com is a one-stop mall of ideas in which people congregate to exchange, discuss, and disseminate the latest news and information from the conservative movement. Townhall.com is committed to inform, educate, and empower the public through this emerging electronic medium. The member organizations and columnists featured on Townhall.com do not necessarily agree on every issue, yet that is why Townhall.com believes its community is of value.

Rebecca Hagelin is the vice president of communications and marketing at The Heritage Foundation. With more than 17 years of experience in developing and implementing comprehensive public affairs and marketing strategies, Hagelin has long been involved in spreading the conservative message in both Washington and around the nation.

The following article was published online on May 12, 2004.

Prisoner Abuse and the Rot of American Culture

Every decent person I know has reacted in horror to the mistreatment of Iraqi prisoners in Al Ghraib prison near Baghdad. When the lewd photos emerged of American soldiers forcing prisoners to engage in sexual acts, and leading them around on leashes with hoods over their heads, and threatening them with electrocution, people were speechless and horrified.

We should be enraged and demand that those involved be severely punished. We must also remember that the vast majority of our brave soldiers are decent human beings who have been willing to sacrifice their very lives to secure freedom for others.

But should we be shocked that some Americans are capable of such barbaric behavior as depicted in the infamous photos?

Consider:

○ Pornography is the No. 1 Internet industry—No. 1. There are well over 300,000 Internet porn sites.

○ American consumers spent an estimated $220 million at such fee-based "adult" sites in 2001, according to Jupiter Media Metrix, a New York Internet research firm. That was up from $148 million in 1999. Jupiter is projecting $320 million by 2005.

○ A comprehensive 2-year study by Alexa Research, a leading Web intelligence and traffic-measurement service, has revealed "sex" was the most popular term for which people searched. According to their online searching habits, people want "sex" more than they want "games," "music," "travel," "jokes," "cars," "jobs," "weather" and "health" combined.

○ A nationwide survey of 1,031 adults conducted by Zogby International and Focus on the Family on March 8–10, 2000, found that "20 percent of respondents—which extrapolates to 40 million adults—admitted visiting a sexually-oriented website. According to the Nielsen Net ratings, 17.5 million surfers visited porn sites from their homes in January of 2000—a 40 percent increase compared with September of 1999."

- Pornography websites earned $1.5 billion in 1999 and more than $2 billion in 2000.
- According to a 2001 report by the American Academy of Pediatrics Committee on Public Education, "by the time adolescents graduate from high school, they will have spent 15,000 hours watching television, compared with 12,000 hours spent in the classroom . . . American media are thought to be the most sexually suggestive in the Western hemisphere. The average American adolescent will view nearly 14,000 sexual references per year, yet only 165 of these references deal with birth-control, self-control, abstinence or the risk of pregnancy or STDs."
- The 2001 pediatric report also said that "56 percent of all programs on American television were found to contain sexual content. The so-called "family hour" of prime-time television (8:00 to 9:00 p.m.) contains on average more than eight sexual incidents, which is more than 4 times what it contained in 1976. Nearly one third of family-hour shows contain sexual references . . ."

And that's just the tip of the iceberg.

The military experts are right when they say we need to discuss how we administer prisons, how we handle foreign detainees and how complaints travel up and down the chain of command. The average soldier receives three hours of training a year on the Geneva Conventions regarding the proper treatment of prisoners of war. Is it possible to deprogram and reprogram soldiers—who come from a culture living the above statistics—in three hours a year?

A recent poll says Americans aren't even overly ashamed of what has gone on. Why? "People out in the hinterlands can keep the perspective of the big picture," the pollster told U.S. News magazine. Oh yeah? What is the big picture? That "everyone does it"? That this was mistreatment, not torture? That these were mere "fraternity pranks"? That the Iraqis are doing far worse to each other and to our soldiers?

Forget defending it. It's indefensible. Since the photos were seen 'round the world, very few folks 'round the world now view America as the country that liberated the Iraqis from Saddam, that rebuilt roads, schools and power stations. They see America as the country that engaged in the exact reprehensible behavior we said we were going to Iraq to stop.

But, with the non-judgmental, sex-crazed, anything-goes culture that we have become at home, it seems that America has set herself up for international humiliation. Our country permits Hollywood to put almost anything in a movie and still call it PG-13. We permit television and computers to bring all manner of filth into our homes. We permit school children to be taught that homosexuality is an acceptable lifestyle. We allow Christianity and the teaching of Judeo-Christian values to be scrubbed from the public square. We allow our children be taught how to use condoms in school, rather than why to avoid sex. We let these things happen. They don't happen on their own.

While hearings take place to examine the horrific behavior that took place in a military prison overseas, it's time to take a cold, hard look at the degradation in our own country—and in our own homes. If there are problems in your home, contact the National Coalition for the Protection of Children and Families, or Focus on the Family, or Web Wise Kids for help.

Presidential Speech

The Speaker: George W. Bush

The forty-third President of the United States, George W. Bush received a bachelor's degree from Yale University in 1968, then served as an F-102 fighter pilot in the Texas Air National Guard. He went on to receive a Master of Business Administration from Harvard Business School in 1975.

The following is a transcript from a speech delivered on May 4, 2004.

President Bush Meets with Alhurra Television on Wednesday

Q: Mr. President, thank you for agreeing to do this interview with us.

Evidence of torture of Iraqi prisoners by U.S. personnel has left many Iraqis and people in the Middle East and the Arab world with the impression that the United States is no better than Saddam Hussein regime. Especially when this alleged torture took place in the Abu Ghraib Prison, a symbol of torture of—

The President: Yes.

Q: What can the U.S. do, or what can you do to get out of this?

The President: First, people in Iraq must understand that I view those practices as abhorrent. They must also understand that what took place in that prison does not represent America that I know. The America I know is a compassionate country that believes in freedom. The America I know cares about every individual. The America I know has sent troops into Iraq to promote freedom—good, honorable citizens that are helping the Iraqis every day.

It's also important for the people of Iraq to know that in a democracy, everything is not perfect, that mistakes are made. But in a democracy, as well, those mistakes will be investigated and people will be brought to justice. We're an open society. We're a society that is willing to investigate, fully investigate in this case, what took place in that prison.

That stands in stark contrast to life under Saddam Hussein. His trained torturers were never brought to justice under his regime. There were no investigations about mistreatment of people. There will be investigations. People will be brought to justice.

Q: When did you learn about the—did you see the pictures on TV? When was the first time you heard about—

The President: Yes, the first time I saw or heard about pictures was on TV. However, as you might remember, in early January, General Kimmitt talked about a investigation that would be taking place about accused—alleged improprieties in the prison. So our government has been in the process of investigating.

And there are two—more than two investigations, multiple investigations going on, some of them related to any criminal charges that may be filed. And in our system of law, it's essential that those criminal charges go forward without prejudice. In other words, people need to be—are treated innocent until proven guilty. And facts are now being gathered.

And secondly, there is investigations to determine how widespread abuse may be occurring. And we want to know the truth. I talked to the Secretary of Defense this morning, by the way. I said, find the truth, and then tell the Iraqi people and the world the truth. We have nothing to hide. We believe in transparency, because we're a free society. That's what free societies do. They—if there's a problem, they address those problems in a forthright, up-front manner. And that's what's taking place.

Q: Mr. President, in a democracy and a free society, as you mentioned, people investigate, but at the same time, even those who are not directly responsible for these events take responsibility. With such a problem of this magnitude, do we expect anyone to step down? Do you still have confidence in the Secretary of Defense?

The President: Oh, of course, I've got confidence in the Secretary of Defense, and I've got confidence in the commanders on the ground in Iraq, because they—they and our troops are doing great work on behalf of the Iraqi people. We're finding the few that wanted to try to stop progress toward freedom and democracy. And we're helping the Iraqi people stand up a government. We stand side-by-side with the Iraqis that love freedom.

And—but people will be held to account. That's what the process does. That's what we do in America. We fully investigate; we let everybody see the results of the investigation; and then people will be held to account.

Q: If your State Department issues a human rights report about practices around the world and abuses, and we call upon countries every once in a while to—

The President: Right.

Q: ——try to put pressure on them to allow International Red Cross to visit prisons and detention center, would you allow the International Red Cross and other human rights organization to visit prisons under the control of the U.S. military?

The President: Of course, we'll cooperate with the International Red Cross. They're a vital organization. And we work with the International Red Cross. And you're right, we do point out human rights abuses. We also say to those governments, clean up your act. And that's precisely what America is doing.

We've discovered these abuses; they're abhorrent abuses. They do not reflect—the actions of these few people do not reflect the hearts of the American people. The American people are just as appalled at what they have seen on TV as the Iraqi citizens have. The Iraqi citizens must understand that. And, therefore, there will be a full investigation, and justice will be served. And we will do to ourselves what we expect of others.

And when we say, you've got human rights abuses, take care of the problem, we will do the same thing. We're taking care of the problem. And it's—it is unpleasant for Americans to see that some citizens, some soldiers have acted this way, because it does—again, I keep repeating, but it's true—it doesn't reflect how we think. This is not America. America is a country of justice and law and freedom and treating people with respect.

Q: Transferring control of Fallujah, in Iraq, to former army officers under Saddam Hussein led many people in Iraq, and even in the Arab world, to believe that the U.S. is lowering its expectation.

The President: Yes.

Q: How would you respond?

The President: Quite the contrary. We're raising expectations. We believe the Iraqi people can self-govern, and we believe the Iraqi people have got the capacity to take care of people who are willing to terrorize innocent Iraqi citizens. And that's what you're seeing in

Fallujah. As a matter of fact, the general in charge of the operation in Fallujah had been imprisoned by Saddam Hussein. So he felt the vindictiveness of the Hussein regime.

And I've got confidence that Iraq will be a peaceful, self-governing nation. And I also have confidence that, with help, the Iraqi security forces will be strong against foreign terrorists and others who are willing to kill, and criminals who are willing to try to wreak havoc in this society. Listen, there are thousands of Iraqi—innocent Iraqis who are dying at the hands of these killers. And we want to help decent, honorable Iraqi citizens bring peace and security to Iraq.

Q: So there is no reversal in policy of de-Baathification?

The President: Oh, no. There are citizens, for example, in the—amongst the teacher ranks in Sunni—parts of Sunni Iraq that were denied the right to teach because they may have been affiliated with the Baathist Party in the past, but who are very important to the future of Iraq because they're teachers. And of course, they are now being let back in the classroom, not to spread political propaganda, but to teach, to teach children.

And obviously, there is a process of balancing those who may have been affiliated with the Baath Party and those who are terrorists and killers. And obviously, terrorists and killers and extremists will not be a part of the government. But people who are by and large peaceful people, who care deeply about the future of Iraq, will be. And that's what you're seeing taking place now.

Q: It's been over a year since Saddam Hussein regime is toppled down, and U.S. allies are in place right now in Iraq. What is your assessment, today, of U.S. allies and the Governing Council and the various factions of the Iraqi government?

The President: Yes, well, first, I think we've made a lot of progress in a year.

Q: Do you still trust them? Do you still——

The President: Well, I trust the Iraqi people. Let me put it to you that way. I believe the Iraqi people want to be free. By far, the vast majority of Iraqi citizens want to have a life that is peaceful, so they can raise their children, see that their children are educated, have a chance for their children to succeed. The business people of Iraq just want a stable environment for them to be able to run their businesses and make a living. People want jobs. I mean, there are normal aspirations in Iraq that give me great confidence in the future of Iraq. People aspire for the same thing in Iraq as we do in America, a chance to succeed.

I also have confidence that the process we're under will work, which is to transfer sovereignty on June 30th. The people of Iraq must understand, sovereignty will be transferred on June 30th. And there's a process now in place to make sure that there's an entity to which we transfer sovereignty. And then there will be elections. And I think the timetable we're on is a realistic timetable; it's one that will be met. And I believe that the elections will help the Iraqi citizens realize that freedom is coming.

Q: If I may ask you my final question on the issue of the peace efforts that you are conducting. You supported Prime Minister Sharon's plan to withdraw from Gaza and you sent senior officials to Israel, and Israeli officials came to Washington and negotiated that plan. Do you think it was a mistake to support a plan before the Prime Minister secured the support of his own party?

The President: I think when you see a step toward peace, it's important for a peaceful nation like America to embrace it. And I felt that a withdrawal from the Gaza by the Israeli Prime Minister, as well as the withdrawal from four settlements from the West Bank by the Israeli Prime Minister, was a step toward peace. And at the time he did so,

I called for the United States and others to seize this moment—the Quartet and the European Union and Russia and the United Nations, and hopefully the World Bank, to seize this moment and to help the development of a Palestinian state that will be at peace with its neighbors; a Palestinian state that will provide hope for long-suffering Palestinian people.

I think this is an historic moment for the world. I think this is a good opportunity to step forth. I am confident that a peaceful Palestinian state can emerge. I'm the first President ever to call for the establishment of a Palestinian state. I still feel strongly that there should be one. I also recognize that we have got a duty, all of us, to fight off the terrorists who are trying to stop the spread of a peaceful Palestinian state, or the creation of a Palestinian state.

And now is the time to make progress. And I believe we can. There was a good statement yesterday out of the Quartet that confirmed our desire for a Palestinian state to emerge. And it's—what the Prime Minister of Israel did was—took a political risk; obviously he did. I mean, his own party condemned the statement—condemned the policy. However, I still believe it was the right thing for him to do. And we support peace in the Middle East. And we support the vision of two states, living side by side in peace.

Q: Thank you very much, Mr. President.

The President: Good job.

Government Document

The Source: The Geneva Conventions

The Geneva Conventions consist of treaties formulated in Geneva, Switzerland, that set the standards for international law for humanitarian concerns. The following are excerpts from the Third Geneva Convention in 1949, which amended the previous 1929 Convention on the treatment of prisoners of war. Nearly all 200 countries of the world have ratified these conventions.

The following is an excerpt from the 1949 conventions.

Geneva Convention (III) Relative to the Treatment of Prisoners of War; August 12, 1949

Article 13

Prisoners of war must at all times be humanely treated. Any unlawful act or omission by the Detaining Power causing death or seriously endangering the health of a prisoner of war in its custody is prohibited, and will be regarded as a serious breach of the present Convention. In particular, no prisoner of war may be subjected to physical mutilation or to medical or scientific experiments of any kind which are not justified by the medical, dental or hospital treatment of the prisoner concerned and carried out in his interest. Likewise, prisoners of war must at all times be protected, particularly against acts of violence or intimidation and against insults and public curiosity. Measures of reprisal against prisoners of war are prohibited.

Article 14

Prisoners of war are entitled in all circumstances to respect for their persons and their honour. Women shall be treated with all the regard due to their sex and shall in all cases benefit by treatment as favourable as that granted to men. Prisoners of war shall retain the full civil capacity which they enjoyed at the time of their capture. The Detaining Power may not restrict the exercise, either within or without its own territory, of the rights such capacity confers except in so far as the captivity requires.

Article 78 [Complaints and Requests]

Prisoners of war shall have the right to make known to the military authorities in whose power they are, their requests regarding the conditions of captivity to which they are subjected.

They shall also have the unrestricted right to apply to the representatives of the Protecting Powers either through their prisoners' representative or, if they consider it necessary, direct in order to draw their attention to any points on which they may have complaints to make regarding their conditions of captivity.

These requests and complaints shall not be limited nor considered to be a part of the correspondence quota referred to in Article 71. They must be transmitted immediately. Even if they are recognized to be unfounded, they may not give rise to any punishment.

Prisoners' representatives may send periodic reports on the situation in the camps and the needs of the prisoners of war to the representatives of the Protecting Powers.

Article 82 [Applicable Legislation]

A prisoner of war shall be subject to the laws, regulations and orders in force in the armed forces of the Detaining Power; the Detaining Power shall be justified in taking judicial or disciplinary measures in respect of any offence committed by a prisoner of war against such laws, regulations or orders. However, no proceedings or punishments contrary to the provisions of this Chapter shall be allowed.

If any law, regulation or order of the Detaining Power shall declare acts committed by a prisoner of war to be punishable, whereas the same acts would not be punishable if committed by a member of the forces of the Detaining Power, such acts shall entail disciplinary punishments only.

*Article 83 [Choice of Disciplinary
or Judicial Proceeding]*

In deciding whether proceedings in respect of an offence alleged to have been committed by a prisoner of war shall be judicial or disciplinary, the Detaining Power shall ensure that the competent authorities exercise the greatest leniency and adopt, wherever possible, disciplinary rather than judicial measures.

Article 84 [Courts]

A prisoner of war shall be tried only by a military court, unless the existing laws of the Detaining Power expressly permit the civil courts to try a member of the armed forces of the Detaining Power in respect of the particular offence alleged to have been committed by the prisoner of war.

In no circumstances whatever shall a prisoner of war be tried by a court of any kind which does not offer the essential guarantees of independence and impartiality as generally recognized, and, in particular, the procedure of which does not afford the accused the rights and means of defence provided for in Article 105.

Article 85 [Offences Committed before Capture]

Prisoners of war prosecuted under the laws of the Detaining Power for acts committed prior to capture shall retain, even if convicted, the benefits of the present Convention.

Article 86 ["Non Bis In Idem"]

No prisoner of war may be punished more than once for the same act or on the same charge.

Article 87 [Penalties]

Prisoners of war may not be sentenced by the military authorities and courts of the Detaining Power to any penalties except those provided for in respect of members of the armed forces of the said Power who have committed the same acts.

When fixing the penalty, the courts or authorities of the Detaining Power shall take into consideration, to the widest extent possible, the fact that the accused, not being a national of the Detaining Power, is not bound to it by any duty of allegiance, and that he is in its power as the result of circumstances independent of his own will. The said courts or authorities shall be at liberty to reduce the penalty provided for the violation of which the prisoner of war is accused, and shall therefore not be bound to apply the minimum penalty prescribed.

Collective punishment for individual acts, corporal punishment, imprisonment in premises without daylight and, in general, any form of torture or cruelty, are forbidden.

No prisoner of war may be deprived of his rank by the Detaining Power, or prevented from wearing his badges.

Article 88 [Execution of Penalties]

Officers, non-commissioned officers and men who are prisoners of war undergoing a disciplinary or judicial punishment, shall not be subjected to more severe treatment than that applied in respect of the same punishment to members of the armed forces of the Detaining Power of equivalent rank.

A woman prisoner of war shall not be awarded or sentenced to a punishment more severe, or treated whilst undergoing punishment more severely, than a woman member of the armed forces of the Detaining Power dealt with for a similar offence.

In no case may a woman prisoner of war be awarded or sentenced to a punishment more severe, or treated whilst undergoing punishment more severely, than a male member of the armed forces of the Detaining Power dealt with for a similar offence.

Prisoners of war who have served disciplinary or judicial sentences may not be treated differently from other prisoners of war.

Article 89 [Forms of Punishment]

The disciplinary punishments applicable to prisoners of war are the following:

(1) A fine which shall not exceed 50 per cent of the advances of pay and working pay which the prisoner of war would otherwise receive under the provisions of Articles 60 and 62 during a period of not more than thirty days.
(2) Discontinuance of privileges granted over and above the treatment provided for by the present Convention.
(3) Fatigue duties not exceeding two hours daily.
(4) Confinement.

The punishment referred to under (3) shall not be applied to officers.

In no case shall disciplinary punishments be inhuman, brutal or dangerous to the health of prisoners of war.

Article 90 [Duration of Punishments]

The duration of any single punishment shall in no case exceed thirty days. Any period of confinement awaiting the hearing of a disciplinary offence or the award of disciplinary punishment shall be deducted from an award pronounced against a prisoner of war.

The maximum of thirty days provided above may not be exceeded, even if the prisoner of war is answerable for several acts at the same time when he is awarded punishment, whether such acts are related or not.

The period between the pronouncing of an award of disciplinary punishment and its execution shall not exceed one month.

When a prisoner of war is awarded a further disciplinary punishment, a period of at least three days shall elapse between the execution of any two of the punishments, if the duration of one of these is ten days or more.

Newspaper Article

The Author: Alfred W. McCoy

Alfred W. McCoy is a professor in the History Department at the University of Wisconsin–Madison. He is the author of several books on Philippine history, two of which have won that country's National Book Award: *Philippine Cartoons* (Manila, 1985) and *Anarchy of Families* (Manila, 1994). Recently, he has completed a book manuscript titled *Closer Than Brothers: Manhood at the Philippine Military Academy* (New Haven, forthcoming, 1999), examining the impact of torture and authoritarian rule upon the country's officer corps.

The following article was published in the *Boston Globe* on May 14, 2004.

Torture at Abu Ghraib Followed CIA's Manual

The photos from Iraq's Abu Ghraib prison are snapshots not of simple brutality or a breakdown in discipline but of CIA torture techniques that have metastasized over the past 50 years like an undetected cancer inside the US intelligence community. From 1950 to 1962, the CIA led secret research into coercion and consciousness that reached a billion dollars at peak. After experiments with hallucinogenic drugs, electric shocks, and sensory deprivation, this CIA research produced a new method of torture that was psychological, not physical—best described as "no touch" torture.

The CIA's discovery of psychological torture was a counterintuitive breakthrough—indeed, the first real revolution in this cruel science since the 17th century. The old physical approach required interrogators to inflict pain, usually by crude beatings that often produced heightened resistance or unreliable information. Under the CIA's new psychological paradigm, however, interrogators used two essential methods to achieve their goals.

In the first stage, interrogators employ the simple, nonviolent techniques of hooding or sleep deprivation to disorient the subject; sometimes sexual humiliation is used as well.

Once the subject is disoriented, interrogators move on to a second stage with simple, self-inflicted discomfort such as standing for hours with arms extended. In this phase, the idea is to make victims feel responsible for their own pain and thus induce them to alleviate it by capitulating to the interrogator's power. In his statement on reforms at Abu Ghraib last week, General Geoffrey Miller, former chief of the Guantanamo detention center and now prison commander in Iraq, offered an unwitting summary of this two-phase torture. "We will no longer, in any circumstances, hood any of the detainees," the general said. "We will no longer use stress positions in any of our interrogations. And we will no longer use sleep deprivation in any of our interrogations."

Although seemingly less brutal, no-touch torture leaves deep psychological scars. The victims often need long treatment to recover from trauma far more crippling than physical pain. The perpetrators can suffer a dangerous expansion of ego, leading to cruelty and lasting emotional problems.

After codification in the CIA's "Kubark Counterintelligence Interrogation" manual in 1963, the new method was disseminated globally to police in Asia and Latin America through USAID's Office of Public Safety. Following allegations of torture by USAID's police trainees in Brazil, the US Senate closed down the office in 1975.

After it was abolished, the agency continued to disseminate its torture methods through the US Army's Mobile Training Teams, which were active in Central America during the 1980s. In 1997, the *Baltimore Sun* published chilling extracts of the "Human Resource Exploitation Training Manual" that had been distributed to allied militaries for 20 years. In the 10 years between the last known use of these manuals in the early 1990s and the arrest of Al Qaeda suspects since September 2001, torture was maintained as a US intelligence practice by delivering suspects to foreign agencies, including the Philippine National Police, who broke a bomb plot in 1995.

Once the war on terror started, however, the US use of no-touch torture resumed, first surfacing at Bagram Air Base near Kabul in early 2002, where Pentagon investigators found two Afghans had died during interrogation. In reports from Iraq, the methods are strikingly similar to those detailed in the Kubark manual.

Following the CIA's two-part technique, last September General Miller instructed US military police at Abu Ghraib to soften up high-priority detainees in the initial disorientation phase for later "successful interrogation and exploitation" by CIA and military intelligence. As often happens in no-touch torture sessions, this process soon moved beyond sleep and sensory deprivation to sexual humiliation. The question, in the second, still unexamined phase, is whether US Army intelligence and CIA operatives administered the prescribed mix of interrogation and self-inflicted pain—but outside the frame of these photographs. If so, the soldiers now facing courts-martial would have been following standard interrogation procedure.

For more than 50 years, the CIA's no-touch methods have become so widely accepted that US interrogators seem unaware that they are, in fact, engaged in systematic torture. But now, through these photographs from Abu Ghraib, we can see the reality of these techniques. We have a chance to join fully with the international community in repudiating a practice that, more than any other, represents a denial of democracy.

Scholarly Article

The Author: Philip G. Zimbardo

Philip G. Zimbardo is an internationally recognized scholar, educator, researcher, and media personality, winning numerous awards and honors in each of these domains. He has been a Stanford University professor since 1968, having taught previously at Yale, NYU, and Columbia. Zimbardo's career is noted for giving psychology away to the public through his popular PBS-TV series, *Discovering Psychology,* along with many text and trade books, among his 300 publications. He was recently president of the American Psychological Association.

The following article appeared in the book *The Social Psychology of Good and Evil,* Chapter 2, published by Guilford Press, 2004.

A Situationist Perspective on the Psychology of Evil: Understanding How Good People Are Transformed into Perpetrators

I endorse the application of a situationist perspective to the ways in which the antisocial behavior of individuals and the violence sanctioned by nations can be best understood, treated, and prevented. This view, which has both influenced and been informed by a body of social-psychological research and theory, contrasts with the traditional perspective that explains evil behavior in dispositional terms: Internal determinants of antisocial behavior locate evil within individual predispositions—genetic "bad seeds," personality traits, psycho pathological risk factors, and other organismic variables. The situationist approach is to the dispositional as public health models of disease are to medical models. Following basic principles of Lewinian theory, the situationist perspective propels external determinants of behavior to the foreground, well beyond the status as merely extenuating background circumstances. Unique to this situationist approach is the use of experimental laboratory and field research to demonstrate vital phenomena, that other approaches only analyze verbally or rely on archival or correlational data for answers. The basic paradigm presented in this chapter illustrates the relative ease with which ordinary, "good" men and women can be induced into behaving in "evil" ways by turning on or off one or another social situational variable.

I begin the chapter with a series of "oldies but goodies"—my laboratory and field studies on deindividuation, aggression, vandalism, and the Stanford prison experiment, along with a process analysis of Milgram's obedience studies, and Bandura's analysis of "moral disengagement." My analysis is extended to the evil of inaction by considering bystander failures of helping those in distress. This body of research demonstrates the underrecognized power of social situations to alter the mental representations and behavior of individuals, groups, and nations. Finally, I explore extreme instances of "evil" behavior for their dispositional or situational foundations: torturers, death-squad violence workers, and terrorist suicide bombers.

Evil can be defined as intentionally behaving, or causing others to act, in ways that demean, dehumanize, harm, destroy, or kill innocent people. This behaviorally focused definition makes the individual or group responsible for purposeful, motivated actions that have a range of negative consequences for other people. The definition excludes accidental or unintended harmful outcomes, as well as the broader, generic forms of institutional evil, such as poverty, prejudice, or destruction of the environment by agents of corporate greed. However, it does include corporate forms of wrongdoing, such as the marketing and selling of products with known disease-causing, death-dealing properties (e.g., cigarette manufacturers or other substance/

The political views expressed in this chapter represent solely those of a private citizen/patriot, and in no way should be construed as being supported or endorsed by any of my professional or institutional affiliations.

drug dealers). The definition also extends beyond the proximal agent of aggression, as studied in research on interpersonal violence, to encompass those in distal positions of authority whose orders or plans are carried out by functionaries. Such agents include military commanders and national leaders, such as Hilter, Stalin, Mao, Pol Pot, Idi Amin, and others whom history has identified as tyrants for their complicity in the deaths of untold millions of innocent people.

History will also have to decide on the evil status of President George W. Bush's role in declaring a pre-emptive, aggressive war against Iraq in March 2003, with dubious justification, that resulted in widespread death, injury, destruction, and enduring chaos. We might also consider a simpler definition of evil, proposed by my colleague, Irving Sarnoff: "Evil is knowing better but doing worse."

We live in a world cloaked in the evils of civil and international wars, of terrorism (home-grown and exported), homicides, rapes, domestic and child abuse, and countless other forms of devastation. The same human mind that creates the most beautiful works of art and extraordinary marvels of technology is equally responsible for the perversion of its own perfection. This most dynamic organ in the universe has served as a seemingly endless source of ever viler torture chambers and instruments of horror in earlier centuries, the "bestial machinery" unleashed on Chinese citizens by Japanese soldiers in their rape of Nanking (see Chang, 1997), and the recent demonstration of "creative evil" in the destruction of the World Trade Center by "weaponizing" commercial airlines. We continue to ask, *why?* Why and how is it possible for such deeds to continue to occur? How can the unimaginable become so readily imagined? These are the same questions that have been asked by generations before ours.

I wish I had answers to these profound questions about human existence and human nature. Here I can offer modest versions of possible answers. My concern centers around how good, ordinary people can be recruited, induced, seduced into behaving in ways that could be classified as evil. In contrast to the traditional approach of trying to identify "evil people" to account for the evil in our midst, I focus on trying to outline some of the central conditions that are involved in the transformation of good people into perpetrators of evil.

Locating Evil within Particular People: The Rush to the Dispositional

"Who is responsible for evil in the world, given that there is an all-powerful, omniscient God who is also all-Good?" That conundrum began the intellectual scaffolding of the Inquisition in the 16th and 17th centuries in Europe. As revealed in *Malleus Maleficarum*, the handbook of the German Inquisitors from the Roman Catholic Church, the inquiry concluded that "the Devil" was the source of all evil. However, these theologians argued the Devil works his evil through intermediaries, lesser demons, and, of course, human witches. So the hunt for evil focused on those marginalized people who looked or acted differently from ordinary people, who might qualify, under rigorous examination of conscience and torture, as "witches," and then put them to death. The victims were mostly women who could be readily exploited without sources of defense, especially when they had resources that could be confiscated. An analysis of this legacy of institutionalized violence against women is detailed by historian Anne Barstow (1994) in *Witchcraze*. Paradoxically, this early effort of the Inquisition to understand the origins of evil and develop interventions to cope with it instead fomented new forms of evil that fulfill all facets of my definition. The phenomenon of the Inquisition exemplifies the notion of simplifying the complex problem of widespread evil by identifying *individuals* who might be the guilty parties and then making them "pay" for their evil deeds.

Most traditional psychiatry as well as psychodynamic theory also locate the source of individual violence and antisocial behavior within the psyches of disturbed people, often tracing it back to early roots in unresolved infantile conflicts. Like genetic views of pathology, such psychological approaches seek to link behaviors society judges as pathological to pathological origins—be they defective genes, "bad seeds," or premorbid personality structures. However, this view overlooks the fact that the same violent outcomes can be generated by very different types of people, all of whom give no hint of evil impulses. My colleagues and I [Lee, Zimbardo, & Berthoff, 1977] interviewed and tested 19 inmates in California prisons who had all recently been convicted of homicide. Ten of these killers had a long history of violence, showed lack of impulse control (on the Minnesota Multiphasic Personality Inventory), were decidedly masculine in sexual identity, and generally extraverted. The other murderers were totally different. They had never committed any criminal offense prior to the homicide—their murders were totally unexpected, given their mild manner and gentle disposition. Their problem was an *excessive* impulse control that inhibited their expression of any feelings. Their sexual identity was feminine or androgynous, and the majority were shy. These "shy sudden murderers" killed just as violently as did the habitual criminals, and their victims died just as surely, but it would have been impossible to predict this outcome from any prior knowledge of their personalities, which were so different from the more obvious habitual criminals.

The concept of an authoritarian personality syndrome was developed by a team of psychologists (Adorno, Frenkel-Brunswick, Levinson, & Sanford, 1950) after World War II who were trying to make sense of the Holocaust and the broad appeal of fascism and Hitler. Their dispositional bias led them to focus on identifying a set of personality factors that might underlie the fascist mentality. However, they overlooked the host of processes operating at political, economic, societal, and historical levels, all of which influenced and directed so many millions of individuals into a constrained behavioral channel of hating Jews and other minority groups, while endorsing and even applauding the views and policies of their dictator.

This tendency to explain observed behavior by reference to internal dispositional factors while ignoring or minimizing the impact of situational variables has been termed the fundamental attribution error (FAE) by my colleague Lee Ross (1977). We are all subject to this dual bias of overutilizing dispositional analyses and underutilizing situational explanations when faced with ambiguous causal scenarios we want to understand. We succumb to this effect because our educational institutions, social and professional training programs, and societal agencies are all geared toward a focus on individual, dispositional orientations. Dispositional analyses are a central operating feature of cultures that are based on individualistic rather than collectivist values (see Triandis, 1994). Thus, it is individuals who are lauded with praise and fame and wealth for achievement and are honored for their uniqueness, but it is also individuals who are blamed for the ills of society. Our legal, medical, educational, and religious systems all are founded on principles of individualism.

Dispositional analyses of antisocial, or non-normative, behaviors typically include strategies for behavior modification, whereby deviant individuals learn to conform better to social norms, or facilities for excluding them from society via imprisonment, exile, or execution. Locating evil within selected individuals or groups carries with it the "social virtue" of taking society "off the hook" as blameworthy; societal structures and political decision making are exonerated from bearing any burden of the more fundamental circumstances that create racism, sexism, elitism, poverty, and marginal existence for some citizens. Furthermore, this dispositional orientation to understanding evil implies a simplistic, binary world of good people, like us, and bad people, like them. That clear-cut dichotomy is divided by a manufactured line that separates good and evil. We then take comfort in the illusion that such a line constrains crossovers in either direction. We could never imagine being like *them,* of doing their unthinkable dirty deeds, and do not admit them into our company because they are so essentially different as to be unchangeable. This extreme position also means we forfeit the motivation to understand how they came to engage in what we view as evil behavior. I find it helpful to remind myself of the geopolitical analysis of the Russian novelist Alexander Solzhenitsyn, a victim of persecution by the Soviet KGB, that the line between good and evil lies in the center of every human heart.

The Transformation of Good People into Agents of Destruction

My bias is admittedly more toward situational analyses of behavior and comes from my training as an experimental social psychologist as well as from having grown up in poverty, in a New York City ghetto of the South Bronx. I believe that dispositional orientations are more likely to correlate with affluence: The rich want to take full credit for their success, whereas the situationists hail more from the lower classes who want to explain the obvious dysfunctional lifestyles of those around them in terms of external circumstances rather than internal failures. I am primarily concerned with understanding the psychological and social dynamics involved when an ordinary, "good" person begins to act in antisocial ways and, in the extreme, behaves destructively toward the property or person of others. I saw, first-hand, my childhood friends go through such transformations, and I wondered how and why they changed so drastically and whether I could also change like that (e.g., they were bullied, failed in school, parents fought all the time, nothing to look forward to). I was similarly fascinated with the tale of the behavioral transformation of Robert Louis Stevenson's good Dr. Jekyll into the murderous Mr. Hyde. What was in his chemical formula that could have such an immediate and profound impact? Even as a child, I wondered if there were other ways to induce such changes, since my friends did not have access to his elixir of evil before they did such bad things to other people. I would later discover that social psychology had recipes for such transformations.

Our mission is to understand better how virtually anyone could be recruited to engage in evil deeds that deprive other human beings of their dignity, humanity, and life. The dispositional analysis has the comforting side effect of enabling those who have not yet done wrong to righteously assert, "Not *me*, I am different from those kinds of people who did that evil deed!" By positing a "me-us-them" distinction, we live with the illusion of moral superiority firmly entrenched in the pluralistic ignorance that comes from not recognizing the set of situational and structural circumstances that empowered others—like ourselves—to engage in deeds that they too once thought were alien to their nature. We take false pride in believing that "I am not that kind of person."

I argue that the human mind is so marvelous that it can adapt to virtually any known environmental circumstance in order to survive, to create, and to destroy, as necessary. We are not born with tendencies toward good or evil but with mental templates to do *either*. What I mean is that we have the potential to be better or worse than anyone who has existed in the past, to be more creative and more destructive, to make the world a better place or a worse place than before. It is only through the recognition that no one of us is an island, that we all share the human condition, that humility takes precedence over unfounded pride in acknowledging our vulnerability to situational forces. If we want to develop mechanisms for combating such malevolent transformations, then it seems essential to learn to appreciate the extent to which ordinary people can be seduced or initiated into the performance of evil deeds. We need to focus on discovering the mechanisms among the causal factors that influence so many to do so much bad, to commit so much evil throughout the globe. (See also the breadth of ideas presented by Baumeister, 1997; Darley, 1992; Staub, 1989; Waller, 2002.)

The Milgram Obedience Experiments

The most obvious power of the experimental demonstration by Stanley Milgram (1974) of blind obedience to authority lies in the unexpectedly high rates of such compliance, with the majority—two-thirds—of the subjects "going all the way" in shocking a victim with apparently lethal consequences. His finding was indeed shocking to most of those who read about it or saw his movie version of the study, because it revealed that a variety of ordinary American citizens could so readily be led to engage in "electrocuting a nice stranger." But the more significant importance of his research comes from what he did after that initial classic study with Yale College undergraduates. Milgram conducted 18 experimental variations on more than a *thousand* subjects from a variety of backgrounds, ages, both genders, and all educational levels. In each of these studies he varied one social-psychological variable and observed its impact on the extent of obedience to the unjust authority's pressure to continue to shock the "learner-victim." He was able to demonstrate that compliance rates of those who delivered the maximum 450 volts to the hapless victim could soar to 90% *or* could be reduced to less than 10% by introducing a single variable into the compliance recipe.

Milgram found that obedience was maximized when subjects first observed peers behaving obediently; it was dramatically reduced when peers rebelled or when the victim acted like a masochist asking to be shocked. What is especially interesting to me about this last result are the data Milgram provides on the predictions of his outcome by 40 psychiatrists who were given the basic description of the classic experiment. Their average estimate of the percentage of U.S. citizens who would give the full 450 volts was fewer than 1%. Only sadists would engage in such sadistic behavior, they believed. In a sense, this is the comparison level for appreciating the enormity of Milgram's finding. These experts on human behavior were *totally* wrong because they ignored the situational determinants of behavior in the procedural description of the experiment and overrelied on the dispositional perspective that comes from their professional training. Their error is a classic instance of the FAE at work. In fact, in this research, the average person does *not* behave like a sadist when an apparently masochistic victim encourages him or her to do so.

Milgram's intention was to provide a paradigm in which it was possible to quantify "evil" by the number of buttons a subject pushed on a shock generator, which allegedly delivered shocks to a mild-mannered confederate, playing the role of the pupil or learner, while the subject enacted the teacher role. Some of the procedures in this research paradigm that seduced many ordinary citizens to engage in evil offer parallels to compliance strategies used by "influence professionals" in real-world settings, such as salespeople, cult recruiters, and our national leaders (see Cialdini, 2001).

Ten Ingredients in the Situationist's Recipe
for Behavioral Transformations

Among the influence principles in Milgram's paradigm for getting ordinary people to do things they originally believed they would not do are the following:

1. Presenting an acceptable justification, or rationale, for engaging in the undesirable action, such as wanting to help people improve their memory by judicious use of punishment strategies. In experiments this justification is known as the "cover story" because it is intended to cover up the procedures that follow, which might not make sense on their own. The real-world equivalent of the cover story is an ideology, such as "national security," that often provides the nice big lie for instituting a host of bad, illegal, and immoral policies.
2. Arranging some form of contractual obligation, verbal or written, to enact the behavior.
3. Giving participants meaningful roles to play (e.g., teacher, student) that carry with them previously learned positive values and response scripts.
4. Presenting basic rules to be followed, which seem to make sense prior to their actual use, but then can be arbitrarily used to justify mindless compliance.

"Failure to respond must be treated as an error" was a Milgram rule for shock omissions as well as for false commissions. But then what happens when the learner complains of a heart condition, wants to quit, then screams, followed by a thud and silence? The learner's apparent inability to respond to the teacher's testing due to death or unconsciousness must be continually challenged by further shocks, since omission equals commission. The proceedings do not make sense at all: How could the teacher be helping to improve the memory of a learner who is incapacitated or dead? All too many participants stopped engaging in such basic, obvious critical thinking endeavors as their confusion and stress mounted.

5. Altering the semantics of the act and action: from hurting victims to helping learners by punishing them.

6. Creating opportunities for diffusion of responsibility for negative outcomes; others will be responsible, or it will not be evident that the actor will be held liable.

7. Starting the path toward the ultimate evil act with a small, insignificant first step (only 15 volts).

8. Increasing each level of aggression in gradual steps that do not seem like noticeable differences (only 30 volts).

9. Gradually changing the nature of the influence authority from "just" to "unjust," from reasonable and rational to unreasonable and irrational.

10. Making the "exit costs" high and the process of exiting difficult by not permitting usual forms of verbal dissent to qualify as behavioral disobedience.

Such procedures are utilized across varied influence situations, in which those in authority want others to do their bidding but know that few would engage in the "end game" final solution without first being properly prepared psychologically to do the "unthinkable." I would encourage readers to engage in the thought exercise of applying these compliance principles to the tactics used by the Bush administration to cajole Americans into endorsing the preemptive invasion of Iraq (discussed further later in the chapter).

Lord of the Flies *and the Psychology of Deindividuation*

William Golding's (1954) Nobel prize-winning novel of the transformation of good British choir boys into murderous beasts centers on the point of change in mental state and behavior that follows a change in physical appearance. Painting themselves, changing their outward appearance, made it possible for some of Golding's characters to disinhibit previously restrained impulses to kill a pig for food. Once that alien deed of killing another creature was accomplished, they could then continue on to kill, with pleasure, both animals and people alike. Was Golding describing a psychologically valid principle in his use of external appearance as catalyst to dramatic changes in internal and behavioral processes? That is the question I answered with a set of experiments and field studies on the psychology of deindividuation (Zimbardo, 1970).

The basic procedure involved having young women deliver a series of painful electric shocks to each of two other young women whom they could see and hear in a one-way mirror before them. Half were randomly assigned to a condition of anonymity, or deindividuation, half to one of uniqueness, or individuation. The appearance of the four college student subjects in each deindividuation group was concealed, and they were given identifying numbers in place of their names. The comparison individuation subjects in the four-woman groups were called by their names and made to feel unique. They were asked to make the same responses of shocking each of two female "victims"—all with a suitable cover story, the big lie that they never questioned.

The results were clear: Women in the deindividuation condition delivered twice as much shock to both victims as did the women in the individuated comparison condition. Moreover, the deindividuated subjects shocked both victims, the one previously rated as pleasant and the other as unpleasant, more over the course of the 20 trials, whereas the individuated subjects shocked the pleasant woman less over time than they did the unpleasant one. One important conclusion flows from this research and its various replications and extensions, some using military personnel: Anything that makes a person feel anonymous, as if no one knows who he or she is, creates the potential for that person to act in evil ways—if the situation gives permission for violence.

Halloween Disguises and Aggression in Children

Outside the laboratory, *masks* may be used to create the anonymity needed to disinhibit typically restrained behavior. For example, people mask themselves at Carnival rituals in many Catholic countries. Children in the United States don masks and costumes for Mardi Gras and Halloween parties. Bringing the laboratory to the party, so to speak, Fraser (1974) arranged for elementary school children to go to a special, experimental Halloween party given by their teacher. There were many games to play and for each game won, tokens were earned that could be exchanged for gifts at the end of the party. Half the games were nonaggressive in nature, and half were matched in content but involved aggression: Physical confrontations between two children were necessary to reach the goal and win the contest. The experimental design was a within-subject (A-B-A) format: in the first phase the games were played without costumes; then the costumes arrived and were worn as the games continued; finally, the costumes were removed and the games went on for the third phase (each phase lasted about an hour). The data are striking testimony to the power of anonymity. Aggression increased significantly as soon as the costumes were worn, more than doubling from the initial base level average. When the costumes were removed, aggression dropped back well below the initial base rate. Equally interesting was the second result: that aggression had negative instrumental consequences on winning tokens—that is, it costs money to be aggressive—but that cost did not matter when the children were anonymous in their costumes. The least number of tokens won occurred during the costumed anonymity phase, when aggression was highest.

Cultural Wisdom of Changing
Warriors' Appearances

Let us leave the laboratory and the fun and games of children's parties to enter the real world, where these issues of anonymity and violence may take on life-and-death significance. Some societies go to war without having the young male warriors change their appearance, whereas others always include ritual transformations of appearance by painting or masking the warriors (as in *Lord of the Flies*). Does that change in external appearance make a difference in how warring enemies are treated? After reading my Nebraska Symposium chapter, Harvard anthropologist John Watson (1973) posed a research question, then went to the human area files to find the answer, then published the data: (1) the societies that did or did not change appearance of warriors prior to going to war, and (2) the extent to which they killed, tortured, or mutilated their victims. The results are striking confirmation of the prediction that anonymity promotes destructive behavior, when permission is also given to behave in aggressive ways that are ordinarily prohibited. Of the 23 societies for which these two data sets were present, the majority (12 of 15, 80%) of societies in which warriors changed their appearance were those noted as most destructive, whereas only one of the eight societies in which the warriors did *not* change appearance before going to battle was noted as destructive. Cultural wisdom dictates that when old men want usually peaceful young men to harm and kill other young men like themselves in a war, it is easier to do so if they first change their appearance by putting on uniforms or masks or painting their faces. With that anonymity in place, out goes their usual internal focus of compassion and concern for others.

The Theoretical Model of Deindividuation
and Bandura's Model of Moral Disengagement

The psychological mechanisms involved in getting good people to do evil are embodied in two theoretical models, the first elaborated by me (Zimbardo, 1970) and modified by input from subsequent variants on my deindividuation conceptions, notably by Diener (1980). The second is Bandura's model of moral disengagement (1998, 2003), which specifies the conditions under which anyone can be led to act immorally, even those who usually ascribe to high levels of morality.

Bandura's model outlines how it is possible to morally disengage from destructive conduct by using a set of cognitive mechanisms that alter (1) one's perception of the reprehensible conduct (e.g., by engaging in moral justifications, making palliative comparisons, using euphemistic labeling for one's conduct); (2) one's sense of the detrimental effects of that conduct (e.g., by minimizing, ignoring, or misconstruing the consequences); (3) one's sense of responsibility for the link between reprehensible conduct and the detrimental effects (e.g., by displacing or diffusing responsibility); and (4) one's view of the victim (e.g., by dehumanizing him or her, attributing the blame for the outcome to the victim).

Dehumanization in Action: "Animals" by Any Other Name Are College Students

A remarkable experiment by Bandura, Underwood, and Fromson (1975) reveals how easy it is to induce intelligent college students to accept a dehumanizing label of other people and then to act aggressively based on that stereotyped term. Four participants were led to believe they were overhearing the research assistant tell the experimenter that the students from another college were present to start the study in which they were to deliver electric shocks of varying intensity to the participants (according to the dictates of a reasonable cover story). In one of the three randomly assigned conditions, the subjects overheard the assistant say to the experimenter that the other students seemed "nice"; in a second condition, they heard the other students described as "animals"; in the third group, the assistant did not label the students in the alleged other group.

The dependent variable of shock intensity clearly reflected this situational manipulation. The subjects gave the highest levels of shock to those labeled in the dehumanizing way as "animals," and their shock level increased linearly over the 10 trials. Those labeled "nice" were given the least shock, whereas the unlabelled group fell in the middle of these two extremes. Thus, a single word—*animals*—was sufficient to incite intelligent college students to treat those so labeled as if they deserved to be harmed. On the plus side, the labeling effect resulted in others being treated with greater respect if someone in authority labeled them positively. The graphed data is also of interest: On the first trial there is no difference across the three experimental treatments in the level of shock administered, but with each successive opportunity, the shock levels diverge. Those shocking the so-called "animals" shock them more and more over time, a result comparable to the escalating shock level of the deindividuated female students in my earlier study. That rise in aggressive responding over time, with practice, or with experience belies a self-reinforcing effect of aggressive or violent responding: It is experienced as increasingly pleasurable.

What my model adds to the mix of what is needed to get good people to engage in evil deeds is a focus on the role of cognitive controls that usually guide behavior in socially desirable and personally acceptable ways. The shift from good to evil behavior can be accomplished by knocking out these control processes, blocking them, minimizing them, or reorienting them. Doing so suspends conscience, self-awareness, sense of personal responsibility, obligation, commitment, liability, morality, and analyses in terms of costs-benefits of given actions. The two general strategies for accomplishing this objective are (1) reducing cues of social accountability of the actor (i.e., "No one knows who I am, nor cares to know"), and (2) reducing concerns for self-evaluation by the actor. The first eliminates concerns for social evaluation and social approval by conveying a sense of anonymity to the actor and diffusing personal responsibility across others in the situation. The second strategy stops self-monitoring and consistency monitoring by relying on tactics that alter states of consciousness (e.g., via drugs, arousing strong emotions or hyperintense actions, creating a highly focused present-time orientation wherein there is no concern for past or future), and by projecting responsibility outside the self and onto others.

My research and that of other social psychologists (see Prentice-Dunn & Rogers, 1983) on deindividuation differs from the paradigm in Milgram's studies in that there is no authority figure present, urging the subject to obey. Rather, the situation is created in such a way that subjects act in accordance to paths made available to them, without thinking through the meaning or consequences of those actions. Their actions are not cognitively guided, as they are typically, but directed by the actions of others in proximity to them or by their strongly aroused emotional states and situationally available cues, such as the presence of weapons.

Environmental Anonymity Breeds Vandalism

It is possible for certain environments to convey a sense of anonymity on those who live in, or pass through, their midst. The people living in such environments do not have a sense of community. Vandalism and graffiti may be interpreted as an individual's attempt for public notoriety in a society that deindividuates him or her.

I conducted a simple field study to demonstrate the ecological differences between places ruled by anonymity versus those conveying a sense of community. I abandoned used but good-condition cars in the Bronx, New York City, and in Palo Alto, California, one block away from New York University and Stanford University, respectively. License plates were removed and hoods raised slightly to serve as ethological "releaser cues" for the potential vandals' attack behavior. It worked swiftly in the Bronx, as we watched and filmed from a vantage point across the street. Within 10 minutes of officially beginning this study, the first vandals surfaced. This parade of vandals continued for 2 days, by which time there was nothing of value left to strip; then they simply began destroying the remains. In 48 hours we recorded 23 separate destructive contacts by individual or groups, who either took something from the abandoned vehicle or did something to wreck it. Curiously, only one of these episodes involved adolescents; the rest of the vandals were adults, many well dressed and many driving cars, so that they might qualify as, at least, lower middle class. Anonymity can make brazen vandals of us all. But what about the fate of the abandoned car in Palo Alto? Our time-lapse film revealed that no one vandalized any part of the car over a 5-day period. When we removed the car, three local residents called the police to say that an abandoned car was being stolen (the local police had been notified of our field study). That is one definition of "community," where people care about what happens on their turf, even to the person or property of strangers, with the reciprocal assumption that they would also care about them.

I now feel that any environmental or societal conditions that contribute to making some members of society feel that they are anonymous—that no one knows or cares who they are, that no one recognizes their individuality and thus their humanity—makes them potential assassins and vandals, a danger to my person and my property—and yours [Zimbardo, 1976].

The Faces of the "Enemy": Propaganda Images Condition Us to Kill Abstractions

We need to add a few more operational principles to our arsenal of variables that trigger the commission of evil acts by men and women who are ordinarily good people. We can learn about some of these principles by considering how nations prepare their young men (admittedly, women are now members of the armed forces in many countries, but it is primarily the men who are sent into combat zones) to engage in deadly wars, and how they prepare citizens to support the risks of going to war, especially a war of aggression. This difficult transformation is accomplished by a special form of cognitive conditioning. Images of "The Enemy" are created by national propaganda to prepare the minds of soldiers and citizens alike to hate those who fit the new category of "your enemy." This mental conditioning is a soldier's most potent weapon, for without it, he could probably never fire his weapon to kill another young man in the cross-hairs of his gun sight. A fascinating account of how this "hostile imagination" is created in the minds of soldiers and their families is presented in *Faces of the Enemy* by Sam Keen (1986; see also his companion video). Archetypal images of the enemy are created by propaganda fashioned by the governments of most nations against those judged to be the dangerous "them"—the outsiders who are also "our" enemies. These visual images create a consensual societal paranoia that is focused on the enemy who would do harm to the women, children, homes, and god of the soldier's nation, way of life, and so forth. Keen's analysis of this propaganda on a worldwide scale reveals that there are a select number of attributes utilized by "homo hostilis" to invent an evil enemy in the minds of good members of righteous tribes. The enemy is aggressive, faceless, a rapist, godless, barbarian, greedy, criminal, a torturer, harbinger of death, a dehumanized animal, or just an abstraction. Finally, there is the enemy as worthy, heroic opponent to be crushed in mortal combat—as in the video game of the same name.

Ordinary Men Murder Ordinary Men, Women, and Children: Jewish Enemies

One of the clearest illustrations of my fundamental theme of how ordinary people can be transformed into engaging in evil deeds that are alien to their past history and to their moral development comes from the analysis of British historian Christopher Browning. In *Ordinary Men: Reserve Police Battalion 101 and the Final Solution in Poland* (1992) he recounts that in March 1942 about 80% of all victims of the Holocaust were still alive, but a mere 11 months later about 80% were dead. In this short period of time, the *Endlösung* (Hitler's "Final Solution") was galvanized by means of an intense wave of mass mobile murder squads in Poland. This genocide required mobilization of a large-scale killing machine at the same time as able-bodied soldiers were needed on the Russian front. Since most Polish Jews lived in small towns and not the large cities, the question that Browning raised about the German High Command was "where had they found the manpower during this pivotal year of the war for such an astounding logistical achievement in mass murder?" (p. xvi).

His answer came from archives of Nazi war crimes, in the form of the activities of Reserve Battalion 101, a unit of about 500 men from Hamburg, Germany. They were elderly family men, too old to be drafted into the army, from working-class and lower middle-class backgrounds, with no military or police experience, just raw recruits sent to Poland without warning of, or any training in, their secret mission: the total extermination of all Jews living in the remote villages of Poland. In just 4 months they had shot to death at point blank range at least 38,000 Jews and had deported another 45,000 to the concentration camp at Treblinka. Initially, their commander told them that this was a difficult mission which must be obeyed by the battalion, but any individual could refuse to execute these men, women, and children. Records indicate that at first about half the men refused, letting the others commit the mass murder. But over time, social modeling processes took their toll, as did any guilt-induced persuasion by buddies who did the killing, until by the end, up to 90% of the men in Battalion 101 had participated in the shootings, even proudly taking photographs of their up-close and personal slaughter of Jews.

Browning makes clear that there was no special selection of these men, only that they were as "ordinary" as could be imagined—until they were put into a situation in which they had "official" permission, even encouragement, to act sadistically and brutishly against those arbitrarily labeled as "the enemy."

Let us go from the abstract to the personal for a moment: Imagine you witnessed your own father shooting to death a helpless mother and her infant child, and then imagine his answer to your question, "Why did you do it, Daddy?"

The War on Iraq: A Spurious Creation of Evil Terrorists and Infusion of National Fears

Fast forward to our time, our nation, our citizenry, and the fears of terrorism instilled by the destruction of the World Trade Center towers since that unforgettable day of September 11, 2001. The initial press and official reaction was to label the perpetrators of this horrific deed as "hijackers," "murderers," "criminals." Soon the label changed to "terrorists" and their deeds described as "evil." *Evil* became the coin of the realm, used repeatedly by the media as fed by the administration, and with an ever-widening net of inclusiveness. Osama bin Laden, the mastermind of 9/11, was the first culprit designated as evil. But when he proved elusive, escaping from the war zone in Afghanistan, it became necessary for the administration's war on terrorism campaign to put a new face and a new place on terrorism. Of course, terrorism works its generation of fear and anxiety by its very facelessness and nonlocal ubiquity. Several countries were labeled by our president as the "axis of evil," with the leader of one of those countries, Iraq, designated as so evil that he, Saddam Hussein, had to be removed from power by all means necessary.

A propaganda campaign was created to justify a preemptive war against Saddam Hussein's regime by identifying the clear and imminent threat to the national security of the United States posed by the alleged weapons of mass destruction (WMD) this evil leader had at his disposal. Then a link was erected between him and the terrorist networks to whom, allegedly, he would sell or gift these WMD. Over time, many Americans began to believe the falsehoods that Saddam Hussein was involved in the 9/11 terrorist attacks, was in complicity with Osama bin Laden, and had ready and operational an arsenal of deadly weapons that threatened U.S. security and well-being. Magazine images, newspaper accounts, and vivid TV stories contributed to the "evilization" of Saddam Hussein over the course of a year.

The vulnerability to terrorism that Americans continued to experience on deep, personal levels—in part, sustained and magnified by the administration's issuance of repeated (false) alarms of imminent terrorist attacks on the homeland—was relieved by the action of officially going to war. The public and Congress strongly supported a symmetrical war of "shock and awe"—to rid Iraq of the feared WMD and destroy Hussein's evil menace. Thus, for the first time in its history, the United States endorsed what the majority believed to be a justified aggressive war that has already cost billions of dollars, untold thousands of deaths (soldiers *and* civilians), totally destroyed a nation, weakened the United Nations, and will enmesh the United States in a prolonged, Vietnam-like, "no exit" scenario for years to come.

When no WMD were uncovered, despite the alleged best intelligence reports and aerial photos of them presented by the Secretary of State to the United Nations, collective cognitive dissonance reduction seeped in to maintain the belief that was still a "necessary" and "good" war against evil (Festinger, 1957). After many months of an all-out, desperately intense search of every part of Iraq, American troops and intelligence forces have not unearthed a single WMD! So the original reason for going to war is being played down and is being replaced by the mantra that Iraq is the new front in our worldwide fight against terrorism, thus it is good we are in control of the destiny of Iraq. But who cares what the truth really is regarding the deceptive reasons for going to war, if the United States is now safer and the president is a commander-in-chief of decisive action—as his image crafters have carefully depicted him in the media. This national mind control experiment deserves careful documenting by unbiased social historians for the current and future generations to appreciate the power of images, words, and framing that can lead a democratic nation to support *and even relish* the unthinkable evil of an aggressive war.

The Socialization of Evil: How the "Nazi Hate Primers" Prepared and Conditioned the Minds of German Youth to Hate Jews

The second broad class of operational principles by which otherwise good people can be recruited into evil is through education/socialization processes that are sanctioned by the government in power, enacted within school programs, and supported by parents and teachers. A prime example is the way in which German children in the 1930s and 1940s were systematically indoctrinated to hate Jews, to view them as the all-purpose enemy of the new (post–World War I) German nation. Space limitations do not allow full documentation of this process, but I touch on several examples of one way in which governments are responsible for sanctioning evil.

In Germany, as the Nazi party rose to power in 1933, no target of Nazification took higher priority than the reeducation of Germany's youth. Hitler wrote: "I will have no intellectual training. Knowledge is ruin to my young men. A violently active, dominating, brutal youth—that is what I am after" (*The New Order*, 1989, pp. 101–102). To teach the youth about geography and race, special primers were created and ordered to be read starting in the first grade of elementary school (see *The New Order*, 1989). These "hate primers" were brightly colored comic books that contrasted the beautiful blond Aryans with the despicably ugly caricatured Jew. They sold in the hundreds of thousands. One was titled *Trust No Fox in the Green Meadows and No Jew on His Oath*. What is most insidious about this kind of hate conditioning is that the misinformation was presented as facts to be learned and tested upon, or from which to practice penmanship. In the copy of the *Trust No Fox* text that I reviewed, a series of cartoons illustrates all the ways in which Jews supposedly deceive Aryans, get rich and fat from dominating them, and are lascivious, mean, and without compassion for the plight of the poor and the elderly Aryans.

The final scenarios depict the retribution of Aryan children when they expel Jewish teachers and children from their school, so that "proper discipline and order" could then be taught. Initially, Jews were prohibited from community areas, like public parks, then expelled altogether from Germany. The sign in the cartoon reads, ominously, "One-way street." Indeed, it was a unidirectional street that led eventually to the death camps and crematoria that were the centerpiece of Hitler's Final Solution: the genocide of the Jews. Thus, this institutionalized evil was spread pervasively and insidiously through a perverted educational system that turned away from the types of critical thinking exercises that open students' minds to new ideas and toward thinking uncritically and close-mindedly about those targeted as the enemy of the people. By controlling education and the propaganda media, any national leader could produce the fantastic scenarios depicted in George Orwell's (1981) frightening novel *1984*.

The institutionalized evil that Orwell vividly portrays in his fictional account of state dominance over individuals goes beyond the novelist's imagination when its prophetic vision is carried into operational validity by powerful cult leaders or by agencies and departments within the current national administration of the United States. Previously I have outlined the direct parallels between the mind control strategies and tactics Orwell attributes to "The Party" and those that Reverend Jim Jones used in dominating the members of his religious/political cult, Peoples Temple (Zimbardo, 2003a). Jones orchestrated the suicide/murders of more than 900 U.S. citizens in the jungles of Guyana 25 years ago, perhaps as the grand finale of his experiment in institutionalized mind control. I learned from former members of this group that not only did Jones read *1984*, he talked about it often and even had a song commissioned by the church's singer, entitled "1984 Is Coming," that everyone had to sing at some services. I will leave it to the reader to explore the similarities between the mind control practices in *1984* and those being practiced on U.S. citizens in the past few years (see Zimbardo, 2003b).

*The Stanford Prison Experiment: A Crucible
of Human Nature Where Good Boys
Encountered an Evil Place*

Framing the issues we have been considering as, in essence, who wins when good boys
are put in an evil place casts it as a neo-Greek tragedy scenario, wherein "the situation"
stands in for the externally imposed forces of "the gods and destiny." As such, we can
anticipate an outcome unfavorable to humanity. In more mundane psychological
terms, this research on the Stanford prison experiment synthesized many of the
processes and variables outlined earlier: those of place and person anonymity that
contribute to the deindividuation of the people involved, the dehumanization of victims, giving some actors (guards) permission to control others (prisoners), and placing it all within a unique setting (the prison) that most societies throughout the world
acknowledge provides some form of institutionally approved sanctions for evil through
the extreme differentials in control and power fostered in prison environments.

In 1971, I designed a dramatic experiment that would extend over a 2-week period
to provide our research participants with sufficient time for them to become fully engaged in their experimentally assigned roles of either guards or prisoners. Having
participants live in a simulated prison setting day and night, if prisoners, or work
there for long 8-hour shifts, if guards, would also allow sufficient time for situational
norms to develop and patterns of social interaction to emerge, change, and crystallize.
The second feature of this study was to ensure that all research participants would be
as normal as possible initially, healthy both physically and mentally, and without any
history of involvement in drugs or crime or violence. This baseline was essential to establish if we were to untangle the situational versus dispositional knot: What the situation elicited from this collection of similar, interchangeable young men versus what
was emitted by the research participants based on the unique dispositions they brought
into the experiment. The third feature of the study was the novelty of the prisoner
and guard roles: Participants had no prior training in how to play the randomly assigned roles. Each subject's prior societal learning of the meaning of prisons and the
behavioral scripts associated with the oppositional roles of prisoner and guard was
the sole source of guidance. The fourth feature was to create an experimental setting
that came as close to a *functional simulation* of the psychology of imprisonment as
possible. The details of how we went about creating a mindset comparable to that of
real prisoners and guards are given in several of the articles I wrote about the study
(see Zimbardo, 1975; Zimbardo, Haney, Banks, & Jaffe, 1973).

Central to this mind set were the oppositional issues of power and powerlessness,
dominance and submission, freedom and servitude, control and rebellion, identity
and anonymity, coercive rules and restrictive roles. In general, these social-
psychological constructs were operationalized by putting all subjects in appropriate
uniforms, using assorted props (e.g., handcuffs, police clubs, whistles, signs on doors
and halls), replacing corridor hall doors with prison bars to create prison cells, using
windowless and clock-less cells that afforded no clues as to time of day, applying
institutional rules that removed/substituted individual names with numbers

(prisoners) or titles for staff (Mr. Correctional Officer, Warden, Superintendent), and that gave guards control power over prisoners.

Subjects were recruited from among nearly 100 men between the ages of 18 and 30 who answered our advertisements in the local city newspaper. They were given a background evaluation that consisted of a battery of five psychological tests, personal history, and in-depth interviews. The 24 who were evaluated as most normal and healthiest in every respect were randomly assigned, half to the role of prisoner and half to that of guard. The student-prisoners underwent a realistic surprise arrest by officers from the Palo Alto Police Department, who cooperated with our plan. The arresting officer proceeded with a formal arrest, taking the "felons" to the police station for booking, after which each prisoner was brought to our prison in the reconstructed basement of our psychology department.

The prisoner's uniform was a smock/dress with a prison ID number. The guards wore military-style uniforms and silver-reflecting sunglasses to enhance anonymity. At any one time there were nine prisoners on "the yard," three to a cell, and three guards working 8-hour shifts. Data were collected via systematic video recordings, secret audio recordings of conversations of prisoners in their cells, interviews and tests at various times during the study, postexperiment reports, and direct, concealed observations.

For a detailed chronology and fuller account of the behavioral reactions that followed, readers are referred to the above references, to Zimbardo, Maslach, and Haney (1999), and to our new website *www.prisonexp.org*. For current purposes, let me simply summarize that the negative situational forces overwhelmed the positive dispositional tendencies. The Evil Situation triumphed over the Good People. Our projected 2-week experiment had to be terminated after only 6 days because of the pathology we were witnessing. Pacifistic young men were behaving sadistically in their role as guards, inflicting humiliation and pain and suffering on other young men who had the inferior status of prisoner. Some "guards" even reported enjoying doing so. Many of the intelligent, healthy college students who were occupying the role of prisoner showed signs of "emotional breakdown" (i.e., stress disorders) so extreme that five of them had to be removed from the experiment within that first week. The prisoners who adapted better to the situation were those who mindlessly followed orders and who allowed the guards to dehumanize and degrade them ever more with each passing day and night. The only personality variable that had any significant predictive value was that of F-scale authoritarianism: The higher the score, the more days the prisoner survived in this totally authoritarian environment.

I terminated the experiment not only because of the escalating level of violence and degradation by the guards against the prisoners that was apparent when viewing the videotapes of their interactions, but also because I was made aware of the transformation that I was undergoing personally (see the analysis by Christina Maslach of how she intervened to help bring light to that dark place and end the study; in Zimbardo et al., 1999). I had become a Prison Superintendent in addition to my role as Principal Investigator. I began to talk, walk, and act like a rigid institutional authority figure more concerned about the security of "my prison" than the needs of the young men entrusted to my care as a psychological researcher. In a sense, I consider the extent to which I was transformed to be the most profound measure of the power of this situation. We held extended debriefing sessions of guards and prisoners at the end of the study and conducted periodic checkups over many years. Fortunately, there were no lasting negative consequences of this powerful experience.

Before moving on, I would like to share parts of a letter sent to me recently (e-mail communication, October 18, 2002) by a young psychology student, recently discharged from military service. It outlines some of the direct parallels between the aversive aspects of our simulated prison many years ago and current despicable practices still taking place in some military boot-camp training. It also points up the positive effects that research and education can have:

> I am a 19-year-old student of psychology [who watched] the slide show of your prison experiment. Not too far into it, I was almost in tears. . . . I joined the United States Marine Corps, pursuing a childhood dream. To make a long story short, I had become the victim of repeated illegal physical and mental abuse. An investigation showed I suffered more than 40 unprovoked beatings. Eventually, as much as I fought it, I became suicidal, thus received a discharge from boot camp. . . .
>
> The point I am trying to make is that the manner in which your guards carried about their duties and the way that military drill instructors do is unbelievable. I was amazed at all the parallels of your guards and one particular D. I. who comes to mind. I was treated much the same way, and even worse, in some cases.
>
> One incident that stands out was the time, in an effort to break platoon solidarity, I was forced to sit in the middle of my squad bay [living quarters] and shout to the other recruits "If you guys would have moved faster, we wouldn't be doing this for hours," referencing every single recruit who was holding over his head a very heavy foot locker. The event was very similar to the prisoners saying #819 was a bad prisoner. After my incident, and after I was home safe some months later, all I could think about was how much I wanted to go back to show the other recruits that as much as the D. I.s told the platoon that I was a bad recruit, I wasn't.
>
> Other behaviors come to mind, like the push-ups we did for punishment, the shaved heads, not having any identity other than being addressed as, and referring to other people as, "Recruit So-and-So"—which replicates your study. The point of it all is that even though your experiment was conducted 31 years ago, my reading the study has helped me gain an understanding I was previously unable to gain before, even after therapy and counseling. What you have demonstrated really gave me insight into something I've been dealing with for almost a year now. Although, it is certainly not an excuse for their behavior, I now can understand the rationale behind the D. I.'s actions as far as being sadistic and power hungry.

The Failure of the Social Experiment of the U.S. Correctional System

As much joy that such personal reactions bring to someone whose vision has always been for psychological research to make a difference in people's lives, I have been saddened by the lack of impact the Stanford prison experiment has had on the correctional system in the United States. When Craig Haney and I recently did a retrospective analysis of our study, with contrasting views of U.S. and California correctional policies over the past 30 years, our conclusions were disheartening (Haney & Zimbardo, 1998). Prisons continue to be failed social experiments that rely on a dispositional model of punishment and isolation of offenders. Gone is any sense of the modifiable situational determinants of crime or of basic rehabilitation practices that might reduce persistently high rates of recidivism. The United States is now the prison center of the universe, with more than 2 million citizens incarcerated, *greater than any other nation,* and growing. Our analysis revealed that prison conditions had significantly worsened in the decades since our study, as a consequence of the politicization of prisons, with politicians, prosecutors, DAs, and other officials taking a hard line on crime as a means of currying favor of an electorate made fearful of crime by media exaggerations. Misguided policies about sentencing for crack cocaine use and sale and the "Three Strikes" rulings have put a disproportionately large number of African American and Hispanic men behind bars for long sentences. There are now more African American men wasting away in the nation's prison system than fulfilling their potentials in our higher educational system.

The Evil of Inaction

Our usual take on evil focuses on violent, destructive actions, but *non*action can also become a form of evil, when assistance, dissent, and disobedience are needed. Social psychologists heeded the alarm when the infamous Kitty Genovese case made national headlines. As she was being stalked, stabbed, and eventually murdered, 39 people in a housing complex heard her screams and did nothing to help. It seemed obvious that this was a prime example of the callousness of New Yorkers, as many media accounts reported. A counter to this dispositional analysis came in the form of a series of classic studies by Latané and Darley (1970) on bystander intervention. One key finding was that people are less likely to help when they are in a group, when they perceive that others are available who could help, than when those people are alone. The presence of others diffuses the sense of personal responsibility of any individual.

A powerful demonstration of the failure to help strangers in distress was staged by Darley and Batson (1973). Imagine you are a theology student on your way to deliver the sermon of the Good Samaritan in order to have it videotaped for a psychology study on effective communication. Further imagine that as you are heading from the psychology department to the video taping center, you pass a stranger huddled up in an alley in dire distress. Are there any conditions that you could conceive that would *not* make you stop to be that Good Samaritan? What about "time press"? Would it make a difference to you if you were late for your date to give that sermon? I bet you would like to believe it would not make a difference, that you would stop and help no matter what the circumstances. Right? Remember, you are a theology student, thinking about helping a stranger in distress, which is amply rewarded in the Biblical tale.

The researchers randomly assigned students of the Princeton Theological Seminary to three conditions that varied in how much time they thought they had between receiving their assignment from the researchers and getting to the communication department to tape their Good Samaritan speeches. The conclusion: Do not be a victim in distress when people are late and in a hurry, because 90% of them are likely to pass you by, giving you no help at all! The more time the seminarians believed they had, the more likely they were to stop and help. So the situational variable of *time press* accounted for the major variance in extending or withholding help, without any need to resort to dispositional explanations about theology students being callous or cynical or indifferent, as Kitty Genovese's nonhelpers were assumed to be—another instance of the FAE, one that needs to be reversed.

The Worst of the Apples in the Evil Barrel: Torturers and Executioners?

There is little debate but that the systematic torture by men and women of their fellow men and women represents one of the darkest sides of human nature. Surely, my colleagues and I reasoned, here was a place where dispositional evil would be manifest: among torturers who did their dirty deeds daily, for years, in Brazil as policemen sanctioned by the government to extract confessions through torturing so-called enemies of the state. We began by focusing solely on the torturers, trying to understand both their psyches and the ways they were shaped by their circumstances, but we had to expand our analytical net to capture their comrades-in-arms who chose, or were assigned to, another branch of violence work—death-squad executioners. They shared a "common enemy": men, women, and children who, though citizens of their state, even neighbors, were declared by "the authorities" to be threats to the country's national security. Some had to be eliminated efficiently, whereas those who might hold secret information had to be made to yield it up and confess to their treason.

In carrying out this mission, these torturers could rely, in part, on the "creative evil" embodied in the torture devices and techniques that had been refined over centuries since the Inquisition by officials of The Church and, later, of the National State. But our current-day torturers added a measure of improvisation to accommodate the particular resistances and resiliencies of the enemy standing before them, claiming innocence, refusing to acknowledge their culpability, or not succumbing to intimidation. It took time and emerging insights into exploitable human weaknesses for these torturers to become adept at their craft, in contrast to the task of the death-squad executioners, who, wearing hoods for anonymity and sporting good guns and group support, could dispatch their duty to country swiftly and impersonally. For the torturer, it could never be "just business." Torture always involves a personal relationship, essential for understanding what kind of torture to employ, what intensity of torture to use on this person at this time: wrong kind or too little; no confession, too much, and the victim dies before confessing. In either case, the torture fails to deliver the goods. Learning to select the right kind and degree of torture that yields up the desired information makes rewards abound and praise flow from the superiors.

What kind of men could do such deeds? Did they need to rely on sadistic impulses and a history of sociopathic life experiences to rip and tear flesh of fellow beings day in and day out for years on end? Were these violence workers a breed apart from the rest of humanity—bad seeds, bad tree trunks, bad flowers? Or, is it conceivable that they were programmed to carry out their deplorable deeds by means of some identifiable and replicable training processes? Could a set of external conditions—that is, situational variables—that contributed to the making of these torturers and killers be identified? If their evil deeds were not traceable to inner defects but attributable to outer forces acting upon them—the political, economic, social, historical, and experiential components of their police training—then we might be able to generalize, across cultures and settings, those principles responsible for this remarkable transformation. Martha Huggins, Mika Haritos-Fatouros, and I interviewed several dozen of these violence workers in depth and recently published a summary of our methods and findings (Huggins, Haritos-Fatouros, & Zimbardo, 2002). Mika had done a similar, earlier study of torturers trained by the Greek military junta, and our results were largely congruent with hers (Haritos-Fatouros, 2003).

We learned that sadists are *selected out* of the training process by trainers because they are not controllable, get off on the pleasure of inflicting pain, and thus do not sustain the focus on the goal of confession extraction. From all the evidence we could muster, these violence workers were not unusual or deviant in any way prior to practicing this new role, nor were there any persisting deviant tendencies or pathologies among any of them in the years following their work as torturers and executioners. Their transformation was entirely understandable as a consequence of (1) the training they were given to play this new role, (2) group camaraderie, (3) acceptance of the national security ideology, and (4) the belief in socialist-communists as enemies of their state. They were also influenced by being made to feel special—above and better than peers in public service—by the secrecy of their duties and by the constant pressure to produce desired results regardless of fatigue or personal problems. We report many detailed case studies that document the ordinariness of these men engaged in the most heinous of deeds, sanctioned by their government at that time in history, but reproducible at this time in any nation whose obsession with national security and fears of terrorism permit suspension of basic individual freedoms.

Suicide Bombers: Senseless Fanatics or Martyrs for a Cause?

Not surprisingly, what holds true for the Brazilian violence workers is comparable to the nature of the transformation of young Palestinians from students to suicide bombers killing Israelis. Recent media accounts converge on the findings from more systematic analyses of the process of becoming a suicidal killer (see Atran, 2003; Bennet, 2003; Hoffman, 2003; Merari, 1990, 2002; Myer, 2003). There have been more than 95 suicide bombings by Palestinians against Israelis since September, 2000. Originally, and most frequently, the bombers were young men, but recently a half dozen women have joined the ranks of suicidal bombers. What has been declared as senseless, mindless murder by those attacked and by outside observers is anything but to those intimately involved. It was mistakenly believed that it was poor, desperate, socially isolated, illiterate young people with no career and no future who adopted this fatalistic role. That stereotype has been shattered by the actual portraits of these young men and women, many of whom were students with hopes for a better future, intelligent and attractive youth, connected with their family and community.

Ariel Merari, an Israeli psychologist who has studied this phenomenon for many years, outlines the common steps on the path to these explosive deaths. Senior members of an extremist group first identify particular young people who appear to have an intense patriotic fervor, based on their declarations at public rallies against Israel or their support of some Islamic cause or Palestinian action. These individuals are invited to discuss how serious they are in their love of their country and their hatred of Israel. They are then asked to commit to being trained in how to put their hatred into action. Those who make the commitment are put into a small group of three to five similar youth who are at varying stages of "progress" toward becoming agents of death. They learn the tricks of the trade from elders: bomb making, disguise, selecting and timing targets. Then they publicize their private commitment by making a videotape on which they declare themselves to be "living martyrs" for Islam and for the love of Allah. In one hand they hold the Koran, a rifle in the other, their headband declaring their new status. This video binds them to the final deed, since it is sent home to the family of the recruit before they execute the final plan. The recruits also realize that not only will they earn a place beside Allah, but their relatives will also be entitled to a high place in heaven because of their martyrdom. A sizable financial incentive is bestowed on their family as a gift for their sacrifice.

Their photo is emblazoned on posters that will be put on walls everywhere in the community the moment they succeed in their mission. They will be immortalized as inspirational models. To stifle concerns about the pain from wounds inflicted by exploding nails and other bomb parts, they are told that before the first drop of their blood touches the ground, they will already be seated at the side of Allah, feeling no pain, only pleasure. An ultimate incentive for the young males is the promise of heavenly bliss with scores of virgins in the next life. They become heroes and heroines, modeling self-sacrifice to the next cadre of young suicide bombers.

We can see that this program utilizes a variety of social-psychological and motivational principles in turning collective hatred and general frenzy into a dedicated, seriously calculated program of indoctrination and training for individuals to become youthful "living martyrs." It is neither mindless nor senseless, only a very different mind set and with different sensibilities than we have been used to witnessing among young adults in our country. A recent television program on female suicide bombers went so far as to describe them in terms more akin to the girl next door then to alien fanatics. Indeed, that very normalcy is what is so frightening about the emergence of this new social phenomena—that so many intelligent young people could be persuaded to envision and welcome their lives ending in a suicidal explosive blast.

To counteract the powerful tactics of these recruiting agents requires the provision of meaningful, life-affirming alternatives to this next generation. It requires new national leadership that is willing and able to explore every negotiating strategy that could lead to peace instead of death. It requires these young people across national boundaries to openly share their values, their education, and their resources and to explore their commonalities, not highlight their differences. The suicide, the murder, of any young person is a gash in the fabric of the human connection that we elders from every nation must unite to prevent. To encourage the sacrifice of youth for the sake of advancing ideologies of the old might be considered a form of evil from a more cosmic perspective that transcends local politics and expedient strategies.

Conclusions

It is a truism in psychology that personality and situations interact to generate behavior, as do cultural and societal influences. However, I have tried to show in my research over the past 30 years that situations exert more power over human actions than has been generally acknowledged by most psychologists or recognized by the general public. Along with a hardy band of experimental social psychologists, I have conducted research demonstrations designed, in part, to provide a corrective balance to the pervasive fundamental attribution error. Nevertheless, the traditional dispositional perspective continues to dominate Anglo-American psychology fueled by reliance on the individualist orientation central in our institutions of medicine, education, psychiatry, law, and religion. Acknowledging the power of situational forces does not excuse the behaviors evoked in response to their operation. Rather, it provides a knowledge base that shifts attention away from simplistic "blaming the victim" mentality and ineffective individualistic treatments designed to change the evil doer, toward more profound attempts to discover causal networks that should be modified. Sensitivity to situational determinants of behavior also affords "risk alerts" that allow us to avoid or modify prospective situations of vulnerability.

Please consider this Zimbardo homily that captures the essence of the difference between dispositional and situational orientations: "While a few bad apples might spoil the barrel (filled with good fruit/people), a barrel filled with vinegar will *always* transform sweet cucumbers into sour pickles—regardless of the best intentions, resilience, and genetic nature of those cucumbers." So, does it make more sense to spend our resources on attempts to identify, isolate, and destroy the few bad apples or to learn how vinegar works so that we can teach cucumbers how to avoid undesirable vinegar barrels?

My situational sermon has several related dimensions. First, we should be aware that a range of apparently simple situational factors can impact our behavior more compellingly than we would expect or predict. The research outlined here, along with that of my colleagues presented in this volume, points to the influential force of numerous variables: role playing, rules, presence of others, emergent group norms, group identity, uniforms, anonymity, social modeling, authority presence, symbols of power, time pressures, semantic framing, stereotypical images and labels, among others.

Second, the situationist approach redefines heroism. When the majority of ordinary people can be overcome by such pressures toward compliance and conformity, the minority who resist should be considered *heroic*. Acknowledging the special nature of this resistance means that we should learn from their example by studying *how* they have been able to rise above such compelling pressures. That suggestion is coupled with another that encourages the development of an essential but ignored domain of psychology—heroes and heroism.

Third, the situationist approach should, in my view, encourage us all to share a profound sense of personal humility when trying to understand those "unthinkable," "unimaginable," "senseless" acts of evil. Instead of immediately embracing the high moral ground that distances us good folks from those bad ones and gives short shrift to analyses of causal factors in the situations that form the context of the evil acts, the situational approach gives all others the benefit of "attributional charity." This means that any deed, for good or evil, that any human being has ever performed or committed, you and I could also perform or commit—given the same situational forces. If so, it becomes imperative to constrain our immediate moral outrage that seeks vengeance against wrongdoers and turn our efforts toward uncovering the causal factors that could have led them in that aberrant direction.

The obvious current instantiation of these principles is the rush to characterize terrorists and suicide bombers as "evil" people, instead of working to understand the nature of the psychological, social, economic, and political conditions that have fostered such generalized hatred of an enemy nation, including our own, that young people are willing to sacrifice their lives and murder other human beings. The "war on terrorism" can never be won solely by the current administration's plans to find and destroy terrorists—since any individual, anywhere, at any time, can become an active terrorist. It is only by understanding the *situational determinants of terrorism* that programs can be developed to win the hearts and minds of potential terrorists away from destruction and toward creation—not a simple task, but an essential one that requires implementation of social-psychological perspectives and methods in a comprehensive, long-term plan of attitude, value, and behavior change.

References

Adorno, T. W., Frenkel-Brunswick, E., Levenson, D. J., & Sanford, R. N. (1950). *The authoritarian personality.* New York: Harper & Row.

Atran, S. (2003, May 5). Who wants to be a martyr? *The New York Times,* p. A23.

Bandura, A. (1998). Mechanisms of moral disengagement. In W. Reich (Ed.), *Origins of terrorism: Psychologies, ideologies, theologies, states of mind* (pp. 161–191). New York: Cambridge University Press.

Bandura, A. (2003). The role of selective moral disengagement in terrorism and counterterrorism. In F. M. Mogahaddam & A. J. Marsella (Eds.), *Understanding terrorism* (pp. 121–150). Washington, DC: American Psychological Association.

Bandura, A., Underwood, B., & Fromson, M. E. (1975). Disinhibition of aggression through diffusion of responsibility and dehumanization of victims. *Journal of Personality and Social Psychology, 9,* 253–269.

Barstow, A. L. (1994). *Witchcraze: A new history of the European witch hunts.* New York: HarperCollins.

Baumeister, R. F. (1997). *Evil: Inside human cruelty and violence.* New York: Freeman.

Bennett, J. (2003, May 30). A scholar of English who clung to the veil. *The New York Times,* pp. A1, A14.

Browning, C. R. (1992). *Ordinary men: Reserve police battalion 101 and the final solution in Poland.* New York: HarperPerennial.

Chang, I. (1997). *The rape of Nanking: The forgotten holocaust of World War II.* New York: Basic Books.

Cialdini, R. B. (2001). *Influence: Science and practice* (4th ed.). Boston: Allyn & Bacon.

Darley, J. M. (1992). Social organization for the production of evil. *Psychological Inquiry 3,* 199–218.

Darley, J. M., & Barson, D. (1973). From Jerusalem to Jericho: A study of situational and dispositional variables in helping behavior. *Journal of Personality and Social Psychology, 27,* 100–108.

Diener, E. (1980). Deindividuation: The absence of self-awareness and self-regulation in group members. In P. B. Paulus (Ed.), *The psychology of group influence* (pp. 209–243). Hillsdale, NJ: Erlbaum.

Festinger, L. (1957). *A theory of cognitive dissonance.* Palo Alto, CA: Stanford University Press.

Fraser, S. C. (1974). *Deindividuation: Effects of anonymity on aggression in children.* Unpublished manuscript, University of Southern California, Los Angeles.

Golding, W. (1954). *Lord of the flies.* New York: Capricorn Books.

Haney, C., & Zimbardo, P. G. (1998). The past and future of U.S. prison policy: Twenty-five years after the Stanford Prison Experiment. *American Psychologist, 53,* 709–727.

Haritos-Fatouros, M. (2002). *The psychological origins of institutionalized torture.* London: Routledge.

Hoffman, B. (2003, June). The logic of suicide terrorism. *The Atlantic Monthly,* 40–47.

Huggins, M., Haritos-Fatouros, M., & Zimbardo, P. G. (2002). *Violence workers: Police torturers and murderers reconstruct Brazilian atrocities.* Berkeley: University of California Press.

Keen, S. (1986). *Faces of the enemy: Reflections of the hostile imagination.* New York: HarperCollins.

Kramer, H., & Sprenger, J. (1971). *The malleus maleficarum.* New York: Dover. (Original work published 1486)

Latané, B., & Darley, J. M. (1970). *The unresponsive bystander: Why doesn't he help?* New York: Appleton-Century-Crofts.

Lee, M., Zimbardo, P. G., & Berthof, M. (1977). Shy murderers. *Psychology Today, 11,* 69–70, 76, 148.

Merari, A. (1990). The readiness to kill and die: Suicidal terrorism in the Middle East. In W. Reich (Ed.), *Origins of terrorism: Psychologies, theologies, states of mind* (pp. 192–200). New York: Cambridge University Press.

Merari, A. (2002, October). *Suicide terrorism.* Paper presented at the First Conference of the National Center for Disaster Psychology and Terrorism, Palo Alto, CA.

Milgram, S. (1974). *Obedience to authority.* New York: Harper & Row.

Myer, G. (2003, May 30). A young man radicalized by his months in jail. *The York Times,* pp. A1, A14.

The new order (The Third Reich). (1989). Alexandria, VA: Time Life Books.

Orwell, G. (1981). *1984.* New York: Signet.

Prentice-Dunn, S., & Rogers, R. W. (1983). Deindividuation and aggression. In R. G. Geen & E. I. Donnerstein (Eds.), *Aggression: Theoretical and empirical reviews—issues in research* (Vol. 2, pp. 155–171). New York: Academic Press.

Ross, L. (1977). The intuitive psychologist and his shortcomings. In L. Berkowitz (Ed.), *Advances in experimental social psychology* (Vol. 10, pp. 173–220). New York: Academic Press.

Staub, E. (1989). *The roots of evil: The origins of genocide and other group violence.* New York: Cambridge University Press.

Waller, J. (2002). *Becoming evil: How ordinary people commit genocide and mass killing.* New York: Oxford University Press.

Watson, R. L., Jr. (1973). Investigation into deindividuation using a cross-cultural survey technique. *Journal of Personality and Social Psychology, 25,* 342–345.

Zimbardo, P. G. (1970). The human choice: Individuation, reason, and order versus deindividuation, impulse, and chaos. In W. J. Arnold & D. Levine (Eds.), *1969 Nebraska Symposium on Motivation* (pp. 237–307). Lincoln: University of Nebraska Press.

Zimbardo, P. G. (1975). On transforming experimental research into advocacy for social change. In M. Deursch & H. Hornstein (Eds.), *Applying social psychology: Implications for research, practice, and training* (pp. 33–66). Hillsdale, NJ: Erlbaum.

Zimbardo, P. G. (1976). Making sense of senseless vandalism. In E. P. Hollander & R. G. Hunt (Eds.), *Current perspectives in social psychology* (4th ed., pp. 129–134). Oxford, UK: Oxford University Press.

Zimbardo, P. G. (2003a). Mind control in Orwell's *1984:* Fictional concepts become operational realities in Jim Jones' jungle experiment. In M. Nussbaum, J. Goldsmith, & A. Gleason (Eds.), *1984: Orwell and our future.* Princeton: Princeton University Press.

Zimbardo, P. G. (2003b). Phantom menace: Is Washington terrorizing us more than Al Qaeda? *Psychology Today, 36,* pp. 34–36.

Zimbardo, P. G., Haney, C., Banks, C., & Jaffe, D. (1973, April 8). The mind is a formidable jailer: A Pirandellian prison. *The New York Times Magazine,* pp. 38 ff.

Zimbardo, P. G., Maslach, C., & Haney, C. (1999). Reflections on the Stanford Prison Experiment: Genesis, transformation, consequences. In T. Blass (Ed.), *Obedience to authority: Current perspectives on the Milgram Paradigm* (pp. 193–237). Mahwah, NJ: Erlbaum.

Credits

Transcript of personal interview with Richard Patrick reprinted by permission of Kim Stallings.

"Jeremy." Words and music by Ed Vedder/Innocent Bystander (ASCAP) and Jeff Ament/Scribing C-Ment Songs/PRI Music, Inc. (ASCAP). Reprinted by permission.

Mission Statement of With Arms Wide Open.

Email exchange between Brian Doherty and the author, September 2002. Used by permission of Brian Doherty.

"Bum Rap," by Brian Doherty from *Reason* Magazine, December 2000. © Reason, www.reason.com. Reprinted by permission.

"George W.'s historical twin," by Benjamin Soskis, *The New Republic*, January 2001. © 2001 The New Republic, LLC. Reprinted by permission of The New Republic.

"There's No Why" by Kristen Baldwin, *Entertainment Weekly*, May 7, 1999. © 1999 Entertainment Weekly Inc. Reprinted with permission.

From "Identifying Bias in News Stories," *How to Identify, Expose & Correct Liberal Media Bias* by Brent Baker, Media Research Center, 1994. Reprinted by permission of Media Research Center.

"Teaching Kids to Kill," by Lt. David Grossman. Reprinted from *National Forum*, Volume 80, Number 4 (Fall 2000). Copyright by David Grossman. Reprinted by permission of the publishers.

From www.keepandbeararms.com. Reprinted by permission.

Mission statement of Drum Major Institute Organization. Reprinted by permission of the Drum Major Institute.

"American Cliché." Words and Music by Richard Patrick. © 2002 EMI APRIL MUSIC INC. and HAPPY DITTIES FROM PARADISE. All rights Controlled and Administered by EMI APRIL MUSIC INC. All Rights Reserved. International Copyright Secured. Used by permission.

"Columind." Words and Music by Richard Patrick. © 2002 EMI APRIL MUSIC INC. and HAPPY DITTIES FROM PARADISE. All rights Controlled and Administered by EMI APRIL MUSIC INC. All Rights Reserved. International Copyright Secured. Used by permission.

". . . the day." Reprinted by permission of C.R. Taylor.

"Suicide." Reprinted by permission of Constantine Maroulis.

"Counting Bodies Like Sheep to the Rhythm of the War Drums." Words and Music by Billy Howerdel and Maynard James Keenan. © 2004 EMI APRIL MUSIC INC., HARRY MERKIN MUSIC and TRANSFIXED MUSIC. All Rights for HAPPY MERKIN MUSIC Controlled and Administered by EMI APRIL MUSIC INC. All Rights Reserved. International Copyright Secured. Used by Permission.

"What Ever Happened to Peace on Earth," lyrics by Willie Nelson. Reprinted by permission of Mark Rothbaum & Associates.

"You're Missing" by Bruce Springsteen. Copyright © 2002 Bruce Springsteen. Reprinted by permission. International copyright secured. All rights reserved.

"American Cliché." Words and Music by Richard Patrick. © 2002 EMI APRIL MUSIC INC. and HAPPY DITTIES FROM PARADISE. All rights Controlled and Administered by EMI APRIL MUSIC INC. All Rights Reserved. International Copyright Secured. Used by permission.

"The Missing." Words and Music by Richard Patrick. © 2002 EMI APRIL MUSIC INC. and HAPPY DITTIES FROM PARADISE. All rights Controlled and Administered by EMI APRIL MUSIC INC. All Rights Reserved. International Copyright Secured. Used by permission.

From *Rich Words* by Richard Patrick found at Filter's official website, www.officialfilter.com. Used by permission of The Firm.

The Google™ homepage is a trademark of Google, Inc. Reprinted by permission.

"The Fight Song." Words by Marilyn Mason. Music by John5. © 2000 EMI BLACKWOOD MUSIC INC., SONGS OF GOLGOTHA, CHRYSALIS MUSIC AND GTR HACK MUSIC. All Rights for SONGS OF GOLGOTHA Controlled and Administered by EMI BLACKWOOD MUSIC INC. All Rights for GTR HACK MUSIC Administered by CHYSALIS MUSIC. All Rights Reserved. International Copyright Secured. Used by permission.

"School War Zone," by Mike Anton, *The Rocky Mountain News*, April 20, 1999. Reprinted with permission of the Rocky Mountain News.

"Up to 25 Die in Colorado School Shooting," by Tom Kenworthy, *The Washington Post*, April 21, 1999. © 1999, The Washington Post Writers Group. Reprinted with permission.

Screen capture from www.safeyouth.org, National Youth Violence Prevention Resource Center. Atlanta: US Centers for Disease Control and Prevention, National Center for Injury Prevention and Control, 2005.

"Facts for Teens: School Violence," Online Documents, National Youth Violence Prevention Resource Center, www.safeyouth.org. Atlanta: US Centers for Disease Control and Prevention, National Center for Injury Prevention and Control, 2005.

"Columbine: Whose Fault Is It?" by Marilyn Manson, *Rolling Stone* Magazine, June 24, 1999. © 1999 Rolling Stone LLC. All Rights Reserved. Reprinted by permission.

"Teen Violence: Does Violent Media Make Violent Kids?" by Teresa Malcolm, *National Catholic Reporter*, May 28, 1999. Reprinted with permission, National Catholic Reporter (www.NCRonline.org).

Transcript of the "Littleton, CO," Elizabeth Farnsworth with Gerald Tirrozi, James Garbarino and Frankin Zimring, broadcast April 21, 1999, *The NewsHour with Jim Lehrer*. Copyright MacNeil-Lehrer Productions. Reprinted with permission.

"Violence Redux: A Brief Legal and Historical Perspective on Youth Violence," by Marshall Croddy, *Social Education*, Vol. 61, No. 5, 1997, pp. 258–264. © National Council for the Social Studies. Reprinted by permission of the NCSS and the author.

"Ironic Literacy: Grasping the Dark Images of Rock and Roll," by Kevin J. Dettmar as appeared in, *The Chronicle of Higher Education*, Vol. 46, No. 39, June 2, 2000. Reprinted by permission of the author.

630   Credits

"U.S. Researchers Lose Edge in Stem-Cell Work," by Scott Allen, *Knight Ridder/Tribune Business News*, February 13, 2004.

"Cloning Gets Closer," by Michael D. Lemonick, et al., *Time*, February 23, 2004. © 2004 TIME, Inc. Reprinted by permission.

"Movie Website Stirs Cloning Controversy," *Reuters*, CNN.com, April 26, 2004.

Adaptation of "The Age of Genetic Technology Arrives," from *Life, Liberty and the Defense of Dignity* by Leon Kass, M.D., Encounter Books, San Francisco, California, © 2002, www.encounterbooks.com. Reprinted by permission.

"The Top Ten Myths about Human Cloning" by Gregory E. Pence. www.humancloning.org. Used by permission of the author, Professor of Philosophy, University of Alabama, Birmingham.

"Cloning as Economic Development," by Neil Munro. Reprinted with permission from *National Journal*, March 6, 2004. Copyright 2005 National Journal. All rights reserved.

"Stem Cell Research: Why Medicine Should Reject Human Cloning," by William P. Cheshire, Jr., M.D., et al. Reprinted with permission from *Mayo Clinic Proceedings*, 2003; 78: 1010–1018.

"Eve Redux: The Public Confusion over Cloning," by Stephen S. Hall, *Hastings Center Report*, Vol. 33, No. 3 (2003). © The Hasting Center. Reprinted by permission of The Hastings Center and the author.

"Intervening with Mother Nature: The Ethics of Human Cloning," by Seymour W. Itzkoff, *The Mankind Quarterly*, Vol. XLIV, No. 1, Fall 2003. Reprinted by permission of the Council for Social and Economic Studies.

"Anti-Terror Bill Becomes Law," The Associated Press, October 26, 2001. Used with permission of The Associated Press, Copyright © 2001. All rights reserved.

Transcript of "Considering the Patriotic Act," with Margaret Warner, broadcast August 19, 2003, *The NewsHour with Jim Lehrer*. Copyright MacNeil-Lehrer Productions. Reprinted with permission.

"Taking Liberties," by Angie Cannon, *U.S. News & World Report*, May 12, 2003, pp. 44–46. Copyright 2003 U.S. News & World Report, L.P. Reprinted with permission.

"The Patriot Act Without Tears," by Andrew C. McCarthy, *National Review*, June 14, 2004. © by National Review, Inc., 215 Lexington Avenue, New York, NY 10016. Reprinted by permission.

"Patriot Spawn," by Julian Sanchez, *Reason* Magazine, April 2004. © Reason Magazine, www.reason.com. Reprinted by permission.

"The USA Patriot Act and the Politics of Fear," by Mark S. Hamm in Ferrell, J., Hayward, K., Morrision, W., & Presdee, M. (Eds.), *Cultural Criminology Unleashed, 1st edition*, 2004, pp. 287–299, London: The GlassHouse Press. Reprinted by permission of Cavendish Publishing Limited.

"Global struggle for women's rights spotlighted at New York meeting," CNN.com, June 4, 2000. Reprinted by permission of CNN.

"Call it Beijing-5," by Paul Bunner, The *Report Newsmagazine (Alberta Edition)*, 7/3/2000. Reprinted by permission of Citizens Centre for Freedom and Democracy.

www.unifem.org. Courtesy UNIFEM, United Nations Development Fund For Women.

"Progress for Women Is Progress for All," United Nations Development Fund for Women found at www.unifem.org. Reprinted by permission.

"A Forty-Year Search for Equality," by Ellen Goodman, *The Washington Post*, June 26, 2004. © 2004, The Washington Post Writers Group. Reprinted with permission.

"Gender Equality & the Millennium Development Goals," www.mdgender.net. Jointly produced by UNDP, UNIFEM, UNFPA, The World Bank and the OECD/DAC Network on Gender Equality. Reprinted by permission.

"United Nations Millenium Declaration," United Nations General Assembly, September 8, 2000. The United Nations is the author of the original material. Reprinted by permission.

"How Effective Is A Human Rights Framework in Addressing Gender-Based Violence?" by Ana Elena Obando, February 2004, originally published by Women's Human Right Net, www.whrnet.org, a project on the Association for Women's Rights in Development (AWID). Reprinted by permission.

"What Is Female Genital Mutilation?", *Female Genital Mutilation: A Human Rights Information Packet*, 1997. © Amnesty International. Reprinted by permission.

"Apologetic Jackson says costume reveal went awry," CNN.com, February 2, 2004. Reprinted by permission of CNN.

"America beats breasts, rends garments over TV boob," *The Australian*, February 7, 2004. Reprinted by permission of Nationwide News.

"Super Bowl Fallout Continues," James Carville, Paul Begala, Robert, Novak and Tucker Carlson, *CNN Crossfire*, February 11, 2004. Reprinted by permission of CNN.

Home page of firstamendmentcenter.org by Ken Paulson, former executive director, First Amendment Center. Reprinted by permission of First Amendment Center.

"Flashpoint: Janet Jackson and government regulation of TV," firstamendmentcenter.org, February 6, 2004. Reprinted by permission of First Amendment Center.

"The Silver Lining of the Janet Jackson Incident: A Demonstration of Democracy-Enhancing Technology, and the Need to Fight the 'Broadcast Flag' Rule," by Lauren Gelman. Used by permission of the author, Associate Director, Stanford Law School Center for Internet and Society.

"What is the Fuss about Janet Jackson's Breast?" by Marjorie Heins, February 2, 2004. The Free Expression Policy Project, Brennan Center for Justice at NYU School of Law. Reprinted by permission of Marjorie Heins.

"Seven severely reprimanded in Iraqi prisoner abuse scandal," by Joseph L. Galloway, *Knight Ridder*, May 3, 2004.

"Arabs Unimpressed by President Bush or Prisoner Abuse," by Naseer Al-Nahr, *Arab News*, May 6, 2004. Reprinted by permission of Arab News.

Transcript of "Iraqi Prisoner Abuse," with Jim Lehrer, broadcast May 4, 2004, *The NewsHour with Jim Lehrer*. Copyright MacNeil-Lehrer Productions. Reprinted with permission.

Web page from www.hrw.org. ©2004 Human Rights Watch. Reprinted by permission.

"Iraq: U.S. Prisoner Abuse Sparks Concerns Over War Crimes," www.hrw.org. © 2004 by Human Rights Watch. Reprinted by permission.

"Signs on the Road to Abu Ghraib," by Sam Smith, *Progressive Review*, May 10, 2004. Reprinted by permission of Sam Smith, editor of the Progressive Review, prorev.com.

"Prisoner Abuse and the Rot of American Culture," by Rebecca Hagelin, May 11, 2004. Reprinted by permission of The Heritage Foundation.

From Geneva Convention (III) Relative to the Treatment of Prisoners of War; August 12, 1949, The United Nations, from http://www.unhchr.ch. The United Nations is the author of the original material. Reprinted by permission.

"Torture at Abu Ghraib followed CIA's manual," by Alfred W. McCoy, *The Boston Globe*, May 14, 2004.

"A Situational Perspective on the Psychology of Evil: Understanding How Good People Are Transformed into Perpetrators," by Phillip G. Zimbardo in *The Social Psychology of Good and Evil*, edited by Arthur G. Miller. Copyright © 2004 Guilford Press. Reprinted by permission.

Index